W9-BDM-230

No End in Sight

No End in Sight

The Continuing Menace of Nuclear Proliferation

Nathan E. Busch

THE UNIVERSITY PRESS OF KENTUCKY

Publication of this volume was made possible in part by a grant from the National Endowment for the Humanities.

Scholarly publisher for the Commonwealth,
serving Bellarmine University, Berea College, Centre College of Kentucky, Eastern Kentucky University, The Filson Historical Society, Georgetown College, Kentucky Historical Society, Kentucky State University, Morehead State University, Murray State University, Northern Kentucky University, Transylvania University, University of Kentucky, University of Louisville, and Western Kentucky University.

Editorial and Sales Offices: The University Press of Kentucky
663 South Limestone Street, Lexington, Kentucky 40508-4008

08 07 06 05 04 5 4 3 2 1

Library of Congress Cataloging-in-Publication Data

Busch, Nathan E., 1971-
No end in sight : the continuing menace of nuclear proliferation / Nathan E. Busch.
p. cm.
Includes bibliographical references and index.
ISBN 0-8131-2323-2 (hardcover: alk. paper)
1. Nuclear nonproliferation. I. Title.
JZ5675.B87 2003
327.1'747--dc22

2003024593

This book is printed on acid-free recycled paper meeting the requirements of the American National Standard for Permanence of Paper for Printed Library Materials.

Manufactured in the United States of America

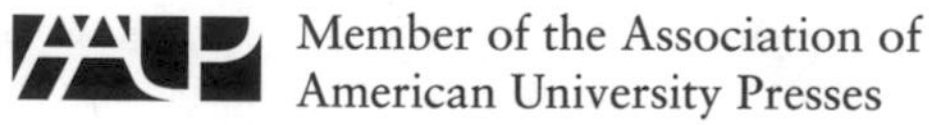

Member of the Association of American University Presses

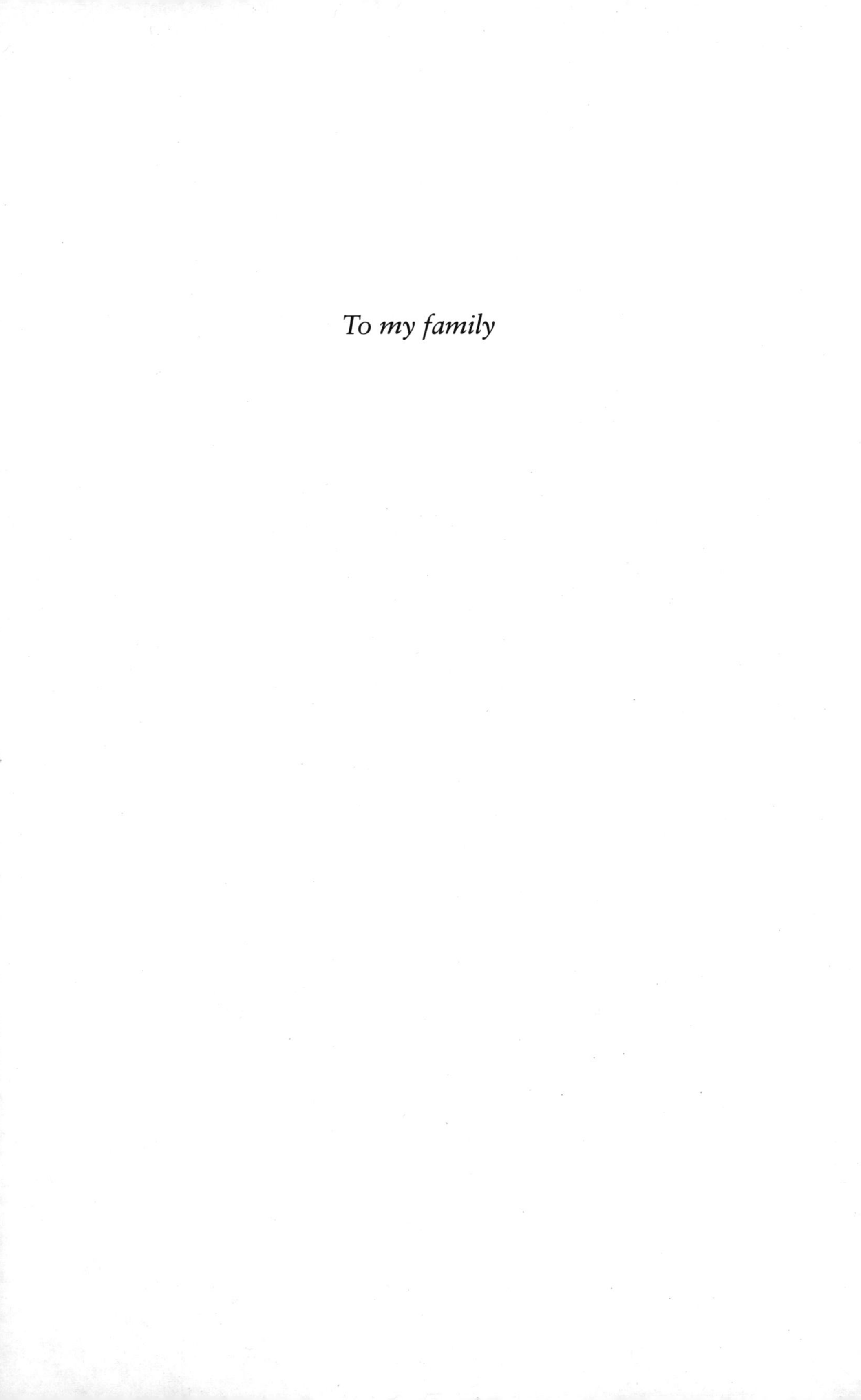

To my family

Contents

Tables and Figures

Tables

Figures

Abbreviations and Acronyms

The following is a list of all the acronyms used in this study. Each acronym is defined the first time it appears in each chapter.

3 I's	isolation, incompatibility, inoperability
3 G's	guards, gates, and guns
ACM	advanced cruise missile
ABM	antiballistic missile system (and treaty)
ADM	atomic demolition munitions
AEC	Atomic Energy Commission (U.S.)
AERB	Atomic Energy Regulatory Board (India)
AFB	Air Force Base
ALCM	air-launched cruise missile
AMAC	aircraft monitoring and control (U.S.)
ASM	air-to-surface missile
ASW	antisubmarine weapon (Russia)
BARC	Bhabba Atomic Research Centre (India)
BCSS	bomber coded switch system (U.S.)
BJP	Bharatiya Janata Party (India)
BMEWS	ballistic missile early-warning system
C^2	command and control
C^3I	command, control, communications, and intelligence
C^4I	command, control, communications, computers, and intelligence
CACE	China Arms Control Exchange
CAEA	China Atomic Energy Agency
CAEP	China Academy of Engineering Physics
CANDU	Canada deuterium uranium reactor
CBMs	confidence-building measures

CCD	coded control device (U.S.)
CCP	Chinese Communist Party
CCS	Cabinet Committee on Security (India)
CHASNUPP	Chasma Nuclear Power Plant (Pakistan)
CHEGET	Russia's "nuclear suitcase"
CINC	Commander-in-Chief
CINCNORAD	Commander-in-Chief, NORAD (U.S.)
CLL	U.S.-China Lab-to-Lab Technical Exchange Program
CNNC	China National Nuclear Corporation
CSS	NATO designation for Chinese nuclear missiles
CTBT	Comprehensive Test Ban Treaty
CTR	Cooperative Threat Reduction (or Nunn-Lugar) program
CWB	Chemical Weapons Branch (Iraq)
D&D	denial and deception
DAE	Department of Atomic Energy (India)
DCC	Development Control Committee (Pakistan)
DF	Dong Feng or "East Wind" (missile) (China)
DMZ	Demilitarized Zone (Korea)
DOD	Department of Defense (U.S.)
DOE	Department of Energy (U.S.)
DPRK	Democratic People's Republic of Korea (North Korea)
DRDO	Defense Research and Development Organization (India)
DSP	Defense Support Program (a satellite early-warning system, U.S.)
ECC	Employment Control Committee (Pakistan)
ENDS	Enhanced Nuclear Detonation Safety (U.S.)
ERDA	Energy Research and Development Administration (U.S.)
ESD	environmental sensing device (U.S., Russia)
FARR	Fail-Safe and Risk Reduction Commission (U.S.)
FRP	fire-resistant pits (U.S.)
GAN	Gosatomnadzor (Russian)
GAO	General Accounting Office (U.S.)
GSLV	Geosynchronous Satellite Launch Vehicle (India)
H-6	Hong-6 bomber (China)
HE	high explosive
HEU	highly-enriched uranium

HUMINT	human intelligence
IAEA	International Atomic Energy Agency
IAEC	Indian Atomic Energy Commission
IAPCM	Institute of Applied Physics and Computational Mathematics (China)
ICBM	intercontinental ballistic missile
IFI	in-flight insertion component (U.S.)
IHE	insensitive high explosive
INF	Intermediate-Range Nuclear Forces Treaty (U.S.-Russia)
INFCIRC	Information Circular (IAEA)
IRGC	Islamic Revolutionary Guard Corps (Iran)
ISIS	Institute for Science and International Security (U.S.)
JDEC	Joint Data Exchange Center (U.S.-Russia)
K-26	Krasnoyarsk-26 (Russia)
KANUPP	Karachi Nuclear Power Plant (Pakistan)
KEDO	Korean Peninsula Energy Development Organization
KGB	Committee for State Security (Soviet Union/Russia)
KMP	key measurement points
LANL	Los Alamos National Laboratory (U.S.)
LCC	Dual Launch Control Center (U.S.)
LDS	Launch-Detection System (U.S. designation for the Russian system)
LEU	low-enriched uranium
LLNL	Lawrence Livermore National Laboratory (U.S.)
LOC	Line of Control (India-Pakistan)
LOW	launch-on-warning
LPAR	large phased-array radar
LUA	launch-under-attack
MB	material balance equation
MBA	material balance area
MC&A	(Fissile) Material Control and Accounting
Minatom	Ministry of Atomic Energy (Russia)
MIRV	multiple independently targetable reentry vehicle
MOD	Ministry of Defense (Russia)
MOX	mixed-oxide nuclear fuel
MPC&A	(Fissile) Material Protection, Control, and Accounting
MUF	"material unaccounted for"

MW(e)	megawatt (electric)
MW(t)	megawatt (thermal)
NATO	North Atlantic Treaty Organization
NCA	National Command Authority
NDA	nondestructive assay
NFU	"no first use" doctrine
NIS	newly independent states
NMD	national missile defense
NMMSS	Nuclear Materials Management and Safeguards System (U.S.)
NNWS	non–nuclear weapons state
NORAD	North American Aerospace Defense Command (U.S.)
NPT	Nuclear Non-Proliferation Treaty
NRB	Nuclear Regulatory Board (Pakistan)
NRC	Nuclear Regulatory Commission (U.S.)
NSC	National Security Council (India)
NSC	National Security Council (U.S.)
NUMAC	Nuclear Material Accounting and Control organization (India)
NWS	nuclear weapons state
OTH	over-the-horizon (radar)
PAEC	Pakistan Atomic Energy Commission
PAL	permissive action link
PAVE PAWS	precision acquisition of vehicle entry phased-array warning system (U.S.)
PES	permissive enable system (U.S.)
PFBR	Prototype Fast Breeder Reactor (India)
PHWR	pressurized heavy-water reactor (India)
PIDAS	perimeter intrusion detection and assessment system (U.S.)
PINSTECH	Pakistan Institute of Nuclear Science and Technology
PLA	People's Liberation Army (China)
PNIs	Presidential Nuclear Initiatives (U.S.-Russia)
PNRA	Pakistan Nuclear Regulatory Authority
PP	Physical Protection
PRP	personnel reliability program
PSLV	Polar Satellite Launch Vehicle (India)
Q-5	Qian-5 bomber (China)
RVSN	Russian Strategic Rocket Forces

SAC	Strategic Air Command (U.S.)
SAC	Second Artillery Corps (China)
SALT I	Strategic Arms Limitation Talks (U.S.-Soviet)
SALT II	Strategic Arms Limitation Treaty (U.S.-Soviet)
SAM	surface-to-air missile
SLBM	submarine-launched ballistic missile
SLCM	sea-launched cruise missile
SLV	Satellite Launch Vehicle
SNM	special nuclear materials
SORT	Strategic Offensive Reductions Treaty (U.S.-Russia)
SRAM	short-range attack missile
SRBM	short-range ballistic missile
SSBN	ballistic missile submarine
SSO	Special Security Organization (Iraq)
START I and II	Strategic Arms Reductions Treaty I and II (U.S.-Russia)
TEL	transporter erector launcher
UNSCOM	United Nations Special Commission (on Iraq)
USSTRATCOM	United States Strategic Command
VMD	video motion detector
WMD	weapons of mass destruction
WPC&A	Weapons Protection, Control, and Accounting
WTO	World Trade Organization

Acknowledgments

This book has been in the works for a number of years, and since it has addressed the nuclear programs in many countries—moving targets, all—it has required numerous updates and revisions. As events change, and the various nuclear programs evolve, not all of the descriptions in this book will remain up to date. I am relieved that throughout all of the revisions and changing events, the basic thesis of this book has remained sound. During the years that this book was underway, however, I have incurred many debts, which I would like to acknowledge now.

This project has spanned several research positions over the years, and I am grateful for the support I have received. Thanks to the Los Alamos National Laboratory, the Belfer Center for Science and International Affairs at Harvard University, and the Center for International Trade and Security at the University of Georgia for providing research positions, financial support, and office space as I was working on this project.

Thanks also to numerous scholars, teachers, and mentors for their wonderful support, advice, and criticism on various drafts of my dissertation and book. These include Samina Ahmed, Gary Bertsch, Jeff Berejikian, Matthew Bunn, George Busch, Peter Busch, Peter Lavoy, and especially Steven Maaranen, Joseph Pilat, and David Welch. I also appreciate the efforts of students and interns at the Center for International Trade and Security and the Department of International Affairs at the University of Georgia, whose efforts in researching and editing were invaluable. These students include Benjamin Bain, Susan Beach, Ethan Beck, Jon Davis, and especially Megan Christ Morgan and Josh Weddle. This book is also much better owing to the efforts of the University Press of Kentucky and its editorial staff, including David Cobb, Gena Henry, Derik Shelor, Robert Swanson, and Steve Wrinn. Thanks also to several reviewers for their insightful comments and criticism. My primary debt, however, is owed my family—my parents, my brother, and my fiancée Elizabeth—for their continual support and encouragement.

Introduction

The Proliferation Debate

One of the highest security priorities of the United States and the international community in the post–Cold War era has been to prevent the proliferation of nuclear weapons to aspiring nuclear states and terrorist groups. The underlying assumption for these efforts is that the proliferation of these weapons of mass destruction is against U.S. and international interests. For example, the second Bush administration has concluded that "Weapons of mass destruction (WMD)—nuclear, biological, and chemical—in the possession of hostile states and terrorists represent one of the greatest security challenges facing the United States. . . . An effective strategy for countering WMD, including their use and proliferation, is an integral component of the National Security Strategy of the United States."[1] In its efforts to prevent the proliferation of nuclear weapons, the United States has encouraged states to sign the 1968 Nuclear Non-Proliferation Treaty (NPT), by which states not already possessing nuclear weapons pledge not to develop nuclear weapons, and current, officially recognized, nuclear weapons states (NWSs)[2] pledge not to assist non–nuclear weapons states (NNWSs) in the development of nuclear weapons. The United States and the international community have also tried to ensure state compliance with NPT requirements, and have attempted to block the development of nuclear weapons programs in so-called rogue states, who seem determined to develop nuclear weapons programs in spite of these efforts.

But this position against the spread of nuclear weapons presupposes an answer to a more fundamental question, one which is hotly contested among academics and scholars of international relations: What are the likely hazards associated with nuclear weapons proliferation? The answer to this question is by no means clear, and the current academic literature differs widely on it. Scholars are divided into roughly two schools: proliferation "optimists," who believe that proliferation can be beneficial and that its associated hazards are not that significant (or are at least surmountable), and proliferation "pessimists," who believe the opposite. The specific hazards in question are largely not contested. As far as I know, for example, no one contests the sheer destructive force of nuclear weapons.[3] What the optimists and pessimists disagree about is the *likelihood* of the use of these weapons, and the *scale* of their use, either intentionally or accidentally, by either a state or non-state group.

The subject of nuclear proliferation has become one of the most pressing ones in international security and U.S. foreign policy in recent years. The issues in the debate were driven home by a series of crises in South Asia, the Middle East, and East Asia during 2002 and 2003. In South Asia, India and Pakistan—both overt nuclear powers since 1998—teetered on the edge of a major war, which could have brought serious risks of escalating into a nuclear war. In Iraq, the United States and Great Britain led a war to disarm the country and replace the Ba'ath regime headed by Saddam Hussein. And, at the same time, serious crises were brewing over North Korea's and Iran's nuclear programs, following Pyongyang's admission in October 2002 that it was pursuing a covert program to enrich uranium and revelations of new and advanced nuclear facilities in Iran in late 2002. These events caused Director of U.S. Central Intelligence George Tenet to predict that the next "domino theory" might be nuclear, citing direct proliferation concerns in Iraq, North Korea, Iran, Libya, and possibly others.[4]

The events of 2002–2003 have forced policymakers, scholars, and populations throughout the world to confront—consciously or unconsciously—the issues in the proliferation debate head on. We have been forced to consider anew the consequences of nuclear proliferation and the justifications (if any) of preventive or preemptive strikes. These questions, of course, were highlighted most vividly in the worldwide, public debates over the legitimacy or necessity for a U.S.-led invasion of Iraq. Although a multitude of arguments were raised for and against military action, some of the most serious focused on the effectiveness of "deterrence" and "containment," which are central themes in the proliferation debate.[5] These issues are very much at the center of questions about how to view, and ultimately address, proliferation in North Korea and Iran as well. Now, as much as at any time since the first detonation of nuclear weapons in 1945, we need to address critically the arguments in the proliferation debate and come to a greater understanding of these issues.

This book helps test the basic theories and assumptions of the optimists and pessimists by examining whether current NWSs have adequate controls over their nuclear arsenals and fissile material stockpiles (highly-enriched uranium [HEU] and plutonium), and by exploring possible reasons why states do or do not implement these controls. It consists of a series of systematic analyses of the nuclear programs in the United States, Russia, China, India, and Pakistan, as well as preliminary studies of the burgeoning programs in Iraq (prior to the U.S.-led invasion in 2003), North Korea, and Iran. These case studies identify the strengths and weaknesses of various systems of nuclear controls in use by current NWSs, and assess what types of nuclear controls the countries with emerging nuclear arsenals are likely to employ. Each case study examines two major topics. The first is "command, control, communications, and intelligence" (C^3I), that is, the technologies and procedures designed to prevent accidental, unauthorized, or inadvertent use.[6] The second major topic is fissile material protection, control, and accounting (MPC&A), which helps prevent proliferating countries and terrorist groups from obtaining fissile materials (for use in nuclear and radiological devices)[7] and helps prevent the sabotage of nuclear facilities.

Part I of this chapter briefly outlines the theoretical disagreement between the optimists and pessimists and explains how the present study fits into their debate. Part II presents the specific research agenda for the current study.

Part I: Critical Issues in the Proliferation Debate

The strategic consequences of nuclear proliferation have been debated almost since the first nuclear weapons were dropped on Hiroshima and Nagasaki.[8] Indeed, only six weeks after the nuclear bombing of Japan, Jacob Vinier argued that it might be desirable for numerous countries to have nuclear weapons.[9] Subsequent scholars made similar arguments in the 1960s and 1970s. Most notably, such scholars as F.H. Hinsley, Richard Rosecrance, and the French theorist Pierre Gallois argued extensively that nuclear proliferation could increase international peace and stability.[10]

The central issue in these, and indeed all, optimist arguments is the notion of deterrence. Deterrence literally means preventing people from doing something by frightening them, particularly through threats of severe consequences.[11] Nuclear weapons, optimists argue, provide one of the very best forms of deterrence, since the potential costs of attacking a nuclear weapons state are extremely high. Due to the deterrent effects that nuclear weapons necessarily bring, optimists conclude that nuclear proliferation can be beneficial because it decreases the likelihood of war.

A number of scholars and policymakers in the 1960s and 1970s disagreed with these arguments, however, initiating what is known as the "nth country" debate. This debate addressed the possibilities of a regional or even a general nuclear war being sparked by an additional, unnamed (or "nth") state that acquired nuclear weapons. Some of these early pessimists argued that because new nuclear powers would not necessarily come in mutually deterring pairs, their relationships would not necessarily be as stable as the U.S.-Soviet relationship. Moreover, after several studies in the late 1950s and 1960s determined that many states, possibly including third-world states, had the technical capability to design and produce a nuclear weapon, some pessimists argued that risks of accidental nuclear war could increase because new nuclear powers might lack the ability to ensure controls over their weapons.[12]

The respective positions of the optimists and pessimists have been laid out most clearly and systematically, however, in the debate between Kenneth Waltz and Scott Sagan. In his 1981 Adelphi Paper, *The Spread of Nuclear Weapons: More May Be Better,* Waltz follows earlier optimists by arguing that rational deterrence theory has demonstrated that nuclear weapons can increase stability among states.[13] Waltz begins his analysis by arguing that states exist in an "anarchic self-help system," wherein they must rely solely upon themselves to maintain their security. Given this system, the best way that a state can prevent an aggressor from attacking is through credible deterrence. Nuclear weapons, Waltz argues, provide exactly such a deterrent.[14] Due to the deterrent effects of nuclear weapons, Waltz argues, states will be extremely cautious and will tend to avoid war. When countries have nuclear weapons (and the capability to retaliate against a nuclear attack), there is no longer any question about whether one can "win" a war: a state is ensured of incurring massive casualties. Moreover, because states act with greater care when potential costs are so high, there will be less risk of blundering into war. In fact, Waltz argues that even the *possibility* of a nuclear retaliation would be sufficient to deter any attack (both conventional and nuclear) by an otherwise aggressive state.[15] As Waltz asks rhetorically, "why fight if you can't win much and might lose everything?"[16] After Waltz published *More May Be Better,* several other scholars, including Bruce Bueno de Mesquita and William Riker, Martin van Creveld, and John Mearsheimer, made similar optimistic predictions about the prospects of a spread of nuclear weapons.[17]

The implicit assumption of Waltz's and other optimists' arguments is that states are unitary, rational actors that consistently act so as to maximize their self-interest.[18] As Waltz confidently argues, "We do not have to wonder whether they [NWSs] will take good care of their weapons. They have every incentive to do so."[19] The premise of this argument is that states always recognize what is in their interest when the stakes are as high as nuclear war, and that their actions will reflect these interests. This is precisely the premise that a new wave of pessimist literature challenged in the late 1980s and 1990s. On the basis of studies they had conducted on the nuclear operations of the United States and the Soviet Union, these pessimists concluded that the arguments of Waltz and other optimists did not square with what was known about the actions of the superpowers.[20] One of the most prominent of these new pessimists—or "neopessimists," as they were sometimes called—was Scott Sagan.[21]

In a well-known article, "The Perils of Proliferation," and later in a 1995 book in which he debated Waltz, Sagan presents "organization theory," which explicitly "challenges the central assumption that states are unitary actors behaving in a self-interested way."[22] According to Sagan, states often encounter severe organizational and bureaucratic obstacles that prevent them from acting in coherent, rational ways. Sagan argues that large organizations such as states function within a "severely 'bounded' form of rationality," employing simplifying mechanisms and routines, such as "standard operating procedures" (SOPs), rigid organizational rules, and "satisficing"—choosing the first option that is minimally satisfying rather than the one that maximizes their utility—rather than strict calculations of the optimal actions in individual circumstances. These constraints on rationality can have serious consequences. For instance, Sagan argues that states will not always create arsenals that can survive a nuclear strike, which undermines deterrence by giving aggressors an incentive to strike first,[23] and that both large organizations and poor countries will necessarily encounter severe obstacles in the command and control of their arsenals.[24] Moreover, Sagan maintains, organizations are made up of highly competitive and self-interested bureaucracies and other subunits that can undermine otherwise "rational" action of the state.[25] Thus, Sagan argues that certain groups, such as the military, might be more likely to use nuclear weapons than civilians,[26] and that parochial interests within certain bureaucracies can preclude systematic implementation of controls and safety measures for their weapons systems.[27]

Subsequent contributions to the debate have largely followed the theoretical frameworks presented by Sagan's and Waltz's characterizations, though the emphasis of later scholarship has focused more directly on potential difficulties that emerging nuclear states such as India and Pakistan, and newly proliferating countries such as Iraq, Iran, and North Korea might encounter.[28] For example, David Karl and Jordan Seng argue that the experiences of emerging or minor nuclear weapons states will be fundamentally different from the experiences of the superpowers during the Cold War. Both scholars argue that greater economic and technical constraints in emerging nuclear states will force them to rely on much smaller nuclear arsenals than those possessed by the superpowers, which would allow them to avoid many of the command-and-control problems predicted by the pessimists.[29] In response, pessimists such as Sagan and Peter Feaver argue that these very economic and technical constraints will weaken command and control in emerging

NWSs. Thus, they argue, one has continuing reason to be pessimistic about the prospects of a spread of nuclear weapons.[30]

Now that we have briefly examined the basic positions of the optimists and pessimists, we need to consider how the present study will illuminate key issues in the debate. In this section, I demonstrate how both C³I and MPC&A are, or should be, central issues in the proliferation debate.

Why Are C³I and MPC&A Important to This Debate?

C³I and Risks of Accidental, Unauthorized, and Inadvertent Use

As Peter Stein and Peter Feaver explain, command and control over nuclear weapons can be characterized as an "always/never" problem: "Nuclear weapons must always detonate when those authorized direct and never detonate when those authorized do not."[31] The "always" side of command and control is achieved by building survivable forces, reliable weapons, and strong communication links. The "never" side is achieved by overcoming two separate threats to the system: *accidental* use and *unauthorized* use. The use of a nuclear weapon would be considered accidental if "everyone is surprised" by its use.[32] Unauthorized use, on the other hand, "refers to the deliberate use by people who have access to the weapon, but who lack authority legitimately to order its use."[33] For example, if a state lacked adequate controls over its nuclear weapons, a crazed soldier or fanatic general could independently decide to use the state's nuclear weapons, even though its central authorities had not ordered their use. Or, alternatively, a terrorist group could steal a nuclear weapon and use the weapon on its own.

Both accidental and unauthorized use must be distinguished from an "inadvertent" use of a nuclear weapon, where the use is intentional and ordered by the people who have legitimate authority to order its use, but the order is based on misinformation. According to the Rumsfeld Commission to Assess the Ballistic Missile Threat, inadvertent use is defined as "one resulting from a mistaken assessment of sensor data, including from ballistic missile early-warning systems, or a misinterpretation of the strategic situation or some combination of the two, especially in times of crisis generated either by domestic or international events."[34] For example, if a state's early-warning system failed, it could launch a nuclear strike against an enemy because it mistakenly thought that the enemy had attacked first.

The various technologies and procedures intended to prevent accidental, unauthorized, and inadvertent use are generally categorized as C³I. It is fairly easy to see why adequate C^3I is necessary for stable deterrence. If a state were accidentally to launch a nuclear weapon against another state, or, for example, a crazed general were to do so, the state runs a high risk of retaliation.[35] The state would run similar risks of retaliation if it launched its weapons as a result of a false alarm or a similar intelligence failure. Any of these events would obviously undermine the very intention of nuclear deterrence, which is to prevent a nuclear attack. In addition, if a state becomes aware that an enemy's arsenal is not secure against accidental or unauthorized use, deterrence can be less effective. A deterrent threat says "if you attack, you will be severely punished."[36] But if a given state's arsenal is not secure, it threatens to harm or destroy other states even if the other states are not contemplating an attack. Another state might have a strong incentive to preempt a strike that could otherwise come at any time.[37]

As we will see, both optimists and pessimists agree that states have a very strong interest in preventing accidental, unauthorized, and inadvertent use, but they disagree over whether or not emerging NWSs will be able to prevent these events from occurring.[38]

Accidental Use

Pessimists argue that nuclear weapons in proliferating states will be susceptible to accidental use because the weapon designs will tend to be relatively crude and the weapons will not have undergone the proper testing to ensure that they are secure.[39] In addition, they argue, it is less likely that these states will have sufficient resources to implement the procedures and technologies necessary for preventing accidental use. The states will therefore be forced to make compromises—cutting corners in critical technologies, or even simply considering safety issues to be less important than the initial development of nuclear arsenals. Safety and control measures will therefore be marginalized, or even largely ignored, as states focus on other priorities.[40]

Optimists such as David Karl argue that emerging NWSs can overcome many of these obstacles by storing their nuclear weapons in a disassembled state.[41] For example, the risks of accidental use can be greatly reduced if the nuclear components in the weapons are stored away from the non-nuclear ones, or if warheads are stored apart from their delivery vehicles. But pessimists respond to such arguments by contending that, first, short flight times for ballistic missiles and concerns about the survivability of nuclear forces will probably cause emerging NWSs to maintain their weapons in an assembled, ready-response mode, just as the United States and Russia do.[42] And second, even if unassembled nuclear weapons are safer during normal, peacetime circumstances, the chances of accidental use could increase dramatically if the state were forced to assemble its weapons rapidly during a crisis.[43]

Unauthorized Use

Both sides of the debate agree that NWSs must have adequate controls to prevent unauthorized use. As we have seen, optimists are confident that NWSs will implement adequate controls against the unauthorized use of their nuclear weapons because it is so clearly in their interest to do so.[44] Moreover, optimists argue that it will be relatively easy for emerging NWSs to ensure proper security for their weapons because their arsenals will be small and their operational systems simple. Because they will have fewer nuclear weapons to control, emerging NWSs will be able to protect their weapons much more effectively, even without the sophisticated command-and-control systems employed by the United States and the Soviet Union.[45] Pessimists argue that use-control devices are still necessary for preventing terrorist seizure of nuclear weapons and unauthorized launches. These problems will remain even if there are fewer weapons to control.[46] In addition, pessimists argue, even though financial constraints will make arsenals smaller, the arsenals will tend to be "untested, unproven, and probably unsafe."[47] And finally, pessimists argue, even though emerging NWSs will initially have smaller arsenals, there is no guarantee that they will remain satisfied with the "minimal deterrence" that small arsenals provide.[48] If the emerging NWSs decide to build up their arsenals, they could then encounter the organizational problems that pessimists have associated with large arsenals.[49]

Inadvertent Use

Optimists and pessimists also agree NWSs must avoid weapon deployments that could lead to inadvertent launches. These include deployments that require rapid response or policies that call for launch-on-warning (LOW), which requires a state to fire its nuclear weapons after an attack is detected but before the incoming nuclear weapons have reached their targets. For example, Kenneth Waltz argues that "survival of forces must not require early firing in response to what may be false alarms."[50] Thus, Waltz acknowledges that if NWSs do in fact tend to develop rapid-response capabilities and policies of LOW, then the risks of inadvertent use would be quite high, since these doctrines greatly reduce the time that leaders have to decide whether to launch their nuclear weapons. But optimists argue that emerging NWSs will *not* develop these capabilities and use-doctrines because they will be able to ensure survivability by dispersing and concealing their nuclear weapons.[51] Instead, optimists argue, emerging NWSs will adopt force doctrines that call for "riding out" a first strike, then engaging in a delayed retaliation.

As a number of pessimists have pointed out, however, a doctrine of ride out and delayed retaliation increases a state's vulnerability to decapitation (where those authorized to order a retaliation are killed or the communication networks necessary for disseminating a launch command are severely disrupted or destroyed) and to counterforce strikes (where large numbers of the state's nuclear forces are destroyed), both of which significantly reduce the state's retaliatory capability. Pessimists have therefore argued that emerging NWSs will not be satisfied with such doctrines, and will instead develop rapid-response capabilities and even adopt policies that allow for LOW.

Fissile Material Protection, Control, and Accounting (MPC&A)

As previously stated, MPC&A is critical both for stopping the proliferation of nuclear weapons to aspiring nuclear states and for preventing nuclear terrorism. I will discuss each in turn.

MPC&A Helps Prevent a Rapid Spread of Nuclear Weapons to Aspiring Nuclear Powers

If states have inadequate MPC&A, then aspiring nuclear states might be able to obtain smuggled or stolen fissile materials, greatly reducing the time it would take to produce nuclear weapons. Even most optimists in fact agree that the spread of nuclear weapons to aspiring states must be both gradual and carefully managed for it to have any stabilizing effects. John Mearsheimer, for example, thinks that some proliferation of nuclear weapons can be beneficial, but that the effects of proliferation "depend upon how it is managed. Mismanaged proliferation could produce disaster, while well-managed proliferation could produce an order nearly as stable as the [Cold War] order."[52] Proponents of such qualified optimist positions give various reasons for their support of only "well-managed" proliferation, citing the problems associated with proliferation in poor states, the inherent instability in the transition to nuclear weapons, and the increased chances of preemptive strikes. Even Waltz argues that "the gradual spread of nuclear weapons is better than either no spread or rapid spread."[53] But unless states have tight and reliable controls over their fissile materials, then proliferating states might be able to obtain stolen materials, greatly reducing the technical obstacles and decreasing the time required for producing nuclear weapons.[54] Thus, if NWSs do not have MPC&A systems to prevent fissile material thefts, the subsequent spread of nuclear weapons could be rapid, and therefore extremely destabilizing.

Moreover, a rapid development of nuclear arsenals could also increase the risks of accidental and unauthorized use, because the emerging NWSs would not necessarily have had time to establish the infrastructures and controls necessary for safe maintenance of their nuclear arsenals. Indeed, Waltz is confident that emerging NWSs will "have time to learn how to care for" their arsenals, because they "can build sizable forces only over long periods of time."[55] But if newly proliferating states have access to sufficient quantities of smuggled or stolen fissile materials, the time it would take to produce a sizable force could be greatly reduced. If NWSs have inadequate MPC&A, then Waltz's argument is much weaker: emerging NWSs would not necessarily have the time to learn about how to ensure the safe care of their nuclear weapons. Thus, the optimists' own arguments imply that adequate MPC&A must be implemented by established and aspiring nuclear weapons states.

MPC&A Helps Prevent Nuclear Terrorism

While the issue of nuclear terrorism has been discussed extensively in government circles for a number of years, it has only been marginally treated in the context of the proliferation debate. As some optimists have noted, however, the chance that a terrorist group could seize nuclear weapons could increase if additional countries developed nuclear weapons, because the number of possible access points would increase.[56] In fact, this is one of the main reasons why John Mearsheimer thinks that proliferation should not be encouraged in poor countries, which might not be able to maintain rigorous controls over their nuclear weapons.[57]

The possibility of a terrorist group obtaining nuclear weapons should be especially troubling to optimists precisely because their arguments are based on deterrence theory. Deterrence can only work if one has an easily identifiable, immobile target, such as a state, against which one can retaliate. Since one cannot necessarily retaliate against terrorist groups in this way, nuclear deterrence may be largely ineffective against them.[58] Because terrorists may not easily be deterrable, it is in the interest of all states to have excellent MPC&A systems in place to ensure that fissile materials cannot be stolen from their nuclear facilities.[59]

The risks of nuclear terrorism have not been taken very seriously by many optimists, in part due to Waltz's arguments that it is unlikely that terrorists would even *want* to develop nuclear capabilities.[60] Waltz's first argument is that the decision to "go nuclear" would require too great an expansion of the terrorist group, which runs counter to the secrecy that terrorists require: "Terrorists work in small groups. Secrecy is safety, yet to obtain and maintain nuclear weapons would require enlarging the terrorist band through multiplication of suppliers, transporters, technicians, and guardians. Inspiring devotion, instilling discipline, and ensuring secrecy become harder tasks to accomplish as numbers grow."[61] In addition, Waltz argues that nuclear weapons do not fit into most terrorist agendas, which are met through "patient pressure and constant harassment. They cannot hope to [reach their long-term goals] by issuing unsustainable threats to wreak great destruction, threats they would not want to execute anyway."[62]

Although Waltz's arguments may have been convincing in the past, it is now clear that the goals of some terrorist groups have changed. The main reason for this change in terrorist goals results from a rise in religious, or "holy," terror, which tends to view such violence "not only as morally justified, but as a necessary expedient for the attainment of their goals."[63] In his latest formulation of his arguments on terrorism, written in 2003, Waltz acknowledges that some terrorists, such as some Islamic groups and "millenarian" groups, do in fact want to cause widespread death and destruction, but he argues that these groups would be likely to choose other, more easily obtainable instruments for carrying out these attacks. For instance, he argues that they could continue to use conventional weapons, or might choose to use chemical or biological weapons instead.[64]

While Waltz's latest arguments on nuclear terrorism are more nuanced than his previous ones, they are still inadequate, since they does not acknowledge that several terrorist groups, in fact, are known to have attempted to acquire nuclear weapons. One such group is the Japanese millenarian cult Aum Shinrikyo. In efforts to bring about their views of the apocalypse, this group is believed to have attempted to purchase nuclear weapons and fissile materials from Russian scientists.[65]

But the more well-known group to have an active interest in nuclear weapons is the Islamic terrorist group al Qaeda. As the U.S. Central Intelligence Agency reported in April 2003, "We also know that al-Qa'ida has ambitions to acquire or develop nuclear weapons and has been receptive to any outside nuclear assistance that might become available."[66] Indeed, Osama Bin Laden has declared obtaining nuclear weapons to be a religious duty and has reportedly attempted to obtain stolen fissile materials on several occasions.[67] Documents seized in al Qaeda hideouts in Afghanistan also reportedly contained crude designs for nuclear weapons and blueprints of U.S. nuclear plants.[68] The September 11, 2001, terrorist attacks on the World Trade Center and the Pentagon clearly demonstrate that Bin Laden and al Qaeda would have few qualms about using such weapons if they were able to acquire them.

While al Qaeda's activities may have been disrupted by U.S. military actions in Afghanistan and elsewhere, it may take years to eradicate al Qaeda's presence. Al Qaeda is believed to have infiltrated nearly sixty countries and has been linked with terror plots in such diverse locations as Egypt, France, Germany, Italy, Singapore, and the Philippines. Furthermore, al Qaeda appears to be much better organized and funded than previously believed, with an established chain of command and numerous sources of funding other than Bin Laden.[69] Therefore, even if Bin Laden is captured or killed, it is possible that al Qaeda could continue to function without him.

Moreover, there are other groups besides al Qaeda that may be interested in nuclear terrorism. According to George Tenet, U.S. Director of Central Intelligence, "Bin Laden's organization is just one of about a dozen terrorist groups that have expressed an interest in or have sought chemical, biological, radiological, and nuclear agents."[70]

Fortunately, building a nuclear weapon from fissile materials is currently beyond the capabilities of most, if not all, terrorist groups.[71] While many scholars have argued that it is relatively easy to make a fission bomb once one has fissile materials,[72] this is probably not the case. One need only look at the difficulties that Iraq had in producing a nuclear weapon—even after devoting extensive money and manpower to the task—to see that producing these weapons is not as easy as many claim.[73] Given the significant hurdles to producing a nuclear weapon, most terrorists interested in WMD would probably attempt to develop chemical or biological weapons instead. Nevertheless, it would clearly be foolish to make the job easier for any terrorists who do wish to develop nuclear weapons by allowing them access to fissile materials. Because we cannot rule out the possibility that terrorist groups might resort to nuclear terrorism, NWSs have an additional incentive to implement adequate measures to prevent thefts of fissile materials.

In addition, there are a number of types of nuclear terrorism other than making or stealing a nuclear weapon. The following terrorist acts should all be classified as nuclear terrorism:

1. Making or stealing a nuclear or radiological weapon for detonation.
2. Making or stealing a nuclear or radiological weapon for blackmail.
3. Sabotaging a nuclear plant for radioactive release.
4. Attacking a nuclear weapons site to spread alarm.
5. Attacking a nuclear plant to spread alarm.
6. Holding a nuclear plant for blackmail.
7. Stealing or sabotaging "things nuclear" for demonstration purposes.
8. Attacking a transporter of nuclear weapons or materials.[74]

Although most of the terrorist activities listed above are relatively clear, a few require further explanation. A radiological device, or "dirty bomb," is a bomb in which radioactive materials are attached to conventional explosives. The explosion of a radiological device could spread radioactive contamination over a relatively large area.[75] Radiological devices may be more properly characterized as weapons of "mass disruption" than mass destruction. The detonation of such a device may not kill a large number of people beyond the effects of the explosive blast itself, but it could cause serious environmental damage, render large areas unusable because of the contamination, and cause public hysteria.[76] Although many commercially available medical or industrial products might be more attractive sources for radioactive material (because they are abundant, often contain highly radioactive material, and are often poorly guarded), any radioactive material—including HEU, plutonium, or the spent fuel from reactors—could be used in a radiological device. If plutonium were used in a well-designed radiological device, the resulting explosion could disperse a cloud of plutonium aerosol, which would be deadly if inhaled.[77]

An effective sabotage of a nuclear power or production reactor could create Chernobyl-like effects, dispersing radiation across large areas.[78] A knowledgeable attacker could damage the reactor cooling system, possibly causing a melting of the reactor core and a steam explosion. The result could be the destruction of the reactor and a release of radioactive materials.[79]

By implementing rigorous MPC&A technologies and procedures at their nuclear facilities, a NWS will help prevent all of the above types of nuclear terrorism. An effective MPC&A system would greatly reduce the likelihood of successful thefts of materials by workers at a nuclear facility, making it much more difficult for terrorists to obtain fissile materials for use in nuclear or radiological weapons. And insofar as the MPC&A system includes an effective physical protection system, it would deter or defeat direct terrorist attacks on nuclear facilities, thereby preventing overt thefts of nuclear materials as well as the capture or sabotage of nuclear facilities.

Part II: Research Agenda

The debate between the optimists and the pessimists focuses largely on whether or not states will implement adequate nuclear controls. Both sides should, and to a certain degree do, agree that it is in states' *interests* to ensure that they have adequate C^3I systems for their nuclear arsenals and adequate MPC&A for their fissile materials. The main point of disagreement between optimists and pessimists is over whether states actually *will* have such rigorous nuclear controls. The debate has too often relied, however, on a competing set of deductions, derived from different theoretical explanations about how states act.[80] Almost every scholar who has contributed to this debate has called for more empirical research to assess whose claims and predictions are correct.[81] The specific value added by this study, therefore, is to provide a more comprehensive, empirical examination of which position has the more realistic understanding of the incentives, capacities, constraints, trade-offs, and subsequent risks that can arise from various nuclear systems and controls.

Toward a "Performance-Based" Approach

How does one determine whether a certain safety or security system is adequate? The best way—and perhaps the only way—to approach this problem is not by asserting that one system is the only acceptable one; instead, we can identify certain objectives that a system must achieve, and examine whether, or to what degree, certain types of systems employed by the NWSs can achieve these objectives. This is generally known as a "performance-based" approach. In each of the major parts of each case study, C^{3}I and MPC&A, the objectives are relatively clear. In the following sections, I will discuss what these objectives are for C^{3}I and MPC&A and the ways in which a performance-based approach can be used to assess whether the various nuclear systems meet these objectives.

"Performance-Based" Approaches and C^{3}I

Although there are no internationally accepted standards for what would constitute adequate C^{3}I, it is still possible to assess the performance of these systems in meeting certain critical objectives that are necessary for stable deterrence. As noted above, both sides of the debate generally agree upon what these objectives are. As Kenneth Waltz has argued, and as the pessimists generally agree, these objectives are: (1) NWSs must develop survivable forces; (2) they must establish reliable command-and-control systems to prevent accidental and unauthorized use; and (3) survival of forces must not require early firing in response to what may be false alarms.[82] The next step is to determine to what degree the various systems in NWSs appear to meet these objectives.

It is necessary to point out, however, that there are significant tensions among these objectives. There is therefore no reason why there *necessarily* is a position that would support the optimists. This is the full implication of the "always/never" dilemma, which states that NWSs are under dual pressures: to ensure that they *always* will be able to use their weapons when they need to, and to ensure that they will *never* be used when they don't want them to be used. On the one hand, states are under pressures to make their forces survivable by dispersing their forces, creating complex command-and-control arrangements, weaponizing and storing their weapons in launch-ready conditions, and adopting policies that allow for LOW. But these procedures and techniques significantly increase the difficulties in ensuring the "never" side: guaranteeing that weapons are not susceptible to accidental, unauthorized, or inadvertent use.

While in *theory* it might not be possible to meet these objectives completely, it might be possible in *practice* to develop systems that more or less satisfy them. So, again, it is necessary to examine the specific systems developed by the NWS to determine how, or whether, they meet these performance-based objectives: ensuring that their arsenals are not vulnerable to accidental, unauthorized, or inadvertent use. In the following sections, we will discuss some of the means by which NWSs can meet these objectives.

Accidental Use

There are two types of accidental use: accidental detonation and accidental launch. An accidental detonation would result from some mishap, such as a plane crash or fire, which causes the warhead to explode, scattering radioactive material or even causing a significant nuclear yield. An accidental launch could result from a technical defect (such as faulty wiring) or unsafe procedures that caused the premature firing of a nuclear-armed missile or release of a nuclear gravity bomb from an aircraft.[83]

Accidental Detonation

There are several possible ways for a state to avoid accidental detonations of its nuclear weapons. The first, and possibly the easiest, way would be for a state to store the nuclear components of the weapons separate from high explosive non-nuclear components during storage and transportation. As we have seen, Karl argues that this is the technique that emerging NWSs will probably use. This approach would reduce many—but not necessarily all—risks of accidental detonation. As pessimists have pointed out, since the weapons would have to be assembled rapidly prior to use, the state might bypass safety procedures in its haste, increasing risks of accidents. The NWSs would therefore need to train its soldiers to assemble weapons rapidly and safely to help avoid some of these risks.

If, on the other hand, a given NWS decides to store its weapons preassembled, there are a number of technological means to help avoid risks of accidental detonation. For example, warheads can be designed to allow for "One-point safety," in which the detonation of the weapon's high explosive at any single point has a very small probability of producing a significant nuclear yield.[84] In addition, the nuclear weapons could be designed to include environmental sensing devices (ESDs), which only allow a weapon to detonate if certain environmental conditions are met, such as certain accelerations, changes in barometric pressures, etc. ESDs would keep a missile from exploding if it accidentally fell off a truck or if a plane carrying nuclear weapons crashed. The nuclear weapons could also be designed to include insensitive high explosive (IHE) to help avoid accidental detonations of the conventional explosive. Depending on the design of the warhead, an accidental detonation of the high explosive could either cause a significant nuclear yield or cause the plutonium to disperse in a deadly aerosol.[85] Use of IHE would reduce this risk. Finally, the nuclear weapon could be designed to include fire-resistant pits (FRP). In an FRP, the plutonium is encased in a metal shell with a high melting point, which is designed to withstand exposure to fires.[86]

Accidental Launch

Again, there are a number of ways to help ensure that accidental launches do not occur. One "low-tech" way to help prevent accidental launches would be to maintain the weapons systems at low states of alert during normal, peacetime circumstances. For example, a state could keep its warheads unmated to the delivery vehicles.[87] If nuclear warheads are not mated to missiles, and gravity bombs are not loaded onto airplanes during peacetime, the risk of accidental launch would be greatly reduced. Again, however, the risks could increase significantly if warheads were mated and the missiles were prepared for launch during crisis situations.

If the warheads are mated to the delivery systems, then the state must employ other means of preventing accidental launches. For example, a state could avoid keeping its missiles continuously targeted against its enemies, or have safety devices such as multiple launch codes to prevent a weapon from being launched by pushing the wrong button. Finally, if an accidental launch were to occur, a state could have integrated into the weapon means of deactivating warheads or aborting the launch.

In order to assess the risk of accidental use, this study will therefore examine the following issues:

- Do NWSs appear satisfied with unassembled weapons, or do they tend to develop assembled weapons, stored in a ready-response mode?
- Are missiles continuously targeted against enemies?
- To what extent do NWSs have integrated safety devices and designs to reduce the risks of accidental detonations and accidental launches?
- Are there means of ensuring that bombers cannot accidentally drop bombs, such as independent locks on their bay doors?
- If the weapons are accidentally released, are there means of deactivating warheads or aborting the launch?

Unauthorized Use

There are a number of ways a state can reduce the vulnerability of its nuclear weapons to unauthorized use, including use-control technologies, administrative procedures, and skilled and reliable employees and guards.[88] This study will therefore assess to what extent NWSs have implemented these command-and-control procedures and technologies.

The first requirement for a command-and-control system would be to establish a clear and reliable chain of command so that any orders from the central authorities are dutifully carried out and there is no possibility for unauthorized personnel to decide to use the weapons on their own. Guards and military officers responsible for handling the weapons must be highly disciplined and should undergo prior screening and personnel reliability testing. They should also be armed to prevent anyone from forcibly seizing the weapons.

NWSs should also have established various procedures for controlling the weapons, such as a "two-person rule," which dictates that every stage in the maintenance, deployment, and use-cycle requires the participation of at least two individuals.[89]

Command-and-control systems that rely heavily on guard forces can work well if procedures such as the two-person rule are strictly followed, and if there is a high level of professionalism in guard forces and military officials handling the weapons, or if there are other means of guaranteeing discipline, such as authoritarian social controls. But command-and-control systems that rely heavily on guard forces can be weakened if the weapons are widely dispersed, or if the state undergoes severe economic, social, and political upheavals. In order to prevent the erosion of central controls under these conditions, the state should therefore have integrated use-control devices on the nuclear weapons, which require a specific code to be entered before the weapons can be launched. Of course, the specific launch codes would also need to be tightly controlled for this method to increase central controls.[90]

This study will therefore assess what measures NWSs have adopted to provide reliable command and control over their nuclear weapons by asking the following types of questions:

- Does each country have a clear, well-established chain of command?
- Are there loyal, armed, well-trained military forces to guard the weapons?
- Do NWSs guarantee high levels of professionalism through rigorous training and personnel monitoring programs?
- Does the country have effective procedures to reduce the risks of unauthorized use, such as a two-person rule whenever anyone must have access to the weapons?
- Is the country politically stable? Do risks of unauthorized use increase during a coup d'etat or other times of political, economic, or social upheaval?
- Are the weapons fitted with reliable use-control mechanisms that require specific codes that must be entered before nuclear-armed missiles can be armed or launched?

Inadvertent Use

As we have seen, both the optimists and pessimists agree that the risks of inadvertent use would be unacceptably high if emerging NWSs adopt policies that require "early firing," such as LOW, because these policies significantly increase risks of panic-launches, false alarms, etc. Based on their respective theories, however, optimists and pessimists disagree over whether emerging NWSs actually will adopt "early firing" policies. Optimists argue that emerging NWSs do not need to adopt such policies because survivability can be maintained through concealment and dispersal of nuclear forces, while pessimists argue that the pressures to build survivable forces will force emerging NWSs to adopt such "early firing" policies. These arguments actually presuppose two questions. First, will dispersal and concealment ensure survivability of both nuclear forces and command structures? This study will attempt to answer this question by examining current assessments of the vulnerabilities of current nuclear forces to nuclear first strikes. And second, regardless of whether or not survivability of nuclear forces and command structures actually *can* be achieved through dispersal and concealment, will NWSs be confident enough in their retaliatory capability to rely on such a policy? This is an empirical question that can be verified by looking at the use doctrines that NWSs are developing or have already adopted. I will therefore attempt to answer this second question by examining the current and emerging capabilities and force doctrines in various NWSs.

But even if NWSs do appear to be moving toward rapid-response capabilities and policies of LOW, it is possible to adopt measures to make inadvertent nuclear war less likely. After all, both the United States and Russia have had policies that allowed for LOW for nearly forty years, and inadvertent nuclear war has not occurred. This was in part due to the presence of reliable early-warning sensors and human intelligence (HUMINT) systems; effective confidence-building measures (CBM), such as hotlines between senior officials on both sides, to reduce risks during crisis situations; and strict policies of restraint, such as avoiding direct military clashes. But it might have also been in part due to luck. This study will examine, first, how successful these measures were during the Cold War.[91] It will then examine whether emerging NWSs appear likely to adopt similar measures to reduce the likelihood of inadvertent nuclear war.

"Performance-Based" Approaches and MPC&A

The objectives that an MPC&A system should achieve are threefold:

1. Prevent the theft of nuclear materials.
2. Prevent the sabotage of a nuclear facility (or a nuclear transport vehicle).
3. Detect the theft of nuclear materials once it has occurred, and, if possible, identify those responsible for the theft.[92]

Finding a standard for MPC&A is generally easier than for C^3I because there is a widely accepted consensus for what procedures and technologies are necessary for achieving these objectives. In particular, the IAEA recommends specific standards for physical protection in INFCIRC/225/Rev.4 and establishes standards for nuclear material control and accounting (MC&A) in INFCIRC/153.[93] These standards are by no means arbitrary; the IAEA has thought very carefully about what would be necessary to achieve these objectives, and the recommendations they put forward reflect consensus among nuclear and arms control experts.[94] (For a more extensive discussion of IAEA-related standards for MPC&A, see the appendix.)

IAEA Standards and Recommendations for MPC&A

MPC&A systems are generally divided into two distinct, though interrelated systems: Physical Protection (PP) and Material Control and Accounting (MC&A). The most straightforward aspect of MPC&A is physical protection. The ultimate purpose of a physical protection system is to prevent the theft of nuclear materials or sabotage of nuclear materials or facilities. These objectives are achieved in two ways: by deterring threats or by defeating them should groups or individuals attempt to steal nuclear materials or sabotage nuclear facilities. This deterrence is achieved by implementing a physical protection system that is *perceived* to be too difficult to overcome. And, of course, if anyone *does* attempt to steal materials or sabotage a facility, the physical protection system must also be able to stop the attempt. An effective physical protection system will use barriers, surveillance systems, alarms, and guards to achieve these goals.[95]

Unlike physical protection systems, which are intended to stop theft or sabotage attempts before they occur, current nuclear material control and accounting (MC&A) systems are used to detect a theft or diversion of nuclear materials once it has occurred. It is only possible to discover whether some materials have disappeared if one knows the exact location and amounts of nuclear materials in a given facility. The material must be effectively "controlled" through technologies and procedures intended to verify easily the precise location and storage condition of nuclear material.[96] In addition, there must be effective "accounting" systems in place to provide "a regularly updated, measured inventory of nuclear weapons usable material, based on routine measurements of material arriving, leaving, lost to waste and remaining within the facility."[97]

IAEA Recommendations and Standards for Designing and Installing MPC&A Systems

A great deal of planning is required to design an effective MPC&A system. The first step in any such system is to determine the types and amounts of nuclear materials stored at given nuclear facilities. The specific MPC&A system will differ at each facility, depending on the "attractiveness" of the materials stored there. The following discussion presents a (very simplified) list of the steps necessary for designing physical protection and MC&A systems and for creating a safeguards culture.

Designing and Installing Physical Protection Systems

The first step in designing a physical protection system is to determine the attractiveness of given fissile materials for theft or diversion. The IAEA has established several different categories for materials stored at nuclear facilities. The specific categories range from Category I (the most attractive) to Category III, depending on the type of material, its physical and chemical form, the degree of dilution, the radiation level, and the quantity of the material present.

(See the appendix, table A.1, for the specific categories for fissile materials established by the IAEA.)

In the next step, the state should identify the specific threats that must be deterred or defeated by the facility's physical protection system. For example, it should determine what domestic and international groups might want to target a given nuclear facility, how well-armed these groups are, and how much time it takes for external armed forces to arrive.

After identifying the potential threats, the state should design and install a physical protection system capable of defeating these threats or delaying the attacking groups until the armed forces can arrive. The IAEA recommends that the physical protection systems for facilities containing Category I materials (substantial amounts of pure plutonium or highly-enriched uranium) be much more robust than for those containing Category III materials (very small amounts of Pu or HEU, or substantial amounts of low-enriched uranium). (See table 1.1 for IAEA recommendations for physical protection of Category I materials.)[98]

Finally, after the state has designed and installed the physical protection system, it should submit the system to thorough performance testing to identify possible weaknesses. These tests should include evaluations of administrative and technical measures, such as detection, assessment, and communications systems, and reviews of the implementation of physical protection procedures. Such evaluations should also include exercises to test the training and readiness of guards and/or response forces. When deficiencies are identified, the state should ensure that facility operators correct the problems.[99]

Designing and Installing MC&A Systems

The state's *material accounting system* must be able to measure materials moving into and out of its nuclear facilities and identify any losses. INFCIRC/153 explicitly outlines necessary requirements for establishing an accounting system at a nuclear facility. The first step in setting up this system is to identify "material balance areas" (MBAs), or key places where the amounts of nuclear material entering and exiting the facility can be measured. The state should then design a system to include the following provisions:

- A measurement system for the determination of the quantities of nuclear material received, produced, shipped, lost, or otherwise removed from inventory, and the quantities on inventory.
- The evaluation of precision and accuracy of measurements and the estimation of measurement uncertainty.
- Procedures for identifying, reviewing, and evaluating differences in shipper/receiver measurements.

Table 1.1. IAEA Recommendations for Physical Protection of Category I Materials During Use and Storage

During use and storage, Category I materials should be contained in at least two complete, distinct, reliable areas, an outer "protected area" and a more secure "inner area." The following are the physical protection recommendations for each of these areas.[a]

Inner area(s):

- All Category I materials should be used or stored within the inner area or inner areas.
- Access to the inner area should be restricted to employees whose duties require access to this area. These employees should carry badges demonstrating authorization.
- There should be a limited number of entrances to the inner area. All emergency exits should be fitted with alarms.
- Fissile materials should be stored in a vault in the inner area. The vault should be protected by alarms and adequate locks, and the issue of keys or key-cards should be closely controlled.
- Whenever persons are present in inner areas, those areas should be under constant surveillance. The surveillance can be effected by mutual observation between two or more coworkers (e.g., a two-person rule).
- Material should be protected by guards at all times. An external and internal patrol should be provided.

Protected area(s):

- The protected area should be under constant surveillance (by a guard or by electronic means). The perimeter of the protected area should normally consist of a physical barrier (a fence, wall, or a similar impediment approved by a security survey) in addition to and outside the walls of the building itself.
- Access to the protected area should be restricted to those whose duties require access to this area.
- Entry of private motor vehicles into the protected area should be minimized and limited to authorized parking areas. Private motor vehicles should be prohibited from access to inner areas.

Note: [a] The requirements outlined in INFCIRC/225 are more extensive than I can describe here. I try to summarize as many of the major points as possible.

- Procedures for taking a physical inventory.
- Procedures for the evaluation of accumulations of unmeasured inventory and unmeasured losses.
- A system of records and reports showing, for each material balance area, the inventory of nuclear material and the changes in that inventory, including receipts into and transfers out of the material balance area.
- Provisions to ensure that the accounting procedures and arrangements are being operated correctly.[100]

The state should also have a *material control system* at each of its facilities to detect the unauthorized movement of fissile materials inside a facility or removal of materials from the facility. IAEA-based material control systems employ portal monitors to detect any materials passing from storage sites and the facility itself, and secure storage containers with tamper-resistant seals and identification codes to detect whether anyone has had access to the materials.[101] These systems also include surveillance cameras and other electronic techniques to monitor and record activities in critical locations and to detect any tampering with measurement equipment or storage containers.[102]

Creating a "Safeguards Culture"

For an MPC&A system to work, it is not enough just to have sensors and alarms installed at nuclear facilities. The country must have an effective "safeguards culture," or a "pervasive, shared belief among political leaders, senior managers, and operating personnel that effective MPC&A is critically important, as manifested in decisions and actions, large and small."[103] This means that every individual must be willing to follow the necessary MPC&A procedures, which are often cumbersome and time-consuming. Managers at nuclear facilities must therefore be willing to sacrifice other important goals (such as meeting production timetables) when necessary in order to ensure that MPC&A is effective.[104] This study will assess whether current NWSs have cultivated safeguards cultures within their nuclear facilities.

Alternative Performance-Based Approaches to MPC&A

The above IAEA standards and recommendations provide very precise measures by which we can judge MPC&A systems in NWSs. But even then, the same arms control experts who put forward these IAEA standards recognize that there are other possible ways to approach the fissile material controls. IAEA standards are heavily weighted toward high-technology means of securing fissile materials. It is possible to develop a system that does not simply rely on these types of controls. For example, there was little concern over possible thefts of fissile materials in the Soviet Union prior to its collapse because it maintained very strict authoritarian controls. As we will see, however, Russia's nuclear controls weakened dramatically after the collapse, in part due to a weakening of the authoritarian controls. Moreover, even if Russia had an MPC&A system like the one recommended by the IAEA, it would still have had serious difficulties controlling its materials after the Soviet collapse. Even a system with the most advanced and carefully designed alarm systems would fail if there were no guards to respond to the alarms.[105]

Moreover, it is possible to design a system that does not require high-technology means of controlling fissile materials. For example, the collaborative U.S.-Russia MPC&A project has developed one system at a Russian facility that places heavy concrete blocks over the openings to fissile material storage areas. Because it requires a large forklift to move these blocks, it would be very difficult to obtain access to these materials without being noticed. But if a state does *not* base its controls on the type of MPC&A system recommended by the IAEA, it is necessary to assess the state's system carefully to determine whether it has instituted other means of ensuring that it can meet the "performance-based" objectives.[106]

In assessing MPC&A systems, we therefore need to ask two questions: first, we must ask whether the state has a system similar to the one recommended by the IAEA, with a corresponding system of guards, gates, and guns to support this system. If *not,* then we need to determine whether the state has an alternate system in place that can adequately meet the performance-based objectives of preventing thefts of fissile materials and sabotage of nuclear facilities. The optimist position would be supported if it were shown that the NWSs generally meet either of these objectives. As I will argue, however, most of the NWSs I examine in this study, with the possible exception of the United States, fall radically short of the IAEA recommendations and regulations, and have done little to find another type of system to meet these objectives other than relying on the "3 G's."

Case Selection

In order to address the research topic outlined above, this book examines the C^3I and MPC&A systems in a number of current and emerging NWSs. It is not exhaustive in its approach, however. Although there are currently five officially recognized NWSs by the NPT (the United States, Russia, China, Great Britain, and France), three de facto nuclear powers (India, Pakistan, and Israel), and several states that have been suspected of pursuing nuclear weapons (including pre-2003 Iraq, North Korea, Iran, Libya, and Syria), this book does not—and cannot—address them all. The individual cases in this book were selected to provide a comprehensive cross section of current and emerging nuclear weapons states. Because this study examines cases that involve countries that vary widely on relevant dimensions, such as wealth, technical capacity, regime type, and political stability, this study will be able to assess what factors affect the ability and willingness of different states to employ various systems of nuclear controls.

Of the recognized NWSs, this book examines the United States, Russia, and China. Each case reveals important information on the types of safety and security mechanisms that have been employed by NWSs. They also reveal some of the serious difficulties involved with maintaining rigorous nuclear safety and security.

The United States is arguably the strongest case for the optimist position. As the state that has had nuclear weapons the longest, the United States has had the longest time to learn how to handle its nuclear weapons. In addition, the United States has the highest level of economic and technical resources for maintaining the safety and security of its nuclear weapons, and the United States has been willing to reveal more information on its nuclear programs than any other of the nuclear states in this study. It is therefore a critical case for identifying the types of difficulties involved with ensuring safety and security for nuclear weapons and materials.

Russia is a critical case for two essential reasons. First, it provides insight into an issue that has not been adequately addressed in the debate, namely what happens when a NWS undergoes economic, political, or social upheavals. In the last decade, severe weaknesses have arisen in Russia's controls over its nuclear arsenal and fissile material stockpile as a direct result of the domestic upheavals that have plagued Russia since the fall of the Soviet Union. These difficulties are due in part to the sheer size of the Soviet arsenal and fissile material stockpile. But they are also partly due to the type of security system that the Soviets adopted, specifically one that relied heavily on personal loyalty of guard forces combined with authoritarian controls. This brings us to the second reason why the Russian case is important: because emerging NWSs will generally face economic and technical constraints, they will tend to develop nuclear control systems that are similar to Russia's, though on a smaller scale. The study of Russia's difficulties will therefore help illustrate the weaknesses in nuclear controls that could arise in emerging NWSs during domestic upheavals and thus help determine what dangers we can expect from the further proliferation of nuclear weapons.[107]

China is another important case for several reasons. First, unlike the

United States and Russia, China has developed a much smaller nuclear arsenal, consisting of roughly 400 nuclear weapons. One might expect it to have fewer difficulties in ensuring safety and security for its nuclear weapons and facilities. On the other hand, China's nuclear security system was based roughly on the Russian model. Its nuclear security systems could potentially encounter similar difficulties during domestic upheavals.

India and Pakistan, in contrast, are important examples of newly proliferating countries. As such, they can help illustrate the nuclear systems and the types of controls that emerging NWSs are likely to adopt. Both optimists and pessimists have made various predictions about what types of systems newly proliferating states will adopt, and India and Pakistan will allow us to test some of these predictions. Moreover, India and Pakistan are critical cases because the two countries have been engaged in intense hostilities prior to and after developing nuclear weapons. They are therefore useful cases for determining the degree to which the spread of nuclear weapons has increased or decreased stability in the region.

The cases of pre-2003 Iraq, Iran, and North Korea are important because, in some ways, they are some of the cases that the entire proliferation debate is about. To the extent that information is available on their nuclear weapons programs, we will be able to apply some of the lessons from the previous cases to these states to determine whether they would be likely to encounter similar—or sometimes unique—risks. The examinations of these countries will have to be speculative at times, since none of them have actually acquired nuclear weapons yet (with the possible exception of North Korea), but we should be able to learn important lessons by examining where they appear (or in the case of Iraq, appeared) to be going.

It is necessary to say a few words about why this study does not examine a few obvious cases, most notably Great Britain, France, and Israel. In addition to space constraints, there are several reasons for this. First, as wealthy, industrialized, capitalist, liberal democracies, Great Britain and France share many key variables with the United States, including similar regime types, economic capabilities, prospects for political stability, etc. In spite of some important differences, they also have similar bureaucratic systems, traditions of responsibility, and technical capabilities. It is not particularly surprising, therefore, that Great Britain and France share many of the same approaches to controlling their nuclear weapons and fissile materials as the United States. Moreover, the United States has shared a great deal of its technologies for ensuring safety, security, and reliability for nuclear weapons with the other two countries.[108] Thus, while these cases would undoubtedly reveal important insights into the debate, they are not examined in the present study. Although Israel's nuclear program would be a fascinating case to examine, the primary reason why it is not discussed here is that the Israeli nuclear effort is so shrouded in secrecy that it is extremely difficult to obtain much reliable information on its nuclear weapons systems.[109]

On the basis of the cases examined in this study, however, we should also be able to identify and examine the ways in which key variables affect state actions, and ultimately affect nuclear safety and security in current and proliferating nuclear weapons states. The following are some of these variables.

What Are the Specific Variables That Can Undermine Nuclear Safety and Security?

To the extent to which available information allows detailed analysis of each of the topics identified in this research agenda, this book will be able to make a significant contribution to the proliferation debate. If it turns out that current NWSs do not have adequate controls over their nuclear arsenals and fissile material stockpiles, we will have some reason to doubt that proliferating states will implement such controls. But because the optimism-pessimism debate is, at its most fundamental level, one over competing theories about how to explain and predict state actions, a simple assessment of whether particular states have implemented adequate controls, while valuable, is not enough to prove that either side is right. I will therefore examine the reasons *why* states did or did not implement rigorous nuclear controls. Because this study examines cases that involve countries that vary widely on relevant dimensions, such as wealth, technical capacity, regime type, and political stability, this study will be able to assess what factors affect the ability and willingness of different states to employ various systems of nuclear controls. It will examine the following issues:

Organizational and Bureaucratic Constraints

As we have seen, optimists claim that states will have adequate nuclear controls because, as unitary, rational actors, they will clearly see it is in their interests to adopt such controls.[110] Pessimists, on the other hand, argue that state action is constrained by organizational difficulties and parochial interests among various bureaucracies. This study will assess the optimists' and pessimists' theories by asking the following questions: If a given state *did* implement rigorous nuclear controls, was it due to a simple rational calculation of its self-interest, as the optimists argue it would be? Was it due to external pressure from the IAEA, the United Nations, or the United States? Did all the state's bureaucracies agree that these controls were necessary, or was there a struggle based on parochial pulling and tugging? If the state did *not* have adequate controls, was this due to bureaucratic parochial interests, "satisficing," or inadequate organizational supervision? Or do other factors determine state decision-making altogether?

Rich vs. Poor Proliferators

In addition, in my sample, I will examine both wealthy, industrialized countries and poor, technologically underdeveloped countries. As we have seen, one of the central issues in the proliferation debate focuses on whether poor countries will have trouble implementing rigorous nuclear controls. I will assess the relative claims of the optimists and pessimists on this issue. The United States is a rich, industrialized country with few financial constraints. It would encounter few, if any, serious financial obstacles that would prevent it from implementing excellent nuclear controls. India and especially Pakistan are good examples of countries with limited resources. Russia and China are somewhat more complicated cases. When Russia was first developing its nuclear weapons (as the U.S.S.R.), it was industrialized and relatively wealthy. Financial constraints should not have affected its implementation of rigorous nuclear controls then. But since its collapse, it has been seriously constrained financially. And while China is desperately poor in many regions, it is relatively industrialized and wealthy in others. In any case, because the current study examines a range of countries in various economic conditions, it will be especially useful for assessing the effects of financial resources in the implementation of nuclear controls.

Political, Economic, and Social Instability

A major objective of the present study is an examination of the effects of domestic upheavals on nuclear controls. Because many of the emerging nuclear states will tend to be less stable than the established NWSs have been, some pessimists have argued that arsenals in emerging NWSs will be particularly susceptible to accidental and unauthorized use, especially during political and social upheavals. Feaver has argued in response to Seng that political instability will tend to undermine the reliability of military personnel (the primary means by which emerging states will control their nuclear forces, since they will have fewer technological controls), and will therefore greatly weaken command and control.[111] This is particularly the case because the weapons in emerging NWSs may tend to have fewer use-control and safety devices than those employed by the superpowers.[112] In response to these arguments, optimists such as Jordan Seng have argued that because emerging

NWSs have fewer nuclear weapons to care for, they will be able to avoid many of the risks of accidental and unauthorized use, even during political crises. In fact, Seng argues that domestic political instability will cause emerging NWSs to employ *stronger* security over their nuclear forces than they otherwise would have, because they will take countermeasures to insulate their nuclear organizations from political fluctuations and ensure the loyalty of the protective forces for their nuclear weapons.[113]

Because a number of the states examined in this study have undergone extreme political, economic, and social upheavals while they possessed nuclear weapons, we should be able to test these predictions. For example, Russia has undergone very severe domestic upheavals in the years following the collapse of the Soviet Union. China has also had a number of severe political upheavals since its first nuclear test in 1964, including the Cultural Revolution and the Tiananmen Square crisis. And Pakistan has experienced an economic collapse in 1998 and a military coup d'etat in 1999. This study will examine whether the specific nuclear controls employed in the NWSs are designed so that they will remain strong during such upheavals.

Opacity

As Avner Cohen and Benjamin Frankel argue, proliferating states can be divided into two categories, visible and opaque. The countries that have proliferated visibly are the five officially recognized nuclear powers (United States, Russia, China, France, and Great Britain), and more recently India and Pakistan (after their 1998 tests). Opaque proliferators are the states that are developing, or already have developed, nuclear weapons capabilities, after the creation of the international non-proliferation regime, embodied above all in the NPT and the International Atomic Energy Agency (IAEA).[114] According to Cohen and Frankel, opaque proliferators are characterized by the following features: no nuclear tests, denial of possession of nuclear weapons, no direct nuclear threats, no nuclear military doctrine, no nuclear military deployment, no open debate about their nuclear weapons programs, and organizational insulation.[115] Opaque proliferators include Israel, India, and Pakistan (prior to their nuclear weapons tests in 1998), and any other states with secret nuclear weapons programs (such as Iran and North Korea still have).[116]

Optimists and pessimists take opposing views on the safety measures that opaque proliferators will take to secure their weapons arsenals. Optimists such as Karl argue that arsenals in opaque states are actually safer than in visible ones, because opaque states often do not assemble their arsenals.[117] Pessimists such as Feaver, however, respond by arguing that opacity decreases both organizational oversight and "nuclear learning" about possible flaws in weapons designs and safety measures.[118]

This study should also shed some light on the debate between the optimists and the pessimists over the nuclear controls implemented by opaque proliferators. Until their nuclear tests in 1998, India and Pakistan were two of the main examples of opaque proliferators. Needless to say, this view of the two countries changed dramatically after their nuclear tests. Nevertheless, India and Pakistan possessed opaque nuclear arsenals for many years, and we can discover a great deal about how opaque proliferators operate by looking at India's and Pakistan's nuclear controls during that time. Indeed, now that they have openly declared their nuclear arsenals, more information about the arsenals has become available than before. In addition, we will now be able to examine a new and extremely important issue in nuclear proliferation: what happens when opaque proliferators become visible proliferators? As the relations between India and Pakistan in the years following their 1998 tests have shown, this transition itself can cause significant regional instability. We are able to learn a great deal about the differences between opaque and visible proliferators by comparing the experiences of India and Pakistan with the three visible proliferators discussed in this study (the United States, Russia, and China).

"Denial and Deception" Techniques Employed by Newly Proliferating States

Because most newly proliferating states will be developing their nuclear programs in the context of nonproliferation and counterproliferation regimes that may oppose proliferation more directly than before, their actions will be directly shaped by these pressures. In particular, due to the serious consequences that could result from revelations about their nuclear weapons programs—such as preventive or preemptive strikes—newly proliferating states will be likely to take greater steps to avoid detection of their WMD programs by U.S. and other states' intelligence systems. These concealment techniques are generally referred to as "denial and deception" (D&D). Although the terms are interrelated, *denial* generally refers to "attempts to block information that could be used by an opponent to learn some truth."[119] It would include active measures such as efforts to conceal WMD through camouflage, electronic emission control, and various forms of physical, personnel, and communications security to conceal the very existence of a clandestine activity.[120] *Deception,* on the other hand, refers to a nation's efforts to cause an adversary to believe something that is not true.[121] Specifically, it uses active or passive measures to convey a false or inaccurate picture of a clandestine activity, such as disguising a biological weapons facility as a vaccine plant.[122]

Although all nuclear states employ some form of D&D, newly proliferating countries will have increased incentives to conceal their programs because they are developing nuclear weapons in the context of strong nonproliferation regimes (established in particular by the NPT). Moreover, the changes in U.S. foreign policy explicitly calling for preventive strikes against WMD proliferators, combined with the U.S.-led invasion of Iraq in 2003, will certainly underscore the necessity of D&D techniques to conceal budding nuclear programs. These techniques can be highly effective in concealing nuclear weapons programs, but they can also create additional difficulties in maintaining strict command-and-control systems and fissile material controls. We will therefore examine whether the D&D techniques employed by newly proliferating countries—particularly Ba'athist Iraq, Iran, and North Korea—create additional difficulties in safety and security.

Policy Implications

Finally, this book will conclude by briefly discussing some possible policy implications for the United States and the international community, based on what we have learned from these case studies. What, in fact, *should* be the United States' and the international community's policies toward proliferation? If this study demonstrates that states do implement adequate nuclear controls, this might suggest that the United States and the international community should relax their stance against proliferation. There is, of course, a difficulty here. It is questionable whether such a reversal of the current stance against proliferation is even possible, given internal pressures from public opinion and external pressures from the nonproliferation regime (which the United States and other major powers helped create). Nor is it likely that the United States would ever have an interest in reversing its opposition to nuclear proliferation. Regardless of whether a spread of nuclear weapons would increase or decrease international stability, such a spread would reduce the United States' ability to project power throughout the world. But a fuller recognition of the effects of nuclear proliferation could cause the United States to modify some aspects of its nonproliferation and counterproliferation policies. While it could still attempt to prevent the spread of nuclear weapons technologies, it might be less likely to undertake preventive military strikes to destroy an emerging NWS's nuclear program (as it did with Iraq in 1998 and 2003). A more complete understanding of the true consequences of nuclear proliferation would therefore be extremely important for shaping future U.S. and other states' foreign policies.

If this study supports the pessimist position, then the United States and other countries should maintain, or possibly strengthen, their opposition to proliferation. Moreover, if this study reveals problems with the nuclear controls in current NWSs, should the United States and others attempt to help them solve some of these problems? If so, what are the obstacles to such efforts?

Both the optimists and the pessimists have made internally consistent arguments for their positions. It is now time to test their theories more fully against the empirical record. Due to the highly sensitive character of this subject, there will necessarily be information gaps in some of the case studies. Nevertheless, I believe there is enough available information to make a definitive pronouncement on the debate. The next chapter will address the strongest case for the optimist position, the United States.

The United States

Why study the United States? As we have seen in chapter 1, optimists such as Kenneth Waltz, John Mearsheimer, and Bruce Bueno de Mesquita and William Riker have pointed to the relative stability that arose between the United States and the Soviet Union during the Cold War as a major source of evidence for their position. They therefore conclude that the U.S. case helps demonstrate that NWSs will control their nuclear weapons safely.[1] But were the specific weapons systems and nuclear controls employed by the United States as safe as the optimists assume? A number of pessimists, such as Bruce Blair, Scott Sagan, and Peter Feaver, have argued that it was not. Furthermore, even if the answer to this first question is "yes," we must also assess whether the U.S. case can help us know whether emerging NWSs would be willing or able to follow the U.S. model. This chapter examines the U.S. weapons systems and nuclear controls in light of these questions to determine whether the U.S. case generally supports the optimist or pessimist position.

The U.S case is also important for several other reasons. First, it is important because the United States has been willing to provide more information on its nuclear systems than other countries. We are therefore allowed better insight into the decision-making process on nuclear issues and into the types of actions that NWSs are likely to take. Second, because the United States has possessed its nuclear weapons the longest, we will be able to understand how—or whether—states engage in "nuclear learning." The longer history will also allow us to look at the difficulties and obstacles that states encounter with their nuclear controls over time. Third, the U.S. case will help us examine why NWSs are motivated to develop certain types of nuclear systems and force deployments. It will therefore help us identify what factors might cause other NWSs to develop certain deployment options and nuclear systems. And finally, the U.S. case study will give us a baseline by which we can judge other NWSs. Unlike several of the cases we will examine, the United States is not significantly constrained by limited resources, authoritarian regimes, or "opaque" nuclear arsenals. It will therefore allow us to isolate some of these variables to determine what factors affect the nuclear controls in NWSs. The United States also provides a baseline because it has arguably devoted more attention to ensuring its nuclear controls than any of the NWSs we will be studying. As such, the United States represents the best case we can reasonably hope for among NWSs. In this study, we will therefore examine the nuclear systems in the United States to determine whether it engaged in risky procedures and whether it had adequate controls over its nuclear forces and fissile materials.

Part I: U.S. Command, Control, Communications, and Intelligence (C^3I)

U.S. Nuclear Arsenal and Delivery Systems

The first nuclear weapons designed by the United States were gravity bombs, delivered by nuclear-capable bombers. The very first nuclear devices were the HEU gun design "Little Boy" and the implosion bomb "Fat Man," which were dropped on Hiroshima and Nagasaki in 1945.[2] After the end of World War II, the United States had components for several additional atomic bombs and several B-29 and B-50 heavy bombers configured to carry them.[3] In 1946, the United States established the Atomic Energy Commission (AEC) to oversee the development of a "war reserve" of nuclear weapons. During the first several years, the stockpile grew very slowly, primarily due to limited fissile materials. In 1946, the stockpile had only nine weapons; in 1947 it had thirteen; and in 1948 it had fifty.[4]

A number of factors influenced the decision to expand the stockpile more rapidly in the late 1940s and early 1950s. First, there was a growth in the supply of fissile materials, combined with several technical breakthroughs that allowed for higher yields with smaller amounts of fissile materials.[5] Second, the United States perceived a greater Soviet threat after the Soviets tested their first nuclear weapon in 1949 and after the outbreak of the Korean War in 1950.[6] As a result, in 1950, President Truman ordered increased production of fission devices and placed the thermonuclear development program on a crash basis.[7] By 1955, the stockpile had grown to 2,250 nuclear weapons and included both strategic and tactical weapons.[8] These weapons were primarily deliverable by aircraft, though nuclear devices were also deployed on atomic artillery projectiles, some short-range missiles, and some atomic demolition units (nuclear land mines).[9]

The peak production years of U.S. nuclear weapons occurred between 1955 and 1967. By 1955, the United States had sufficient fissile material production capability to sustain a rapid development of nuclear weapons. It is estimated that between 1955 and 1967, 30,000 new warheads entered the stockpile, swelling its number to over 32,000.[10] The U.S. arsenal included both fission and thermonuclear weapons,[11] deliverable by bombers, tactical missiles, and new strategic ballistic missiles.[12]

In the mid-1960s, the United States restructured its nuclear forces. Tactical weapons began to dominate the stockpile. Strategic inventories were reduced as intercontinental ballistic missiles (ICBMs) and submarine-launched ballistic missiles (SLBMs) became operational and older bomber forces were phased out.[13] The United States now had a "triad" of capabilities: long-range strategic aircraft, land-based ICBMs, and SLBMs.

The number of U.S. nuclear weapons decreased through the 1970s, primarily due to the retirement of large numbers of bombs, U.S.-based air defense warheads, and some tactical air- and sea-launched missiles.[14] By the early 1980s, the U.S. nuclear arsenal had been reduced to approximately 25,000 warheads of air-, sea-, and land-based weapons systems, and atomic demolition units.[15] At this point, the United States and the Soviet Union began negotiations for arms reduction treaties. The following sections will discuss the series of arms limitation and reduction treaties undertaken by the United States and the Soviet Union (and later Russia) during the 1970s, 1980s, and 1990s.

Nuclear Arms Limitation Treaties, Reduction Treaties, and Presidential Initiatives

Recognizing the extreme dangers and economic costs of the massive arms buildups during the Cold War, the United States and the Soviet Union began negotiations in the early 1970s for limiting strategic nuclear weapons deployments. These negotiations culminated in the Strategic Arms Limitation Talks (SALT I) and the Strategic Arms Limitation Treaty (SALT II). SALT I was a collection of agreements, including a treaty to limit antiballistic missile systems (the ABM Treaty)[16] and an Interim Agreement to limit strategic offensive arms. SALT II, on the other hand, was a treaty that limited the weapons on each side to specific numbers. Although both sides observed SALT II limits, it was never ratified by the U.S. Senate.[17]

Intermediate-Range Nuclear Forces (INF) Treaty

In 1983, U.S. president Ronald Reagan and Soviet premier Leonid Brezhnev began negotiations on a treaty to remove intermediate-range missiles from their forces. These negotiations gained momentum in 1984 after Mikhail Gorbachev came to office, and both sides signed the Intermediate-Range Nuclear Forces (INF) Treaty in 1987. The INF Treaty required complete elimination of all deployed U.S. and Soviet land-based missiles with ranges of 300 to 3,400 miles and banned production, storage, or deployment of such systems thereafter. The treaty also established a system of on-site inspections to verify compliance with INF regulations.[18]

Strategic Arms Reduction Treaty (START I)

Negotiations for the first Strategic Arms Reduction Treaty (START I) began in 1982 and were completed in the early 1990s. Both sides signed the treaty on July 31, 1991, but it did not enter into effect until 1995. START I limits each side to 1,600 strategic delivery vehicles, and a total of 6,000 accountable warheads for those delivery vehicles. In addition, the treaty requires a reduction of deployed heavy ICBMs, namely the Soviet SS-18s, from 308 missiles to 154.[19] On December 5, 2001, both the United States and Russia had met the requirements of the treaty.[20]

1991–1992 Presidential Nuclear Initiatives (PNIs)

On September 27, 1991, President George H.W. Bush announced a series of arms reduction initiatives that were intended to reflect the changing security environment brought about by the end of the Cold War. These initiatives included the withdrawal of U.S. Army nuclear weapons from overseas bases and the elimination of approximately 3,000 nuclear artillery shells and short-range Lance missile warheads.[21] Bush also eliminated numerous naval tactical nuclear missions and ordered the withdrawal of tactical nuclear weapons from surface ships and attack submarines.[22] In response to these initiatives, Russian president Michael Gorbachev announced a similar series of nuclear arms reduction initiatives later in 1991. In 1992, Russian president Boris Yeltsin announced reductions that slightly expanded those of his predecessor.[23]

START II

In 1992 Presidents Bush and Yeltsin began negotiations for a further reduction of strategic nuclear weapons, and both sides signed the START II treaty in January 1993. START II required the reduction of deployed warheads to 3,500 and the removal of all ICBMs with multiple independently targetable reentry vehicles (MIRVs). It also limited the total warheads deployed on submarine-launched ballistic missiles (SLBMs) to 1,750 for each side. START II originally called for the force reductions to be completed no later than

Table 2.1. U.S. Strategic Force Reductions in Accordance with START I &II

	FY1990[a]	FY1999[b]	START I (Dec. 5, 2001)[c]	START II (Dec. 31, 2007)[d]
ICBMs	1,000	550	550	500
Attributed Warheads on ICBMs	2,450	2,000	Not over 2,000	500
SLBMs	568[e]	432[f]	Not over 432	336
Attributed warheads on SLBMs	4,864[e]	3,456[f]	Not over 3,456	Not over 1,750
Ballistic Missile Submarines	31[e]	18[f]	Not over 18	14
Attributed Warheads on Ballistic Missiles	7,314[e]	5,456[f]	Not over 4,900	Not over 2,250
Heavy Bombers	324	115[g]	97[g]	97[g]

Source: Federation of American Scientists, "United States Nuclear Forces."

Notes: [a] These are the numbers of strategic forces outlined in an original Memorandum of Understanding (MOU) between the United States and Russia, which stated the total number of strategic forces in each country's arsenal. [b] These are the numbers to which the strategic forces had been reduced by FY1999. [c] These are the total number of strategic nuclear weapons allowed by START I. Both the United States and Russia had met these limits by December 5, 2001. [d] These are the total number of strategic forces that would have been allowed by START II. This treaty was rendered null and void after the United States withdrew from the ABM Treaty. [e] Excludes five decommissioned submarines (and associated missiles/warheads) that were still START accountable. [f] Excludes two Benjamin Franklin–class SSBNs converted to Special Operations Forces that are still START accountable. [g] Excludes 93 B-1s that are devoted entirely to conventional missions. B-1s are still accountable as a nuclear bomber under START I, but would not have been accountable under START II.

January 1, 2003, but in their March 1997 meeting in Helsinki, Presidents Clinton and Yeltsin agreed to extend the deadline to December 31, 2007. They stipulated, however, that systems that would be eliminated under START II had to be deactivated by December 31, 2003.[24]

Although the U.S. Senate ratified START II in January 1996, the Russian Duma delayed consideration of START II several times in the late 1990s, including delays in January 1998 in protest over the bombing of Iraq by the United States and Great Britain and in 1999 in protest over the NATO bombing of Yugoslavia. The Duma finally ratified START II on May 4, 2000, shortly after the election of Russian president Vladimir Putin.[25] The Duma's ratification was contingent on the United States' not abrogating the ABM Treaty, however. In response to the U.S. withdrawal from the ABM Treaty so that it could create a national missile defense (NMD), the Russian Duma declared on June 14, 2002, that it was no longer bound by START II.[26]

The Strategic Offensive Reductions Treaty, 2002

On November 13, 2001, at the beginning of a three-day U.S.-Russian summit, President George W. Bush pledged to reduce the deployed U.S. strategic nuclear arsenal to between 1,700 and 2,200 warheads over the next ten years. Russian president Vladimir Putin announced that he would try to "respond in kind."[27] Russian officials, however, pushed for these reductions to be codified in a formal treaty to prevent arms buildups in the future. On May 24, 2002, both sides signed the Strategic Offensive Reductions Treaty (SORT), also known as the "Moscow Treaty," which would require the United States and Russia to reduce their deployed strategic nuclear arsenals to between 1,700 and 2,200 warheads each by the end of 2012.[28] This treaty has been criticized, however, since it does not require either side to destroy the warheads that have been removed from alert status. Indeed, the Bush administration reportedly plans to store thousands of the removed warheads in an "inactive" or "hedge" arsenal. The hedge arsenal, which currently includes about 3,000 warheads, could increase to about 4,000 warheads.[29] The U.S. Senate approved the treaty unanimously on March 6, 2003. Although the Russian Duma tabled the treaty in March 2003, citing security concerns over the U.S. invasion of Iraq, it ratified the treaty on May 14, 2003.[30]

Current U.S. Nuclear Forces

As of May 2003, the total U.S. nuclear stockpile consisted of over 10,000 weapons. Of these weapons, approximately 7,650 are operational, while the remaining weapons are retained in the "hedge" stockpile to provide extra warheads for reconstitution of part of the force in case arms control expectations failed to materialize.[31] (See table 2.2 for a list of current U.S. nuclear forces.)

Table 2.2 U.S. Nuclear Forces, 2003

Type	Name	Launchers/ SSBNs	Range (km)	Year Deployed	Warhead x Yield (kiloton)	Warheads Active /spares
ICBMs						
LGM-118A	MX/Peacekeeper[a]	40	9,600+	1986	10 W87 x 300 (MIRV)	400/50
LGM-30G	Minuteman III: Mk-12 Mk-12A	50 300	9,600+	1970 1979	3 w62 X 170 (MIRV) 3 w78 X 335 (MIRV	150/15 900/20
	Minuteman III Mk-12	150	9,600+		1 W62 x 170	150
Total		540				1,600/85
SLBMs						
UGM-96A	Trident I C-4[b]	96/4	6,400+	1979	6 W76 x 100 (MIRV)	576
UGM-133A	Trident II D-5 Mk-4 Mk-5	288/12	6,400	1992 1990	8 W76 x 100 (MIRV) 8 W88 x 475 (MIRV)	1,920/156 384/16
Total		432/18				2,880/172

Table 2.2 U.S. Nuclear Forces, 2003

Bombers						
B-2	Spirit	21/16[c]	9,600 (unrefueled)	1994	B61-7/-11, B83 Bombs	800/45[d]
B-52	Stratofortress	94/56[c]	14,080 (unrefueled)	1961	ALCM/W80-1 x 5-150 ACM/W80-1 x 5-150[e]	430/20 430/20
Total		115/72				1,660/85
Non-Strategic Forces						
Tomahawk SLCM		325	2,500 (nuclear)	1984	1 W80-0 x 5-150	325
B61-3, -4, -10 bombs		n/a	N/A	1979	.3-170	800/40
Total		325				1,125/40
Other Weapons						
Hedge/Reserve						≈3,000
GRAND TOTAL						**≈10,265/382**

Sources: Norris et al., "U.S. Nuclear Forces, 2003," p. 76; Greg Webb, "United States: Large Reductions Made Recently," *Global Security Newswire*, December 7, 2001; "Trident Fleet Ballistic Missile," web factsheet, United States Navy Factfile, <http://www.chinfo.navy.mil/navpalib/factfile/missiles/wep-d5.html>; "Tomahawk Cruise Missile," web factsheet, United States Navy Factfile, <http://www.chinfo.navy.mil/navpalib/factfile/missiles/wep-toma.html>; "B-52 STRATOFORTRESS," U.S. Air Force Fact Sheet, <http://www.af.mil/factsheets/factsheet.asp?fsID=83>; "B-2 SPIRIT," U.S. Air Force Fact Sheet, <http://www.af.mil/factsheets/factsheet.asp?fsID=82>; Center for Defense Information, "Nuclear Weapon Database: United States Arsenal," <http://www.cdi.org/issues/nukef&f/database/usnukes.html>.

Notes:

a Currently being removed from the U.S. arsenal.

b Will be removed from the U.S. arsenal in 2005.

c The first figure is the total inventory (including backup aircraft and those used for training/testing). The second figure is the "primary mission inventory," comprised of the operational bombers that could be used in conventional or nuclear bombing missions.

d This number includes the total number of B61-7, B61-11, and B83 gravity bombs and spares.

e Bombers are loaded in a variety of ways, depending on their mission. B-2s do not carry ALCMs or Advanced Cruise Missiles (ACMs).

Nuclear Weapon Storage and Deployment

Since 1992, the United States has been consolidating its nuclear forces. As of 1998, it had withdrawn nuclear weapons from 13 states and stored its nuclear weapons at twenty-four main depots in fourteen states.[32] The United States currently deploys 200 Minuteman ICBMs at Malmstrom Air Force Base (AFB) in Montana; 150 Minuteman ICBMs at Minot AFB, North Dakota; and 150 Minuteman ICBMs and 40MX missiles at Warren AFB in Wyoming (though the MX missiles are currently being phased out and will be completely removed from the arsenal by 2006).[33] Sixteen ballistic missile submarines (SSBNs) operate from bases in Bangor, Washington, and Kings Bay, Georgia, with approximately two-thirds at sea at any given time.[34] The United States also maintains a stockpile of approximately 320 Tomahawk sea-launched cruise missiles (SLCMs) and their warheads at the Strategic Weapons Facilities in Bangor and Kings Bay.[35]

At the height of the Cold War, the United States also deployed approximately 10,311 nuclear weapons in seventeen foreign countries.[36] Since the end of the Cold War, the United States has withdrawn these weapons from many of these countries. As of 2003, it still deployed approximately 150 nuclear weapons at nine U.S. bases in six European NATO countries. All of these weapons are B61 strike bombs, controlled by the U.S. Air Force.[37]

The only facility for assembly and disassembly of U.S. nuclear weapons is the Pantex Plant, located seventeen miles northeast of Amarillo, Texas. Due to the major weapons reductions in the last decade, the United States has been retiring about 1,300 warheads per year. Approximately 350 nuclear weapons are present at this facility at any given time, though most of these weapons are awaiting dismantlement.[38] Plans are reportedly underway, however, to expand the capacity of the Pantex facility to meet a planned workload of approximately 600 warheads (assembled or dismantled) per year.[39] Between October 1986 and September 1996, Pantex disassembled 12,514 warheads. At the end of 1997, there were approximately 10,750 "pits"—the nuclear cores of dismantled warheads—in storage at Pantex.[40]

The U.S. C³I System

Launch-on-Warning (LOW)

As the vulnerabilities of decapitation or destruction of large numbers of nuclear U.S. forces increased, the U.S. command system became increasingly geared toward the capability of launching the majority of the nuclear forces before Soviet weapons reached their targets. By the early 1980s, official U.S.

policy therefore reportedly allowed for the option of launch-on-warning (LOW).[41] Although this policy allowed for greater survivability of U.S. forces, it significantly increased the requirements for C³I. The option of LOW required that the majority of U.S. nuclear forces be placed on high alert, which allowed the weapons to be launched within fifteen minutes of the detection of an incoming Soviet attack. It also required a high reliance on early-warning sensors to detect an attack and a command system that could disseminate a launch command very rapidly. At the same time, precautions had to be taken to ensure adequate command and control over the nuclear forces to prevent accidental or unauthorized use. The following sections discuss the C³I system that evolved to provide simultaneously the dual needs of operational readiness and command and control.

Early-Warning Systems

In order to ensure that it could detect an incoming Soviet attack, the United States developed an intricate system of early-warning sensors to observe the launching and transit of Soviet strategic delivery vehicles. In the early 1950s, the United States constructed an extensive chain of radar installations in Alaska, Canada, and Greenland to detect Soviet bombers en route to North America.[42] The United States expanded its early-warning radar system in the 1960s to include over-the-horizon backscatter (OTH-B) radars, which bounce their radio signals from the ionosphere and thus are able to detect objects at much longer distances.

As the Soviets developed ICBM capabilities in the 1950s and 1960s, the United States also constructed a ballistic missile early-warning system (BMEWS), which employed radars to detect incoming ballistic missiles.[43] These radars were located at three main sites along Soviet ICBM corridors: Clear, Alaska; Thule, Greenland; and Flyingdales, England. The United States later expanded and improved its BMEWS to detect possible Soviet SLBM launches. This new system employed long-range phased array radars (called PAVE PAWS[44]) located on the east and west coasts.[45]

The United States also developed an advanced early-warning system, known as Defense Support Program (DSP), which uses satellites to detect infrared energy radiated from the exhaust of a missile's rocket engine when launched from anywhere on the Earth's surface.[46] For most of the DSP's history, three geostationary satellites provided continual surveillance of most of the Earth's surface.[47] The current DSP system reportedly employs five geostationary satellites, with the two extra satellites providing additional surveillance of areas of concern, particularly Russia and China. These additional satellites allow for greater accuracy in determining missile launch trajectories.[48]

The information from the satellites and the PAVE PAWS radars is forwarded to Cheyenne Mountain Air Station in Colorado Springs, the National Military Command Center, and the U.S. Strategic Command (USSTRATCOM).[49] The data from all other early-warning sensors is fed only to Cheyenne Mountain, which serves as the primary center for the North American Aerospace Defense Command (NORAD), the organization responsible for assessing and processing early-warning information. If the early-warning stations at NORAD determined that an attack might be headed toward the United States or its allies, they would notify the Commander-in-Chief of NORAD (CINCNORAD) at the nearby Peterson AFB. If CINCNORAD were also to determine the possibility of an attack, he or she would then convene a "threat assessment conference" with more senior personnel, such as the chairman of the Joint Chiefs of Staff.[50] If the threat were to persist, the final action would be to convene a "missile attack conference," which brings in all senior personnel, including the president, to decide on U.S. options.[51] This entire assessment—from the initial detection to the final decision—would occur extremely rapidly, taking place over approximately fifteen minutes.

Command Structure

Under normal circumstances, the U.S. president is the only person authorized to command the use of nuclear weapons.[52] If the president were to decide to use nuclear weapons, he or she would order the decision to be transmitted down the chain of command, through the secretary of defense to the appropriate and specified regional combatant commanders.[53] The president would then transmit the launch order from his black bag "football," which follows the commander-in-chief at all times. The football presumably contains authenticating codes, which identify the launch command as emanating from him, and possibly the enabling codes necessary for launching U.S. nuclear weapons. In order to prevent a decapitation strike, however, the authentication and enabling codes are almost certainly also held at other layers in the chain of command. If the president were to issue a launch command, he would presumably activate the football by a code card that he carries on his person.[54]

At this point, the order from the National Command Authority (which includes the president, secretary of defense, and the Chairman of the Joint Chiefs of Staff) would be relayed to the U.S. Strategic Command (USSTRATCOM), which would pass the order to the U.S. alert forces. In the event that the underground USSTRATCOM center became inoperable, control of strategic forces would be transferred either to the CINC Mobile Consolidated Command Centers (MCCCs), consisting of a series of electrically shielded shelters mounted on semi-trailers, or to the USSTRATCOM Airborne Command Post, which is ready to become airborne twenty-four hours a day.[55]

Line of Succession

If the president were incapacitated or killed, the authority to order the use of nuclear weapons would be transferred down a specified chain of command. The line of succession for the presidency is clearly established by the Constitution and subsequent succession laws passed by Congress. The current succession order is the following: vice president, speaker of the House, president pro tempore of the Senate, and the cabinet secretaries in chronological order of establishment of their departments.[56] In order to prevent the elimination of the entire line of succession, current U.S. procedures prevent all of these people from being in the same place at a given time. In the event of a decapitation strike that killed a number of the people in the line of succession, however, it is likely that this line of succession would be preempted at some point by the National Command Authority (NCA), either out of necessity or by pre-arranged plans. Although the legality of such a preemption would be questionable, Peter Feaver points to some evidence that U.S. plans did call for such a devolution of authority to the NCA.[57]

Predelegation of Launch Authority

A number of scholars have argued that U.S. presidents, beginning with Dwight D. Eisenhower, delegated to key military commanders the authority to use nuclear weapons under certain circumstances.[58] This "predelegation" of launch authority would enable the United States to respond with nuclear weapons even if the president were unable to order their use in a timely manner. In particular, predelegation would allow the United States to retaliate in the event of a surprise Soviet attack that "decapitated" the civilian command authority.

Recently declassified documents in the National Security Archive confirm that Eisenhower did approve predelegation instructions in late 1959 to the commanders-in-chief of the Atlantic Command, European Command, and Strategic Air Command.[59] These instructions authorized commanders "to expend nuclear weapons in defense of the United States, its Territories, possessions and forces when the urgency of time and circumstances does not permit a specific decision by the President or other person empowered to act in his stead."[60] Other declassified documents in the National Security Archive indicate that Presidents Kennedy and Johnson adopted predelegation instructions that were "basically the same" as Eisenhower's.[61] Information on predelegation arrangements made by President Johnson after March 1964 or by his successors remains classified, but Bruce Blair cites some evidence suggesting that predelegation continued at least through the late 1980s.[62]

Control Structure: Security Procedures and Use-Control Devices

In order to help prevent thefts or unauthorized use of its nuclear weapons, the United States developed a number of procedures and use-control devices for its nuclear weapons. One such measure was implementing a personnel reliability program (PRP) to ensure that only individuals who meet the highest suitability and reliability standards are assigned to nuclear duty positions.[63] In addition, the United States strictly enforces a "two-person rule," which requires a minimum of two authorized personnel to be present during any functions where people come into contact with nuclear weapons or code materials related to their release.[64]

As the number of nuclear weapons deployed in Europe increased, the United States began exploring ways to ensure control over nuclear weapons committed to NATO use.[65] To this end, the United States reportedly developed a "two key" system for NATO weapons, so that two people would be necessary to launch any of these weapons. One key was to be in the possession of a European officer, and the other was to be in the possession of a U.S. officer. There proved to be problems with this system, however. In June 1959, Congressman Charles Porter reportedly visited a *Thor* missile base at Feltwell, England, and found that the British missile control officer possessed both keys necessary for launching the weapons.[66] In addition, the United States reportedly feared that if major divisions were to arise among NATO countries, a European country could take the U.S. officer's key by force.[67]

These concerns prompted the United States to try to ensure more effective decoupling of the possession of U.S. nuclear weapons from the ability to use them. In 1958 and 1959 Fred Iklé of the U.S. Air Force Project at RAND had recommended that a "combination lock" be placed on U.S. nuclear weapons. At about the same time, John Foster of Lawrence Livermore National Laboratory (LLNL) and Harold Agnew of Los Alamos National Laboratory (LANL) were proposing improved safety and control measures for U.S. nuclear weapons. When the Joint Committee on Atomic Energy became concerned about the security of nuclear forces deployed in Europe, U.S. laboratories had already designed prototypes for electromagnetic, remote-controlled combination locks to be inserted into the nuclear weapon circuitry. The first versions of these locks were incorporated into bombs and missiles, while the Army's artillery-fired atomic projectiles were stored in special storage containers with rugged standard combination locks. In 1962, President Kennedy issued National Security Memorandum 160, which required more effective PAL designs to be placed on nuclear weapons based in Europe.[68]

There are reportedly several different PAL designs on U.S. nuclear weapons, known as Category (CAT) A, B, D, and F. CAT A PALs were the first electromechanical, remote-controlled locks. The mechanism was inserted into the arming circuits for the weapon and prevented it from being activated until the proper four-digit enabling code was inserted. To insert the code, a portable control box was attached to the weapon and a dual code was inserted by a two-person team. CAT B PALs were similar to CAT A, but were reportedly built with a greater economy of input wires, which also allowed them to be controlled from an airplane cockpit. The CAT D PAL was completed in the mid to late 1970s. It incorporates a six-digit coded switch and a "limited try" feature, which irreversibly locks the switch if the wrong code is entered too many times.[69] CAT F PALs appear to be similar to CAT D PALs, but require a twelve-digit code.[70] Newer warhead designs also reportedly include a membrane that can detect penetration or entry attempts and disable the weapon.[71]

The military at first opposed the incorporation of PALs into nuclear weapons because they thought PALs would reduce operational readiness.[72] Nevertheless, in 1967, the United States decided to extend the use of PALs to weapons carried by Strategic Air Command (SAC) bombers.[73] Nuclear-capable aircraft were fitted with an "Aircraft Monitoring and Control" (AMAC) system, which permits the pilot to monitor and control a nuclear weapon's safety systems as well as its arming and fusing. PAL codes are transmitted through AMAC.[74]

The United States also reportedly placed use control devices, called Permissive Enable Systems (PESs), on its ICBMs in the late 1970s. According to Peter Feaver, this system is similar to PALs, with one difference: "Whereas PALs block the nuclear detonation in a bomb or artillery shell, PES inhibits a missile launch and does not affect the nuclear warhead at all."[75] The PESs prevent a launch crew from launching an ICBM until they insert a specific code. This code is presumably tightly controlled and transmitted to the launch crews along with the launch command.[76] In addition, U.S. ICBMs reportedly also contain a launch control system called a "Dual Launch Control Center" (LCC), which requires that when a two-member ICBM crew transmits a launch signal, another crew in the squadron must confirm the signal before the launch can take place.[77]

For many years, however, PALs (or their equivalents) were not incorporated into weapons deployed on Navy ships or submarines because the Navy argued that the SLBM force could become ineffective if command centers were destroyed or if communications to submarines were interrupted.[78] During this time, unauthorized launches were reportedly prevented by a series of procedures that involved most of the submarine crew.[79] According to open-source reports, if a transmission to launch naval nuclear weapons were received, the transmission would be announced to the entire crew and verified by two teams of officers. Special keys would then be issued to those responsible for pre-launch and launch sequences, so that a series of "permission" switches could be closed in a prescribed sequence. The entire crew would be informed of each step in these procedures.[80]

In 1992, however, the Department of Defense's Commission on Fail-Safe and Risk Reduction (FARR) recommended that PALs or PAL-equivalents be incorporated into all U.S. nuclear forces, including naval nuclear weapons.[81] The 1995 Department of Defense Nuclear Posture Review indicated that continued implementation was needed for completing the Trident Coded Control Device (CCD) and providing for system-level CCDs or PALs on all U.S. nuclear weapons by 1997.[82] These provisions were reportedly implemented in either 1996 or 1997.[83] Once CCDs were placed on the Trident SLBMs, all nuclear weapons in the U.S. arsenal reportedly contained PALs or equivalent use-control devices.

Risks of Accidental Use

In the early years of its nuclear weapons program, the United States ensured that the risks of accidental detonation were small by keeping the fissile materials separated from the non-nuclear detonation devices during storage and transportation. The nuclear weapons reportedly had a separable capsule containing the fissile materials. Crew members would insert this capsule into the bomb during flight. This early system was cumbersome and time consuming, however, and required the crew to manhandle the materials into place.[84] In the early 1950s, an automatic in-flight insertion (IFI) component was developed that allowed the crew to insert the capsule automatically during flight.[85]

The United Stated changed this system once it began producing hydrogen bombs and tactical nuclear weapons in the early 1950s. Hydrogen bombs require reliable fission devices as triggers for the larger fusion detonations. In order to make the yields of fission devices more reliable and predictable, scientists at LANL devised a technique called "boosting." In a boosted device, a mix of deuterium and tritium gases is introduced into the nuclear system, which produces higher, more reliable yields. This process, however, required a "sealed-pit design," where the nuclear materials are permanently positioned within the high explosives. As a result, the safety precaution of separating the fissile materials from the high explosives had to be abandoned and other means for preventing accidental detonations and accidental launches had to be found.[86]

Risks of Accidental Detonation

In order to reduce the likelihood of accidental detonations of the sealed-pit designs, safety systems were reportedly incorporated into the warhead and bomb electrical systems.[87] For instance, the firing signals were kept away from the critical components by an air gap, and critical cables were isolated from each other. These designs were intended to prevent the transmission of any accidental signals to detonate the warhead.[88] Pre-flight operations reportedly included pre-arming the warheads by inserting arming plugs; removing "safing" wires that prevent closure of release switches; and connecting "pull-out wires" that pull out when the bomb is released, activating the switches. Prior to release of the bomb, the pilot would activate a reversible arm-safe switch. Other safety devices included environmental sensing devices (ESDs), which automatically arm the bomb only after certain environmental conditions are met. These conditions are only produced by the flight of a bomb, such as close-to-zero accelerations, changes in barometric pressures, and decelerations from the bomb's parachute.[89] One of the most important safety designs incorporated into U.S. nuclear weapons was the "one-point safety" design. In a one-point safety design, if the weapon's high explosive is detonated at any single point, the probability of producing a nuclear yield exceeding four pounds TNT equivalent is less than one in a million.[90]

During the 1950s and 1960s, a series of accidents involving nuclear weapons reportedly focused the debate on nuclear weapons safety.[91] The most serious of these reported accidents involved the U.S. bomber forces, a large percentage of which were constantly in flight in case the Soviet Union launched a preemptive strike against the United States or its allies. The following are a few of the most famous incidents:[92]

- *Kirtland AFB, New Mexico*: On May 22, 1957, while a B-36 bomber was approaching the base at an altitude of 1,700 feet, a bomb fell from its bomb bay, taking the bay doors with it. The high explosive in the weapon reportedly detonated on impact, completely destroying the weapon and making a crater approximately twenty-five feet in diameter and twelve feet deep. The capsule containing the fissile materials was on board the aircraft but was not inserted into the weapon. A nuclear detonation was not possible.[93]

- *Florence, South Carolina*: On March 11, 1958, a bomber from Hunter AFB accidentally jettisoned an unarmed nuclear weapon because of a malfunction of the plane's bomb-lock system. The weapon's conventional explosive detonated on impact, but no capsule of nuclear materials was present in the weapon or on the aircraft.[94]
- *Goldsboro, North Carolina*: On January 24, 1961, during a B-52 airborne alert, the structural support of the right wing of a bomber collapsed, which ultimately caused two weapons to separate from the aircraft during aircraft breakup at 2,000 to 10,000 feet altitude. One bomb's parachute opened, and that weapon received little damage from impact. The other bomb broke apart on impact, though no explosion occurred.
- *Palomares, Spain*: On January 17, 1966, a B-52 and a KC-135 collided during a routine high altitude air refueling. Both aircraft crashed. The B-52 was carrying four nuclear weapons. Two bombs were recovered, but the high explosives on the other two bombs exploded on impact, scattering low-level radiation over a small area.[95]
- *Thule, Greenland*: On January 21, 1968, a B-52 crashed and burned seven miles from the runway of Thule AFB, Greenland. The bomber carried four nuclear weapons, all of which were destroyed by fire.[96] Some radioactive contamination occurred from the accident.[97]

The U.S. government reportedly learned some important lessons from these accidents. First, the majority of the serious nuclear weapons accidents involved the airborne alert of the B-52 bomber force. Although the Defense Department had already planned to discontinue routine airborne alerts because the U.S. ICBM force was making such alerts unnecessary, these accidents (particularly the 1966 Palomares accident) reportedly caused the DOD to cancel the peacetime B-52 airborne alerts earlier than planned.[98] Second, weapons designers learned that accidents frequently mimic the delivery method for the weapons. Safety devices would therefore need to prevent accidental detonations under conditions that were similar to weapons' delivery methods. And third, designers reportedly learned that wire insulation and printed circuit boards become unpredictable during fires, and it therefore becomes relatively "easy" to get electrical charges across the terminals of a safety device.[99]

As a result, weapons designers renewed their efforts to design safety devices that would prevent accidental detonations in all abnormal environments. Because a number of the accidents involved fires, Lawrence Livermore and Los Alamos National Laboratories developed a high explosive that is less sensitive to abnormal environments, called insensitive high explosive (IHE). Although the "one-point safety" designs make it highly unlikely that a detonation of the high explosive would result in a significant nuclear yield, such a detonation could result in the spread of radiation or, in more severe cases, in the release of a deadly plutonium aerosol.[100] Because IHE is less powerful than the HE used in older weapons, however, it was reportedly not used in the W76 or W88 warheads in order to maximize the military capabilities of the Trident I and II SLBM.[101]

LANL and LLNL also developed fire-resistant pits (FRPs).[102] In an FRP, the plutonium is encased in a metal shell with a high melting point, designed to withstand exposure to a jet fuel fire of 1,000 degrees Celsius for several hours. Because FRPs are only useful if the high explosive does not explode, they are most likely to be effective in weapons equipped with IHE. In addition, FRPs would probably not be able to withstand rocket-propellant fires, which generally burn much hotter than aircraft fuel fires.[103]

Enhanced Nuclear Detonation Safety (ENDS) System

In 1972, Sandia National Laboratories developed the Enhanced Nuclear Detonation Safety (ENDS) system, which isolates the electrical elements critical to detonation, to prevent premature arming of a nuclear weapon subjected to abnormal conditions.[104] In the ENDS system, the warhead is reportedly designed to meet three characteristics, called the "3 I's." First, the critical components are to be *isolated* from their surroundings by placing them within an energy barrier. The barrier blocks all forms of energy at levels sufficient to cause a nuclear yield of greater than the equivalent of four pounds TNT. When the proper signal is transmitted, an "energy control element" is opened to allow energy into the exclusion region.[105]

Second, the deliberate action that passes through the barrier must be *incompatible* with naturally occurring signals, energy types, or levels. In order to open the energy control element, a complex pattern of binary pulses is transmitted, which opens the lock for the energy control element. Typically, U.S. nuclear weapons contain two safety devices, and each safety device is operated with a different binary pattern.[106]

And, third, some of the components needed for nuclear detonation must become *inoperable* in the event of an accident.[107] At some level of exposure to abnormal environments, the barrier becomes ineffective. In such events, the nuclear device is reportedly designed so that certain key components are more vulnerable to abnormal environmental conditions than others. Under such conditions, these components, known as "weaklinks," will become irreversibly inoperative.[108] "Stronglinks," on the other hand, are the components necessary for safing and arming the weapon, and are designed to withstand severe environmental conditions.[109] The combination of weaklinks and stronglinks helps ensure that the components necessary for detonating the weapon fail before the stronglinks do, ensuring that the weapon "fails safely." For example, capacitors are generally used as weaklinks and are designed to melt at relatively low temperatures. Thus, in the event of a fire, the weaklinks will melt before the safety device or the barrier fails from thermal exposure, thereby rendering the weapon inoperative.[110]

Possible Continuing Safety Problems (1990–present)

Although the above list of safety devices and designs is very impressive and provides very high safety standards for U.S. weapons, some of the weapons in the U.S. arsenal reportedly do not contain all of these safety devices. As a result, several Congressional studies in the 1990s determined that some parts of the U.S. arsenal did not meet the most modern safety standards. In Congressional testimony before the Drell Committee on Nuclear Safety, the directors of the three weapons laboratories testified about continuing safety problems with the short-range nuclear attack missile, SRAM-A. The Drell report criticized the United States for retaining weapons in its arsenal that did not meet the safety standards established in 1968.[111] In light of this testimony, the United States soon discontinued the SRAM-A. But the Drell Committee also identified problems with the W76 and W88 warheads, which are used on the Trident I and II SLBMs. According to the Drell report, in order to maximize the range of the missiles with their full payloads (up to eight warheads), neither of these warheads contains IHE or FRPs.

In addition, the Drell report also argued that there was a potential safety problem with the propellant for the Trident I and II missiles. In order to maximize their range, these missiles use a propellant that could detonate, rather than simply ignite.[112] The Trident missiles' eight warheads are adjacent to and surround the third-stage rocket motor (in order to meet the geometric constraints of a submarine hull and at the same time achieve maximum range). The report concluded that if the third-stage motor were to detonate in a submarine loading accident, it might detonate the high explosive surrounding the nuclear pit in one or more of these nuclear warheads and lead to plutonium dispersal or possibly to a nuclear yield.[113]

In a follow-up report to Congress, R.E. Kidder reported that some procedural precautions were undertaken to alleviate some of the potential dangers identified in the Drell report. In particular, a procedural change was made in the manner in which the Trident missiles are loaded onto submarines. "The warheads are no longer mated to the missile until *after* the missile has been loaded into the launch tubes. This eliminates the possibility that the accidental detonation of a missile's propellant, during loading of the missile into a launch tube could result in the detonation of any (or all) of the missile's warheads."[114] But the Kidder report also emphasized that some safety problems with the W76 and W88 warheads identified in the Drell report still remained. Because these warheads did not contain IHE or FRPs, both warheads were given a grade of "C" in their safety evaluation. The report stressed that this does not necessarily mean that the warheads are unsafe, but that they do not meet modern U.S. safety standards. It did, however, indicate that the safety of these weapons could possibly be improved by replacing their warheads with other warheads that did contain IHE and FRPs, such as the W87 warhead or the W89 SRAM-II, and by replacing the third-stage propellant on the Trident missiles with a non-detonable propellant.[115]

The U.S. arsenal still reportedly contains the W76 and W88 warheads. If the W88 warhead were to be redesigned to contain IHE, it would reportedly require additional (though moderate) tests.[116] The United States never conducted these tests, however, and the warheads still appear to lack IHE. In addition, the U.S. arsenal still contains the W62 warhead on the Minuteman III ICBM. Because the W62 reportedly lacks IHE, FRPs, and ENDS, it received a "D" in the Kidder report's safety evaluation.[117] This warhead is scheduled for retirement and has slowly been removed from the arsenal, but roughly 300 W62 warheads remained on Minuteman III ICBMs as of May 2003.[118] According to the 2002 Nuclear Posture Review, the W62 warhead will be retired in 2009.[119]

Risks of Accidental Launch

During its nuclear history, the United States has had relatively few incidents that involved the accidental release of a nuclear gravity bomb or missile. But such accidents did occur.[120] Most of these accidents involved the accidental release of gravity bombs during the period when a portion of SAC bombers were in constant air alert. In order to help prevent future accidental bomb releases, SAC reportedly adopted safer procedures and developed additional safety devices for bombers. Perhaps the most important change was to take strategic bombers off continual airborne alert in 1968.[121] In addition, after the accidental release over Florence, North Carolina, bomber crews were reportedly ordered to lock in nuclear bombs during flight, which significantly decreased the risk that they could be dropped accidentally.[122] SAC also adopted a bomb release mechanism for strategic aircraft, called the bomber coded switch system (BCSS). The BCSS will not allow an armed

Table 2.3 Safety and Control Devices on U.S. Nuclear Weapons				
Warhead/Weapon	**Control Feature**	**IHE**	**FRP**	**ENDS**
W62 Minuteman III (mk-12)	PED, Dual LCC	No	No	No
W76 Trident I, Trident II (mk-4)	Trident CCD	No	No	Yes
W78 Minuteman III (Mk-12A)	PES, Dual LCC	No	No	Yes
W80-0 Tomahawk SLCM	Cat D PAL	Yes	No	Yes
W80-1 ALCM/ACM	Cat D PAL	Yes	No	Yes
W87 MX/Peacekeeper[a]	PES, Dual LCC	Yes	Yes	Yes
W88 Trident II (Mk-5)	Trident CCD	No	No	Yes
B61 Gravity bomb	Cat D PAL/AMAC	Yes	No	Yes
B83 Gravity bomb	Cat D PAL/AMAC	Yes	Yes	Yes

Sources: Norris and Arkin, "U.S. Nuclear Weapons Safety and Control Features," p. 49; Norris and Kristensen, "U.S. Nuclear Forces, 2003," p. 74.

Note: [a] Currently being removed from the U.S. arsenal.

nuclear bomb to be dropped until the aircraft commander inserts a proper code to unlock the bomb bay release system.[123]

Because the United States employs numerous launch controls for its nuclear missiles, the risk of accidental launches is very small. For example, because enabling codes for ICBMs must be transmitted by the National Command Authority and entered by the launch crews prior to launch, U.S. ICBMs cannot be accidentally launched by pushing the wrong button.

Nevertheless, there have been some reports of accidental launches of nuclear missiles. On September 19, 1980, during routine maintenance in a Titan II silo in Damascus, Arkansas, an Air Force repairman accidentally dropped a heavy wrench socket, which fell toward the bottom of the silo. The socket bounced and stuck the missile, causing a leak from a pressurized fuel tank. The missile complex and the surrounding area were immediately evacuated. The fuel vapors within the silo eventually ignited and exploded. The missile burst through the silo door (which reportedly weighed 740 tons) and landed about 1,000 feet away.[124] Although this accident was certainly very serious, it is highly unlikely that the missile would have followed its normal launch trajectory, even if the heavy silo door had not been present.

There have been additional, though less reliable, accounts of accidental launches or near-launches of nuclear missiles. For example, Shaun Gregory reports the following incidents:

- On November 19, 1980, a Titan missile drill reportedly started a missile on a real launch sequence that was prevented only by one of the crew shutting the missile down.[125]
- In 1984 a computer malfunction at a Minuteman missile silo indicated that the missile was about to launch itself.[126]
- There were two reported incidents in which "nuclear-tipped anti-aircraft missiles" were launched by accident.[127]

Conclusions about Accidental Use

Overall, the United States has devoted a great deal of research and resources to guaranteeing the safety of its nuclear arsenal. These efforts have largely paid off. By most accounts, the U.S. arsenal is currently the safest in the world. Nevertheless, over the years, the United States made a number of decisions that provided less-than-optimal safety. Some of these decisions led to serious accidents (though never to a full-scale nuclear detonation). As we have seen, the most serious of these accidents arose from the decision to maintain a continual airborne alert for its nuclear bombers, and the risks of accident were significantly reduced once the United States eventually took the bombers off airborne alert. But even in its recent history, the United States has chosen to retain warhead designs—and even introduce new warheads—that reportedly do not meet its own (admittedly very rigorous) safety standards. Thus, U.S. nuclear history demonstrates the constant tension between pressures to maintain deterrence or strategic capabilities and those of ensuring safety. We will need to keep this issue in mind when we assess the risks that emerging NWSs might take.

Unauthorized Use

Throughout its nuclear history, the United States has gone to great lengths to prevent an unauthorized use of its nuclear weapons. Due to the extensive system of physical protection, security procedures (such as the two-person rule), launch controls, and use-control devices, the risks of unauthorized use of U.S. nuclear weapons are currently very small.

In the past these risks were somewhat greater. Before U.S. weapons contained PALs, the U.S. controls relied heavily on security procedures and physical protection. These controls ultimately depended on the reliability of the guard forces and personnel responsible for handling the nuclear weapons. Because the U.S. personnel reliability programs were very good, these controls were probably quite sound, especially when the U.S. arsenal was relatively small. The deployment of large numbers of nuclear weapons in Europe did raise some concern over a weakening of central controls, however. This problem was largely resolved by including PALs on U.S. weapons deployed in NATO countries.

As we have seen, however, naval nuclear weapons lacked sophisticated use-control devices until the late 1990s. While the procedures on naval forces were probably sufficient to prevent a single officer from using the nuclear weapons, critics have argued that the procedures could not prevent a so-called *Hunt for Red October* scenario, in which a submarine would be capable of launching its nuclear weapons if a large portion of the crew—or at least its officers—collaborated. In addition, the use-control procedures on naval nuclear weapons would not have prevented the crew from launching their nuclear weapons if they had determined that the United States had been attacked (for example, if communications between the central command and the ship were to break down). Nor would they have prevented the crew from launching their nuclear weapons if they faced a situation where they had to use their nuclear weapons to save their own lives. It is necessary to stress that these risks were probably quite small (especially because the naval forces were more survivable than other U.S. forces), but they apparently did exist.[128]

Now that all U.S. weapons contain some form of sophisticated use controls, the risks of unauthorized use have been greatly reduced. It would be very difficult for forces possessing U.S. nuclear weapons to use them without authorization from higher up in the command chain. Nevertheless, the predelegation of launch authority does increase the risks of unauthorized use. As we have seen, predelegation must involve providing the authenticating and enabling codes to senior military officers for use under specified circumstances. But, depending on Department of Defense predelegation procedures, these same officers could potentially authorize a launch on their own.[129] In addition, predelegation could produce serious difficulties in controlling or terminating a nuclear exchange once it had begun and could increase the possibility of inadvertent war resulting from a warning or assessment error during a crisis.[130] Because there is no available information on whether the United States still predelegates launch authority, however, it is impossible to determine whether this risk still pertains today. In any case, since the authority to order a launch has probably been given to only a few reliable officers, the risks of unauthorized use arising from predelegation would probably be fairly small.

One other possible weakness in the U.S. controls against unauthorized use involves nuclear weapons in transit. During transportation, the physical protection of nuclear weapons would be weakest. Because a great number of nuclear weapons were transported during the 1950s and the early 1960s, when U.S. nuclear weapons lacked PALs, there probably was some risk that these weapons could have been seized by terrorist groups. The introduction of PALs on weapons deployed in NATO countries helped reduce the risks of unauthorized use if the weapons were seized during transit. But these risks remained for the road transportation of naval nuclear weapons until the late 1990s. And these risks still do not appear to have been eliminated for U.S. ICBMs. If the reports on the use-control devices on U.S. ICBMs are correct, the ICBMs currently lack PALs on the warheads themselves. While the risks of unauthorized launch of deployed ICBMs are minimal due to the PES (which only allows a launch of an ICBM after a specific enabling code is entered), the risks could increase if these weapons were involved in accidents or were stolen during transit.[131] Because the United States maintains very good physical controls over nuclear weapons in transit, however, the risks of theft of U.S. nuclear weapons during transit are probably quite small. In addition, critical safety devices such as ESDs provide some degree of use control over weapons that lack PALs. Because the weapons can only be detonated under conditions that imitate the flight of the ICBMs, they would still be very difficult to detonate, even in the unlikely event of their theft.[132]

Inadvertent Use

As we have seen, the United States employs a large nuclear arsenal, deployed in a manner that allows for rapid response, and a use-doctrine that allows for launch-on-warning. This deployment option increases the survivability of U.S. nuclear forces, but, as a number of scholars have argued, it also significantly increases the risks of inadvertent nuclear war.[133] I will not attempt to address this issue in greater detail than these scholars already have. But it is necessary to discuss the main ways that inadvertent use is possible.

False Alarms

One of the main potential causes of inadvertent use would be a false alarm generated by the U.S. early-warning systems. As we have seen, the United States relies heavily on a sophisticated system of early-warning radars and satellites to detect possible attacks. But the U.S. early-warning sensors reportedly have experienced a number of false alarms. The following are several such reported incidents:

- The original U.S. BMEWS had serious defects. Its resolution was poor and its computers were unable to handle heavy traffic or unexpected events. In October 1960, several radars detected a Soviet ballistic missile attack. Although panic ensued, the United States did not respond because redundant sensors did not detect an attack.[134]
- On October 3, 1979, radar for detecting SLBM attacks picked up a low orbit rocket body that was close to decay and generated a false launch and impact report.[135]
- On November 9, 1979, missile crews received a warning that a massive nuclear strike from the Soviet Union was on its way. It turned out that a training tape that simulated all the signals of a massive Soviet first strike had mistakenly been loaded into a computer at Cheyenne Mountain. The mistake was discovered only after U.S. leaders also viewed the data from early-warning satellites, which detected no missile launches.[136]
- On June 3, 1980, the SAC command post indicated that two SLBMs had been launched toward the United States. Eighteen seconds later, the display systems showed an increased number of SLBM launches. SAC command post personnel contacted NORAD personnel, and the NORAD personnel indicated that they had no indication of launched SLBMs. Shortly after the initial indication, the SAC duty control officer directed all alert crews to move to their aircraft and start their engines in case they needed to take off in order to survive. After a short period, the SAC sensors cleared, indicating that there were no missile attacks. The SAC aircraft crews were directed to shut down their aircraft but remain in their aircraft. But then, after another brief period, the warning display at SAC indicated that Soviet ICBMs had been launched toward the United States. After another interval, the National Military Command Center (at the Pentagon) received notification that SLBMs were launched. Within a few minutes of the alarm, all of the command posts had reportedly concluded that the data was erroneous because NORAD's sensors had not detected any launches and because the information received from NORAD did not follow any logical pattern or sequence. In the end it was discovered that the false alarms were caused by a faulty circuit in the communications system that transmitted information from NORAD to U.S. command centers.[137]
- CIA director James Woolsey related a case in which the U.S. BMEWS mistook the rising moon for a Russian ICBM attack. NORAD experts quickly concluded that the data could not be true, because Soviet premier Nikita Khrushchev was actually in the United States at the time.[138]

These and similar reported incidents are very troubling. After the false alarm in 1980, however, NORAD did reportedly revise its rules for threat evaluation.[139] In addition, as the above incidents also demonstrate, the United States has redundant early-warning systems that can help corroborate or challenge the information from a given set of sensors. Moreover, the United States also weighs the information based on human intelligence gathering and assessments of the strategic situation. If other sources of information indicate that an attack is unlikely, U.S. early-warning centers will be much more likely to doubt the data from one set of sensors. For this reason, the risks of inadvertent war are greatest during times of crisis, when experts at U.S. early-warning centers would be more likely to suspect an attack.

Unfortunately, according to open-source reports, several false alarms have also occurred during times of crisis. For example, Scott Sagan has argued that several false warnings occurred during the Cuban missile crisis. In each of the false alarms, the officers involved reportedly believed that war had begun, but in none of the cases were irreversible steps taken.[140]

- On October 25, 1962, a figure was seen climbing the fence at the Duluth Sector Direction Center in Minnesota. Because U.S. personnel had been warned about possible sabotage attempts at command-and-control facilities, the guard forces sounded the sabotage alarm. Unfortunately, the alarm was faulty. Instead of the sabotage alarm sounding, the Klaxon went off, ordering an immediate launch of the aircraft at nearby bases. As the aircraft began to taxi down the runway, the pilots reportedly believed that nuclear war had started. Before the aircraft were able to take off, however, an officer from the command post drove to the runway and signaled the aircraft to stop.[141]
- On October 28, only minutes before Khrushchev announced his willingness to withdraw missiles from Cuba, radar operators at Moorsetown, New Jersey, detected what appeared to be a missile launch from Cuba against the United States. The radar operators immediately notified the NORAD command center. After verifying the sensor information, NORAD officers relayed the warning information to the Strategic Air Command in Omaha. It was only after the missile was supposed to have reached its target and no detonation was detected that NORAD discovered that a training tape was mistakenly feeding into the Moorsetown monitors.[142]
- On October 31, 1962, the radar system at U.S. Air Force control and warning centers in Ontario detected that two unidentified planes had crossed the Mid-Canada Line of NORAD radars. In response, full base defense plans were reportedly implemented, and all personnel were noti-

fied to expect an impending attack. Because the two aircraft never materialized, however, the two air force bases affected by the warning returned to DEFCON 3 readiness (the heightened alert status maintained throughout most of the Cuban missile crisis) after forty minutes.[143]

Organizational Difficulties and Inadvertent Use

Proliferation pessimists have also argued that serious organizational problems can significantly increase the risks of inadvertent war during crisis situations. During periods of heightened alerts, it becomes much more difficult for states to prevent events from spinning out of control.[144] For example, studies of the Cuban missile crisis have reported several serious mishaps and organizational difficulties that occurred during the crisis and which could have possibly triggered a nuclear war. The following are some of these reported incidents:

- On October 26, 1962, as the crisis reached its crescendo, SAC launched a Titan ICBM from Vandenberg AFB in accordance with its predetermined flight-test schedule. Although this missile did not carry a nuclear warhead, the Air Force had mated the warheads to the other ICBMs at the base and had placed them on alert. If the Soviets had detected the launch and had been aware of the alert status of the other ICBMs at Vandenberg, they could have easily misinterpreted the launch as part of a nuclear attack.[145]
- On October 27, 1962, an American U-2 reconnaissance plane on a routine air-sampling mission inadvertently strayed into Soviet airspace. As Soviet MiG fighters attempted to intercept the plane, U.S. F-102s also flew to escort the plane back to its base and prevent the MiGs from entering U.S. airspace. The F-102s were carrying live nuclear anti-aircraft missiles because of the heightened alert. If a dogfight had occurred between the U.S. and Soviet aircraft, the U.S. planes might have detonated nuclear weapons in or near Soviet airspace. Fortunately, the Soviet MiGs failed to intercept the U-2 and the plane was successfully led back into U.S. airspace.[146]

During normal, peacetime circumstances, the numerous controls on U.S. weapons and redundant early-warning information make the risks of inadvertent war highly unlikely. But crisis situations increase the likelihood that false alarms might be interpreted as real, and that operations that would otherwise be interpreted as benign might be misinterpreted as aggressive. Since the end of the Cold War, it has probably become less likely that nuclear crises will arise. Nevertheless, given a reported worsening of U.S.-Russian and U.S.-Chinese relations leading up to and following the 2003 invasion of Iraq, one necessarily cannot rule out the possibility that nuclear crises will arise in the future. During such crises, the risks of inadvertent nuclear war can increase significantly.

Part II: The United States' MPC&A

U.S. Fissile Material Stockpile and Production Facilities

Current Stockpiles

At the end of 1999, the U.S. military fissile material stockpile contained an estimated 100 metric tons of plutonium and 635 metric tons of weapons-grade uranium. It is also estimated to possess 4 to 5 metric tons of separated plutonium from its civil power reactors.[147]

The United States has declared 52.5 metric tons of plutonium and 174 metric tons of HEU to be in excess of its military purposes.[148] It has made arrangements for the disposition of these materials. The HEU will be down-blended to low-enriched uranium (LEU). The blend-down will be carried out by the DOE's Savannah River Site and the Y-12 Plant at Oak Ridge, Tennessee, as well as several private sector companies.[149] Surplus plutonium, on the other hand, will be burned as mixed oxide (MOX) fuel in existing, domestic commercial reactors. Two facilities at the Savannah River site are being constructed to disassemble U.S. nuclear weapons components, separate the plutonium from the weapons, and prepare the MOX fuel. After the MOX fuel is prepared, it will be shipped to the commercial reactors, where it will be irradiated. The irradiation process will convert the plutonium into a form that cannot be used easily in nuclear weapons. The resulting spent fuel from the reactors will then be taken to a high-level waste storage facility.[150]

Fissile Material Production Facilities

During the Manhattan Project, scientists developed two different designs for nuclear weapons. Little Boy was a gun-design weapon using uranium as its nuclear fuel. Fat Man, on the other hand, was an implosion device with a plutonium core. In order to produce fissile materials for these weapons, the United States constructed a small-scale plutonium production reactor and a large uranium enrichment facility at Oak Ridge in 1943.[151] In the same year, the United States also constructed a plutonium production facility at the Hanford site near Richmond, Washington.[152]

Between 1947 and 1952, the U.S. Atomic Energy Commission initiated the construction of several new facilities to increase U.S. fissile material production capabilities. These new facilities included three additional gaseous diffusion plants (for enriching uranium) at Hanford; gaseous diffusion plants at Paducah, Kentucky, and Portsmouth, Ohio; five additional reactors for producing plutonium at the Hanford facility; and several reactors for producing tritium and plutonium at a new site at Savannah River, South Carolina.[153]

The United States stopped production of fissile materials for use in nuclear weapons in 1988. HEU production for nuclear weapons ended in 1964 when the K-25 site at Oak Ridge stopped producing the material (though the facility was not shut down until 1987).[154] Weapons-related plutonium production ended in 1988 when the United States shut down the production facilities at Hanford and Savannah River. The Hanford facility was closed due to safety concerns raised by the 1986 Chernobyl accident, while the Savannah River facility was shut down because it was judged that the U.S. stockpile had more than enough fissile materials.[155] On July 14, 1992, U.S. president George H.W. Bush officially announced a unilateral moratorium on fissile material production for nuclear weapons or other explosive devices.[156]

Weapon Assembly/Disassembly Facilities

In the early years, Los Alamos National Laboratory constructed nuclear weapons from fissile materials shipped from U.S. fissile material production facilities. In the early 1950s the United States decided that LANL should focus on the development of new weapons designs rather than weapon production. It therefore established the Rocky Flats facility in Colorado in 1951 to manufacture triggers, or "pits," from fissile materials, though Los Alamos also retained some pit production capabilities.[157] After 1965, Rocky Flats became the only pit production facility in the United States. After fabricating the pits, Rocky Flats then sent them to the Pantex Plant near Amarillo, Texas, to be incorporated into nuclear weapons.[158]

Rocky Flats was shut down in December 1989 due to severe safety and environmental problems. Although the United States briefly considered resuming operations at Rocky Flats in 1990 to produce W88 warhead pits for the Trident II missile, it has never done so.[159] Instead, Rocky Flats has been permanently shut down, and U.S. efforts at the facility have focused on environmental clean-up and the protection of the large amounts of fissile materials remaining in the facility.

Although President George H.W. Bush announced in February 1992 that no more W88 warheads would be built, small-scale production of W88 pits was resumed at the TA-55 facility at Los Alamos to replenish pits destroyed in reliability testing.[160]

Early Fissile Material Controls

From 1947 to 1954, all special nuclear materials (SNM)[161] in the United States was owned by the government and was generally held by the Atomic Energy Commission and its contractors, who ran government-owned or government-controlled plants and laboratories.[162] Early nuclear material controls were provided by the military, which played a critical role in the protection of information and nuclear materials through the use of troops, multiple fences, and other traditional military security procedures.[163] The U.S. safeguards system was mainly understood to be a matter of economics, and fissile materials were controlled primarily because of their intrinsic value, rather than concerns about proliferation or terrorism.[164] As a result, however, there were often serious weaknesses in U.S. fissile material controls. For example, early on, it was perfectly legal to ship kilogram quantities of plutonium through commercial freight, or to store separated plutonium in facilities without twenty-four-hour guard forces.[165]

Increased attention was paid to risks of proliferation and subnational terrorism in the 1960s and 1970s, however, with the introduction of the Atoms for Peace Program and the Nuclear Non-Proliferation Treaty, and as incidents of non-nuclear terrorism increased worldwide. In 1966, the AEC established a safeguards advisory panel that raised the issue of safeguards against subnational threats posed by criminals and terrorists. As a result, the AEC increased its efforts to improve physical protection systems for national security nuclear facilities and private-sector power reactors.[166]

In 1974, the Energy Research and Development Administration (ERDA) and the Nuclear Regulatory Commission (NRC) replaced the AEC. The NRC assumed responsibility for the private sector nuclear industry, while the ERDA oversaw national security programs and research and development activities. Although the ERDA was soon replaced by the Department of Energy (DOE) in 1977, the years that it existed were critical for assessing and improving the safeguards systems in the United States. The ERDA oversaw a number of detailed assessments of the U.S. safeguards system to identify and fix any weaknesses or vulnerabilities. In 1976 a joint ERDA-NRC Task Force on Safeguards produced a report on the current status and future prospects for U.S. MPC&A. While these assessments found that most facilities were generally in compliance, improvements were needed to assure the capability to counter the defined threat levels. The most prevalent issues dealt with controls over access to stored and in-process fissile materials, exit search procedures, and security force response capabilities. As part of efforts to improve U.S. fissile material controls, ERDA supported research and development activities to provide advanced techniques for modeling, assaying, assessing, and protecting nuclear materials.[167]

During the first years after the DOE replaced the ERDA, research and development activities in safeguards and security flourished. In 1979, the DOE established the Office of Safeguards and Security to develop policy and support safeguards and security applications to assure the nuclear materials inventory at contractor facilities. For physical protection, new concepts in commercially available technologies were applied to provide advanced systems. Safeguards systems also benefitted from advances in computing technologies and nonintrusive measurement systems. Security forces personnel were increasingly replaced by automated monitoring and alarm systems, and complex wet chemistry analyses for nuclear material accountability measurements were replaced with automated destructive and nondestructive assay systems.[168]

In spite of these advances, however, a series of scathing Congressional hearings in the 1980s identified a number of problems with the protection of fissile materials throughout the DOE complex.[169] In 1982, the House Subcommittee on Oversight and Investigation found that "the DOE was simply not protecting its critical nuclear weapons facilities from a host of real threats," including those of thefts of nuclear materials and sabotage.[170] In a second set of hearings in 1986, the same subcommittee found that serious problems still remained at some of the DOE's nuclear weapons sites. It reported that "the DOE's own internal inspection reports show that plutonium and highly enriched uranium are still highly vulnerable to theft and sabotage at these locations."[171] The 1986 hearings identified several specific examples to illustrate its findings. For example, inspections revealed that there were no portal monitors to prevent nuclear material from being carried out at some of the exits at the Pantex facility, perhaps the most sensitive facility in the entire U.S. complex.[172] The Congressional hearings also reported that during a test at the Pantex facility, an insider was able to smuggle a pistol and explosives into the facility to be used several days later in a successful attempt to steal bomb parts containing plutonium.[173] In addition, the hearings reported that during a test at the Savannah River site, the guard force reportedly failed to prevent a mock terrorist force from gaining access to the facility and making off with mock plutonium. The guard force was reportedly still shooting at one another twenty minutes after the adversary force had left the facility.[174]

In a summary of its 1986 findings, the House Subcommittee identified the following general problems with the DOE's safeguards and security program:

- Inadequately trained guard forces.
- Inadequate protection against insider threat.
- Conflicting state laws over whether guards can use deadly force to prevent thefts of materials.

- Inability to track and recover fissile materials and nuclear weapons in the event that they are stolen from the DOE.
- Reduction of funds for safeguards and security upgrades.[175]

In additional follow-up Congressional hearings in 1989, the Subcommittee found that the DOE had made some advances in safeguards and security. It reported that "guard forces at the Hanford Nuclear Reservation, the Savannah River plant, and Oak Ridge are generally well trained and have state-of-the-art weapons and equipment. DOE and its contractors have improved their protection of special nuclear materials and classified documents." But the Subcommittee also found that serious problems still remained at some facilities. For example, Edward McCallum, the director of the DOE's Office of Security Evaluations, reported "serious deficiencies" at Lawrence Livermore National Laboratory, including incidents where Category I quantities of SNM[176] were routinely "left unattended in unalarmed rooms during offshift hours" and incidents where "Category 1 quantities of material were often left, between process steps, with only one person or unattended."[177] The Subcommittee concluded that "protecting its nuclear weapons and classified programs is still not a high priority for the Department [of Energy]."[178]

In part due to these hearings, funding for the DOE's Safeguards and Security Program was more than doubled, and hundreds of millions of dollars were spent on a "crash program" to build a host of new security systems, from fences and razor ribbon to high-technology perimeter intrusion detection and assessment systems.[179] More advanced computing systems were developed to improve materials accountability and to assess potential vulnerabilities in security systems. The DOE also implemented a human reliability program in 1985, which would help reduce potential insider threats by requiring everyone who had access to significant quantities of SNM to undergo extensive medical reviews and drug testing.[180]

Current U.S. MPC&A Systems

A given MPC&A system in the United States is designed to meet the unique requirements of the facility at which it is installed. There are, however, general guidelines with which all MPC&A systems must comply. U.S. MPC&A systems are based on a notion of graded controls, which are designed to provide different levels of protection based on the attractiveness level of the materials present at a given facility. The attractiveness of the material contained in U.S. facilities is determined according to specific criteria. (See table 2.4 for the graded safeguards categories for given amounts of fissile materials. See table 2.5 for the recommended MPC&A integration measures for each category of fissile materials.)

U.S. MPC&A systems are generally divided into physical protection and material control and accounting (MC&A) systems. As we have seen in chapter 1, physical protection systems are intended to deter and defeat attempted attacks on nuclear facilities, while MC&A systems are designed to detect thefts of fissile materials. All aspects of U.S. MPC&A systems are designed to provide "defense in depth," where there is a degree of redundancy in the systems, so that the failure of one part of the system does not result in the failure of the entire system.[181] The current physical protection and MC&A systems will be discussed separately.

Current Physical Protection Systems

Protective Personnel

Protective personnel are employed at all U.S. facilities containing nuclear materials. These personnel include security officers and security police officers. These personnel form the core of the "active" protective system, which ensures that the facility operation complies with its license. The qualifications and authority for protective personnel at DOE and DOE-contractor facilities are clearly established in official U.S. government regulations.[182] These regulations specify which facilities require protection by security officers, and which require security police officers, depending on what category materials are present in the facility.[183] A protective force consisting of security police officers is required at facilities possessing Category I and/or Category II quantities of fissile materials.[184]

Personnel Identification Systems

Entry into a "Restricted Access" area or facility is based on prior authorization and local, live-time validation of the identity of the individual attempting access to the area. Several methods are used to verify personnel identities. One common approach employs a photographic identification card that is checked by a security police officer. In addition, several types of automated access systems have been developed, including systems that require the person seeking access to insert his or her magnetically encoded card and type in a unique personal identification number, and systems to identify personal characteristics, such as hand geometry or patterns in the retina of the eye.[185]

Table 2.4. U.S. Graded Safeguards Categories

	Attractive-ness Level	Pu/U-233 Category (quantities in kgs)				Contained U-235 Category (quantities in kgs)			
		I	II	III	IV	I	II	III	IV
Weapons[a]	A	All	N/A	N/A	N/A	All	N/A	N/A	N/A
Pure Products[b]	B	≥2	≥0.4<2	≥0.2<0.4	<0.2	≥5	≥1<5	≥0.4<1	<0.4
High-Grade Materials[c]	C	≥6	2<6	≥0.4<2	<0.4	≥20	≥6<20	≥2<6	<2
Low-Grade Materials[d]	D	N/A	≥16	≥3<16	<3	N/A	≥50	≥8<50	<8
All Other Materials[e]	E	N/A	N/A	N/A	Reportable Quantities	N/A	N/A	N/A	Reportable Quantities

Source: Control and Accountability of Nuclear Materials, Office of Safeguards and Security, U.S. Department of Energy, DOE 5633.3B, September 7, 1994, p. I-7.

Notes:

[a] Includes assembled weapons and test devices.

[b] Includes pits, major components, button ingots, recastable metal, directly convertible metals.

[c] Includes carbides, oxides, solutions (^{3}25g/L), nitrates, etc., fuel elements and assemblies, alloys and mixtures, UF4 or UF6 (^{3}50% U-235).

[d] Includes solutions (1g to 25g/L), process residues requiring extensive reprocessing, moderately irradiated material, Pu-238 (except waste), UF4 or UF6 (^{3}20%<50% U-235).

[e] Includes highly irradiated forms, solutions (<1g/L), uranium containing <20% U-235 (any form, any quantity).

Table 2.5. Recommended MPC&A Integration for Each Category of SNM		
Material Category and Attractiveness Level	**Threat Level**	**Recommended MPC&A Elements**
Category I-A Category I-B Category II-B Category I-C	High	Inner Area within Protected Area Exterior and Interior Intrusion Detection Rapid Assessment for Intrusion Detection Substantial Delay Repositories and Vaults Vault Storage of Material When Not in Use Authorized Access Control Two-Person Rule or Equivalent Surveillance Key and Combination Control Staffed SNM and Metal Portal Monitoring Material Measurement and Measurement Control Physical Inventory ProgramWaste Monitoring Daily Administrative Checks Robust Guard Response within Delay Times Protection of Guard Response Force Location Guard Communications Hardened Central Alarm Station/Possible Secondary
Category II-C	Medium	Protected Area Exterior and Interior Intrusion Detection Assessment for Intrusion Detection Adequate Delay Repositories and Vaults Vault Storage of SNM When Not in Use Authorized Access Control Two-Person Rule or Equivalent Surveillance Key and Combination Control Staffed SNM and Metal Portal Monitoring, if necessary Material Measurement and Measurement Control Physical Inventory Program Waste Monitoring Acceptable Guard Response within Delay Times Guard Communications Protected Central Alarm Station
Category II-D Category III	Low	Random Guard Patrol or Minimal Intrusion Detection Material Secured When Not in Use Key and Combination Control for Authorized Personnel Minimal Material Control and Accountability Program Acceptable Guard Response
Category IV	Low	Locked Room Key Control for Authorized Personnel

Source: Guidelines for Material Protection, Control and Accounting Upgrades at Russian Facilities, Los Alamos National Laboratory, September 28, 1998, p. 8. Although this document is intended for use in MPC&A upgrades in Russian facilities, it essentially summarizes the MPC&A system used in the United States. For a discussion of the joint U.S.-Russian program to upgrade MPC&A systems at Russian facilities, see chapter 3.

Barriers

Barriers include physical constructs and administrative procedures, both of which have the same goal: restricting access, movements, and activities in restricted areas and facilities to those persons and activities that have been previously authorized. Common physical barriers to control access include razor-wire fences, reinforced walls and doors, and metal gratings over windows.[186] Administrative barriers are maintained by specific policies and by promulgation of instructions, codes, and orders.

Numerous studies have been conducted to assess how well physical barriers provide resistance to forcible assault. These studies have found that a determined and well-equipped adversary can defeat any physical barrier if given enough time. Physical barriers are thus generally regarded as delaying devices intended to prevent an intruder from achieving his or her goal before guard forces can arrive. Because the delays provided by passive barriers such as fences, walls, and doors are surprisingly small, a number of "activated" barriers have been designed to increase delay times. These activated barriers can include some of the following:

- Coils of concertina or barbed wire are suspended near the ceiling in critical rooms and corridors. When an alarm is sounded, the coils are dropped to the floor to impede the intruder's progress.
- Chemical smoke is dispensed to restrict the intruder's visibility.
- Aqueous foam is created and released to fill the room containing the intruder or his target, thus inhibiting visibility.
- Sticky foam is dispensed to make it difficult for the intruder to detach the materials or himself from the area. Sticky foam has also been built into some walls and is used to fill any hole created in the walls by explosives.[187]

Detection Devices

The United States currently uses a number of devices to detect unauthorized personnel, materials, and actions in its nuclear facilities. There are two general types of detection devices: intrusion detectors are used to detect unauthorized personnel in a facility, while contraband detectors are used to detect the introduction of unauthorized materials (weapons, cameras, etc.) into a facility or the unauthorized removal of materials (nuclear materials, detection equipment, etc.) from a facility.

Interior and exterior intrusion detectors are either used by protective personnel or are installed within the facility to detect motion. Protective personnel employ various equipment to detect unauthorized personnel in a facility, such as closed-circuit television and night-vision devices. Video motion detector (VMD) systems employ television cameras and monitors to observe critical areas. If the VMD systems detect motion in these areas, they trigger an audible alarm and often initiate a video recorder to preserve a picture of the event or motion that caused the alarm.[188]

Additional exterior intrusion detectors are strategically located in a cleared area inside the outer security fence of the area being protected. Several detection devices are often used in conjunction to reduce the frequency of unwanted alarms. These detectors include some of the following devices:

- A taut-wire fence, consisting of several tightly strung horizontal wires located at points from near ground level to above normal human height. A small amount of pressure against any of the wires is sufficient to trigger an alarm.
- An electric field fence is used to detect any disturbance in the electric field created by charged wires in the fence.
- Buried-line intrusion detectors are similar to electric field fences, but they detect any disturbance in the electric field created by charges wired under the ground.
- Infrared and microwave detectors send electromagnetic radiation from a set of transmitters on one post to a set of receivers on another post some distance away. An intruder crossing between the posts would trigger an alarm.
- Seismic detectors are generally buried at specified intervals and produce an alarm if they sense vibrations caused by the footsteps of an intruder.[189]

Contraband detectors, on the other hand, are generally located at strategic access points, such as the entrances and exits of a facility. Most of these devices are used in "portal monitors," through which anyone entering or exiting a facility must pass. They are also generally available in handheld devices for use by guards. Contraband detectors include explosives detectors, metal detectors, radiation detectors, and X-ray package inspection devices.[190]

Communications Systems

Communications systems are critical for the success of physical protection systems. In an integrated system, intrusion detector alarms must be received by a security force communications center, which in turn must communicate with the facility's guard forces and possibly with local law-enforcement agencies. The communication system generally relies on phone lines, coaxial cables, or fiber optics, and various radio devices. It is critical that facilities have redundant networks to prevent the entire communications system from failing if one set of communications fails.[191]

Current Fissile Material Control and Accounting (MC&A) Systems

Material Accounting

Nuclear materials accountability programs must ensure that all nuclear materials are accounted for and that theft or diversion has not occurred.[192] It must therefore meet three objectives: to provide assurance that all material quantities are present in the correct amount, to provide timely detection of a material loss, and to estimate the amount of any loss and its location.[193]

Material Balance Areas

For material control and accounting purposes, nuclear facilities are divided into material balance areas (MBAs). An MBA is defined such that all movement of material into and out of the area and periodic inventories of materials within the area are measured and recorded through key measurement points (KMPs). KMPs are strategic locations where nuclear material appears in a measurable form that allows determination of the material flow or inventory. The KMPs therefore include input, output, and inventories in MBAs, including discards and storage.[194]

Accounting Systems

Each facility must have a system that provides for tracking nuclear material inventories, documenting material transactions, issuing periodic reports, and assisting with the detection of unauthorized system access, data falsification, and material gains or losses.[195] An accounting system must begin with proper documentation based on a material balance equation. The conservation of mass would indicate that:

Ending Inventory - Beginning Inventory = Input Transfers - Output Transfers

Because there will be some uncertainties in measurement amounts, there must be some specified allowable margins of error on these calculations. The material balance equation (MB) therefore states that:

MB = "beginning inventory" - "ending inventory" + "input transfers" - "output transfers"

The quotation marks around the units indicates acceptable margins of error in measurements. If the MB is positive, it indicates an apparent loss of materials; if it is negative, it indicates apparent gain of materials. If the MB value exceeds an acceptable range, then immediate action is necessary to discover what caused the imbalance.[196]

The materials balance equation includes all of the material movements across the MBA boundary during the period between two successive inventory determinations. The MBA must be capable of being updated daily or on demand for all nuclear transactions. The material balances are carefully logged into an accounting database, and the data is sent to a national database, the Nuclear Materials Management and Safeguards System (NMMSS).[197]

Physical Inve ntories

In order to verify that the actual amounts of fissile materials in the facility equal the amounts stated in the accounting database, each facility must conduct periodic physical inventories of its fissile materials. In MBAs where the material quantities are in the form of discrete items (such as a storage vault for cans of uranium oxide), material accounting may take the form of item control, by which the identity and integrity of the individual items can be confirmed. In such item control areas (ICAs), the material is confirmed either by verifying that a sealed container or other form of containment has remained intact since the last inventory (e.g., through a tamper-indicating seal), or by a measurement that verifies that the item has physical characteristics (such as weight or radiation emissions) consistent with the accounting records.[198] For facilities that contain bulk materials or non-discrete items such as fluids, the physical inventories must be taken through direct measurement (such as balances or dip-tube manometers), analytical methods applied to samples (such as measuring weight), or by radiation emissions.[199]

The most straightforward method of determining the quantity of SNM in a well-defined item would be to measure the mass of the object of which the SNM is a part, then to conduct a careful destructive analysis of a small sample to determine the chemical or isotopic composition of the object. But this process is time-consuming, and may be impossible for some types of materials. For this reason, other measurement techniques have been developed. The most effective of these techniques are those that employ nondestructive assay (NDA) of the sample material. NDA techniques obtain mass values for the SNM content of an item without opening or otherwise disturbing the item or its container.[200] There are a number of different NDA techniques, including "passive" NDA, which measures spontaneous gamma or neutron emissions, and "active" NDA, which derives is primary information from the interaction of an external radiation source with the sample.[201]

Measurement and Measurement Control

All facilities are also required to implement strict measurement and measurement controls to establish material values and to assure the quality of the data. First, the facilities must establish what measurement methods will be used and when the measurements are to be taken. Second, they must also ensure that the personnel conducting the measurements are properly trained and qualified. Third, they must ensure any sample measured is representative of the bulk of the material that is being tested. And finally, they must ensure that the measurement equipment is calibrated regularly. The regulations for all these areas must be carefully documented and strictly followed.[202]

Material Transfers

Each facility must also have a program to control and account for internal and external facility transfers of nuclear materials. They must have documented procedures that specify the requirements for authorization, documentation, tracking, verification, and response to abnormal situations that may occur during the transfer of nuclear materials. For example, Category I and II quantities of fissile materials transferred between facilities must be measured independently by the shipper and the receiver to ensure that no materials were stolen or diverted while the materials were in transit. Movements of fissile materials within a facility, such as from one MBA to another, must also be carefully documented and verified, though they only require one transfer check.[203]

Material Control Indicators

The management in each facility is also required to implement a program for assessing the various material control indicators (such as differences between shipping and receiving inventory measurements and discrepancies in inventory measurements) to provide assurance that losses or unauthorized removals of nuclear materials are detected. If there is a difference between the material balances calculated by shippers and receivers, or the material balances calculated when material is moved within a facility, the facility must be able to determine whether the difference is statistically significant and, if so, what the cause of the difference is.[204] Each facility must also have specific procedures for documenting and reporting any significant differences in material balances.[205]

Current Fissile Material Control Systems

Nuclear control programs must control nuclear materials in a manner sufficient to prevent or deter loss or misuse. The general requirements for MC&A systems are thoroughly outlined in official government documents.[206] These documents divide material control into four functional performance areas: access controls, material surveillance, material containment, and detection and assessment. The requirements in each of these areas depend on the attractiveness level of materials contained in each facility.

Access Controls

Each facility containing SNM is required to have a graded program for controlling access to nuclear materials; nuclear materials accountability, inventory, and measurement data; and data-generating equipment and other items or equipment where misuse or tampering could compromise the safeguards system. This program requires that only authorized personnel have access to these materials and equipment, and that the equipment include tamper-indicating devices.[207]

Material Surveillance

Each facility's management must establish a graded surveillance program for monitoring nuclear materials and detecting unauthorized activities, as well as procedures for reporting the status of the material and the facility. Material surveillance may be carried out through some of the following mechanisms:[208]

- Intrusion alarms: Alarms provide detection capabilities for personnel entering at times when the area should be unoccupied.
- Area surveillance by personnel: The two-person rule is a commonly used personnel surveillance method that can be enhanced by supervisor surveillance and monitored closed-circuit television.
- Automated area surveillance: Automated surveillance methods that rely on computer control alone or computer control in conjunction with human supervision.
- Shelf monitors: A shelf monitor continuously measures and reports on a physical characteristic, such as weight or radioactive emissions, of an item that is placed on a shelf.
- Item motion detectors: A transponder-equipped device containing a sensitive accelerometer is placed on top of an item and emits a signal if the item is moved.

- Digital image processing: Digital image processing can be used to detect the movement of a single item or large numbers of items.[209]
- Automated means through monitoring devices, sensors (such as portal monitors), or other instrumentation to detect anomalies and to report alarm conditions.
- Visual surveillance, either through the two-person rule or monitoring by external personnel to assess SNM material movements or inventory status.
- Through process logs, inventory records, or other information to indicate anomalies and trigger investigations.

Material Containment

A critical part of material containment is the division of facilities containing nuclear materials into protected areas, materials access areas, and materials balance areas. Category I quantities of fissile materials must be used, stored, or processed only within a materials access area that is contained within a protected area. Category II quantities of materials must be used, processed, or stored at least within a protected area. Both of these categories of materials must be stored in a vault when the materials are not in use.[210]

Each facility must also have controls to ensure that nuclear materials are controlled, processed, or stored within an MBA. These controls must ensure that materials are removed from the MBA only via authorized pathways or portals and that they are subject to transfer and verification procedures.[211]

Detection and Assessment

Each facility must also have the capability to detect and assess the unauthorized removal of nuclear materials. This system should be interfaced with the facility's physical protection system so that protective forces are notified when unauthorized removals occur. These detection systems should include some of the following elements:[212]

- Tamper-indicating devices. These include seals on containers for fissile materials, monitoring equipment, and gauges and other measuring devices.[213]
- Portal monitors. Portal monitors should be placed on all possible exits to the facility and possibly on all exits to a given MBA. These monitors should be carefully maintained and their performance checked. Measures should be taken to prevent unauthorized access to portal monitor instrumentation and cabling.

- Waste monitors. All liquid, solid, and gaseous waste streams leaving an MBA should be monitored to detect thefts or diversion. These monitors could include gamma/neutron radiation detectors.

These detection systems should be tested regularly to ensure that they have not been modified in any unauthorized way.

Integration of the Individual Elements in MPC&A Systems

As previously noted, the entire MPC&A system must be carefully integrated so that all the parts work in conjunction. This requires that the specific objectives of the MPC&A system are identified, the MPC&A system is carefully designed, and the system is extensively performance tested to ensure that the system works as an integrated whole.[214]

Continuing Problems with U.S. MPC&A

Owing to continual improvements in safeguards and security procedures and technologies, U.S. MPC&A programs are probably the most stringent and effective in the world.[215] Nevertheless, assessments in the mid- and late-1990s continued to identify problems with U.S. MPC&A. Although many of the problems identified in these assessments were due to historical problems arising from statistical measurements conducted over numerous years, some of them raised ongoing problems with the security systems and accounting procedures at some DOE facilities.

Large Quantities of "Materials Unaccounted For" at U.S. Nuclear Facilities

In 1996, the United States declassified information about the plutonium produced and held at U.S. production facilities.[216] In the resulting report, the United States indicated the "inventory differences" recorded at those sites. These inventory differences, which are defined as the book inventories less the physical inventory, were recorded at the facilities during the years they were in operation. Presumably, annual physical inventories were taken at the sites and compared with the book inventories.[217] The inventory differences are usually referred to as "material unaccounted for" (or MUF, in the standard terminology used by the IAEA). As shown by table 2.6, as of 1996 the MUF reported at U.S. production facilities was quite large, over 2,700 kilograms.

According to the DOE, the factors that have contributed to the inventory differences include the following:

Table 2.6. Total Pu Inventory Differences at U.S. Production Facilities, 1996	
Site	**Quantity (in kilograms)**[a]
Hanford Reservation	+1,266.0
Rocky Flats	+1,191.8
Savannah River	+232.0
Los Alamos National Laboratory	+47.5
Lawrence Livermore National Laboratory	+5.5
Argonne National Engineering Laboratory	-3.4
Idaho National Engineering Laboratory	-5.6
Other Sites	+16.7
Total	**+2,750.5**

Source: Albright et al., *Plutonium and Highly Enriched Uranium, 1996*, p. 46.

Note: [a] The "+" or "-" denotes whether the book inventory exceeds (+) or falls short (-) of the physical inventory.

(1) high measurement uncertainty of plant "holdup"; (2) measurement uncertainties because of the wide variations of the matrix containing the materials; (3) measurement uncertainties due to statistical variations in the measurement itself; (4) in the early years, technology had not been developed to measure the material adequately; (5) measurements for waste are still very uncertain because often small quantities of plutonium or uranium are mixed with a variety of other materials so variable that it is not possible to make accurate calibration sources for measurements; (6) losses from operations, such as accidental spills where accurate measurements were not made before the spill; (7) corrections of human errors in the input of data into accounting systems; and (8) rounding errors.[218]

As the DOE report indicates, a large amount of the MUF is believed to be due to "holdup," where fissile materials are trapped in pipes, joints, etc., throughout the facilities. Because most of these facilities are generally well-protected and typically employ systems (such as portal monitors) to detect unauthorized removals of fissile materials, there is a reduced risk that these materials could be stolen. In addition, most of the inventory differences reportedly arose from activities in the 1950s, 1960s, and early 1970s, before tighter measurement and accounting requirements were enforced, or even technologically achievable.[219] Nevertheless, with such significant account imbalances, it would have been nearly impossible to verify whether or not thefts have occurred, particularly during the time that the less advanced measurement and accounting systems were used.

Security Difficulties at Rocky Flats

In the mid-1990s, the security at Rocky Flats came under severe criticism. As noted above, Rocky Flats was shut down in 1989 due to serious environmental and safety concerns. While the facility was not producing new fissile materials in the 1990s, it still contained large amounts of fissile materials, much of which remained in pipes and joints throughout the facility due to "holdup." Thus, even though Rocky Flats was not producing fissile materials, it was critical to maintain strict security at the facility while cleanup operations took place. Unfortunately, the security at this facility was frequently found to be seriously deficient.

In early 1997, David Ridenour, the security chief at Rocky Flats, quit in "disgust," complaining that he could not guarantee security at the site.[220] At the time of Ridenour's resignation, the secretary of energy acknowledged that "significant" security problems existed at the site.[221]

Rocky Flats's physical protection systems have had a history of "marginal" or "unsatisfactory" ratings from the DOE, and a series of tests over the years have resulted in knowledgeable individuals successfully removing mock plutonium from the facility without authorization or detection. In 1997, shortly before Ridenour resigned from his position, the DOE rated the facility's physical protection as "unsatisfactory." The facility received its first "satisfactory" rating in September 1997, though a DOE report in mid-1997 argued that there was "reason for skepticism" about the improvements because Rocky Flats "has a long history of improving its protective systems only to allow them to degrade once again when priorities shift or external pressures abate." It is therefore probably not surprising that a November 1997 DOE review described security at Rocky Flats as again "less-than-adequate." The review indicated that "DOE protective standards were not being met with respect to the protection of special nuclear materials against theft," and it pointed to "on again, off again" management attention to physical protection at the facility.[222] In part due to this criticism, significant efforts were made to improve the security at Rocky Flats. DOE officials reported that most of these problems had been addressed by the late 1990s,[223] and most of the cleanup had been completed by late 2001.[224]

Office of Oversight Reports in the Late 1990s

The DOE's Office of Independent Oversight and Performance Assurance performed reviews in 1995 and 1998 that found significant problems with the DOE's fissile material assurance programs.[225] In the 1995 report, the Office of Oversight found that no accurate inventories exist for thousands of kilograms of scrap plutonium and HEU in the U.S. complex, and that even though physical protection was generally found to be reliable, "an accurate inventory is necessary for continued assurance against theft of diversion."[226]

The 1998 follow-up report identified "notable progress" in improving the problems identified in 1995, but reported that "many weaknesses in fissile material assurance remain, and the DOE has not yet achieved an acceptable level of confidence in its nuclear material inventory."[227] The 1998 report found that the weaknesses were similar to the problems identified in 1995. The report identified the following general types of weaknesses:

- Significant quantities of fissile materials that have never been measured.
- Inventory values that are not defensible because the measurement techniques were inadequate or not repeatable, or because the inventory value is based on an estimate.
- Materials that have indefensible values because of inadequate or lost records.
- Items that cannot be measured because they are inaccessible (e.g., in a high-radiation area).
- Failure to conduct required physical inventories.
- Physical inventories that do not encompass all materials or that do not provide sufficient data to determine whether materials are accounted for.
- Inventory measurements that do not provide assurance that materials have not been diverted.
- Inappropriate inventory practices, such as not updating accounting records after inventory measurements indicate significant differences between the actual amounts of materials and the recorded amounts.
- Incomplete or inappropriate inventory sampling plans.
- Failure to include holdup in accountability records after it has been identified and/or measured.[228]

The serious criticisms in the 1995 and 1998 reports spurred significant efforts within the DOE to address these problems. In November 2000, the Office of Oversight conducted another follow-up report on the DOE's MPC&A programs. This report found that the DOE's MPC&A programs had improved significantly since 1998. The report found that while some corrective actions are still ongoing at several sites, Independent Oversight inspections indicated that most sites now have satisfactory MPC&A programs.[229] The report did note, however, that there are significant remaining weaknesses in MC&A at the Y-12 Plant at Oak Ridge and in accounting programs for irradiated nuclear fuel, including enriched fuel returned from foreign countries.[230]

There have been additional reports of possible ongoing difficulties with U.S. systems, however. According to information acquired by a nongovernmental watchdog group in the United States, security flaws reportedly exist at nuclear weapons facilities around the country, which may leave U.S. weapons-grade nuclear material vulnerable to theft and sabotage by terrorists.[231] Citing this report and internal Department of Energy (DOE) documents, U.S. Rep. Edward J. Markey submitted a letter to the DOE in January 2002 identifying inadequate security at several U.S. nuclear weapons sites.[232] Although some of Markey's allegations may have been overstated, there have been additional criticisms of the nuclear security within the DOE and the National Nuclear Security Administration (NNSA)—a separately organized agency within DOE responsible for nuclear security at the major U.S. nuclear weapons laboratories. In a May 2003 report, the Government Accounting Office detailed several fundamental difficulties in the NNSA's management of its Safeguards and Security Program. The GAO noted, first, that the NNSA had problems defining and coordinating clear roles and responsibilities for NNSA headquarters and site operations. Second, it reported problems in the NNSA's oversight of contracting agents responsible for day-to-day security. And third, the GAO reported shortcomings in the expertise and training of staff and security specialists.[233]

Part III: Conclusions

Although proliferation optimists point to the United States as one of the primary examples supporting their position, the evidence on this point is far from conclusive. In fact, the experience of the United States should give us more reason for pessimism than optimism about the safety and security consequences resulting from further proliferation. I will first discuss the conclusions that can be drawn from the U.S. case study in the areas of command and control and MPC&A.

Conclusions about Command and Control

The U.S. case study demonstrates very vividly the level of effort that is required to successfully address what Peter Feaver calls the "always/never dilemma." NWSs are under simultaneous pressure to ensure that their nuclear weapons "always" work when they need them to, but are "never" used when they do not want them to be used. U.S. strategies for achieving the "always" side have included making technical advances on triggering designs, designing resilient command systems that protect against decapitation, developing large arsenals with the capabilities for rapid response, adopting (at least in the early years) a continual air alert for air forces, predelegating launch authority, adopting a use doctrine that allows for LOW, and developing advanced early-warning systems. These systems have helped ensure that the U.S. arsenal is survivable and resistant to decapitation, but they also make the "never" side of the dilemma extremely difficult to solve.

Through extensive efforts, the United States has made great achievements in reducing the likelihood of accidental, unauthorized, and inadvertent use. As we have seen, U.S. weapons include sophisticated safety designs and use-control devices, and the U.S. early-warning system contains numerous redundant sensors to minimize false alarms. Nevertheless, this study has identified a number of risky procedures, accidents, risks of unauthorized use, and false alarms that have weakened U.S. efforts to solve the "never" side of the dilemma.

Because the United States has corrected many (though not all) of these procedures, the U.S. arsenal is now generally considered to be relatively safe. But the U.S. case study should cause us to be very concerned about the further proliferation of nuclear weapons. As we have seen, the greatest risks occurred during the early years of the U.S. nuclear weapons program, before it made significant advances in its weapons designs and use-control devices. But emerging NWSs may have to pass through a similar developmental stage. While they might be able to avoid some difficulties because many of the necessary technologies are now available on the open market, many other necessary technologies are not available or are very expensive. As we have seen, it requires extensive efforts and resources to ensure adequate C^3I systems, and it will probably be beyond the capabilities of most emerging NWSs to achieve standards similar to what the United States has. Setting aside the technical requirements for producing resilient command-and-control systems, the cost of such systems is extraordinarily high. To put some of these expenses in perspective, a perimeter intrusion detection and assessment system (PIDAS) for the physical protection of facilities containing Category I materials costs nearly $1,000 per foot, and a typical Cat D PAL device on U.S. weapons costs an estimated $50,000.[234] It is highly unlikely that emerging NWSs will be able, or willing, to spend limited resources on similar control systems. As a result, emerging NWSs might tend to encounter more severe difficulties in preventing accidental, unauthorized, and inadvertent use than the United States did.

Conclusions about U.S. MPC&A

In the first years of its nuclear program, the United States maintained security through the "3 G's." As the worldwide terrorist threats increased, however, these controls were found to be radically inadequate for protecting against overt and covert (insider) thefts of fissile materials and sabotage of nuclear facilities. Especially during the early years, U.S. government agencies generally did not devote enough serious attention to safeguards and security because their efforts were much more focused on rapid fissile material production.[235]

Over the years, however, the United States did significantly improve its MPC&A. The Department of Energy currently spends approximately $800 million every year on safeguards and security in the DOE nuclear complex, and its MPC&A systems are now probably the best in the world.[236] But this progress was typically achieved in fits and starts, often due to scathing investigations by independent agencies and the U.S. Congress. This fact alone should cause us to doubt that emerging NWSs will make similar efforts to achieve similar fissile material controls, because it is unlikely that their nuclear programs will allow for similar transparency and oversight.

In addition, we must doubt that emerging NWSs will be able to devote close to the same resources to ensuring adequate MPC&A. As we have seen, *even after* the United States incorporated extensive detection and alarm systems, implemented rigorous requirements for training and security forces, and designed its systems to provide a high level of accounting and control, its MPC&A systems were sometimes *still* found to have serious deficiencies. This demonstrates the extreme difficulties involved with MPC&A, and we should doubt whether emerging NWSs will be able or willing to design and implement similar MPC&A systems.

Will Emerging NWSs Be Likely to Learn from the U.S. Experience?

Through extensive efforts over numerous years, the United States has managed to develop a number of ways to control its nuclear arsenal and fissile material stockpile. While, in some ways, this case could be interpreted as a qualified support of the optimist position, such a conclusion hinges upon whether or not emerging NWSs will learn from the U.S. experience. To a large degree, we will have to keep this question in mind as we turn to the other cases in this book, but there are nevertheless reasons to question the extent to which emerging NWSs will in fact learn from the U.S. experience.

Emerging NWSs will only be able to learn from the U.S. experience if they recognize any problems that the United States had with its nuclear safety and control systems; engage in an open examination of their own programs to identify similar problems; and either avoid adopting systems that lead to such problems, or failing that, implement similar or equivalent solutions to the problems. But there are at least two reasons to doubt that emerging NWSs will do so. First, as Cohen and Frankel argue, the nuclear programs in emerging NWSs will tend to be "opaque," where there is no open debate about the nuclear programs and very little independent oversight of safety and security procedures.[237] As we have seen, these were critical elements in identifying weaknesses in U.S. safety and security measures and in spurring efforts to correct these weaknesses. If emerging NWSs do not have such open debate or independent oversight, it is doubtful that they will correct similar problems in their own programs.

Second, as we have seen from the U.S. case, there is a significant tradeoff between developing survivable forces, which require larger forces and dispersed deployments, and maintaining rigorous controls over nuclear weapons. In the early years of its nuclear history, the United States attempted to develop survivable forces and command structures, but in the process adopted procedures and deployments that increased risks of accidents and loss of central control over its nuclear weapons and fissile materials. The United States eventually corrected many of these problems by developing very expensive command-and-control and MPC&A systems. If emerging NWSs attempt to develop survivable forces by increasing their force sizes and weapons dispersals, they too will need to develop reliable systems for controlling their nuclear weapons and fissile materials. However, the limited resources in emerging NWSs will probably prevent them from being able to afford command-and control and MPC&A systems similar to those employed by the United States.

It is possible that emerging NWSs will find alternative ways of addressing the safety and security issues highlighted in the U.S. case study. We will examine to what extent they have done so in subsequent chapters. But it is worth noting that these remain very difficult problems to address. If emerging states do not find alternate methods of solving these issues, their nuclear arsenals and fissile material stockpiles could be much more vulnerable than those in the United States. In particular, if emerging NWSs depend on low-cost security systems that rely heavily on guards, gates, and guns, their nuclear controls could become particularly vulnerable during political, social, and economic upheavals. In the next chapter, we will identify more clearly the ways that such upheavals can undermine nuclear controls by examining the effects they have had on the nuclear controls in Russia.

3 Russia

Why study Russia? In early rounds of the debate, Waltz and other optimists pointed to the relative stability that arose between the superpowers during the Cold War as evidence for their position.[1] In response, a number of pessimists in the early 1990s argued that the Cold War was not as stable as the optimists would like to think because the superpowers had actually encountered significant command-and-control difficulties over the years, and that the spread of nuclear weapons would be destabilizing because emerging nuclear weapons states (NWSs) would likely experience more severe command-and-control difficulties than the superpowers did.[2] Thus, in the early rounds of the debate, both sides acknowledged the importance of Russia, but they took opposing positions as to what the case of Russia proved.

The character of the proliferation debate changed, however, with the publication of the articles by David Karl and Jordan Seng.[3] In these articles, Karl and Seng maintain that the Russian case is not applicable to the overall question of whether emerging NWSs will have reliable nuclear controls, because the small arsenals and simple command structures in emerging NWSs will allow them to avoid the command-and-control difficulties encountered by the superpowers. As a result of these articles, little more has been said about Russia in the context of the proliferation debate, as scholars turned to examine risks associated with the smaller arsenals of emerging NWSs.[4]

This chapter demonstrates that the Russian case remains relevant to the proliferation debate and that it continues to reveal serious difficulties with the optimist position. The Russian case provides insight into an issue that has not been adequately addressed in the debate, namely what happens when a NWS undergoes economic, political, or social upheavals. In the last decade, severe weaknesses have arisen in Russia's controls over its nuclear arsenal and fissile material stockpile as a direct result of the domestic upheavals that have plagued the nation since the fall of the Soviet Union.

During the Cold War, the Soviet Union had massive numbers of nuclear weapons deployed in Eastern-bloc countries and many of the Soviet republics. After the fall of the Berlin Wall in 1989 and the subsequent breakup of the Soviet Union, many of these weapons initially remained in the Eastern-bloc countries and several of the newly independent states (NIS) other than Russia. Recognizing the extreme risk of a loss of control over these weapons, Moscow (with U.S. assistance) engaged in a massive effort to remove its nuclear weapons from these countries. All the weapons deployed in Eastern Europe were reportedly returned to Russia in 1989,[5] but many nuclear weapons remained in the NIS for several years.[6] Although Russia negotiated and carried out the removal of the nuclear weapons from many of the NIS relatively easily,[7] it had much more difficulty arranging for the removal of thousands of strategic and tactical nuclear weapons deployed in Belarus, Ukraine, and Kazakhstan. In 1992, however, the leaders of these countries signed the Lisbon Protocol, in which they agreed to return the nuclear weapons deployed on their territories.[8] All the tactical weapons were returned to Russia by the end of 1992, and all the warheads for the strategic weapons were returned by the end of 1996.[9] But the dangers were not over yet.

In the decade following the Soviet collapse, Russia has continued to encounter serious difficulties in maintaining nuclear controls, due to the deterioration of nuclear infrastructures, serious economic constraints, and the weakening of systems for controlling its nuclear weapons and fissile materials. This chapter will examine these weaknesses in great detail.

Part I: Russia's C³I and the Risks of Accidental, Unauthorized, and Inadvertent Use

Russia's Nuclear Arsenal and Delivery Systems

Russia's current nuclear arsenal contains an estimated 22,500 warheads. Of these warheads, roughly half are believed to be mated to delivery systems.[10] Until the end of the Cold War, the Soviet Union had extremely powerful conventional and nuclear forces. In recent years, however, Russia's conventional forces have largely collapsed, due to a lack of money to pay soldiers or replace aging equipment.[11] As a result, Russia's military plans for the next decade have called for an increased reliance on nuclear forces.[12] However, the same economic problems that have hurt Russia's conventional forces have also hurt Russia's nuclear forces. Russia's arsenal is still enormous and extremely powerful, but its strength increasingly lies in its land-based strategic rocket forces, and even those forces are decaying rapidly.[13]

Nuclear Arms Control Treaties

SALT, INF, START I

As discussed in chapter 2, the United States and Russia negotiated several important arms control treaties in the 1970s and 1980s. These negotiations culminated in SALT I and II, the Intermediate-Range Nuclear Forces (INF) Treaty, and the first Strategic Arms Reduction Treaty (START I).[14]

1991–1992 Presidential Nuclear Initiatives (PNIs)

In 1991–1992, the United States and Russia both undertook unilateral initiatives to reduce their tactical nuclear arsenals.[15] In October 1991, Mikhail Gorbachev announced the Tactical Nuclear Weapon Reduction Initiatives, and in January 1992 Boris Yeltsin confirmed and slightly expanded them. Taken together, these initiatives state the following:

- Complete elimination of warheads for tactical land-based missiles, artillery shells, and mines.
- Elimination of one half of the warheads for antiballistic missiles and anti-aircraft missiles; the remaining warheads will be stored at central facilities.
- Elimination of one-third of the warheads for surface ships and submarines with the exception of SLBMs; the remaining warheads will be stored at central facilities.
- Partial elimination of the warheads for naval aircraft; the remaining warheads will be stored at central facilities.
- Elimination of half of the warheads for tactical air force aircraft.[16]

In 1996, Russia announced that these measures were scheduled to be completed by the year 2000. Because the PNIs contain no verification guidelines, it is impossible to be certain of the extent to which they have actually been implemented, but informed estimates of Russia's current tactical nuclear arsenal have ranged from 3,500 to 8,000 weapons.[17] Some of these tactical weapons are deployed (mated to delivery vehicles), and some are non-deployed (stored at central storage facilities).[18]

START II

As stated in chapter 2, although the United States and Russia have both ratified START II, the Russian Duma has declared itself no longer bound by

START II due to the U.S. withdrawal from the ABM Treaty.[19] Certain aspects of START II have been superseded by the Strategic Offensive Reductions Treaty, however.

Strategic Offensive Reductions Treaty (SORT)

The United States and Russia signed the Strategic Offensive Reductions Treaty (SORT), or the "Moscow Treaty," in 2001, which requires them to reduce the size of their strategic nuclear arsenals to between 1,700 and 2,200 warheads. Although the United States ratified the treaty in March 2003, the Russian Duma delayed ratifying it until May 2003.[20]

Regardless of whether the Duma had ratified SORT, however, Russia almost certainly would have had to reduce its number of nuclear weapons to roughly the levels called for by the treaty because many of its nuclear forces are deteriorating and will soon need to be removed from service. Some Russian analysts, like their U.S. counterparts, have argued that 1,500 weapons might be the most that Russia can really sustain.[21] In 1998, Russia's first deputy prime minister, Yuri Maslyukov, stated that in the near future the most Russia could hope for is several hundred nuclear charges.[22]

Russia's C^{3}I System

Russia's C^{3}I system has evolved significantly over the years.[23] The initial command-and-control system relied on the physical separation of nuclear warheads from their delivery vehicles, but this system was fundamentally changed in the latter part of the 1960s when the Soviets became concerned about the survivability of their nuclear forces and command structure, given the increasing accuracy and rapid flight times of U.S. missiles. Because of these concerns, the Soviets adopted a planning requirement that allowed for the option of launch-on-warning (LOW) and placed their missiles on a permanent alert.[24]

LOW

Under the LOW system, the Soviets would be able to detect an incoming nuclear attack and launch a massive retaliation before the incoming U.S. missiles could reach their targets.[25] LOW would help ensure both that the Soviet intercontinental ballistic missile (ICBM) arsenal would not be destroyed by a U.S. strike, and that the Soviet nuclear force would not be "decapitated," that is, that its command, control, and communications (C^3) would not be destroyed or so completely disrupted that they would be unable to

Table 3.1. Russia's Nuclear Weapons, 2004

Type (NATO Designation)	Range (km)	Warheads x Yield	No. of Weapons (START I MOU/Current)[a]	No. of Warheads (START I MOU/Current)
Intercontinental Ballistic Missiles (ICBMs)				
SS-18 (Satan)	11,000	10 x 550/750 kt (MIRV)	204/138	2,040/1,380
SS-19 (Stiletto)	10,000	6 x 550 kt (MIRV)	170/134	1,020/804
SS-24 M1 (Scalpel)	10,000	10 x 550 kt (MIRV)	43/36	430/360
SS-25 (Sickle)	10,500	1 x 550 kt	430/342	234/342
SS-27 (Topol-M)	10,500	1 x 550 kt	30	30
Total			680	2,916
Submarine-Launched Ballistic Missiles (SLBMs)				
SS-N-18 M1 (Stingray)	6,500	3 x 550/750 kt (MIRV)	224/96	672/288
SS-N-20 (Sturgeon)	8.300	10 x 200 kt (MIRV)	120/40	1,200/400
SS-N-23 (Skiff)	9,000	4 x 100 kt (MIRV)	112/96	448/384
Total			232	1,072

Bombers (Strategic)				
Tu-95 MS6 (Bear H6)	6,500-10,500	6 AS-15A ALCMs or bombs	27/34	162/204
Tu-95 MS16 (Bear H16)	6,500-10,500	16 AS-15A ALCMs or bombs	55/30	880/480
Tu-160 (Blackjack)	10,500-13,200	12 AS-15B ALCMs, AS-16 SRAMs, or bombs	15/15	180/180
Total			79	864
Sea-Launched Cruise Missiles (SLCM) (Tactical)				
SS-N-3B (Sepal)	460	1 x 350 kt (dual capable)		Total SLCM warheads: ≈ 240
SS-N-9 (Siren)	110	1 x 200 kt(dual capable)		
SS-N-12 (Sandbox)	550	1 x 350 kt(dual capable)		
SS-N-19 (Shipwreck)	550	1 x 500 kt(dual capable)		
SS-N-21 (Sampson)	3,000	1 x 200 kt(dual capable)		
SS-N-22 (Sunburn)	110	1 x 200 kt(dual capable)		
Surface-to-Air Missiles (SAM) (Tactical)				
SA-10/SA-N-6 (Grumble)	45/75/90	Unknown (dual capable)		Total SAM warheads: ≈ 1,200
SA-5B (Gammon)	150	1 x 25 kt		

Bombers and Fighters (Tactical)				
Tu-22M (Backfire)	1,500-1,850	AS-4 ASM	150[b]	Total warheads: ≈ 1,730[b]
Su-24 (Fencer)	2,500-3,000	AS-16 ASM, bombs	330[b]	
Anti-Submarine Weapons (ASW) (Tactical)				
SS-N-14 (Silex)	55	1 x 5 kt		Total ASW warheads: ≈ 210
SS-N-15 (Starfish)	45	1 x 200 kt		
SS-N-16 (Stallion)	100	1 x 200 kt		
TOTAL WARHEADS				**≈ 8231[c]**

Sources: Robert S. Norris and Hans M. Kristensen, "Russian Nuclear Forces, 2003," *Bulletin of the Atomic Scientists* 59, no. 4 (July/August 2003), pp. 70-72; Robert S. Norris, William M. Arkin, Hans M. Kristensen, and Joshua Handler, "Russian Nuclear Forces, 2002," *Bulletin of the Atomic Scientists* 58, no. 4 (July/August 2002), pp. 71-73; *Jane's Fighting Ships*, 1998-1999 (London: Sampson Low, Marston and Co., 1999), pp. 545-611; "U.S. and Russian/Soviet Strategic Nuclear Forces," *Arms Control Today*, October 2001; "Nuclear Weapons Database: Russian Nuclear Forces," Center for Defense Information, <http://www.cdi.org/issues/nukef&f/database/rusnukes.html>; Hans M. Kristensen, "Russian Nuclear Forces, January 2003," Sipri Project on Nuclear Technology and Arms Control, <http://projects.sipri.se/nuclear/russia.pdf>; "Table of USSR/Russian Strategic Bomber Forces, 1956-2002," Archive of Nuclear Data, Natural Resources Defense Council, <http://www.nrdc.org/nuclear/nudb/datab8.asp>.

Notes:

[a] Under START I, the United States and the Soviet Union committed to sharing information on their strategic nuclear arsenals. Twice per year, each side provides a memorandum of understanding (MOU), which states the number of their strategic nuclear weapons. The first number in this column indicates the number reported in the original 1990 MOU. The second number indicates the current arsenal size.

[b] This number includes the tactical aircraft assigned for both air force and naval missions.

[c] Russia is also believed to have approximately 8,000–10,000 tactical and strategic warheads in storage, either awaiting disassembly or in reserve.

launch a retaliatory strike. According to Bruce Blair, these were legitimate concerns, because during most of the Cold War a first strike by the United States might in fact have been capable of destroying a large number of Soviet ICBMs or decapitating the Soviet C³I system.[26] LOW was therefore implemented (at least in part) to help ensure a credible retaliatory capability.[27] Thus, although the capability for LOW introduces inherent dangers (such as an increased chance of inadvertent nuclear war), it was implemented to reduce very real risks and help maintain credible deterrence.

In order to carry out LOW, the Soviets needed both to establish a reliable early-warning system that could detect an incoming nuclear attack and to develop the ability to launch their ICBMs within fifteen minutes of the warning's being received.

Russia's Ballistic Missile Early-Warning System (BMEWS)

The Soviets began research on their ballistic missile early-warning system (BMEWS) in the late 1950s as part of its antiballistic missile (ABM) system, which was designed to protect critical command-and-control centers in Moscow from a ballistic missile attack. Eventually, however, BMEWS became a critical part of the Soviet launch-on-warning capability. Plans for a comprehensive BMEW system were approved in 1972. This comprehensive system would include long-range radar, over-the-horizon radar, and satellite-based BMEWS.

Long-Range Radar

The Soviet Union's domestic BMEW system officially began operation on February 15, 1971, when the first two surveillance radars, located near Murmansk and Skrunda, were put on alert status.[28] Both of these posts used Dnestr-M long-range radar, which could detect approaching ballistic missiles at distances of up to 5,000 kilometers.[29] During the next several years, the Soviets built a number of Dnestr-M and higher-voltage, upgraded Dnepr long-range surveillance radars (both of these radars are usually called "hen houses" by U.S. intelligence experts). In the mid-1970s, the Soviet Union began constructing a new type of long-range radar called Daryal radars (usually called "large phased-array radars" or "LPARs" by U.S. intelligence experts). By the mid-1980s, they had completed several LPARs and had begun construction on several more.

After the breakup of the Soviet Union, however, most of these BMEWS remained outside of Russia, causing a major disruption in the BMEW system. In addition, the construction of many of the LPARs has never been completed, and many of the remaining early-warning radar facilities (especially the hen houses) will soon need to be retired because they are reaching the end of their service lives. Russia will probably have extreme difficulty building many more of these radar stations, given its current economic shortages. In order to help fill the gap left by the closing and disassembly of the radar station located in Skrunda, Latvia, Russia commissioned an additional early-warning station in Baranovichi, Belarus, in 2000. The system was put on experimental duty in December 2003 and, after being tested for several months, was placed on full combat duty in October 2003.[30] Azerbaijan also reportedly ratified an agreement in March 2002 to lease the Liaki (also known as the Gabala) radar station to Russia for ten years.[31] Nevertheless, Russia's early-warning radar system is still far from comprehensive and will probably continue to deteriorate as the aging radar stations reach the ends of their service lives and are retired. (See table 3.2 for the current status of Russia's early-warning radars, figure 3.1 for the locations and reconnaissance zones for hen house radars, and figure 3.2 for the locations and reconnaissance zones for LPARs.[32])

Over-the-Horizon Radars

In an attempt to increase the advance warning times for their early-warning radars, the Soviets attempted to install a system of over-the-horizon radars, which reflect short-wave radio waves off the Earth's ionosphere. An over-the-horizon radar would therefore detect a missile launch sooner than the regular long-range radars would. The Soviets began an over-the-horizon radar project in the late 1940s, but it was suspended until the end of the 1950s due to technical difficulties. By the mid-1970s, Russia had built two over-the-horizon radars, located near Pripyat and near Bolshaya Kartel in Khabarovsk Kray (although the Bolshaya Kartel radar was not put on alert status until 1982). These radars remained on alert status until 1990, when they were shut down and partially dismantled.[33]

Satellite-Based BMEWS

Research into satellite-based early-warning systems began in the late 1960s and continued through much of the 1970s. Actual deployment of this early-warning system began in 1977. The initial system, called Launch Detection System-1 (LDS-1) in the United States, employs satellites traveling in overlapping high elliptical orbits that detect the infrared radiation from a ballistic missile launch against the background of space. This system became operational in 1978 (after six satellites were in orbit), and it was placed on

Table 3.2. Russia's Ballistic Missile Early-Warning Radars		
Radiotechnical Center	**Radars**	**Comments**
Murmansk	Hen House	Reaching end of service life
Olenegorsk	LPAR	Experimental receiver model
Mishelevka	2 Hen Houses LPAR	Reaching end of service Operational
Pechora	LPAR	Operational
Krasnoyarsk	LPAR	Operational
Skrunda, Latvia	2 Hen Houses LPAR	Operation stopped in 1998 Radar eliminated in 1995
Nikolayev, Ukraine	Hen House	Negotiations over control never completed. Reaching end of service life.
Mukachevo, Ukraine	Hen House LPAR	Negotiations over control never completed. Reaching end of service life. Construction stopped in 1991
Liaki (Gabala), Azerbaijan	LPAR	Agreement reached in 2002 for Russia to lease for ten years. Operational.
Sary Shagan, Kazakhstan	2 Hen Houses LPAR	Reaching end of service lives Radar never incorporated into BMEW system
Baranovichi, Belarus	LPAR	Placed on full combat duty in October 2003. Operational.

Sources: Podvig et al., *Russia's Strategic Nuclear Weapons*, p. 410; "Belarus Early Warning System to Be Tested," *Interfax*, August 2, 1999; "Azerbaijan Ratifies Radar Deal," *Russia Journal*, March 19, 2002; "Russian Radar Put into Operation in Belarus," *Pravda* (Russia), October 1, 2003.

Figure 3.1. Locations and Reconnaissance Zones of "Hen House" Radars

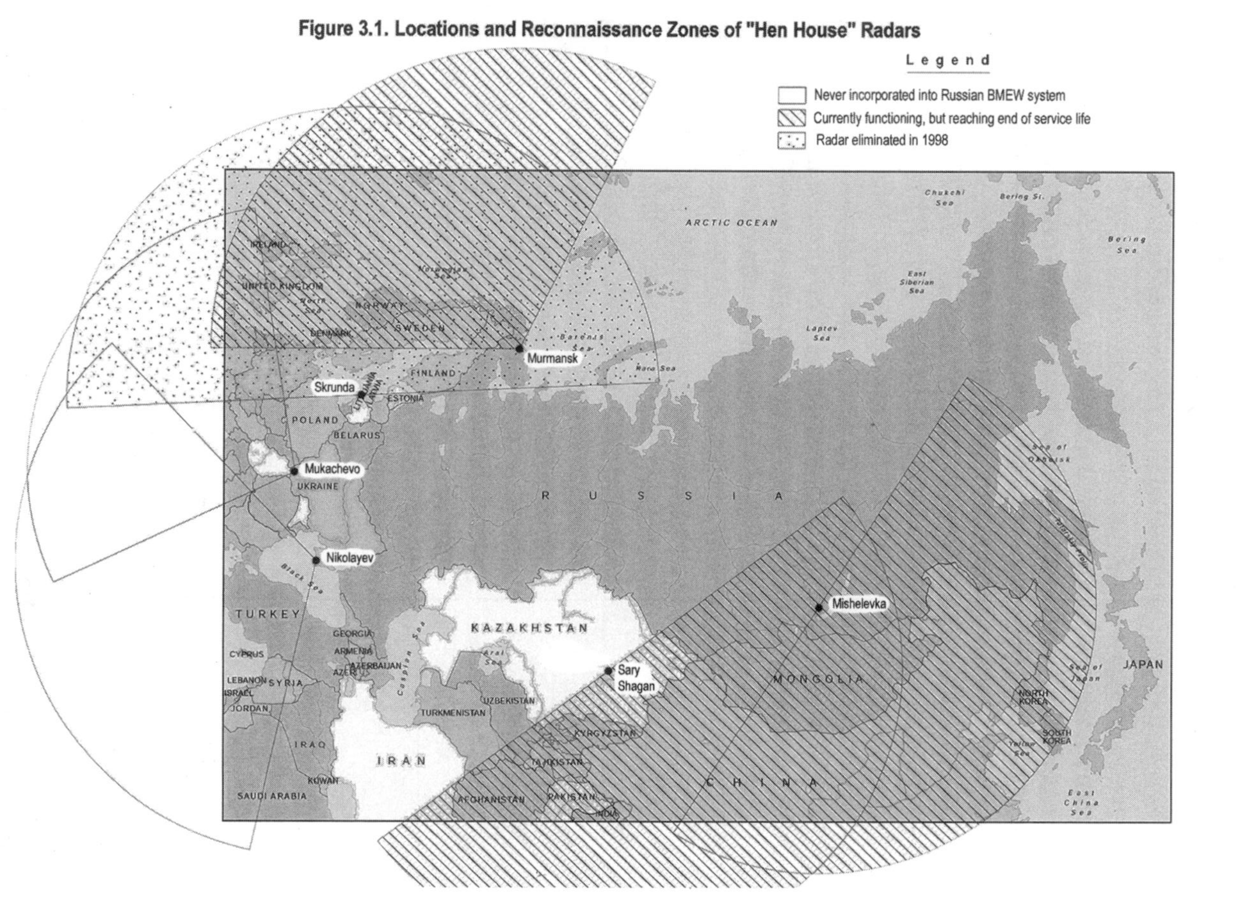

Figure 3.2. Locations and Reconnaissance Zones of LPARs

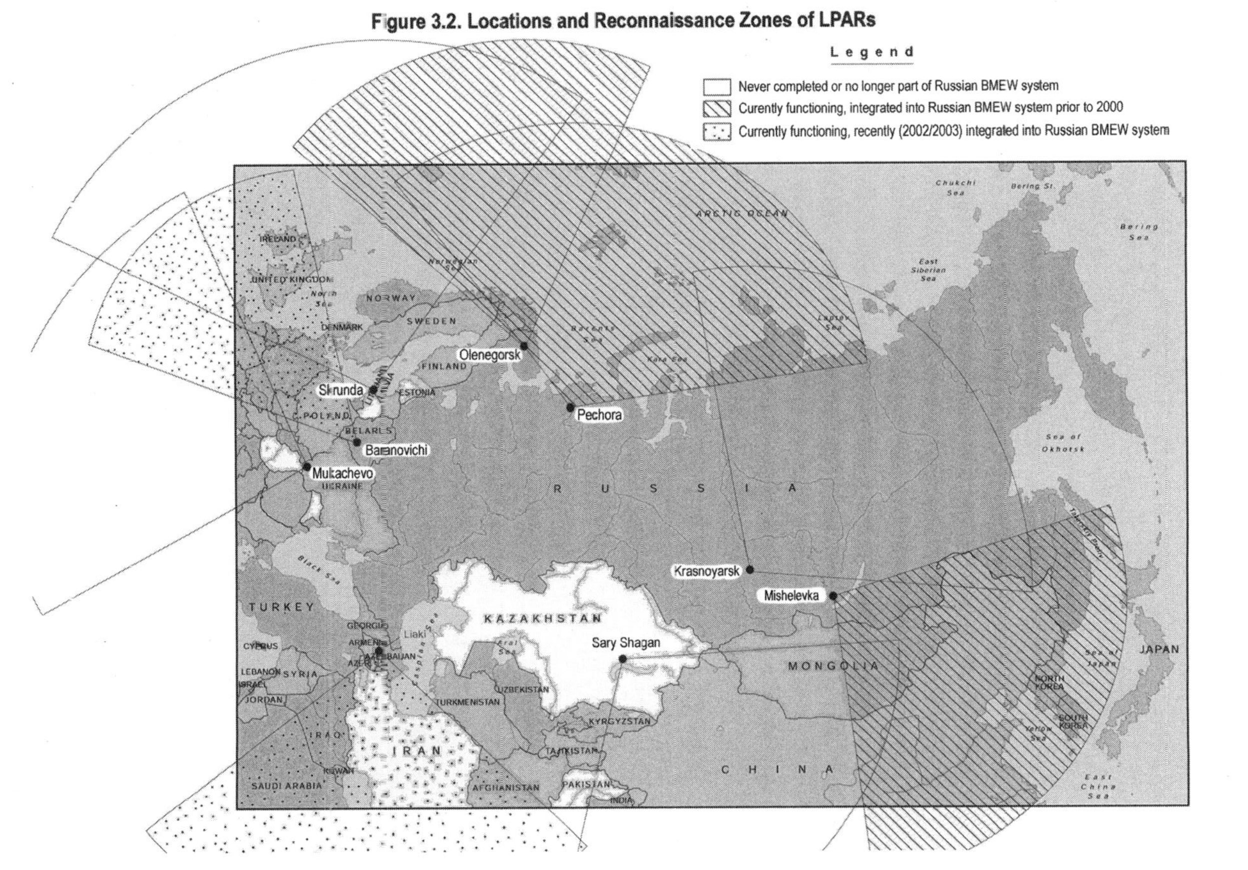

alert status in 1982. Although at its peak the Soviet system consisted of nine satellites with overlapping orbits, through the 1990s satellites began to fail without being replaced.[34]

In 1984 the Soviet Union began launching geostationary satellites for a second orbital BMEW system, called Launch-Detection System-2 (LDS-2) in the United States.[35] Between 1984 and 1998, the Soviets and Russians launched nine geostationary satellites, but a number of these satellites proved to have defects that caused them to fail soon after they were launched. In September 1997, Russia had only two functioning geostationary satellites remaining. Russia launched another geostationary satellite on April 29, 1998, but it reportedly failed only a few months later.[36] Russia's final two functioning geostationary satellites are believed to have failed in 1998.[37] For nearly three years, Russia had no functioning geostationary satellites, until Russia launched one geostationary satellite in 2001.

The Current Status of Russia's BMEWS

Russia's BMEW system has seriously deteriorated since the collapse of the Soviet Union. As noted, many Soviet early-warning radar stations are no longer under Russian control, and many of the remaining radars are reaching the ends of their service lives. In addition, Russia's satellite systems have been failing rapidly. In 1997, Russia had seven functioning high-elliptical satellites. In 1998, this number reportedly dropped to three. The two remaining geostationary satellites had helped to fill some of the gaps in Russia's satellite surveillance, but even these satellites stopped working in 1998.[38] Russia launched an additional non-geostationary satellite in 1999, raising the number to four, but Russia's high-elliptical satellite coverage was reportedly blind for at least seven hours each day and possibly much more.[39]

Russia's BMEW system was dealt a near-fatal blow on May 11, 2001, when a fire ravaged an important ground relay to Russian satellites, interrupting or breaking communications with all four of Russia's remaining early-warning satellites. Three of these satellites were ultimately lost, though one was brought back into operation in September 2001. This means that for nearly four months, Russia had no functioning satellite based early warning system at all.[40]

In efforts to repair some of the damage to the early-warning constellation, Russia subsequently launched one high-elliptical satellite in April 2001 and one geostationary satellite in August 2001, but the high-elliptical satellite never reached sufficient altitude to function properly.[41] As of late 2002, Russia therefore had only one functioning high-elliptical satellite and one geostationary satellite.

Table 3.3. Russia's Early-Warning Satellites (Launched after 8/28/1990)		
Satellite	**Launch Date**	**Estimated End of Life**
Kosmos-2097	August 28, 1990	April 1995
Kosmos-2105	November 20, 1990	April 1993
Kosmos-2176	January 24, 1992	April 1996
Kosmos-2196	July 8, 1992	June 1994
Kosmos-2217	October 21, 1992	April 1993
Kosmos-2232	January 26, 1993	June 1998
Kosmos-2241	April 6, 1993	January 1997
Kosmos-2261	August 10, 1993	March 1998
Kosmos-2222	November 28, 1993	December 1996
Kosmos-2286	August 5, 1994	March 1998
Kosmos-2312	May 24, 1995	December 1997
Kosmos-2340	April 9, 1997	May 2001
Kosmos-2342	May 14, 1997	May 2001
Kosmos-2351	May 7, 1998	May 2001
Kosmos-2368	Devember 27, 1999	Operational, as of May 2002
Kosmos-2388	April 1, 2002	Never reached operational altitude
Geostationary Satellites		
Kosmos-2133	February 14, 1991	December 1995
Kosmos-2155	September 13, 1991	June 1992
Kosmos-2209	September 10, 1992	November 1996
Kosmos-2224	December 17, 1992	June 1999
Kosmos-2282	July 7, 1994	December 1995
Kosmos-2345	August 14, 1997	February 1999 (moved off station in 1998)
Kosmos-2350	April 29, 1998	June 1998
Kosmos-2379	August 24, 2001	Operational, as of May 2002

Sources: Pavel Podvig, "History and the Current Status of the Russian Early-Warning System," *Science and Global Security* 10, no. 1 (2002), pp. 38-39; Podvig et al., *Russia's Strategic Nuclear Weapons*, pp. 416-417; Bogatrev, "Russian Antimissile Defense Cracks," p. 2; Woolf, "Nuclear Weapons in Russia," p. 5; Zaloga, "Russia's Strategic Forces Stumble," pp. 13-14; Clark, "Decline of the Russian Early Warning Satellite Programme," p. 17.

The deterioration of the Russian BMEW system has created great concern that Russia would be unable to identify and correctly characterize missile and rocket launches.[42] To help avoid problems that might arise from the deteriorating system, in the June 2000 summit meeting, Presidents Bill Clinton and Vladimir Putin agreed to establish a permanent Joint Data Exchange Center (JDEC) near Moscow to share information about nuclear launches.[43] For several years, however, little progress has been made, as the proposed plan became mired in details—the Russians have reportedly said that Russian law requires Americans to pay taxes on equipment brought into the country and to assume liability for construction, while the U.S. side did not want to set a precedent that would affect larger aid programs.[44] In 2002, Congress authorized funding for the JDEC but decided to withhold 50 percent of the funds until Russia and the United States reach a cost-sharing agreement and an agreement on taxes and liability for the United States and U.S. participants. In their joint summit meeting in May 2002, Presidents Bush and Putin did reaffirm their commitment to opening this center, but by late 2003 little or no progress had been made on this issue.[45]

Russia's Command-and-Control Structure: Launch Procedures and Use-Control Devices

Russia's main nuclear weapon command-and-control system is called the Kazbek system. In this system, the links in the chain of command for transmission of an order to launch nuclear weapons are completely disengaged under normal conditions. It would generally require a preliminary command from the president and defense minister to engage these communication links. While these communication links are disengaged, it is impossible for a launch command to be transmitted accidentally or by an unauthorized party.[46] In addition, both civilian and military authorities are able to override unauthorized efforts to launch missiles and sever communications with sites receiving unauthorized information.[47]

In the event of detection of a nuclear attack by satellite sensors or early-warning radar, Russia's early-warning center would send a warning to the headquarters of the defense minister, the General Staff, and the Strategic Rocket Forces, as well as a special warning to the president, defense minister, and chief of the General Staff through their nuclear suitcases (or Chegets).[48] The president, defense minister, chief of the General Staff, the nuclear commanders-in-chief, and the head of the early-warning center would then confer on special communication lines to assess what the threat is. If they received secondary verification of an incoming attack and judged that the technical warning was not in error, then the president and defense minister would transmit a "preliminary command" via their Chegets, which would engage the communication links necessary for subsequent launch commands.[49]

If this detection of a nuclear attack took place during a nuclear crisis (or if the Russians were launching a first strike), the leaders would have already retired to reinforced command centers, from which they could issue the preliminary command directly.[50] In these cases, the nuclear suitcases would be superfluous.[51]

While it generally requires the command from the president and minister of defense to engage these communication links, Podvig et al. note that "some steps required to raise the level of readiness could also be taken on the orders from the General Staff."[52]

If the leaders decided to give an actual launch command, they would relay the command to the General Staff and strategic force commanders.[53] The General Staff would then disseminate the appropriate orders and launch codes to the branches of the armed forces, which in turn would relay the launch command and enabling codes necessary for launching the nuclear weapons. Or, alternatively, the General Staff could deliver the launch orders for strategic weapons directly to the launch platforms, which (after a several-minute delay) would automatically launch the weapons from silos or truck launchers.[54]

Some assessments of Russia's command-and-control structure suggest that the president, defense minister, and the chief of the General Staff are not actually necessary for the launch of Russian nuclear weapons. If these assessments are correct, the authorization codes conveyed by the suitcases are merely proof of the *approval* of the Cheget-holders, while the General Staff controls the actual codes required for the launch of Russian strategic missiles.[55]

ICBMs

The level of alert status and the corresponding combat-readiness of Russian ICBMs have changed fundamentally over the years. In 1960, three levels of alert status were instituted in Russia's Strategic Rocket Forces (RVSN). Under normal circumstances, Russian missiles were kept in a state of "permanent readiness." In this state, the missiles were stored in silos without the nose sections mated. (In the case of the R-12 missile, the gyros were also not attached.) During a "red alert," the intermediate alert status, the nose section (and the gyros on the R-12) were attached to each missile. In a "full alert," the highest alert status, the missiles were fueled and aimed. It reportedly took several hours to prepare the missiles for launch under this system.[56] When the Soviets adopted a launch-on-warning policy, however, they had to reduce dramatically the launch times for their missiles. They therefore changed the alert status of their missile forces to a "permanent red alert," during which the missiles were stored fully fueled, with their reentry vehicles (including the warhead) mated.[57] In this new system, the ICBMs could be launched in less than fifteen minutes.

Russian ICBMs and ICBM silos have sophisticated use-control devices. First, it appears that Russian missile warhead detonation systems are deactivated during normal circumstances and require a separate command to activate them.[58] This command cannot be given before the communication links are engaged by the preliminary command. It is possible that an authorization code must be entered in order to activate the warhead detonation systems.

If the General Staff chose to have the launch crews launch the ICBMs, they would first send a message to the Strategic Rocket Forces headquarters containing the command to unlock specific launchers and the unlocking codes for those launchers. The launch crews would then enter the authorization codes and launch the missiles.[59] Only those launchers designated for immediate launch need be unlocked. They automatically lock again if they are not launched in a short period of time.[60] In addition, Russian missile silos are equipped with sensors that would detect an unlawful entry or an attempt to defeat the locks on the missiles. In either of these cases, the launch mechanism for the ICBM would be automatically disabled.[61]

SLBMs

According to one account of early Soviet launch procedures for SLBMs, targeting information was contained in a General Staff package that was opened after the submarine received the order to institute red alert status. The launch codes were contained in an additional package that was kept in the personal safe of the submarine's commanding officer. These codes were only entered into the missiles after the commanding officer and his senior watch officer both verified the authenticity of the launch order.[62] In the early 1970s, the launch codes were no longer contained on the submarine itself, but were transmitted to the submarine along with the order to launch the missiles.[63] This system is still used by Russia today.[64]

On early Russian submarines, the pre-launch procedures were mostly conducted manually and took about an hour to perform. On modern submarines, these procedures are automated and take two or three minutes.[65] SLBMs can be launched either from submarines on patrol or from submarines in port.[66] It is possible that the SLBMs on submarines in port are connected to the Kazbek system and can be launched automatically in the same way ICBMs can.

According to a 1996 report by the *Washington Times,* the use-control devices on Russian submarines were quite weak at that time. The report states that "some submarine crews probably have an autonomous launch capability for tactical nuclear weapons and might have the ability to employ SLBMs as well."[67] If this information is true, then the Russian central command would have been unable to stop a rogue submarine attack.[68] However, Russian command and control over its submarine-launched nuclear weapons has apparently been improved since 1996. Russian submarines apparently no longer have the ability to launch nuclear weapons without receiving enabling information from the General Staff.[69]

ALCM and Gravity Bombs

There are three levels of alert for Russia's strategic air forces. During peacetime, nuclear weapons are stored away from the bombers in facilities near the airfields.[70] In the second level of readiness (alert condition 2), the planes would be prepared for takeoff and nuclear munitions would probably be loaded on them.[71] Under red alert (alert condition 1), the planes would be fully prepared for takeoff and might even have their engines running.[72]

Bomber crews would probably receive a preliminary command to use nuclear weapons (along with the command to load the weapons on the bombers) and a final command to use the weapon after takeoff. The bombers might also be equipped with locks to prevent an accidental or unauthorized missile launch or bomb release. The unlocking codes for these locks would probably be transmitted along with the final command to use the nuclear weapons. If an actual order to use the nuclear weapons were given, the planes would fly to designated launch points and launch their weapons. The bombers are equipped with a system of locks that prevent their cruise missiles or bombs from being released from anywhere except these designated launch points.[73]

Although the nuclear-capable bombers contain relatively sophisticated use-control devices, it has been reported that the bombs contain relatively crude locks and that the cruise missiles have no adequate controls at all.[74] Blair refers to Russian sources, which state that "a captured cruise missile armed with a nuclear payload could be readily launched from a variety of planes and would produce a nuclear detonation."[75] It is possible, however, that the weapons for Soviet heavy bombers contain a mechanical lock or an electronic PAL that must be unlocked with codes transmitted by the General Staff and the national command authority before they can be armed and employed by the bomber crews.[76]

Tactical Weapons

Russia promised to destroy all land-based tactical nuclear weapons—including land-based tactical ballistic missiles, artillery shells, and mines—in the

1991–1992 PNIs. In these same initiatives, Russia also committed to removing tactical nuclear weapons from its naval forces.[77] If Russia is complying with these commitments, then there will not be any launch procedures for these weapons because they will already be in long-term storage. If the Russians are not complying with the initiatives or if they decide to re-deploy tactical nuclear weapons, it is not clear what their launch procedures would be.

According to the PNIs, the only tactical nuclear weapons that will be deployed are the gravity bombs and short-range cruise missiles for tactical bombers.[78] In the event of a nuclear crisis, guards must receive special authorization to unlock the weapons and move them to the bombers.[79] Although it is not clear what use-control devices or launch procedures exist for tactical bombers, they are probably similar to those for strategic bombers.[80]

A number of experts have expressed concern over whether Russia has adequate command and control of its tactical nuclear weapons. Because most of Russia's tactical nuclear weapons are contained in storage facilities, the security of these weapons is only as good as the level of security of the storage facilities. It is not clear that Russia has been willing or able to provide the necessary resources for the secure storage of its nuclear weapons.[81]

To make matters worse, it is not clear that Russia's tactical nuclear weapons are equipped with very sophisticated use-control devices. Some land-based tactical nuclear weapons may be equipped with PALs, but the quality of the PALs may vary among different types of tactical weapons, and some older weapons may not have them at all.[82]

The use-control devices for sea-based tactical nuclear weapons are reportedly even worse than those for land-based ones. According to Woolf, "some of these weapons, such as the nuclear-armed torpedoes on attack submarines, may not contain PALs. Instead, the Soviet Union had instituted organizational procedures to complicate the unauthorized launch of tactical nuclear weapons by a ship or submarine captain."[83] If the sea-based tactical nuclear weapons have been removed from the naval vessels, however, then there would be no organizational procedures to maintain any command and control over these weapons.

Contrary to all these negative reports about Russian protection of its tactical nuclear weapons, General Eugene Habiger, head of the U.S. Strategic Command at the time, gave a very positive assessment of Russian controls in 1998. He argued that Russia did an excellent job of protecting all of its nuclear weapons, including the tactical ones.[84]

Perimeter System

In addition to the Kazbek system, Russia has a second, reserve command-

and-control system known as the Perimeter system. This newer battle management system became operational in 1985.[85] Designed to reduce the risk of decapitation, the Perimeter system uses rockets to transmit launch orders directly to strategic missile launchers. These rockets are launched by the central command station (or a reserve command station). The rockets fly over missile positions, continuously transmitting the launch command and authorizing codes.[86] It appears that ICBMs can be launched either by launch crews, who enter the transmitted codes, or automatically, by remote transmission of the launch codes to the missile launchers themselves.[87] The signals transmitted by the rockets could also be received directly by submarines and bombers (or transmitted to them by relay stations).[88]

In order to launch Russian ICBMs with the Perimeter system, one must both be able to launch the communications rockets and know the ICBM launch codes that will be transmitted by the Perimeter rockets. It is possible that if the president and the minister of defense work together, they have the ability to launch Russia's ICBMs using the Perimeter system.[89] There is some question whether or not the General Staff can also launch Russia's ICBMs using the Perimeter system. According to Blair, the General Staff does have this ability, although Podvig et al. do not make a similar suggestion.[90] Judging by most of Russia's controls, it is likely that the communication rockets for the Perimeter system require authorization codes to be entered before they can be launched. It is not clear, however, whether the president and minister of defense have sole control over these codes, or whether the General Staff also has access to them.[91]

"Dead Hand"

It appears that the Perimeter system was also designed to allow for the semiautomatic launch of Russia's strategic nuclear weapons. This capability has been called the "Dead Hand" because it would allow the leadership to ensure the launch of Russia's weapons even if it were destroyed by a nuclear attack. If the Russian president expected an attack or if an attack was actually detected, he could order the activation of the Perimeter system and possibly distribute the launch codes to an underground command node outside Moscow.[92] If the command node did not receive an order to stop the combat algorithm within a given period of time, the command rockets would launch automatically.[93] The staff of the combat node would then transmit the launch command and the launch codes via the command rockets.[94]

There have been some reports that the communication rockets for the Perimeter system can only be launched if special seismic sensors detect the detonation of nuclear weapons on Russian territory.[95] If this is the case, then the Perimeter system could not be used to launch a first strike. Podvig et al., however, do not appear to indicate that the detection of nuclear detonations is necessary for the launch of the communication rockets.[96]

Podvig et al. argue that the "Dead Hand" was never actually deployed because it was determined to be too dangerous. However, there does seem to be a fair amount of evidence that this system was or could still be deployed.[97]

The Deterioration of Russia's Command-and-Control System

A number of reports have argued that Russia's command-and-control system is collapsing due to the combined effects of aging systems and severe economic hardship. The articles refer to a number of incidents to illustrate their case:

- The Kazbek system has been in continual use since 1983, even though it was only intended to last ten years. Due to a lack of funding for maintenance and modernization, the system is reportedly falling into disrepair.[98]
- On a number of occasions in the last several years, critical communication links to nuclear submarines were cut off and the operations at some nuclear weapons centers were severely disrupted when thieves tried to "mine" communications cables for scrap metal.[99]
- The service lives have expired for a great number of Russia's nuclear weapons. Although Russia has attempted to extend the service lives for a number of the weapons, it is not clear how much Russia can extend them without compromising the safety and reliability of the weapons.[100]
- Local utility managers have repeatedly shut off the power to various nuclear weapons installations after the military authorities there failed to pay their electric bills. Power was shut off at Gadzhievo naval base and weapons storage facilities on September 21, 1995; at the military shipyard Sevmorput on September 26, 1995; and at bases for air defense and Strategic Rocket Forces in the Khabarovsk territory on July 20, 1999. And on June 27, 2000, troops from the Strategic Rocket Forces base in Sibirskiy were forced to stage a commando raid on a neighboring power company after it threatened to shut off its electricity.[101]
- The equipment that controls nuclear weapons reportedly malfunctions frequently, and critical electronic devices and computers sometimes switch to a combat mode for no apparent reason.[102]

Although this list is quite troubling, Russia's command-and-control technologies and procedures have been fairly resilient so far. What is particularly unnerving about this list is that it indicates trends that could undermine Russia's command and control in the future.[103]

The Risks of Accidental Use

The use of a weapon would be considered accidental if "everyone is surprised" by its use.[104] The following are the risks of accidental use of Russian nuclear weapons.

Accidental Detonation

Russia has instituted several technical and procedural means of protecting against the accidental detonation of its nuclear weapons. First, according to Bruce Blair, some Soviet warheads or delivery systems were equipped with environmental sensing devices (ESDs), which ensured that the warheads would only detonate if specific environmental conditions were met. He alleges that electronic devices on a Soviet strategic missile warhead monitor the missile's acceleration, the surrounding barometric pressure, and the missile's deceleration to determine whether to arm itself for detonation.[105] Although Blair only specifies that the ESDs were implemented on Soviet strategic missile warheads, they have presumably been carried over into some Russian warhead designs as well.

A second way that the Russians protect against accidental detonation is by removing some components necessary for detonation from their warheads during transportation and perhaps even while they are deployed in the field. As part of the Cooperative Threat Reduction Program, the United States helped research and fund improvements on the railway transportation system for Russian nuclear weapons.[106] In order to help the United States design improvements to railcars designated for transporting Russian nuclear weapons, the Russians allowed the United States to ship one of their railcars to Sandia National Laboratory. Inside the railcar was a locked compartment where the components necessary for warhead detonation would be stored.[107] There is some indication that these components are kept separate from warheads while the nuclear weapons are deployed in the field.[108] Podvig et al. perhaps refer to the same safety procedures when they state that the warhead detonation systems on Russia's ICBMs are disengaged during normal circumstances.[109] While these detonation systems are disengaged, it would be much harder for an accidental detonation to occur.[110] Because these detonation systems would probably be engaged if Russia's nuclear forces were put on a higher state of alert, however, the chance of accidental detonation would correspondingly increase during a nuclear crisis.

Finally, the Russians reduce the risk of accidental detonation by trying to design their warheads, as the United States does, to be "one-point safe." Such warhead designs greatly reduce the chance that a significant nuclear yield would result if the high explosives in a warhead were accidentally ignited.[111] The Russians initially claimed that their regulations on the probability of an accidental warhead detonation under abnormal conditions are more stringent than U.S. regulations. After they were questioned about these regulations, however, it became clear that Russian calculations include not only the probability of a nuclear yield given the accidental ignition of high explosives, but also the probability of such an accident occurring in the first place. Because U.S. requirements for "one-point safety" only consider the probability of a significant nuclear yield *after* an accidental detonation of the insensitive high explosives has occurred, they are probably more stringent than Russian regulations.[112] It is impossible to tell for certain, however, because the Russians have been unwilling to reveal either their specific regulations or the specific method of analyzing compliance with these regulations.

There is some evidence, however, that the Russians do not generally use insensitive high explosives (IHE) in their nuclear weapons. During a meeting conducted under an international agreement in 1997, John Dallman (a high explosives expert at Los Alamos National Laboratory) and other members of the U.S. team got the impression that IHE only has limited use in the Russian nuclear program, based on personal conversations and the topics the Russians discussed in their papers.[113] Under some accident circumstances, there could be a greater likelihood that the conventional explosives in a nuclear weapon will detonate if it contains HE instead of IHE.[114] An accidental detonation of conventional explosives could disperse plutonium in a deadly aerosol or even cause a significant nuclear yield if the nuclear weapons are not properly one-point safe. Given that Russian regulations for one-point safety appear to be less rigorous than U.S. regulations, the risks of a nuclear yield during an accident might be higher than many experts would like for them to be.

It is also possible that some risks of accidental detonation could arise from Russia's aging weapons. A U.S. document on the DOE Stockpile Stewardship Program reports that as stockpiled weapons age, a number of physical changes can take place that can affect nuclear weapon safety, performance, and reliability.[115] These changes include:

- Degradation of organic high explosives.
- Cracks and voids developing in or among components.

- Aging of plutonium, producing a buildup of impurities.
- Changing of material characteristics, with subsequent dimensional changes (often referred to as "creep").[116]

Although this document focuses specifically on U.S. nuclear weapons, one could presume that similar changes would occur in aging Russian warheads, and that the safety, performance, and reliability of Russian warheads could be affected in similar ways. Aging can produce changes in high explosives that could have unknown effects on detonation properties. Changing detonation properties in turn can affect both the likelihood of HE detonation and the likelihood of a nuclear yield in the event of an accident. The United States does not currently know of any effects of aging that could increase the likelihood of HE detonation, but this is a relatively new field and much more research is necessary.

Risks of Accidental Launch

Accidental ICBM Launch

Russia has instituted a number of technical and procedural controls that greatly reduce the chance of an accidental ICBM launch. First, the communication links for the Kazbek system are disconnected under normal circumstances. A command to launch the missiles cannot be transmitted accidentally during these times. Second, because the warhead detonation systems on Russian ICBMs appear to be disengaged during normal circumstances, if an ICBM were accidentally launched during these times, it would probably not result in a nuclear yield.[117] Third, because Russia's ICBMs require authorization codes to be entered before they can be launched, no one can accidentally launch an ICBM by pushing the wrong button.

In May 1994, U.S. president Bill Clinton and Russian president Boris Yeltsin agreed to stop aiming strategic missiles at each other. Although this detargeting agreement was highly touted by the Clinton administration, it is likely that it had only a marginal effect in reducing the nuclear danger. Although the Russians claimed that it would take over ten minutes to retarget the missiles,[118] some extremely reliable U.S. sources—including James Woolsey, former Director of Central Intelligence—argue that the retargeting of Russian ICBMs would take less than a minute.[119] If this is true, then the detargeting agreement would therefore not dramatically reduce the dangers of an inadvertent launch that accompany the quick decision-making necessary for launch-on-warning military postures.[120]

However, the detargeting agreement could reduce the catastrophic consequences of an *accidental* launch if the missile defaults were set to launch a missile harmlessly toward the ocean. But there are conflicting accounts of whether the default settings on Russian missiles have been reprogrammed in this way. According to Blair, in the event of an accidental or unauthorized launch, Russian ICBMs would revert to their old Cold War targets.[121] On the other hand, James Woolsey argues that the detargeting *would* render the Russian missiles harmless in these circumstances.[122]

One thing is certain, however: if an accidental launch were to occur, Russia probably would not be able to destroy the missile in mid-flight. According to Colonel General Vladimir Yakovlev, the former commander of the Russian Strategic Rocket Forces, although Russian test missiles are fitted with a self-destruct mechanism, the actual combat missiles are not.[123] If the defaults on Russia's missiles are still set for their old Cold War targets, there would be no way to stop a missile from hitting the United States in the unlikely event of an accidental launch.[124]

Nevertheless, as we have seen, there are in fact a number of procedures and controls for Russian ICBMs that would protect against accidental launches. For this reason, the most careful and reliable assessments of Russia's strategic nuclear systems have determined that the risk of an accidental ICBM launch is currently quite small.[125]

Accidental Gravity Bomb/Cruise Missile Release

The risks of accidental bomb releases or air-launched cruise missile (ALCM) launches appear low for a number of reasons. First, during normal, peacetime circumstances, nuclear bombs and cruise missiles are stored in guarded storage areas away from the bombers.[126] If this is the case, then the risk of an accidental release of a gravity bomb or ALCM launch during peacetime is quite small. Second, in the highest level of alert, bombers are sitting on runways with their nuclear weapons loaded and perhaps with their engines running. Even in the event of hostilities, Russian nuclear bomber forces would not fly combat patrol missions.[127] Third, the bombers are equipped with locks that prevent a release of their weapons unless the pilot follows a specific flight pattern and enters a specific unlocking code that would probably be transmitted along with the final command to use the nuclear weapons.[128]

There is, however, one trend that seems rather troubling. Russia's economic crisis in the late 1990s hit the Air Force quite hard, and the Air Force had to cut back the amount of training that pilots receive. In 1998, the Russian Air Force only received 15 to 40 percent of its normal flight training.[129] In order to ensure that these nuclear missions are safely conducted, the pilots of nuclear bombers would need to be carefully trained in all the safety procedures for flying military missions with nuclear weapons. But it is not clear that Russian pilots are receiving this kind of training. Unless Russian nuclear bomber pilots have received significantly more training than the average pilots, or unless their training has significantly increased in recent years, they could make serious mistakes—including crashing their planes (which could cause a dispersal of fissile material or even a nuclear yield). As long as the procedures for nuclear bombers remain the same, however, the risk of an accidental nuclear bomb release or nuclear ALCM launch will remain quite small.[130]

Accidental Submarine-Launched Ballistic Missile (SLBM) Launch

In general, there is not a major risk associated with accidental launches of SLBMs. There is a high degree of centralization on Russian SSBNs, so any procedures will probably have a high degree of supervision. In addition, there appear to be use-control devices on Russian SLBMs that would prevent their launch except by the direct command of the Russian authorities.

Although it is possible to fire the SLBMs from submarines in port,[131] it is not exactly clear how these would be launched. If these weapons are launched in the same way as when the submarine is at sea, then the same kinds of procedures and use-control technologies would help prevent an accidental launch. If the SLBMs on submarines in port can be launched automatically by the Kazbek system, they are also probably subject to the same (low) risks of accidental launch as Russia's ICBMs.[132]

The Russian Navy is encountering the same problems with poorly trained forces as the Air Force. Because the Navy lacks the necessary funds to keep its submarines running, naval officers are not receiving the amount of training they used to receive. To make matters worse, morale is extremely low among the naval forces because of sporadic payment of wages and deteriorating social conditions. This forces many officers to leave the Navy in search of better financial opportunities. The increased turnover rates further reduce the average training of the naval officers. As a result of the decreased training of naval officers and the reduced routine maintenance and repairs of the ships, the safety levels on both decommissioned and operating naval ships are being severely compromised.[133]

It is very difficult to say what effect the poorly trained submarine crews will have on the risk of accidental launches. Because there does seem to be a high degree of centralization on the SSBNs, it is not clear whether the submarine commanders will be as poorly trained as the general submarine crews. Probably the greatest risk associated with poor training of submarine crews would be accidentally sinking the submarine and causing an environmental disaster.[134]

Accidental Use of Land-Based and Sea-Based Tactical Nuclear Weapons

In the 1991 PNIs, President Gorbachev committed to destroying tactical land-based ballistic missiles, artillery shells, and mines, and to removing all tactical nuclear weapons from Russia's Naval forces.[135] If Russia has complied with these initiatives, then the risk of accidental use of Russia's tactical nuclear weapons is currently quite small. Because there are no verification guidelines for this treaty, however, it is impossible to know to what degree Russia has complied with them.[136] But even while these weapons were deployed, the risk of their accidental use was relatively small during peacetime circumstances, because the standard procedure for these weapons from the Soviet era to the present was to store the warheads separately from their delivery systems.[137] While the weapons are stored this way, the chance of accidental launch remains small. It is not clear, however, whether there are any controls to prevent accidental launch once the warheads are mated to the delivery vehicles.

Conclusions about the Risks of Accidental Use

Overall, Russia's current controls have kept the risks of accidental launches of its nuclear weapons quite small. It is not clear, however, that Russia's controls will remain as secure as they have been. Severe economic and political hardships have caused several dangerous trends that could erode Russia's controls and thereby increase the chance of accidental use.[138]

First, Russian troops are poorly trained and might be less able to handle nuclear weapons safely.[139] So far, Russia's current procedures and use-control devices have probably prevented the poor training of its troops from significantly increasing the risk of accidental use, but it is difficult to foresee how this will affect risks in the longer term.

Second, Russian warheads, missiles, and command-and-control equipment are all aging, and it is not clear that Russia is willing or able to spend the necessary funds to renew these systems. Most indications seem to be that the Russian system would fail safely, but it is very difficult to predict what the effect of aging missiles and warheads will be. In all likelihood, it will simply make them inoperative, but aging circuitry or aging high explosives could increase the risk of an accidental missile launch or warhead detonation.[140]

The Risks of Unauthorized Use

The unauthorized use of a nuclear weapon "refers to the deliberate use by people who have access to the weapon, but who lack authority legitimately to order its use."[141] For example, if a state had inadequate controls over its nuclear weapons, a crazed soldier or fanatic general could independently decide to use the nuclear weapons, even though the state's central authorities had not ordered the use. Or, alternatively, a proliferating country or terrorist group could steal a nuclear weapon and use the weapon on its own.

Most of Russia's nuclear weapons systems have some form of protection against unauthorized use, and some of the controls are very good. According to U.S. National Intelligence Officer for Strategic and Nuclear Programs Robert Walpole, an unauthorized launch of one of Russia's ICBMs is "highly unlikely."[142] While the 1998 Rumsfeld Commission agrees with Walpole, it notes that this situation could change dramatically if Russia's political situation were to continue to deteriorate.[143] Nevertheless, it is important to note that these conclusions relate only to Russia's ICBMs (and probably their SLBMs). The risk of the unauthorized use of other nuclear weapons in Russia's arsenal, such as ALCMs or tactical weapons, could be significantly greater because these weapons often lack sophisticated use-control devices.[144]

Several scenarios of unauthorized use have been discussed in the literature on Russia's nuclear arsenal, including a breakdown of control at the top of the command chain, a revolt by a regional leader or military commander, and the theft of a nuclear weapon.[145] I will discuss each of these scenarios in turn.

Loss of Control at the Apex of Power

In this scenario, there is a loss of legitimate control over nuclear weapons at the very top of the chain of command. The most likely scenario of such a loss of control would be if the General Staff attempts to seize control over the nuclear weapons. A great deal depends on whether or not the General Staff has the technical ability to launch the nuclear weapons without the participation of the Cheget-holders.

For the General Staff to use the Kazbek system, they would need to activate the communication links necessary for issuing a launch command, then transmit the authorizing codes necessary for launching the nuclear weapons. Although the General Staff might be able to activate the communication links on its own,[146] there is still some question whether the General Staff controls the authorizing codes. If they do (as many open-source assessments indicate), then they probably could seize control of Russia's nuclear weapons. But even if they do not, it might be possible for them to override the Kazbek system.[147] In all likelihood, however, this would require a fair amount of time and probably could only be carried out during a large-scale, organized coup d'etat. Of course, such a coup d'etat did occur in 1991, and it is generally agreed that there was a serious weakening of Russia's nuclear controls.

In the August 1991 coup, communist hard-liners at the very highest governmental levels attempted to oust President Mikhail Gorbachev and restore the old order. The coup plotters included the defense minister and possibly the chief of the General Staff, the two Cheget-holders other than the president.[148] During the coup attempt, Gorbachev was arrested and his nuclear suitcase was seized. Russia's nuclear controls were thus severely strained during the coup, but most assessments indicate that they were not completely compromised.[149] One of the main reasons for this is that the commanders-in-chief of the strategic forces (Navy, Air Force, and Strategic Rocket Forces) decided to disobey all orders from the coup plotters and were reportedly capable of blocking a launch command when the Kazbek system was in the manual mode.[150] In addition, the acting president during the coup, Gennady Yanayev, probably did not have the technical ability to use the Cheget because Gorbachev's nuclear suitcase was rendered useless before it was taken and loyalists in the General Staff refused to give Yanayev the ability to use any additional Chegets.[151] This incident is very troubling, however, and has caused analysts to wonder what might happen in a similar, better-coordinated coup attempt.[152]

Risk of a Regional Leader or Military Commander Revolting

Russia's many regional governors have become increasingly autonomous over the last decade, and there is increasing concern that the central government will be unable to maintain control.[153] If these trends continue, it is possible that a regional leader, or a high-level regional military commander, might decide to revolt against the central government. During such a revolt, a leader might be quite tempted to seize the nuclear weapons located in his region.[154]

Such a revolt would probably require the collaboration of the regional military units. But the military units might in fact be tempted to join such a revolt, because they appear to be increasingly loyal to the regional governments and increasingly discontent with the central government. The military was hit particularly hard by the economic crisis in the late 1990s, and the regional governments have generally done more to ease the plight of the military units in their territories than has the central government.[155] According to Daniel Gouré, a former Pentagon official and now vice president of the Lexington Institute, because military allegiance is increasingly linked regionally, there is a significant risk that the center will not hold.[156]

Since a rebellious regional leader or military commander would almost certainly want to target the nuclear weapons against Moscow, he would probably prefer to seize tactical nuclear weapons, rather than strategic ones. And it would probably be easier for him to use the tactical weapons, because Russia's strategic weapons generally contain sophisticated use-control devices, while some tactical weapons reportedly contain only very crude devices, and others might not contain any at all.[157] If a region were to rebel and that region contained a tactical nuclear weapon storage facility, there could be an extreme risk that the central government would lose control of these weapons.

Theft of Nuclear Weapons

While the risk of theft of Russia's *deployed* strategic nuclear weapons is still relatively small, many of Russia's strategic and tactical nuclear weapons located in central storage facilities could be at some risk of theft. In addition, due to the START and SORT initiatives, Russia is presumably moving a number of nuclear weapons to its serial production facilities for dismantlement and destruction. Nuclear weapons are at greatest risk during transportation and require extensive security to ensure that they are properly protected. Most available information indicates that Russian nuclear weapons are still relatively safe,[158] but there are a number of troubling indications that the security of these weapons may be eroding.

Most of these central nuclear weapon storage facilities were built thirty to forty years ago, and many reportedly require reconstruction.[159] In 1996, the Russian Ministry of Defense (MOD, the agency responsible for Russian nuclear weapons) reported that the reserves for technical maintenance of these facilities were nearly exhausted. That year, the MOD requested 640 billion rubles for security operations and R830 billion for the development and purchase of physical protection equipment, but it only received R110 billion for security operations and R53 billion for physical protection equipment.[160] While the MOD might have exaggerated the amount of money it needed, one cannot help being troubled by the large gap between the funding requested and the funding actually delivered. Moreover, one can only suspect that the situation worsened during Russia's economic crisis in 1998, and it is not clear whether the Russian government has subsequently increased funding to the MOD.

One can also draw some conclusions about the security of Russian nuclear weapons from the current projects in the U.S.-sponsored Cooperative Threat Reduction (CTR) program. One part of CTR is the Weapons Protection, Control, and Accounting (WPC&A) program, which helps Russia ensure the security of its nuclear weapons during transportation, storage, and dismantlement.

In the early years of the CTR program, U.S. assistance focused on helping Russia consolidate its nuclear forces. It therefore helped Russia improve the security of Russian nuclear weapons during transportation to centralized storage sites. Between 1992 and 1996, the United States provided Russia 3,020 armored blankets and 150 "supercontainers" to improve protection of warheads during shipment, modification kits to improve security for 100 nuclear weapon railcars, and 15 guard railcars.[161] The U.S. Defense Department also delivered emergency response training and equipment "in the event of a nuclear weapons transportation incident."[162] Although these efforts are significant, it is not clear that they are enough to ensure the security of Russian nuclear weapons during transport. According to Vladimir Orlov, director of the Center for Political Research in Russia, and editor-in-chief of the Russian nonproliferation journal *Yaderny Kontrol,* in 1997 Russian military units had only 17 percent of the cargo trucks the military needed for transportation of nuclear weapons.[163] Orlov also reports that between 1993 and 1996, 223 special railcars for nuclear warhead transport were retired and only 38 railcars were supplied to replace them.[164] This shortage of transportation vehicles could cause dangerous delays in the shipment of nuclear weapons.

In the later years of the CTR program, the focus has shifted to improving the security of Russian storage facilities. The WPC&A program is helping Russia design computer tracking systems for warheads and has provided software for assessing storage site vulnerabilities.[165] It is also helping the MOD improve the security of over fifty storage facilities,[166] providing fences and sensors as "quick fixes" for security problems.[167] The fact that the U.S. DOD feels that these improvements are necessary indicates that there are problems with the security of Russia's nuclear weapon storage facilities, and the fact that the DOD calls these upgrades "quick fixes" implies that the security problems might in fact be relatively severe. It is necessary to emphasize that Russia's current security for its nuclear weapons is still probably fairly strong, but given the evidence of Russia's deteriorating facilities and security systems, one must wonder whether it will remain strong in the future.

The consequences of the theft of nuclear weapons could be quite serious. As noted, although Russia's strategic nuclear weapons contain sophisticated use-control devices, some of its tactical weapons might not. But even if stolen weapons *do* contain these use-control devices, the theft would still be very serious. Even if a proliferating country or terrorist group were unable to detonate a stolen weapon, it could still obtain the nuclear material from the weapon for use in a radiological device or for use in a new nuclear bomb, and it might also be able to use the stolen weapon to gain design information for its own weapon.[168]

Conclusions about the Risks of Unauthorized Use

There do seem to be increased risks of a loss of central control over Russia's nuclear weapons, especially during times of acute economic or political crisis. And while the risks are still relatively small (except perhaps for the theft of nuclear weapons), they could increase suddenly and dramatically if Russia's political and economic difficulties worsen.[169]

Moreover, if the deterioration of the Kazbek system continues, Russia might decide to adopt a more "delegative" command system, where authorization codes are distributed to officials further down the chain of command in order to reduce pressures in the command system that might arise during crisis situations.[170] Such a command system could significantly increase risks of unauthorized use, because greater numbers of people would have access to the launch codes for Russia's nuclear weapons.[171]

Because relations between Russia and the United States improved significantly during 2001–2002, Russia may be much less inclined to adopt such a delegative system.[172] But this is by no means certain, since relations between the two countries cooled dramatically after Russia opposed the U.S. efforts to gain approval by the United Nations Security Council for an invasion of Iraq and reports surfaced that Russia provided Iraq with anti-tank guided munitions, night-vision goggles, and satellite-jamming devices; spied on British prime minister Tony Blair for Saddam Hussein; and even provided the Iraqi regime with lists of assassins available for "hits" in the West.[173] These events have strained relations between United States and Russia so much that they have been described as approaching the "chilliest since the Cold War."[174]

One must keep in mind, however, that the loss of central control over a nuclear weapon does not necessarily mean that the weapon will be used.[175] But the use of nuclear weapons as tools in a domestic political struggle is bound to have a destabilizing effect, both domestically and internationally, and could increase the likelihood of preemptive nuclear strikes, panic-launches, and nuclear accidents.[176] In addition, the theft of nuclear weapons by proliferating states or terrorist groups could be extremely destabilizing because those groups would not have the experience or capabilities necessary for handling these weapons safely.[177]

Inadvertent Use: Russia's Aging Early-Warning System

Both accidental and unauthorized use must be distinguished from an "inadvertent" use of a nuclear weapon, where the use is intentional and ordered by the people who have legitimate authority to order its use, but the order is based on misinformation. The risk of an inadvertent launch of Russia's nuclear forces has increased significantly in recent years. As we have seen, there are currently large gaps in surveillance by Russia's early-warning satellites, and there is a great risk that Russia would not be able to correctly identify a launch of U.S. ICBMs or SLBMs. In addition, because there are very few early-warning radar stations in Eastern Europe, Russia would have even less time to decide whether or not to launch its missiles before an attack arrived. This serious time constraint, combined with Russia's option of LOW, greatly increases the chance that Russia might inadvertently retaliate against a supposed missile attack that never actually occurred.

To make matters worse, Russia's deteriorating BMEW system can no longer give much redundant information about a missile attack. Thus, if one sensor detects a missile launch, Russia's early-warning centers would be less able to verify whether or not the detection is mistaken. Moreover, multiple radar sensors increase confidence in the data that is used to calculate the trajectory of the missile or rocket. With fewer sensors, there is increased risk that Russia's early-warning centers could conclude that a missile was heading for Russia when it actually was not.

These kinds of miscalculations are not merely far-fetched scenarios. There actually have been cases where Russia's early-warning sensors mistakenly detected an incoming missile attack. In one case, on September 26, 1983—soon after Russia's BMEW system became active—one of Russia's early-warning satellites falsely detected a launch of five U.S. Minuteman ICBMs. After several tense minutes, the officer on duty decided that the satellite detection was a mistake.[178]

A second, rather famous example of a failure in Russia's early-warning system is the Black Brant XII incident.[179] On January 25, 1995, the United States and Norway jointly launched the Black Brant XII, a rocket designed to study the Northern Lights. However, Russia's early-warning radars misidentified this rocket as a possible U.S. SLBM, and the crew at the radar station notified central early-warning stations of a possible missile launch. These early-warning stations, in turn, alerted the highest levels of the Russian command by sending a message to their nuclear suitcases.[180] At that point, President Boris Yeltsin, Defense Minister Pavel Grachev, and Chief of the General Staff Mikhail Lolesnikov had a telephone conference about what action to take. While it is not exactly clear what they decided to do, there is some evidence that the Russian forces were put on a higher alert level during this crisis. Nikolai Devyanin, chief designer of the Russian nuclear suitcase, reportedly said that Russia's command-and-control system was placed in combat mode.[181] If this is true, then the Cheget-holders may have issued the preliminary command, activating the communication links for the Kazbek system.

Although some analysts have argued that the Russian BMEW system performed as it was supposed to during this incident,[182] others have questioned why it identified the launch as a possible missile attack when the rocket trajectory was headed *away* from Russia.[183] Whatever the case may be, an early-warning system that cannot distinguish between a benign rocket launch and an actual nuclear missile attack—combined with a policy that allows for LOW—poses serious risks of inadvertent launches.[184] And these risks have probably increased since the 1995 incident, as Russia's early-warning system has continued to deteriorate.[185]

Conclusions about Inadvertent Use

The deterioration of Russia's early-warning radar and satellite systems has undeniably increased the likelihood of an inadvertent launch of Russia's nuclear weapons. These risks are smaller than they might otherwise be, however, because the Russian early-warning system takes into account general political circumstances in addition to the technical information from radars and satellites to assess whether there is an incoming missile attack. Because Russian leaders have stated repeatedly that they believe there is a greatly reduced likelihood of a nuclear attack from the United States, they would be more likely to question the information from early-warning sensors.[186]

Nevertheless, the diminished number of early-warning sensors has further reduced the time Russian leaders would have in which to decide whether or not a detected attack is real before they would need to launch their own missiles. If the Russian BMEW system were to continue to deteriorate, the danger of inadvertent launch would probably increase.

If current plans to build a joint U.S.-Russia early-warning station are implemented, some risks of inadvertent launches would be reduced. But the greatest dangers associated with Russia's deteriorating BMEW system could still arise if relations between the United States and Russia were to sour again. Obviously, the Russians would be less likely to trust the information from a joint early-warning station if they feared that the United States might attack them. Thus, if relations between the United States and Russia were to worsen, or if Russia feared that the United States was trying to capitalize on a situation of acute civil strife in Russia, the risk of an inadvertent launch of Russia's nuclear forces could significantly increase.[187]

Part II: Russia's MPC&A

As far as is known, nuclear materials were very secure during the Soviet era. The Soviet system was quite simple: it maintained very strict controls over its population and relied on the presence of guards, gates, and guns at its nuclear facilities. Military nuclear facilities were generally inside the closed cities, which were located in remote areas and were surrounded by heavily guarded fences. Access to the cities was strictly controlled, and only authorized personnel were permitted to enter.

Most experts believe that the physical protection of Soviet nuclear facilities was excellent. There was very little risk of an outsider attack on a facility because the nuclear cities were too well guarded and the society was too closely controlled. There was also very little risk of insiders stealing materials from nuclear facilities. The highly privileged and patriotic personnel working at the nuclear cities had little incentive to steal nuclear materials in the first place. But even if an insider *had* wanted to steal materials, he would have found it extremely difficult to sell them because the KGB monitored everyone's actions very closely.

After the collapse of the Soviet Union, however, things changed dramatically. According to Matthew Bunn, "A security system designed for a single state with a closed society, closed borders, and well-paid, well-cared-for nuclear workers has been splintered among multiple states with open societies, open borders, desperate, underpaid nuclear workers, and rampant theft and corruption."[188] The MPC&A at Russian nuclear facilities was simply not designed to protect materials in this new political and economic situation. As a result, the personnel at nuclear facilities now had greater incentives and greater opportunities to steal nuclear materials. And some personnel gave in to this temptation. Russian prime minister Mikhail Kasayanov admitted in September 2000 that twenty-one attempts to steal registered nuclear materials occurred between 1991 and 1999.[189] Several of these attempts resulted in the theft of fissile materials, including 1.5 kilograms of HEU from the "Luch" facility in Podolsk, Russia, in 1992; 1.8 kilograms of HEU from the Andreeva Guba naval base in July 1993; 4.5 kilograms of HEU from the Sevmorput naval shipyard in November 1993; over 360 grams of Pu, seized in a German "sting" operation on a plane from Moscow, in August 1994; and 2.73 kilograms of HEU, seized in Prague in December 1994.[190] While the frequency of incidents seemed to taper off in the mid-1990s, there have been renewed incidents in recent years. For example, in December 1998 employees at a Chelyabinsk facility reportedly were stopped just as they were about to steal 18.5 kilograms of weapons-usable fissile materials,[191] and in November 2001 two men were reportedly arrested in Turkey attempting to sell over a kilogram of highly-enriched uranium believed to have originated in Russia.[192] On November 13, 2001, Yuri Volodin, head of the safety department at the Russian nuclear regulatory agency, reported a serious, previously undisclosed security violation sometime in the past two years. While

Volodin refused to provide further details, he said the incident was of "the highest possible consequence."[193] It is also impossible to rule out the possibility that additional attempted or successful thefts have occurred, but were never discovered or never confirmed by the Russian government.[194]

Current Fissile Materials Stockpiles

Although precise amounts have never been confirmed, the Soviet Union is believed to have produced hundreds of metric tons of highly-enriched uranium (HEU)[195] and plutonium (Pu). Approximately half of these amounts are contained in weapons, while the remaining fissile materials (as much as 800 metric tons) are stored in nearly 400 buildings in over 50 sites across Russia.[196] These amounts of stored fissile materials will undoubtedly increase as Russia continues dismantling its nuclear weapons, according to START commitments. The following is a summary of the different types of sites believed to contain fissile material and the Russian agencies responsible for fissile material security.[197]

Defense Facilities

During the Cold War, the Soviet Union created a massive nuclear complex for its nuclear weapons program. At least 221 facilities were built as part of the Soviet nuclear weapons complex, with a large percentage located in Russia. Most of the Russian defense facilities are located in the ten formerly closed, or secret, cities. These facilities engaged in a number of different activities, including mining and milling uranium ore, uranium enrichment, producing and processing plutonium, assembling nuclear weapons, and disposing and storing nuclear waste.[198] Some of these facilities are still used as part of Russia's defense complex, while others have been shut down.[199] Massive amounts of fissile materials are still located at most of these facilities.

Naval Fuel

Because the Russian Navy uses HEU for its nuclear-powered ships (enriched between 20 and 90 percent U-235), there are large amounts of very attractive fissile materials located at some of Russia's naval bases, particularly at the bases for its Northern and Pacific Fleets.[200] Fresh nuclear fuel rods are shipped by rail, then stored until needed in land-based facilities and storage ships.[201] These sites have received a great deal of attention since 1993, when 4.5 kilograms of uranium (enriched to 20 percent U-235) was stolen from a Northern Fleet storage facility.[202]

Civilian Facilities

The concept of a "civilian" nuclear complex is somewhat new to Russia. During the Soviet era, many nuclear reactors (such as the plutonium production plants) were used both to produce heat and electricity and to produce weapons-grade fissile materials. In recent years, however, Russia has made efforts to distinguish between its defense and civilian nuclear facilities. Some of the civilian facilities produce or use only low-enriched uranium (LEU), which cannot be used to make nuclear weapons, but some of them use HEU. While all of Russia's civilian nuclear facilities could be targets for nuclear terrorism, a number of them also contain highly attractive materials for theft.

Russian Agencies That Have Authority over Fissile Materials

The Russian Ministry of Defense (MOD) has responsibility for monitoring "nuclear and radiation safety of nuclear weapons and nuclear power units of military designation."[203] The MOD is therefore responsible for the security of all deployed nuclear weapons, all nuclear warheads, and all naval nuclear fuel (primarily HEU). Within the MOD, the 12th Directorate has responsibility for all security of all assembled nuclear weapons. It therefore oversees the security of deployed nuclear weapons, nuclear weapon storage facilities, and nuclear weapons during transport.[204]

Russia's Ministry of Atomic Energy (Minatom) has authority over all defense-related fissile materials. It is therefore responsible for security of weapons-related processing plants and Russia's serial production facilities (where warheads are assembled and disassembled).[205]

The nuclear regulatory agency Gosatomnadzor (GAN) has authority over all civilian nuclear fuel. It therefore has responsibility for security of fissile materials at Russia's nuclear power plants.[206] GAN is also responsible for nuclear safety at Russia's civilian nuclear facilities.

Specific Weaknesses in Russia's MPC&A after the Soviet Collapse

The system of fissile material security at the former-Soviet nuclear facilities was severely weakened after the collapse, as guard forces weakened and the strict societal controls largely disappeared. The MPC&A system that Russia inherited from the Soviets simply did not come close to meeting Russia's new MPC&A needs. A resilient MPC&A system must be strong in two distinct areas: physical protection, and material control and accounting (MC&A). Physical protection systems are designed to deter or defeat any external attacks by groups or individuals who want to steal nuclear materials or sabotage nuclear facilities. MC&A systems, on the other hand, are designed to detect a theft of nuclear materials once it has occurred. Such systems accomplish this by keeping very close measurements of the amounts of materials in each facility and by detecting whether any materials are moved or taken.[207] The following is a description of the some of the weaknesses in Russia's MPC&A in both these areas.

Physical Protection

The physical protection of Russian nuclear facilities often varied widely. While the protection at nuclear weapon assembly and storage facilities was still fairly good, the protection of many of Russia's production reactors and naval facilities were often reported to be quite weak. For example, many facilities containing HEU and Pu had open first floor windows with no bars on them; there were often large holes cut into the walls for ventilation; the doors on the buildings and the vaults were often made of wood; and the fences around nuclear facilities were often dilapidated or damaged, and many contained large holes.[208]

Many buildings were also not equipped with surveillance or alarm systems.[209] And even when a building did have an alarm, the system was typically quite old and often no longer operational.[210] According to Vladimir Orlov, 70 percent of the available security equipment at Russian facilities was obsolete as of 1997, and 20 percent had been working two to three times its service life.[211] In addition, because the Soviets had not engaged in extensive designing and testing of their physical protection systems, it was often possible to bypass or defeat alarm systems.[212]

As noted, the physical protection of Soviet facilities was mainly based on an extensive guard force. After the collapse of the Soviet Union, however, many facilities were forced to cut costs by reducing the number and quality of guards at their sites. Many facilities reportedly refused to enter into expensive contracts for guard forces with the Ministry of Internal Affairs. Instead, they hired cheaper but often poorly trained civilian guard forces.[213] There were typically no guards at the individual buildings in a nuclear facility, though there were usually guards around both the city and the perimeter of the nuclear facility. To make matters worse, guards stationed at Russian facilities were typically not equipped with radios.[214] Any guard on patrol must have a radio to notify a central guard station if he sees anything unusual. As it was, if a guard needed to report anything, he would need to run back to the guard station, often located up to a kilometer away.

In a 1993 report on fissile material security, Russia's nuclear regulatory agency, Gosatomnadzor (GAN), identified many of these same problems with Russia's physical protection:

- Lack of physical protection standards.
- Focus on the protection of a site's outer perimeter and inadequate defenses of buildings and facilities inside the fence.
- Inadequate protection of guards from small-arms fire (lack of bulletproof guard posts or protected bunkers).
- Lack of vehicle barriers.
- Lack of portal monitors to detect fissile materials, explosives, or weapons.
- Inadequate communication between individual guards, between patrol units and the central alarm station, and between the facility and the off-site law-enforcement force.
- Inadequate manpower and low salaries of security personnel.[215]

MC&A

The MC&A at Russian nuclear facilities was often even worse than the physical protection. In fact, many facilities did not have a precise MC&A system at all, because the Soviet fissile material production plants were focused on producing large amounts of fissile materials and had little time for precise MC&A procedures.[216]

Most facilities did have massive paper records of the fissile materials produced, but these records were not very precise. Indeed, they were never intended to keep an exact inventory of the materials produced or stored at a given facility. Instead, they used an accounting system based on the financial value of the materials rather than their specific amounts.[217] But even if these records *had* been accurate, it still would have been nearly impossible to detect a theft of materials, since one would have had to track the amounts of materials through hundreds of pages of records.[218]

In fact, Russian facilities often did not even know what category of nuclear material they had stored there.[219] This is a basic fact that is necessary for designing an MPC&A system, for it determines the attractiveness of the material for theft and therefore determines what kinds of controls must be in place. The IAEA, for example, recommends that facilities containing Category I materials (substantial amounts of pure Pu or HEU) have much stronger MPC&A than those containing Category III materials (very small amounts of Pu or HEU, or substantial amounts of low-enriched uranium).[220] Nuclear material shipped to Russian facilities typically contained a "manufacturer's passport" value, which states the type and amount of nuclear material in each container, but this measurement system did not work well for materials that were not in a convenient itemized form, such as small pellets, liquids, or powders.[221] In addition, the passport values were often incorrect, due to measurement errors, time constraints, or intentional overstatements.[222] When materials entered a facility, typically there was no independent verification of passport values; they were simply assumed to be correct.[223]

To make matters worse, because a production plant and its personnel were subject to harsh penalties if the plant did not meet its production quotas, there was usually a back room in production facilities where extra HEU or plutonium was stored in case the facility did not meet the quota for a particular month. Because there were no precise records of these materials, they could be stolen without anyone noticing. And over time, facilities would often lose track of where they put these materials.[224]

As a result of these procedures, most Russian nuclear facilities did not have any accurate idea of the amounts of materials they contained after the Soviet collapse.[225] This is the very first step in creating an MC&A system—if one does not know the precise amounts of materials in a given facility, one cannot know if any is missing.

In addition, there were no procedures for tracking materials once they were inside a given facility. Russian nuclear facilities did not have material balance areas (MBAs), which are the foundation for the accounting systems typically used in Western MC&A systems.[226] In the Western system, nuclear materials are measured (by radiation and mass measurements) whenever they are moved from one designated MBA to another. Thus, if any material is missing, one can tell when and where the loss occurred. In Russian sites, however, there was generally free movement of materials throughout a facility, except when the materials were placed in a storage vault. It would therefore have been very hard to detect a theft of materials or track down the people who might have stolen it. Moreover, even the materials stored in vaults were seldom counted or measured to verify that none was missing.

Finally, Russian nuclear facilities rarely had material control equipment in place to ensure that materials could not be moved or stolen without detection. There were rarely any portal monitors to detect if someone tried to leave a nuclear facility with nuclear materials.[227] The seals on material storage containers were generally made of wax or a soft lead and could be easily removed and replaced with another seal. There were typically no tamper-indicating seals or identification codes on the containers to show if any seals had been broken or replaced.[228]

In the 1993 report on nuclear safety and security, GAN summarized these problems in Russia's MC&A:

- Material loss limits often are not substantiated and do not exclude unaccounted losses within the authorized limits.
- The principle of personal responsibility often is not enforced.
- Measurement of nuclear materials in the process of inventory taking and in transfers of materials between facilities are inadequate.
- Measurements of waste, scrap, and hold-up of nuclear materials are inadequate.
- There are no uniform accounting procedures or computerized accounting systems.[229]

The Early History of U.S.-Russian MPC&A Collaborations

As reports of potential weaknesses in Russia's nuclear security began surfacing in the early 1990s, U.S. officials determined that it was in the U.S. interest to help Russia secure its nuclear weapons and fissile materials. Shortly after the 1991 coup attempt, Senators Sam Nunn and Richard Lugar attempted to gain congressional support for a program that would help improve Russian nuclear security.

The Cooperative Threat Reduction (CTR) or the "Nunn-Lugar" Program

In November 1991, the U.S. Congress passed the bill sponsored by Nunn and Lugar allocating $400 million of Defense Department funds to assist the newly independent states (NIS) with the "transportation, storage, safeguarding, and destruction of nuclear and other weapons [and with] the prevention of weapons proliferation."[230] This bill gave rise to the Cooperative Threat Reduction (CTR) program (also called the Nunn-Lugar program, after its sponsors). In addition to providing funding and assistance for the elimination of delivery systems, the CTR program also helped Russia with the security of its nuclear weapons, especially during disassembly, and helped install MPC&A systems at civilian nuclear institutes in Russia.[231]

Negotiations for the Nunn-Lugar program began at a March 1992 meeting between representatives of the Russian and U.S. governments. Unfortunately, these negotiations progressed slowly and were characterized by frustrating delays. Although there were significant problems on both sides, the main responsibility for these delays appears to lie with the Russian government.[232] One problem was that there were organizational problems within the Russian government as to what bureaucracy was responsible for the various parts of the nuclear program.[233] Moreover, the Russian Ministry of Atomic

Energy (Minatom), the main organization responsible for Russia's nuclear materials, was often unwilling to relinquish any authority because this would reduce its power.[234] Indeed, there are numerous instances of "turf battles" between Minatom and the newly created nuclear regulatory agency GAN over which agency should have authority over given projects.[235]

The most serious obstacle in the Nunn-Lugar negotiations, however, was that both the Russian government and Minatom refused to admit that there was a problem with their nuclear material security, since doing so would in effect be an admission of incompetence.[236] This obstinacy made it very difficult to justify the millions of dollars allocated to the CTR program and caused great delays in the implementation of many CTR projects.

After a frustratingly slow start, however, the CTR program did eventually overcome many of the negotiation obstacles, but this was not before a second approach for improving Russia's nuclear security had been developed.[237]

U.S.-Russia Lab-to-Lab Collaborations and the MPC&A Program

In 1993 and 1994, scientists at Los Alamos National Laboratory (LANL) began discussing with their counterparts at Russian scientific laboratories the possibilities for laboratory-level scientific collaborations to improve Russian MPC&A. In 1994, the Department of Energy allocated $2 million for these collaborations, and a delegation from LANL went to Russia to negotiate and sign contracts for improving Russian MPC&A systems.[238] Once these contracts were approved by the central governments in each country, the U.S. and Russian nuclear laboratories began implementing the MPC&A upgrades. These collaborations quickly took on lives of their own and were eventually organized into an overall MPC&A program overseen by the Department of Energy.[239]

The lab-to-lab program achieved almost immediate successes, in large part because it was able to avoid many of the bureaucratic obstacles that delayed the CTR program.[240] The main reason for this was that the lab-to-lab negotiations were based on mutual trust among U.S. and Russian scientists, built up through previous scientific collaborations in the early 1990s.[241] As a result, the Russian scientists were more willing than their government to admit that there was a problem with Russia's fissile material control. Nevertheless, even then, it was not until June 1994 that scientists at Arzmas 16 admitted to Sigfried Hecker (director of LANL at the time) that there was a problem—more than two years after he had broached the subject to them.[242]

An Example of MC&A Upgrades: The Plutonium Production Facility at Krasnoyarsk-26

Krasnoyarsk-26 (or K-26) is one of the former-Soviet "nuclear cities."[243] It was established in 1950 to produce plutonium for Soviet nuclear weapons and currently has a population of nearly 100,000. The actual Pu production facility is a huge underground complex located roughly ten miles from the residential area. It consists of three Pu production reactors; a water cooling plant; and chemical, uranium and graphite reactors. Two of the Pu production reactors at K-26 were shut down in 1992, but the third is still being used to produce heat and electricity for the city. (Russia is not believed to be using any of this new Pu in its nuclear weapons program.) K-26 contains large amounts of HEU (enriched to 90 percent U-235) and Pu. The underground complex contains two fissile material storage vaults, one for HEU and one for Pu.

In order to identify the risks of material diversion and the role of the MPC&A program, we will need to discuss how this facility works. All technical information about the Pu production plant at Krasnoyarsk-26 was related in an interview on May 25, 1999, with Dr. Konstantin Dorofeev, head of the Russian MC&A program at K-26.

The plutonium is produced by passing many 3"x 1.5" HEU pellets through a reactor. After they are passed through the reactor, these pellets contain Pu, which needs to be separated from the rest of the materials in the pellets.[244] The pellets are then moved to the radiochemical plant, where the Pu is removed by a Purex process. In the Purex process, spent fuel is passed through a series of large tanks, where a variety of solvents are used to separate the plutonium from the other substances.[245]

After the Pu is removed, it is still in a liquid solution. It is moved to the Calcination Room, where it is dried. The result is a relatively pure Pu oxide powder. This powder is then placed into containers and moved to the Pu storage vault.

Proliferation Risks at K-26 before the MC&A Program

The following are the procedures and process that placed the fissile materials at risk. According to Konstantin Dorofeev, these MC&A weaknesses were typical of most nuclear facilities in the Russian nuclear complex.

The HEU was shipped to the facility in roughly one-foot square boxes. There were somewhere between ten and twenty HEU pellets per box. Before the U.S.-Russia MPC&A program began, there were no tamper-proof seals or bar codes on the boxes. In fact, there were not even any locks on the boxes; the seals on the boxes could be removed with a screwdriver.

Before the MC&A upgrades, the accounting system for the facility was not very precise. There were no identification codes on the HEU pellets or the boxes. Accounting was conducted by paper and pencil. According to Dorofeev, the accounting was about as precise as at any standard industrial production plant. There was a separate group that was responsible for accounting, but according to Dorofeev, this was not enough since the accounting personnel were not scientifically trained and did not know advanced scientific accounting techniques, such as nondestructive assay or radiation measurement.

The facility did do some verification of the materials as they passed through the production process. They knew how much Pu should be produced in the reactor, and the containers in the calcination room were weighed to make sure that roughly the correct amount of Pu was being produced. These scales were relatively crude, however, and could not obtain very precise measurements.

In Dorofeev's opinion, the containers used to store Pu were not properly accounted for. There were no bar codes on these containers or locks with separate ID codes. The locks on the containers consisted of a thin wire and a lead lock. According to Dorofeev, if someone wanted to, he could cut the wire on the lock, steal the material, and put a new lock on the empty container. Since neither the containers nor the locks had ID codes, no one would notice that the materials were missing unless they weighed the containers. But this probably would never be done because there were no thorough verification techniques to ensure that no material had been stolen after the containers had been placed in storage. The facility did conduct periodic inventories of the nuclear materials, but this was done by counting the number of containers on the shelves in the storage vault. There was no way to detect whether someone had removed materials from the containers.

Some of the MC&A Upgrades at K-26

In order to help reduce these risks, the U.S.-Russian program instituted the following MPC&A upgrades to the facility:

- Special technical accounting groups are being integrated directly into each technical department at the facility. The accounting personnel are now scientists conversant with modern, scientific accounting techniques.
- Bar codes and tamper-proof seals have been placed on the boxes of HEU pellets and plutonium. The locks on the plutonium containers have identification codes so that it is possible to verify that a given lock has not been cut and replaced with another lock.
- The liquid storage tanks in the radiochemical plant are being fitted

with tank volume measurement (TVM) equipment to measure the exact volume of the liquid in the tanks.
- New, high-precision electronic scales are being installed in the calcination room and the storage vaults to help verify that no nuclear material has disappeared.
- A video surveillance and alarm system is being installed in the storage vaults.
- Portal monitors are being installed at all possible exits. The portal monitors will sound an alarm if anyone tries to remove radioactive materials from the facility.
- A computer system is being implemented to keep track of the amounts and locations of all the nuclear materials at the facility. The computer system also records who applied the tamper-proof seals on the storage containers, when the seals were applied, when they were last checked, and when they were destroyed.
- Because the Pu storage vault is now full, the U.S. is helping the Russians build another storage vault.

Assessing the MPC&A Program: Significant Progress, but Enduring Problems

Since 1994, the MPC&A program has made continual progress. As of February 2000, it has completed MPC&A upgrades at 113 buildings in Russia and the newly independent states, and is currently installing systems at an additional 72 buildings.[246] But a tremendous amount still needs to be done. A recent Harvard University study reported that "by the end of fiscal year (FY) 2002, only about 37% of the potentially-vulnerable nuclear materials in Russia was protected by initial, 'rapid' upgrades, and less than one-sixth of Russia's stockpile of HEU had been destroyed."[247] In addition, a number of problems have made it difficult to ensure that Russian nuclear materials are fully secure.

Physical Protection

Although significant progress has been made in upgrading physical protection, much more still needs to be done. According to William Potter, director of the Monterey Center for Nonproliferation Studies, "at many of the central storage facilities, which are bursting at their seams with weapons-grade material, there are [still] no perimeter fences, armed guards, vehicle barriers, operational surveillance cameras, and metal detectors at entrances."[248]

What is perhaps even more troubling is that even when the modern surveillance and alarm systems have been installed at Russian facilities, they are often not used. At one facility, a new infrared intrusion detecting system was rendered ineffective because the grass was not mowed.[249] At other facilities, high-quality surveillance systems were made useless when the facilities shut off their electricity in order to reduce their power bills.[250] There are also numerous reports of guards shutting off security and monitoring systems because they decided there were too many false alarms.[251]

But even if the surveillance and alarm systems have not been shut off, it is not clear that anyone would respond to an alarm at some facilities. Many facilities cannot afford to pay the guards and officers responsible for security, and there have been many reports of guards leaving their posts to look for food or refusing to respond to alarms because they lacked adequate winter clothing.[252]

MC&A

Throughout the MPC&A program, MC&A upgrades at Russian facilities lag behind physical protection upgrades. These delays are due in part to a limited Russian acceptance of the possibility of insider theft (even though to date all reported nuclear material thefts from former-Soviet facilities have been carried out by insiders), and in part to the fact that it has been easier to justify physical protection upgrades to the U.S. Congress.[253] According to Matthew Bunn, hundreds of tons of fissile materials is still stored in buildings that are not equipped with portal monitors.[254]

Moreover, most Russian facilities still have not finished conducting a comprehensive physical inventory of their nuclear materials (the first step in creating an MC&A system), and therefore still do not have an accurate assessment of the categories or amounts of materials they contain.[255]

The MPC&A program has also had difficulties establishing a "safeguards culture" in Russia, where everyone from high-level politicians to the lowest-level guard recognizes the importance of rigorous MPC&A procedures and technologies.[256] For example, Russians often still do not follow the "two-person rule," a basic procedure that forbids any single person to be alone with nuclear materials. To help enforce the two-person rule, all vaults should have at least two locks on their door, and no individual should have access to both keys. The Russians have long insisted that they follow the two-person rule, but their enforcement of this procedure has often been relatively lax. In fact, even at Russian facilities that have received MPC&A upgrades, U.S. program participants have often observed "exceptions" made to the two-person rule during their visits, in order to speed up access to a secure area.[257] There have also been a number of cases in which the director of a nuclear facility and other high-level managers had master keys that could open any vault.[258] U.S. scientists have extensively emphasized the necessity for these procedures and have made some progress in convincing the Russians to follow them, but the progress can often be frustratingly slow.

Conclusions about the MPC&A Program

Although the MPC&A program has made significant progress in improving Russia's nuclear security and controls, the enduring problems identified above are significant cause for concern. There appear to be several fundamental reasons for these problems. First, the scale of the problem is much bigger than early estimates indicated. Although it was initially believed that 80–100 buildings contained weapons-usable fissile materials, it turned out that there are nearly 400 buildings containing these materials, and most are in need of upgrades.[259] Many frustrating problems, such as the fact that physical inventories have not been completed at many sites, can be traced to the sheer magnitude of the dilemma. Second, Russia often does not have the technological infrastructure (including domestic industry capable of producing reliable spare parts, resources for purchasing critical technologies, or sufficient numbers of highly trained technical experts for operating equipment) necessary to sustain the new equipment installed at its nuclear facilities.[260] Therefore, although some progress has been made toward implementing modern high-technology solutions, some of the most appropriate and effective upgrades have proven to be "low tech," such as strengthened doors, locks, and bars on windows, in part because they do not require the infrastructure to maintain them.[261] Third, many facilities are proving to be unwilling or unable to pay for the operation and maintenance of the new technologies once they are installed. Finally, and most troubling, the Russians often do not understand, or simply do not see the necessity for, the new MPC&A technologies and procedures.[262]

These problems have created significant obstacles to the continued success of the MPC&A program. But given the serious consequences of fissile material theft and nuclear terrorism, continued effort should be devoted to improving Russia's fissile material controls. Further steps in the MPC&A program should include efforts to solve the specific problems outlined above by consolidating materials to fewer locations, improving Russia's technological base, and cultivating a safeguards culture at Russian nuclear facilities.[263]

Part III: Conclusions

The Russian case gives us important empirical evidence by which we can improve our understanding of the effects of domestic upheavals on nuclear controls. It provides insight in two fundamental areas. First, the Russian case demonstrates how domestic upheavals can weaken command structures, communication networks, and early-warning systems. In the most extreme cases, domestic upheavals can erode the allegiance of military units possessing nuclear weapons, and could even lead to nuclear coups.[264] Alternatively, the country can fragment, creating new nuclear powers that have inadequate experience controlling nuclear weapons.[265] But even in less severe cases, domestic crises can undermine necessary resources and manpower for the maintenance and repairs of command networks and early-warning systems. These factors can significantly increase risks of accidental, unauthorized, and inadvertent use of nuclear weapons.

Second, the Russian case demonstrates how domestic upheavals can significantly increase the risks of "nuclear leakage," in which nuclear weapons or fissile materials are stolen for sale on the black market. Although nuclear leakage has not been directly addressed in the context of the proliferation debate, these risks are very serious and are thus directly relevant to the debate. As we have seen, in order to prevent nuclear leakage, NWSs must have effective WPC&A systems at their nuclear weapon storage facilities, and MPC&A at their production facilities and fissile material storage facilities.[266] As part of their MPC&A, NWSs should also have resilient physical protection systems, which would help prevent the capture or sabotage of nuclear facilities. But the case of Russia gives us significant reason to doubt that they will. The Soviets relied heavily on the "3 G's"—guards, gates, and guns—for protecting their nuclear materials, and this system proved to be fragile after the Soviet collapse.[267] Due to the domestic crises that have plagued Russia since the collapse, there is significant evidence that Russian nuclear facilities are vulnerable to insider thefts and terrorist attacks, thus causing them to be a potential and actual source of nuclear leakage.[268]

It could be, however, that these problems are unique to Russia. In the following chapters, we will examine the evidence from other NWSs to determine whether their nuclear systems could potentially reveal similar weaknesses.

China

Why is China an important case to study? China has had a nuclear weapons arsenal since its first nuclear test in 1964, and like the United States and Russia, it is officially recognized as a nuclear weapons state by the Nuclear Non-Proliferation Treaty (NPT). Although China is clearly one of the most important states to examine when assessing the probable actions of NWSs, there have been no systematic studies of China's nuclear program in the context of the optimist-pessimist debate. It is an important case to study for the following reasons.

First, a major issue in the debate is whether or not *new* NWSs will have done all the planning, conducted all the tests, and implemented all the technologies necessary for a resilient command-and-control system. The assumption of this argument is that established NWSs, by the mere fact that they are established rather than new, *do* have resilient command-and-control systems.[1] Because China has possessed nuclear weapons for nearly forty years, it is a useful case with which to test this assumption. If the nuclear optimists are correct, we would expect that China would have a very secure system of controls against accidental and unauthorized use.

Second, another topic in the debate concerns whether opaque nuclear programs will cause additional problems for emerging NWSs. While this might be true, it is useful to examine whether or not the *visible* proliferators, such as China, have resilient nuclear controls. As we have seen, some research suggests that the nuclear controls in the United States and Russia might not have been as resilient as most optimists assume, but very little work has been done on China.

Third, China is a relatively poor country.[2] It would be useful to examine whether or not economic constraints have affected China's ability to implement adequate nuclear controls. David Karl and Jordan Seng have argued that because poor countries will have small arsenals, potential command-and-control problems will be easier to solve. We will examine whether this was the case in China.

Fourth, Seng argues that countries with potential political instability will actually tend to have *stronger* command and control over their nuclear weapons than other NWSs. Because China has seen a great deal of political turmoil since its revolutionary beginnings in 1949, it would be particularly useful to determine whether there were weaknesses in China's command and control during these crises and whether China has taken additional precautions to protect against unauthorized seizure or use of its nuclear weapons since then.

Finally, because China's fissile material controls appear to have been modeled after the Soviet system, many experts have been concerned that the Chinese system could reveal the same weaknesses as the Soviet system during similar crises. It is therefore necessary to assess the risks arising from China's current system for controlling fissile materials at its nuclear facilities. This chapter identifies a number of potential weaknesses in China's MPC&A.

Part I: China's C³I and Risks of Accidental, Unauthorized, and Inadvertent Use

China's Nuclear Arsenal

China's nuclear arsenal is currently believed to contain about 400 warheads. Of this number, about 250 are believed to be strategic weapons in a triad of long-range land-based missiles, bombers, and submarine-launched ballistic missiles, and about 150 are believed to be "tactical" weapons, presumably lower-yield bombs for tactical aircraft, artillery shells, atomic demolition munitions (ADMs), and short-range missiles.[3] However, China is currently believed to be modernizing and expanding its nuclear arsenal, and has warned that it will expand its arsenal size by a much larger amount if the United States deploys a national missile defense (NMD).[4] Each type of delivery system is discussed briefly below.

Nuclear-Capable Aircraft

China's first nuclear weapon delivery means was by aircraft, which could drop gravity bombs. China's current nuclear-capable air force includes the Hong-6 (a modified Soviet Tu-16) and the Qian-5 bombers. Each of these aircraft is able to carry one nuclear gravity bomb. Because of the greater vulnerability of aircraft during delivery, China has placed less emphasis on improving its nuclear-capable bombers than it has on developing its nuclear missiles. As of mid-2004, the People's Liberation Army (PLA) inventory basically contained aircraft of obsolete designs with short flight radiuses and limited capabilities for delivering nuclear bombs to targets.[5]

Nuclear Submarines and Submarine-Launched Ballistic Missiles (SLBMs)

China currently has one Daqingyu (Xia)-class nuclear submarine, believed to be based in the North Sea Naval Fleet in Qingdao.[6] The submarine is deployed with twelve Julang-1/CSS-N-3 SLBMs. The missiles use a solid-fuel propellant and have a range of 1,700 kilometers with a payload of 200–300 kilotons.[7] China is also developing second-generation nuclear submarines, armed with a new type of SLBM. "A new generation of nuclear powered submarines (Type 094) reportedly are scheduled for construction after the year 2000 and would carry 16 JL-2 missiles."[8] The JL-2 missiles are still being developed, but they will have a range of 8,000 kilometers and will allow China's submarines to target the United States from locations near China's coast.[9] (See table 4.1 for details on China's SLBMs.)

Land-Based Ballistic Missiles

China began its missile program in 1956 and initially received assistance from the Soviets. In that year, the Soviets sold China two R-1 missiles. Since this missile was quite primitive, however, the Soviets supplied China with two R-2 missiles in 1957. In 1958, the Soviets supplied technical blueprints and engineers to build the R-2. This missile was successfully flight-tested in 1960 and was renamed the Dong-Feng-1. There are currently no DF-1 missiles deployed in China's nuclear arsenal, however.[10]

In 1965, China embarked on the "Eight-Year Plan for the Development of Rocket Technology." The goal of this plan was to develop missiles with ranges capable of hitting four different American targets (either U.S. bases or the United States itself). The DF-2 was designed to strike Japan, the DF-3 was designed to strike the Philippines, the DF-4 was designed to strike Guam, and the DF-5 was designed to strike the continental United States.[11] By 1971, China had achieved its goal (although some of the missiles were not deployed until much later).[12] After 1981, China focused on improving its land-based rocket technologies. In 1985, China successfully flight-tested the DF-21, a two-stage, solid-fueled missile. This missile is a modified JL-1 submarine-launched ballistic missile (SLBM). As of 2001, China had only about 20 DF-5 missiles, and another 100 missiles with ranges from about 1,800 to 4,750 kilometers.[13]

In order to increase the survivability of its nuclear arsenal, China began the research and development of a second generation, mobile long-range ballistic missile system in the early 1980s. To make the missiles mobile, however, China needed to miniaturize their nuclear payloads and switch from liquid to solid propellants.[14] As of May 2004, China was continuing to convert its missile arsenal to mobile systems. It currently has three types of road-mobile, solid-propellant missiles: the DF-21 (CSS-5),[15] a medium-range ballistic missile (MRBM); and two types of tactical missiles (see below). In the first decade of the twenty-first century, China is expected to begin deployment of two long-range road-mobile ICBMs: the DF-31, with an estimated range of about 8,000 kilometers, and the DF-31A, with an estimated range of about 12,000 kilometers.[16] China reportedly flight-tested the DF-31 in 1999, twice in 2000, and once (reportedly unsuccessfully) in January 2002.[17] It is possible that both the DF-31 and DF-31A will be equipped with multiple independently targetable reentry vehicles (MIRVs).[18] (See table 4.1 for details on China's land-based missiles.)

Tactical Weapons

China currently has two tactical missiles, the DF-15 (CSS-6) and the DF-11 (CSS-7). The DF-15 has a range of 600 kilometers and the DF-11 has a range of 280 kilometers.[19] Both missile types are road-mobile, contain a solid propellant, and can carry either nuclear or conventional warheads. They are intended both for use in China's own arsenal and for export.[20] China is believed to have exported the DF-11 (although it was called the M-11) to Pakistan in 1991.[21] There is also some evidence that China possesses nuclear artillery shells and ADMs for use on the battlefield.[22] It is not currently known whether China's tactical nuclear weapons are deployed in the field along with their delivery systems or kept in storage.[23] If they are deployed in the field, they are probably placed under the control of regional commanders.[24]

China's Nuclear Weapon Storage and Deployment

China has been unwilling to divulge much information about how or where its nuclear weapons are stored. This secrecy is presumably to help assure the safety and security of its arsenal, given the arsenal's limited size and China's storage methods for its nuclear weapons. China must maintain secrecy about the location of its nuclear weapons in order to ensure the survivability of its arsenal.

Many of China's warheads are located at assembly and storage facilities. Of China's deployed nuclear weapons, some ICBMs are deployed in silos,

Table 4.1. Chinese Nuclear Weapons							
Type	NATO Designation	No.	Year Deployed	Range (km)	Warhead x yield	No. of warheads	Technical Description
Aircraft[a]							
Hong-6	B-6	100	1965	3,100	1-3 x bomb	100	
Qian-56	A-5	30	1970	400	1 x bomb	30	
Land-Based Missiles							
DF-3A	CSS-2	40	1971	2,800	1 x 3.3 MT	40	Single stage, storable liquid
DF-4	CSS-3	20	1980	4,750	1 x 3.3 MT	20	Two stage, storable liquid
DF-5A	CSS-4	20	1981	13,000	1 x 4-5 MT	20	Two stage, storable liquid
DF-21A	CSS-5	48	1986	1,800	1 x 200-300 kt	48	Two stage, solid fuel, road mobile
DF-31	CSS-X-10	0	2005 ?	8,000	MIRV x ?	?	Three stage, solid fuel, road mobile
DF-31A	CSS-?	0	2010 ?	12,000	MIRV x ?	?	Three stage, solid fuel, road mobile

SLBMs							
Julang-1	CSS-N-3	12	1986	1,700	1 x 200-300 kt	12	Two stage, solid fuel, sea-based version of DF-21
Julang-2	CSS-N-4	0	2010 ?	8,000	1 x 200-300 kt	?	Three stage, solid fuel, sea-based version of DF-31
Tactical Weapons							
DF-15 (M-9)	CSS-6	?		60	Nuclear capable 1 x low kt	Total Tactical warheads ≈120	Solid fuel, road mobile
DF-11 (M-11)	CSS-7	?		280	Nuclear capable 1 x low kt		Solid fuel, road mobile
Artillery/ ADMs		?			Low kt		

Sources: Norris et al., "Chinese Nuclear Forces, 2001," p. 71; Norris and Kristensen,"Chinese Nuclear Forces, 2003," p. 77; Cirincione et al., *Deadly Arsenals*, p. 143-144; Lewis and Hua, "China's Ballistic Missile Programs," pp. 9-11.

Note: [a] Figures for bomber aircraft are for nuclear-configured versions only. Hong-5 bombers previously had a nuclear role, but have been retired. For more than a decade, China has been developing a supersonic fighter-bomber, the Hong-7, but it will reportedly not have a nuclear role. Aircraft range is equivalent to combat radius. Assumes 150 bombs for the air force, with yields estimated between 10 kt and 3 MT.

but most are kept hidden in caves and deep canyons. The following is the available information on China's nuclear weapons storage system.

Nuclear Weapon Storage, Assembly, and Research Facilities

China is believed to store some of its warheads in storage facilities at multiple locations across the country. A major storage facility is believed to be the Lop Nur test site, which might contain as many as 150 tactical nuclear weapons.[25] Chinese nuclear weapons are also probably located at several nuclear weapon assembly facilities.[26] Information on the specific facilities is scarce, but nuclear weapons are believed to be assembled at the Jiuquan Atomic Energy Complex in Gansu, Harbin in Heilongjiang, and Plant 821 in Sichuan. It is also likely that some warhead prototypes are built at some of China's nuclear weapon research facilities, such as the Mianyang facility.

Nuclear-Capable Bombers and Gravity Bombs

Not much is known about China's nuclear-capable bomber force. According to Norris et al., "It is believed that [China's] bomber force is assigned nuclear and conventional missions and is deployed at regular air bases and also on rotation to numerous contingency bases."[27] It is not clear whether the nuclear-capable bombers are organized into independent units, or whether they are integrated into the same units as conventional bombers. It does appear that each major unit (up to an air division) is assigned to one air base, which is responsible for all aspects of operations, training, maintenance, and repair.[28] If China's bombers are assigned nuclear missions, one might conclude that some nuclear gravity bombs are stored at air force bases, but this has never been verified. Jack Anderson quotes a Defense Intelligence Agency report as saying that "only one national stockpile site and no regional sites have been observed in China. Thus if nuclear weapons for air delivery are deployed to air bases, they have been effectively hidden."[29]

Nuclear Missiles Deployed in Caves and Silos

China's first-generation missiles have been stored either in caves or silos. The Dong Feng-4 (DF-4), for example, is still stored in caves. The cave-storage method, however, causes significant problems in China's ability to respond quickly to nuclear attacks. The Dong Feng-4 is stored horizontally in the caves, but its skin is too thin for it to be filled with propellants in this position without causing serious body damage (even though it reportedly uses a storable liquid fuel).[30] Large, liquid-fueled missiles such as the DF-4 therefore need to be prepared inside the cave, rolled outside, then erected and filled before they can be fired.[31]

DF-5 missiles, the only missiles capable of striking the United States, are stored in silos.[32] As of 1992, only four DF-5A missiles had been deployed in silos, though more are almost certainly deployed now.[33] Although these missiles use a storable liquid fuel, they can only be kept fueled for about twenty-four hours because the fuel is highly corrosive and the missiles could leak.[34] The DF-5 missiles are therefore stored unfueled, with fuel storage tanks located nearby.

China's method of storing weapons in silos could also cause some problems. It is not clear that these silos have been sufficiently hardened to survive a nuclear strike.[35] In order to make its silo-stored missiles more survivable, China reportedly built a large number of bogus silos.[36] According to a June 2000 report by the U.S. Department of Defense, China had built eighteen DF-5 missile silos.[37] Although some reports have suggested that China deploys the DF-5 in silos at three separate locations, more recent reports indicate that the sole base for DF-5 missiles is located near Luoning, in the Henan province.[38]

China's Transition to a Mobile Ballistic Missile System

The small number of missiles in China's arsenal, combined with its storage method for these missiles, raised concerns in China about the survivability of its arsenal in the event of a nuclear attack. In order to increase the survivability of its nuclear arsenal, China has been developing a mobile ballistic missile system since the early 1980s. Once China has completed the transition to a mobile system, it is not clear how or where China will deploy its missiles, but it will have the capability to deploy its missiles in a launch-ready condition, in which the missiles are stored fully fueled and with their warheads mated.[39] Indeed, missiles using solid propellants *must* remain fueled during storage.[40] In addition, if the missiles will be mobile, the warheads will probably need to be kept near the missiles. Since continual transportation of both the de-mated warheads and the missiles is difficult and time-consuming, it is quite possible that the warheads will be kept mated to the missiles, or will be mated in periods of increased alert.[41]

C3I (Command, Control, Communications, and Intelligence)

Chain of Command—The Roles of the Chinese Communist Party (CCP), the Central Military Commission (CMC), and the Second Artillery Corps (SAC)

There is little question that the Chinese command-and-control structure is designed so that the CCP has the ultimate authority over the use of China's nuclear weapons. In 1929, Mao Zedong stated that "Our principle is that the Party controls the gun and the gun shall never be allowed to control the Party," and it is unlikely that this principle has changed.[42] If a decision were made to launch China's missiles (or to prepare them for launch), the command would probably originate in the Central Committee of the CCP Politburo. The command would then be relayed to the CMC, the association that has direct authority over all armed forces of the People's Republic of China.[43] The CMC would then relay the launch command to the senior leadership in the PLA.

The central command-and-control center for all PLA forces, including the Second Artillery, is Xishan, in the hills west of Beijing, where strategic operational orders originate. The Second Artillery is responsible for the command and control of China's nuclear and conventional missile forces.[44] A launch command would pass from Xishan to the Second Artillery headquarters and its communications regiment. The command would then be sent directly to China's six launch bases, bypassing China's military region commands.[45] The launch base command centers would, in turn, communicate with their respective launch brigades. Each launch base is directly subordinate to the Second Artillery commander in Qinghe, although they do receive support from the military regions.[46]

Nuclear Force Doctrine: Minimal vs. Limited Deterrence

For many years, China has relied on a doctrine of "minimal deterrence." This doctrine requires only a small number of strategic weapons to inflict unacceptable damage to a few of an enemy's cities. Such a doctrine does not allow for a disarming first strike; rather, it requires the NWS to "ride out" a nuclear strike and then engage in a delayed retaliation. China maintained such a force doctrine until at least the late 1990s. For example, it has an official doctrine of "no first use" (NFU) of nuclear weapons and a small

ICBM force stored that cannot be readied and fired rapidly. However, in recent years, China has appeared to be evolving toward a force doctrine of "limited deterrence." A limited deterrence doctrine calls for some counterforce and warfighting elements, with intended targets including enemy missile bases, C^3I centers, and strategic warning assets.[47] Chinese strategic analysts argue that limited deterrence requires a greater number of smaller, more accurate, survivable, penetrable ICBMs and SLBMs; a ballistic missile defense capability to protect its limited deterrent force; space-based early-warning and command-and-control systems; and anti-satellite assets to hit enemy military satellites.[48] Some Chinese analysts have also argued that China's first response must be immediate and extremely rapid. As Iain Johnston points out, while this response would still be a reaction to an aggressive action taken by the enemy (and therefore probably still in accordance with China's doctrine of NFU),[49] it is not at all clear that China's forces should wait until after this initial action is complete. "In other words, there are intriguing hints of interest in launch-on-warning or launch-under-attack."[50] Until recently, China's capabilities fell far short of what would be required by a doctrine of limited deterrence.[51] But recent advances in China's C^3I have brought the nation much closer to this goal.[52]

China's C^3I Modernization

Improved Ballistic Missile Capabilities

China's current generation of missiles does not allow for anything approaching limited deterrence. These missiles are fairly inaccurate, which limits their utility in precision strikes of hardened targets, and they are stored unfueled with their warheads unmated, which prevents rapid response and survivability. The newer generation of missiles solves many of these problems, however. For example, according to the U.S. Pentagon, China is using the Global Positioning System to make "significant improvements" in the accuracy of its newer missiles. In addition, if the missiles are stored with their warheads mated, they could allow for rapid response. Indeed, most sources indicate that the launch times for the DF-31 and DF-31A could be under fifteen minutes and under five minutes, respectively.[53] The number of strategic missiles in China's arsenal would prevent a limited deterrent posture for some time, however. Nevertheless, China is reportedly planning to increase significantly the number of missiles in its arsenal, especially if the United States deploys NMD.[54]

Upgrades of China's Command System

C^{3}I modernization has been one of China's top priorities since 1979, and they have made significant improvements in this area. As Gill and Mulvenon point out, however, some of the reported "breakthroughs" suggest that the past level of command-and-control structures was not particularly advanced. For example, the official *People's Liberation Army Daily* in early 1998 noted that the Second Artillery Corps (SAC) "after three years of arduous work" developed a new digital microwave communications system, which now allows for secure "all-weather" communications for missile launch. "With the new system," the article notes, "the Second Artillery will no longer be affected by natural conditions such as weather."[55]

Nevertheless, according to a 1998 report by the U.S. Department of Defense, China's command-and-control facilities are located in an extensive network of hardened, underground shelters that would be very resistant to attack. The communication system is carried by a number of redundant transmission systems, and has been determined to be "survivable, secure, flexible, mobile, and less vulnerable to exploitation, destruction or electronic attack."[56] The DOD report concludes that the command-and-control systems are capable of supporting military operations within China and would probably survive attempts at decapitation.

Intelligence: Improving Early-Warning and Satellite Capabilities

The PLA has long suffered from antiquated air defenses and intelligence networks. Specifically, the PLA Air Force (PLAAF) has lacked decent early-warning radars, early-warning satellites, and automated intelligence handling and transmission facilities. Since the first Gulf War, however, Chinese policymakers have placed a high priority on upgrading their overall air defense capability in order to protect strategically critical points.[57] A comprehensive air defense network is reportedly being designed to counter air and missile attacks. The network is composed of numerous segments, including early-warning radars and satellites, rapid data processing and command centers, air defense weapons, and offensive counter-air and counter-space weapons.[58] China is reportedly close to achieving the capability to develop early-warning systems. As Mark Stokes notes, "China has a well-established technology base in infrared sensors, which, when placed on satellites, can detect a missile almost immediately after launch by detecting the infrared radiation from its engine motor plume. Technical writings indicate the space industry is working to master specific technologies associated with missile early-warning satellites."[59]

In 1975, China reportedly dismissed the option of a launch-on-warning system because it was unable to build a reliable early-warning system.[60] Were China to achieve a reliable early-warning system, it might adopt a doctrine of limited deterrence, possibly including a policy of launch-on-warning.[61] China is believed to be much more likely to adopt such doctrines if the United States develops and deploys NMD.[62]

Use-Control Devices and "Negative Controls"

Although there is a frustrating lack of information on the subject, evidence exists that China's nuclear weapons lack sophisticated use-control devices to ensure central controls. For example, China's weapons reportedly lacked PALs in 1987,[63] and it is not believed that this situation has changed during the intervening years.[64] Although there have been reports that China has improved its command-and-control system in recent years, these improvements appear to have been primarily in communications systems. As Bates Gill and James Mulvenon note, these changes improve the leadership's "positive control" over its nuclear forces by increasing the survivability of the missile forces and command systems.[65] However, the changes do not appear to improve China's "negative control," or the element of command and control that prevents the accidental or unauthorized use of the nuclear weapons. Instead, China reportedly maintains negative controls through guard forces, separate storage of warheads and missiles, and procedures such as the two-person rule.[66]

The Risks of Accidental Use of Chinese Nuclear Weapons

Given China's current missile systems and deployment procedures, it is considered unlikely that China will accidentally launch a nuclear ballistic missile. According to Robert D. Walpole, the U.S. National Intelligence Officer for Strategic and Nuclear Programs, an unauthorized or accidental launch of a Chinese nuclear missile is highly unlikely, as long as current security procedures and systems are in place, because China keeps its missiles unfueled and without warheads mated.[67] In fact, under the best circumstances, it would take China several hours to prepare these unassembled missiles for launch.[68] While its missiles are stored in this condition (i.e., during peacetime), there is virtually no chance of any typical accidental-launch scenario occurring.

Of course, the fact that China keeps most of its missiles unfueled and its warheads unmated does not completely remove any chance of an accidental launch. If China found itself in a situation in which it decided to bring its missiles to a launch-ready condition, it might need to assemble them in an extreme hurry. Unless China had rigorously trained its personnel to assemble the weapons under these conditions, they might be more likely to make mistakes, possibly leading to an accidental launch. It is not clear whether China has in fact trained its personnel to act under such crisis situations, but we do know that China has not done the extensive training and tests that the United States and Russia have.[69] Thus, the chance of China's accidentally launching its missiles is quite low during peacetime, but it might in fact be significantly higher during crisis situations.[70]

Although China's mobile missile system could reduce the chance of a successful preemptive strike against China, this system could also introduce new risks of accidental launch. As we have seen, it is quite possible that the warheads will be kept mated to the missiles, or will be mated in periods of increased alert. If China's missiles were stored in this launch-ready condition, the risks of accidental launches could increase significantly. Indeed, one must recall that China already has some road-mobile, nuclear-capable, tactical missiles. If the warheads are continuously mated to these tactical missiles, then there might be a chance that China could accidentally launch a nuclear missile against a neighbor.[71]

The Risks of Unauthorized Use of Chinese Nuclear Weapons

The chance of an unauthorized use of China's nuclear weapons may be significantly greater than the chance of an accidental use. China's current system of command and control relies heavily on the presence of the "3 G's": guards, gates, and guns. There is, however, a significant weakness in a command-and-control system that relies heavily on guard forces: if there were a breakdown in the chain of command, the guards might follow the orders of someone who is disobeying the commands of the central authorities.

Because Chinese weapons appear to lack sophisticated use-control devices equivalent to U.S. PALs, China would not have any technological means of ensuring control over its nuclear arsenal during a domestic political crisis. In these cases, the chance of an unauthorized use of nuclear weapons could increase significantly. It is this weakness in particular that led Terry Hawkins, director of the Nonproliferation and International Security Division of Los Alamos National Laboratory, to say, "China's command and control over its nuclear weapons possibly is not as good as we'd like it to be."[72] According to Robert Walpole, the unauthorized use of Chinese nuclear weapons is highly unlikely "as long as current security procedures and systems are in place."[73] But in times of political crisis, the command-and-control system in China would not necessarily stay in place. Indeed, there is reason to suspect that China's command-and-control structure has demonstrated significant weaknesses during more than one political crisis.[74]

The Cultural Revolution

The Cultural Revolution was a time of extreme political turmoil for China. As the entire country collapsed into chaos, political purges, uprisings, revolts, and riots were commonplace. Although Nie Rongzhen, head of China's overall strategic weapons program, managed to isolate the nuclear weapons program from this revolutionary frenzy for a time, it was impossible to hold off the effects of the political crisis forever. During the Cultural Revolution, there were several incidents that involved China's nuclear weapons.

October 1966: Red Guards Conducted an "Unauthorized" Nuclear-Armed Missile Test

In 1966, at the peak of the Cultural Revolution, the Second Artillery launched an armed nuclear warhead over Chinese population centers, apparently contrary to the orders of Nie Rongzhen.[75] Evan Feigenbaum reports this incident in his Ph.D. dissertation:

> In part because strategic weapons tests had powerful patriotic and ideological appeal, weapons testing became increasingly identified with mobilizational fanaticism when the Cultural Revolution broke out in military industry. Red Guards in Beijing and rebel factions among the workers on the test bases adopted weapons tests as a cause celèbre of their movement, explicitly suggesting a "bond between the creative force of Mao's radicalism and the force of the [atomic] bomb" (Lewis and Xue, 1988a, p. 202). When the Second Artillery Corps decided to test a DF-2 missile on October 27, 1966, by launching it, armed with a live warhead, over population centers against a ground zero in Xinjiang, Nie [head of NDSTC, which had de facto control over the Second and Seventh Ministry systems]—powerless to halt the test—attempted to at least control its potentially disastrous effects by taking personal charge of safety procedures. On the 25th, he flew to the Shuangchengzi launch base (Base 20) to demand briefings on safety procedure. After the test, a relieved Nie flew to the impact zone to assess the missile's accuracy and to demonstrate his authority.[76]

Although the missile hit its target and detonated without any mishap, this case demonstrates the lack of a resilient command-and-control structure in China at that time. Granted, this was only an unauthorized test launch of an armed nuclear missile; it was not a launch against another country. But this test launch shows us two things. First, if the soldiers in the Second Artillery who decided to launch the missile had decided—in a similar revolutionary or patriotic frenzy—to launch the nuclear missile against another country, they could have. It is clear that in 1966 China had few—if any—reliable controls against the unauthorized use of its nuclear weapons.

Second, this incident shows that the people who have control over nuclear weapons do not always make rational decisions about the use of these weapons. This was reportedly only the second test launch of any DF-2, and the first test of a DF-2 missile armed with a nuclear warhead. And it was only China's fourth nuclear test altogether.[77] The Second Artillery took a very great risk when it launched this missile *over China's own territory.* In his memoirs, Nie Rongzhen emphasized the extreme danger of this test: "if by any chance the nuclear warhead exploded prematurely, fell after it was launched, or went beyond the designated target area, the consequences would be too ghastly to contemplate."[78]

January 1967: Mao Yuanxin Led Attack on Lop Nur

In January 1967, staff members of the Nuclear Weapons Test Base defied orders and invited radicals from the Red Rebellious Corps from the Harbin Military Engineering Institute (HMEI) to Xinjiang to engage in revolutionary activities and attack "bourgeois" personnel. Mao Yuanxin (Mao Zedong's nephew) led a group of radicals on a 4,000-kilometer trip to attack the Lop Nur test base. By the time they arrived, Nie Rongzhen had prepared the base's defenses and had the radicals arrested as they attacked.[79]

December 1967: Regional Military Commander Threatened to Take Over Lop Nur Test Site

In 1967 General Wang En-Mao, military commander of the Chinese province of Xinjiang, reportedly threatened to take over the Lop Nur nuclear weapons testing site during a dispute with Mao Zedong. Since Lop Nur is believed to be a major nuclear weapons storage site, this threat also entailed seizing control over the nuclear weapons stored there. As the military commander of the region, Wang probably would have been able to seize control over the nuclear weapons if he had wanted to.[80] This dispute was resolved peacefully, and the threat was never carried out.

1971: The Lin Biao Affair

Near the end of the Cultural Revolution, a growing disagreement between Mao Zedong and his then-designated successor, Defense Minister Lin Biao, occurred over the political role of the People's Liberation Army (PLA). Because of this disagreement, Mao eventually removed Lin from his position as successor. As it was becoming clear that he was losing Mao's favor, however, Lin increasingly turned to his other main power base—the PLA. These political events came to a head when Lin, Ch'en Po-ta (another prominent political figure), and five top-ranking military officials challenged Mao, first openly at the Second Plenum of the Ninth Central Committee, and then clandestinely by plotting a coup d'etat to remove Mao from power. By September 1971, however, it became clear that the coup plans had failed, after Mao managed to gain assurances of loyalty from regional military leaders in preparation for a final showdown with Lin. When Lin learned of this, he reportedly attempted to flee the country by flying to the Soviet Union. He never made it. Lin died, along with his wife and son, when their plane crashed in Mongolia (either because it was shot down or because it ran out of gas).[81]

The Lin Biao affair was above all "a struggle between a Mao-led civilian party and a Lin-led Army for control of China's political system."[82] Both the Lin Biao affair and the subsequent purges resulting from it created deep tensions between the PLA and the governing party.[83] This struggle is especially troubling because the PLA had—and still has—custody over China's nuclear weapons, and because these weapons did not contain PALs. As Dan Caldwell suggests, this affair must have raised the question in Chinese leaders' minds about the necessity for use-control devices on nuclear weapons.[84] In fact, it appears that the Chinese discussed PAL technologies with the United States sometime after these events took place.[85] It is reasonable to conclude that they probably had in mind some of the risks that arose during the Lin Biao affair.

The Tiananmen Square Crisis

At the time of the Tiananmen Square crisis, there was a great deal of speculation about a possible breakdown in Chinese command arrangements that would then have spurred a loss of central control over China's nuclear forces.[86] Since there was not much evidence in the public domain at the time to confirm these speculations, however, it was generally concluded that the Chinese command structure was probably more resilient than previously believed.[87] In recent years, however, there has been renewed speculation that there was in fact a significant weakness in China's command and control over its nuclear weapons during the Tiananmen Square crisis. Indeed, Chinese officials appear to have all but admitted this to be the case. China reportedly expressed interest in U.S. PAL technology in 1994 because during the Tiananmen Square crisis Beijing's leaders had feared their army might split over the decision to crush student protests, causing the central government to lose control of its nuclear arsenal. American PALs, the Chinese said, would reduce any such risk in the future.[88] It is therefore worthwhile to examine what might have happened during the Tiananmen Square crisis, because it can shed light on the consequences of any continuing weaknesses in China's command-and-control structure.

The weakness in China's command-and-control structure during the Tiananmen Square crisis appears to have been caused principally by a significant weakness in the central government's authority over the PLA, combined with an apparent lack of technical means of authentication and central control over China's nuclear forces.

There is strong evidence of factional conflict in the PLA. During the crisis, a number of military units were quite reluctant to use force against the students. A major factor in determining whether or not a given military unit in the PLA remained loyal to the central government was personal loyalty to high-ranking military leaders. In particular, a number of high-ranking military officers signed publicly distributed letters opposing the use of force. It appears that many units of the PLA were more loyal to these officials than to the central government, especially when the officials had had some personal connection with the units.[89] It is likely that at least some members of the Second Artillery were influenced by personal relationships, just as the rest of the PLA was. Indeed, a number of high-ranking military officials who were influential with the Second Artillery opposed the use of force against the students.

One of these influential military figures was the minister of defense, Qin Jiwei. After the imposition of martial law in Beijing, approximately 300 military officers, including Qin Jiwei, signed a letter opposing the use of force against the protestors.[90] In addition, the political stances taken by Nie Rongzhen and Zhang Aiping, two prominent (though retired) military officials and heroes of China's nuclear weapons program, may have influenced members of the Second Artillery. Both of these men publicly opposed the use of force against the students.[91] Nie Rongzhen had been the head of the strategic weapons program during China's push to build the bomb.[92] Zhang Aiping was an ex-minister of defense[93] and had overseen China's first test of its atomic bomb. Both of these men were public heroes, and were probably especially revered in military units such as the Second Artillery that were most directly affected by their past work.

Because the Second Artillery controls almost all of China's nuclear weapons, it is central to the chain of command. Ultimately, if there were weaknesses in China's chain of command at the time of the crisis, they probably involved questions about whether the Second Artillery would remain loyal to the central government if the government ordered a crackdown on the protesting students.[94] Since Chinese nuclear weapons did not contain PALs (or equivalent use-control devices) during the crisis, a revolt by the Second Artillery would probably have constituted a loss of central control over China's nuclear weapons.

Possibilities of Future Political Instability in China

The above cases demonstrate how political instability can potentially undermine China's nuclear controls. These lessons are particularly relevant, because it is not clear that China will be able to avoid severe political instability in the future. China has been changing fundamentally in a number of ways in recent years. These changes have been sources of significant instability, and it is not yet clear that the regime will survive these changes. Indeed, it appears that the Chinese Communist Party (CCP) is rapidly losing influence in China. This is partly due to the liberalization of China's economy, partly due to the CCP's increasing inability to solve many of China's internal difficulties, such as the separatist movements and the pressures of liberalization, and partly due to the large dissatisfaction in the populace with widespread government corruption. After years of being denied by the government and the government-controlled press, these problems have become severe enough that the CCP has recently been forced to admit them. According to a June 2, 2001, article in the *New York Times,* "A startlingly frank new report from the Communist Party's inner sanctum describes a spreading pattern of 'collective protests and group incidents' arising from economic, ethnic and religious conflicts in China and says relations between party officials and the masses are 'tense, with conflicts on the rise.'"[95] The following sections discuss these sources of instability in greater detail.

Economic Changes and Political Stagnation

The most fundamental changes have resulted from China's transition to an open economy. With a reported sustained yearly growth rate of nearly 8 percent, China's economy has grown dramatically in the last decade.[96] China's entry into the World Trade Organization (WTO) will essentially guarantee that China's economy will continue to open up in the future.[97] But these economic changes, and in particular China's entry into the WTO, will almost certainly create severe shocks to the political system in both the short term and the long term. As Minxin Pei, a senior associate at the Carnegie Endowment for International Peace, has argued, "in both the short and long term, China's entry into the WTO—and the radical economic reforms likely to accompany it—will generate powerful shocks to the country's existing political system. . . . It remains highly uncertain, however, whether the Chinese regime is resilient enough to withstand such shocks."[98]

China's economic restructuring has only benefited a small, highly educated elite and has actually worsened conditions for workers in traditional industries and for rural farmers.[99] The worsening economic conditions in these two groups, combined with increasing frustration with widespread corruption in the CCP, have caused these groups to become immense reservoirs of social discontent. In recent years, there have been an increasing number of riots over government corruption, excessive taxation, and the CCP's inability to ease the economic hardships among industrial workers and rural farmers. According to some reports, there were over 100,000 protests in China in 1999, many of which led to violent clashes.[100] It has been estimated that the number of protests may have risen to as high as 200,000 in 2002.[101] The following are just a few examples of such incidents:

- In the largest labor protests since 1949, tens of thousands of displaced workers protested every weekday in March 2002 in Daqing in China's northeast.
- On April 20, 2001, more than 600 police and paramilitary troops stormed the village of Yuntang in the Jiangxi province, which was rebelling against rising taxes and official corruption.
- In August 2000, up to 20,000 farmers rioted for five days in the Jiangxi province in southern China, with some attacking government buildings and looting officials' homes in protest over government fees and taxes.
- In February 2000, tens of thousands of workers staged a violent protest at China's largest nonferrous metal mine, burning cars and holding police at bay for several days. The workers were protesting against what they said was an unfair and corrupt handling of the mine's bankruptcy.
- On October 18, 1999, more than 2,000 protesters took over a Sichuan railway station in protest over government handling of funds invested in illegal companies. The protesters were angry that the city government of Chongqing, which had earlier shut down several illegal investment companies, was not planning to return the invested funds immediately.
- In late 1998, the people of Shao village in southern Hebei rioted for the right to vote, and more than 700 riot police surrounded the village.[102]

Numerous scholars have expressed concern that this growing discrepancy between the rapid economic reforms and the lack of political reforms could be a major source of political upheavals and possibly even collapse the regime.[103] According to Hua Di, "the real threat to the PRC's current regime comes not from foreign military intervention . . . but from the Chinese people's pervasive dissatisfaction with the regime's corruption."[104] Hua concludes that "unless a political reform is launched and succeeds, in which the current regime in China takes initiative to change itself from a one-party dictatorship to a multi-party democracy, the corruption will not end but the regime will be finished."[105]

Increasing Regionalism and Separatist Movements

There are also numerous reports of increasing regionalism and separatist movements that could threaten to break China apart. For example, there are large economic disparities between the rich, southeastern provinces and poor, western provinces. Chinese leaders are reportedly worried that the southeastern provinces will someday refuse to finance the poor, western provinces and attempt to leave China.[106] But some western provinces are even more likely to want to break away from China. There are several separatist movements within China, most notably in Tibet and the western province of Xinjiang.[107] The separatist movement in Xinjiang has been particularly violent. Members of its predominantly Islamic Uighur population reportedly have received arms and training in places such as Afghanistan and Pakistan, then returned to oppose Beijing.[108] Although Beijing has engaged in severe crackdowns on these movements—Western-based monitoring groups have recorded more than 200 death sentences and 200 executions of Xinjiang separatists since 1997—the government has been surprisingly unsuccessful in quelling the unrest.[109]

There is also reported ethnic unrest in Inner Mongolia that could develop into a full-fledged separatist movement. China is quite worried that if one area were to achieve independence, the other areas would increase their efforts to secede. For example, the sheer resilience of the Xinjiang separatist movement has reportedly helped encourage Tibetans and Mongolians in their struggles against the central government.[110] This is reportedly a major reason why Beijing is so determined to prevent Taiwan's separation from mainland China.[111]

Conclusions about Unauthorized Use

The events during the Cultural Revolution and the Tiananmen Square crisis suggest a troubling weakness in China's command and control over its nuclear weapons. China's command-and-control structure seems to work well enough under normal, peaceful circumstances, but has proven to be vulnerable in times of acute political crisis. During these times, the risk of unauthorized use of Chinese nuclear weapons may have increased significantly. This fact seems especially disturbing, as China has experienced a great deal of political turmoil since its revolutionary beginning in 1949, including the Great Leap Forward in 1958–1960, the Cultural Revolution from 1966–1971, Lin Biao's attempted coup d'etat in 1971, and the Tiananmen Square crisis in 1989. And, one must recall, a number of these incidents occurred while China possessed nuclear weapons.

Moreover, as we have seen, there are continuing possibilities of serious economic, political, and social upheavals in China in the future. Given China's current system of nuclear controls, this political instability could have very severe consequences. According to Jones et al., "the possibilities run the spectrum from a breakup of China into multiple states, the breakdown of central authority and the rise of regional warlords, or a steady deterioration of central authority that would increase the opportunity for theft and smuggling of nuclear materials or weapons."[112]

The Risks of Inadvertent Use

The current risks of inadvertent use of Chinese nuclear weapons are probably fairly low because China keeps its missiles unfueled and its warheads unmated. Because China has only a limited ability to respond rapidly, it would be much more likely to "ride out" a nuclear strike and hope that enough of its nuclear weapons survive to allow it to retaliate. Nevertheless, because it is not at all certain that any of China's strategic nuclear weapons would survive a first strike, it is quite possible that China would prepare its weapons for launch during a crisis.

If China were to assemble its nuclear weapons during a crisis, however, an adversary could misinterpret these actions as an indication that China was actually planning to launch its weapons. Given the long preparation times for China's strategic missiles and the excellent reconnaissance satellites of potential enemies, such as the United States, China's enemies might be able to learn that it was assembling its weapons and the locations of these weapons.[113] This might cause an enemy to panic and engage in a preemptive nuclear strike before China's missiles were ready to be fired.[114]

Some scholars have also expressed concern that the preparation of China's weapons would create a "use them or lose them" scenario. Because China's current generation of long-range missiles use a highly corrosive liquid fuel, they need to be fired within twenty-four hours after they are fueled. And since it is virtually impossible to take the fuel out of the missiles again without damaging them, any deterrent effect China has from its nuclear weapons would be eliminated roughly twenty-four hours after China fueled its weapons. These conditions could create very strong pressures for China to use its weapons once they are fueled.[115] Of course, these pressures would be balanced by the very strong pressures for China *not* to launch its weapons because of the consequences of a nuclear retaliation. Perhaps a more serious "use them or lose them" scenario would arise due to the vulnerability of China's nuclear weapons to a disarming first strike by an adversary, such as the United States. If, during a crisis, China had prepared its weapons for launch and believed that a U.S. attack was imminent, it might decide to use its weapons first, thereby ensuring that its weapons would not be destroyed.[116]

Moreover, the risks of inadvertent use could increase significantly if China were to move to a force doctrine of "limited deterrence." As we have seen, such a doctrine would require advanced early-warning systems and some counterforce capabilities. Some of China's military analysts have argued that China should develop rapid-response capabilities and possibly even a policy of launch-on-warning.[117] If China does adopt such a system, the risks of inadvertent war could become fairly high, especially during crises. Because the decision to use the nuclear weapons would need to be made very rapidly, there would be much higher risks of panic-launches and launches due to misinformation or false alarms.

Part II: China's MPC&A

Current Fissile Materials Stockpiles

Although China is believed to have ended production of HEU in 1987 and weapons-grade plutonium in 1991, it is believed to have a significant stockpile of weapon-usable fissile materials.[118] According to most unclassified estimates, China is believed to have accumulated between 2 and 6 metric tons of plutonium and between 15 and 25 metric tons of highly-enriched uranium (HEU) by the end of 1994.[119]

China is believed to store its stocks of fissile materials at a number of civilian and military nuclear facilities across the country. Historically, the same facilities have been used for both civilian and military programs, but several years ago China began a process of converting large sections of its nuclear complex to strictly civilian use.[120] According to some estimates, approximately fourteen sites associated with China's nuclear weapons program contain significant quantities of weapons-usable fissile material.[121] The primary locations of non-weaponized fissile materials are believed to be China's plutonium production and uranium enrichment facilities, nuclear weapons research institutes, and other nuclear fuel cycle facilities.[122] (See table 4.2 for a list of the Chinese facilities believed to contain fissile materials.)

Chinese Agencies That Have Authority over Fissile Materials

It is difficult to determine which agencies have responsibility for the protection of fissile materials. There are several reasons for this. First, the division of authority is confusing to outside observers because China has made public very little information about its nuclear industry. Second, in 1998 and for the next several years, China conducted a major restructuring of its nuclear bureaucracies, and it is not clear that the dust has completely settled.[123] Finally, although "formal authority," determined by one's bureaucratic position, is probably the most important factor in determining responsibility for fissile materials, "informal authority," determined by personal connections, can also play an important role.[124] Nevertheless, the following are the agencies that are believed to have responsibility for fissile material controls.

Before China restructured its nuclear industry in 1998, the China National Nuclear Corporation (CNNC) was responsible for the control of nuclear materials for the whole country. Within the CNNC, the National Office of Nuclear Material Control was responsible for the implementation aspects of MPC&A.[125] The China Academy of Engineering Physics (CAEP) also apparently had some responsibility for production, storage, and control of fissile materials intended for military purposes.[126] After the restructuring, the responsibility for MPC&A for civilian and military fissile materials was given to the China Atomic Energy Agency (CAEA).[127] Within the CAEA, the Bureau of Nuclear Material Control is the main institution that regulates fissile materials.[128]

Defining the Threats to Chinese Nuclear Facilities

All states with nuclear facilities, civil or military, need a strong system of MPC&A because these facilities can be vulnerable to nuclear terrorism. China is no exception. Terrorists are becoming increasingly international. If they want to obtain fissile materials, they may choose to target the weakest MPC&A system.[129] Of course, international terrorist groups would have difficulties operating in China because foreigners typically stand out visually, do not speak Chinese well, and would be easy to spot in the remote areas where most of China's nuclear facilities are located. But as China's borders continue to open up, international terrorism might become more of a problem.

Perhaps a greater current risk than international terrorists attempting to acquire fissile materials from Chinese nuclear facilities is an increasing risk of domestic terrorism in China. In particular, Muslim separatists in Xinjiang have engaged in a number of acts of domestic terrorism. These terrorist ac-

Table 4.2. Chinese Facilities Believed to Store Weapons-Usable Fissile Materials [a]

Name/Location of Facility	Type/Status
Nuclear Weapons Complex	
Northwest Nuclear Technology Institute, in the Scientific Research District near Malan, Xinjiang	Archive on nuclear explosions, warfare, and weapons research and design; associated with testing at Lop Nur.
Jiuquan Atomic Energy Complex (Plant 404), Subei, Gansu	Fabrication of fissile materials into bomb core, and final weapons assembly; possibly closed down and being decommissioned.
Lop Nur Nuclear Weapons Test Base, Xinjiang	Nuclear weapons test site and possible nuclear weapons stockpile.
Chinese Academy of Engineering Physics (CAEP), Mianyang, Sichuan	Nuclear weapons research, design, and technology complex; called the "Los Alamos of China"; 11 institutes, 8 located in Mianyang.
Institute of Applied Physics and Computational Mathematics, Beijing	Research on nuclear warhead design computations for CAEP.
Harbin, Heilongjiang	Possible warhead assembly and production site.
Plant 821, Guangyuan, Sichuan	Nuclear weapons assembly facility; possibly closed down.
Plutonium Production Reactors	
Plant 821, Guangyuan, Sichuan	Light water cooled graphite moderated reactor (LWGR), natural uranium (U), 1,000 megawatt (MW); largest plutonium (Pu) production reactor in China; possibly shut down.
Jiuquan Atomic Energy Complex (Plant 404), Gansu	LWGR, natural U, 400-500 MW; shut down.

Table 4.2. Chinese Facilities Believed to Store Weapons-Usable Fissile Materials	
Research Reactors	
High Flux Engineering Test Reactor (HFETR), Nuclear Power Institute of China, Chengdu, Sichuan	Tank, light water (LW); HEU (90%), 125 MW; operational.
HFETR critical, Nuclear Power Institute of China, Chengdu, Sichuan	Critical assembly, LW; HEU (90%), 0 MW; operational.
Ming Jiang Test Reactor (MJTR), Nuclear Power Institute of China, Chengdu, Sichuan	Pool, LW; HEU (90%), 5 MW; operational.
MNSR IAE, China Institute of Atomic Energy, Tuoli, near Beijing	Tank in pool, LW; HEU (90%), 0.027MW; operational.
MNSR-SD, Shandong Geology Bureau, Jinan, Shandong	Tank in pool, LW; HEU (90%), 0.027MW; operational.
MNSR-SZ, Shenzhen University, Guangdong	Tank in pool, LW; HEU (90%), 0.027MW; operational.
Zero Power Fast Critical Reactor, Southwest Research Institute, Chengdu, Sichuan	Critical fast; HEU (90%), 0 MW; operational.
PPR Pulsing Reactor, Nuclear Power Institute of China, Chengdu, Sichuan	Pool, HEU (20%), 1 MW; operational.
HWRR-II, China Institute of Atomic Energy, Tuoli	Heavy-water, LEU (3%), 15-MWt; operational. Under IAEA safeguards.
Uranium Enrichment	
Heping Uranium Enrichment Plant, Heping, Suchuan	Gaseous diffusion plant estimated to produce 750-2,950 kg HEU/year; operational.
Lanzhou Nuclear Fuel Complex, Lanzhou, Gansu	Gaseous diffusion plant estimated to produce at least 150-330 kg HEU/year; operational.

China Institute of Atomic Energy, Tuoli, near Beijing	Laboratory-scale gaseous diffusion; developed enrichment process later installed at Lanzhou.
Russian-supplied centrifuge enrichment plant, Chengdu, Sichuan	Large-scale enrichment facility; under construction; capacity 200,000 SWU/yr; will probably only produce LEU. First stage completed in 1998; second stage completed in 2001; final stage is expected to be completed in 2005. Under IAEA safeguards.
Plutonium Reprocessing	
Jiuquan Atomic Energy Complex (Plant 404), Subei, Gansu	Large-scale reprocessing plant; 300-400 kg Pu/year, pilot reprocessing plant and nuclear fuel processing plant for refining plutonium into weapons-usable metals; closed.
Plant 821, Guangyuan, Sichuan	China's largest plutonium separation facility; 300-400 kg Pu/year; closed.
Nuclear Fuel Component Plant (Plant 812), Yibin, Sichuan	Plutonium fuel rod fabrication and plutonium production and processing for nuclear weapons; operations.
Lanzhou Nuclear Fuel Complex, Lanzhou, Gansu	Pilot-spent fuel reprocessing plant, nominal capacity of 100 kg heavy metal per day; completion expected in 2002.
Nuclear Power Reactors	
Guangdong-1, Daya Bay, Shenzhen, Guangdong	PWR, 944 MWe, operational.
Guangdong-2, Daya Bay, Shenzhen, Guangdong	PWR, 944 MWe, operational.
Lingao-1, Daya Bay, Shenzhen, Guangdong	PWR, 935 MWe, operational.
Qinshan-1, Zhejiang	PWR, 935 operational, under IAEA safeguards.
Qinshan 2-1, Zhejiang	PWR, 944 MWe, operational.

Table 4.2. Chinese Facilities Believed to Store Weapons-Usable Fissile Materials

Nuclear Power Reactors	
Qinshan 3-1, Zhejiang	PHWR, 935 MWe, operational, under IAEA safeguards.
Qinshan 3-2, Zhejiang	PHWR, 935 MWe, operational, under IAEA safeguards.
Lingao-2, Daya Bay, Shenzhen, Guangdong	PWR, 935 MWe, under contruction, expected completion 2003.
Qinshan 2-2, Zhejiang	PWR, 935 MWe, under contruction, expected completion 2004.
Tianwan 1 (Lian Yungang-1) Jiangsu	PWR, 935 MWe, under contruction, expected completion 2004.
Tianwan 2 (Lian Yungang-2) Jiangsu	PWR, 935 MWe, under contruction, expected completion 2005.

Sources: Jones et al., *Tracking Nuclear Proliferation*, pp. 65-67; "Chinese Nuclear Power Reactors," Power Reactor Information System, IAEA website, <http://www.iaea.org/programmes/a2/>; "China's Nuclear Power Reactors," Nuclear Threat Initiative, <http://www.nti.org/db/china/pwrrctr.htm>; Cirincione et al., *Deadly Arsenals*, pp. 158-161.

Note: [a] The weapons-usable fissile materials listed here include HEU and plutonium, including reactor-grade plutonium. The plutonium at the nuclear power reactors would presumably be unseparated from spent fuel, however, which would make it a less attractive target for theft.

tivities reached their peak in 1997, but they have reportedly continued in recent years. The possibility that these separatists might want to sabotage a nuclear facility or obtain fissile materials for terrorist purposes cannot be ruled out.[130]

One intriguing incident did reportedly occur in March 1993 at the Lop Nur site, located in Xinjiang.[131] On this occasion, around 1,000 protestors stormed the site in protest over China's nuclear testing. They were dispersed after the PLA fired shots. A spokesman for the Chinese Defense Ministry reportedly described the protestors as "barbarians" and claimed that they had done serious damage to the test site.[132] Additional reports, from Uighur sources citing the Chinese language paper *Singtao,* suggested that military equipment, airplanes, and tanks were also destroyed in the fighting that ensued between the Uighurs and the PLA. These sources also alleged that the attackers had stolen radioactive material from the test site, though this claim has proved impossible to substantiate.[133] While it is quite likely that radioactive material does exist at the Lop Nur site, it is unclear whether the attack took place near any sensitive locations. Given the size and the defenses at the site, it seems more likely that this incident was a violent protest and trespass action in clear contempt of Chinese authorities, rather than a dedicated attack or a credible threat to the security of Chinese nuclear materials or facilities.

The ethnic unrest in Tibet and Inner Mongolia could also eventually erupt into domestic violence.[134] While the Tibetan independence movement certainly has not erupted in the terrorism that has characterized the Xinjiang conflict, one cannot be certain that it never will. There are nuclear facilities and military bases located in provinces near Tibet that could be targets for terrorism.

China and International MPC&A Standards

Because China is officially recognized as a nuclear weapons state by the NPT, it is not bound by most of the IAEA regulations for control over fissile materials. Thus, to a large degree, China is responsible for implementing its own standards for fissile material control. However, China has voluntarily bound itself to some IAEA standards.

In 1988, China signed an agreement with the IAEA to place some of its facilities under IAEA safeguards. This agreement is published in INFCIRC/369.[135] China currently has five facilities under IAEA safeguards: the Qinshan-1 power reactor; Qinshan 3-1 and 3-2 (which are Canadian deuterium uranium, or CANDU, power reactors that became operational in 2002 and 2003); the HWRR-2 research reactor at the China Institute of Atomic Energy (CIAE); and a gas-centrifuge uranium enrichment plant, which was purchased from

Russia and will be used to produce low-enriched uranium (LEU).[136] Operation of the first stage of the uranium enrichment facility began in 1998 and the second in 2001. The third and final stage of the enrichment facility is expected to be completed in 2005.[137]

In addition to its voluntary agreement to place some facilities under IAEA safeguards, China has also signed several international agreements that relate to the controls over nuclear materials. The first of these was the 1979 Convention on the Physical Protection of Fissile Materials (codified in INFCIRC/274/Rev.1).[138] Although this agreement is important, it has a relatively limited scope. It applies only to transports of fissile materials used for peaceful purposes across international borders. It is silent about both defense-related fissile materials and physical protection inside a country's borders. In addition, the treaty contains no method of verification or enforcement.

Another important international standard that China signed is the *Guidelines for the Management of Plutonium* (INFCIRC/549).[139] These guidelines establish requirements for the management and disposition of civil plutonium and other plutonium deemed no longer required for defense. They establish MC&A standards similar to INFCIRC/153 and say that states should implement physical protection regulations "taking into account" INFCIRC/225/Rev.3.[140] These guidelines are limited, however, by the fact that they do not *require* the physical protection regulations established by INFCIRC/225. Nor do they say anything about the management of uranium or plutonium that is not used for peaceful purposes.[141]

Overall, the international arrangements to which China has committed are of relatively limited use in establishing rigorous and enforceable MPC&A standards in China. Let us now examine whether China has created a domestic legal infrastructure for effective MPC&A.

China's Domestic Regulations for MPC&A

China's legal framework for the protection of fissile materials is established in two documents: the 1987 "Regulations on Nuclear Materials Control of the People's Republic of China" (hereafter: 1987 "Regulations") and the 1990 "Rules for Implementation of the Regulations on Nuclear Materials Control of the People's Republic of China" (hereafter: 1990 "Rules"). In the following two sections, I discuss the MPC&A measures required by these two documents.

MC&A Measures Required by Chinese Law

From the 1960s to the late 1980s, the Chinese used a "nuclear material led-

Table 4.3. International Agreements Relating to Chinese Fissile Materials

International Agreement	Date	Requirements and Types of Materials Covered
Convention on the Physical Protection of Fissile Materials (codified in INFCIRC 274/Rev.1)	1979	Applies to transports of fissile materials for peaceful purposes across international borders.
INFCIRC/369	1988	Places certain facilities under IAEA safeguards.
Guidelines for the Management of Plutonium (codified in INFCIRC/549)	1997	Applies only to civil and other plutonium deemed not for defense. Recommends implementing physical protection systems for these materials "taking into account" INFCIRC/225.

ger system" in its nuclear facilities. Under this system, paper records documented the amounts of nuclear materials.[142] By 1990, however, China's MC&A regulations had become much more systematic. The 1987 "Regulations" established laws requiring strict licensing procedures for nuclear facilities. Before the license is granted, the facility must "establish and maintain a nuclear materials balance system and an analysis and measurement system, and use the approved analysis and measurement method to attain specified requirements of measuring error."[143]

The 1990 "Rules" gave the CNNC responsibility for "establishing the accounting system of nuclear materials of the whole country."[144] It also clarified the MC&A requirements that nuclear facilities must satisfy. It required a new accounting system that calculates MUF (materials unaccounted for) in the same way as that required by IAEA INFCIRC/153. The 1990 document also established regulations that define what is an acceptable standard error of MUF in Chinese nuclear facilities.[145]

In addition to these legal requirements, China revised its nuclear materials accounting forms in 1991. These forms now conform to those used internationally. The new forms are the following:

- NMF-R01: Nuclear Material Transfer (similar to U.S. DOE form 741)
- NMF-R03: Nuclear Material Inventory Change (similar to IAEA Form ICR)
- NMF-R04: Physical Inventory (similar to IAEA Form LPI)
- NMF-R05: Nuclear Material Balance (similar to IAEA Form)
- NMF-R06: Annotation
- NMF-R07: Nuclear Material Accident[146]

Physical Protection Measures Required by Chinese Law

By and large, China's legal framework incorporates the physical protection standards established by INFCIRC/225. These documents not only use the same method of categorization of fissile materials as INFCIRC/225, but they also require similar physical protection measures.[147] See table 4.4 for the specific physical protection measures that these documents require for each category of fissile materials.

China's legal regulations match international standards for MPC&A fairly well. If China's nuclear facilities met these regulations, its MPC&A would probably be adequate. Unfortunately, most reliable sources indicate that China's actual MPC&A is characterized by rigorous laws but lax enforcement. Indeed, according to Wen Hsu, a China expert at Sandia National Laboratories, while the two documents that regulate China's nuclear controls specify the materials to be regulated, the responsibilities of the supervising authorities, the licensing process, how nuclear material accounting should be performed, and guidelines on the physical protection of nuclear materials, they do not specify how these measures should be enforced, who would enforce them, or the criteria by which compliance should be measured.[148] As a result, there is significant evidence that China's actual MPC&A typically falls far short of its legal regulations.

China's Actual System of MPC&A

It has become clear that China protects its nuclear facilities and controls its fissile materials primarily by means of the "3 G's" guards, guns, and gates.[149] This system mainly controls fissile materials by using guards and intimidation to keep out anyone who might attempt to steal nuclear materials. "In Russia and China, in particular, [fissile material control systems] were designed to keep 'the outside out' rather than 'the inside in,' and they relied heavily upon totalitarian instruments of social control."[150]

Because China is a member of the IAEA, and has some facilities under IAEA safeguards, it must certainly have a general knowledge of what is re-

Table 4.4. Physical Protection Standards Established by Chinese Law

For Using or Storing Category I Nuclear Materials

- Materials must be contained in at least two complete, reliable physical barriers. Actual materials must be stored in a vault or special security container.
- Alarm or surveillance protection equipment.
- Technical protection system with alarming and monitoring installations, etc.
- 24-hour armed guards.
- Special passes or badges for all people entering the site; strict control of non-site personnel's entrance with the procedure of registration, and full-time escort by the site personnel after access.
- A "double men and double lock" regime.[a]

For Using or Storing Category II Nuclear Materials

- Two physical barriers; one barrier must be complete and reliable. Actual materials must be stored in a "strong room"–type storage area.
- Alarm or surveillance protection equipment.
- 24-hour guards (preferably armed).
- Special passes for all people entering the site.

For Using or Storing Category III Nuclear Materials

- A complete and reliable physical barrier.
- Material should be placed in security containers or someone should be assigned to watch material.

Source: 1990 "Rules," pp. 10–13.

Note: [a] This is equivalent to the "two-person rule," by which no one is permitted to have access to nuclear material without another person present. To help enforce this procedure, the doors to nuclear material storage vaults require two keys and no single person is supposed to have both keys.

quired for a modern MPC&A program. In addition, it has purchased several nuclear power facilities from France that contain modern MPC&A systems. But there is little evidence that the Chinese have designed or implemented modern MPC&A systems in their indigenous nuclear facilities.

Fissile Material Control and Accounting (MC&A)

China reportedly developed a computer accounting system for its nuclear fuel in 1996 to help detect the loss or theft of fissile materials.[151] China claimed that this system met international standards for accountability. These computer systems have reportedly been installed at roughly a dozen nuclear facilities.[152] If this information is true, this number of systems may not be enough to improve China's material accountability significantly, because there are many more than twelve facilities in China that contain fissile materials. It is possible that more than twelve facilities have computerized systems for material accountancy, but China's nuclear materials accountability will necessarily be limited by the number of computer systems it purchases for this purpose.

In addition, these computer systems are really only useful to the extent to which Chinese facilities have been set up to isolate strategic monitoring points, where one can measure the amounts of fissile materials moving through the facilities. And it is not clear that the Chinese facilities are designed to allow for this. According to Annette Schaper, nuclear facilities in China (and other NWSs) "may lack designs that specifically facilitate an overview of material flows, define strategic points, provide access for taking samples, designate measurement points, contain installations that enable the application of tags and seals, and restrict human entry."[153] No matter how good a country's accounting computers are, its MC&A will be seriously defective unless its facilities are designed so that the amounts of fissile materials contained in them can be measured easily and frequently. It is not clear that China's facilities are designed in such a way. Indeed, given its reliance on a Soviet-style system, there is no reason to believe it would have designed its facilities in this manner.

In addition, although the Chinese probably have knowledge of the specific equipment necessary for a modern, Western-style MC&A system, it is not clear that they have installed much of this equipment at their own facilities.[154] Nor is it clear that China has undertaken the extensive designing and testing necessary to assemble MC&A equipment into an integrated system that is capable of detecting the theft of fissile materials. This was a major weakness in the Soviet system, and is probably a weakness in the Chinese system as well.

To the extent that China has no systematic MC&A, it presumably has only a limited ability to detect theft by insiders. Indeed, because Chinese nuclear facilities were probably not designed so that reliable physical inventories could be taken, China probably does not even have a precise inventory of the amount of nuclear materials in its facilities. This is the most basic step in any MC&A system, for without this knowledge there is no way to detect if any material has disappeared. Instead, China mainly trusts that its social control is such that no insider would steal any nuclear materials.

Physical Protection Systems

The most important aspect of a physical protection system is the assessment of whether a given nuclear facility can deter or defeat any potential threat. In order to do this, a state needs to carry out five steps:

1. Design a basic physical protection system.
2. Create scenarios for the possible kinds of attack on a given nuclear facility.
3. Test to make sure that the facility's current defenses can counter the attack.
4. Fix any weaknesses discovered in the tests.
5. Repeat steps three and four until the defenses can defeat all types of attack.

While there is a small but growing body of literature on China's MPC&A, there is very little specific information on the physical protection of Chinese facilities. We simply do not know whether China has engaged in such systematic designing and testing of its physical protection systems. Nor do we know whether China has created a legal structure that specifically outlines how a facility would put a physical protection system into place. Given the Soviet model for China's physical protection, however, it is unlikely that China has taken either of these critical steps in the design and implementation of Western-style physical protection systems. We therefore cannot be certain that physical protection systems at Chinese nuclear facilities would be able to repel a dedicated attack.

As noted above, China's physical protection has mainly relied on the presence of guards at its nuclear facilities to deter and defend against attacks. The guards at smaller nuclear facilities are provided by the facility itself, while the guards at major facilities are members of China's armed forces.[155] It is simply not known whether China has taken all appropriate steps to ensure that these guards are properly armed or trained.

Until recently, there were few concerns about the weakness of physical protection systems at Chinese nuclear facilities. Like the Soviet Union before its collapse, China's central authorities maintained massive social controls that pervaded every aspect of the society. Just as no one was worried about people stealing fissile materials in the Soviet Union, there was relatively little reason to fear that people would attempt to steal these materials in China. But this has changed in recent years. Since China began to make economic reforms in the 1970s, there has been a significant erosion of societal controls and central government authority. Crime rates in China have soared in recent years, and people in China, including local government officials, routinely evade government dictates.[156]

Moreover, recent governmental restructuring and budget cutbacks have cost many governmental officials their jobs, including many in the nuclear sector and the military.[157] It is difficult to determine how these cutbacks will affect the nuclear sector, but the result could be a larger pool of disgruntled people who might be tempted to steal nuclear materials and sell them, who might be vulnerable to recruitment by terrorist or organized crime groups, or who might provide information on security measures to support an attack.[158] These problems are probably much less severe than the problems in the Russian nuclear complex (e.g., people are probably still getting paid regularly), but they do exist in an incipient form. Chinese nuclear materials still probably remain under tight central government control, but these problems are clearly widespread in other sectors of the Chinese economy and government and could eventually spread to the nuclear sector.

Because China's major nuclear weapons facilities are located in isolated areas, however, they will tend to be less affected by the weakening of societal controls.[159] It would therefore be easier for the government to maintain strict oversight of these facilities and much more difficult for outsiders to attack the facilities. Still, the general loosening of societal controls is troubling because China has relied heavily on these controls to discourage any attacks on its nuclear facilities.

Conclusions about China's MPC&A

China's current system of MPC&A apparently has worked well so far, but there is no guarantee that it will do so in the future. As we have seen, there are terrorist groups that might attack China's nuclear facilities. In addition to international terrorists who might be interested in obtaining nuclear materials, there are angry and disenfranchised groups within China that could be interested in engaging in a broader range of terrorist activities against the central authorities. Given the current evidence of the protective measures at

China's nuclear facilities, it is possible that a well-organized terrorist attack could be successful.

But the most significant weaknesses in China's system of MPC&A could become critical in times of political and economic crisis. Clearly, the experience in Russia shows the limitations of an authoritarian type of control during such crises. China has had its share of crises in the past and might have additional ones in the future.[160] If such crises were to occur, China's controls over its fissile material stockpiles could become significantly weaker.[161]

Several different kinds of crises could undermine China's controls over its fissile material stockpiles. If China underwent a severe economic downturn, it could face the same kinds of problems that Russia is now facing. If the wages of the scientists and guards at Chinese nuclear facilities were reduced, they might be tempted to supplement their incomes by selling fissile materials on the black market.[162] Given China's lack of a systematic MC&A system, it probably would not be able to detect this kind of insider theft.

A second way that China's MPC&A could collapse is if there were a decentralization of power in China. As we have seen, a number of scholars have argued that regionalism is increasing in China, and that the Chinese Communist Party is losing its influence.[163] China has relied heavily on strict social controls to deter any insider theft or terrorist attempts. As these societal controls weaken, we could see a dramatic increase in these illicit activities. A similar pattern in Russia and the newly independent states appeared following the collapse of the Soviet Union.

Finally, a sustained leadership conflict or political crisis could undermine China's MPC&A. As we have seen, the Cultural Revolution disrupted nuclear production and caused violent clashes in Chinese military research facilities. While another political crisis on the scale of the Cultural Revolution may never occur again in China, a significant leadership conflict could distract attention and interfere with close supervision of the Chinese nuclear complex.

The U.S./China Lab-to-Lab Collaborative Program 1995–1998

In part in an effort to better understand and to address some of the above proliferation concerns, a formal letter exchange was begun in 1995 among the directors of nuclear laboratories in the United States and China, following informal contacts under careful government oversight the previous year. It was determined that Department of Energy nuclear laboratories and their counterpart research facilities in China have many mutual scientific interests, and that laboratory-level collaboration was desirable in specific areas.[164] These discussions resulted in the "U.S.-China Lab-to-Lab Technical Exchange Program" (CLL), or as it was renamed in 1998, the China Arms Control Exchange (CACE).[165] The CLL program covered topics ranging from nuclear materials management (including MPC&A), to verification technologies critical to the Comprehensive Test Ban Treaty (CTBT), to additional efforts in export controls. This discussion will focus specifically on MPC&A collaborations.

CLL Meetings and Workshops on MPC&A, 1995–1998

The first meeting at which U.S. and Chinese scientists discussed MPC&A technologies occurred in 1995. In this meeting, American scientists from Lawrence Livermore, Sandia, and Los Alamos National Laboratories met with Chinese scientists from the China Academy of Engineering Physics (CAEP) and the Institute of Applied Physics and Computational Mathematics (IAPCM). A second round of discussions began in January 1996, when American scientists from Livermore, Sandia, and Los Alamos met with Chinese scientists at the IAPCM for a workshop on MPC&A technologies. During the workshop, scientists from both countries presented papers discussing the current MPC&A practices, technologies, and methodologies used in each country.

In 1997, Sandia National Laboratories held a two-week-long course in China on physical protection system design for nuclear facilities. It was held at the China Institute of Atomic Energy in Beijing from March 29–April 10. These workshops helped train Chinese scientists in Western methods for designing and installing integrated physical protection systems.

In 1998, Sandia National Laboratory held a workshop in China on MC&A techniques. This workshop helped the Chinese develop strategies for identifying strategic monitoring points, installing measurement gauges, etc. If implemented in Chinese nuclear facilities, these MC&A procedures and technologies would help the Chinese take precise physical inventories of the fissile materials in their nuclear facilities and subsequently detect any theft of these materials.

U.S.-China Integrated Demonstration of MPC&A, July 1998

The principal Los Alamos activity, and a flagship CLL project, was to build a model MPC&A system in China to demonstrate Western-style MPC&A techniques and technologies. Work on this project began in 1996 and was completed in 1998. The opening of the demonstration took place in July

1998. The purpose of this MPC&A demonstration was to "provide an important foundation for building future activities for nuclear materials management in China."[166] It was hoped that the model facility would help China and the U.S. achieve this end "through development of common approaches and deployment of integrated systems of modern technologies."[167]

A great deal of modern MPC&A technology was installed at this facility. The new equipment included access-control devices, such as motion detectors, cipher-activated locks, magnetic card readers, and hand-geometry readers. Screening and monitoring devices were installed, such as metal detectors, portal radiation detectors, and an NTvision camera remote-monitoring system. Equipment for materials measurement and tracking systems were also installed, including gamma spectrometers for nuclear materials assay, a complete barcode inventory system, and tamper-resistant seals.[168] The United States provided most of the equipment except the facility itself, the security fence, and the nondestructive assay equipment, which were provided by China.

These China Lab-to-Lab collaborations were designed to help create a "safeguards culture" in China by showing them the advantages of modern MPC&A systems. The CLL program made some progress in this area, but it is clear that more still needs to be done.

Espionage Allegations and the Cessation of Contacts under the CLL Program

In 1998, policymakers and arms control experts hoped that the CLL program would help build a strong foundation of trust and mutual cooperation between the United States and China on issues of nonproliferation and arms control. CLL collaborations were to encourage increased transparency and mutual understanding of the nuclear programs in both countries (while protecting their respective national security interests) and help build a strong basis for future MPC&A programs in China.[169]

The aftermath of the controversial 1999 Cox report[170] and its allegations of Chinese espionage targeted against U.S. nuclear facilities, however, gave rise to a complete cessation of contacts under CACE. Although the CACE program was cleared of any involvement in the espionage scandal,[171] previously planned visits were canceled and no new events have yet been scheduled. As a result, the continued existence and nature of the program are very uncertain at this time. Indeed, in spite of continuing interest among parts of the U.S. government in the continuation of the program, no authorization exists for renewing lab-to-lab contacts with China.[172]

Obstacles to China's MPC&A Modernization

While it is possible that the Chinese have continued to upgrade MPC&A on their own, there is reason to doubt that they have made significant improvements without U.S. cooperation—even though China knows many of the basic requirements for rigorous MPC&A systems. There are several reasons for this. First, in spite of its economic growth over the last decade, China remains a resource-limited country.[173] Stringent physical protection regulations are very expensive to implement.[174] Although expenses would presumably be lower in China than in the United States, Chinese scientific facilities are often underfunded and therefore may have difficulties meeting the physical protection regulations established by Chinese law.

In addition, Chinese officials often have difficulty justifying the high cost of modern MPC&A systems typically in use by Western countries. Because China is a comparatively poor country, it could either use its resources to feed its citizens, strengthen its economy, and improve its military, or it could use them to improve its MPC&A. China's limited financial resources have often caused it to place safety and security as lower priorities than other objectives.

Furthermore, the Chinese may not have improved their MPC&A because historically there has been a lack of coordinated policy among the different bureaucracies that have responsibility over China's nuclear complex. One could characterize the Chinese nuclear complex as "stove-piped," without much communication among the different bureaucracies or coordination of their nuclear policies. According to Wen Hsu, "the government departments [in China's nuclear establishment] have continued to act as fiefdoms that jealously guard their prerogatives, to the extent that their possessiveness has discouraged interdepartmental exchanges."[175] Moreover, each of the bureaucracies has limited resources, and each might be unwilling to pay for MPC&A technologies that it believes another agency should pay for.

But the main reason that China may not have improved its MPC&A significantly in recent years is that many Chinese officials simply have not seen the need for the stringent MPC&A implemented by Western countries. The Chinese have stated publicly that their method of MPC&A is "similar to that of the Russians," which was mostly dependent in the past on security personnel.[176] Although it has become clear that such a system can become particularly weak during political and economic crises, the Chinese consider these methods to be adequate for now because, they maintain, their current political, social, and military situation is relatively stable.[177]

The U.S.-China collaborative programs worked to help change these perspectives on nuclear security and promoted significant progress in security upgrades at Chinese facilities. Without these or similar programs, it is likely that potential vulnerabilities will remain at Chinese nuclear facilities, at least for some time.

Part III: Conclusions

Available information indicates that China may not have sufficiently implemented adequate controls over its nuclear arsenal and fissile material stockpile. In particular, both China's command and control and MPC&A could potentially become vulnerable during extreme economic and political crises. On the basis of the information we have seen in this case study, the following conclusions probably can be drawn about China's nuclear controls.

- *While the risks of accidental launches of China's nuclear weapons are currently quite low, they could increase in the near future.* Since China currently stores most of its missiles unfueled and without their warheads mated, there is currently very little risk of an accidental launch of China's nuclear weapons during normal, peacetime circumstances. However, the risk of accidental launch could be significantly higher during a nuclear crisis if China were to fuel the missiles and mate the warheads to bring its arsenal to a state of launch-readiness. Moreover, the risks of accidental launches could increase once China completes its transition to a mobile, solid-fueled missile system. The new missiles will be stored fully fueled, and due to necessity for increased missile mobility, it is also quite possible that China will begin storing its missiles with their warheads mated. If China's new missile system is stored in this state of launch-readiness, the risk of an accidental launch of a Chinese nuclear weapon could significantly increase.
- *The risk of the unauthorized use of China's nuclear weapons could be high during political and economic crises.* Because China's command-and-control system relies primarily on guards, gates, and guns, the chain of command over China's nuclear weapons could potentially erode during extreme political or economic crises. There appear to have been significant problems with discipline in the PLA in the past, and these problems could arise again during domestic upheavals. In addition, there is evidence of increasing regionalism and general dissatisfaction with the central government, which could undermine China's central controls. These risks are particularly troubling because China's nuclear weapons do not appear to contain use-control devices,

such as PALs or equivalent launch codes that need to be entered before the nuclear weapon can be launched.

- *China's MC&A may be incapable of detecting an insider theft of nuclear materials.* Although many Chinese nuclear facilities have some MC&A equipment, this equipment does not appear to have been integrated into an effective system. An intelligent insider might therefore be able to defeat the system and smuggle nuclear materials out of a nuclear facility. While China's authoritarian regime would still probably discourage anyone from deciding to steal nuclear materials, China's strict societal controls are loosening. During an economic or political crisis, an insider could therefore be tempted to steal China's nuclear materials for sale on the black market or for other purposes.
- *It is not clear that the physical protection of Chinese nuclear facilities could repel a dedicated attack.* While the physical protection of Chinese nuclear facilities is probably superior to their MC&A, it is not clear that it would be able to defend against an outsider attack. China does not appear to have installed carefully designed, integrated security systems at its nuclear facilities or performed rigorous performance tests of these systems to determine whether they could defeat possible attacks. Without these measures, there is little way for China to be certain its physical protection system can withstand credible threats. Although information is sketchy, it is also not clear that the guards at Chinese nuclear facilities are highly trained or heavily armed. For the physical protection of its nuclear facilities, China mainly relies on its societal controls and on the isolation of the facilities. But it is not clear that these will be adequate for physical protection in the future, especially during political crises. Chinese facilities could therefore be potentially vulnerable to a dedicated attack, whether it is conducted by terrorists, rogue elements within the Chinese military, or even another country.
- *It appears unlikely that China will improve its MPC&A without U.S. encouragement.* Although the MPC&A for Chinese nuclear facilities appears to fall short of both international standards (such as those recommended by the IAEA) and China's own legal standards, most evidence indicates that China does not see much urgency in improving its MPC&A. Many Chinese officials who talked to U.S. scientists have reportedly said their nuclear materials are secure because no one steals in China. But this appears to be changing as China's societal controls loosen. While the United States is quite concerned that China's controls will eventually no longer be adequate, Chinese officials have generally not demonstrated the same level of concern. The United States

must continue working with the Chinese to help create a safeguards culture in China in which everyone from high-level politicians to the lowest-level guard recognizes the importance of rigorous MPC&A procedures and technologies.

These conclusions give us reason to be pessimistic about the risks associated with the proliferation of nuclear weapons. As we have seen, this case study has identified a number of potential weaknesses in China's controls over its nuclear weapons arsenal and fissile material stockpile as well as potential risks of accidental, unauthorized, and inadvertent use.

The Chinese case is particularly troubling because China has had plenty of time to improve its controls, but for various reasons has been unable or unwilling to do so. Because emerging NWSs will probably encounter many of the same constraints that China has, we should have serious doubts whether they will be likely to develop rigorous nuclear controls. In the following chapter, we will examine the nuclear controls and nuclear risks in two emerging NWSs, India and Pakistan, to determine how serious these concerns should be.

India and Pakistan

Why study South Asia? India and Pakistan are critical cases for the optimist-pessimist debate. They are important for two essential reasons. First, because India and Pakistan have a history of conflict, they are useful for determining whether or not the spread of nuclear weapons increases or decreases stability. Indeed, optimists have generally argued that nuclear weapons have increased stability in the region.[1] Pessimists, on the other hand have argued that nuclear weapons have increased tensions and the risks of nuclear war.[2] As we will see, a close examination of the history of the tensions in the region and the directions that the nuclear programs in India and Pakistan are taking reveals greater support for the pessimists' arguments.

The second reason why India and Pakistan are essential cases for the proliferation debate is that they help illustrate the nuclear systems and the types of controls that emerging NWSs are likely to adopt. Seng and Karl, in particular, point to these countries as examples of why emerging NWSs will probably have safer arsenals than the superpowers because they will remain satisfied with small, non-weaponized nuclear forces. To a certain degree, some of these optimistic predictions have been disproved by the dual tests conducted by India and Pakistan in 1998. Neither country remained content merely with an "existential" deterrent, though they now are somewhere in a no-man's-land between existential and minimal deterrence. Although it is not yet clear what types of weapons systems and deployment options the two countries will choose to adopt, this chapter identifies a number of troubling trends in Pakistan and India toward weaponization and deployment.

Unlike previous chapters, which focused on a single NWS, this chapter will focus on both India and Pakistan. This is partly because the issues affecting each country are so intertwined that it is easier to deal with them together. But it is also partly due to the fact that there is much less available information on Indian and Pakistani nuclear controls.

It is also the case that a great deal is still undetermined in India's and

Pakistan's nuclear programs. For example, it remains to be seen whether these countries will actually weaponize their nuclear devices and deploy them in the field. As we will see, however, most indications are that they probably will develop these capabilities. If they continue in the direction they are currently headed, the primary question is *when,* not *if,* they will develop these capabilities. In this chapter, we will also examine whether available information indicates that India and Pakistan have adequate command-and-control and MPC&A systems in place. Although there are admittedly significant gaps in information, and the character of the nuclear programs in South Asia is still somewhat undetermined, this chapter will argue that most indications appear to be that the South Asian case generally supports the pessimist position.

Part I: Indian and Pakistani C^3I and the Risks of Accidental, Unauthorized, and Inadvertent Use

History of the South Asian Nuclear Rivalry: "The Most Dangerous Place on Earth"

South Asia is a particularly unstable region for a number of reasons. Regional tensions remain high due to ongoing political dynamics between India and Pakistan, the ongoing conflict over Kashmir, the 1998 nuclear tests and subsequent missile tests, and the October 1999 military coup in Pakistan.[3] In addition, India cites the threat from Chinese strategic forces and China's nuclear modernization effort as additional justifications for its nuclear program.[4] The relations between India and China increase the tensions between India and Pakistan because Pakistan views any improvement in New Delhi's deterrent capability vis-à-vis China as an additional threat to itself. India, meanwhile, views China's continued assistance to Pakistan's nuclear and missile programs as an effort to undermine India's security. When these sources of regional tension are coupled with the history of violence and extreme mistrust between India and Pakistan, the resulting environment is extremely volatile. In the following sections, I will examine the history of conflict between India and Pakistan, and why it led President Bill Clinton to describe South Asia as "the most dangerous place on Earth."

India and Pakistan have fought three interstate wars since 1947. This number rises to four if one considers the 1999 Kargil conflict a war. Because the number of people killed in the 1999 conflict was more than 1,000 on each side, it exceeds the level typically categorized as a war.[5] Since their independence, relations between the two countries have been constantly fraught with mistrust and conflict. Soldiers on both sides continually shoot at each other across the Line of Control (LOC) in Kashmir, and several incidents—including Brasstacks (1986–1987), the Kashmir crisis (1990), and the Kargil war (1999)—ran serious risks of nuclear escalation.

Brasstacks (1986–1987)

In November–December 1986, India began field simulations for a large-scale military exercise, code-named "Brasstacks." The field simulations took place in the desert of Rajasthan, roughly one hundred miles from the Pakistani border. This location is reportedly an ideal staging point for an invasion of the Pakistani state of Sind, which would effectively cut Pakistan in half.[6]

Based on its own intelligence, Pakistan feared that India was planning to convert the exercise into an attack.[7] These fears were heightened because India provided incorrect information about how long the exercises would last.[8] Pakistan was ending its own annual exercises at the time. Instead of immediately removing his forces to their peacetime locations, the commanding general, Khalis Muhamud Arif, deployed his armored units north of the Sutlej River to ensure that his troops would be optimally positioned defensively if Indian troops attacked. Although Arif deliberately positioned his troops in such a way as to allow Indian reconnaissance to recognize their defensive posture, to his surprise, his troop movements went unnoticed for two weeks. When the Pakistani troops were finally located by Indian intelligence, their defensive positioning went unnoticed, and near-panic ensued in New Delhi as Indian officials feared that Arif was preparing for an attack.[9]

This incident dramatically increased tensions in the region and led to mobilization of troops on both sides, border skirmishes, and exchanges of fire between Indian and Pakistani troops.[10] Because both India and Pakistan reportedly had a crude nuclear weapons capability at this time, if the incident had escalated into a larger-scale military conflict, the conflict could have had a nuclear dimension. According to Mario Carranza, "by providing Pakistan with the wrong information about the duration of a gigantic military exercise on its border, and deploying its military forces in a provocative manner, India precipitated a crisis that could have led to a nuclear confrontation."[11]

The crisis reached its height on January 24, 1987, when both sides made several saber-rattling declarations and Indian troops advanced to the border because Pakistan had not withdrawn its troops from front-line positions. On January 28, Indian and Pakistani troops exchanged fire in Kashmir, while leaders in both countries announced diplomatic negotiations to solve the crisis. The two countries began high-level negotiations on January 31, and a sector-by-sector pullout of troops deployed along the international border began on February 4.[12]

Although some optimists have argued that this incident actually demonstrates that nuclear deterrence restrained both sides because the incident did not escalate into a full-scale border war,[13] both sides took very serious risks during the incident. According to Mario Carranza, a minor incident in this highly charged environment could have triggered a major military conflict, which could easily have escalated into a nuclear conflict.[14]

Kashmir (1990)

In 1989, terrorists sparked a conflict that again almost brought India and Pakistan to the brink of war. The origins of the conflict can be traced to Indian prime minister Rajiv Gandhi's attempts to manipulate the outcome of state elections in 1987. Gandhi's efforts sparked a wave of terrorism, which resulted in the kidnapping of the Indian home minister's daughter in late 1989. Although she was released unharmed, India accused Pakistan of supporting the Kashmiri Muslim insurgency.[15] Both sides again engaged in a series of threats, most likely including nuclear threats.[16] Again, large numbers of troops were deployed on each side of the border.[17] During the crisis, the United States reportedly intercepted a message to the Pakistan Atomic Energy Commission ordering it to assemble at least one nuclear weapon.[18] As tensions mounted, Pakistani foreign minister Sahabzada Yaqub Khan flew to New Delhi, where he held a strained meeting with his counterpart, Inder Gujral. The United States was sufficiently concerned that it sent a high-level delegation under Deputy National Security Advisor Robert Gates to mediate.[19]

Optimists have again argued that nuclear deterrence restrained the countries from going to war.[20] More recent assessments, however, indicate that India did not take seriously the possibility of a nuclear threat from Pakistan.[21] Instead, Indian leaders were primarily concerned about avoiding a conventional war with Pakistan, but "neither India nor Pakistan seemed able or willing to defuse the situation. They had talked themselves into corners from which domestic and interstate politics would not allow them to escape."[22] As with many of the incidents between India and Pakistan, this crisis demonstrates how mutual mistrust, domestic factors, and non-state actors create situations that run a high risk of spiraling out of control. According to Neil Joeck, the 1990 crisis contradicts "the confident argument that central decision-makers are able to control behaviour on the ground in Kashmir and therefore prevent war."[23]

Kargil (1999)

Confident that its conventional and nuclear forces would deter a large-scale retaliation and hoping to gain international attention for the Kashmir issue,

Pakistan sent several thousand Islamic militants and Pakistani troops across the LOC into the Indian-controlled Kargil heights during the winter of 1999.[24] Meeting no resistance in the unoccupied mountainous region, the infiltrators pushed farther into Kargil and dug in. From their positions, Pakistani troops threatened not only Highway 1A, the lifeline between Kashmir and Ladakh, but also India's hold on Saichan.[25] India discovered the infiltrators in May 1999 and responded by sending troops into the region. Several weeks of intense fighting ensued, which included heavy artillery and air attacks. By mid-1999, the Vajpayee administration threatened to extend fighting beyond the LOC if Pakistan did not withdraw its troops from Indian-controlled Kashmir.[26] India signaled its intent to escalate the conflict by massing its troops along the LOC and the international border and dispatching naval ships in preparations for a naval blockade of Pakistani ports.[27] U.S. satellites also reportedly detected elements of the Indian Army's main offensive "strike force" loading tanks, artillery, and other heavy equipment onto flatbed rail cars.[28]

As outbreak of a larger conflict appeared imminent and Pakistan increasingly came under severe international criticism, Pakistani prime minister Nawaz Sharif asked the United States' President Clinton to mediate between the two sides. A meeting took place between Sharif and Clinton, along with members of the U.S. National Security Council (NSC), on July 4. Clinton stated the U.S. position clearly: an immediate Pakistani withdrawal back across the LOC. In an intriguing paper describing this meeting, former NSC member Bruce Reidel relates details of this meeting.[29] One striking feature of this meeting was that Sharif seemed astonished when Clinton informed him that U.S. intelligence had detected preparations by the Pakistani military to deploy nuclear weapons.[30] In the end, Sharif agreed to withdraw. On July 11, the Indian and Pakistani Directors-General of Military Operations met and reached an agreement on Pakistan's withdrawal. Pakistani troops began to withdraw by mid-July.[31]

During the conflict, Pakistan threatened to use the "ultimate weapon"; warned of "irreparable losses" if India crossed the LOC;[32] and, according to U.S. intelligence, was preparing its nuclear weapons for possible use.[33] According to some reports, India also put its nuclear forces on alert during the conflict.[34] Most alarmingly, retired admiral L. Ramdas, former chief of staff of the Indian Navy, has reported that over a dozen people in responsible positions on both sides advocated the use of nuclear weapons during the conflict.[35] It is hard to predict what would have happened if the United States had not intervened, or if Indian forces had not gained a military advantage before the U.S. intervention, but it is quite likely that the conflict would have escalated further, greatly increasing the risks of a nuclear exchange.

Renewed Tensions after September 11, 2001

In the events following the September 11, 2001, terrorist attacks on the United States, tensions again heightened between India and Pakistan. Soon after the United States declared a war on terrorism and Pakistani president general Pervez Musharraf agreed to support U.S. bombing in Afghanistan, Muslim terrorists began a new wave of attacks in Indian-controlled Kashmir, as well as in India and Pakistan. Although the United States said that its war on terrorism included opposition to attacks in Kashmir, Indians viewed the U.S. statements as belied by its actions. Instead of increasing pressure for Pakistan to stop supporting cross-border terrorism, the United States instead removed economic sanctions against Pakistan and even renewed possibilities of military trade.[36]

In October and November 2001, tensions between India and Pakistan mounted as the cross-border terrorism continued, including an attack on October 1 outside the State Assembly building in Kashmir that killed thirty-eight people.[37] After this attack, India rejected the first of two offers by Pakistan to hold talks to settle the Kashmir issue. In an attempt to de-escalate the violence, U.S. secretary of state Colin Powell visited India and Pakistan in October. But on October 15, the eve of Powell's visit, India shelled eleven Pakistani posts across the LOC with heavy mortar, rocket, and machine-gun fire.[38] During the next week Indian and Pakistani troops fired on each other at several points along the LOC, and violence continued in Kashmir.[39] In the midst of this violence, on October 22, India's Prime Minister Vajpayee rejected a second Pakistani bid for talks on Kashmir, stating that "in this situation, there is no point in talking to Pakistan."[40] Terrorist attacks in Kashmir continued, including clashes on November 2 that killed thirty-one people.[41]

The situation became even worse after December 13, 2001, when five militants attacked the Indian parliament, killing eight people before being killed themselves.[42] After the attacks, Indian officials stated that they had evidence linking the attacks to two Pakistani-based Islamic groups, Lashkar-e-taiba and Jaish-e-Muhammad. Indian police and intelligence officials also claimed that the Pakistani Inter-Services Intelligence Agency (ISI) helped coordinate the attacks.[43]

After the December 13 attack, India began massing troops along the LOC and threatened to invade unless Pakistan stopped supporting cross-border terrorism. Over the next several months, the countries deployed a combined total of over a million troops and heavy artillery along the LOC. India, and possibly Pakistan, also deployed missiles along the international border, though it was unclear whether these missiles were armed with nuclear warheads.[44]

During a speech on January 12, Musharraf outlawed several militant groups and vowed to crack down on Pakistani-based militant groups. Over the next few weeks, he arrested an estimated 2,000 militants (though he later granted a number of them amnesty).[45] India, however, questioned the seriousness of Musharraf's commitment to ending the terrorism. As proof of their seriousness, India asked Pakistan to hand over twenty militants and criminals, refusing to discuss a de-escalation until Pakistan did so.[46] To date, Pakistan has refused to give up any of the people on the list.

George Tenet, the Director of U.S. Central Intelligence, stated that the chances of large-scale war between the two countries were higher during the 2001–2002 crisis than at any point since their last major war in 1971.[47] The most immediate risks of war were defused after India began withdrawing troops from the border, followed by a withdrawal by Pakistan. But U.S. intelligence agencies remain quite concerned about the prospects for stability in South Asia because the underlying cause of the tension remains unchanged and the cycles of tension between India and Pakistan are growing shorter.[48] Indeed, tensions between the two countries increased yet again after an attack by suspected Pakistani-backed militants killed twenty-four Hindu civilians in March 2003.[49]

Confidence-Building Measures and Crisis Stability

India and Pakistan have instituted a number of confidence-building measures (CBMs) over the years, which were intended to increase trust, stabilize relations, and improve crisis stability. Between 1965 and 1992, India and Pakistan agreed to the following principal CBMs:

- Hotline between Military Operation Directorates (1965);
- Agreement on the Prohibition of Attack against Nuclear Installations and Facilities (1988, ratified in 1992);
- Hotline between Prime Ministers Benezair Bhutto and Rajiv Gandhi (1989);
- Measures to Prevent Air Space Violations and to Permit Overflights and Landing by Military Aircraft (1992).[50]

These CBMs have had highly mixed results, at best. Their success has been severely constrained by a deep mistrust on both sides, combined with a lack of use, or even misuse, of the measures. For example, although the Prohibition of Attack against Nuclear Installations and Facilities was constructive in theory, it failed in its objectives due to suspicions on both sides. According to the agreement, both sides would provide lists of their major nuclear facilities, but immediately after the two sides exchanged lists, both sides accused each other of concealing key installations. Neither side had the ability to verify the other's declarations, and without a previous record of reliable confidence-building, this measure was unable to alleviate the mistrust.[51]

Even more troubling, the various channels that had been established to improve communication links between both sides were seldom used. Although several hotlines were established between the two sides, they have rarely been used during crises—precisely the times when they were most needed. For example, although a hotline between the Military Operation Directorates had existed since 1965, it was not used during the height of the Brasstacks crisis. According to Bajpai et al., "when the possibility of war loomed large, CBMs were distrusted or misused by one or both sides: at crucial moments, India resisted giving information to the Pakistani side out of fear that the information might somehow be used to its disadvantage, and both sides stopped using the . . . hotlines after December 8."[52] After the Brasstacks incident, both sides agreed to an additional series of CBMs, including a hotline between the prime ministers. But the hotlines were not used during the 1990 Kargil crisis (only one year after the hotline between the prime ministers was established), during the 1999 Kargil war, or during the 2001–2002 crisis.[53]

In 1999, the two sides expressed intentions to improve their strategic situation by implementing wide-ranging CBMs in the Lahore Declaration. In this agreement, Prime Ministers Vajpayee and Sharif reaffirmed the declarations they had made after their 1998 tests, including commitments to resolve all issues, including Kashmir; refrain from interfering in each other's internal affairs; intensify bilateral dialogue; take steps to avoid accidental and unauthorized use; and "condemn terrorism in all its forms." In addition, in an attached Memorandum of Understanding, the prime ministers agreed to the following specific measures:

- To engage in bilateral consultations on security concepts, and nuclear doctrines, with a view to developing CBMs in the nuclear and conventional fields.
- To provide each other with advance notification in respect of ballistic missile flight tests.
- To undertake national measures to reducing the risks of accidental or unauthorized use of their nuclear weapons and to notify each other immediately in the event of any accidental, unauthorized, or unexplained incident.
- To abide by their respective unilateral moratorium on conducting fur-

ther nuclear test explosions unless either side, in exercise of its national sovereignty, decides that extraordinary events have jeopardized its supreme interests.

- To conclude an agreement on prevention of incidents at sea in order to ensure safety of navigation by naval vessels and aircraft belonging to the two sides.
- To review periodically the implementation of existing CBMs and, where necessary, set up mechanisms to monitor and ensure effective implementation of these CBMs.
- To undertake a review of the existing communication links (e.g., between the respective Directors-General, Military Operations) with a view to upgrading and improving these links, and to provide for fail-safe and secure communications.
- To engage in bilateral consultations on security, disarmament, and non-proliferation issues.[54]

This agreement was highly praised and created a great deal of hope that the two sides could end their extreme mutual mistrust and begin setting the stage for a stable deterrent relationship.[55] Unfortunately, the hopes connected with Lahore were short-lived. Within months of the declaration, war between India and Pakistan broke out in Kashmir. Indeed, it quickly became clear that Pakistani insurgents were inside Indian-controlled Kashmir *while the Lahore Declaration was being negotiated.*[56] When this became clear, Indian officials justifiably felt outraged and betrayed.

Due to the sharp downturn in Indo-Pak relations after the Kargil war, few of the measures in the Lahore Declaration were ever realized. In fact, for a year and a half after the war, the Indian government refused to have any official contact with Pakistan until the latter stopped supporting terrorists in Kashmir.[57] Prime Minister Vajpayee and General Musharraf did hold their first summit meeting in July 2001, but the meeting ended in acrimony and was followed by the attack on India's parliament six months later.[58] After the attack on its parliament, India severed all diplomatic ties, recalling its ambassador from Pakistan and requesting that Pakistan do the same. Overall, the CBMs outlined in Lahore may have actually done more harm than good, as India now views any such commitment from Pakistan with suspicion. (One notable exception, however, is that both sides have generally notified each other before conducting missile tests, though Pakistani officials claimed that India never notified them before their March 26, 2003, launch).[59]

More recently, however, India and Pakistan may have made some tentative steps in improving their relations. In May 2003, India's Prime Minister Vajpayee declared that India would make a last effort at peace with Pakistan, adding that "at least in my life this is the last time I will be making an attempt to resolve the Indi-Pak dispute."[60] After a positive response from Pakistan, the two sides have made some steps toward improving relations. Both sides announced steps to restore full diplomatic relations, which had been severed since 2001.[61] Moreover, on May 18 Pakistan released Indian soldiers that had been imprisoned for over two years, and on May 27 India stated that it would resume cross-border bus service with Pakistan and would release seventy Pakistani fishermen and sixty other civilians in Indian custody.[62]

Whether these steps will make any significant breakthroughs remains to be seen. A great deal depends on whether Musharraf will be willing or able to end Pakistan's support of cross-border terrorism. If he does end the terrorism, the stage may be set for significantly improved relations between India and Pakistan. But current indications are not promising. In spite of his promises, Musharraf continues to support militants and fundamentalist Islamic political groups.[63] Indeed, even as these measures were being implemented, Indian soldiers reportedly killed twelve militants as they tried to slip into Indian-controlled Kashmir from Pakistan.[64] In the event of additional terrorist attacks by Islamic militants in India or Kashmir, Vajpayee's ultimatum might end the hopes for a resolution of tensions and may even force India to take military action against Pakistan. If the latter were to happen, it is unclear that the two countries would be able to avoid a major war, which would run serious risks of becoming a nuclear confrontation.[65]

Unstable Deterrence: Misapplied Lessons from the Cold War

Although India and Pakistan have adopted the language of deterrence that was used during the Cold War, it is not clear that they understand it in the same way that the United States and the Soviet Union did. During the Cold War, the United States and the Soviet Union engaged in proxy wars in *other* countries, but never against each other. The risks of an escalation into direct conventional war against each other were thus relatively small, except during acute incidents, such as the Cuban missile crisis and the 1973 Middle East crisis.[66] India and Pakistan, however, have engaged in both extended proxy wars and direct interstate wars on each other's territory, and the risks of escalation into a full-scale conventional war have at times been quite large.[67]

India has adopted a policy of "no first use," but it maintains a military doctrine that includes waging limited conventional wars with nuclear-armed foes.[68] Pakistan, on the other hand, has maintained that it will use nuclear weapons in response to either conventional or nuclear attacks from India. While the United States also maintained a first-use policy in response to a conventional attack from the Soviet Union against the United States or Western Europe, there are significant differences in the way India and Pakistan approach deterrence. Since 1989 Pakistan has intensified support for its proxy war in Kashmir in the belief that its nuclear weapons effectively countered India's conventional superiority.[69] Once Pakistan demonstrated its nuclear capability in 1998, Pakistani security managers were even more convinced that they could deter India's conventional forces. Indeed, according to most accounts, in the 1999 Kargil war, the Pakistani military intervened across the LOC into Indian-administered Kashmir precisely because it was confident its nuclear weapons would deter India.[70] Even during the conflict itself, a senior Pakistani official stated that "The Indians cannot afford to extend the war to other areas in Kashmir, leave aside launching an attack across international boundaries" because of the "risk of nuclear conflagration."[71] But Indian officials had the opposite opinion. They, in turn, were confident that their conventional superiority was sufficient to counter Pakistan's nuclear capability.[72] These divergent opinions brought the two countries to the brink of a full-scale war.

The 1999 Kargil war clearly demonstrates how the Indian and Pakistani understandings of the role of their nuclear weapons have increased the likelihood of armed conflict and the risks of nuclear war. And yet, even then, both sides appear to have drawn the wrong lessons from the conflict. On the Pakistani side, the military regime claims that the Kargil conflict demonstrates the effectiveness of nuclear deterrence because it prevented an Indian conventional military attack.[73] On the Indian side, political leaders claim that Pakistan's nuclear capability only deters the use of nuclear weapons, and threaten to resort to a limited conventional war should unrest in Kashmir continue at present levels.[74] India has therefore increased efforts to improve its conventional and nuclear capabilities vis-à-vis Pakistan.[75]

India's and Pakistan's Current Nuclear Capabilities and Delivery Systems

Indian and Pakistani Nuclear Capabilities

After nearly twenty-five years of "opaque" nuclear programs, both India and Pakistan decisively demonstrated their nuclear capabilities in a series of reciprocal tests in 1998. On May 11 and 13, India shocked the world by testing five nuclear devices and subsequently declaring itself a nuclear-weapons power. (See table 5.1 for a summary of India's nuclear tests.) Although India had previously demonstrated its nuclear capability in May 1974 by detonat-

Table 5.1. Nuclear Tests by India and Pakistan

Location	Date	Yield
	India's Nuclear Sites	
Pokhran, Rajasthan	May 18, 1974	15 kt
Pokhran, Rajasthan	May 11, 1998	43 kt thermonuclear, though disputed 12 kt fission sub-kiloton
Pokhran, Rajasthan	May 13, 1998	0.2 kt 0.6 kt
	Pakistan's Nuclear Tests	
Chagai Hills	May 28, 1998	Pakistan claims that its five tests were of a combined explosive force of 40-45 kt of which one was in the 30-35 kt range.
Chagai Hills	May 30, 1998	Claimed yield was 15-18 kt

Source: Table prepared by Carnegie Non-Proliferation Project, quoted in Neil Joeck, "Nuclear Relations in South Asia," in Joseph Cirincione, ed., *Repairing the Regime* (New York: Routledge, 2000), p. 135.

ing a nuclear device in what it called a "peaceful nuclear experiment," this new series of tests marked a turning point in India's nuclear program and constituted an official declaration of its status as a nuclear power. Following the tests, an Indian spokesman stated that India now had "a proven capability for a weaponized nuclear program."[76] India claims that this capability includes the potential for sub-kiloton and thermonuclear devices, though international experts have contested this claim.[77]

India's 1998 tests triggered a Pakistani response two weeks later, when Pakistan detonated six nuclear devices. (See table 5.1 for a summary of Pakistan's nuclear tests.) In the months that followed the tests, relations between the two countries worsened significantly and both countries conducted a series of missile tests.

Delivery Systems for Nuclear Weapons

India and Pakistan both have bombers that could deliver nuclear weapons, though India has a significant superiority. Pakistan reportedly has about 50 front-line nuclear-capable bombers, while India has roughly 230–300.[78] A large proportion of these aircraft are based close to the border between the two countries (near Lahore and New Delhi).[79]

Both countries have also engaged in extensive missile programs. In effect, a slow-speed nuclear and missile arms race is currently underway between the two countries.[80] In the following sections, I will examine the burgeoning missile capabilities in each country.

Indian Ballistic Missiles

Prithvi-I (SS-150), Prithvi-II (SS-250), Prithvi-III (SS-350 or Dhanush)

There are three versions of this short-range missile, each of which is mobile and nuclear-capable.[81] The Prithvi is liquid-fueled and uses basic propulsion technology from the Russian SA-2 surface-to-air missile. The Prithvi-I has a range of 150 kilometers and a payload of 1,000 kilograms and has been produced for use by the Indian Army.[82] In 1994, the Army ordered seventy-five Prithvi-I missiles, and twenty to fifty are believed to have been delivered to the 333d Missile Group.[83] The Prithvi-I was most recently tested on March 26, 2003.[84] The Prithvi-II has a 500-kilogram payload and a range of 250 kilometers and was designed for use by the Air Force.[85] The Prithvi-III, also called the Dhanush, is similar to the Air Force version and is intended to be launched from a surface vessel. The Dhanush was unsuccessfully flight-tested in April 2000, but was successfully tested in September 2001.[86]

The Prithvi is essentially a Pakistan-specific weapon and can target half of Pakistan. One major drawback of the Prithvi is that it uses a highly volatile liquid fuel, which has to be loaded immediately prior to launch.[87] The Prithvi's fuel significantly reduces its usefulness as a mobile missile and has caused some analysts to doubt that the Prithvi would be used to carry nuclear warheads.[88] According to some reports, however, more stable solid-fuel versions of the Prithvi may also be under development.[89]

Agni-I

This medium-range, nuclear-capable missile has an estimated range of 2,000 kilometers with a 1,000-kilogram warhead.[90] Because of the Agni's longer range, it would be able to target all of Pakistan, as well as many key targets in China.[91] The Agni-I is a two-stage missile, using both solid and liquid fuel. The first stage reportedly uses the same first-stage solid-fueled booster as that used on India's Satellite Launch Vehicle-3 (SLV-3),[92] while the second stage is believed to be a modified liquid-fueled Prithvi-I.[93] If this is true, then the liquid fuel used in the Agni-I is probably the same volatile fuel used in the Prithvi, which means that it must also be fueled immediately before use.

Agni

On January 25, 2002, and January 9, 2003, India flight-tested a shorter-range variant of the Agni-I missile, called simply the Agni. This single-stage, solid-fueled missile is estimated to have a range of 700–750 kilometers.[94] It is believed to be the first stage of the Agni-I. Because the new Agni-variant uses solid fuel, it may be intended to replace the Prithvi. Since it does not use a volatile and corrosive liquid fuel, it is possible to prepare the missile for launch much more safely and rapidly. Its solid fuel would also allow India to fire the missile from rail- and road-mobile platforms and possibly allow India to adopt a rapid-response capability (where the warheads are stored assembled and mated to ballistic missiles).[95] Thus, this missile could increase the safety and survivability of India's nuclear forces, but it could also increase instability and risks of accidental, unauthorized, and inadvertent launches.

Agni-II

The Agni-II is a two-stage, rail-mobile, solid-propulsion missile with a range of approximately 2,000–2,500 kilometers. It was successfully tested on April 11, 1999, and January 17, 2001.[96] India has announced that it has begun production of the Agni-II and will place it under the control of the Army.[97]

Agni-III

India is also reportedly attempting to develop a longer-range Agni missile, which will be called Agni-III. This missile is believed to have a possible range between 3,500–5,000 kilometers with a 1,000-kilogram warhead. According to some sources, one possible option for the Agni-III would be to modify the Agni-II by adding an additional booster with thirty-six tons of propellant.[98]

Sagarika SLBM

India is also developing a submarine-launched ballistic missile with Russian assistance.[99] This missile reportedly will have a range of approximately 320

Table 5.2. Indian Ballistic Missile Capabilities					
Type	**First Tested**	**Range (km)**	**Payload (kg)**	**Technological Characteristics**	**Comments**
Land-Based Ballistic Missiles					
Prithvi-I (Army)	Feb. 1988	150	1,000	Single stage, liquid fuel, road mobile	In 1994, the Army ordered 75, of which 20-50 have been delivered to the 333d Missile Group. Most recently tested, March 2003.
Prithvi-II (Air Force)	Feb. 1996	250	500	Single stage, liquid fuel, road mobile	In 1994, the Air Force ordered 25.
Agni-I	May 1989 (failed); Feb. 1994	2,500	1,000	Two stage, liquid and solid fuel, first stage used SLV-3, second used Prithvi-I	Tested to a range of 1,400 km. Successfully validated India's reentry vehicle technology and basic guidance systems.
Agni	Jan. 2002	700-750		Single-stage, solid fuel, rail and road mobile	Believed to be the first stage of Agni-I. Tested in Jan. 2003

kilometers and is intended to be launched from the "Advanced Technology Vessel" nuclear submarine.[100]

Space Launch Vehicles

Finally, India has also made a number of much longer-range rockets, which could be used as the basis for longer-range ballistic missiles. The Augmented Space Launch Vehicle (ASLV), a second-generation rocket, successfully put a spacecraft into a 450-kilometer orbit in 1992. The five-stage rocket uses

Table 5.2. Indian Ballistic Missile Capabilities					
Type	First Tested	Range (km)	Payload (kg)	Technological Characteristics	Comments
Land-Based Ballistic Missiles					
Agni-II	April 1999	2,500–3,000	1,000	Two stage, solid fuel, rail mobile	Tested to a range of 2,000 km on Pairl 11, 1999, and Jan. 17, 2000.
Agni-III	N/A	3,500	1,000	?	To be developed using PSLV technology
Sea-Based Ballistic Missiles					
Prithvi-III (Dhanush)	April 2000 (failed)	350	500	Single stage, liquid fuel [a]	Sea-launched naval version. Successfully tested in Sept. 2001.
Sagarika	N/A	200-300 ?	500 ?	?	Submarine-launched. Russian aid in development

Sources: Table prepared by Carnegie Non-Proliferation Project, quoted in Joeck, "Nuclear Relations in South Asia," p. 139; U.S. Department of Defense, *Proliferation: Threat and Response*, pp. 21-30; Sanjeev Miglani, "India Tests Nuclear Capable-Missile," *Reuters*, January 17, 2001; Wagner, "India Tests Short-Range Agni Ballistic Missile."

Note: [a] Although the Carnegie Non-Proliferation Project indicates that the Dhanush might possibly be solid-fueled, the U.S. Department of Defense indicates that the Dhanush is similar to the Prithvi-II, which is believed to be liquid-fueled. Cf. Table prepared by Carnegie Non-Proliferation Project, quoted in Joeck, "Nuclear Relations in South Asia," p. 139, and U.S. Department of Defense, *Proliferation: Threat and Response*, p. 25.

solid fuel for all stages. If this rocket were used as a ballistic missile, it is estimated that it would have a range of 4,000 kilometers.[101] The ASLV program led to other, more advanced rocket projects: the Polar Satellite Launch Vehicle (PSLV) and the Geosynchronous Satellite Launch Vehicle (GSLV).

The PSLV, a four-stage rocket, has solid-fueled first and third stages, liquid-fueled second and fourth stages, and six solid-fueled strap-on boosters. In 1996, this missile placed a 1,770-pound remote-sensing satellite into a 900-kilometer orbit.[102] The GSLV has not been tested yet, but if it is successful it will be significantly more powerful than the PSLV. It appears to be a two-stage rocket with the same first-stage as the PSLV (but the PSLV's strap-on boosters will be replaced by four more powerful boosters derived from the PSLV's second stage). The GSLV's second-stage will use a cryogenic rocket engine purchased from Russia.[103] Both the PSLV and GSLV could be converted into intercontinental-range ballistic missiles. If they were converted into missiles, the PSLV would have a range of at least 8,000 kilometers, and the GSLV would have a range of 14,000 kilometers. All the SLVs would be powerful enough to carry nuclear warheads

Pakistani Ballistic Missiles

Pakistan has made significant progress developing and producing ballistic missiles, largely through foreign assistance, primarily from China and North Korea. Although China pledged in 1996 to stop assisting Pakistan's nuclear and missile programs, the U.S. CIA reported that these activities actually increased after the 1998 nuclear tests.[104] China again formally committed to stop exporting missile components forbidden by the Missile Technology Control Regime (MTCR) on November 21, 2000, and announced new missile-related export controls in August 2002, but as of June 2003, U.S. intelligence agencies nevertheless continued to believe that Chinese firms remained key suppliers of missile technologies to Pakistan.[105] The following discussion summarizes Pakistan's current missile capabilities.

Hatf-I, Hatf-II (Abdali)

During the 1980s, Pakistan launched a ballistic missile program. By the late 1980s, this program had produced the Hatf-I, a short-range ballistic missile with a range of 80–100 kilometers and a payload of 500 kilograms.[106] The Hatf-I has reportedly been deployed with the Pakistani army since the mid-1990s.[107] Pakistan's early missile program also produced the second-generation Hatf-II with Chinese assistance.[108] The Hatf-II (sometimes also called the Abdali), reportedly has a range of 180 kilometers and was tested in May 2002.[109]

Haft-III (Ghaznavi, M-11)

Between 1991 and 1994, Pakistan received eighty-four M-11 short-range ballistic missiles from China.[110] This nuclear-capable missile reportedly has a range of 290 kilometers with an 800-kilogram payload. According to some reports, these missiles are currently stored at the Sargodha Air Force Base.[111] A missile production unit was reportedly set up at Fateh Jung with Chinese assistance.[112] In early 1997 some of these missiles, now called the Hatf-III or the Ghaznavi, were reportedly made operational and deployed with the 155 Composite Rocket Regiment of the Second Army Artillery Division, Attock.[113] The Hatf-III was also reportedly tested in May 2003.[114]

Haider-I

Pakistan is reportedly close to testing a new short-range ballistic missile called the Haider-I. It is a nuclear-capable, solid-fueled, single-stage missile with a range of approximately 350 kilometers. It is reportedly being developed with Chinese assistance.[115]

Shaheen-I

Pakistan has also developed the solid-fueled, road-mobile Shaheen-I SRBM, which was successfully flight-tested in April 1999. According to Pakistani officials, this nuclear-capable missile has a range of 600–700 kilometers and a payload of 500 kilograms.[116] In 2001, Pakistani officials announced that serial production of these missiles had begun and that the missiles had been inducted into the army.[117] The missile was reportedly tested again in October 2002.[118]

Shaheen-II

Pakistani officials have stated that a longer-range Shaheen-II is currently under development. According to some reports, a pair of Shaheen-II ballistic missiles were displayed during the Pakistan Day parade in Islamabad on March 23, 2000.[119] One of the missiles was carried on a twelve-wheel transporter erector launcher (TEL), while the other missile was carried on a missile transporter. During the parade, it was claimed that the Shaheen-II surface-to-surface missile had a range of 2,000 kilometers.[120] Successful development of this missile will require continued assistance from Chinese entities or other potential sources.[121]

Ghauri-I and -II

This road-mobile, nuclear-capable missile has (at its longest) a range of 1,500 kilometers.[122] When launched toward India (roughly south), it would have a range of 950 kilometers.[123] Successfully tested in April 1998 and 1999,[124] this missile is widely accepted to be North Korea's No Dong MRBM.[125] According to some reports, China might have provided missile guidance technology (an area where North Korea is known to be weak) and other forms of assistance in support of the Ghauri program.[126] Although Pakistani officials have claimed that the Ghauri has a range of 1,500 kilometers and is capable of carrying a 700-kilogram payload, its range is probably 1,300 kilometers, the range of the No Dong.[127] In January 2003, the Ghauri was formally handed over to the military. It is not clear how many missiles have been delivered, but it is believed that serial production of the Ghauri-I has already started.[128] Pakistan is also developing a longer-range Ghauri-II, which has an estimated range of 2,000 kilometers. The Ghauri-II was reportedly tested in May 2002.

Expected Deployment Systems

Both India and Pakistan are believed to have designed nuclear gravity bombs that could be delivered by aircraft. In both countries these weapons are generally believed to be stored unassembled. According to the U.S. Department of Defense, India could assemble and deploy a few nuclear weapons within a few days to a week, while Pakistan could probably assemble its weapons "fairly quickly."[129] Some scholars, however, have speculated that India and Pakistan may maintain some assembled nuclear weapons as well.[130] During a crisis, the nuclear components would presumably be assembled and loaded onto bombers.

As we have seen, both countries are also developing ballistic missiles as possible delivery vehicles for their nuclear weapons. While India is probably still not able to deploy warheads on its missiles, it may be able to do so in the near future.[131] India's August 1999 draft nuclear doctrine shows that India is moving toward weaponization and deployment of significantly more advanced weapon systems. This doctrine lays the foundation for a "survivable" arsenal of several hundred warheads deployed on missiles, aircraft, and ships; "robust" command-and-control procedures and technologies; nuclear weapons stored in a high state of alert; and even a space-based early-warning system.[132] This draft doctrine has not been officially accepted or rejected by the Indian government.[133] Whether or not India adopts this specific doctrine, the current direction of India's nuclear policy is clearly toward deployment and more advanced weapons systems.[134]

If India does deploy nuclear warheads on missiles, Pakistan is likely to follow suit, to the extent that it can.[135] Pakistan may also adopt such a deployment strategy due to independent considerations, such as the vulnerability of Pakistani weapons and command-and-control structures to conventional or nuclear attacks from India (especially given recent advances in India's intelligence-gathering and precision-strike capabilities).[136] Given these vulnerabilities, Pakistan will probably adopt a mobile missile system.[137] Both Pakistan's liquid-fueled Ghauri and solid-fueled Shaheen missiles feature mobile launchers, and it is likely that if Pakistan chose to deploy nuclear

Table 5.3. Pakistani Ballistic Missile Capabilities

Type	First Tested	Range (km)	Payload (kg)	Technological Characteristics	Comments
Land-Based Missiles					
Hatf-I	April 1988	80-100	500	Single stage, solid fuel	Developed with Chinese assistance. In service.
Hatf-II (Abdali)	April 1988	180	500	Single stage, solid fuel	Tested May 2002, in production.
Hatf-III (Ghaznavi)	May 2002	290	500	Single stage, solid fuel	Based on a Chinese M-11 missile. 30+ stored in canisters at Sargodtha Air Force Base near Lahore; some possibly deployed in 155 Composite Rocket Division of the Second Army Artillery Division.
Haider-I	Under development	350	?	Single stage, solid fuel	Being developed with Chinese assistance.
Shaheen-I (Hatf IV)	April 14, 1999	600-700	1,000	Single stage, solid fuel, road mobile?	In service. Tested in October 2002.
Shaheen-II	Under development	2,000-2,500	400-500	Two stage, solid fuel, road mobile	
Ghauri (Hatf-V)	April 6, 1998	1,300-1,500	700	Single stage, liquid fuel, road mobile	Tested to 1,100 km. North Korean No Dong MRBM. In service. Tested in May 2002.
Ghauri II (Hatf-VI)	April 14, 1999	2,000	1,000	Single stage, liquid fuel	Tested to 1,165 km. Based on North Korean No Dong. In development. Tested in April 2002.

Sources: Lavoy and Smith, "The Risk of Inadvertent Nuclear Use between India and Pakistan," p. 3; Cirincione et al., *Deadly Arsenals*, pp. 213-14; CIA, *Acquisition of Technology Relating to Weapons of Mass Destruction and Advanced Conventional Munitions, 1 January through 30 June 2002*; Table prepared by Carnegie Non-Proliferation Project, quoted in Joeck, "Nuclear Relations in South Asia," p. 140; U.S. Department of Defense, *Proliferation Threat and Response*, p. 30; "Pakistan to Test-Fire Ballistic Missiles," *Dawn*.

warheads on these missiles, they would be deployed in mobile configurations.[138] These systems increase the survivability of the nuclear forces, but they significantly increase command-and-control difficulties. It is also quite possible that Pakistan will need to predelegate the authority to launch the nuclear weapons.[139] Such a predelegation would increase the likelihood of unauthorized or inadvertent use, as greater numbers of people would be authorized to use the nuclear weapons.

Some accounts have questioned India's missile capabilities, however. According to some reports, Indian security experts are questioning the effectiveness of indigenously developed and produced Agni and Prithvi missiles.[140] Other analysts have argued that Indian warheads will not be able to be deployed on missiles without further nuclear tests.[141] If these assessments are correct, then Pakistan's missile capability is probably more advanced than India's, because Pakistan has reportedly relied upon foreign warhead and missile designs, which have already been successfully tested.[142] But it is important not to underestimate India's missile capabilities. Some assessments by Indian think tanks and defense panels have reportedly urged speeding up India's indigenous missile programs.[143] In addition, Russia has reportedly been helping India with its missile program.[144]

Before we can know for certain what weapon deployments India and Pakistan will adopt, if any, we have to wait and see what actions India takes. India does appear to be pushing for some kind of weapon deployment, but whether nuclear weapons will be deployed on missiles depends on what India's missile capabilities really are.

Nuclear Command-and-Control Structures in India and Pakistan

Neither India nor Pakistan yet has a well-established command-and-control network for its nuclear weapons, though both countries have recently made strides in establishing command structures and decision-making bodies for policy planning and for authorizing the use of nuclear weapons. As we will see, however, their approaches are quite different. In India, the top command structure lies firmly in the hands of civilian leaders, while in Pakistan control over nuclear weapons has always been maintained by the military. The following sections examine their command structures in greater detail.

India's Nuclear Command Structure

In India, the civilian government and the nuclear establishment have maintained exclusive control over Indian nuclear weapons. This was long assumed to be India's official policy, though it was not made explicit prior to

2003. Prior to India's establishment of the nuclear command structure in 2003, there was no formal structure for nuclear decision-making. Instead, key decisions on nuclear policy were formulated by top leadership and the nuclear establishment.

Command Structure Prior to 2003

Although India created the National Security Council (NSC) in April 1999—a body comprising top ministers and intended to plan long-range nuclear strategy—it never met. The military had recommended that a National Command Authority be established as a high-level command institution, with a National Strategic Nuclear Command reporting to it and comprising military and technical personnel.[145] But this proposal was never accepted by the government. According to K. Subrahmanyam, the convener of India's National Security Advisory Board, the NSC was "stillborn."[146] During this time, nuclear policymaking presumably remained controlled by a few top politicians and the nuclear establishment.

A number of scholars highlighted the potential difficulties that could have been caused by the tightly controlled nature of India's command structure during this time. Prior to 2003, the Indian military was completely excluded from engaging in any strategic nuclear planning or preparations for ensuring adequate command and control if the nuclear weapons were to be transferred to the military. Although this arrangement was set up to reduce risks of unauthorized and accidental use (by keeping warheads isolated from the military), as well as to isolate decision-making from potentially hawkish military planning, it did produce a number of potential risks. Because the military had little or no experience handling nuclear weapons, this arrangement could have actually increased some risks of accidental or unauthorized use once the weapons were transferred to the military, presumably during a crisis.[147]

Moreover, tightly controlled decision-making can cause leaders to make mistakes and carry out actions that are not properly thought through. According to Neal Jocck, "Excessively-controlled decision-making also poses potential problems. The *Brasstacks* exercise, for example, was planned by a small circle of officials who apparently did not carefully consider how Pakistan would respond to such a massive show of force. This restricted decision-making was followed by Prime Minister Rajiv Gandhi's exclusion from the loop when the issue reached crisis proportions."[148]

Finally, India's tightly controlled command structure could have caused serious difficulties if anything had happened to the few people in charge of nuclear decision-making. The lack of an adequate Indian command structure was highlighted in October 2000 when Indian prime minister Atal Behari Vajpayee underwent knee surgery. During the surgery, the one person known to be authorized to launch India's nuclear weapons was temporarily put out of commission.[149]

As we will see, however, some of these potential difficulties were subsequently addressed by India's formalization of its command structure in January 2003.

Command Structure after 2003

On January 4, 2003, the office of the Indian prime minister announced a decision by the Cabinet Committee on Security (CCS) that established an official command structure for Indian nuclear weapons.[150] The doctrine establishes a National Command Authority, which is composed of a Political Council and an Executive Council. India's prime minister chairs the Political Council, which is the sole body that can authorize the use of nuclear weapons. The Executive Council is chaired by the national security advisor. It "provides inputs for decision making in the National Command Authority and executes the directives given to it by the Political Council."[151] The 2003 nuclear doctrine called for the establishment of a "credible nuclear deterrent," a posture of no first use, and a policy of no nuclear use against non-nuclear states. It did, however, reserve the right for India to use nuclear weapons to retaliate against chemical and biological weapons.[152]

That same day, the CCS also approved the appointment of a commander-in-chief of the Strategic Forces Command (SFC) to take charge of India's nuclear arsenal. This step made official a June 2002 decision to place India's command-and-control system under the SFC. The 2002 decision formed an Army Strategic Rocket Command (ASRC) to handle surface-based nuclear weapons.[153]

This series of decisions made India's command structure much clearer, though it did leave a few questions about some of the specifics of India's command structure. According to the Ministry of External Affairs, the CCS "approved the arrangements for alternate chains of command for retaliatory nuclear strikes in all eventualities," which might refer to cases in which the prime minister was incapacitated during a nuclear crisis. It remains unclear what the alternate chains of command might be and whether they are civilian or military.[154]

Moreover, an important question that remains unclear is who will exercise physical control over the nuclear weapons during peacetime. The previous command arrangement clearly ensured that the nuclear warheads remained under the control of the nuclear establishment, particularly the

Defense Research and Development Organization (DRDO) and the Indian Atomic Energy Commission (IAEC). It is not clear whether the 2003 decision will transfer the physical control to the SFC during normal, peacetime operations, or whether it will be transferred to the military only during crises.[155] Most suggestions appear to be that for the time being the military will not have operational control of the warheads, but that this sets the stage for operational readiness and eventual deployment of India's nuclear weapons.[156]

Nevertheless, India's 2003 nuclear doctrine does resolve a number of the potential risks that had previously existed prior to India's formalization of the command structure. Key elements of the military will exert a greater influence in military planning and will now have a greater role in establishing specific command-and-control arrangements. It is necessary to underscore, however, that this decision took place nearly four and a half years after India's 1998 tests of its nuclear weapons, and nearly thirty years after it first crossed the nuclear threshold. It will also presumably take some time for India to set in place specific command-and-control structures within the military and train its personnel in the safe and secure handling of nuclear weapons. It is possible, though, that this command structure had previously existed in secret, which may have allowed India to begin addressing some of these issues.[157]

Pakistan's Nuclear Command Structure

Pakistan created a National Command Authority (NCA) in February 2000, following India's creation of the NSC, to facilitate the command and control of its nuclear weapons. The NCA is reportedly composed of two committees, the Employment Control Committee (ECC) and the Development Control Committee (DCC).[158] The Army chief and head of the military regime (currently General Pervez Musharraf) will head each of the committees.[159] Other members of the Employment Control Committee will be the ministers of foreign affairs, defense, and interior; the chairman of the joint chiefs of staff committee; and the chiefs of the armed forces. The DCC will include the chairman of the joint chiefs of staff committee, the chiefs of the armed forces, and a "representative of the strategic organization and scientific community."[160] On November 28, 2000, all strategic organizations, including the Khan Research Laboratories, the National Development Complex, and the Pakistan Atomic Energy Commission, were placed under the control of the NCA.[161]

The organization of the NCA is dominated by high-level members of Pakistan's military, and it is generally assumed that the military controls Pakistan's command-and-control structure as well as its entire nuclear infrastructure. As the head of both the civilian government and the military, General Musharraf presumably has the final authority to order a launch of Pakistan's nuclear forces.

This focused command structure has its advantages and disadvantages. Because nuclear decision-making is tightly controlled and focused, it should be fairly well-coordinated. But because the nuclear command structure is dominated by the army chief, heading the military regime, it could fall into the wrong hands if the regime were to topple.[162] If this were to happen and the power vacuum were not filled by a stable civilian regime, Pakistan's nuclear weapons could fall into the hands of Muslim radicals. According to General Anthony Zinni, former commander-in-chief of the U.S. Central Command, "My worry is that Musharraf may be the last hope. We could have fundamentalists [in power] and another fundamentalist state that looks like Iran. That could be dangerous for obvious reasons. Or, we could have complete chaos and something that looks like Afghanistan."[163]

The nuclear controls in Pakistan also probably would not remain as centralized as they are now if India and Pakistan were to weaponize their arsenals. Because of the vulnerability of Pakistan's nuclear forces to decapitation or elimination during a first strike, Pakistan would probably choose to predelegate the authority to launch its nuclear forces.[164]

Specific Command-and-Control Procedures and Technologies

As Karl and Seng have noted, all things being equal, the smaller size of the arsenals in India and Pakistan decrease some of the risks of accidental and unauthorized use. But the size of the arsenal is not the only factor that affects nuclear controls. As we have seen in Russia, even though its controls have weakened, many of the risks of unauthorized use are reduced because many of its nuclear weapons have sophisticated use-control devices. This is not the case in India and Pakistan. Most available information indicates that neither of these countries has advanced command-and-control systems in place for their nuclear weapons.[165] In particular, most assessments indicate that their nuclear weapons lack sophisticated use-control devices to prevent unauthorized use.[166] Instead, both countries rely largely on the presence of guards, gates, and guns for the security of their nuclear weapons.

Because both Indian and Pakistani nuclear controls rely heavily on the "3 G's," it is critical that they ensure that the guard forces at their nuclear facilities are reliable. As Scott Sagan notes, however, there are currently no programs in India or Pakistan to ensure the reliability of guards, civilians, and military officers at nuclear facilities.[167] Without such programs in place, India and Pakistan run the risk that some guards or workers might steal nuclear weapons or fissile materials, or sabotage their nuclear facilities.

There is also some evidence that, at least at certain times, these countries may not have placed command and control as their highest priorities. For example, it has been reported that in order to avoid detection by spy satellites or their own security forces prior to the 1998 nuclear tests, India did not increase the security forces for guarding the nuclear weapons while they were being moved to the Pokhran test site or while they were being prepared for testing.[168] The weapons were reportedly moved at night with only five to six guards per truck.[169] While these procedures successfully avoided detection, they were potentially quite dangerous.[170] If any of the many people involved with the procedures had alerted groups interested in obtaining Indian nuclear devices, India's defenses would have had serious difficulties in defeating an organized attack.

India has also reportedly designed a number of nuclear devices in addition to the ones used in the 1998 tests. Moreover, because the weapons were ready for testing within a few weeks of the Bharatiya Janata Party's election, this indicates that the weapons were probably built prior to the election. This raises questions about where these weapons were stored and how they were protected, whether only five nuclear devices were manufactured, whether other devices are ready for further tests or for weaponization and deployment, and whether these warheads are stored at locations that are secure from external attack or sabotage.[171] Unfortunately, nothing is known for certain about how the Atomic Energy Commission is ensuring the physical safety of these nuclear devices and their components.[172]

Lack of Safety Cultures in India and Pakistan

Pessimists have raised concerns that limited resources and rudimentary technologies will cause the nuclear systems in emerging NWSs to be unreliable at best, and unsafe at worst. These concerns have been specifically raised about the nuclear programs in India and Pakistan. For example, Indian scholars Praful Bidwai and Achin Vanaik have raised concerns about what they call "ramshackle deterrence" in South Asia.[173] Citing numerous serious mishaps in the testing and designs of Indian military technology, they highlight the "disaster-prone character of a good deal of Indian (and Pakistani) military as well as civilian infrastructure and hardware, marked as it is by frequent accidents, component failures, substandard designs, poor maintenance and unsafe operational practices."[174] They conclude that the "poor safety culture is bound to affect the working of all the hardware and software involved in any possible command, control, communications, and intelligence systems India and Pakistan may build in the future."[175]

Safety of Indian Nuclear Facilities

There is significant evidence that the Indian nuclear program has not placed safety as a high priority. Indeed, all nine of India's nuclear power reactors that were operational in 1996 were among the 50 least reliable of the 399 reactors monitored by the IAEA.[176] According to a 1996 report by India's Atomic Energy Regulatory Board (AERB), as many as 130 safety issues were identified at Indian nuclear power plants.[177] The most serious of the safety problems identified by the AERB are at nuclear power plants located in the southern city of Madras and the western state of Rajasthan, both of which have outmoded systems for preventing a catastrophic core meltdown.[178] According to A. Gopalakrishnan, the former director of AERB, India's Department of Atomic Energy (DAE) continually ignored the AERB's recommendations to improve the safety of India's nuclear plants.[179] Moreover, as of April 2000, the DAE now forbids the AERB any access whatsoever to India's nuclear facilities.[180]

According to some reports, the safety culture at India's nuclear weapons facilities is even worse than at India's nuclear power facilities. Although most information about India's weapons facilities is tightly controlled, there are nevertheless several reports of horrible problems at the Bhabba Atomic Research Centre (BARC), India's primary nuclear weapons facility. For example, in 1991, the Dhruva reactor reportedly operated for almost a month with a malfunctioning emergency cooling system. And in 1995, huge amounts of water reportedly drained from the wet storage block containing submerged uranium fuel rods after an inlet hose was disconnected. If someone had not noticed the reduced water level, the radioactive fuel would have been exposed to open air, potentially causing a major disaster.[181]

Similar Safety Concerns in Pakistan

Similar concerns have been raised about the safety of Pakistani nuclear facilities. In 1994, Pakistan established the Nuclear Regulatory Board (NRB), which was intended to oversee safety procedures in Pakistani nuclear facilities, but it was reportedly merely an appendage of the Pakistan Atomic Energy Commission (PAEC) and therefore provided no independent oversight.[182] Pakistan has replaced the NRB with the Pakistan Nuclear Regulatory Authority (PNRA),[183] but the PNRA will probably provide only marginally better oversight than the NRB. Four main aspects of Pakistan's nuclear program—power generation, medical use, agricultural use, and educational facilities—remain under the authority of the military-controlled PAEC and are shrouded in secrecy.[184] It is therefore doubtful that the PNRA can provide any coherent, independent evaluation of safety standards in Pakistan's nuclear program.[185]

This lack of independent oversight has raised serious concerns about the safety of Pakistani nuclear facilities. For example, the Chasma Nuclear Power Plant (CHASNUPP), which was connected to a power grid in June 2000, is reportedly built in a location that some experts have warned is earthquake-prone.[186] Because the power plant is built on the banks of the River Indus, a major water lifeline for Pakistan, a major accident could have devastating effects on the country. Moreover, the CHASNUPP plant is based on the designs of China's Qinshan reactor, which reportedly is seriously flawed. The faulty design in the Qinshan reactor caused a serious accident in 1998 and forced the reactor to be shut down for a year.[187] The CHASNUPP has undergone simulation tests, but there are concerns that the tests only evaluated basic scenarios and might not have been designed to test serious design problems, such as the one that caused the failure at the Qinshan reactor.[188]

There are also some questions about whether Pakistan has taken the necessary measures to ensure the safety of its nuclear weapons. On April 10, 1988, a massive explosion occurred at the Ojheri ammunition depot located in a heavily populated area in the twin cities of Rawalpindi and Islamabad.[189] The explosion sent heat-seeking missiles, rockets, and projectiles into population centers in both cities, causing massive destruction and hundreds of casualties. The damage caused a temporary breakdown of telecommunications in the federal capital and at military headquarters, and caused widespread rumors of an Indian attack on the Kahuta nuclear facility, which is located nearby.[190] If any of the missiles had struck the Kahuta facility, it could have caused a massive release of radioactivity in the region. While the ammunition depot did not contain nuclear weapons, it raises questions about the emphasis that Pakistan places on ensuring that its weapons are stored safely, and one must wonder whether they might take risks with their nuclear weapon storage.[191]

The lack of safety cultures in India and Pakistan, while troubling in themselves, also point to more fundamental dangers that probably run through the entire nuclear programs in both countries. In particular, they justify pessimists' concerns that emerging NWSs will tend to marginalize safety and control measures in their single-minded pursuit of their weapons programs.[192] India and Pakistan have demonstrated that they are willing to risk serious accidents and potential catastrophes in some parts of their nuclear programs.

We cannot be at all confident that they will not run similar risks in other parts of their programs, including the safety and security of the nuclear weapons themselves.

Risks of Accidental Use of Nuclear Weapons

Because both India and Pakistan reportedly store their nuclear weapons in unassembled states, the risks of accidental use are currently relatively small. But a great deal depends on whether India decides to weaponize its arsenal and deploy nuclear weapons. As the 1999 draft nuclear doctrine demonstrates, nuclear hawks in India are pushing for deployment and rapid-response capabilities. If India were to adopt this doctrine or a similar one, the warheads would be mated to delivery systems. When weapons are stored in this state, the risks of accidental detonations could increase significantly. Because it is very unlikely that India has designed its nuclear weapons to allow for one-point safety, or to use insensitive high explosives (IHE) or fireproof pits,[193] the risks of an accidental detonation could be relatively high in the event of a fire or a mishap involving a nuclear weapon (such as a nuclear weapon falling off a truck or an accident involving a vehicle carrying nuclear weapons).

In addition, because the Indian military currently has little experience handling nuclear weapons, the risks of accidental use could be very high during a crisis situation, at least for some time to come. If the order were given to prepare India's nuclear weapons for possible use, the military (perhaps in conjunction with India's nuclear scientists) would need to assemble the warheads rapidly; mate them to the delivery vehicles (gravity bombs or missiles); and prepare them for use, either by loading them into bombers or by aiming the missiles and preparing them for launch. All these procedures require training and precision, and, given the early stages of India's new command-and-control arrangements, it is not at all clear that the Indian military would be able to carry them out safely under extreme time constraints.[194]

If India decided to develop a rapid-response capability, some of these dangers would be lessened, but more serious dangers would be introduced. In particular, there would be a significantly increased risk of an accidental launch of nuclear-armed missiles. India would need to engage in a great deal of additional research into safety mechanisms to prevent such an accidental launch, and it is simply not known how much effort India is devoting, or will devote, to this area.[195] Because the Prithvi and the two-stage Agni-I missiles contain a nonstorable liquid fuel, it would be impossible to deploy the current configuration of either missile to allow for a rapid response. This significantly reduces the likelihood of these missiles being launched accidentally during normal circumstances, though the risks of accidental launches would probably increase significantly if they were fueled during a crisis situation. As noted, however, India has conducted several successful flight tests of the Agni and Agni-II missiles. Because these missiles use a solid fuel, they could be deployed in a rapid-response state. If India were to choose such a deployment option, the risks of an accidental launch could increase significantly. These risks would depend on the extent to which India integrates use-control devices into its weapons to prevent accidental launches, but there is little evidence that India is currently devoting significant efforts to develop such use-control devices.[196] Furthermore, even if India intends to develop such use-control devices, if a nuclear crisis were to arise before India had developed them, it still might be tempted to mate warheads on its missiles.

If India does decide to weaponize its arsenal, it still remains to be seen what type of deployment option it would choose. According to a statement in November 1999 by India's foreign minister, Jaswant Singh, India would not keep its weapons on a "hair-trigger alert," though he did suggest that these weapons would be dispersed and made mobile to improve their chances of surviving a first strike.[197] If this statement is true, then the risks of accidental launch would be relatively small during normal circumstances.[198] But these risks would increase significantly during crisis situations, when India would presumably mate the warheads to the missiles.[199] If the military still has not been given physical control over the warheads, this would further reduce risks of accidental use during peacetime, though the transfer of nuclear weapons to the military during a crisis could significantly increase the risks of an accident due to the military's inexperience in handling the nuclear weapons.[200]

What deployment option Pakistan might adopt depends in part on India's weapon deployment. It appears that if India were to adopt a rapid-response option, Pakistan would probably adopt a similar missile deployment, thereby increasing the risks of an accidental launch of its nuclear weapons as well. But even if India were to deploy its weapons (in field positions) without the warheads mated, concerns about survivability might nevertheless cause Pakistan to adopt a rapid-response capability. If such an event were to occur, the risks of Pakistani accidental missile launches could be quite high, especially because it is unlikely that Pakistan currently has the technical capacity to integrate sophisticated launch controls into its missile designs.

Just as in India, it is also unlikely that Pakistan's nuclear devices are designed to minimize risks of accidents.[201] Because Pakistan's warheads are based on an early Chinese warhead design, they probably do not contain one-point safety designs, IHE, or fire-resistant pits. If Pakistan were to assemble its nuclear warheads, there could be an unacceptable risk of an accidental detonation of its nuclear weapons. Moreover, if Pakistan were to mate nuclear warheads to its missiles, either because it chose to establish a rapid-response capability or because of an ongoing nuclear crisis, then similar concerns would exist about accidental launches of Pakistani nuclear weapons.

Risks of Unauthorized Use

The current risks of unauthorized use of nuclear weapons in India and Pakistan are probably relatively small because they have a very small number of nuclear weapons and those weapons are tightly controlled by their nuclear establishments. But there are a number of factors that could increase risks of unauthorized use in the future.

Although both India and Pakistan currently possess nuclear weapons that could be delivered by aircraft, and are both actively developing nuclear-capable ballistic missiles, none of their weapons appear to contain sophisticated use-control devices to prevent unauthorized use. Instead, the nuclear controls in both countries appear to be based on guards, gates, and guns. As we have seen in the Russian and Chinese cases, while the "3 G's" might be sufficient during normal circumstances, they are particularly vulnerable during political, economic, and social upheavals.

The Russian case has demonstrated that severe domestic upheavals can undermine central controls and weaken the infrastructures that previously maintained the security for nuclear weapons. In particular, such upheavals can undermine the loyalty of guards and workers at nuclear facilities, especially if the state collapses economically and can no longer afford to pay those employees. Neither India nor Pakistan appears to have taken the necessary steps to prevent such weaknesses from arising in their nuclear controls. Because Indian and Pakistani nuclear controls rely on the "3 G's" while reportedly lacking personnel reliability programs, there could be a significant risk of thefts of nuclear weapons during severe upheavals.

The Russian analogy is particularly relevant in the Pakistani case. The Pakistani state is far from stable. After the nuclear tests in 1998 and the military coup in 1999, the Pakistani economy came close to collapsing and remained quite unstable for the next several years.[202] In the aftermath of the September 11, 2001, terrorist attacks, the United States removed economic sanctions and approved nearly $1 billion in international foreign aid to Pakistan. But with a debt burden of nearly $39 billion, massive economic disparities, and continuing low levels of foreign investment, there still is significant cause for concern about the prospects for Pakistan's long-term political and economic stability.[203] If the Pakistani state were to fail, there could be significant risks of a collapse in its nuclear controls. Were such an event to occur, there could be an extreme risk of thefts of nuclear weapons or of nuclear weapons falling into the hands of Islamic militants.[204]

In the events following the September 11 attacks and President Musharraf's decision to support U.S. military strikes in Afghanistan, there were serious concerns about a potential collapse of Pakistani nuclear controls. These concerns were spurred by reports of public riots, a close affiliation among some elements of the Pakistani military and intelligence community with the Taliban regime and al Qaeda, and the tenuous hold that Pakistani president Musharraf appears to have in Pakistan.[205] In October 2001, President Musharraf took significant steps to centralize his control by removing high-level military and intelligence officers with ties to the Taliban, but analysts have nevertheless continued to raise concerns about Musharraf's ability to maintain control.[206] Due to the seriousness of these risks, President Musharraf ordered an emergency redeployment of Pakistan's nuclear arsenal, and the United States has offered to advise Pakistan on methods for securing its nuclear stockpile.[207] If the U.S. military strikes in Afghanistan had extended for a longer period, Musharraf might have found it increasingly difficult to remain in power and reign in the more extreme elements in his country.

One also cannot rule out the possibility that terrorists might choose to target nuclear facilities in India and Pakistan, especially if domestic instability were to increase. Both India and Pakistan have serious problems with domestic terrorism.[208] These terrorists are increasingly well-armed and have targeted critical infrastructures and military bases in the past.[209] Although current defenses at both Indian and Pakistani nuclear weapons storage facilities are probably sufficient to defend against most terrorist attacks,[210] the physical protection systems at other nuclear facilities might be less effective.[211] Moreover, if the defenses at the most sensitive facilities were weakened by domestic upheavals, then the risks of successful terrorist attacks—either for purposes of theft or sabotage—could increase significantly.

But even if such extreme events did not occur, the tightly controlled decision-making and underdeveloped command-and-control structures in both India and Pakistan could potentially allow unauthorized use, particularly during crises. In India, some of these risks have been minimized by the formalization of its command structure, though the military units are still fairly inexperienced with handling these weapons.[212] Moreover, because India probably still lacks clearly defined, detailed operational procedures and established, resilient communication channels, there would still be a fairly high risk of unauthorized use arising from confusion or miscommunication during a crisis. These concerns will probably remain for some time to come, though the specific risks could eventually be improved, depending on the training the military receives and the degree of professionalism among the troops.

Because Pakistan is currently under military rule, and its nuclear weapons are controlled by the military, one would expect a better coordination of nuclear decision-making and command-and-control systems. Nevertheless, there are potential problems with Pakistani command and control as well. The lack of a clear operational use doctrine, combined with inadequate C^3I, could increase the risks of unauthorized use during crises: "there is no enunciated nuclear doctrine, nor are there decision-making and communications systems adequate for either strategic or tactical command and control in the nuclear environment. Nuclear targeting information could not be passed in time to be of use in a rapidly changing situation, which would increase the probability of own-troop strikes by tactical [nuclear] missiles."[213]

The risks of unauthorized use would increase if India and Pakistan were to deploy their weapons on ballistic missiles. Risks of decapitation and questions about the survivability of the nuclear forces would probably cause both India and Pakistan to deploy mobile systems if they were to operationalize their nuclear forces. These systems would significantly increase difficulties in command and control, especially because their weapons lack use-control devices.[214] In addition, because of the risks of decapitation, Pakistan is likely to adopt a "delegative" system, where the authority to launch nuclear weapons is given to a number of military officials.[215] As the number of people authorized to launch nuclear weapons increases, so does the risk of a use of nuclear weapons that has not been commanded by the central authorities.[216]

Inadvertent Use

The greatest concerns have been raised about a possible inadvertent use of nuclear weapons in South Asia. The combined effects of mutual mistrust, very short flight times for missiles, continual armed conflicts along their borders, and few reliable CBMs make the risks of inadvertent use quite severe, especially during crisis situations. According to George Perkovich, a South Asia expert at the Carnegie Endowment for International Peace, "Kargil proved that having nuclear weapons would not deter new conflicts. It also showed that unless such conflicts themselves were prevented, the possibility of an accidental or deliberate nuclear exchange would also increase given both states' relatively poor systems of intelligence surveillance and nuclear command and control."[217]

Due to continual mistrust between the two countries, each would be likely to misinterpret military movements, missile tests, or accidental detonations as an impending attack by the other side. The risks of misinterpreting each other's motives are compounded by the vulnerability of their nuclear forces and the short flight times of the forces to key targets. For example, because the runways at Pakistani Air Force bases could be destroyed by a conventional air strike or nuclear attack,[218] India could effectively eliminate Pakistan's nuclear bomber capability. During an acute crisis, Pakistan might be faced with a "use them or lose them" dilemma, in that it would need to attack rapidly or lose its ability to retaliate altogether. For this reason, Pakistani officials would be extremely suspicious of any Indian actions that could be interpreted as preparations for an attack. Because the flight time of Indian bombers is approximately ten minutes, Pakistani leaders would have a very limited amount of time to decide whether to launch their own attack.[219] These conditions thus create an ongoing environment in which inadvertent use is quite possible.

In addition, both countries have unreliable intelligence systems, which have repeatedly misinterpreted the other's intentions. For example, during the Brasstacks incident, Pakistani intelligence reported that India's exercise was merely a cover for an attack. Meanwhile, Indian intelligence overlooked the defensive nature of the Pakistani troops' position. These intelligence failures caused each side to escalate the tensions unnecessarily. In addition, their intelligence systems have sometimes failed to detect major troop movements altogether. As we have seen, during the Brasstacks crisis, Indian surveillance planes did not detect Pakistani troops positioned at their border for two weeks. And in the 1999 Kargil war, Indian intelligence failed to detect the Pakistani invasion until several months after they had positioned themselves at strategic locations in the Kargil heights. These intelligence failures could have two consequences. First, if either side were surprised by comparatively benign actions (such as Pakistan's defensive positioning during the Brasstacks crisis), it would be more likely to overreact and mistakenly conclude that an attack is imminent. And second, if one side (especially Pakistan) is confident that an invasion would not be detected at first, it might be more likely to launch attacks across the border. Each of these scenarios would greatly increase the risks of nuclear escalation.[220] Presumably owing to the massive intelligence failure prior to the 1999 Kargil war, however, India has recently made significant investments in its intelligence-gathering capabilities, which could reduce risks of such failures by India in the future.[221]

The dangers of miscalculations and intelligence failures are increased by the crude early-warning systems employed by both countries, particularly Pakistan. Several incidents serve to illustrate this point. First, prior to

Pakistan's nuclear tests in 1998, Pakistan reported that it had detected an air force attack on its radars and warned that it had mated a number of warheads to its Ghauri missiles.[222] While this report might have been circulated in order to justify their nuclear tests, circulating such a report could have caused India to mate weapons to its missiles, greatly increasing the risks of inadvertent use (as well as accidental and unauthorized use).

Another, perhaps more troubling, incident occurred prior to the U.S. missile strike on Afghanistan in August 1998. The United States sent a high-level U.S. official to Pakistan because it feared Pakistan would detect the missile and interpret it as an Indian strike. Pakistan never even detected the missile, however. Scholars have pointed out that this incident emphasizes not only the U.S. concern about inadvertent nuclear war between India and Pakistan, but also that Pakistan's early-warning system "has serious flaws, and such shortcomings are more likely to foster nervousness than calm. To the extent that they lack reliable early-warning systems, India or Pakistan could base launch decisions on unreliable sources, increasing the chance of mistakes."[223]

But even if India and Pakistan *had* reliable early-warning systems, the risks of inadvertent war would still be extremely high. If Indian or Pakistani radars detected aircraft headed toward them, they would have very little time to decide what to do before the aircraft reached their targets. In addition, because there would be a great deal of uncertainty about whether attacking bombers carried conventional or nuclear weapons, the attacked side (especially Pakistan) could face a "use them or lose them" scenario and be tempted to launch a nuclear attack to ensure that its nuclear capability was not destroyed.[224] Thus, even if India and Pakistan do not deploy nuclear weapons on missiles, the risks of an inadvertent use in these circumstances could be extremely high.

If India and Pakistan were to deploy their nuclear weapons on missiles (a scenario that is quite likely, given the vulnerability of Pakistani airfields and India's stated need for deterrence against the People's Republic of China), the risks of inadvertent use would become even worse. Because the flight time for ballistic missiles between the two countries is less than five minutes,[225] Indian and Pakistani leaders would have virtually no time to decide what action to take (or perhaps even to launch a retaliatory strike) before the missiles hit their targets.[226] The psychological effect on the two countries would be tremendous. According to François Heisbourg, once theater missiles are deployed in South Asia, the strategic situation will resemble the Cuban missile crisis, except that it "would be permanent rather than temporary, would occur without adequate C^3I in place, and with political leadership located less than five minutes from mutual Armageddon."[227]

The risks of inadvertent war are further increased by the fact that India and Pakistan have minimal CBMs to decrease such misinterpretations. As we have seen, even though the two sides have negotiated a series of CBMs, including hotlines between the heads of the Indian and Pakistani governments, they are rarely used, even during times of escalated tension.[228] With the moves to restore diplomatic relations in May 2003, there may be improved communication links between the two countries, but these tentative, positive steps forward could quickly evaporate in the event of renewed hostilities. Indeed, since Prime Minister Vajpayee has made it clear that this is his last effort at easing tensions, the next crisis could be the most severe we have seen yet.

The combination of these factors has created a situation in which the risk of inadvertent use is extremely high. Because both sides deeply mistrust each other, they are likely to misinterpret each other's actions and escalate tensions unnecessarily. As George Perkovich argues, the fundamental lesson of the Brasstacks crisis is that "neither Indian nor Pakistani leaders intended to wage war against each other, yet India's exercise and Pakistan's defensive countermeasures signaled threats that heightened the other's insecurity and could have escalated to a war that neither wanted."[229]

The accidental explosion at the Ojheri ammunitions depot in Pakistan also demonstrates how tightly controlled nuclear programs, mutual mistrust, and serious accidents can raise the risks of inadvertent nuclear war.[230] In the discussion following the Ojheri explosion, top military officials admitted that the existence of the depot was known only to military dictator General Zia ul-Haq and Inter-Services Intelligence, which controlled the clandestine operation of supplying arms to the Afghan resistance. According to Ahmed and Cortright, "The combination of the three factors—the proximity of the military headquarters, the federal capital, and the Kahuta facility; the breakdown in communications; and a weak command-and-control structure—could have created a chain of misperception and miscalculation leading to accidental or inadvertent war. Since both Pakistan and India were nuclear capable by 1988, such a conflict could have included a nuclear dimension."[231] As it was, the incident caused widespread rumors that India had attacked Pakistan's Kahuta nuclear facility and command-and-control centers.[232] If a similar accident were to occur during an acute crisis, such as a conflict similar to the 1999 Kargil war, Pakistan almost certainly would conclude that it was an attack—particularly if both sides have operational nuclear weapons.

Conclusions about Command and Control: Impossible Deterrence?

Many of the problems we have identified relate to the lack of adequate command-and-control procedures and technologies in India and Pakistan. As we have seen, the lack of these systems could make the risks of accidental, unauthorized, and inadvertent war quite high, especially if the two countries push forward with weaponization and deployment of their nuclear weapons. But even if the two countries were to establish clearer command structures and develop sophisticated use-control devices and early-warning systems, it would still be very difficult for India and Pakistan to maintain stable deterrence. Because the two countries share an international border, the flight times for nuclear bombers and missiles are very short. It would therefore be very difficult for the two countries to avoid the risks of accidental, unauthorized, or inadvertent use during crisis situations.

Some scholars have recommended that the United States assist India and Pakistan with their command-and-control systems in order to minimize the risks of accidental and unauthorized use.[233] There are, however, significant political and technical obstacles to such assistance. First, it would run counter to U.S. NPT obligations. Such assistance would, in effect, condone the nuclear weapons programs in India and Pakistan and could therefore encourage other aspiring NWSs to develop nuclear weapons.

In addition, while such assistance would decrease some risks, it could increase others. In particular, such assistance could help India and Pakistan overcome some of the difficulties in the designs of their nuclear weapons and missile systems. It could also increase Indian and Pakistani confidence in their abilities both to prevent a crisis situation from spinning out of control and to launch their nuclear weapons rapidly if such a crisis did escalate. Given the history of conflict between India and Pakistan and the short flight times for delivery systems, such confidence would significantly increase the risks of inadvertent use.

The best way to minimize nuclear dangers in South Asia would be to encourage India and Pakistan to refrain from deploying their weapons, to cap their nuclear programs, and, if possible, to set the stage for an eventual withdrawal of nuclear weapons from the region. While such actions would be extremely difficult to carry out, they would be the ones most likely to reduce the very real risks of nuclear war between India and Pakistan.[234] For such objectives to have any chance of success, the perceived political and military threats on each side would first need to be addressed. This can only be achieved by encouraging India and Pakistan to improve their bilateral relations. Interim goals should include encouraging the two countries to return to the (largely abandoned) prescriptions outlined in the Lahore Declaration, and increasing international pressure on Pakistan to reign in cross-border terrorism.

Part II: India's and Pakistan's MPC&A

Indian and Pakistani Nuclear Facilities

India

India has a fairly large infrastructure for producing fissile materials, including thirteen nuclear reactors, uranium mines and processing plants, and facilities to extract plutonium from spent fuel.[235] All of these facilities are operated by the Indian Department of Atomic Energy, and there is generally little distinction between military and civilian nuclear programs in India.

India's main nuclear weapons development establishment is the Bhabba Atomic Research Centre (BARC), which is located near Trombay.[236] India's main plutonium production reactors are the Cirus and Dhruva reactors. To produce weapons-grade plutonium, BARC converts uranium into metallic reactor fuel, irradiates that fuel in the Dhruva and Cirus reactors, then processes the spent fuel to extract weapons-grade plutonium.[237] By 1999, the Cirus reactor had produced an estimated total of 240–336 kilograms of plutonium, and the Dhruva reactor had produced an estimated 280 kilograms of plutonium.[238]

In the 1970s, India also began research into fast-breeder reactors, which can rapidly produce weapons-quality plutonium.[239] As part of this program, the IAEC built the pilot-scale, Fast Breeder Test Reactor (FBTR) in Kalpakkam. Some analysts believe that the plutonium produced in this reactor has been used in India's nuclear weapons program.[240] The IAEC announced in 1997 that it would soon break ground for a 500-MW(e) Prototype Fast Breeder Reactor (PFBR), also located at Kalpakkam.[241] India claimed that the PFBR would be completed in 2007.[242]

India also has fourteen nuclear power reactors, located in numerous locations across the country, and it is currently building eight more.[243] (See figure 5.1 for the locations of India's power reactors.) Of these reactors, only four are currently under IAEA safeguards.[244] The remaining reactors could be used as sources for reactor-grade plutonium, which could be used as part of India's nuclear weapons program. India also has several plutonium reprocessing facilities, which can extract plutonium from spent fuel produced at India's unsafeguarded commercial reactors. These reprocessing facilities are located at Tarapur, Trombay, and Kalpakkam.[245] The plutonium extracted from spent fuel can be used in nuclear weapons, though this reactor-grade plutonium is not as desirable as weapons-grade plutonium, due to the low concentration of Pu-239.[246] India has also recently built eight unsafeguarded pressurized heavy-water reactors (PHWR), Madras I and II, Narora I and II, Kakrapar I and II, and Rajasthan III and VI, which are reportedly ideal for production of high-quality plutonium in spent fuel because they involve a short uranium burn-up period, which ensures a higher Pu-239 concentration.[247]

BARC also has the capability to enrich natural uranium to produce HEU using two ultracentrifuges, located in Mysore and Rattehali.[248] The HEU could be used to produce fission weapons, though India is more likely to use it to fuel a nuclear submarine, increase the yield of a hydrogen bomb, or fuel "boosted" nuclear weapons.[249]

Finally, New Delhi has also signed a deal with Russia to purchase two lightweight reactors, which are planned to be built in southern India.[250] These facilities will reportedly be under facility-specific IAEA safeguards.[251]

Pakistan

Pakistan's main uranium enrichment facility is located in Kahuta. The facility is based on German Urenco G-1 and G-2 designs that were reportedly stolen by A.Q. Khan, the "father" of Pakistan's nuclear weapons program.[252] The enrichment plant has an estimated 3,000 centrifuges in operation, which can produce 55–95 kilograms of HEU per year. The Kahuta site may also be the location where HEU is formed into weapon cores. Pakistan also has several smaller facilities that could be used to produce HEU. Golra Sharif and Sihala, both located near Islamabad, reportedly contain small, unsafeguarded centrifuge plants.[253]

Pakistan also possesses a capability to produce small amounts of weapons-grade plutonium. In 1998, Pakistan announced that the Khushab reactor had started operating. This reactor could make enough plutonium for a few nuclear weapons per year.[254] The New Laboratories at the Pakistan Institute of Nuclear Science and Technology (PINSTECH) contain a plutonium reprocessing facility. Although the facility began as an experimental-scale reprocessing plant, it was reportedly upgraded and expanded during the 1990s and is believed to be able to reprocess all the irradiated fuel produced at the Khushab reactor.[255]

There are also several research and commercial reactors in Pakistan. Because these facilities are under IAEA safeguards, they are not currently part of Pakistan's nuclear weapons program. Nevertheless, they are a potential source of spent fuel (which could be reprocessed for the reactor-grade

Figure 5.1. Selected Indian Nuclear Facilities

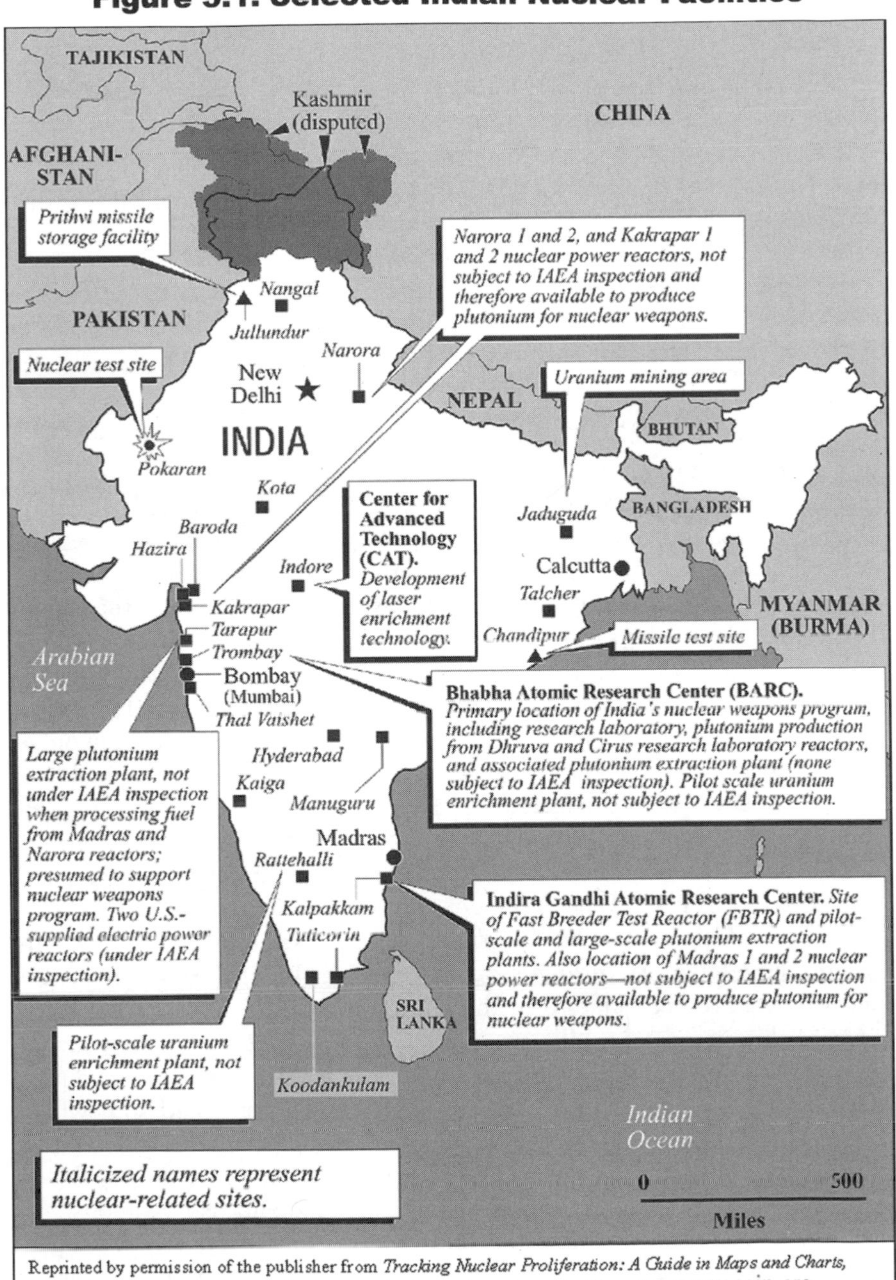

Reprinted by permission of the publisher from *Tracking Nuclear Proliferation: A Guide in Maps and Charts, 1998* (Washington, DC: Carnegie Endowment for International Peace, 1998), p. 126. www.ceip.org

plutonium it contains). Two small research reactors at PINSTECH are the main centers of Pakistan's open nuclear research and development program. One of these reactors (known as PARR-1) is a 10-MW pool-type research reactor supplied by the United States in 1965, and the other (PARR-2) is a Chinese-supplied 27-KW(t) pool-type reactor.[256] Pakistan has one operating commercial reactor at Karachi. This plant is a fully safeguarded 137-MW(e) CANDU heavy water reactor, supplied by Canada. This plant became operational in 1998.[257]

Fissile Material Production Capabilities and Current Stockpiles

Because India and Pakistan have never provided independent confirmation, there is a great deal of uncertainty about their current stockpile sizes. Current estimates of India's fissile material stockpile are based on the production capability of weapons-grade plutonium in the Cirus, Dhruva, and power reactors (subtracting estimates of the materials used in the nuclear tests, production losses, and civil-uses of the weapons-grade plutonium). These estimates conclude that India's fissile material stockpile was probably somewhere between 240 and 395 kilograms of weapons-grade plutonium at the end of 1999, with the median estimate being 310 kilograms.[258] This stockpile is estimated to allow for approximately sixty-five nuclear weapons.

Unlike India, Pakistan's nuclear weapons reportedly contain HEU, rather than plutonium. Although Pakistan reportedly declared a moratorium on its production of HEU in 1991, it is generally assumed that it has resumed full-scale production of HEU since the 1998 tests. A.Q. Khan also announced soon after the tests that Pakistan had never stopped producing HEU, though this claim has been greeted skeptically. Whether or not Pakistan stopped producing HEU in 1991, however, does not make a significant difference in the size of Pakistan's current HEU stockpile, because Pakistan was accumulating a large quantity of low-enriched uranium (LEU) during this period and would have been able to further enrich the LEU fairly rapidly. Thus, even if Pakistan did cease HEU production in 1991, it probably has roughly the same amount of HEU now as it would have had if it never stopped producing HEU.[259] According to current estimates, Pakistan had somewhere between 585 and 800 kilograms of weapons-grade uranium at the end of 1999, with a median estimate at 690 kilograms.[260] This amount of HEU is estimated to be enough for approximately thirty-nine nuclear weapons.[261]

In 1998, Pakistan announced that the Khushab reactor had started operating. This reactor gives Pakistan the capability to produce enough weapons-grade plutonium for a few nuclear weapons per year. Because the reactor probably did not operate well during its early period, however, it is only

Figure 5.2. Selected Pakistani Nuclear Facilities

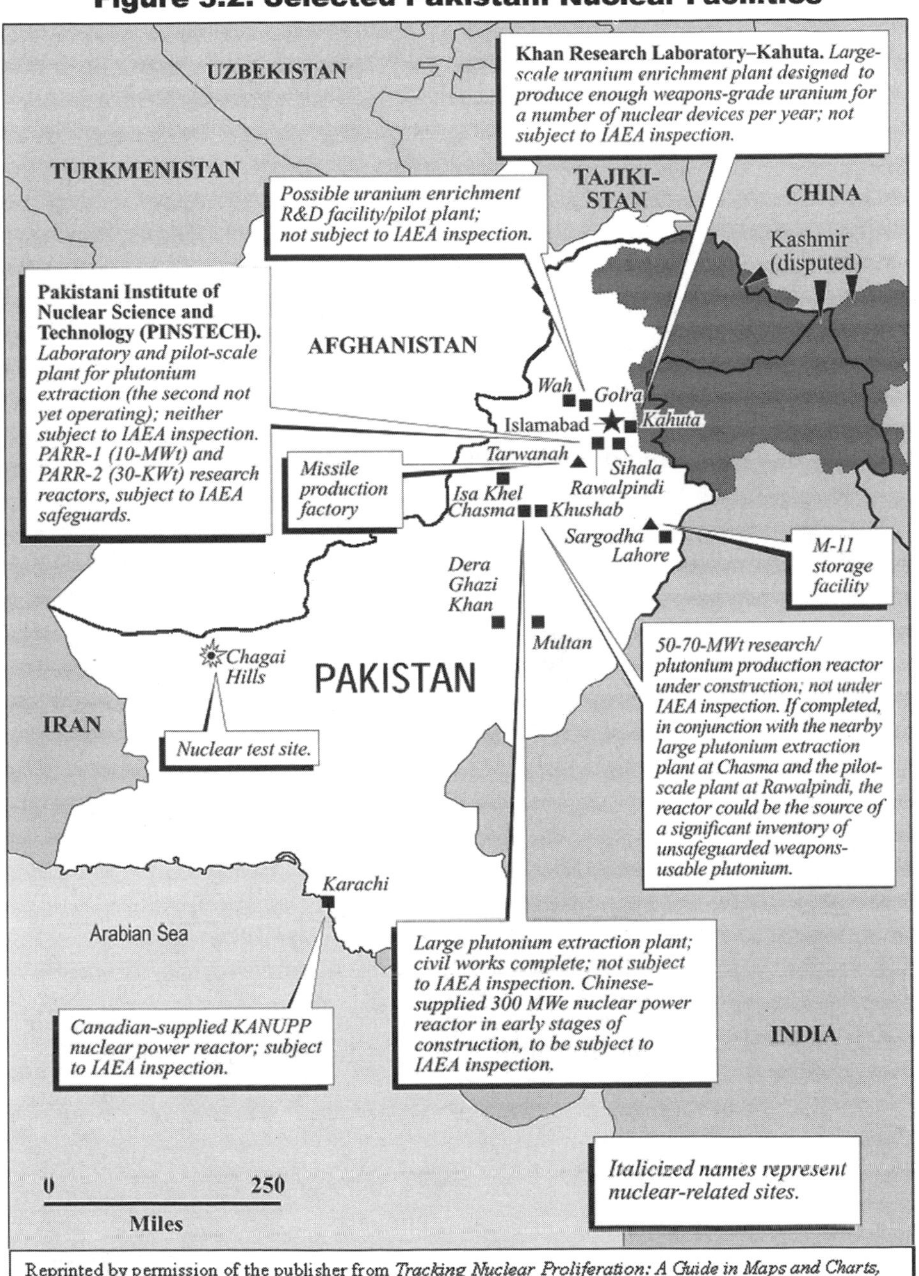

Reprinted by permission of the publisher from *Tracking Nuclear Proliferation: A Guide in Maps and Charts, 1998* (Washington, DC: Carnegie Endowment for International Peace, 1998), p. 126. www.ceip.org

estimated to have produced approximately 5.5 kilograms of weapons-grade plutonium by the end of 1999.

Both countries are believed to be trying to increase their fissile material stockpiles as rapidly as possible.[262] As part of this effort, India may be considering using its civil power reactors to increase its stock of weapons-grade plutonium. In addition, it is possible that India might use reactor-grade plutonium for its nuclear weapons.[263] Some assessments suggest that one of the devices tested in 1998 used reactor-grade plutonium, though these assessments are contested.[264] If India were to use reactor-grade plutonium in its weapons, its stockpile would be significantly larger than previously estimated. India is estimated to have approximately 800 kilograms of unsafeguarded separated reactor-grade plutonium and 3,400 kilograms of unsafeguarded reactor-grade plutonium that is not separated from spent fuel.[265]

MPC&A Systems at Indian and Pakistani Nuclear Facilities

While there is very little available information on Indian and Pakistani fissile material controls, there is reason to conclude that their fissile material security systems lack adequate MPC&A technologies. Indeed, according to high-level U.S. government officials, India and Pakistan largely rely on institutional structures for the security of their fissile materials, rather than sophisticated MPC&A systems.[266] The following is as precise a description of Indian and Pakistani fissile material security as possible, given the scarcity of open-source information on these systems.

Physical Protection

There is fairly strong reason to conclude that Pakistan does not have modern physical protection systems at its indigenous nuclear facilities. For instance, at a 1997 conference on MPC&A, the Pakistani representative discussed at length the military defenses at Pakistan's primary uranium enrichment facility at Kahuta. These defenses include extensive military forces and surface-to-air missiles to defend against an Indian air strike. But he was completely silent about any advanced security systems, portal monitors, or access control systems at the facility, which are essential elements of modern MPC&A systems.[267] Similarly, in a speech at the 2001 Carnegie International Non-Proliferation Conference, the Pakistani foreign minister stated that Pakistan has "administrative and legal mechanisms," and "institutional controls" over fissile materials, but did not mention any technological means for controlling the materials.[268]

In the absence of evidence to support a different conclusion, we cannot assume that sophisticated physical protection systems exist in Pakistan.

There are several additional reasons to doubt that Pakistan has developed these MPC&A technologies. First, it is unlikely that Pakistan has the technological or industrial capability to produce the equipment necessary for a sophisticated MPC&A system on its own. As we saw in chapter 3, without an established technological infrastructure, Russia has had significant difficulty building indigenous portal monitors and nondestructive assay equipment, and it is likely that Pakistan would have similar difficulties. Second, Pakistan would have been unable to buy this equipment from any of the industrial countries that do produce MPC&A equipment. Because this equipment would be incorporated into Pakistan's nuclear program, none of the participants in the Nuclear Supplier's Group would be allowed to sell it to Pakistan. And finally, due to the assistance that Pakistan received from China in most aspects of its nuclear program, including the designs of its nuclear facilities, there is reason to suspect that Pakistan's fissile material controls on its indigenous facilities would closely resemble China's, which are generally based on the "3 G's."[269]

Pakistan does have several nuclear facilities that are under IAEA safeguards, however. These facilities presumably have more sophisticated MPC&A systems that probably meet IAEA standards. For example, the KANUPP reactor, used for civilian power, is currently under Canadian-IAEA safeguards, which were left in place after Canada withdrew assistance on the reactor. Another reactor under IAEA safeguards is the CHASNUPP reactor, currently being installed with Chinese assistance. It will reportedly possess Chinese-IAEA safeguards.[270]

Some analysts have also raised serious concerns about the physical protection systems at Indian facilities. In 1988, Paul Leventhal and Brahma Chellancy argued that "there is an urgent need for upgrading physical protection systems at dozens of nuclear reactors, laboratories, fuel fabrication and reprocessing plants, and research institutes scattered across India."[271] India's MPC&A technologies may have improved somewhat since then, as its facilities reportedly include intrusion alarms, portal monitors, and multiple-layered access controls.[272] According to one report, Indian facilities include the following physical protection measures:

- When necessary (depending on the materials present), a double-barrier system is used, which is equipped with intrusion alarms and TV cameras under the control of security staff inside the facility.

- Internal security guards are not armed, but backup is provided by special armed state police forces, which are kept at close proximity to the facility but keep a low profile. Commandos from the National Security Guard are available if needed.
- Access to such facilities is controlled by monitors, magnetic cards, turnstiles, etc. India is currently developing a fingerprint access system.
- Reprocessing plants are co-located with power plants and R&D reactors to minimize transportation risks.[273]

Although this physical protection system sounds fairly impressive, some high-level U.S. government officials have questioned the adequacy of this system and have maintained that it probably falls short of international standards.[274] Moreover, according to A. Gopalakrishnan, the former head of India's nuclear regulatory agency, India's security plans do not include performance testing of this physical protection system to ensure its effectiveness.[275] Without such performance testing, it is impossible to identify or correct any weaknesses in a given physical protection system.[276] For this reason, the latest IAEA physical protection standards recommend performance testing as a critical element in physical protection systems.[277] Because India has not tested its physical protection system, it could include serious defects that have simply gone unnoticed.

MC&A

It is also unlikely that India and Pakistan have implemented accurate material control and accounting (MC&A) systems to measure and track fissile materials moving through their nuclear facilities. According to Annette Schaper, a senior research associate at the Frankfort Peace Research Institute (PRIF), because the majority of their facilities were not designed with international safeguards in mind, they may lack designs that specifically facilitate an overview of material flows, provide access for taking samples, designate measurement points, contain installations that enable the application of tags and seals, and restrict human entry.[278]

As we have seen, high-level U.S. government officials have confirmed this assessment. These officials argue that India and Pakistan largely rely on institutional structures for the security of their fissile materials, rather than sophisticated MC&A.[279] Furthermore, A. Gopalakrishnan possibly gave some additional support for this suggestion, at least regarding India's MC&A. In correspondence with the author, Gopalakrishnan recommended that the United States engage in collaborations on MC&A technologies with India.[280]

It should probably be concluded from his statements that India's MC&A falls short of international standards.

Are Sophisticated MPC&A Systems Even Necessary in India and Pakistan?

Because India and Pakistan have relatively small stockpiles of fissile materials, it is worth examining whether sophisticated MPC&A systems are even necessary in India and Pakistan. Indeed, some U.S. officials have maintained that because these stockpiles are small and tightly controlled, sophisticated MPC&A is not necessary.[281] But, as I will argue, such MPC&A systems are necessary for several reasons.

First, both India and Pakistan currently produce fissile materials at several different facilities spread across their respective countries. Moreover, both India and Pakistan are building additional production facilities for producing fissile materials. Because of the diverse locations of these facilities, it is in fact harder to control the materials than it might seem, given the small size of their arsenals and stockpiles.

Second, it is generally believed that both countries are expanding their fissile material stockpiles as quickly as possible.[282] As the amounts of fissile materials produced by these numerous facilities accumulate, it will be increasingly difficult to maintain the institutional controls that they have so far maintained.

The lack of safety cultures in India and Pakistan also raises questions about the adequacy of their "safeguards cultures." As we have seen in the Russia case study, unless a NWS has exerted a great deal of effort cultivating a safeguards culture, in which everyone from high-level politicians to the lowest-level guard recognizes the importance of rigorous MPC&A procedures and technologies, the directors and workers at nuclear facilities are often willing to bypass security procedures in order to achieve other goals, such as meeting production schedules.[283] A number of analysts have drawn an analogy between safety cultures and safeguards cultures, because the same motivations can undermine both.[284] As we have seen, without independent regulatory agencies to enforce safety procedures, Indian nuclear facilities have had shoddy safety records. Indeed, A. Gopalakrishnan maintains that the physicists who measure radiation levels avoid reporting safety problems because the reports could delay production schedules.[285] It is likely that the same constraints would prevent reporting of violations in safeguards procedures, especially because both India and Pakistan are currently trying to produce fissile materials as rapidly as possible. Although one Indian analyst has argued that an independent organization called Nuclear Material Accounting and Control (NUMAC) oversees MC&A, it is unlikely that NUMAC actually is independent of India's Department of Atomic Energy (DAE). If this is the case, then the DAE could ignore the regulations established by NUMAC, just as it has with the safety regulations established by the AERB, the agency responsible for nuclear safety.[286]

There is also reason to suspect that Pakistan would have similar problems with the enforcement of its fissile material procedures. Because Pakistani fissile materials are controlled by the military, there is little reason to believe that any independent authority is responsible for enforcement of safeguards procedures.

Without sophisticated MPC&A systems or rigorous safeguards cultures to help track and control fissile materials, it is possible that insiders could steal these materials from Indian or Pakistani nuclear facilities.[287] This reportedly occurred in India in 1994, when police in the eastern Indian state of Meghalya arrested four men for smuggling uranium. This uranium was reportedly stolen by a scientist employed by India's Department of Atomic Energy. Officials from India's Atomic Energy Commission later confirmed that 2.5 kilograms of "semi-processed" uranium, as well as 95 kilograms of "unprocessed" uranium, had been recovered. While it is unlikely that these materials could be used to make a nuclear device, it does indicate that some personnel at India's nuclear facilities are willing to steal materials for sale on the black market.[288]

Another incident, though of a different nature, occurred in India in November 2000. Indian police reportedly seized fifty-seven pounds of uranium from a home in Hyderabad, a city in southern India, and arrested two men who had been trying to smuggle the material out of the country. The men had apparently discovered the uranium when they bought a large quantity of scrap from a local hospital. The hospital had reportedly used the material to treat cancer patients and was supposed to have returned the material to BARC.[289] While this material does not appear to have been weapons-usable, it does raise serious questions about BARC's material accounting systems, since BARC apparently did not notice that the uranium had not been returned.

Greater risks of insider theft probably exist in Pakistan. In addition to thefts motivated by economic gain, some insiders at Pakistani nuclear facilities might also have ideological reasons for stealing materials. Pakistan has long maintained close connections with terrorist groups and Muslim countries, particularly Afghanistan. And while Pakistan officially severed its connections with the Taliban and some domestic militant groups, many Pakistani citizens retain loyalties to them. It is therefore possible that some sympathizers within Pakistan's nuclear program might be tempted to steal materials for Islamic terrorist groups.[290] Recent incidents highlight these concerns. In November 2001, two Pakistani nuclear scientists were arrested for possible connections with the Taliban and al Qaeda. One of these scientists, Sultan Mahmood, was a nuclear engineer who reportedly played an important role in Pakistan's programs to produce highly-enriched uranium and plutonium. The scientists reportedly admitted to having briefed Bin Laden and his associates several times on nuclear, biological, and chemical weapons.[291] Although neither scientist appears to have particular experience in building these weapons, this incident highlights concerns about possible connections between some members of Pakistan's nuclear industry with Islamic fundamentalist groups. Moreover, according to some reports, the United States has investigated new leads on possible contacts between Pakistani nuclear scientists and the Taliban or al Qaeda. While there are few details on the new investigations, these nuclear scientists may have actual experience in the production of nuclear weapons and related technologies.[292]

Because Pakistani fissile materials are controlled by the military, it is possible that their materials are more tightly controlled than those in India. As we have seen, however, Pakistan's fissile materials are almost certainly controlled primarily through guards, gates, and guns. But, as the Russian case has demonstrated, the "3 G's" can be particularly weak during political, economic, and social upheavals.[293] Similar domestic upheavals could undermine fissile material controls in Pakistan. Although Pakistan has fewer fissile materials than Russia does, a breakdown in Pakistani fissile materials controls would still be very serious. Because members of Pakistan's nuclear program may have allegiances to fundamentalist Islamic groups, there might be greater opportunities for sale to groups that might be interested in obtaining fissile materials.

It is quite possible that Pakistan could encounter such political or economic upheavals. Because the Pakistani economy remains far from stable, it could encounter renewed financial difficulties in the near future. Moreover, as mentioned above, numerous scholars were concerned that political upheavals after President Musharraf's decision to support U.S. military strikes in Afghanistan could weaken Pakistani nuclear controls. Since the United States achieved a rapid victory in Afghanistan, it is likely that Pakistan has weathered the worst of the storm. But these incidents do raise questions about Pakistan's ability to maintain control of its nuclear assets during future crises. It would be hasty to conclude that no similar crises will ever occur in Pakistan again. For example, prior to U.S.-led war in Iraq, widespread public opposition forced Musharraf to openly oppose the war. If the United States were to extend its military campaign to other Islamic countries (such as Iran), there still could be a political backlash within Pakistan. Moreover, although some of the most militant Islamic groups have now been outlawed, the regime reportedly continues to support Islamic militants.[294] If U.S. pressure forced Musharraf to carry out a more severe crackdown on these Islamic groups, it could create divisions within the military or possibly even cause a coup.

Furthermore, as a direct result of recent actions by the military regime, Pakistan's Islamic parties have gained an increased foothold in the country. Prior to the flawed December 2002 elections, the military crippled Pakistan's main political parties, but in doing so allowed the Islamic parties to gain a greater foothold in the country. According to Šumit Ganguly, these actions "gave a foothold to the numerous previously marginalized religious parties, which have now come to the fore. Now these parties and the religious zealots who are attracted to their fold may become a threat to the regime's stability because of their profound reservations about the U.S.-led war and the overall alliance with the United States."[295]

U.S. officials have continued to express concerns about potential weaknesses in Pakistani nuclear controls. In March 2002, U.S. Senator Richard Lugar proposed to expand the Cooperative Threat Reduction Program to include efforts to help Pakistan and India secure their nuclear assets. Moreover, in September 2002, U.S. Undersecretary of Defense Douglas Feith and dozens of U.S. officials spent a week in Pakistan to discuss security cooperation. According to U.S. officials, these talks failed to address the issue of joint efforts to improve Pakistani nuclear security, however, despite ongoing concerns "that the country's small but shrouded nuclear weapons complex may be at risk of theft or leakage."[296]

Part III: Conclusions

This chapter has identified a number of serious potential and actual dangers associated with the nuclear programs in India and Pakistan. Of all the cases examined in the current study, the risks of a nuclear exchange are probably the highest in South Asia. Since developing their nuclear capabilities, India and Pakistan have had a number of nuclear crises, fought a small-scale conventional war, and, more recently, engaged in the largest military buildup in decades. This situation will only become more volatile if India and Pakistan deploy their weapons on missiles. Unfortunately, both countries appear to be moving in that direction. Once their weapons are deployed in this manner, they will have created a situation in which the risks of inadvertent use—and even intentional use—could be quite possible.

Moreover, even though both countries have made significant progress in their missile programs, they appear to have made less progress in designing advanced command-and-control systems, developing and promulgating specific operational use-doctrines, and training their armies in procedures and techniques for handling their weapons safely. As a result, the risks of accidental or unauthorized use could be quite high for some time to come, particularly during crisis situations.

And finally, because both countries largely rely on the "3 G's" for control over their nuclear weapons and fissile materials, there is little assurance they will be able to prevent insiders from stealing fissile materials or even selling nuclear weapons on the black market. Furthermore, as we have seen, this system of controls can erode or collapse during domestic upheavals. As the events following the U.S. bombing campaign in Afghanistan demonstrate, these risks may be particularly severe in Pakistan. But, given their security systems, the nuclear controls in either country could be undermined during political, social, or economic upheavals, greatly increasing dangers of thefts of nuclear weapons or fissile materials.

Because it still remains to be seen exactly where India and Pakistan will go with their nuclear programs, it is impossible to be certain that worst-case scenarios will result. If they refrain from weaponizing and deploying their nuclear weapons, *or* if they design and implement sophisticated C^3I and MPC&A systems, establish reliable confidence-building measures and other means for improving crisis stability, refrain from deploying their weapons on missiles, and make significant progress in resolving the Kashmir issue, they may be able to reduce or avoid some of the greatest risks identified in this study. But so far, most indications appear to be that they are not consistently taking either of these paths. Instead, they appear to be moving toward deployed missile systems without adequate C^3I systems to help reduce risks of accidental, unauthorized, or inadvertent use and without MPC&A systems to help prevent thefts of fissile materials or sabotage of nuclear facilities. Thus, while India and Pakistan could eventually fix many (though probably not all) of the problems identified in this study, the situation is likely to become worse before it gets better—if it gets better at all.

Newly Proliferating States
Iraq, North Korea, and Iran

The issue of WMD proliferation came to dominate international politics in 2002 and 2003. Although the United States and Western intelligence agencies have long believed that "rogue states" such as Iraq, North Korea, Iran, and Libya were pursuing nuclear weapons, these issues developed into crises in 2002.[1] For most of 2002 and early 2003, the United States, Great Britain, and other key allies pushed for a war to disarm Iraq and replace the regime headed by Saddam Hussein. After a short period of inspections overseen by the United Nations, the United States led the invasion of Iraq in April 2003. At the same time, however, it became increasingly clear that North Korea and Iran were pushing forward with covert nuclear weapons programs in violation of their NPT commitments.[2] During 2002 and 2003, the United States and the international community deliberated over what the proper response to this new surge in proliferation should be. The world was sharply divided over whether the U.S.-led invasion of Iraq was justified and whether Saddam Hussein could be deterred.[3] Similarly, a great deal of attention has been paid to what the true risks posed by nuclear weapons in North Korea and Iran really are. The United States has not ruled out military force or other means, such as strong international sanctions and increased support of opposition groups, to force "regime changes" in these countries as well.

In this chapter, we will examine the extent to which the issues discussed in the previous chapters apply to newly proliferating states. We will also identify potentially unique risks that newly proliferating states might encounter. In order to identify some of these risks, we will examine the nuclear programs and domestic political situations in Ba'athist Iraq, North Korea, and Iran. This chapter argues that some of the difficulties in nuclear controls that we have seen in the previous cases are likely to be encountered by newly proliferating states if they are allowed to pursue their nuclear weapons programs unimpeded. This will be likely for several reasons: first, the denial and deception methods employed by newly proliferating countries will be likely to create problems with security and careful tracking of materials. Second, it is likely that these states will employ low-technology systems to control their nuclear weapons and materials, relying primarily on guards, gates, and guns. As we have seen, however, these systems are particularly weak during domestic upheavals because such unrest can disrupt central oversight and undermine the reliability of guard forces and personnel at nuclear facilities. Third, although this point is more tentative, because there are increased prospects of preventive military strikes by the United States and its allies, newly proliferating states might be more inclined to emphasize survivability over safety and security, dispersing their weapons systems and possibly deploying them in configurations that could allow for rapid responses or even launch-on-warning.

Given a general lack of information about these programs, rapidly changing events, and the fact that these programs are (or were) in their early stages, it will be impossible for this chapter to provide an exhaustive treatment of these issues. Although this chapter will raise important issues that are directly relevant to this overall study, in a number of key areas it will be forced to present these issues as topics for further research. Indeed, much of this discussion will be somewhat speculative, since much will depend on specific decisions that the proliferating states will take as their programs develop. But it will be possible to identify likely and important trends that will allow us to make some predictions about potential risks in these proliferating countries.

Increasing Threats of Preventive Strikes

Unlike the other states studied in this book, newly proliferating states will have to beware of preventive strikes. To a degree, proliferating states have always had to worry about preventive strikes, since such strikes would delay or eliminate the state's nuclear weapons program at a time when the state would be unable to retaliate with nuclear weapons.[4] For example, the United States reportedly considered preventive strikes against both the Soviet Union and China during the early stages of their nuclear programs, and Israel engaged in a preventive strike against Iraq's Osirak reactor. But such strikes are now much more likely, given changes in U.S. foreign policy after September 11, 2001. Indeed, this is now officially part of U.S. nonproliferation and counterproliferation policies.[5]

The Role of Denial and Deception Techniques

Because most newly proliferating states will be acting within a framework that may oppose proliferation more directly than before, many of their actions will be shaped by these nonproliferation and counterproliferation regimes. In particular, due to the serious consequences that could result from revelations about their nuclear weapons programs, such as preemptive strikes, newly proliferating states will be likely to take greater steps to avoid detection of their WMD programs by U.S. and other states' intelligence measures by employing various "denial and deception" (D&D) techniques. Although the terms are interrelated, denial generally refers to "attempts to block information that could be used by an opponent to learn some truth."[6] It would include active measures, such as efforts to conceal WMD via camouflage, electronic emission control, and various forms of physical, personnel, and communications security that help hide the very existence of a clandestine activity.[7] Deception, on the other hand, refers to a nation's efforts to cause an adversary to believe something that is not true.[8] Specifically, it involves the use of active or passive measures to convey a false or inaccurate picture of a clandestine activity, such as disguising a biological weapons facility as a vaccine plant.[9]

Proliferating states will be likely to use various D&D techniques to conceal their nuclear programs. For example, Iraq, North Korea, and Iran all have concealed their nuclear weapons programs in numerous facilities, often hidden underground. The steps that these countries have taken will be useful for examining the general denial and deception approaches that other proliferating states might take. But, also, proliferating states will have extensive reasons for dispersing, hiding, or having the capability for rapid movement of materials. For example, Iraq relied on mobile facilities for WMD production, when possible. Because nuclear facilities are less mobile than chemical and biological facilities, however, this will be less of an option for nuclear proliferators. But proliferating states will adopt other approaches to counteract this. First, in order to conceal fissile material stockpiles from inspectors, retain some amounts of the stockpiles in the event of detection, and protect them from attack, proliferators may have multiple storage facilities for fissile materials and may have the capability of moving the stockpiles rapidly. Second, because it is easier to strike reactors, proliferators might opt for uranium enrichment instead, which allows for numerous, dispersed, more easily concealed facilities.[10] This appears to be the pattern in Iraq, Iran, and North Korea. Third, they might opt for developing extensive dual-use facilities that allow them to acquire nuclear expertise without violating the NPT, but which allow for rapid "break out" capabilities.

Marginalized Safety and Security Due to Economic and Technical Constraints

Lack of Sophisticated Security Systems

There are likely to be significant economic and technical constraints in proliferating countries, particularly in key proliferating countries, such as Iran, North Korea, Libya, Syria, etc. Because these countries are resource-limited, they will generally be unable to afford expensive security systems. It is therefore likely that these states will employ low-technology systems to control their nuclear weapons and materials, relying primarily on guards, gates, and guns. As we have seen in the other case studies, these systems are particularly weak during domestic upheavals because such upheavals can disrupt central oversight and undermine the reliability of guard forces and personnel at nuclear facilities.

Potential Shortcomings in Safety Systems

As we have seen, there have been concerns about the safety of nuclear facilities in current nuclear powers.[11] As Jeffrey Knopf has argued, the safety problems are likely to be even more severe in newly proliferating states: "Many of the more recent nuclear acquisition efforts have occurred in countries that have troubled economies, less modern technology, and unstable or authoritarian governments. It is unlikely that workers or the public in these countries will be well protected against the hazards of nuclear weapons production."[12] It is possible that some proliferating countries could avoid some of these risks because parts of their nuclear programs could be based on, or diverted from, existing reactors and other nuclear facilities. Nevertheless, even these states would need to build additional facilities, such as those for reprocessing spent fuel, for storing radioactive waste and separated fissile materials, and possibly for enriching uranium, that might lack adequate safety systems.

Moreover, as pessimist scholars have argued, limited economic and technical resources might reduce the capability of proliferating states to carefully design and test their nuclear weapons systems to ensure that they provide a high level of safety. As Lewis A. Dunn has argued, newly proliferating states might marginalize safety and security because they are using all of their available resources in acquiring the nuclear weapons in the first place.[13]

Potential Risks Arising from Rapid-Response Deployments

Because preemption is likely to be a major component of U.S. foreign policy, it is likely that newly proliferating states will disperse and deploy their weapons in ways that provide greater survivability. They will therefore be likely to deploy their arsenals in numerous locations, possibly in rapid-strike configurations. They might also be inclined to move military equipment in order to defeat any intelligence leads by Western powers concerning the location of the weapons. Due to the increased risks of preventive strikes, proliferating states may also have increased pressures to adopt launch-on-warning (LOW) capabilities.[14] Some analysts have speculated that Iraq may have adopted this approach with some of its WMD in the years between 1998 and 2002, due to concerns about a preventive strike by the United States, though it is now quite unclear what Iraq's WMD capabilities were during this period.[15]

We will now examine these issues in as much detail as possible by analyzing the nuclear programs of Iraq, North Korea, and Iran.

Iraq

In March 2003, the United States began a military operation to overthrow the regime headed by Iraqi president Saddam Hussein and his Ba'ath Party. Although Iraq is no longer pursuing nuclear weapons after the regime change, we can learn a great deal about how newly proliferating states go about pursuing their nuclear programs by examining Iraq's nuclear weapons program prior to and after the 1991 Gulf War.

The Iraqi Nuclear Weapons Program

It is widely believed that Iraq was only a few months away from developing a nuclear weapon prior to the 1991 Gulf War. After the war, weapons inspectors in the United Nations Special Commission on Iraq (UNSCOM) discovered a major covert nuclear weapons program, consisting of at least twenty-five major facilities and employing over 20,000 people.[16]

Although Iraq ratified the NPT in 1969, it maintained a covert nuclear weapons program since the early 1970s, most notably marked by its acquisition of the Osirak reactor from the French in 1974. The Osirak reactor, which would have been under International Atomic Energy Agency (IAEA) safeguards, was secretly intended to provide the technical expertise to allow Iraq to build another, secret reactor to provide plutonium for nuclear weapons.[17] Following Israel's destruction of the Osirak reactor in 1981, however, the Iraqi program focused primarily on developing implosion devices using highly-enriched uranium (HEU) as their nuclear fuel.[18]

Iraq's uranium enrichment program employed virtually every approach for enriching uranium, including high magnetism, gaseous diffusion, and centrifuges.[19] While the program had achieved the most success with high magnetism and gas diffusion, it had reportedly acquired the designs and much of the equipment for 20,000 modern centrifuges by the time of Iraq's invasion of Kuwait.[20]

Questions about a Continuing Nuclear Weapons Program after 1998

In 1998, UNSCOM inspectors became increasingly frustrated by a lack of Iraqi cooperation, reporting that they were unable to continue with their inspection work.[21] The inspectors were withdrawn in December 1998, and the United States and Great Britain launched the Desert Fox bombing campaign, which targeted suspected WMD and other military facilities. After these events, it was clear that Iraq would not allow the inspectors back in. According to U.S. intelligence agencies, Iraq intensified its efforts to produce nuclear weapons after the expulsion of UNSCOM inspectors. Intelligence estimates in 2001 and 2002 predicted that if Iraq's efforts had gone undetected and unimpeded, it could probably have acquired nuclear weapons in the second half of the decade.[22]

Following the resumption of inspections in November 2002, IAEA director Mohammed ElBaradei reported, however, that the United Nations Monitoring, Verification and Inspection Commission (UNMOVIC) and IAEA inspectors had found no evidence of ongoing nuclear weapons programs in Iraq. In fact, the IAEA found problems with the two main pieces of evidence that the Bush administration had cited as proof of Iraq's continuing nuclear ambitions: evidence that Iraq had tried to acquire aluminum tubes for use in centrifuges and that it had tried to import natural uranium from Niger.[23] According to the IAEA and some independent arms control specialists, the aluminum tubes would be difficult, if not impossible, to use in centrifuges.[24] Moreover, after bringing in handwriting analysts, the IAEA concluded that the documents purporting to reveal the efforts to import natural uranium from Niger had been forged.[25]

The Bush administration and U.S. intelligence agencies nevertheless continued to maintain that Iraq was still pushing forward with its nuclear weapons program.[26] For example, George Tenet reported in February 2003 that "Iraq has established a pattern of clandestine procurements designed to reconstitute its nuclear weapons program. These procurements include—but also go well beyond—the aluminum tubes that you have heard so much about."[27] There may be some reason to believe this, since it seems unlikely that Iraq would simply have abandoned these efforts after the expulsion of weapons inspectors in 1998. Moreover, one should recall that the IAEA also gave Iraq a clean bill of health until 1991, when inspections following the Gulf War demonstrated conclusively that Iraq in fact had a massive nuclear weapons program. The lack of evidence found by UNMOVIC and IAEA inspections in 2002–2003 could therefore only merely demonstrate the effectiveness of Iraqi denial and deception techniques rather than a lack of a program.

Nevertheless, even after the U.S.-led invasion toppled the Ba'ath regime in April 2003, U.S. and British inspections teams have so far been unable to find any evidence that Iraq had an active nuclear weapons program. Several findings, however, have raised suspicions that Saddam Hussein had not abandoned his nuclear ambitions. Dr. David Kay, head of the Iraq Survey Group (ISG), which was given responsibility for searching Iraq for WMD following the invasion, reported to the U.S. Congress that his team did in fact find indications that there was interest beginning in 2002 in renewing a centrifuge enrichment program. Evidence has also emerged that Iraq sought to preserve much of its technological capability from its pre-1991 nuclear weapons program through several means. For example, at the direction of senior Ba'ath Party government officials, many of the scientists involved in Iraq's pre–Gulf War nuclear weapons programs concealed research-related documents and equipment from UN/IAEA inspectors. One of these scientists, moreover, told the ISG that it was a "common understanding" among the scientists that the hidden material would later be used to resume nuclear weapons–related work. In addition, documents and testimony of Iraqi scientists indicate that some of the key technical groups from the pre-1991 nuclear weapons program were preserved intact and conducted work on nuclear-relevant, dual-use technologies, possibly with the intention of maintaining readiness for future reassignment to nuclear weapons–related activities.[28]

Still, the lack of concrete evidence of a renewed Iraqi nuclear weapons program renders any conclusions highly speculative. Additional information on whether Iraq continued to have an active nuclear weapons program may be revealed as investigators continue to sift through intelligence documents and interrogate scientists who may have been involved in the programs, but as time goes on, this possibility seems less likely.

Iraq's Denial and Deception Techniques

Because proliferating countries might use similar approaches to conceal their nuclear weapons programs, it is useful to examine some of the deception and denial techniques used by Iraq prior to, and after, the 1991 Gulf War.[29] Iraq hid its nuclear program through a number of means, including numerous, dispersed facilities; complex layouts and multiple designs for facilities; diminished or hidden defenses; and the ability to move equipment, materials, and documents rapidly.[30]

Because Iraqi officials knew some details about Western intelligence collection methods, including satellite surveillance, they attempted to conceal their facilities in ways that would not be detected by these methods. For instance, they knew that two important pieces of evidence were the power lines and defenses at various facilities. As a result, after the 1991 Gulf War, it was discovered that the Tarmiya nuclear site, located about thirty kilometers northwest of Baghdad, had underground cables running electricity from power stations located several kilometers away. The facility itself also lacked military defense systems or multiple guard fences. Instead, the facility was located inside a much larger military exclusion zone.[31]

An additional technique that Iraq employed to hide its WMD facilities is to place them underground. Indeed, a defector from Iraq reported that he had helped build over twenty secret facilities associated with Iraqi chemical, biological, and nuclear weapons programs. According to the defector, these sites were hidden in underground wells, private villas in residential areas, and under the largest hospital in Baghdad.[32] Other defectors have reported that a massive underground tunnel system, originally designed for a subway system, was converted to conceal WMD programs.[33]

U.S. intelligence agencies believe that Iraq continued to employ similar denial and deception techniques for its nuclear weapons programs after the 1998 expulsion of weapons inspectors. Assistant Secretary of Defense Paul Wolfowitz stated in January 2003, "We have many reports and other evidence of WMD material being relocated to agricultural areas and private homes, hidden beneath mosques or hospitals. Furthermore, according to these reports, the material is moved constantly, making it difficult to trace or find without absolutely fresh intelligence."[34]

It is a logical assumption that Iraq would have employed similar approaches to concealing its nuclear weapons and fissile materials if it indeed had restarted its nuclear weapons program after 1998. As we will see, however, while these techniques are effective methods for concealing weapons and weapon-related materials—and preventing their being eliminated in a first strike—they do reduce the ability to track and protect these materials, especially if the central government controls or military discipline were to weaken.

Iraq's Nascent Use Doctrine

Because Iraq never completed its efforts to develop nuclear weapons, we can only speculate about what its use doctrine for nuclear weapons would have been. But we may be able to obtain some insight into what it might have been like by looking at Iraq's use doctrines for chemical and biological weapons. Also, some important insights are revealed about a nascent use doctrine for tactical nuclear weapons in a recently declassified Iraqi military document seized during the 1991 Gulf War. As we will see, the use-doctrines for its strategic and tactical weapons appear to be quite different.

Iraqi Use-Doctrine for Strategic Chemical, Biological, and Possibly Nuclear Weapons

Iraq developed strategic chemical weapons, mainly for use on the medium-range Al Hussein missiles, primarily to be used to deter Israel. It also experimented with spray tanks on Mirage F-1 aircraft and remote-controlled MiG-21 jet fighters and other remotely piloted aircraft for delivery of biological agents against Israel.[35]

According to Iraqi officials, Iraq's use-doctrine for its strategic chemical and biological weapons appeared to be primarily defensive in nature. In various speeches, Saddam Hussein and other officials have indicated that the strategic weapons were to be used primarily in a second-strike capability. In 1990, when relations with Israel were at a particularly low point, Saddam indicated that he predelegated authority for certain military leaders to use the weapons in the event of a nuclear attack from Israel.

Iraqi officials have also indicated that during the first Gulf War military commanders were similarly given predelegation to launch the chemical weapons in the event of a nuclear strike by the United States, Israel, or other U.S. allies. McCarthy and Tucker note that seven fully fueled Al-Hussein missiles appear to have been retained as a strategic reserve during the war, probably for delivery of strategic chemical or biological weapons.[36] Moreover, according to information later revealed by Iraqi generals, the predelegation may have extended not only to use in response to a clear nuclear strike, but also in the event of a cessation of all communications with Baghdad.[37]

It is likely that Saddam may have viewed strategic nuclear weapons in the same manner: primarily as a defensive weapon to deter a WMD attack by Israel. Norman Cigar has argued, however, that Iraq viewed Israeli strategic deterrence as only applying because Israel was the only state in the Middle East possessing nuclear weapons. It is therefore possible that Saddam would have viewed a sufficient strategic arsenal as effectively neutralizing Israel's deterrent capability, thereby allowing Iraq to attack Israel.

Use Doctrine for Tactical WMD

Tactical chemical and biological weapons were to be used on the battlefield, and chemical weapons were used extensively in the 1980–1988 Iran-Iraq war. The Iraqi arsenal for chemical and biological weapons mainly consisted of artillery and mortar shells, short-range Scud-B ballistic missiles, aerial bombs, and air-to-surface rockets (mounted on helicopters).[38]

The Iraqi Army's Chemical Weapons Branch (CWB) was responsible for developing the operational doctrine for chemical and biological weapons, though the Ba'ath Party's Military Bureau probably had final authority over operational plans.[39] Iraqi military doctrine emphasized the tactical use of chemical weapons: "to demoralize and provoke fear in an enemy is as important as causing battlefield casualties."[40] To this end, they were used with great effectiveness during the Iran-Iraq war. Although the weapons did not kill large numbers of Iranian soldiers—it has been estimated that chemical weapons caused approximately 50,000 casualties and 5,000 deaths out of the estimated 1 million casualties during the war—Iraq's chemical weapons had a disproportionate effect on the Iranian military, creating widespread panic and demoralization among Iranian troops.[41]

Similarly, biological weapons were viewed as effective tactical weapons for delivering lethal or nonlethal doses to overburden the enemy and damage troop morale. The use doctrine for biological weapons, outlined in two documents published in 1984 and 1987, emphasized the use of biological agents to incapacitate soldiers, who would then require extensive medical supplies and treatment facilities, sapping the enemy's attention and resources. The 1987 document also may suggest using covert biological attacks behind enemy lines.[42]

Iraq's use-doctrine for chemical and biological weapons match fairly well with what now appears to have been a nascent use-doctrine for tactical nuclear weapons on the battlefield. This doctrine is outlined in a newly declassified document that was originally seized during the 1991 Gulf War. The document, entitled *Pamphlet: The Operational Use of Weapons of Mass Destruction; Volume 2; Part 2; Foundations for the Use of Nuclear Weapons in War,* is dated 1988. Because Iraq never acquired nuclear weapons, this use-doctrine was necessarily anticipatory. As such, it is not certain that the military would have adopted this use-doctrine. Nevertheless, as Norman Cigar notes, this is the third draft of the document, which shows somewhat refined planning for the use-doctrine. The document appears to have been created for distribution to the general military.

Overall, the Iraqi military thinking viewed nuclear weapons as a "practical warfighting tool rather than only as a doomsday deterrent with a largely political significance."[43] In fact, the document suggests that nuclear escalation would have been nearly automatic and was to be expected.[44] At most, mutual nuclear deterrence might have played a role in limiting where the contending sides targeted their weapons, but it would not limit their battlefield use. The document views nuclear warfare as quite probable and "even something not to be avoided, given the assumed advantages it could provide."[45] A major thrust of the document is that nuclear war is survivable and in fact could be winnable.[46]

The document discusses the use of nuclear weapons in both a defensive and an offensive mode, but "with a pronounced emphasis on the offensive."[47] A nuclear weapon was essentially viewed merely as a "bigger bomb" that could create greater casualties. As such, nuclear weapons would change the specific tactics used in a war, though the war would not change in its fundamental character: "Ordinarily, there is no clear distinction between nuclear war and non-nuclear war. . . . The nature of battle will reflect the traditional earlier concept." The document recognizes the potentially devastating effects from nuclear weapons and calls for limiting their effects, but it mainly emphasizes protecting friendly forces by constraining the geographic locations in which the weapons would be used. But it also emphasized tactics to recover from nuclear exchanges rapidly and capitalize on the disorder that they caused among one's enemy.

Command and Control

Because Iraq never successfully acquired nuclear weapons, it is impossible to say for certain what Iraq's command-and-control arrangements for nuclear weapons might have been, but it is possible to speculate on what some of the general features may have been based on Iraq's command-and-control arrangements for its other WMD and other available information.

Iraqi officials have reported that in preparation for the 1990 Persian Gulf War, Iraq filled thousands of tactical artillery shells with chemical agents and had approximately seventy-five warheads for longer-range, Al Hussein missiles containing chemical and biological agents.[48] As McCarthy and Tucker argue, Iraq had distinct command-and-control arrangements for strategic and tactical unconventional weapons.[49]

Given the unreliability of Iraq's other strategic delivery systems, Iraq's strategic unconventional weapons would probably have been delivered by the Al Hussein missile. The primary organization responsible for these missiles was the military's Unit 224, but the Special Security Organization (SSO)—

the main intelligence organization that oversaw the rest of the state security and intelligence institutions—appears to have controlled the chemical and biological warheads and possibly some missiles and launchers.[50] UNSCOM officials reportedly concluded from statements by Iraqi officials that for conventional missile operations, Unit 224's command link ran through the General Staff Headquarters, but for the unconventional operations it ran through the SSO.[51]

There were several storage depots and several additional "interim" storage sites for chemical and biological weapons. All warheads were reportedly kept within one hundred kilometers of Baghdad, presumably due to concerns of coups or rebellions. Some degree of centralized control over Iraqi chemical weapons was maintained by not forward-deploying these weapons to the troops until the order for their use was given.[52] Once the warheads were deployed, the First Missile Maintenance Battalion from Unit 224 retained physical control over the warheads at the various dispersal sites. There were reportedly no special procedures for launching missiles armed with chemical and biological weapons. "The Unit 224 commander would receive an order and a target and then communicate this information to field units. A warhead or warheads would be moved to one of the mating sites, uploaded onto a missile by Unit 224 troops, driven to a surveyed site onboard a TEL (mobile transporter-erector), and launched."[53]

Iraqi officials have reported that the authority to launch chemical and biological weapons was predelegated to certain field commanders during the 1991 Gulf War in the event of a first use of nuclear weapons by Israel or allied forces.[54] According to some reports, Saddam gave the SSO units orders to launch chemical and biological weapons against Israel if contact with him were severed and the SSO officers believed that the communications links were lost due to a nuclear attack against Baghdad.[55]

Although there is little information about Iraq's intended command-and-control arrangements for strategic nuclear weapons, the arrangements might have followed similar patterns. In order to retain survivability during a military strike, Iraq's strategic nuclear weapons would probably have been dispersed. It is unlikely that at least early Iraqi nuclear weapons would have had use-control devices. (Given the rush to produce a nuclear weapon before the Gulf War began, it is likely that Iraqi efforts focused more on the basic technical elements for producing a nuclear yield than on integrating any use-control devices into the warhead design.) As with the chemical and biological weapons, command and control over the nuclear warheads may have been maintained by not distributing the weapons to troops until shortly before they were to be used, or perhaps the SSO would launch them itself.

There is a little more information on possible command-and-control arrangements for tactical nuclear weapons. According to the Iraqi manual discovered after the 1991 Gulf War, the commander of the army would oversee the actual allocation of tactical nuclear weapons, distributing them to his subordinate corps on a limited basis, "either for a specific phase of operations or enough for several days' use."[56] Division commanders could then distribute them to their own subordinate brigades, although this measure is considered "an exception," to be undertaken only when the brigades are operating in isolation of "distant fronts" or in "movements of a fluid nature."[57]

Cigar notes, however, that there is a tension within the doctrine as to whether the launch and targeting authority would be centralized or decentralized. In some places, the document suggests that "final targeting selection and prioritization is to be the responsibility of the area commander and the operations and intelligence staffs," which suggests a more centralized decision-making process.[58] But in other places, the document suggests a decentralized command structure as a way to capitalize on rapidly changing contingencies on the battlefield: "The doctrine elsewhere puts a premium on 'decentralized command,' arguing that subordinate commanders need to have the ability to use nuclear weapons in order to take advantage of 'rapid changes' in a timely manner on a dispersed battlefield (pp. 42–43). In fact, emphasizing the need for a high tempo and flexibility in the attack for friendly formations (which may not be able to mass if, in turn, they want to avoid becoming a target of nuclear strikes), decentralization is offered as a solution, as long as the commanders' intent is understood by subordinates (p. 88)."[59]

Iraq and Deterrence

In the months leading up to the 2003 war, it was intensely debated whether Saddam was deterrable.[60] For example, John Mearsheimer and Steven Walt argued that the United States did not actually try to deter Saddam prior to his occupation of Kuwait. Instead, they argue, messages conveyed by the State Department and the U.S. ambassador, April Glasby, gave the impression that the United States would not intervene if Iraq invaded Kuwait.[61] Moreover, there is evidence that during the 1991 Gulf War Saddam was deterred from using chemical weapons due to clear U.S. threats of "terrible consequences" if he did. Mearsheimer and Walt therefore concluded that, since Saddam was deterrable, the 2003 war with Iraq was wholly unnecessary.

In fact, Mearsheimer and Walt argue that Saddam Hussein was not a "serial aggressor," intent on dominating the Persian Gulf. Instead, they argue that Iraq's attacks on Iran in 1980 and Kuwait in 1990 were instigated by perceived threats to the Iraq regime. In 1980, Iraq was responding to Iranian efforts to encourage Iraq's Kurdish and Shiite populations to revolt against the regime. And, they contend, Iraq's invasion of Kuwait was an effort to deal with Iraq's continued vulnerability after the Iran-Iraq war. "An important cause of Iraq's difficulties was Kuwait's refusal both to loan Iraq $10 billion and to write off debts Iraq had incurred during the Iran-Iraq War. Saddam believed Iraq was entitled to additional aid because the country helped protect Kuwait and other Gulf states from Iranian expansionism." Moreover, they note, Kuwait was producing oil in excess of the quotas set by the Organization of Petroleum Exporting Countries, driving down oil prices.[62]

There do appear to be some difficulties with this argument, however. First, it is by no means clear that the United States essentially gave Saddam a "green light" to invade Kuwait, as Walt and Mearsheimer contend. According to Kenneth Pollack, a former senior CIA specialist on Iraq, Tariq Aziz told reporters that at the time of the invasion, Saddam believed that the United States would not tolerate an Iraqi invasion of Kuwait.[63] Moreover, President George H.W. Bush stated in a letter to Saddam (delivered by Secretary of State James Baker to Foreign Minister Tariq Aziz on January 9, 1991) that the United States "would not tolerate" the destruction of Kuwaiti oilfields and threatened "the strongest possible response" if the oilfields were destroyed.[64] Iraqi troops nevertheless destroyed 700 oil wells in several Kuwaiti oilfields as they were pushed out of Kuwait.[65] As Kenneth Pollack argues, therefore, it does appear that the United States tried to deter Saddam in several ways and that the deterrence was ineffective.

Second, while available evidence does suggest that Saddam may have been deterred from using chemical weapons during the first Gulf War, he was not deterred from ordering the launch of thirty-nine Scud missiles against Israel, in spite of the possibilities of a massive Israeli retaliation.[66]

And third, Saddam appears to have had greater ambitions than just occupying Kuwait prior to the Gulf War, contrary to what Walt and Mearsheimer claim. As soon as Iraqi troops invaded Kuwait, U.S. intelligence agencies were alarmed by the rapid deployment of troops into positions that would have allowed a rapid invasion of Saudi Arabia.[67] Indeed, according to Richard Butler, the former head of UNSCOM, it was later discovered that Saddam had already produced car license plates that contained the phrase "Iraqi Saudi."[68] Saddam reportedly viewed nuclear weapons as a sufficient means of deterring the United States from intervening in such invasions.[69] According to Kenneth Pollack, Saddam's half-brother and former chief of intelligence, Barzan al-Tikriti, stated that Iraq needed nuclear weapons because it wanted "a strong hand in order to redraw the map of the Middle East."[70]

In the most likely scenario, if Saddam had acquired nuclear weapons and sufficient delivery systems (particularly ballistic missiles), he could have used them to deter the United States (and Israel) by threatening critical strategic targets (such as Saudi oilfields or Israel). This would have emboldened him to invade his neighbors or at least seize their key oilfields, particularly those in Kuwait, Saudi Arabia, or Iran, without fears of a significant U.S. response.

These scenarios cast some doubt on the optimists' contention that nuclear weapons would reduce international conflict. Such events would almost certainly have caused Iraq's neighbors (such as Saudi Arabia and Iran) to scramble to produce nuclear weapons themselves, if possible.[71] But it is unlikely that they would have been able to acquire these weapons before Iraq invaded. It is possible, in this event, that the United States could have attacked Saddam conventionally and used its nuclear weapons to deter Iraq's nuclear weapons. But this is not the "stability-instability paradox," where nuclear states only engage is small-scale war and are deterred from large-scale war by the presence of nuclear weapons—it would be a large-scale war, which would run serious risks of nuclear escalation.

These risks of nuclear escalation are underscored by the available information on Iraq's nascent nuclear doctrine. The recovered Iraqi document outlining a use-doctrine suggests that Iraqi military planning appeared to have a fairly low threshold for nuclear use. As Norman Cigar suggests, "Iraqi leaders have approached the possibility of a nuclear battlefield with an equanimity that has long disappeared in the West."[72] If true, then, this document has tremendous significance to the proliferation debate. Cigar assesses the implications of this document for the optimist position:

> The basic assumption of this view has been that the incipient threat of nuclear war would cause countries to consider any type of major war as too dangerous and costly in light of the potential to escalate to an unthinkable nuclear holocaust. However, the doctrine studied here suggests that Iraqi thinking on the nuclear issue has been at odds with this assumption, given Iraq's focus on nuclear weapons as a theater asset and Baghdad's apparent consideration of a lower threshold for their use than had been the case for the U.S. or USSR, at least in the later stages of the Cold War.[73]

Again, because Iraq has never successfully developed nuclear weapons, this issue will remain speculative. On the one hand, it is hard to see that Saddam would be willing to risk annihilation in a nuclear war, and his restraint from using chemical weapons during the first Gulf War (and possibly during the second one as well, if he did in fact possess them then) does appear to support this position. But troubling questions remain about the degree to which Saddam would have practiced the nuclear restraint exercised by other nuclear powers (such as the United States and the U.S.S.R. during the Cold War), given some of the risks that Pollack identifies, combined with Iraq's nascent use-doctrine—which assumed that deterrence is not stable and emphasized instead offensive use of nuclear weapons as the means of winning a nuclear war.

In addition to questions about whether it would have been possible to deter Saddam, there are other important issues that are worth raising about Iraq's nuclear program, including the alleged link between Iraq and terrorists, potential safety risks at Iraqi facilities, and potential risks of accidental, unauthorized, and inadvertent use.

Iraq's Alleged Link with al Qaeda

The Bush administration and Western intelligence agencies alleged that there were ties between Saddam Hussein and various terrorist groups, including al Qaeda. Administration officials argued for some time that Bin Laden and Hussein were, in some ways, natural allies. Although Hussein's regime was far from religious, the two leaders had a common interest in attacking the United States. But for much of the time that they were making these arguments, the Bush administration provided little evidence to support these connections. However, in February 2003, U.S. officials made their case somewhat more clear.

According to George Tenet, some connections between the Iraqi regime and al Qaeda had gone on since the mid-1990s: "Iraq has in the past provided training in document forgery and bomb-making to al-Qa'ida. It also provided training in poisons and gasses to two al-Qa'ida associates; one of these associates characterized the relationship he forged with Iraqi officials as successful."[74] But the clearest alleged connections appear to center on a terrorist cell headed by Abu Musab al-Zarqawi.

In his February 5 speech to the UN Security Council, Colin Powell outlined the U.S. intelligence information on this connection. Al Zarqawi is an alleged associate of Osama Bin Laden and reportedly ran a terrorist training cell in Afghanistan until the collapse of the Taliban regime in 2001. After that, he escaped to northern Iraq and established a training camp in the territory controlled by the radical Islamic group Ansar al-Islam. Al Zarqawi was also reportedly supported by the Iraqi regime. In May 2002, Zarqawi reportedly went to Baghdad for medical treatment, residing there for two months. In his speech, Powell stated that nearly two dozen extremists converged on Baghdad while Zarqawi was there, and established a base of operations. "These al-Qaida affiliates now coordinate the movement of people, money, and supplies into and throughout Iraq for [Zarqawi's] network, and they have now been operating freely in the capital for more than eight months."[75] But, if true, the connections may go deeper than just allowing the extremists to remain in Baghdad. Powell also maintained that the Iraqi regime provided al Qaeda operatives direct training in techniques for developing biological and chemical weapons.

Based on this information, Western intelligence agencies were quite concerned that Iraq might decide to provide WMD, possibly including nuclear weapons, to al Qaeda. In spite of this circumstantial evidence, however, these links do appear a bit tenuous. There are questions about the degree to which Iraq was actively assisting Ansar al-Islam, rather than just harboring terrorists. Documents have come to light since the 2003 Gulf War, however, that do appear to suggest at least some connections between Hussein's regime and al Qaeda. According to intelligence reports found by the *London Telegraph* in the headquarters of the Mukhabarat (Iraq's intelligence service), a meeting took place in 1998 between senior Iraqi intelligence officials and an al Qaeda envoy. The objective of the meeting was to establish a relationship between Baghdad and al Qaeda, "based on their mutual hatred of America and Saudi Arabia."[76] The meeting reportedly went so well that it was extended by a week and ended with arrangements being made for Bin Laden to visit Baghdad himself.[77] Moreover, in November 2003, an intelligence memorandum from Undersecretary of Defense Douglas J. Feith to the Senate Intelligence Committee was leaked to the conservative journal the *Weekly Standard*. This memorandum detailed fifty items of intelligence from multiple sources and agencies pointing to cooperation between Iraq and al Qaeda. The memo indicates that such cooperation included an Iraqi agreement not only to provide safe haven to al Qaeda operatives, but also to provide them with money and weapons.[78] If true, these intelligence items indicate a substantial, operational connection between the Ba'ath Party and al Qaeda. These reports do not, however, indicate whether Iraq was willing to provide any assistance to al Qaeda in developing WMD. It also remains quite questionable whether Hussein would have been willing to provide nuclear weapons technologies to fairly unreliable terrorists if Iraq had acquired these weapons.[79]

Safety Risks at Iraqi WMD Facilities

The safety and environmental standards of the Iraqi WMD programs typically fell far short of Western standards, and the Iraqi intelligence agencies even capitalized on these marginal safety standards to deceive Western intelligence agencies.[80] According to Jonathan Tucker, the Iraqis "were prepared to cut corners on worker safety and environmental protection to an extent unthinkable in the West."[81] For example, Tucker notes, a lack of biocontainment measures at the Al Hakam factory led many UNSCOM inspectors to conclude that BW agents could not have been produced at the facility, due to the high risk of contaminating workers and the surrounding environment—and yet the site nevertheless was used to produce thousands of tons of anthrax spores and botulinum toxin.[82] Tucker further notes that Iraq's chemical weapons program was just as cavalier toward safety and security, where soldiers routinely handled chemical munitions without protective masks or suits.[83] Although there are few specific details, similar safety deficiencies appear to have existed in Iraq's nuclear weapons complex. According to Peter Zimmerman, "even by Manhattan Project standards their precautions were primitive and inadequate to protect the majority of workers."[84]

Possible Risks of Accidental, Unauthorized, and Inadvertent Use

Since Iraq never acquired nuclear weapons before the Ba'athist regime was overthrown by the U.S. military operation, there were never any risks of accidental, unauthorized, or inadvertent use of these weapons. But it is possible to speculate on what some of these risks may have been by examining information on Iraq's nuclear program and warhead designs revealed by the UNSCOM inspections; Iraq's deployment and use-doctrines for chemical and biological weapons, particularly during the 1991 Gulf War; and evidence of ongoing deception and denial techniques employed by Iraq. Because Iraq could have employed different techniques as its nuclear program matured, however, this section can only raise potential difficulties based on extrapolation from available information.

Accidental Use?

There are serious concerns about whether Iraq's nuclear weapons would have been adequately tested or carefully designed to prevent accidental detonations. Prior to the first Gulf War, as they were rushing to develop a nuclear weapons capability, Iraqi weapons designers were still struggling with the basic warhead configurations. Iraq had reportedly only performed about twenty detonation experiments related to their implosion design by May 31, 1990, the last date referred to in UN-held reports. In the final months before the Gulf War, Iraq engaged in a rush program to develop nuclear weapons. Even after seizing the HEU at its two reactors, however, there was only enough fissile materials for possibly one nuclear weapon. No material would have been left over for testing the warhead design.[85] The Iraqi program was also reportedly experiencing difficulties in miniaturizing the warheads, making effective use of fissile materials, and enhancing yields.[86]

There are also serious questions about the safety of the actual Iraqi warhead design.[87] According to UNSCOM inspectors, Iraq risked producing a weapon that was highly vulnerable to shock and accidents: "The inspectors found out one other thing about the Iraqi bomb—it is highly unstable. The design calls for cramming so much weapon-grade uranium into the core, they say, that the bomb would inevitably be on the verge of going off—even while sitting on the workbench. 'It could go off if a rifle bullet hit it,' one inspector says, adding: 'I wouldn't want to be around if it fell off the edge of this desk.'"[88]

If Iraq had successfully acquired nuclear weapons, there would also have inevitably been concerns about accidental launches, depending on what operational plans the Iraqi military adopted. Due to risks of preemptive strikes, the Iraqi military might have dispersed their weapons and assembled the weapons in rapid-strike configurations, especially during crisis situations. We may never know what their specific operational plans would have been, however.

Unauthorized Use?

Again, depending on the military plans that Iraq adopted, there could also have been risks of unauthorized use. If the nuclear weapons were deployed to military combat units, it might have been difficult to guarantee that unauthorized use did not occur. For example, it is highly unlikely that the Iraqi designs for nuclear weapons would have contained any significant use-control devices, especially at first. Given the rush to produce a nuclear weapon before the first Gulf War began, it is highly unlikely that any efforts were devoted to integrating use-control devices into the Iraqi nuclear warhead design. Instead, the majority of Iraqi efforts focused on the basic technical elements for producing a nuclear yield.

Because Iraq's chemical weapons were generally not delivered to normal combat units prior to orders for use, however, some risks of unauthorized use were reduced, though the Iraqi use-doctrines did not always spell out the conditions for use. The Iraqi document outlining a nascent tactical nuclear weapons doctrine suggests similar command-and-control methods for nuclear weapons: troops would only be given weapons on a limited basis, "either for a specific phase of operations or for several days' use." But, as noted above, in certain places, the document recommends a "decentralized command," by which subordinate commanders would be granted license to use the nuclear weapons on their own authority to capitalize on rapid changes on the battlefield.[89] If this is true, it does leave significant questions about the possibility of unauthorized use of at least Iraq's tactical nuclear weapons.[90]

Inadvertent Use?

Because we do not know for certain what Iraq's operational plans or deployments for nuclear weapons would have been, it is impossible to determine what the risks of inadvertent nuclear use would have been. But some light may again be shed by looking at some of the risks of inadvertent use of Iraqi chemical and biological weapons. The predelegation of authority to use Iraqi chemical weapons may have increased some of these risks. As we have seen, SSO officers had been ordered to launch chemical and biological weapons against Israel if the United States or Israel used nuclear weapons against Iraq. Scott Sagan notes two incidents during the 1991 Gulf War that could have created precisely such a misconception. The first occurred on January 28, 1991, when the United States bombed a large ammunition bunker outside of Basra. The resulting explosion was so large that both the Israelis and the Russians contacted the United States to see if it had detonated a nuclear weapon. The second incident occurred on February 7, 1991, after U.S. forces detonated a BLU-82 "Daisy Cutter" bomb. A British commando reportedly announced on an open radio frequency that the United States had just "nuked Kuwait." If Iraqi generals had witnessed either of these incidents or heard the British radio transmission, they might have retaliated with chemical weapons.[91]

Moreover, if the reports are true that the preauthorization extended to circumstances in which all communications with Baghdad had been severed, the risks of inadvertent use could have been significantly higher. As Amatzia Baram notes, several different events could have led to a communications breakdown, including "occupation of Baghdad by Allied forces; a bombing raid that killed Saddam and other top Iraqi leaders; or perhaps even an effective siege of the city."[92] If Iraq had had nuclear weapons at the time and had followed similar predelegation procedures for these weapons, there could have been similar risks of inadvertent use of nuclear weapons. It must be noted, of course, that we may never know what Iraqi military plans would have been for the nuclear weapons.

Risks of Weakened Security during Political Upheavals

In the event of a preventive military strike, the controls over WMD weapons and related materials can become completely disrupted. In addition to increasing risks of intentional, unauthorized, or inadvertent use, such strikes can dramatically increase risks of thefts or loss of these materials. In the 2003 U.S.-led invasion of Iraq, the highest priority was to locate, destroy, or control all WMD and materials as soon as possible. Most importantly, this strategy was intended to prevent these weapons from being used against U.S. soldiers or their allies and to vindicate the Bush administration's decision to go to war to disarm Iraq. But many analysts have also feared "that the chaos of the Iraqi government's fall would give an opening to Iraqi scientists or security officials inclined to seize and sell special weapons for profit or revenge."[93] There were also concerns that inadequately guarded materials could be stolen by looters. The risks of unstable controls following a preventive strike were highlighted when the U.S. military found a large stockpile of unenriched uranium at Iraq's Tiawatha facility, which had been abandoned by the Iraqi Republican Guard. Three warehouses at the facility held over 2,500 barrels of uranium and had reportedly been completely unguarded for several days while looters had repeatedly raided the site. Since it was natural (unenriched) uranium, this material could not have been used in a nuclear weapon (it was Iraq's only stockpile of nuclear material sanctioned and monitored by IAEA). But the incident raised questions about other WMD stockpiles that might have been hidden in Iraq and were similarly unguarded.[94]

Even in less extreme political circumstances than invasion, however, there could be risks of thefts of materials. Although the U.S.-led invasion and subsequent regime change has probably put an end to Iraqi WMD programs for the foreseeable future, it was not always certain that there would be an invasion. If, instead, Hussein had been allowed to pursue his WMD programs unimpeded, or if a longer-term inspection regime had been put in place, Baghdad could have employed similar deception and denial methods to hide its WMD programs. But these methods could create serious difficulties in tracking and controlling the materials, especially during domestic upheavals.

For example, if current D&D methods are any indication, it is unlikely that many of the places that Iraq would hide its nuclear facilities, weapons, or fissile materials would have rigorous security systems. Extensive security at a mosque or hospital would surely be seen as suspicious. Moreover, if Saddam were to continually move his fissile material stockpiles, as he appears to have done with his chemical and biological stockpiles, it would be impossible to design measurement or alarm systems for these facilities.

Some of these potential risks are vividly illustrated by the examples of Iraqi deception and denial techniques listed above. For instance, in order to avoid arousing suspicion of the Tarmiya site, Iraq had no security fences or military defenses at the site because it was located within a much larger military exclusion zone. But the difficulties in controlling a given area increase significantly as the size increases. It becomes much harder to control the perimeter of these areas; while large areas would make it much more difficult for any detected intruder to reach any sensitive locations before being apprehended, it is much more difficult to detect and defend against intruders in the first place. For example, it would be prohibitively expensive for any country to install significant intrusion detection systems around large areas of many kilometers.

And while it is true that Hussein maintained a near-total control over his population—especially the more elite military units and the scientists involved in his WMD programs—the security of these weapons and materials depended entirely on Hussein's continued ability to maintain these controls. Given the fluidity of the situation in Iraq, it would be foolish to assume that this would always have been the case. If Hussein's central authority had begun to weaken at one point or another—an explicit goal of U.S. foreign policy since 1998—or were directly collapsed by foreign invasion, the risks of thefts of sensitive materials could have increased dramatically.[95]

Lessons for Other Proliferating States

Other proliferating states are going to draw important lessons from Iraq. Most obviously, they are going to see that the United States and key allies, such as Great Britain and Australia, are willing to engage in preemptive strikes against proliferating countries. This could mean that states will be less likely to develop nuclear weapons in the first place, since they would have seen the serious consequences that could result. On the other hand, they may be likely to draw almost the opposite conclusions. For starters, given the widespread public outcry and the failure of the United States to garner UN support for the military action, they may very well recognize how difficult it would be for the United States to garner support for further military actions against proliferating states. Moreover, proliferating states might see the need for rapidly acquiring nuclear weapons in order to deter the United States from attacking them.[96]

But there are other important lessons that proliferating countries will learn from the Iraqi case. They will note the highly publicized and quite successful Iraqi experience in concealing its WMD programs, facilities, and materials. Because these methods were so successful, it is quite likely that other states will tend to adopt similar denial and deception techniques. There will inevitably be some differences, of course. For example, as Jonathan Tucker notes, few other proliferators will have the financial and technical resources to match the extensive D&D techniques employed by Iraq, but he predicts that countries such as Iran and North Korea will employ similar methods, though perhaps on a smaller scale.[97] As we will see, this pattern generally holds true. But, as we will also see, some proliferating countries may attempt to stay more explicitly within the constraints of the NPT for a longer time while they acquire the expertise to develop facilities indigenously.

North Korea

The Democratic People's Republic of Korea (DPRK) has long been one of the most isolated and oppressive regimes in the world. Tensions between North Korea and South Korea and the United States have lasted since before the Korean War in 1959. Following World War II, the Korean Peninsula was officially divided into communist North Korea, which was supported by the Soviet Union and China, and South Korea, which was supported by the United States. Since then, intense hostilities have existed between the two countries along the Demilitarized Zone (DMZ), the 2.5-mile-wide, 151-mile-long demarcation between the two countries. After the collapse of the Soviet Union in 1991 and the reduction of support from the Soviet and Chinese regimes, North Korea has spiraled into a severe economic crisis. The regime was ruled by Kim Il Song until his death in 1994; since then it has been ruled by his son, Kim Jong Il. Although tensions have remained high throughout the regime's history, they have been punctuated by extreme crises, most notably in 1993–1994 and 2002–2003, which were sparked by the DPRK's pursuit of nuclear weapons.[98]

NPT Accession and the 1993–1994 Nuclear Crisis

North Korea acceded to the NPT on April 18, 1985, but did not complete negotiation of a safeguard agreement until April 19, 1992, after the United States declared that it would withdraw its nuclear weapons from South Korea as part of a global nuclear withdrawal. Initial inspections of North Korea's nuclear facilities began the following May to verify the accuracy of Pyongyang's declarations about its nuclear program. The IAEA conducted six inspections of North Korea's nuclear facilities from 1992 to 1993. A great deal of these inspections focused on North Korea's plutonium separation facilities. North Korea had declared that it had performed a one-time removal of ninety grams of plutonium from several "damaged" fuel rods in 1989, but IAEA chemical analysis of samples of this plutonium found that North Korea had extracted plutonium on four separate occasions, beginning in 1989.[99]

The IAEA findings sparked a crisis, beginning with the IAEA's request to perform inspections of two suspected waste sites on February 11, 1993. North

Korea refused to grant access to these sites and announced on March 12 that it was exercising its right to withdraw from the NPT, which would take place in ninety days (in accordance with NPT stipulations). Although Pyongyang subsequently agreed to suspend its withdrawal from the NPT on the eighty-ninth day after it made its announcement, it continued to constrain IAEA inspections of its facilities for the next nine months. In December 1993, IAEA director Hans Blix announced that IAEA safeguards were unable to provide any assurance that North Korea was not diverting plutonium into a nuclear weapons program.[100]

This crisis reached its peak in May 1994, when Pyongyang announced that it would remove the fuel rods from its 5-MW reactor, potentially providing enough plutonium for several nuclear weapons. The United States responded to these events by circulating a proposal to the United Nations Security Council to impose a new round of sanctions on North Korea. The United States was also considering a military strike to destroy North Korean nuclear facilities.[101]

In efforts to ease these tensions, former U.S. president Jimmy Carter met with North Korean president Kim Jong Il on June 16–17, 1994.[102] This meeting led to the 1994 Agreed Framework, which successfully eased the crisis for the time being.

The 1994 Agreed Framework

The core of the Agreed Framework was a deal by which the United States would provide a package of nuclear, energy, economic, and diplomatic benefits to North Korea in return for Pyongyang's freezing the operations and infrastructure development of its nuclear program. North Korea would freeze the operation of graphite-moderated reactors and related facilities (including a large fuel fabrication facility and small-scale reprocessing plant), halt the construction of several additional reactors and a major plutonium reprocessing facility, and allow the IAEA to verify these measures.[103] The United States, along with Japan, South Korea, and other countries, also agreed to provide two light-water reactors to compensate for the loss of the power output of the graphite-moderated reactors, and established the Korean Peninsula Energy Development Organization (KEDO) to oversee construction of the reactors. Prior to the completion of the reactors, the United States agreed to provide heavy oil to North Korea. Since 1996, the United States has provided about 500,000 tons of heavy oil per year.[104] North Korea was found to be in violation of this agreement in October 2002, sparking a serious nuclear crisis.

The 2002–2003 Nuclear Crisis

In October 2002, the United States accused North Korean officials of pursuing a secret uranium enrichment program in violation of the 1994 Agreed Framework.[105] According to U.S. intelligence agencies, North Korea received the enrichment technology from Pakistan.[106] In a surprise move, North Korea apparently admitted that it was continuing with its nuclear weapons program, though there have been some questions about whether it actually admitted its enrichment program.

In subsequent months, North Korea expelled IAEA inspectors and withdrew from the NPT,[107] restarted its 5-MW(e) reactor at Yongbyon,[108] and moved trucks into position to remove spent fuel rods, which store enough plutonium for several nuclear weapons.[109] The DPRK has also stated that it will restart all nuclear operations that were halted by the Agreed Framework. North Korea has claimed that it is restarting its nuclear reactors in order to produce electricity, but U.S. officials and nuclear experts have challenged these claims because the reactors are not connected to power grids and could therefore provide little electricity.[110]

In response to these moves, KEDO halted shipments of oil to North Korea in December 2002, and the IAEA found North Korea to be in breach of its NPT obligations in February 2003.[111] Diplomatic negotiations quickly reached an impasse over the crisis, with Pyongyang calling for bilateral talks between North Korea and the United States, and the United States calling for multilateral talks, which would also include South Korea, Japan, and China.

In clear moves to escalate the crisis, the DPRK began limited tests of surface-to-ship missiles. The United States responded by halting food assistance to North Korea (though it subsequently stated that it would resume shipments), deploying bombers in Guam, moving two aircraft carriers into the area, and reviewing war plans for strikes on North Korean nuclear facilities.

In late April 2003, China coordinated trilateral talks among the United States, North Korea, and China, to be held in Beijing. These talks were viewed as marking a breakthrough in the multilateral vs. bilateral impasse between Washington and Pyongyang. The talks broke down soon after they started, however, when a North Korean official told U.S. representatives that Pyongyang already possessed nuclear weapons, had completed the reprocessing of plutonium from spent fuel rods removed from a 5-MW reactor at Yongbyon, and would be willing to sell nuclear weapons or other nuclear technologies abroad.[112]

August 2003 saw talks resume, this time involving Japan, South Korea, and Russia, as well as China, the U.S., and the DPRK. The six-party talks produced no concrete results, as North Korea threatened to test and deploy nuclear weapons if the U.S. refused to enter into a nonaggression pact. Nevertheless, all parties involved confirmed their willingness to continue diplomatic negotiations in the future.[113]

In the following months, the DPRK claimed to have completed reprocessing all 8,000 of the spent fuel rods removed from its reactors, which experts estimate would produce enough weapons-grade plutonium for the eventual construction of roughly twenty warheads.[114] Intelligence analysts were unable to substantiate these claims and continue to argue over just how many bombs the DPRK is likely to possess. The IAEA asserts that North Korea has likely reprocessed enough plutonium to make two new nuclear bombs, while officials in the Bush administration believe that the North has reprocessed between an eighth and a third of its nuclear fuel rods into weapons-grade plutonium.[115] Charles Pritchard, who served as the State Department special envoy for North Korean nuclear issues until the summer of 2003, called it a "distinct possibility" that North Korea now has eight or more nuclear weapons.[116]

In one of the few positive developments in the dispute, in October of 2003, President Bush proposed a multilateral agreement in which the U.S., Japan, Russia, China, and South Korea would pledge to guarantee the DPRK's security in exchange for the DPRK's complete dismantling of its nuclear weapons program, shipping all nuclear material out of the country, and granting inspectors full access to all facilities. The North Koreans promised to evaluate the offer.[117] Diplomatic efforts thus appear to be gathering some momentum, but any resolution likely will have to contend with adamant disagreements from both sides over the appropriate sequence of concessions. This sign of at least the possibility of an eventual diplomatic breakthrough came at a crucial time, since the CIA informed Congress in August 2003, "We assess that North Korea has produced one or two simple fission-type nuclear weapons and has validated the designs without conducting yield-producing nuclear tests."[118] The report states that "North Korea would not require nuclear tests to validate simple fission weapons."[119] To date, however, no real diplomatic breakthroughs have occurred, and negotiations have remained at an impasse.

Primary Nuclear Facilities

Yongbyon

North Korea's key nuclear weapons facilities are located at the Yongbyon complex, located about one hundred kilometers north of Pyongyang. The Yongbyon complex includes a small research reactor, a 5-MW(e) gas-graphite moderated reactor, an unfinished 50-MW(e) reactor, a fuel fabrication complex, a spent fuel reprocessing facility, and waste storage sites.

Taechon

There is also a 200-MW(e) nuclear reactor under construction in Taechon, in the North Pyongan Province, but work on it was frozen under the Agreed Framework of October 1994. In February 2003, North Korea declared the intention to resume the construction of this reactor and the 50-MW(e) reactor.

Sinpo

As part of the 1994 Agreed Framework, the United States, South Korea, and Japan were constructing two light-water reactors at Sinpo. Although 2003 was set as the "target date" for completion of the facilities, construction fell significantly behind schedule. The concrete for the foundations was poured in August 2002, and the completion date for the first reactor was set back to 2008, barring further delays.[120] Construction on the facilities was halted following the revelations of North Korea's covert uranium enrichment program.

Suspected Facilities

North Korea is suspected of having constructed additional underground facilities as parts of its nuclear weapons program. One of the most significant of these facilities is the Kumchangni underground complex. In 1996, U.S. intelligence agencies detected extensive tunneling activities within Mount Kumchangni and suspected North Korea of constructing a possible nuclear weapons facility there. The site was believed to be large enough to contain a nuclear reactor or reprocessing facility.[121] After nine months of negotiation, the United States and North Korea reached an agreement on March 16, 1999, by which U.S. experts would be allowed to inspect the facility in exchange for 500,000 metric tons of food aid to North Korea.[122] Two visits to the site subsequently took place in May 1999 and May 2000. Administration officials declared that no evidence of nuclear activity had been found, but previous reports indicated that North Korea had removed equipment from the facility.[123] Some analysts have concluded that the DPRK had engaged in the tunneling activities at the site in order to raise concerns about a nuclear program and ultimately set the stage for additional economic and political assistance.[124]

But North Korea is suspected of having possibly constructed other secret enrichment and reprocessing facilities as well.[125] For instance, intelligence analysts reportedly do not know the location of North Korea's enrichment facility (or facilities), though they suspect it is buried underground.[126] There are also several additional underground sites in North Korea that are suspected of being part of the nuclear program, though it is not always clear what purposes they serve. (See table 6.1 for a summary of North Korea's nuclear weapons facilities.)

Ongoing Proliferation Efforts and Fissile Material Production Capabilities

In the April 2003 trilateral talks, North Korea claimed that it possessed nuclear weapons and had already reprocessed the plutonium from the spent fuel rods that were removed from the 5-MW(e) reactor, which would have provided enough plutonium for several more weapons. Although intelligence analysts disagree over how far the DPRK has progressed in its reprocessing efforts, there is little doubt that the North did begin reprocessing its spent fuel rods in mid-2003. U.S. intelligence detected emissions of the reprocessing byproduct krypton-85 gas from the Yongbyon reprocessing facility in July of 2003.[127] Sensors set up on North Korea's borders also detected traces of the gas that appear to have originated from a second, secret reprocessing facility, perhaps buried in the mountains.[128] The existence of such a second plant is yet to be confirmed. The possible existence of a second reprocessing plant greatly complicates the efforts of intelligence experts to determine the DPRK's total reprocessing capability. If the main plant at Yongbyon is fully operational, Pyongyang will be able to separate enough plutonium for approximately 1.3 nuclear weapons per month.[129] Of course, the existence of a second plant would increase this capacity.

North Korea restarted its 5-MW(e) reactor in February 2003. This reactor has a relatively slow irradiation rate, but would be able to produce approximately fifteen kilograms of plutonium after running for two years, enough for approximately three nuclear weapons. The spent fuel would need to be cooled for several months in a storage pond before it could be reprocessed.[130] The 50-MW(e) nuclear reactor at Yongbyon was about two years from completion when its construction was frozen by the Agreed Framework in 1994. It would still probably take the same amount of time to be completed. Once completed, this reactor would produce about 55 kilograms of plutonium each year, enough for eleven nuclear weapons per year.[131] The 200-MW reactor at Taechon was at least two years from completion when its construction was frozen in 1994, and would take several years before it could become operational. This reactor could produce approximately 220 kilograms of plutonium per year, enough plutonium for forty-four nuclear weap-

Table 6.1. North Korea's Nuclear Weapons Facilities

Name/Location	Type	IAEA Safeguards?
Power Reactors		
Sinpo (Kumbo)	2 light water, 1,000 MWe; under construction prior to 2002	Yes [a]
Yongbyon	Gas-Graphite, nat. U, 5 MWe; reactivated in 2003	No [b]
Yongbyon	Gas-Graphite, nat. U, 50 MWe; construction frozen until 2003	No [b]
Taechon	Gas-Graphite, nat. U, 200 MWe; contruction frozen until 2003	No [b]
Research Reactors		
Yongbyon	Pool-type, HEU, 4 MWt; operating	No [b]
Yongbyon	Critical Assembly	No [b]
Pyongyang	Subcritical Assembly	No [b]
Reprocessing Facilities		
Yongbyon	Partially completed; operations possibly reactivated in 2003	No [b]
Pyongyang	Soviet-supplied laboratory-scale "hot cells"	No
Uranium Processing		
Pyongsan	Uranium mining; status unknown	N/A
Pakchon	Uranium mining; status unknown	N/A
Pyongsan	Uranium milling; status unknown	N/A

Pakchon	Uranium milling; status unknown	N/A
Yongbyon	Uranium purification (UO2) facility; operating	Yes
Yongbyon	Fuel fabrication facility; possibly reactivated in 2003	Yes
Yongbyon	Pilot-scale fule fabrication facility; dismantled, according to North Korean officials	No
Suspected Facilities		
Taechon	Possible production of highly-enriched uranium, possible reprocessing and storage of plutonium; underground site	No
Hagap	Possible production of highly-enriched uranium, possible reprocessing and storage of plutonium; underground site	No
Kumchangri	Unknown; underground site	No
Pakchon	Possible production of highly-enriched uranium, possible reprocessing and storage of plutonium; underground site	No
Yongjo-ri	Possible uranium enrichment facility	No
Academy of Sciences	Possible uranium enrichment facility	No

Sources: Joseph Cirincione, et al., *Deadly Arsenals: Tracking Weapons of Mass Destruction* (Washington, D.C.: Carnegie Endowment for International Peace, 2002), p. 253; "North Korea Nuclear Profile," Center for Nonproliferation Studies, available on the Nuclear Threat Initiative website, <http://www.nti.org>.

Notes:

[a] As part of the 1994 Agreed Framework, the United States, Japan, and South Korea were building these light-water reactors to replace North Korea's other nuclear facilities. Construction was frozen in 2002.

[b] The IAEA verified a freeze in operations, in accordance with the 1994 Agreed Framework, until inspectors were expelled in 2002.

ons per year.[132] North Korea announced in December 2002 that it was resuming the construction of both of these reactors.[133]

More questions remain about North Korea's uranium enrichment capabilities. U.S. intelligence agencies believe that Pyongyang has been attempting to acquire an enrichment capability for at least several years. According to the Department of Defense, "in 2001, North Korea began seeking centrifuge-related materials in large quantities. It also obtained equipment suitable for use in uranium feed and withdrawal systems. North Korea's goal appears to be a plant that could produce enough weapons-grade uranium for two or more nuclear weapons per year when fully operational."[134]

There are few publicly available details about where North Korea's uranium enrichment facilities are located or exactly how advanced this enrichment program really is. Assistant Secretary of State James Kelly stated on March 12, 2003, however, that North Korea might be quite far along in this project: "The enriched uranium issue, some have assumed, is somewhere off in the fog of the distant future. It is not. . . . It is only probably a matter of months and not years behind the plutonium."[135]

If North Korea were to complete these unfinished reactors and achieve the capability to enrich uranium, it would have a large-scale fissile material production capability. Just the three reactors alone would be able to produce about 280 kilograms of plutonium per year, or enough for about fifty-six nuclear weapons per year, though it would take several years to reach this level of production.[136] It is currently unclear how much uranium the enrichment program would be able to provide once it is completed.

Ballistic Missile Capabilities

North Korea has a fairly advanced ballistic missile program, which would allow it to deliver WMD throughout much of Asia. It is also developing significantly longer-range ballistic missiles that would allow North Korea to strike Alaska and possibly parts of the west coast of the United States. It is also a major exporter of ballistic missiles.

The DPRK's primary method of delivering nuclear weapons would be via these ballistic missiles.[137] But there are some questions about the capability of North Korea to deliver nuclear warheads by its current missiles. Until North Korea achieves this capability, it would probably rely on aircraft or unconventional means (such as special operations forces, terrorists, etc.) to deliver the weapons.[138]

In 1999, Pyongyang announced that it would refrain from testing ballistic missiles for the time being, and it reconfirmed this moratorium in writing in 2000. North Korea restarted testing some surface-to-ship missiles in February and March 2003, though as of early December 2003 it had yet to test any of its advanced ballistic missiles.[139]

It is not known how these missiles are or will be deployed. But since North Korea's primary military plans call for rapid, overwhelming, surprise attacks, it is likely that WMD warheads and missiles will be deployed near each other.[140]

Scud B and C

North Korea has produced, deployed, and exported two versions of the Russian-designed Scud missile: the Scud-Mod B, which has a 320- to 340-kilometer range with a 1,000-kilogram payload, and the Scud-Mod C, which has a 500-kilometer range with a 700- to 1000-kilogram payload.[141] North Korea is believed to possess over 500 Scud missiles in its inventory.[142]

No Dong

The No Dong is a medium-range ballistic missile with a range of 1,300 kilometers and a 700- to 1000-kilogram payload, which would enable it to strike targets throughout the peninsula and most of Japan.[143] A more advanced variant of the Scud, these missiles use a storable but highly corrosive liquid fuel. North Korea is believed to have produced enough No Dong missiles for its own use, as well as for export to various countries, including Pakistan and Iran.[144]

Taepo-Dong I

In 1998, North Korea test-launched the Taepo-Dong I space launch vehicle missile, and the flight path passed over Japanese territory. The advanced, three-stage design of the rocket came as a surprise to the Western intelligence community. Even though its third stage failed to boost the payload into orbit, it indicated that North Korea was close to developing an intercontinental-range ballistic missile. With such a design, North Korea would be able to strike all of South Korea and Japan, as well as large portions of China and Russia. With a light payload, the three-stage missile could potentially strike the United States, though with very poor accuracy.[145]

Taepo-Dong II

North Korea is also reportedly conducting research on an additional, longer-range three-stage ballistic missile, the Taepo-Dong II, which would potentially deliver a several-hundred-kilogram payload to Alaska and Hawaii, or a lighter payload to the western half of the continental United States.[146] This missile has never been tested, however.

Denial and Deception Techniques

As the most tightly closed and isolated country on earth, North Korea naturally poses tremendous challenges to foreign intelligence agencies attempting to find out anything about the regime, let alone the status and locations of its WMD facilities. All information within the country is strictly controlled, and Kim Jong Il limits any sensitive information to a small circle to which U.S. diplomats are generally denied access. Moreover, with closed borders and no U.S. embassy in North Korea, there are few opportunities for placing intelligence operatives in the country.[147] Western intelligence agencies have therefore been forced to rely much more heavily on longer-range intelligence-gathering methods, such as electronic eavesdropping and satellite surveillance, to find out information about North Korea. And Pyongyang is a master of manipulating and defeating these intelligence methods.[148]

One of North Korea's primary ways of concealing its WMD and other weapons programs from satellite surveillance has been to hide them in numerous underground shelters. As Lynn M. Hansen notes: "No state in the world is better at tunneling into mountainsides and hiding things than North Korea. Tunnels hide virtually all aspects of their military forces, especially artillery and missile systems. Frequently dummy pieces of equipment are visible to confuse or deceive. [The DPRK] has one of the better understandings of U.S. overhead intelligence capabilities and is extremely proficient at implementing denial and deception practices."[149]

Military Strategy and Potential Nuclear Weapon Deployments

North Korea's military doctrine has centered on the notion of a massive surprise attack to overwhelm U.S. and South Korean forces deployed along the Demilitarized Zone (DMZ).[150] To achieve this end, the majority of its military force is "forward-deployed" along the DMZ and has the capability for carrying out rapid strikes with little advance mobilization, transportation, or preparation. Because North Korea's military cannot compete with the modernized U.S. and South Korean forces, Pyongyang's military plans have for twenty years emphasized the use of WMD to catastrophically damage U.S. and South Korean forces, allowing North Korea's outdated but extensive equipment and weapons to be effective.[151]

Pyongyang's military plans currently call for extensive use of chemical and possibly biological weapons to achieve this end. Any nuclear weapons that North Korea might have are probably reserved for use on longer-range ballistic missiles against off-peninsula targets and would probably be reserved until the regime faces certain destruction and defeat.[152] But as North Korea's nuclear arsenal increases in size, it "may be inclined to use some against South Korea early in the conflict to demonstrate its power and rapidly achieve some military objectives."[153]

Due to the necessity of maintaining secrecy, particularly in the event of a surprise attack, North Korea would almost certainly have its nuclear weapons deployed in configurations that would allow rapid-strike capabilities. Because transportation of weapons and other supplies to the front lines would almost certainly arouse suspicion, the nuclear weapons and their delivery vehicles would be likely to be stored together. North Korea's current missiles, including the short-range No Dong and the longer-range Taepo-Dong I and II missiles, all appear to contain a corrosive liquid fuel, however, so they may be unable to regularly store their missiles in a fueled state. They would more likely be fueled and mated to warheads only during crisis situations or immediately prior to use.

Command and Control

North Korea does appear to have a command structure in place for the security of WMD. According to Joseph S. Bermudez, decisions to use nuclear weapons would be centralized around Kim Jong Il and a small coterie of decision-makers in the DPRK leadership. All nuclear weapons, biological weapons, and special warheads for ballistic missiles are under the protection of the State Security Department and Political Security Bureau.[154] Given the tendencies toward a highly centralized command structure, it may be unlikely that the DPRK leadership would predelegate authority to its subordinates, except possibly during wartime situations or prior to an attack.[155]

North Korea appears to rely almost entirely on its authoritarian controls and security agencies to ensure the security of its WMD facilities, weapons, and military, rather than advanced security systems, alarms, military defenses, or advanced measurement and accounting systems. This is due in part to the prohibitive cost of these security systems,[156] as well as the fact that such systems would highlight the facilities and storage depots as targets. But, above all, such systems are simply unnecessary, given the total control that the regime has over its population. "Nuclear, biological, and chemical activities are organically secure and do not exhibit the telltale security measures apparent in Western or Third World countries (e.g., extensive multilayered barrier fences or fortified bunkers). In the DPRK, simple roadblocks, fences, and internal security forces are sufficient to ensure security."[157]

Safety Risks at North Korean Nuclear Facilities

Not much is known about safety risks at nuclear facilities in the DPRK, though there are a few pieces of revealing information on the safety of the facilities. North Korea is known to have experienced significant environmental and safety problems in the main nuclear weapons complex in Yongbyon.[158] For starters, the designs of the site did not take into account the seasonal flooding of the nearby Kuryong River. As a result, the basement rooms of the site are regularly flooded. In fall 1995, the basements of the critical assembly and the nuclear fuel storage facilities were completely flooded.[159] According to Jeffrey Knopf, IAEA inspectors and other observers "have expressed concern about the potential for accidents at the site and about the physical security of its nuclear materials. IAEA officials have also indicated that North Korea's radiation shielding systems are 'inferior to those of the advanced countries.'"[160]

Moreover, IAEA inspectors discovered in 1994 that the spent fuel rods that were removed from the 5-MW(e) reactor were improperly stored to prevent corrosion of the cladding around the uranium metal fuel. The fuel rods were stored in a cooling pond near the reactor, and North Korea reportedly did "little to slow the corrosion of the fuel cladding, or even to clean the water sufficiently to allow visual inspection of the fuel to check for cladding corrosion."[161] If the corrosion had created holes in the cladding, radionuclides in the uranium fuel would have escaped into the environment. In addition, under certain conditions, the uranium metal can ignite spontaneously if exposed to air, potentially causing a serious radiation accident. Due to concerns that North Korea would reprocess the spent fuel, the U.S. government sent a team of nuclear engineers to put the spent fuel in corrosion-resistant canisters.[162]

North Korea and Risks of "Loose Nukes"

If North Korea pushes forward with its fissile material and nuclear weapons programs, it could become a major supplier to terrorists or other proliferating countries. According to Richard Armitage, U.S. deputy secretary of state, one of the primary concerns about North Korea's nuclear weapons program is that it might sell nuclear weapons, fissile materials, or related technologies to "a non-state actor or a rogue state."[163] Indeed, North Korea has traditionally been a major proliferator of missile technologies, willing to sell these technologies to the highest bidder. It is quite likely that it would be willing to sell its nuclear technologies in a similar way, especially if it viewed such sales as necessary for the survival of its economy. According to Stephen W. Bosworth, former U.S. ambassador to the Republic of Korea, "It has no friends. It, in its view, has no meaningful connection with countries around it, nothing that it is not willing to sacrifice. And it has no shame, nor any guilt. Its only objective is regime survival."[164] If its survival were threatened, there is little reason to doubt that the DPRK would be willing to sell nuclear materials to the highest bidder. The North Korean official's threats during the April 2003 trilateral meeting that Pyongyang would be willing to export its nuclear technologies certainly drive home these risks.[165]

There is also a significant risk that Pyongyang would be unable to control its weapons and materials during domestic upheavals or regime collapse.[166] Given the central importance North Korea places on its nuclear facilities, the regime's strong central controls, and the small stocks of fissile materials and possibly nuclear weapons present in North Korea, we can probably assume that Pyongyang is currently able to maintain careful oversight over its nuclear assets. Nevertheless, if North Korea were to acquire larger stockpiles of fissile materials as it pushes forward with plutonium production and uranium enrichment, this could become a critical issue in the future. As with several other countries examined in this study, North Korea's nuclear controls could therefore become vulnerable during times of domestic instability. And, as we will see, North Korea is far from stable.

Possibilities of Severe Instability or Regime Collapse

North Korea has revealed many signs of a growing domestic crisis over the last decade.[167] It is desperately impoverished, large portions of its population are malnourished or starving, and tens of thousands of refugees have attempted to escape the country.[168]

As Scott Snyder has argued, there are several possible sources of regime-threatening instability in North Korea, including a weak and unstable economy; widespread famine and refugee flows; potential internal pressures; and international reactions to North Korea, including reduced foreign assistance.[169] Any of these factors, or a combination of them, could cause significant instability or even regime collapse.

Steady Economic Decline

North Korea has experienced a slow descent into economic collapse over the last decade, after the collapse of the Soviet Union and the end of heavily subsidized trade with both the Soviets and China. The DPRK's economic output is currently 40 percent of what it was in 1990.[170] As Stephen Bosworth has argued, the DPRK may not be far away from political collapse, since its economy has in effect already collapsed.[171]

Despite the clear necessity for opening up the economy, the regime is well aware that doing so would unleash "turbulent and unpredictable forces" that could easily spin out of control.[172] The regime has seen clearly the lessons from the political and economic reforms in the U.S.S.R. and, more recently, in China. In 2002, Pyongyang announced plans to introduce limited economic reforms. As part of these economic reforms, the DPRK also announced plans for creating a small, contained, capitalist economic zone and selected the Chinese businessman Yang Bin to oversee the district.[173] Local inhabitants would be removed from the capitalist zone, and the area would be fenced off from the rest of the country.[174] This plan lost steam, however, after China arrested Yang on charges of tax evasion and corruption in October 2002, and little further action appears to have been taken along these lines.[175] Moreover, what limited reforms the regime took in 2002 have only made the country's economic matters worse, by driving up inflation without increasing individual incomes or pay scales.[176]

Famine and Refugees

Ill-planned agricultural policies and droughts brought about a desperate famine in North Korea in 1995–1996. Recent foreign estimates suggest that more than 2 million North Koreans starved to death during the famine.[177] International aid workers have reported widespread malnourishment, including stunted growth and inhibited mental development.[178] Despite a good harvest in 2001, the nation still faces its ninth year of food shortages "because of a lack of arable land; collective farming; weather-related problems, including major drought in 2000; and chronic shortages of fertilizer and fuel."[179] Although the country has avoided a repeat of the mass starvation of the mid-1990s—mainly through massive international assistance of 1.5 million tons of grain annually—the population remains vulnerable to prolonged malnutrition and deteriorating living conditions.[180]

The widespread food shortages have caused massive refugee flows out of North Korea into South Korea and especially China. It is estimated that between 140,000 and 300,000 North Koreans are hiding in China.[181] But many refugees are stopped at the border and returned to North Korea, where they are severely punished, killed, or sent to one of North Korea's slave labor camps.[182] Refugee flows have reportedly increased in recent months, as Pyongyang's limited economic reforms in 2002 drove up the price of basic staples as much as 400 percent, putting food even further out of the reach of the general population.[183]

To date, the food shortages have not caused severe regime instability, because the population is too weak to mount significant protest against the government. Indeed, some analysts have suggested that the regime uses food as a weapon against the population to keep them weak and dependent on the state.[184] Moreover, the military and ruling elites have been shielded from the food shortages in part by siphoning off food assistance instead of allowing the food to reach the general population.[185]

Nevertheless, if the food shortages became severe enough, they could potentially begin to threaten the regime. Significant increases in refugee flows or food riots could cause the regime to engage in severe crackdowns on the population, sparking a "vicious cycle leading to further destabilization" or a general collapse.[186] Because the population is so completely crushed by poverty and famine, however, there are some questions about whether it would be able to mount any significant resistance, no matter how desperate the situation becomes.

Instability within the Elite and Military

In recent years, there has been accumulating evidence of growing dissatisfaction within North Korea's governing elite and military, the key pillars of support for the regime. Increasing anecdotal evidence suggests that Kim's rule is increasingly subject to private criticism inside North Korea's political elite.[187] This dissatisfaction among the elite is also demonstrated by a number of high-level defections in recent years.[188] Indeed, there have been reports of numerous defections of North Korea's military and scientific elite in 2002 and 2003, including key nuclear specialists.[189]

So far, Kim Jong Il has managed to suppress any direct opposition within the elite and military by maintaining strict supervision and by purging any potential opposing group. He has also managed to balance a number of competing elements within the elite, including the Party versus the Army, and the old guard versus the younger hopefuls.[190] But if this delicate balance is disrupted for any reason, "Pyongyang's power elite will slip into a centrifugal spiral, followed by internecine power struggles and the collapse of the regime."[191] For instance, if Kim were to disappear from the scene, through accident, illness, or any other reason, factional cleavages could spin out of control.[192] Even if Kim remains healthy and in power, however, other factors could disrupt the regime's delicate balance. By maintaining the divergent and competing elements within the regime to balance against each other, the potential for disrupting power cleavages will remain and will be increasingly difficult to balance indefinitely.[193] Moreover—and this may ultimately prove the most threatening for the regime's survival—if North Korea's economic and food situations were to worsen to the extent that they began to deny vital resources to the key pillars on which the regime's power rests, including the military, security systems, and the top echelons of the Party, there could be significant resistance to Kim's rule, resulting in severe instability, a coup, or a complete collapse of the regime.[194]

Reduction of Foreign Assistance

As Nicholas Eberstadt has suggested, one reason why North Korea's economic tailspin has not caused the regime to collapse is that North Korea has managed to extract significant foreign assistance from the United States, Japan, South Korea, China, and various humanitarian groups.[195] Increasing aggressive actions from North Korea could cause the various groups to cut off the assistance. Indeed, in the 2002–2003 nuclear crisis, the United States has pushed the other countries to take a tougher stance toward North Korea. If North Korea were to become completely isolated, it would quite likely collapse.

The United States halted shipments of heavy oil to North Korea after Pyongyang admitted it was pursuing a covert nuclear weapons program. On February 25, 2003, the Bush administration decided to resume food assistance to North Korea after a two-month hiatus, but at a reduced level and only under close supervision. The total amount of proposed food aid would be 40,000 metric tons, with a possible additional 60,000 tons later, if the food appeared to be going to the right places. This amount is down from 157,000 metric tons the previous year. According to Colin Powell, the U.S. government wanted assurances that the food aid would not be used to prop up the elite or the regime.[196] Some administration officials have reportedly also stated that they wanted to see China use its aid programs to pressure Pyongyang to give up its nuclear programs.[197]

It is fairly unlikely that China would take dramatic steps to isolate the DPRK, however, due to concerns that such steps could collapse the regime, sparking regional instability and causing massive refugee flows across the Chinese–North Korean border.[198] Nevertheless, China views North Korea's belligerent actions during the April 2003 meeting in Beijing to be a major embarrassment. Although the meeting failed to bring about any significant breakthroughs in the crisis, some analysts have argued that it will cause China to take a stronger stance against Pyongyang.[199]

There have also been significant differences between the U.S. and South Korean positions on North Korea. The South Korean position is in sharp divergence from the positions taken by the United States and even Japan, which is now taking a harder-line stance on the situation.[200] South Korea's former president, Kim Dae Jung, had long sponsored a "Sunshine Policy" toward North Korea, which emphasized engagement and humanitarian assistance.[201] Kim Dae Jung's successor, Roh Moo Hyun, was elected on a platform that called for expanding cooperation with North Korea beyond Kim Dae Jung's policies and that opposed economic sanctions or military strikes.[202] South Koreans have long been worried that a stronger stance against North Korea would only incite Pyongyang to take even more provocative responses and that a further isolation of the regime, including multilateral sanctions, could cause the regime to collapse—a result that could mean disaster for South Korea's economy. South Korea's position was thrown into question, however, due to aggressive actions taken by North Korea, including a missile test on the same day as Roh's inauguration, as well as Pyongyang's belligerent actions in arms talks and its declarations that it already had nuclear weapons.[203] If it is confirmed that North Korea does, in fact, already possess nuclear weapons, or if the regime takes steps to test or export nuclear technology, it will be increasingly hard for South Korea to maintain a policy of continued engagement with North Korea.[204]

Conclusions about Domestic Instability

The ongoing surprise is that, contrary to widespread, ongoing predictions, the regime has not collapsed yet. But it is also clear that the current system is not sustainable. Although some scholars have argued that North Korea would be able to "muddle through" for some time by depending on foreign assistance, even these scholars have suggested that the DPRK's "muddling through" period is reaching an end.[205] The ongoing strain of feeding the masses, while keeping the military satisfied, may be too much for the system to handle indefinitely.[206]

While the regime may eventually collapse regardless of international pressure, North Korea's recent actions have begun to solidify international opinion on the need for stronger stances against the regime. At the very least, North Korea's main providers of international assistance, the United States, China, South Korea, and Japan, may be less willing to support the ailing regime, making its survival even less certain.

If the communist regime does collapse, its controls over its nuclear materials could collapse as well, particularly given the type of central controls on which the regime relies. But a great deal would depend on the manner of the regime's collapse—whether it is a soft or hard landing. If it dies peacefully, integrating with South Korea, the risks of losses of nuclear materials would be lessened (though probably not eliminated altogether). If it is a "hard landing" brought about by sanctions, a military strike, or even a full-scale war with South Korea, then the risks of losses of nuclear materials could be very great indeed.[207]

Iran

U.S. intelligence agencies have long suspected Iran of engaging in a large-scale, covert nuclear weapons program. They maintain that Iran is attempting to acquire expertise on nuclear production and facility designs through an elaborate system of military and civilian organizations.[208] Although Iran ratified the NPT in 1970, Iranian interest in nuclear weapons (and other WMD) is believed to have begun in earnest in the 1980s during the Iran-Iraq War, after widespread Iraqi use of chemical weapons. The prospect of an Iraq armed with WMD continued to weigh heavily among Iranian defense planners after the Iran-Iraq War and even following the 1991 Gulf War, but Iran also likely viewed nuclear weapons as a means of deterring U.S. or Israeli attacks.[209] This latter concern has undoubtedly been a major motivation after the U.S.-led invasion of Iraq in 2003.

U.S. officials argue that Iran is trying to acquire the capability to produce both plutonium and highly-enriched uranium for use in nuclear weapons.[210] While Iranian officials have repeatedly denied the existence of any nuclear weapons programs, international suspicions led the IAEA to demand a comprehensive declaration of all nuclear activities in October of 2003. In the resulting report, Iran admitted to having conducted various uranium enrichment efforts, and shortly thereafter the IAEA issued a report revealing the existence of a covert Iranian nuclear program dating back to 1986. Iranian officials insisted that the program was solely for the development of peaceful nuclear technologies, but the United States and others contest this claim, citing for instance that the Tehran Nuclear Research Center produced small amounts of plutonium between 1988 and 1992.[211] Plutonium production is normally only associated with nuclear weapons production.[212]

Iran showed some willingness to respond to the heightening international concerns over its nuclear programs by reaching an agreement with British, French, and German diplomats on October 21, 2003, in which Iran promised to sign and ratify the IAEA Additional Protocols. The Additional Protocols would allow for unannounced inspections and unrestricted access to Iran's nuclear facilities. Iran also pledged to suspend uranium enrichment for an unspecified interim period.[213]

The revelation of Iran's secret program prompted the IAEA to issue a resolution on November 10, 2003, declaring that Iran has repeatedly breached its safeguard obligations under the NPT.[214] The resolution stopped short of referring the violation to the U.N. Security Council for punitive action, however, and commends Iran for its "active cooperation and openness" in agreeing to a new policy of full disclosure.[215] Furthermore, the resolution carefully articulates that there is no evidence to date that Iran's covert nuclear activities were part of a weapons program, but it proceeds to state, "given Iran's past pattern of concealment, it will take some time before the Agency is able to conclude that Iran's nuclear programme is exclusively for peaceful purposes."[216]

Nuclear Facilities

In many ways, Iran appears to be drawing important lessons from Iraq's and North Korea's denial and deception techniques for their clandestine nuclear programs. Like the other countries, Iran is believed to be using its declared nuclear facilities to acquire capabilities for developing nuclear weapons facilities on its own and has hidden several key nuclear facilities underground. As John Wolf, assistant secretary of state for nonproliferation, stated in April 2003, "Despite the professions of transparency and peaceful intent, Iran is going down the same path of denial and deception that handicapped international inspections in North Korea and Iraq. We have seen the pattern of cheat and retreat before—of begrudging compromises on process but obstinacy on real disclosure."[217]

Bushehr Reactor

In 1979, the revolutionary regime of Ayatollah Khomeini came to power and inherited two partially completed German-supplied power reactors at Bushehr. Khomeini froze the construction of these reactors once he came to power, and they were severely damaged by Iraqi bombing during the 1980–1988 Iran-Iraq war.[218]

In 1995, Russia and Iran signed an agreement to repair and finish construction on one of the Bushehr reactors, build an additional power reactor, and provide a heavy-water system to Iran, much to the frustration of the United States.[219] The United States managed to convince Russia to cancel several of these contracts and arrange for the removal of the spent fuel to Russia, but construction of the Bushehr reactor proceeded as originally planned.[220] It is estimated that the reactor will become operational in the second half of 2004.[221] U.S. intelligence agencies have argued that Iran would use this reactor to help it acquire at least the technical expertise for a nuclear weapons program, and possibly as a source for plutonium. Russia maintained that this reactor was allowed by the NPT, since Iran had signed the NPT and the Bushehr reactor would be under IAEA safeguards. In order to provide additional assurances, Russia would provide the low-enriched uranium fuel and remove the spent fuel from Iran. This last part of the agreement was thrown into question, however, when Iran announced that it would enrich uranium for the facility and construct a reprocessing facility to remove plutonium from spent fuel.

Natanz

In August 2002 an Iranian opposition group, the National Council of Resistance to Iran, disclosed information on two possible Iranian nuclear sites, including a facility located near Natanz, a town located 200 miles south of Tehran. In February 2003, the Institute for Science and International Security (ISIS) released satellite photographs of Natanz that revealed a possible pilot-scale uranium enrichment facility. According to the satellite images, the Natanz site consisted of three main areas: the first includes three large underground structures and an underground vehicle tunnel leading to the structures; the second includes six large buildings; and the third includes what might be the main administrative building.[222]

In February 2003, the IAEA announced that it would inspect the suspect facilities. The inspection took place at the end of February 2003 and revealed a large-scale uranium enrichment facility under construction. The Natanz site included a pilot-scale enrichment plant containing 160 centrifuges. More startling, in surrounding buildings, Iranian workers were constructing 1,000 additional centrifuges and had acquired the equipment for 4,000 more. Iran continues to maintain that these centrifuges are intended for civilian use, but there are serious questions about this claim. For example, environmental sampling discovered traces of weapons-grade uranium both at Natanz as well as at the Kalaya Electric Company just outside of Tehran. Iranian officials claimed that the traces arrived on imported enrichment equipment. Even if these claims are true, the discovery reveals further deception since Iran never declared its imports of these technologies, claiming instead to have developed its centrifuge technology indigenously.[223] What is even more suspicious about this discovery is the fact that Iran's 1995 Bushehr agreement with Russia established that Russia would provide the uranium for Iran's nuclear reactors. Once completed, Iran's centrifuges would allow it to produce enough HEU for roughly two nuclear weapons per year.[224]

Other Known and Suspected Nuclear Facilities

The National Council of Resistance to Iran also indicated that another site might be located near Arak. In the satellite imagery it acquired of the site, ISIS confirmed that the Arak facility appears to be a construction site for a heavy-water plant. Heavy water, which is ordinary water enriched in the hydrogen isotope deuterium, is used as a moderator in one type of nuclear reactor.[225]

Iran might be constructing additional facilities as part of its nuclear program as well. According to senior officials, Iran is constructing numerous underground sites, which are believed to be part of the nuclear weapons program.[226] Some of these facilities are undoubtedly the ones at Natanz, but there may be additional ones as well.

Closing the Fuel Cycle

Iran also officially announced in February 2003 that it would close its fuel cycle, mining uranium for its reactors and reprocessing the spent fuel afterward.[227] Although Iranian officials have continued to maintain that these steps would be solely for civilian use, U.S. officials believe that these steps are intended to allow Iran the capability to produce nuclear weapons.[228] Although Russia and Iran had apparently agreed that the spent fuel would be returned to Russia, Iranian officials stated in March 2003 that this agreement remained unsigned.[229] Moreover, the head of the Iranian Atomic Energy Organization, Gholamreza Aghazadeh, stated that Iran also intends to open a uranium-conversion plant at Isfahan, one of whose products will be uranium metal. This announcement prompted further questions about Iranian nuclear ambitions because the metal has few civilian uses but is an important component of nuclear weapons.[230]

Missile Capabilities

Due to significant assistance from entities in the former Soviet Union, North Korea, and China over the years, Iran has made significant progress toward becoming self-sufficient in the production of ballistic missiles.[231]

Scud-B and -C

Iran is believed to possess about 300 Scud-B missiles with a range of 300 kilometers and a 1,000-kilogram payload, and approximately 100 Scud-C

Table 6.2. Iran's Nuclear Infrastructure		
Name/Location	**Type**	**IAEA Safegaurds?**
Power Reactors		
Bushehr I	Light Water, LEU, 1,000 MWe; damaged by Iraqi air strikes, currently under construction with Russian assistance.	Planned
Bushehr II	Light Water, LEU, 1,300 MWe; damaged by Iraqi airstrikes. Facility remains unfinished, and project currently suspended.	Planned
Research Reactors		
Tehran	Light Water, HEU, 5 MWt; operating.	Yes
Esfahan	Miniature neutron-source reator, 900 grams of HEU, 27 kW, operating.	Yes
Reprocessing Facilities		
Tehran	Laboratory-scale hot cells; may not be operational.	No
Uranium Enrichment		
Natanz	Pilot-scale centrifuge enrichment facility containing roughly 160 centrifuges; unclear whether operating.	No
Natanz	Large-scale centrifuge facility under construction, may contain as many as 5,000 centrifuges when completed.	No
Tehran	Alleged uranium centrifuge research program, Sharif University of Technology	No
Uranium Processing		
Yazd Province	Discovery of uranium deposits announced in 1990.	N/A
Tehran	Uranium ore concentration facility; incapacitated.	N/A
Esfahan	Planned uranium conversion plant that could produce UF4, UF6, and UO2. China cancelled its assistance in 1997.	Planned
Suspected Facilities		
Arak	Possibly heavy-water production plant; under construction.	No

Sources: Joseph Cirincione, et al., *Deadly Arsenals: Tracking Weapons of Mass Destruction* (Washington, D.C.: Carnegie Endowment for International Peace, 2002), p. 268; David Albright and Corey Hinderstein, "Iran Building Nuclear Fuel Cycle Facilities: International Transparency Needed," *ISIS Issue Brief*, December 12, 2002, <http://www.isis-online.org/publications/iran/iranimages.html>.

missiles with a 500-kilometer range. With assistance from North Korea, Iran has acquired the capability to manufacture Scuds.[232]

CSS-8

Iran purchased approximately 200 Chinese-supplied CSS-8 short-range missiles in 1989. These missiles have an estimated range of about 150 kilometers and a payload of 190 kilograms.[233]

Shahab-III, -IV, and -V

Iran has also tested the medium-range Shahab-III in July 1998 and July 2000. This missile is a derivation of the North Korean No Dong missile, with an estimated range of 1,300 kilometers and a payload of approximately 750 kilograms. Iran is now believed to have the capability to deploy limited numbers of the Shahab-III.[234] In addition, Iranian officials have publicly acknowledged the development of a longer-range Shahab-IV and have mentioned a Shahab-V missile.[235]

Possible Deployments and Command-and-Control Structure

As Iran nears the threshold for nuclear weapon production, it will inevitably need to begin thinking about command-and-control systems, deployment options, and use-doctrines for its nuclear weapons. Some light may be shed on these issues by examining the ways that Iran appears to be addressing them for its other weapons of mass destruction.

Gregory Giles notes that Iran's acquisition and use of chemical weapons during the 1980–1988 Iran-Iraq War was largely defensive in nature, and suggests that Iran may not be the first to use WMD during a conflict, but may opt instead for a second-strike posture.[236] But there is also some evidence that the military doctrine of Iran's Islamic Revolutionary Guard Corps (IRGC), the military organization responsible for acquiring, controlling, and using chemical and biological weapons, may allow for first use of chemical weapons. "The IRGC's emerging maritime doctrine for chemical and biological weapons apparently is intended as an asymmetric escalation option, either to preempt or respond to a high-technology conventional attack. The prospect that the IRGC might use chemical and biological weapons at sea before the actual onset of hostilities with the United States cannot be dismissed."[237]

The IRGC is an organization that was established as a highly trained corps that could more reliably handle Iran's chemical and biological weapons than the regular military corps. It is possible that, were Iran to acquire nuclear weapons, the IRGC might be given responsibility for controlling these weapons. Or, as Giles notes, "Iran's clerical leadership might create a new organization for nuclear weapons—one that is more professional and reliable than either the regular military or the IRGC."[238]

Although the size of Iran and the regular army units deployed along the borders might allow the country to maintain a more centralized system for controlling its WMD, increasing threats of preemptive strikes by the United States or Israel would probably require Iran to disperse its WMD capabilities and adopt a more "delegative" command-and-control system.[239] Such a system could increase "the risk of inadvertent escalation resulting from false warnings or unauthorized use—that is, the system could 'fail deadly.'"[240] Some of these risks could be mitigated somewhat, however, if Iran were to create a more disciplined organization responsible for controlling the country's nuclear weapons.[241]

The extent of these risks will depend on the systems that Iran chooses if and when it acquires nuclear weapons. Nevertheless, because the risks of preemptive strikes by other states has probably increased, particularly from the United States, Iran may be forced to emphasize survivability over centralized control in its WMD deployments.

Potential for Significant Political Instability

The Iranian Islamic Revolution led by the Ayatollah Khomeini in 1979 saw the Islamic clergy seize control of all political, judicial, educational, and media institutions and systematically silence all opposition.[242] The eight-year war with Iraq that followed, from 1980–1988, devastated the Iranian people and their economy, and by the time Khomeini died in 1989, many initial supporters of the revolution had become disillusioned with the excesses of the Islamic regime.[243]

This disillusion persists today and has materialized into a viable reform movement as "attempts by the ruling clergy to control personal and public space and suppress dissent in the name of Islam have been countered by the rise of a middle class that demands greater liberalization and reforms."[244] Dispute between the dissatisfied reformists who seek popular sovereignty within a more open society and the unelected conservatives who desperately cling to their power under the current system has created substantial sociopolitical instability. The potential for this instability to erupt into a popular uprising led Director of Central Intelligence George Tenet to declare in February 2003, "we take the prospect of sudden, regime threatening unrest seriously and continue to watch events in Iran with that in mind. For now, our bottom line analysis is that the Iranian regime is secure, but increasingly fragile."[245]

The potential for domestic upheaval in Iran thus appears substantial. The election of the reformist Mohammad Khatami as president in 1997 and his reelection in 2001, both with a majority of some 70 percent,[246] indicate the mounting discontent of the Iranian people with life under the tight grip of conservative clerical rule. Since his election, however, Khatami's ability to effect significant reform has been constrained. The conservative Supreme Leader Ayatollah Sayyed Ali Khamenei and conservative clerical councils retain ultimate authority over most issues and have thus impeded his efforts. Over the past five years, the clash between the entrenched conservatives and increasingly popular reformists has been marked by protests that could erupt into popular revolt in the foreseeable future.

Economic Stagflation and Increasing Public Frustration

Iran's worsening economic crisis has inflamed public discontent and increased pressures for reform. A soaring inflation rate of over 30 percent, a stagnant market, and a recession compounded by low oil prices have dragged the economy to a near standstill.[247] Meanwhile, the state's efforts to ameliorate the crisis have failed, and its mismanagement of the country's resources "is now resulting in a potentially wealthy nation sliding into poverty and decline."[248] The current regime's economic incompetence has particularly alienated Iran's younger generation (65 percent of the population is under thirty), many of whom were already dissatisfied with the government's strict social controls.[249]

The election of Khatami brought high hopes both for reformists, who hoped he would help to alleviate economic woes, and for conservatives, who hoped his election would calm the dissatisfied youth. Khatami's inability to boost the faltering economy during his seven-year tenure, however, has dashed these hopes and led many Iranians to accuse the president of neglecting economic reforms in his quest to liberalize politics.[250] In fact, experts have argued that "even if Khatami showed leadership qualities and expertise in the economic area, it is doubtful whether he would be able, or be permitted, to carry out the necessary reforms."[251] Rescuing Iran's economy necessitates fundamental structural changes that would require conservatives in power to relinquish their tight grip on economic institutions and allow widespread privatization.[252] Since these conservatives refuse to accept the necessary reforms, the current economic crisis, discontent among the population, and resulting domestic instability are likely to persist.

Election of Khatami and the Reform Movement

Khatami's election came as a shock to the Iranian regime. The victory of a reformist candidate was highly unlikely given that the Guardian Council of Elections, controlled by conservative clerics, must approve all candidates before they may appear on the ballot.[253] Due to Khatami's relative political obscurity at the time, however, the Guardian Council failed to consider him a serious threat to win the election and thus included him on the ballot despite his reformist views.[254] As the only reformist on the ballot, Khatami succeeded in drawing support from a wide array of groups discontent with the ruling establishment, and despite staunch efforts by hard-line factions to tarnish his reputation, the widespread public disillusionment propelled him to victory.[255]

Khatami's popularity has emerged largely from his moderate position that the Islamic Iranian state must be reformed but not disbanded.[256] He holds that Iran must remain an Islamic Republic but must become "gentler, kinder, and more tolerant and transparent."[257] Unlike the radical reformists that have comprised the majority of opposition groups since the 1979 revolution, Khatami leads a reform movement that seeks to maintain a system of clerical rule while developing a civil society based on the rule of law and an open political system. The vehement opposition that these proposed reforms have encountered stems from the decreased power that they would necessarily bring to conservatives who currently control the economy, judiciary, and armed forces.[258] A stark ideological divide also separates the conservative opposition from the reformists. A key tenet of the dispute is the extent to which the Supreme Leader should wield political power from his position as spiritual leader in a modern nation-state that invests its authority in the constitution.[259] Reformists argue for popular sovereignty, while conservatives insist on the right of the clerics to rule all aspects of society. Adding to the ideological divide is Khamenei's view of liberalism and globalization as subversive forces that must be resisted through an Iranian isolationist posture. Khatami and his reformists, on the other hand, assert that engagement and dialogue with the West are essential in an era of rapid modernization.[260] The clash between reformists and conservatives over these central issues has "polarized [Iran's] politics and society to an unprecedented and dangerous level,"[261] and the conflict has sparked numerous protests.

Protests in 1999

Since Khatami's election, Iranian hardliners have taken drastic measures to curb the growth of the surging reform movement and have repeatedly resorted to violence against reform activists. In 1998, members of the Ministry of Intelligence, under the direct control of Khamenei, assassinated several opposition activists, while numerous others were arrested and imprisoned.[262] Moreover, conservative forces have repeatedly attacked the liberal newspapers that have emerged to challenge the traditionally state-controlled media, resulting in the closure of over thirty publications in the latter part of 2002 alone due to their alleged opposition to Islam and the Islamic Republic.[263] In the summer of 1999, when Khatami's most supportive publication, the daily *Salam,* was shut down, students reacted with peaceful protests. Vigilante groups and security forces under Khamenei's control violently broke up the demonstrations, attacking students in their dormitories and killing two. This excessive display of force by conservative forces prompted mass protests and riots that offered a vivid portrait of Iran's increasing domestic unrest.

Protests in 2002

In late 2002, tensions between reformists and conservatives sparked mass protests that again brought Iranian society ever closer to widespread domestic revolt. This time, the catalyst was the death sentence of popular reformist scholar Hashem Aghajari on charges of blasphemy after he gave a speech supporting the separation of church and state and arguing for reform within the clerical hierarchy.[264] Outraged students gathered outside the Amir Kabir University in Tehran to protest the decision and to voice their discontent with the conservative regime and President Khatami's continued inability to implement promised reforms.[265] The students demanded a referendum to address Iran's future political status, an effort that hardliners assailed as an attempt to undermine the Islamic system and replace it with a secular government.[266] The protests eventually erupted into violent clashes with conservative forces, with both sides using tear gas and over 200 students and monarchists being arrested.[267]

Following the confrontation, students for the first time received a massive showing of popular support when over 10,000 demonstrators gathered outside Tehran University to voice solidarity with the students' cause.[268] This demonstration likewise resulted in violence as police resorted to beatings and pepper spray in attempts to quell the crowd.[269] Similar gatherings that followed in five other major cities[270] brought Iran perilously close to domestic upheaval once again.

February 2003 Elections

The municipal elections held on February 28, 2003, offered a powerful illustration of just how disillusioned the public has become with the failure of recent reform efforts. While the reformists officially lost the election to the somewhat obscure, moderately conservative Abadgaran Party, the elections proved a decisive victory for no one, as the official news agency IRNA reported a voter turnout of less than 25 percent in the capital and only slightly higher elsewhere.[271] Other sources, in fact, cite the turnout in Tehran as actually less than 12 percent of the electorate.[272] Regardless of the exact statistics, Iranian voters succeeded in powerfully displaying their disenchantment with the current system that has failed to produce reforms despite the electorate's repeated reform mandate in recent years.

Conclusions on Risks of Instability in Iran

Iranians clearly displayed their apathy toward the 2003 elections with their record low turnout, but the implications of this apathy regarding the extent of public unrest and the potential for domestic upheaval remain disputed. Some foreign diplomats inside Iran and even some Iranian reformists have argued that the hardliners have mollified some segments of the society by granting meager reforms, such as allowing couples to hold hands in public and letting women wear coats that show their figures.[273]

It may be true that such minor reforms temporarily calmed some Iranians' discontent; however, they have proven ineffective pacifiers. On June 10, 2003, the streets of Tehran again erupted with demonstrations demanding political reforms. Many of the demonstrators called for the death of Supreme Leader Khamenei, and some even demanded that President Khatami resign due to his inability to promote reform. The protests quickly swelled to become the largest and most violent to date, with unrest and sporadic violence persisting for over a week. Once again, conservative vigilantes, many belonging to the Islamist organization Ansar Hezbollah, sought to crack down on the demonstrations, beating pedestrians with clubs, firing machine guns into the air, wielding knives, and even breaking into university dormitories to attack sleeping students.[274] The widespread turmoil led Khamenei to issue a warning to protesters that continued disruptions would lead to a harsh response by security forces similar to that of July 1999, which left two students dead.[275]

Less than a month later, on July 9, 2003, demonstrations again swept the country to commemorate the anniversary of the 1999 crackdown and to call for increased freedom. The scale of the demonstrations is difficult to determine, however, because a press ban issued by the government in anticipation of the protests stifled most foreign press coverage. State-owned Iranian news sources ignored the unrest, but other Iranian news outlets reported extraordinarily broad disturbances, including numerous large clashes and violent attacks on several police headquarters.[276] Accounts indicate that security forces again resorted to firing shots in the air and releasing tear gas to disperse the crowds.[277] The government also deployed the armed forces to protect government buildings, and military helicopters flew over the capitol in an attempt to intimidate the demonstrators.[278]

These frequent and powerful displays against the Islamic regime clearly illustrate the continued dissatisfaction and volatility of the populace. The showing of apathy in recent elections thus most likely indicates frustration with the inability of elected reformists to prompt change rather than an increasingly widespread lack of interest among Iranians concerning their government. The fact remains that "the accumulation of grave domestic problems, including unemployment, inflation, economic mismanagement, corruption and restrictive social policies, have brought the Islamic republic to the verge of breakdown,"[279] and Iranians' tolerance continues to wane. Although the mullahs have managed to maintain control so far, it is clear that their hold on power is slipping.

It remains to be seen if this widespread public dissatisfaction will succeed in consolidating public opinion against the regime. The possibility remains, after all, that the conservatives could launch a comprehensive crackdown on the reform movement, since the regime has already shown its willingness to call on the military to quell demonstrations. Such a crackdown could succeed in crushing the reform movement, but it could likewise create a cycle of violence leading to chaos and completely destabilizing the regime. Finally, violent repressive actions against the reformists could create an impetus for an intervention by the United States or other major powers. In fact, reports have already emerged that, given the emerging crisis over Iran's nuclear program, the United States may increase its efforts to destabilize the regime, possibly including funding opposition groups in Iran and launching covert operations.[280] What is critical for this study, however, is that few would be confident that the Iranian regime will remain stable over the coming years. Thus, the risks of domestic instability weakening central controls over nuclear weapons and fissile materials are extremely relevant to the case of Iran.

Conclusions

Although it is impossible to determine with certainty what the specific risks might be in the newly proliferating countries, the available information does reveal a number of troubling trends.

Preventive Strikes

The U.S.-led toppling of Saddam Hussein's Ba'ath regime in 2003 obviously highlights the issue of preventive strikes against proliferating countries. And the United States has not ruled out the possibility of preventive strikes against North Korea or Iran. These events clearly support Scott Sagan's predictions that the spread of nuclear weapons could actually increase international instability by creating incentives for preventive strikes. Although there are ongoing questions about what Iraq's WMD capabilities actually were before the second Gulf War, and there were justifications for the war other than Iraq's WMD programs, it is highly unlikely that the United States would have invaded Iraq without the strong conviction that Saddam was concealing the WMD. Moreover, because preemption will be a concern for Iran and North Korea, they will use various deception and denial techniques to hide their programs and weapons, and they will have much stronger incentives to deploy their weapons in launch-ready conditions, potentially creating increased risks of accidental, unauthorized, or inadvertent use.

Potential Risks of Accidental, Unauthorized, and Inadvertent Use

It is too soon to determine what the specific risks would be in these areas, since Ba'athist Iraq never successfully acquired nuclear weapons, Iran has not acquired them yet, and North Korea may not have yet acquired reliable delivery systems for its weapons. The evidence surveyed here does reveal some concerns in these areas, however.

First, due to the risks of preventive strikes, all three countries have strong incentives to disperse and conceal their weapons. They do appear to employ somewhat different approaches to hiding their weapons, though. Iraq reportedly moved its chemical and biological weapons frequently, though most of them were stored in the near proximity of Baghdad to maintain control during potential uprisings. North Korea, on the other hand, largely employs caves to hide its unconventional weapons. Less is known about Iran's systems for concealing and dispersing its weapons of mass destruction. There have, however, been reports that "Iran has created shelters and tunnels in its coastal areas which it could use to store Scud and other missiles in hardened sites and reduce their vulnerability to air attack."[281] Presumably, it has adopted similar techniques for its WMD stockpiles as well.

All three countries do appear to have maintained fairly strong controls over their unconventional weapons, relying primarily on internal security systems to do so. There was some contrary evidence on this, however. Saddam Hussein appears to have given some form of preauthorization for chemical weapons during the first Gulf War, and there were discrepancies on the extent to which military officials in the field would have had authorization to use nuclear weapons in the battlefield.

Some evidence suggests that the necessity of maintaining central control would prevent the countries from deploying their weapons. All three counties are or were developing missiles as their preferred WMD delivery systems, but given the types of missiles (all use SCUD derivatives), they would be unable to store them in a fully fueled condition for very long periods without needing to clean and refuel them. But, as we have seen, all three countries have strong incentives for acquiring the capabilities for first use, or preemptive strikes. For instance, if the information on Iraq's operational plans for tactical nuclear weapons is correct, Iraqi military planners viewed nuclear weapons as an effective means for war fighting. Gregory Giles also pointed to evidence that Iran's chemical weapons could be employed in preemptive strikes. And North Korea's military doctrine explicitly calls for rapid, heavy casualties, delivered by an overwhelming first strike with both conventional and unconventional weapons.

Finally, there are serious questions about the safety of warhead designs for the nuclear weapons in these proliferating states, potentially leading to concerns about accidental detonations. Given the risks of preemption, all three countries have or had extremely strong incentives to develop their weapons rapidly, possibly emphasizing the acquiring of deliverable nuclear weapons rather than careful safety designs. Iraq's reportedly unsafe nuclear weapon design clearly helps confirm this concern.

Safety Risks

In addition, we have seen solid evidence supporting Lewis Dunn's contention that newly proliferating countries may marginalize safety in their push to acquire nuclear weapons capabilities. Iraq and North Korea have both had serious safety problems in their nuclear facilities. All assessments of their nuclear facilities have indicated that their safety standards fall far short of Western standards, creating risks of environmental contamination and exposure of workers to radiation.

Of the three countries, there is the least information on the safety of Iran's nuclear programs. There are, however, reports of lax safety standards at Iran's main chemical weapons storage site, which caused the deaths of hundreds of workers.[282] Since Iran has received more directed assistance from Russia in constructing its nuclear facilities, it might have fewer difficulties in this area. There are some remaining questions about the safety of the uranium enrichment plants. Overall, there are fewer safety concerns about enrichment facilities, since these sites cannot have massive meltdowns like nuclear reactors, but they can still cause serious environmental and health risks.[283] The IAEA conducted inspections of the facilities at Natanz and Arak in 2003 both to assess the safety conditions at the sites and to determine whether Iran was violating the NPT. There is no publicly available information on whether the IAEA detected any safety problems, however.

Weakened Controls During Political Instability

The greatest potential risks center on the risks of breakdowns in central control during political upheavals. None of the countries studied in this chapter—Iraq, Iran, and North Korea—had or have very promising prospects for political stability. These risks, coupled with their denial and deception techniques, create unique risks of losses of nuclear materials. As we have seen in the case of Iraq—the most extreme case of political instability—the overthrow of a regime can cause a dramatic severing of central controls. This is in some way obvious, of course, since the U.S.-led invasion removed what had been the pillar of central control in Iraq for several decades, the Ba'ath Party. The controls over Iraqi nuclear facilities essentially evaporated overnight as Republican Guard forces abandoned the sites when U.S. forces approached. Since preventive strikes are a continuing possibility with other proliferating countries, potentially including Iran, North Korea, Syria, and even Libya (if it is determined that Moammar Gaddafi has not completely abandoned his nuclear ambitions), further proliferation—and the responses to the proliferation—could significantly increase risks that nuclear materials could be stolen and sold on the black market.

What is equally important from the Iraqi case is the widespread looting that took place after the Ba'ath regime fell. If other proliferating regimes were to collapse, either from external military invasion or by indigenous forces, similar looting could result. Currently, the most likely proliferators, such as North Korea, Iran, Syria, and Libya, all have authoritarian regimes that have long oppressed their populations. Sudden release from these authoritarian controls would be likely to spark similar looting.

As we have seen in Iran and North Korea, there are very real possibilities of precisely such instability. Widespread political upheavals are a very real near- to mid-term possibility in each country. In North Korea, the regime has long teetered on the brink of collapse, as its economy experienced a slow spiral into insolvency. The pillars of stability in the regime, including the military and the elite, have so far stayed in place, but if the economic difficulties and food shortages begin to affect them as well, the regime will be finished. Moreover, if North Korea's aggressive statements and actions lead to greater isolation of the regime, drying up sources of food, economic, and fuel assistance to the regime, the regime will be unable to stay afloat.

Unlike in North Korea, where the population is too weak to mount any domestic opposition, in Iran the population is the most likely threat. Given the widespread public dissatisfaction with the rule of the conservative clerics, combined with frustration with Khatami's reform movement, the situation could soon escalate into a violent resistance to the regime. This opposition movement will reportedly receive assistance from the United States in efforts to destabilize the government (particularly due to U.S. claims that Iran is harboring al Qaeda operatives).[284] In addition, the United States may be spurred to intervene if the mullahs order widespread crackdowns on the opposition groups.

These cases therefore strongly support a contention that we have seen throughout this book, that domestic upheavals can cause losses of central control over nuclear weapons and related materials, increasing risks of thefts and sales to other countries or terrorist groups. This issue will remain an enduring concern if further proliferation occurs.

Sales of Nuclear Materials and Possible Connections with Terrorist Groups

U.S. officials have been long concerned that Iraq, Iran, and North Korea would provide nuclear weapons or fissile materials to terrorist groups. This was a stated reason for the military intervention in Iraq, and it does remain a potential concern with Iran and North Korea.

As we have seen, prior to the war with Iraq, Bush administration officials and U.S. intelligence agencies made numerous accusations that Saddam's Ba'athist regime had established connections with al Qaeda and had even provided the group assistance in developing chemical and biological weapons. While the U.S. officials provided some circumstantial evidence to support these charges, they were justifiably received with some degree of suspicion. More evidence has surfaced since the war that does appear to draw some connections between the Ba'ath Party and al Qaeda operatives, though as of yet these recovered documents do not address any WMD assistance that Iraq may have provided.

Similar concerns may pertain to the case of Iran as well. In fact, the Iranian regime may have greater ideological connections with al Qaeda than Iraq's Ba'ath Party did. The Ba'athist regime was essentially secular, though Iraqi officials' rhetoric was often religious in its character. The U.S. State Department has labeled Iran as "the world's most active supporter of terrorism."[285] Iran has funded, trained, and armed numerous terrorist groups throughout the world, including the Palestinian terrorists groups Hamas and Islamic Jihad, and the Lebanese terrorist group Hezbollah.[286] Due to their sharing radical forms of Islam, there might be a natural synergy between

Iran and al Qaeda, in spite of the fact that the two groups are associated with different sects of Islam (the Iranian clerics are Shi'ite, while al Qaeda is more directly connected with Sunni Islam).

In fact, it appears that the Shi'ite-Sunni divide is proving to be a less significant impediment to cooperation than many scholars previously believed. Al Qaeda has successfully forged significant ties with the Iranian-funded Shi'ite terrorist group Hezbollah.[287] There have also been reports that Iran's Qods (or Jerusalem) Force, one of the five branches of the Islamic Revolutionary Guard Corps, has had ties with al Qaeda for more than a decade. According to U.S. and European intelligence officials, this group reportedly formed a tactical alliance with al Qaeda in the early 1990s and strengthened these ties after the fall of Afghanistan.[288] The U.S. allegations in 2003 that Iran is sheltering al Qaeda operatives are therefore particularly troubling,[289] though there is currently no evidence that Iran has assisted al Qaeda with any WMD. Although it may be unlikely that Iran would decide to provide terrorists with nuclear weapons, we cannot entirely rule this possibility out. What is probably more likely, however, is that the regime would almost certainly use nuclear weapons to deter any major retaliations as it continued to fund and sponsor terrorism.

North Korea poses a different type of threat. There are clearly no ideological connections between the quasi-Communist regime and Islamic militants, and the North Korean regime is not known to have supported any terrorist acts since 1987.[290] The greatest concern is that North Korea would be willing to sell nuclear materials to any ready buyer, especially since North Korean officials have explicitly threatened that they would be willing to export nuclear weapons and related materials. Because the regime desperately needs money and considers itself bound by no external obligations, it may at some point be willing to sell nuclear materials to proliferating states or terrorist groups.

Now that we have concluded the final empirical case studies, we are in a position to draw together the lessons from the range of cases examined in this work and relate them to the theoretical arguments presented in the proliferation optimism-pessimism debate. I will address this topic in the final chapter.

7 Conclusions

The evidence from the case studies examined in this project suggests that there is significant reason to be pessimistic about the further spread of nuclear weapons. In these conclusions, I return to the various arguments and predictions of the optimists and pessimists outlined in chapter 1. Part I of this chapter examines what these case studies have taught us about the proliferation debate, and Part II discusses some steps that the U.S. government and the international community might take to prevent the further spread of nuclear weapons and to reduce nuclear dangers among current NWSs.

Part I: Returning to the Optimist-Pessimist Debate

Assessing the Various Predictions of the Optimists and Pessimists

Optimists and pessimists each have made a number of predictions about the nuclear systems and corresponding nuclear controls that will be employed by emerging NWSs. This study has checked the various predictions against the record by assessing key aspects of the nuclear systems in NWSs. It has examined a range of cases that vary widely in their economic resources, technical capabilities, and regime types, and includes the "best case" (specifically the United States) to establish a baseline—one which itself does not unqualifiedly support the optimist position. Both sides in the debate generally agree on what criteria would determine whether or not the spread of nuclear weapons would be beneficial. As we have seen, Kenneth Waltz establishes several requirements for stable deterrence: first, NWSs must develop survivable forces; second, they must establish reliable command-and-control systems to prevent accidental and unauthorized use; third, they must avoid developing systems that require rapid decision-making, which could lead to inadvertent use.[1] In addition, for the optimist position to be convincing, emerging NWSs must develop and implement sophisticated MPC&A systems to help prevent the theft of fissile materials and the sabotage of nuclear facilities. Optimists are generally confident that NWSs will satisfy each of these criteria and are therefore confident that the spread of nuclear weapons will increase international stability. In the following discussion I will summarize the conclusions we can draw about each of the predictions made by each side in the debate. As we will see, *although the risks did vary widely among the individual cases, the accumulated evidence from these cases generally supports the pessimist position.*

Will Emerging NWSs Create Survivable Forces?

The evidence concerning the likelihood of NWSs developing survivable forces is somewhat mixed. On the one hand, it is very difficult to build survivable forces. The United States and the Soviet Union exerted tremendous efforts to develop systems that would be capable of surviving a first strike. These systems included resilient command and communications systems; extensive forces, deployed in rapid-response configurations that allowed for launch-on-warning; sophisticated early-warning systems; and hardened shelters for political leaders. Still, some analysts have questioned whether their nuclear forces and command structures were, in fact, survivable.[2]

China's nuclear forces have also been vulnerable to a first strike, since for many years they relied on a deterrence based on an outdated ICBM force of roughly eighteen missiles capable of striking the United States. Because it would require several hours of preparation with the missiles exposed before their weapons could be launched, China's forces would be highly vulnerable to a nuclear first strike by NWSs with advanced surveillance systems, such as those possessed by the United States. India and Pakistan also rely on small forces and rudimentary command and communication structures that could be destroyed by a first strike.[3] In addition, analysts have argued that a conventional or nuclear strike by India could destroy the launch strips at Pakistani air force bases, thereby eliminating or significantly weakening Pakistan's current retaliatory capability.[4] Because it is very difficult to create survivable forces, there are risks that nuclear powers might engage in a nuclear first strike and that vulnerable nuclear powers will face a "use them or lose them" dilemma.

On the other hand, pressures to build survivable forces are likely to cause NWSs to develop larger and more advanced arsenals, dispersed weapon deployments, and more complicated command structures. Of the established NWSs, the United States, Russia, Great Britain, and France all developed these capabilities fairly early. And China appears to be developing similar capabilities. Although China initially stored its missiles unfueled and without the warheads mated, concerns about survivability are causing China to move to a mobile system, in which the missiles will be stored fully fueled, possibly with mated warheads.[5] Moreover, both India and Pakistan appear to be moving in a similar direction. Whether or not India adopts a system similar to the one called for in its 1999 draft nuclear doctrine, it is moving toward weaponization and deployment of mobile missile systems that could allow for a rapid-response capability. Pakistan, as well, appears to be moving toward mobile systems, and might very well adopt a rapid-response capability, a launch-on-warning policy, and predelegation of launch authority.[6] Thus, virtually every nuclear power so far has yielded—or is yielding—to pressures to build larger, more robust, more *complex* nuclear systems, and it is reasonable to expect that other emerging NWSs will behave similarly.[7] Larger and more complex systems might be more survivable (though they still might be vulnerable to a nuclear first strike), but they also significantly increase command-and-control difficulties, as we will see in the next section.

Will Emerging NWSs Develop Resilient Command-and-Control Systems to Prevent Accidental and Unauthorized Use?

These case studies very clearly illustrate Peter Feaver's arguments about the always/never dilemma.[8] In the early stages of their nuclear programs, the United States, the Soviet Union, China, India, and Pakistan relied on unassembled weapons. But the pressures to build survivable forces have led, or are currently leading, these states to move toward assembled weapons and dispersed deployments. These systems require advanced weapons designs and safety devices to avoid accidental detonations, and sophisticated command-and-control systems to prevent accidental and unauthorized use. Although it is possible that proliferating countries could find alternative ways to compensate for some of these risks, the cases in this study suggest reasons to doubt, at least, that emerging NWSs will consistently develop advanced safety and command-and-control systems.

Accidental Detonations

Both the United States and the Soviet Union moved to systems employing assembled warheads in the early 1960s. While the United States has devoted a great deal of effort to minimizing risks of accidental use, it also chose a number of deployment options, such as the continual air alert for its bomber forces, that increased risks of accidental use. As a result, the United States did have several accidents that led to accidental detonations of the high explosives in nuclear weapons, causing serious radiation dispersals (though the risks of nuclear yields resulting from these accidents were minimal). Since then, the United States has integrated numerous safety features into its weapons designs to help prevent accidental detonations, such as one-point safety, insensitive high explosives (IHE), fire-resistant pits (FRPs), and enhanced nuclear detonations safety (ENDS) systems.[9] Nevertheless, for many years the United States retained weapons systems that did not meet its highest safety standards.[10] In fact, several weapons systems in the U.S. nuclear arsenal reportedly still lack IHE, FRPs, and even ENDS (though these weapons systems are scheduled for deactivation in the near future).[11]

The safety standards for Russian nuclear weapons appear to be less rigorous than those for U.S. weapons. For example, while Russian weapons do employ designs to reduce the likelihood that an accidental detonation of the high explosives would result in nuclear yields, there is some evidence to suggest that these weapons do not come close to U.S. requirements for one-point safety. Because Russian nuclear weapons also do not appear to use insensitive high explosives, the risks that an accident could detonate the high explosives in Russian nuclear weapons—leading to radiation dispersals or even to nuclear yields—also appear to be higher than in the United States.[12] These risks of accidental detonation could further increase as Russian nuclear weapons continue to age.[13]

There is relatively little information about the safety devices on Chinese nuclear weapons, but knowledgeable analysts have argued that Indian and Pakistani nuclear weapons lack sophisticated safety designs and safety devices necessary for preventing accidental detonations.[14] Although the risks of accidental detonations of Indian and Pakistani nuclear weapons have probably been fairly small so far because they reportedly store their weapons in unassembled states, these risks could increase significantly if they carry out their plans for weaponized deployment.[15]

Because Iraq never became a nuclear power, and Iran and North Korea have probably not yet become nuclear powers, it is not clear what the risks of accidental detonations would be. It is possible that they could have avoided, or still will avoid, many of these risks by not assembling their warheads during peacetime circumstances. Nevertheless, what information is available raises questions in this area as well. Given the high risks of preventive and preemptive strikes by the United States or other countries, they would have very strong incentives to assemble their weapons, at least during crises. The pressures to create (and possibly deploy) their nuclear weapons rapidly could cause proliferating states to marginalize safety designs. For example, the reports that Iraq was pushing forward as rapidly as possible to acquire nuclear weapons capability without having conducted a large number of tests on its warhead detonation systems, combined with UNSCOM officials' reports that the Iraqi warhead design would have been highly vulnerable to shocks and accidents, suggest that at least the first-generation of Iraqi nuclear weapons could have had significant risks of detonating accidentally.[16]

Accidental Launches

Overall, the current risks of accidental launches of nuclear weapons appear to be fairly small. Although the United States and Russia store their nuclear weapons in launch-ready conditions, both countries have advanced use-control devices that are highly effective in preventing accidental launches. And because China, India, and Pakistan do not currently mate their warheads to delivery vehicles, the risks of accidental launches of their nuclear weapons are also currently quite small.

Nevertheless, the risks of accidental launches of Chinese, Indian, and Pakistani nuclear weapons would be significantly higher during crisis situations, when they would presumably mate their warheads to delivery vehicles. Because none of these countries appear to employ sophisticated use-control devices for their weapons, the risks of accidental launches of their nuclear weapons would be significantly higher if they were to assemble their weapons during crises. This would especially be the case in India and Pakistan because they currently have only crude command-and-control systems and limited experience with nuclear weapons.[17]

Moreover, China, India, and Pakistan are all moving toward mobile, solid-fueled missile systems. And because of the perceived necessity for increased missile mobility, it is also quite possible that they will begin storing their missiles with their warheads mated. If new missile systems in China, India, and Pakistan are stored in this state of launch-readiness, the risks of accidental launches of their nuclear weapons could significantly increase. This is especially the case because their weapons do not appear to contain integrated launch controls similar to those used in the United States and Russia.

Unauthorized Use

These cases have given us reason to doubt that emerging NWSs will have adequate controls to prevent unauthorized use. During the early years of their nuclear programs, every NWS we examined relied on guards, gates, and guns to prevent unauthorized use. These controls can work fairly well to prevent unauthorized use, depending on what procedures the state employs to control the weapons and whether the weapons are deployed. But as the size of the arsenal increases and as the weapons are deployed, these controls can reveal serious weaknesses.

In the 1940s and early 1950s, the United States maintained controls over its nuclear weapons through the "3 G's." As the United States began deploying nuclear weapons in Europe, however, it could no longer be certain that these controls were sufficient for preventing unauthorized use. The United States eventually strengthened its command-and-control system by integrating PALs into its weapons deployed in Europe. But even then, it was not until 1996 or 1997 that it placed use-control devices on the nuclear weapons controlled by the navy. In addition, critics have argued that procedures such as the predelegation of launch authority weaken the central, civilian controls over U.S. nuclear weapons,[18] though because the military has a strong tradition of professionalism, the likelihood of unauthorized use is probably fairly small.

At first, the Soviet Union also controlled its nuclear weapons through the "3 G's." As its arsenal expanded in the 1960s, however, it began placing use-control devices on many of its nuclear weapons. But serious weaknesses in these controls arose after the Soviet collapse. It was only through tremendous efforts (and U.S. assistance) that Russia was able to bring the weapons deployed in Eastern Europe and the newly independent states back onto Russian territory. But the country's serious political and economic difficulties have continued to erode Russia's ability to maintain central control over its nuclear weapons in the last decade. Because Russia's main command-and-control system, the Kazbek system, is deteriorating, Russia might have to adopt a more "delegative" system, whereby authorization and enabling codes are distributed to lower levels in the command chain.[19] Such a system could significantly increase the risks of unauthorized use, as larger numbers of people would gain access to the launch codes for Russia's nuclear weapons.[20] In addition, because troops in Russia's regional military units and the Strategic Rocket Forces are very poorly paid, there is an increased risk of nuclear coups, rebellions of regional leaders or military commanders, and thefts of nuclear weapons.[21] Since many of Russia's tactical weapons reportedly lack use-control devices equivalent to PALs, the theft of any of Russia's tactical nuclear weapons could constitute a complete loss of central control over these weapons.

The Russian case also yields important lessons about possible weaknesses in Chinese, Indian, and Pakistani nuclear controls. Most evidence suggests that all three of these states rely primarily on the "3 G's" for their nuclear controls. As the Russian case demonstrates, these systems can become particularly weak during domestic upheavals because such upheavals undermine the reliability of guard forces and personnel at nuclear facilities.[22]

While the use-control devices on most (though probably not all) of Russia's nuclear weapons increased assurances that Russia's nuclear controls had not collapsed, emerging NWSs will probably tend to lack such use-control devices on their weapons, especially at first. Because China, India, and Pakistan currently appear to lack such use-control devices, if any of them were to experience serious political, economic, or social upheavals, its nuclear controls could become severely compromised or could collapse altogether.

The available evidence from Iraq, North Korea, and Iran suggests similar risks. It is fairly unlikely that these countries would have use-control devices integrated into their nuclear weapons designs, at least at first. For example, given how quickly Iraq was pushing to develop functioning nuclear weapons in 1990–1991, it is highly unlikely that any effort was devoted to integrating use-control devices into their warhead design. Nor is it very likely that North Korea would have the economic or technical resources for use-control devices. If these countries were to adopt similar command-and-control arrangements for their nuclear weapons as they have for their chemical and biological weapons, they would be more likely to rely on internal security systems and loyalty of distinct military units to prevent unauthorized use. These systems can function fairly well during normal circumstances, but do have the potential to become weakened during crises and domestic upheavals.

Will Small Arsenals and Simple Command Structures Be Sufficient for Maintaining Nuclear Controls?

Both David Karl and Jordan Seng argue that the nuclear weapons in developing countries will be relatively easy to control, even without sophisticated use-control devices, because their arsenals will be small and their command systems simple.[23] But there are serious problems with this argument. First, as we have seen, there is little evidence to suggest that emerging NWSs *will* remain satisfied with small arsenals and simple command structures. Instead, most evidence suggests that they will tend to develop larger, more complex systems, which increase organizational difficulties and will be much harder to control. As the Russian case demonstrates, complex systems can deteriorate during economic crises due to a lack of resources for maintenance and repairs.

Moreover, even if some emerging NWSs do keep their arsenals small and simple, their controls could *still* be severely weakened during domestic upheavals. The most serious weaknesses in Russia's controls were caused less by the size of its nuclear arsenal or the complexity of its command structure than by the *type* of nuclear controls that it inherited from the Soviet

Union. To be sure, the scope of Russia's problems has been exacerbated by size and complexity, but because Russia's nuclear controls relied heavily on guards, gates, and guns, Russia still would have had difficulties maintaining its nuclear controls *even if its nuclear system had been much smaller.* Emerging NWSs probably will have problems similar to Russia's during political upheavals because they are likely to rely on the "3 G's" for their nuclear command-and-control systems. Indeed, we have seen that the arsenals in China, India, and Pakistan are potentially vulnerable to accidental or unauthorized use, even though they are comparatively small.

For example, although information on the incidents that occurred during the Cultural Revolution and the Tiananmen Square crisis is incomplete, these incidents do appear to be important counterexamples to Karl's and Seng's arguments. There were several close calls in China during the Cultural Revolution (including what could be interpreted as an unauthorized test launch of a nuclear weapon in 1966), even though China's arsenal ranged from twenty to one hundred warheads during these incidents.[24] It is also quite possible that China could experience severe instability in the future. There are widespread reports of increasing dissatisfaction with the high levels of corruption in the Chinese Communist Party (CCP), increasing regionalist movements, and skyrocketing crime rates. These factors have led a number of analysts to argue that the regime could experience severe instability or even collapse.[25]

The prospects for political and economic stability have been even worse in Pakistan. Between 1998 and 2001, Pakistan's economy teetered continually on the brink of collapse. While the U.S. decision to remove economic sanctions in September 2001 has improved the prospects for Pakistan's economy, an economic recovery is by no means guaranteed.[26] If Pakistan were again to encounter severe economic stresses, it could experience difficulties in controlling its nuclear weapons and fissile materials that are similar to those experienced in Russia. Although Pakistan's nuclear complex is obviously much smaller than Russia's, so are its economy, technical capabilities, organizational infrastructures, and experience with nuclear weapons. Thus, it is possible that Pakistan could experience an even more severe breakdown in its nuclear controls than Russia has experienced if its economy were again to become unstable.

Moreover, during the U.S. military campaign in Afghanistan, numerous scholars expressed concerns that political upheavals could undermine Pakistani nuclear controls.[27] Although the political instability appears to have been less severe than many feared it would be, it might have worsened significantly if the bombing campaign had lasted longer than it did.[28] The widespread public opposition to the U.S.-led invasion of Iraq in 2003, along with the military regime's strengthening of Pakistan's radical Islamic parties in late 2002, suggests that we could yet see regime-threatening instability in Pakistan.[29] Given the type of nuclear controls on which Pakistan relies, these controls could become severely weakened during extreme political upheavals.

As these accounts suggest, the risks of accidental and unauthorized use could be very high in emerging NWSs, particularly during nuclear crises or periods of domestic instability. The prospects for proliferation are therefore especially disturbing because emerging NWSs will tend to be more unstable than the established NWSs have been.[30] For example, all three of the emerging nuclear powers examined in this study—Iraq, Iran, and North Korea—have had significant risks of domestic instability. Although Saddam Hussein proved able to crush any opposition, he did experience a number of coup attempts (the most serious in 1992), as well as repeated riots and uprisings (in 1991, 1995, 1996, and 2000) during his time in power.[31] And once an external invasion took place, all central authority evaporated quite rapidly.[32] The risks of regime-threatening upheavals are much greater, however, in North Korea and Iran than in Ba'athist Iraq. As we have seen, neither of these countries has great prospects for political stability in the near- to mid-term.[33] In the event of severe upheavals or regime collapse, they could experience a rapid deterioration of their central controls over their nuclear weapons and related materials.

Nor is it clear that simple command structures in emerging NWSs will significantly reduce the risks of accidental or unauthorized use, as Seng and Karl contend. Indeed, as several analysts have argued, the rudimentary command-and-control structures in India and Pakistan increase the likelihood of accidental or unauthorized use, particularly during crises. The Indian military currently has little experience in handling nuclear weapons. If India's nuclear weapons were given to the military during a crisis, they would be as inexperienced in preventing their use as they would be in using them.[34] Moreover, because Pakistan currently lacks an enunciated nuclear doctrine, reliable decision-making or communications systems, or explicit targeting information, there is an increased likelihood that Pakistan's own troops might undertake strikes on their own.[35] These are risks that any emerging NWS would likely experience as they worked to develop nuclear weapons, formulate use-doctrines, and establish command-and-control systems. But since many of the countries most likely to develop nuclear weapons in the foreseeable future would have to consider the chances of preventive strikes as quite high, they might choose to deploy (or be forced to deploy) their nuclear weapons before they have all these issues sufficiently worked out. In these instances, the simple command structures would not necessarily prevent accidental or unauthorized use, and in fact could increase these risks.

Will Emerging NWSs Be Likely to Avoid Inadvertent Use?

This study has demonstrated that the further spread of nuclear weapons would probably increase the risks of inadvertent use. As we have seen, the risks of inadvertent use are relatively high among current NWSs, and there is little reason to think that emerging NWSs will avoid these risks. The pressures to build survivable forces caused both the United States and Russia to develop systems that allowed for launch-on-warning. In order to allow for LOW, they placed their nuclear weapons on permanent alert in the early 1960s, which would allow the weapons to be launched within fifteen minutes from a detected attack. They also developed sophisticated early-warning systems to detect incoming nuclear attacks. As pessimists have argued, the policies of LOW require rapid decision-making, which significantly increases the risks of panic-launches due to miscalculation or false warnings.

While early-warning systems in the United States and Russia were intended in part to reduce inadvertent nuclear war by ensuring that the nuclear weapons in each country would only be used in the event of a verified attack, the early-warning systems in both countries have reportedly experienced numerous false alarms, which, combined with their LOW doctrines, could have led to inadvertent launches. Overall, the risks of inadvertent launches of either state's weapons have remained relatively small during normal, peacetime circumstances because both countries base their decisions on factors beyond those indicated by the early-warning sensors—including the political relations between the two countries at the time and whether it would be at all *likely* that the other country would be attacking. But these risks would be much higher during crisis situations. And several false alarms also reportedly occurred during crises, causing many analysts to conclude that the risks of inadvertent launches during these crises were quite high.[36]

Moreover, Russia's deteriorating early-warning system, combined with its continuing deployment of weapons in a rapid-response mode, has further increased risks of inadvertent war. Because Russia's early-warning sensors are reportedly blind for several hours per day,[37] Russian leaders would potentially have very little time to decide whether or not a detected attack is real before they would need to launch their own missiles. If the Russian BMEW system continues to deteriorate, the danger of inadvertent launches would probably increase, especially if relations between the United States and Russia were to become more strained.[38]

Of the cases studied, the current risks of an inadvertent launch of Chinese nuclear weapons are possibly the lowest, because China stores its missiles unfueled, with their warheads unmated. But, again, the risks of inadvertent launch would probably increase significantly during crisis situations, when Chinese missiles would presumably be fueled and the warheads would presumably be attached to the missiles. In addition, China is currently developing mobile missile systems that use solid fuel (which means they would be stored fully fueled) and could be stored with their warheads mated. If China does choose such a deployment option, the risks of inadvertent launch could significantly increase.

The risks of inadvertent use of Indian and Pakistani nuclear weapons are probably the highest of the cases examined in this study. Owing to the rapid flight times for aircraft, India and Pakistan would have to make decisions to use their nuclear weapons with little or no advanced warning. This situation will only become more dangerous if and when they decide to deploy their weapons on missiles.[39] Thus, the geographical proximity of India and Pakistan creates a situation in which the risks of panic-launches and launches based on misinformation are extremely high. Neither country has a reliable early-warning system, but given their geographical proximity, it is not even clear that early-warning systems would help reduce the risks of inadvertent launches. In addition, severe mistrust, combined with notoriously bad intelligence systems, has caused the two states to misinterpret each other's intentions on numerous occasions.[40]

Thus, while the risks of inadvertent use do vary from case to case, these cases demonstrate that the risks of inadvertent use are very real. We have yet to see what approaches newly proliferating states will take in their nuclear programs, but pressures for ensuring survivable forces will certainly exist, particularly in the face of opponents such as the United States that can strike from great distances with little warning. In order to address these risks, proliferating countries could adopt launch-on-warning capabilities or predelegate launch authority (as Saddam did with his chemical weapons in 1991). And in order to address very clear asymmetries between their military capabilities and those of their adversaries, they may also adopt military doctrines calling for rapid, full-scale, and even preemptive strikes (as North Korea's military plans do, and Iran's military plans may allow for). Given that many potential proliferators—such as Iran, North Korea, Iraq (before March 2003), Syria, and Libya—will also be likely to have questionable intelligence, early-warning, and communications systems, these types of policies could create significant risks of inadvertent use.

Will Emerging NWSs Develop Adequate MPC&A Systems?

We also have reason to doubt that fissile materials will be adequately controlled in emerging NWSs. All the states examined in this study have relied on guards, gates, and guns for their fissile material security and controls for at least part of their nuclear history. Of these cases, only the United States moved to more advanced MPC&A systems, and only after repeated investigations identified significant vulnerabilities in its earlier type of fissile control to insider thefts and terrorist attacks. The system of guards, gates, and guns can only work well if there is a strict authoritarian regime or a strong culture of professionalism to reinforce these controls. And, as the Russian case has vividly demonstrated, systems that rely heavily on guards, gates, and guns can break down during severe political, economic, and social upheavals. The Chinese case also demonstrates the potential weaknesses in this type of fissile material control. China's current system is probably much stronger than Russia's (in spite of U.S.-Russian efforts to improve Russian controls) because its political system has not yet undergone severe domestic upheavals the way Russia's has. But China's fissile material controls have the potential to reveal weaknesses similar to Russia's, due to the weakening of the Chinese Communist Party, skyrocketing crime, and high levels of corruption among government officials.

Because India and Pakistan also rely primarily on "institutional controls" for their fissile materials, their fissile material stockpiles are vulnerable in similar ways. As we have seen, their nuclear facilities are vulnerable to terrorist attacks and insider thefts. Moreover, there is a significant risk that Pakistan could undergo domestic upheavals that are similar to Russia's. Thus, the Russian model is also important for identifying the vulnerabilities in Pakistani fissile material controls.

Obviously, Russia's MPC&A difficulties have been exacerbated by the sheer size of its fissile material stockpile, but if emerging NWSs were to divert fissile materials from indigenous nuclear reactors over a number of years into covert, or "opaque," nuclear programs, they too could accumulate relatively large fissile material stockpiles.[41] In addition, if they were to adopt the Soviet system of guards, gates, and guns, which does not require investment in high technology but has proven to be vulnerable during domestic upheavals, then emerging NWSs could experience the same problems with the security of fissile materials encountered by Russia. And indeed this is quite likely to happen. It is very expensive to create an MPC&A system that provides "defense-in-depth," whereby the security of fissile materials is not compromised if one part of the security system fails. Emerging NWSs will often be unable to afford, or unwilling to justify the expense of, the equipment and designs necessary for resilient MPC&A systems, and thus they are likely to rely on Soviet-style MPC&A.

What is equally troubling is that most of the countries examined in this study have demonstrated little interest in improving their MPC&A. In Russia, even after the United States has helped them upgrade the MPC&A at their facilities, there have been repeated instances of personnel bypassing safeguards procedures and even turning off alarm systems because they were perceived to be nuisances. China has demonstrated similar reluctance to improving its MPC&A. Chinese leaders have often argued that because China is currently relatively stable, there is no urgency in improving its MPC&A right now.[42] Similar trends appear to be the case in India and Pakistan, where fissile material production is often viewed as a higher priority than safety and safeguards, and where both countries have refused any assistance in improving their MPC&A systems.[43] All of these countries appear to lack developed "safeguards cultures," where all personnel at a nuclear facility view fissile material controls as a higher priority than other objectives, such as meeting production timetables.

Because there is no evidence that emerging NWSs will view MPC&A as a higher priority than current NWSs have, it is quite likely that a further spread of nuclear weapons will increase risks that fissile materials will be stolen or diverted, and will increase opportunities for the sabotage of nuclear facilities. In fact, the evidence from pre-2003 Iraq, North Korea, and Iran suggests that they may view issues such as safety and security as lower priorities than the current NWSs. In order to conceal the existence of their nuclear programs, these countries have adopted denial and deception techniques that could provide even greater obstacles to rigorous fissile material controls. By dispersing their WMD programs in numerous, often underground facilities, reducing or concealing their security systems, and moving WMD materials to conceal them from inspectors or from an adversary's military planners, the newly proliferating countries have managed to hide their programs fairly well. But it is less clear that they would be able to guarantee the security of these materials, particularly during times of domestic instability. As a result, a further spread of nuclear weapons would be likely to increase risks of thefts of materials, which could lead to a rapid, destabilizing spread of nuclear weapons and possibly increase the opportunities for nuclear terrorism.[44]

Intentional Sales of Nuclear Materials and State-Sponsored Terrorism

Finally, we have seen some evidence that some newly proliferating countries might be willing to sell their nuclear materials to other proliferating states or possibly even to terrorists. For example, there is strong evidence that Pakistan provided North Korea, Iran, and Libya with uranium enrichment technologies in exchange for missiles or money.[45] There are also very serious concerns that North Korea would be willing to sell nuclear weapons to the highest (or any) bidder, including proliferating states and terrorist groups.[46] Such intentional sales of nuclear weapons technologies could lead to rapid nuclear proliferation across many countries, an event that optimists admit would be destabilizing.[47]

Furthermore, though this is more speculative, we cannot rule out the possibility that some proliferating states might be willing to provide nuclear weapons, fissile materials, or radioactive materials to terrorists in order to assist them in carrying out nuclear terrorism against mutual enemies. While there is currently no evidence that any state has been tempted to engage in such activities, various Bush administration officials and U.S. intelligence agencies have alleged that Iraq assisted al Qaeda operatives in developing certain chemical and biological weapons.[48] At the very least, the states that sponsor terrorism could use their nuclear weapons to help prevent major retaliations for their continued funding of terrorist groups. Pakistan has used its nuclear weapons in this manner to allow it to continue sponsoring terrorism against India and Indian-controlled Kashmir, and it would be likely that other state-sponsors of terrorism, such as Iran or Syria could follow a similar pattern.

It is also possible that some states, or subgroups within these states' nuclear weapons programs, might be tempted to provide nuclear weapons or related materials to terrorists for ideological purposes. For example, some Pakistani nuclear scientists reportedly met with Osama Bin Laden and briefed him on chemical, biological, and nuclear weapons.[49] It is possible that other countries, such as Iran—or certain workers within Iran's nuclear weapons program—could have similar ideological motivations for helping terrorists carry out nuclear or radiological attacks against such countries as Israel and the United States.

Assessing the Fundamental Assumptions of the Optimists and Pessimists

As Scott Sagan correctly points out, the optimist-pessimist debate is, most fundamentally, a debate over "how best to explain and predict the behavior of states."[50] The entire optimist argument rests on the premise that NWSs will always behave "rationally," or consistently act so as to maximize their self-interest. Because it is so clearly in the interests of NWSs to build safe, secure, and reliable nuclear systems, optimists are confident they will.[51] Pessimists, on the other hand, assume that organizational, bureaucratic, and economic factors will prevent states from pursuing what could otherwise be interpreted as their "objective" interests.[52] In this study, we have seen much greater support for the pessimist assumptions. The following sections will discuss the various factors that prevent states from identifying and pursuing what is in their interests.

What Factors Prevent States from Pursuing Otherwise "Rational" Objectives?

Organizational and Bureaucratic Constraints

In the U.S. case study, we have seen how individual organizations, such as the Department of Energy, can view certain objectives (such as meeting production timetables) as higher priorities than safety and security.[53] But these constraints are much more noticeable in the other case studies. In Russia, we saw how Russian bureaucracies have often been unwilling to implement fundamental changes in fissile material controls because doing so would be admitting incompetence. In addition, the negotiation and implementation of the CTR and MPC&A programs were—and still are—often delayed by "turf battles" among various bureaucracies within Russia's nuclear complex.[54] Similar constraints have affected state action in China, where bureaucratic infighting limited the extent to which China was able to modernize its MPC&A system as part of the U.S.-China lab-to-lab program.[55] These constraints are most prominent in India and Pakistan, where tightly controlled nuclear programs and lack of oversight have dramatically weakened safety and security for their nuclear systems.

Economic and Technological Constraints

This study has also generally supported the pessimist argument that economic and technological constraints will limit safety and security measures undertaken by NWSs. Although most observers would agree that resilient command-and-control and MPC&A systems are in the interests of every NWS, almost every one of the states examined in this study has had difficulties developing the technologies necessary for such systems. In addition, where the technologies are available on the open market, the prohibitive costs involved with the implementation of such systems have undermined the controls established by almost every state examined in this study, with the exception of the United States.

Denial and Deception (D&D) Techniques

As we have seen in the studies of Iran, Iraq, and North Korea, proliferating states will be very likely to employ denial and deception techniques to conceal their nuclear programs. These techniques include multiple, dispersed facilities; various measures to conceal the presence of these facilities, such as hiding the facilities underground or concealing WMD facilities within dual-use facilities or civilian buildings and populations; concealing or reducing security measures at the facilities; and continually moving critical technologies and materials. All states used D&D techniques to conceal their intentions, military facilities, and related weapons technologies.[56] But emerging NWS will have even greater incentives to use extensive D&D techniques, given the changes in U.S. counterproliferation policies that call explicitly for preventive strikes against WMD proliferators.[57] These techniques create additional difficulties for controlling and accounting for nuclear materials. Given these techniques, proliferating states could have extreme difficulties in maintaining central control of these materials if their central authority were disrupted by military strikes or domestic instability.

Opacity

Emerging NWSs will probably rely on "opaque" nuclear arsenals, especially at first, whereby their weapons remain untested, there are no nuclear military doctrines, there are no weapons deployed, and there is no open debate about their nuclear weapons.[58] The cases in this study have generally supported the pessimist argument that opacity decreases both organizational oversight and "nuclear learning" about possible flaws in weapons designs and safety measures.[59] As we have seen, U.S. controls were often improved only after independent agencies and congressional investigations revealed significant weaknesses in U.S. nuclear safety and security. Because emerging NWSs will tend to have opaque nuclear programs, they will be more likely to rely on unsafe weapons designs and will tend to regard safety and security as lower priorities than weapons production.

A critical examination of the nuclear programs in India and Pakistan generally supports this argument. The lack of transparency in their nuclear programs has prevented independent oversight of safety and safeguards procedures. As a result, India continues to operate nuclear facilities with safety features that may be inadequate to prevent catastrophic core meltdowns. Pakistan, as well, has had serious accidents, which have risked damaging their nuclear facilities.[60] Because India and Pakistan have demonstrated that they are willing to risk serious accidents and potential catastrophes in some parts of their nuclear programs, it is likely that similar problems exist throughout their nuclear programs, including the safety and security of their nuclear weapons themselves.[61] Both countries have generally attempted to hide any difficulties in these areas behind the veil of "national security interests."[62] In addition, the lack of independent oversight of Indian and Pakistani nuclear programs makes it very unlikely that either country has developed "safeguards cultures" to help prevent thefts of fissile materials from their nuclear facilities.[63]

This study has also revealed heightened risks of war, once emerging NWSs move from opaque to "visible" nuclear programs. After their 1998 tests, India and Pakistan openly declared themselves nuclear powers and began moving toward weapon deployments. The nuclear tests and subsequent events significantly increased tensions between the two states. Since the time they became "visible" proliferants, they have engaged in a small-scale war, repeatedly issued nuclear threats, and engaged in a massive military buildup in 2001–2002.[64] But these actions all took place when neither state had yet established either military nuclear doctrines or command-and-control systems. As a result, the move to visible nuclear status has significantly increased instability in the region. And there is little evidence that emerging NWSs will remain satisfied with an opaque status. Of the current nuclear powers, only Israel has been satisfied with an opaque nuclear program.

Political, Economic, and Social Upheavals

One of the most important lessons from this study is that severe domestic upheavals can seriously undermine nuclear controls. Thus, these cases reveal serious difficulties with Jordan Seng's argument that the risk of domestic political conflict would actually cause a state's leaders to maintain *stronger* controls over the state's nuclear weapons.[65] As the Russian case clearly demonstrates, severe domestic crises can create new circumstances that were not adequately foreseen. During economic, political, and social upheavals, the nuclear controls in any NWS are likely to be strained to the breaking point. Extensive economic resources and reliable manpower are required to maintain nuclear controls during such upheavals, and these are precisely what such upheavals tend to undermine.

Chinese nuclear controls have also demonstrated potential and actual weaknesses during domestic upheavals. Indeed, China has experienced a number of domestic crises during its nuclear history. China's control over its nuclear weapons was relatively weak during these crises and there was a definite risk that central authorities could have lost control over Chinese nuclear weapons. Granted, there is evidence that China expressed interest in improving its command and control after the Tiananmen Square crisis, but this was only after the fact. And it is likely that China *still* does not have PALs on its nuclear weapons.[66] The evidence from China therefore suggests that Seng is too optimistic in concluding that the risk of domestic conflict will actually increase the measures a state will take to ensure control over its nuclear weapons.

NWSs Might Simply Not See the Necessity for Rigorous Safety and Security Measures

As we have seen, both optimists and pessimists do, or should, acknowledge that it is in the interests of every NWS to maintain safety and security for their nuclear weapons and fissile materials. And yet, the cases in this study suggest that NWSs, or certain groups within NWSs, simply may not see the necessity for rigorous safety and security measures. In particular, emerging NWSs will tend to marginalize such measures in their single-minded pursuit of their weapons programs.[67] This is the most fundamental weakness in the optimists' arguments, since they assume that states will always clearly understand—and pursue—their interests.[68]

For example, we have seen extensive evidence that India and Pakistan have underdeveloped safety and safeguards cultures.[69] Both countries have been willing to risk accidents and potential catastrophes in numerous areas of their nuclear programs, and neither state has been willing to correct these problems. The marginalizing of safety and security is not unique to India and Pakistan. For example, even after Russian facilities encountered severe difficulties with fissile material security and the United States assisted them with MPC&A upgrades, many facilities *still* do not choose to follow the procedures or use the technologies necessary for fissile material security. We have seen similar problems in China. Although Chinese officials have admitted that their fissile material controls are based on the Russian model, they have demonstrated little interest in improving their fissile material controls because, they argue, China is currently stable. But since China has had severe domestic upheavals in the past and could have more in the future, this position appears unjustified. Because it is highly unlikely that emerging NWSs would see their self-interests any more clearly than have the current NWSs, we have reason to side with the pessimist position.[70]

Will Emerging NWSs Learn the Lessons of the Past?

Optimists often argue, implicitly or explicitly, that emerging NWSs will avoid some of the difficulties that current NWSs may have encountered because they will learn from the current NWSs' mistakes.[71] Indeed, in the 1990s, many scholars argued that South Asia was taking a different, and arguably, safer route than that taken by the Superpowers.[72] But the events of the last several years have proven that these predictions were overly optimistic. As we have seen, both states are moving toward assembled weapon systems and much larger deployments (though their arsenals will clearly be much smaller than those of the Superpowers).[73] In fact, insofar as India and Pakistan have learned any lessons from the Cold War, they have learned many of the *wrong* lessons. Although they have adopted the language of deterrence used in the Cold War, they have not demonstrated the same levels of restraint that the United States and the Soviet Union did. Instead, they have supported proxy wars in each other's territories and have even gone to war with each other. If India and Pakistan are at all representative of emerging NWSs, their actions should give us little confidence that "nuclear learning" will take place in emerging NWSs.

Moreover, we have also seen strong evidence that emerging NWSs will be unlikely to learn from the lessons in Russia. In spite of the clear evidence that nuclear controls based on the "3 G's" are highly vulnerable during domestic upheavals, China, India, Pakistan, and even Russia itself have been reluctant to adopt more advanced command-and-control and MPC&A systems. There is very little reason for confidence that emerging NWSs will be more likely to learn from Russia's difficulties than these states have been. Rather, the evidence supports the opposite conclusion.

Indeed, it is much more difficult than one might think for "learning" to take place on institutional or state levels. As Jack Levy has argued, very different processes occur when an institution learns than when an individual learns.[74] In particular, learning on an institutional or government level can only take place if individuals' inferences from experience become embedded in organizational memory and procedures, and this process can be blocked by any number of factors, including organizational resistance to change as well as domestic, economic, or bureaucratic constraints.[75] As the Indian and Pakistani cases demonstrate, all of these factors have limited the extent to which India and Pakistan have been able or willing to learn from the experiences of the other NWSs and adopt specific procedures and technologies to minimize dangers in their nuclear systems. In addition, the highly controlled nuclear programs in India and Pakistan have prevented open debate over nuclear policies and the advantages or disadvantages of various nuclear systems, creating serious obstacles to "nuclear learning."[76]

Would These Dangers Be Solved by Providing Command-and-Control Technologies to Emerging NWSs?

Optimists have argued that many of the difficulties identified by the pessimists could be solved if the United States were to provide emerging NWSs with command-and-control technologies.[77] Indeed, because a major focus of this study has been on whether or not NWSs will develop command-and-control and MPC&A technologies, it is necessary to address this contention.

There are, in fact, a number of reasons against providing emerging NWSs with technologies to help them control their burgeoning nuclear weapons programs. Setting aside such significant questions as whether emerging NWSs would be willing to provide the United States information about their weapons designs and capabilities, such a policy would be a "non-starter" among policymakers in Washington, and for good reason. First, it is doubtful that the United States would want to commit its efforts and resources to helping *additional* countries solve their nuclear difficulties. The United States appropriated $940 million of the FY2004 budget to helping Russia improve its nuclear controls.[78] While it might be desirable to work with officially recognized NWSs, such as Russia and China, to improve their nuclear controls, it does not make much sense to encourage further proliferation, only to devote additional resources to helping the new NWSs in such endeavors.[79] Second, the United States would be unlikely to be willing to help emerging NWSs develop safe weapons designs and command-and-control systems because such assistance could significantly improve their military capabilities. As Peter Feaver has argued, regardless of whether one is an optimist or pessimist in the proliferation debate, it is not in the U.S. interest to help emerging NWSs improve their nuclear capabilities. Such a policy would dramatically undermine the U.S. ability to project its power abroad and would tend to embolden other states to resist U.S. efforts to impose its will.[80]

More fundamentally, it is also unlikely that providing such assistance would reduce many of the risks identified in this study. While improved command-and-control technologies could reduce some risks of accidental and unauthorized use, they would also tend to increase other risks. Improved command-and-control technologies could encourage emerging NWSs to deploy their weapons at higher states of readiness, increasing the regional tensions and the likelihood of inadvertent and intentional use.[81]

Advanced command-and-control technologies may also increase the confidence among emerging NWSs that they can "handle" any situation that arises, and therefore could make them more willing to engage in "risky" activities. To illustrate this case, one need only look at the 1999 Kargil war. Would advanced command-and-control technologies have reduced the likelihood of such an event occurring? The answer to this is decisively no. As it was, Pakistan invaded Indian-controlled Kashmir in 1999 because it was convinced that its nuclear capabilities would prevent a large-scale Indian retaliation. An advanced, mobile missile system deployed in a configuration that allowed for a rapid-response capability would probably have only emboldened Pakistan even more.

Furthermore, such assistance would also implicitly condone the nuclear programs in emerging NWSs, undermine U.S. nonproliferation commitments, and cause serious damage to the nonproliferation regime. The Nuclear Non-Proliferation Treaty (NPT), the cornerstone of the nonproliferation regime, forbids such assistance. If the United States were to abandon its NPT commitments, the entire nonproliferation regime would begin to unravel. Additional states with nuclear aspirations could thus be encouraged to develop nuclear weapons. Given the risks that could result from the rapid spread of nuclear weapons, such events could seriously undermine international stability.[82]

The question remains, however, whether the United States should help emerging NWSs design and implement MPC&A systems. To a certain degree, such assistance would be unnecessary because many of these safeguards technologies are available from the IAEA.[83] U.S. scientists could, however, help instruct emerging NWSs in techniques for designing and implementing MPC&A systems. But, as we have seen, there is little evidence that emerging NWSs would even be interested in developing MPC&A technologies, given the costs of such systems. For example, Chinese officials have demonstrated little interest in improving their MPC&A, in spite of U.S. encouragement and willingness to work with them on this agenda, and U.S. scientists have given numerous briefings on MPC&A techniques to Indian and Pakistani scientists, with little success.[84]

Summing Up: Will the Further Spread of Nuclear Weapons Be Better or Worse?

This study has revealed numerous reasons to be skeptical that the spread of nuclear weapons would increase international stability by helping prevent conventional and nuclear wars. Because there is reason to suspect that emerging NWSs will not handle their nuclear weapons and fissile materials any better than current NWSs have, we should conclude that the further spread of nuclear weapons will tend to undermine international stability in a number of ways. First, because emerging NWSs will probably rely on inadequate command-and-control systems, the risks of accidental and unauthorized use will tend to be fairly high. Second, because emerging NWSs will tend to adopt systems that allow for rapid response, the risks of inadvertent war will also be high, especially during crisis situations. Third, because emerging NWSs will tend to adopt MPC&A systems that are vulnerable to overt attacks and insider thefts, the further spread of nuclear weapons could lead to rapid, destabilizing proliferation and increased opportunities for nuclear terrorism.

Finally, there is reason to question whether nuclear weapons will in fact increase stability. Although nuclear weapons can cause states to be cautious about undertaking actions that can be interpreted as aggressive and can prevent states from attacking one another, this may not always be the case. While the presence of nuclear weapons did appear to help constrain U.S. and Soviet actions during the Cold War, this has generally not held true in South Asia. Many analysts conclude that Pakistan invaded Indian-controlled Kargil in 1999, at least in part, because it was *confident that its nuclear weapons would deter a large-scale Indian retaliation.* The Kargil war was thus in part *caused by* the presence of nuclear weapons in South Asia. Thus, the optimist argument that nuclear weapons will help prevent conventional war has not always held true. Moreover, this weakness in the optimist argument should also cause us to question the second part of their argument, that nuclear weapons help prevent nuclear war as well. Conventional wars between nuclear powers can run serious risks of escalating to nuclear war.[85]

Based on a careful examination of nuclear programs in the United States, Russia, China, India, and Pakistan, as well as preliminary studies of the programs in Iraq, North Korea, and Iran, this book concludes that the optimists' arguments about the actions that emerging NWSs will probably take are overly optimistic. While it is impossible to *prove* that further nuclear proliferation will necessarily precipitate nuclear disasters, the potential consequences are too severe to advocate nuclear weapons proliferation in hopes that the stability predicted by the optimists will indeed occur.

Part II: Policy Implications

The theoretical discussion of the proliferation debate is not merely "academic"; it has direct policy implications. Because optimists understate the dangers of proliferation, they weaken support for international nonproliferation objectives, including efforts to prevent the further spread of nuclear weapons and programs designed to help current NWSs reduce proliferation risks arising from weakened nuclear controls. The theoretical conclusions of this study indicate, however, that the United States and the international community should take further steps in precisely these areas. The case studies in this book suggest a series of appropriate policies that the United States and the international community might undertake to promote these nonproliferation objectives. Because the primary objective of the present study is not to identify policy recommendations, however, the following sections will only briefly outline the general directions that U.S. and international policy should probably take, but will not discuss specific recommendations in great detail.

Strengthen Efforts to Prevent a Further Spread of Nuclear Weapons

Because nuclear proliferation is likely to be dangerous and destabilizing, it is in the interests of the United States and the international community to develop a consensus on strengthening the international nonproliferation regime and ensuring compliance with it. As part of a strengthened regime, IAEA safeguards need to be based on full and effective implementation of new and existing authorities for the IAEA, which will help prevent diversion of fissile materials from declared nuclear facilities and increase assurances that there are no opaque nuclear programs. A critical step in ensuring these additional authorities are adopted would be to encourage a greater number of states to ratify the Additional Protocol, which would allow for greater access to suspected nuclear facilities and allow IAEA inspectors to conduct environmental monitoring to detect hidden nuclear facilities.[86]

Moreover, the world should maintain strong pressures on Iran and North Korea to eliminate their nuclear programs. There are, of course, many important reasons for maintaining these efforts anyway—such as potential risks of accidental, unauthorized, and inadvertent use, and dangers that these countries could export their nuclear materials to other proliferating countries or terrorist groups—but it is also worth considering more subtle reasons for preventing such proliferation, such as the potential vulnerabilities that could eventually arise in Iran's or North Korea's nuclear controls.

In the case of Iran, it is critical that the United States and other countries work with the IAEA to ensure that inspections proceed with truly unfettered access to all suspected facilities, but they should be prepared to use military force in the event of any delays or attempts to conceal these programs. Iran has continually maintained that it is pursuing only civilian nuclear programs and is not violating its NPT obligations. As we have seen, this claim is highly suspect, since it makes little sense for Iran to be spending billions on nuclear power when it has some of the largest oil reserves in the world, and since Iran only declared its uranium enrichment facility at Natanz to the IAEA after Iranian opposition groups notified the international community of its existence. But if this is Iran's claim, then it should be willing to adopt the Additional Protocols to provide the IAEA with greater access and monitoring capabilities. If Iran continues to refuse these measures, which is likely, then the international community should be willing to take stronger steps to block Iran's nuclear program. First, the United States should apply greater pressure on Russia to stop assisting Iran in building the Bushehr reactor.[87] Second, the United States and other countries should increase efforts to isolate the regime through increased sanctions. Third, the United States and other major powers should also continue supporting Iranian opposition groups in their efforts to bring about reforms or overturn the regime. Finally, the United States should not rule out the possibility of some form of military action, either to strike Iran's known nuclear facilities or even to bring about a regime change.

In the case of North Korea, the large presence of conventional and unconventional weapons that could be used to strike South Korea will probably prevent any military action to disarm the North, but it may be possible to use strong diplomatic means to achieve disarmament. The United States has taken the correct steps to further isolate North Korea by refusing to provide the shipments of oil that were arranged for in the Agreed Framework. It is also critical to maintain a united front with Japan and South Korea against yielding to North Korea's demands for oil, food, and money.[88] In addition, the United States must continue to work with China, North Korea's closest ally, to maintain a strong condemnation of Pyongyang's nuclear program. As scholars have noted, the loss of shipments of oil, money, and other international support will strongly impact North Korea, and this can be the starting point for productive negotiations.[89]

But even if these steps are taken, many worldwide nuclear risks remain, and the United States and the international community should do what they can to help reduce these risks.

Further Cuts in U.S. and Russian Nuclear Forces

A number of scholars have discussed possible ways to reduce dangers arising from the U.S. and Russian nuclear arsenals. The first steps they suggest are further reductions in the U.S. nuclear weapons program and fissile material stockpiles. Due to START I, the U.S. and Russian nuclear arsenals have both been significantly reduced in recent years. But many scholars argue that more should be done. The reductions outlined in Strategic Offensive Reductions Treaty (SORT) are a significant step, though some scholars have criticized the timetable for these reductions.[90] Since the cuts will take place over ten years, neither side appears to be in any particular hurry to reduce their arsenals. The two sides should also make progress in resolving their disputes over the U.S. "hedge" arsenal, which could also cause Russia to retain a permanent hedge arsenal in return—an arsenal it can ill afford to retain.

Given the risks that this study has identified, particularly with Russia's deteriorating nuclear controls, the United States and Russia should increase efforts for further—and more rapid—nuclear arms reductions.

The United States should also explore the possibilities for bilateral accords on the elimination of large numbers of tactical nuclear weapons in the U.S. and Russian arsenals.[91] While START limits the redeployment of strategic weapons, the tactical weapons reductions on both sides have only been limited by nonbinding unilateral declarations.[92] Because many of Russia's tactical weapons reportedly do not contain use-control devices, thefts of these weapons could be especially serious. Efforts to negotiate further tactical nuclear weapons reductions have reportedly not achieved much success, however, because Russia reportedly views its tactical nuclear forces as a necessary countermeasure to the recent technological breakthroughs by the United States in costly, advanced conventional arms.[93]

Increase Assistance to Russia

One of the most pressing threats to U.S. and global security is the danger arising from Russia's deteriorating nuclear systems. As we have seen, the deterioration of Russia's C^{3}I system has increased the dangers of accidental, unauthorized, and inadvertent use. One way to help reduce some of these dangers would be for the United States and Russia to finish the construction of the Joint Data Exchange Center (JDEC) as soon as possible, so that the two countries can share early-warning information on potential nuclear launches.[94] This center would help reduce risks of inadvertent launches, especially if relations between the United States and Russia do not deteriorate. The United States and Russia should therefore move rapidly to resolve their ongoing disputes over the center, so that the U.S. Congress will release the remaining funding.[95] Some analysts have also recommended that the United States provide financial and technical assistance to help Russia improve its ballistic missile early-warning (BMEW) system.[96]

Other analysts, most notably Bruce Blair, have also recommended dealerting U.S. and Russian nuclear weapons.[97] Many of the risks of inadvertent launches are due to the combined effects of Russia's deteriorating BMEW system and the high alert status (or "hair-trigger" alert) of U.S. and Russian nuclear weapons. If the weapons were taken off their high alert status, then at least some of these risks would be reduced. Although the Moscow Treaty includes provisions to remove a large number of weapons from alert status, these provisions will only be implemented over ten years; a significant number of weapons (1,700–2,200) will remain on high alert; and the provisions could be reversed rapidly, since the treaty does not forbid states to retain large hedge stockpiles.[98] Advocates of such proposals have suggested various ways for de-alerting the nuclear weapons, including removing warheads from missiles and storing them separately, removing launch keys from control centers, and erasing targeting information from computer systems.[99] These proposals are not without their critics, however. Officials in the governments and militaries in both the United States and Russia have often objected to such suggestions because they feel it would reduce security too much.[100] Critics have also argued that de-alerting could greatly *increase* instability during crises, because both sides would have great incentives to engage in dangerous re-alerting of massive numbers of weapons very quickly.[101]

Given the seriousness of the risks associated with a loss of control over Russia's nuclear weapons and fissile materials, continued emphasis must also be placed on improving Russia's nuclear security. The United States and the international community should therefore increase funding and support for the CTR and MPC&A programs. A January 2001 bipartisan report argued that current efforts in U.S.-Russian nuclear security should be significantly expanded. The report recommended that the United States should invest $30 billion over the next ten years in this critical area.[102]

The Bush administration can and should place efforts to help Russia improve its controls among its highest priorities. Unfortunately, the administration's policies on U.S.-Russia nonproliferation programs did not get off to a propitious start. Despite President Bush's pledges to increase support for these programs prior to his election, the Bush administration started its term by proposing to cut the program's budget by $40 million compared to the previous year's budget and nearly $100 million compared to the FY2002 budget envisioned by the Clinton administration.[103]

In the aftermath of the September 11, 2001, terrorist attacks, however, there has been renewed urgency to improving Russia's nuclear controls. After their November 2001 summit meeting, Presidents Bush and Putin issued a joint statement, which called for "improving the physical protection and accounting of nuclear materials for all possessor states." Following on these provisions, U.S. Department of Energy secretary Spencer Abraham and Russian minister of atomic energy Alexander Rumyantsev announced an agreement on November 29, 2001, to expand and accelerate efforts to improve MPC&A.[104]

The funding for these programs has also been significantly increased in the last several years. Although the FY2002 budget provided $173 million to MPC&A programs, roughly the same as 2001 levels,[105] the proposed FY2003 budget included $233 million for the MPC&A program.[106] Moreover, in December 2001, the U.S. Congress allocated $226 million in emergency supplemental funding for nonproliferation and nuclear security programs in Russia and the former Soviet Union. This money was part of a $20 billion supplemental allocation attached to the defense appropriations bill. In the FY2004 budget, Congress approved a total of $255 million for MPC&A programs in the former Soviet Union, $36 million more than was requested.[107]

Furthermore, on June 27, 2002, the Group of 8 (G-8) industrialized countries met in Canada to discuss a "Global Partnership Against the Spread of Weapons and Materials of Mass Destruction."[108] This initiative, also called "10 plus 10 over 10," calls for the United States to provide $10 billion over the next ten years to assist Russia in securing its nuclear weapons and materials, and calls for the other G-8 states to provide an additional $10 billion over the same period. If carried out, this initiative will not only greatly increase the funding and assistance to Russia, but will also provide much-needed *international* commitment to addressing this problem. There are, however, some questions about the extent to which the G-8 countries will be able to deliver on these commitments, due to worldwide economic stagnation.[109]

In addition to funding issues, the United States and Russia appear to have made progress on another major obstacle to the MPC&A program. Due to the sensitivity of the issues involved, U.S. personnel had long been denied access to many critical sites and were therefore unable to determine what improvements were necessary at these sites. In late September 2001, however, Russia agreed to grant access to the majority of Minatom sites, thereby setting the stage for major work to get under way at the remaining sensitive facilities.[110]

In addition to these efforts, it is also possible that the scope of the MPC&A program might be dramatically expanded. With the recent government and media attention on the possibility that Bin Laden might posses a radiological device (a "dirty bomb"), there may be efforts to control not only plutonium and HEU, but also other types of radioactive substances, such as spent fuel and uranium enriched to below 20 percent U-235 (the amount necessary for a nuclear explosion).[111]

For the CTR and MPC&A programs to be successful in the long term, however, they must ensure the "sustainability" of the security upgrades to Russian facilities. The reports of facilities being unable to maintain equipment once it is in place or of facilities simply being willing to bypass security procedures are very troubling indeed. There are several ways for the CTR and MPC&A programs to help ensure that security upgrades are effective in the future, including promoting indigenous Russian MPC&A technologies and providing funding for certain aspects of the operation and maintenance of the MPC&A technology until Russia can take over.[112]

But for these collaborative projects truly to be successful, they must address Russia's security and safeguards culture more directly. A recent study by the University of Georgia's Center for International Trade and Security outlines several basic prerequisites for nurturing Russia's nuclear security culture, including encouraging Russia's political leadership and top executives to promote the principles of nuclear security in allocation of resources; making instructions and regulations more user-friendly and understandable; improving nuclear site recruitment and training procedures; and changing how nuclear site personnel perceive the level of threat to fissile materials.[113] Western states and nongovernmental organizations can provide a great deal of assistance in these areas and should work with Russia to implement programs to help achieve these objectives as soon as possible.

Explore Possibilities for Renewed Collaboration with China to Improve Nuclear Controls

Any accidental or unauthorized launch of nuclear weapons or any theft of nuclear weapons or fissile materials constitutes an unacceptable threat to the United States and the international community. The United States therefore has a vital interest in encouraging China to improve the command-and-control system for its nuclear weapons and the MPC&A for its nuclear facilities. The best way for the United States to pursue this interest would be to continue the lab-to-lab collaboration with China.[114]

Increased scientific collaborations will improve the trust between the two countries on nuclear issues. This greater trust could increase transparency and mutual understanding of the nuclear establishments in the two counties. It is only from such a position of trust that the United States could hope to encourage China to improve its command-and-control structure.

The United States must ensure that its assistance in improvements to China's command-and-control system does not also improve China's nuclear capabilities. For example, although specific technical information about some types of use-control devices should not be given China because it would also reveal important information about U.S. warhead designs,[115] there are a number of U.S. use-control technologies and procedures that have little to do with weapon designs. With care, the United States should be able to help China improve its command and control while still protecting its national security interests.

But perhaps even more importantly, the lab-to-lab collaborations seem to be the best way we could hope to encourage China to improve its MPC&A. As we have seen, weak MPC&A systems can increase the risks of nuclear weapon proliferation and nuclear terrorism. Despite the uncertainties that remain in our knowledge about Chinese MPC&A, the risks of losing material, as well as the opportunities for improved controls, strongly suggest that the United States should take a vital interest in encouraging China to improve the MPC&A for its nuclear facilities. The United States must also help create a safeguards culture in China, where everyone from high-level politicians to the lowest-level guard recognizes the importance of rigorous MPC&A procedures and technologies.

The most direct way to address these potential threats would be to restart MPC&A collaborations with China. There have been few prospects for such cooperation in recent years, but an improvement in U.S.-China relations after the September 11, 2001, attacks may allow opportunities for reintroducing such a program in the future. U.S. and Chinese officials have stated that they "stand side-by-side" in the war on terrorism and have committed to promoting international antiterrorism cooperation.[116] This position may provide an opportunity to renew lab-to-lab collaborations in the context of the antiterrorism campaign.

These efforts will have to proceed carefully, however, in order to allay Chinese suspicions that this is a merely cynical approach to gain information on China's nuclear program. Also, China will need some reassurance that such cooperation will not trigger future espionage scandals. By including the U.S.-China MPC&A program among the various programs intended to bolster the war on terrorism, however, it may be possible to avoid some of the political difficulties that affected the CACE program last time around—for instance, to strictly segregate the MPC&A program from other issues of nuclear cooperation to make it more palatable to political authorities on both sides.[117]

As a first step to renewing MPC&A collaborations, the United States should attempt to reestablish the contacts with officials within the CNNC and the CAEA that were severed after the publication of the Cox report. This step can be achieved by renewing engagement with officials at international conferences, and by inviting Chinese officials to the United States to meet with U.S. policymakers, scientists, and academics.

The United States could also consider initiating other lab-to-lab collaborations dealing with less sensitive issues. These collaborations could focus on safety and security issues at civilian facilities, for instance. They could engage, at least at first, such Chinese agencies as the National Nuclear Safety Administration (NNSA).[118] If these programs were to achieve success, then U.S. and Chinese officials could consider expanding them to include all of China's nuclear facilities.

A difficulty with such an approach, however, is that the largest stockpiles of HEU and separated plutonium are presumably located at China's military facilities. This approach would therefore mean that the most attractive materials for theft would be the last to be dealt with. Thus, while this approach would be the most likely to be acceptable to leaders on both sides, it should be expanded as soon as politically feasible. In the meantime, however, beginning with civilian facilities would by no means be wasted time. First, improving MPC&A at China's civilian and research reactors would reduce risks of sabotage and help protect the sensitive materials at these facilities. Second, by beginning with civilian facilities, China could become more familiar with Western approaches to designing and installing MPC&A systems, thus setting the stage for rapid progress when the program is expanded to military facilities.[119]

Pursue More Consistent Non-Proliferation Policies and Support Improved Nuclear Security in South Asia

India and Pakistan are currently at critical crossroads in their nuclear programs. Both countries have demonstrated their nuclear weapons capabilities, but neither has yet moved down the path toward weaponization and deployment. If the United States and the international community take advantage of this window of opportunity, they could stop the movement toward weaponization and deployment before it is too late.

Such an undertaking will obviously be very difficult and will require able diplomacy, as well as a successful strategy of incentives and international pressure. In the past, the United States has pursued inconsistent nonproliferation policies in South Asia, which it was often willing to compromise when they became inconvenient.[120] The United States should learn from these lessons and pursue more consistent nonproliferation policies in the region.

In the near term, however, there are significant obstacles to renewed nonproliferation objectives. In the aftermath of the September 11, 2001, terrorist attacks, the United States removed most of its economic sanctions and eased its nonproliferation pressure, since it needed Pakistan as a base for attacks on Afghanistan and later on al Qaeda operatives in the region.[121] It has also opened the possibility for future military sales to Pakistan. While it may have been necessary for the United States to make some compromises in light of the vital need to remove the imminent danger of terrorist attacks, these actions will make nonproliferation objectives in South Asia more difficult.

It is important not to forget previous nonproliferation commitments as the United States focuses on its war on terrorism. The United States should therefore work with the international community to encourage both countries to sign and ratify the Comprehensive Test Ban Treaty (CTBT) and refrain from producing weapons-grade fissile materials. To change India's and Pakistan's cost-benefit analysis on weaponization, the United States should warn the two countries that nuclear weapons deployment will result in stringent unilateral and international diplomatic and fiscal sanctions.[122] In addition, the United States and the international community should continue working to prevent India and Pakistan from acquiring technologies that would assist in missile production and weapons deployment. They should therefore work to strengthen compliance with current nonproliferation export-control regimes, such as the Missile Technology Control Regime (MTCR).[123]

The United States and the international community must also work to help resolve the critical flashpoint of Kashmir. Although India has refused to allow third-party mediation over the issue of Kashmir, the United States can work with the two states in improving crisis stability. The steps taken by the two countries in May 2003 to improve relations are positive developments, and the United States and others should work to help India and Pakistan reestablish the confidence-building measures outlined in the Lahore Declaration.[124] But the success of these measures depends on Pakistan's willingness to reign in cross-border terrorism. The United States should be very clear that it opposes Pakistan's support of Islamic militants and should encourage Musharraf to follow through with the crackdown on militants. Pakistan's support of Islamic militants has been a major source of the tensions between India and Pakistan, a cause of many of the problems in Afghanistan, and a continuing obstacle to long-term stability within Pakistan itself.

Given the potential risks of nuclear thefts and sabotage identified in this study, the United States and the international community should also encourage India and Pakistan to improve their nuclear security systems. Although a number of scholars have recommended that the United States provide command-and-control technologies, such as PALs or equivalent systems, such assistance would both conflict with U.S. nonproliferation obligations and could increase the likelihood that India and Pakistan would operationalize their nuclear weapons. A more feasible option would be for the United States to provide general information on how to design security systems and establish personnel reliability programs. The United States should also encourage both countries to work with the IAEA to implement MPC&A systems at their nuclear facilities. For example, they could work with the IAEA's International Physical Protection Advisory Service for assistance in designing physical protection systems.[125] Because both India and Pakistan are currently members of the IAEA, this may be a viable option for improving nuclear security in India and Pakistan without openly condoning their nuclear weapons programs. The United States should also consider establishing contingency plans for emergency assistance to Pakistan if domestic upheavals were to threaten the security of Pakistani nuclear weapons.[126]

Improve Nuclear Security at Worldwide Civilian Reactors

Finally, the United States and the international community should work with the IAEA to encourage improvements in nuclear security at civilian reactors throughout the world. The IAEA reported that thefts of nuclear materials around the world have increased in recent years.[127] Because materials produced at civilian reactors could be used in nuclear weapons or radiological devices, they are a serious concern. The IAEA and its participating countries should therefore strengthen international requirements for physical protection systems at nuclear reactors and enrichment facilities.

On December 7, 2001, the IAEA held a meeting in Vienna to consider expanding the 1980 Convention on Physical Protection of Nuclear Material to include requirements that member states pass legislation implementing IAEA guidelines for physical protection of nuclear facilities.[128] The meeting stalled, however, apparently because some members were reluctant to amend the convention. After a follow-up meeting in March 2002, the IAEA did approve a program to help states improve the MPC&A at their nuclear facilities. The program allows for a member state to request for the IAEA to provide a team of experts to conduct assessments of MPC&A at given facilities, give advice on security upgrades, and, in rare cases, provide some small types of equipment for these upgrades.[129] While this new program may help improve the MPC&A systems in certain states, however, it does not require states to meet any international standards for MPC&A. Given the risks of nuclear terrorism, more needs to be done to improve legal standards for MPC&A at nuclear facilities throughout the world.

Part III: The Perils of Abstract Theorizing

Until now, the proliferation debate has largely taken place on an abstract, theoretical level. No doubt this orientation partly reflects perfectly legitimate scholarly concerns: in order to improve our understanding of international affairs, we of course need to establish theories to explain and predict state action. Participants in the proliferation debate have gone astray, however, in placing theorizing at the beginning, rather than at the end of their thinking. Instead of building theories on solid evidence gathered from rigorous empirical studies, they have too often predicted future state actions only on the basis of preexisting theories. From a scholarly point of view, one of the most important lessons from the present study is that we cannot afford anything other than a relentlessly empirical foundation for—and testing of—social science theory.

While abstract theorizing can be found on both sides of the debate, it is especially common among the optimists. Rather than asking how NWSs actually *do* act, optimists have begun with theories of how states *should* act—that is, in accordance with supposedly "realist" rational-actor models—and predicted the actions of states on that basis. One need only recall Waltz's confident statement, "We do not have to wonder whether they [NWSs] will take good care of their weapons. They have every incentive to do so."[130] On the contrary, the proper approach to theory would *begin* with wonder about whether states do, in fact, always act with such rational incentives in mind. As the present study has demonstrated, there is little empirical support for such an optimistic position where nuclear proliferation is concerned. While realist theories may be useful for explaining certain types of state actions, they are inappropriate models for predicting specific policies and actions that NWSs will take.

Having oversimplified the causes and motivations of state action, the optimists make highly inappropriate policy recommendations regarding nuclear proliferation. Indeed, those recommendations go beyond what the optimists' own theories could possibly support. In a context *other* than the proliferation debate, Waltz argues that his theories cannot predict specific policies or particular actions by individual states; instead, he maintains, they can predict only general trends.[131] But, as Jeffrey Knopf has pointed out, when one is advocating a further proliferation of nuclear weapons, predicting general trends is not enough: one must be certain that one's theories are correct *all of the time*.[132] It is likely that a certain awareness of the special dangers attending nuclear weapons policy leads Waltz to misapply his own realist theory and predict that NWSs will act rationally without exception. But that awareness must be replaced by fully conscious practical reasoning. Empirically grounded theories, combined with the prudence of the policymaker, would lead to policy recommendations that are more sound.

Absent a nuclear exchange, or a series of nuclear exchanges, we will lack conclusive proof that a further spread of nuclear weapons will lead to nuclear catastrophes. May such a proof never be forthcoming. In the meantime, however, I hope this study will contribute to more nuanced and accurate theorizing about state action—theories acknowledging that while states sometimes act rationally, they often fail to do so when constrained by certain political, bureaucratic, economic, and other factors. I also hope this study will contribute to better-informed policymaking on nuclear issues. Although continued study of the historical record and future developments will surely provide additional relevant information, it is already fairly clear that U.S. and global interests lie in preventing a further spread of nuclear weapons and reducing nuclear dangers among current NWSs as much as possible. If the United States takes the lead in these areas, we will make progress toward making the world a safer place.

Appendix
Current IAEA-Related Standards for MPC&A

One of the major issues this book examines is the adequacy of the MPC&A programs in the NWSs. It is therefore critical that we establish a standard by which we can judge whether or not a given MPC&A program is "adequate." What, then, would an "adequate" MPC&A system look like? This is not an easy question to answer. Before we can answer this question, however, we need to examine what objectives an MPC&A program should try to achieve.

An effective MPC&A system serves up to four different objectives:

1. Prevent the theft of nuclear materials.
2. Prevent the sabotage of a nuclear facility (or a nuclear transport vehicle).
3. Detect the theft of nuclear materials once it has occurred.
4. Detect the diversion of nuclear materials by a given state from its peaceful nuclear program to an opaque nuclear weapons program.

In order to achieve these objectives, MPC&A systems are generally divided into two distinct, though interrelated systems: Physical Protection and Material Control and Accounting (MC&A). A physical protection system is designed to prevent the theft of nuclear materials or sabotage of nuclear materials or facilities.[1] These objectives are achieved in two ways: by deterring threats or by defeating them should groups or individuals attempt to steal nuclear materials or sabotage nuclear facilities.[2] This deterrence is achieved by implementing a physical protection system that is perceived to be too difficult to overcome. And, of course, if anyone does attempt to steal materials or to sabotage a facility, the physical protection system must also be able to stop the attempt. An effective physical protection system will use barriers, surveillance systems, alarms, and guards to achieve these goals.

Nuclear material control and accounting (MC&A) systems, on the other hand, are used to detect a theft or diversion of nuclear materials once it has occurred. It is only possible to discover whether some materials have disappeared if one knows the exact location and amounts of nuclear materials in a given facility. The material must be effectively "controlled" by means of portal monitors to detect any materials passing from nuclear material storage sites, secure containers for nuclear material, tamper-resistant seals, and identification codes that make it possible to verify easily the location and storage condition of nuclear material.[3] In addition, there must be effective "accounting" systems in place to provide "a regularly updated, measured inventory of nuclear weapons usable material, based on routine measurements of material arriving, leaving, lost to waste and remaining within the facility."[4]

The MC&A systems required by the International Atomic Energy Agency (IAEA) are used to detect whether a NNWS has diverted nuclear materials from its peaceful nuclear programs into a nuclear weapons program. The MC&A systems in the NWSs, on the other hand, are primarily intended to detect a theft of nuclear materials for use by (or sale to) either a terrorist group or a country that wants to build nuclear weapons. While a physical protection system might be very useful in opposing an attempt by an outsider to steal fissile materials, MC&A is a means of detecting such attempts by insiders. While MC&A is mainly useful in detecting a theft after it has occurred, it can also serve as a deterrence against the insider threat, because it will often be possible to trace who the insider was once it has been discovered that nuclear materials have disappeared.

Now that we have seen what an MPC&A program is supposed to do, we can examine what specific requirements are necessary in order to achieve these goals. This is an issue that the International Atomic Energy Agency has spent a great deal of time attempting to answer. Since its inception, the IAEA has been responsible for facilitating the use of nuclear energy for peaceful purposes and implementing a system of audits and on-site inspections, collectively known as "safeguards," to verify that nuclear facilities and materials are not being diverted for nuclear explosive purposes.[5] As part of its responsibilities, the IAEA has helped create recommendations and standards for MPC&A systems. Although the IAEA regulations apply only to peaceful nuclear materials, they also give us a good idea of what a complete MPC&A system for nuclear materials would look like. They therefore give us a standard by which we can judge the adequacy of the MPC&A in the NWSs.

It is necessary to explain the general background for IAEA regulations. In Parts I and II below, I therefore briefly describe the IAEA-related treaties that establish the laws and norms for MC&A, then discuss the specific requirements for MC&A that arise from these treaties. I follow the same procedure in Parts III and IV below for physical protection standards.

Part I: IAEA Treaties That Help Establish Standards for MC&A

Limited-Scope Safeguards (covered under INFCIRC/66)

The very first IAEA safeguards system was outlined in INFCIRC/26. The document required inspections of the reactors, but "except in the case of an incident requiring a 'special inspection,' at least one week's notice was to be given of each inspection; the notice must include the name(s) of the inspector(s), the place and time of arrival in the State concerned and the items to be inspected."[6] Although significant for being the first safeguard system, INFCIRC/26 left much to be desired. Its first and most obvious shortcoming was that it only applied to reactors producing less than 100 MW(t). In addition, because of the political battles during its negotiation, the final document was "one of the most convoluted pieces of verbal expression in history."[7] In February 1963, the Board of Governors of the IAEA unanimously agreed that INFCIRC/22 needed to be clarified, and its safeguards extended to cover reactors of any size.[8]

It took until June 1965 to reach unanimous agreement in favor of INFCIRC/66, which applied safeguards to all sizes of nuclear reactors. It was later revised, so that safeguards would be applied to reprocessing plants (in INFCIRC/66/Rev.1 in 1966) and fuel fabrication plants (in INFCIRC/66/Rev.2 in 1968). INFCIRC/66 established what came to be called "limited-scope" safeguards. These safeguards are placed on individual plants, shipments of nuclear fuel, or supply agreements between importers and exporters of nuclear fuel or technology.[9]

INFCIRC/66 does not explicitly require a system for accounting and control (MC&A), but it does require a "system of records" and a "system of reports," which together would essentially require an MC&A program.[10] It says nothing about any standards for physical protection for nuclear facilities.

Under INFCIRC/66, it is possible for a nation to have both safeguarded and unsafeguarded nuclear facilities. Limited-scope safeguards are currently still applied to the states that have not signed the Treaty on the Non-Proliferation of Nuclear Weapons (NPT): India, Israel, and Pakistan.

Treaty on the Non-Proliferation of Nuclear Weapons (NPT)

The NPT is the cornerstone for current international efforts in nuclear nonproliferation. It was opened for signature in 1968 and entered into force in

1970. As of November 2002, every country in the world had signed the NPT except India, Israel, and Pakistan, though North Korea withdrew from the treaty in January 2003.[11] The NPT essentially says that the nuclear weapons states (NWSs) will help non–nuclear weapons states (NNWSs) with their peaceful nuclear programs as long as the NNWSs promise not to use these technologies as part of an opaque nuclear program.[12] In addition, Article VI of the NPT says that each party to the treaty will undertake to work toward nuclear disarmament.

Article I of the NPT forbids any nuclear weapons state (NWS) party to the treaty from transferring "to any recipient whatsoever nuclear weapons or other nuclear explosive devices or control over such weapons or explosive devices directly or indirectly; and not in any way to otherwise acquire nuclear weapons or other nuclear explosive devices, or control over such weapons or explosive devices." Thus, the NPT also implies that the NWSs should have strict fissile material protection, control, and accounting (MPC&A), since inadequate controls could increase risks of thefts of fissile materials, which could ultimately allow aspiring nuclear powers to develop nuclear weapons. Of course, MPC&A in the NWSs is not the most direct purpose of the NPT. It focuses much more on intentional transfers of nuclear weapons technologies from the NWSs to the NNWSs and on the illicit diversion of nuclear materials and technologies from peaceful nuclear programs in the NNWSs.

Article II of the NPT says that each NNWS party to the treaty agrees not to receive or develop any nuclear weapons technologies, either directly or indirectly. In order to verify this commitment, Article III of the NPT says that the NNWSs should undertake to accept IAEA safeguards "for the exclusive purpose of verification of the fulfillment of its obligations assumed under this treaty." The NPT therefore provides the basis for full-scope international safeguards, but it does not specify in detail how the safeguards are to be implemented in each NNWS or the techniques and methods to use. The specific details for full-scope safeguards were later laid out in INFCIRC/153.

Full-Scope Safeguards (covered under INFCIRC/153)

INFCIRC/153 established a system of safeguards to help verify that NNWSs fulfill the commitments they undertook in the NPT not to divert nuclear materials into opaque nuclear weapons programs. As such, it places no specific requirements on the NWSs. This fact, however, was the cause of intense debate for several years after the NPT entered into force. Many of the NNWSs were concerned that the full-scope safeguards would give the NWSs a competitive advantage in their peaceful nuclear programs. In order to appease these concerns, President Johnson offered to apply safeguards to all nuclear activities in the U.S. other than those with direct national security significance. The offer took effect in 1980. Since then, the United Kingdom, France, and Russia have made similar offers.[13] But there are still no safeguards on the nuclear weapons programs in the NWSs.

Part I of INFCIRC/153 outlines the general principles governing the rights and obligations of the parties to the NPT. In order to verify that no nuclear material has been diverted into nuclear weapons programs, it is critical that the IAEA know exactly how much nuclear material a state has at each stage of its nuclear cycle. INFCIRC/153 therefore makes specific requirements for nuclear material control and accounting (MC&A) in the NNWSs: "The Agreement should provide that the State shall establish and maintain a system of accounting for and control of all nuclear material subject to safeguards under the Agreement, and that such safeguards shall be applied in such a manner as to enable the Agency to verify, in ascertaining that there has been no diversion of nuclear material from peaceful uses to nuclear weapons or other nuclear explosive devices, findings of the State's system."[14] Part II of INFCIRC/153 explains the requirements for the MC&A program in much greater detail. I will discuss these specific requirements in my own Part II below.

INFCIRC/153 also makes provisions for the IAEA to conduct inspections of declared nuclear facilities in the NNWSs. The agency must conduct an initial (ad hoc) inspection to determine the amount of nuclear materials that a given state possesses in its declared nuclear facilities. After that, the Agency can make routine inspections to verify that that State's "reports are consistent with its records" and to verify "the location, identity, quantity and composition of all nuclear material subject to safeguards under the Agreement."[15] The agency can also conduct "special inspections" if it "considers that information made available by the State, including explanations from the State and information obtained from routine inspections, is not adequate for the Agency to fulfil its responsibilities under the Agreement."[16] In both these cases, the IAEA must give the State prior notification that it will conduct the inspections.[17]

Strengthened Safeguards System (Programme 93+2) and "Integrated Safeguards"

Although the full-scope safeguard system has done a fairly good job at verifying the safeguards agreements undertaken in the NPT, it has some serious shortcomings. Its greatest shortcoming is that the IAEA is only given the authority to inspect the inventories of *declared* nuclear facilities to ensure that nuclear material had not been diverted to weapons programs. Full-scope safeguards simply do not apply to any nuclear materials produced or stored at undeclared nuclear facilities. The 1991 Persian Gulf War revealed the weakness of the full-scope safeguard system. It came to light that Iraq had an extensive opaque nuclear weapons program and had come very close to making a nuclear weapon. It was later discovered that North Korea had also engaged in an opaque nuclear weapons program. Iraq and North Korea were violating the NPT, since they had promised not to develop nuclear weapons when they signed the treaty. But the IAEA was unable to detect these violations, since they occurred at undeclared nuclear facilities. As a result of these evident weaknesses in the full-scope safeguards system, the IAEA undertook a study to determine ways to strengthen the safeguards system. This study was known as the 93+2 Program, and gave rise to a two-part Strengthened Safeguards System.

In 1995, the IAEA's Board of Governors approved Part I of the Strengthened Safeguards System. Part I provides for the following measures:

- Non–nuclear weapons states are now required to provide IAEA with additional information about nuclear activities undertaken prior to entry into force of their safeguards agreements.
- IAEA's inspectors are now allowed to perform environmental sampling at facilities and locations where they currently have access.
- IAEA is increasing its access to all declared nuclear and nuclear-related locations and will employ the use of unannounced inspections.
- IAEA is testing new safeguards measurement and surveillance systems that can operate unattended and can transmit safeguards data remotely.
- IAEA is increasing its cooperation with state and regional systems of accounting and control, including those in the European Union, performed by the European Atomic Energy Community (EURATOM), and those between Brazil and Argentina.[18]

Part II of the Strengthened Safeguards System was passed by the Board of Governors in May 1997, and was codified in INFCIRC/540, the *Model Protocol Additional to the Agreement(s) between State(s) and the International Atomic Energy Agency for the Application of Safeguards,* or the Model Additional Protocol. The Model Additional Protocol measures include the following:

- IAEA will gather information about all aspects of a state's nuclear fuel cycle, including information about research and development on the nuclear fuel cycle, the manufacture and export of sensitive and other key nuclear-related equipment, and all buildings on a nuclear site.

- IAEA inspectors will be provided access to all aspects of a state's nuclear fuel cycle including: facilities at which nuclear fuel-cycle research and development is carried out; manufacturing and import locations; and all buildings on a nuclear site, including undeclared or suspect sites. This is to provide, among other things, a deterrent to the co-location of clandestine and peaceful activities. IAEA may exercise this right through short-notice inspections on sites where nuclear material is located and at other locations. This access will include the right to take environmental samples.
- IAEA inspectors will be provided access to conduct "wide-area" environmental monitoring, that is, collecting environmental samples beyond declared locations when deemed necessary.
- States will improve their administrative arrangements for designating inspectors and issuing multiple-entry visas to facilitate unannounced/short-notice inspections and permit access to modern means of communication.[19]

As of November 11, 2003, the Additional Protocols had been signed by seventy-eight states and had entered into force in thirty-eight states.[20]

Most of the IAEA's current and future work on the Strengthened Safeguards System continues to be that of integrating traditional nuclear material verification activities with new strengthening measures.[21] This endeavor is now called Integrated Safeguards. Many of the details on Integrated Safeguards have yet to be determined, but the new IAEA authorities could allow for a redefinition of traditional safeguards activities. In particular, if the IAEA were able to obtain a positive conclusion on the absence of undeclared nuclear material activities in a given state as a whole, particularly on activities related to enrichment and reprocessing, it might be able to reduce current levels of traditional safeguards verification efforts on undeclared nuclear materials.[22]

Part II: Specific MC&A Standards set by INFCIRC/153

To a certain degree, the IAEA safeguards are intended to serve a different purpose than the MC&A programs in the weapons states would. The goal of the IAEA safeguards is to detect whether any NNWS is diverting nuclear materials from a peaceful nuclear program into an opaque nuclear weapons program. This is simply not a concern for the NWSs. In the NWSs, we are concerned with the possibility of theft of nuclear materials, especially by insiders. But the only way to detect whether anyone has illegally obtained nuclear materials from the NWSs is if the NWSs have adequate MC&A systems. Thus, the standards for MC&A established by INFCIRC/153 will be an excellent measure by which we can judge the adequacy of the MC&A in the NWSs.

INFCIRC/153 explicitly requires the State signatories to establish a state system of accounting and control (SSAC) for nuclear materials.[23] The first step in setting up this system is to identify "material balance areas," or key places where the amounts of nuclear material entering and exiting the facility can be measured. In addition, INFCIRC/153 requires the following provisions:

1. A measurement system for the determination of the quantities of nuclear material received, produced, shipped, lost, or otherwise removed from inventory, and the quantities on inventory.
2. The evaluation of precision and accuracy of measurements and the estimation of measurement uncertainty.
3. Procedures for identifying, reviewing, and evaluating differences in shipper/receiver measurements.
4. Procedures for taking a physical inventory.
5. Procedures for the evaluation of accumulations of unmeasured inventory and unmeasured losses.
6. A system of records and reports showing, for each material balance area, the inventory of nuclear material and the changes in that inventory, including receipts into and transfers out of the material balance area.
7. Provisions to ensure that the accounting procedures and arrangements are being operated correctly.
8. Procedures for the provisions of reports to the Agency.

INFCIRC/153 requires that State signatories be able to calculate "material unaccounted for" (MUF) with the following formula:

MUF = BI (beginning inventory) + A (additions) - EI (ending inventory) - R (removals) - KL (known loss)

In order to ensure an accurate MUF, the state should establish a specific records system, which will consist of *accounting records* of all nuclear material subject to safeguards, and *operating records* for facilities containing such nuclear material.

The *accounting records* should consist of:

- All inventory changes, so as to permit a determination of the book inventory at any time.
- All measurement results that are used for determination of the physical inventory.
- All adjustments and corrections that have been made in respect of inventory changes, book inventories, and physical inventories.
- Any differences between shipper and receiver reports.
- For all of these inventory changes and physical inventories, the records should show the material identification, batch data, and source data for each given batch of nuclear material.

The *operating records* should consist of:

- Those operating data which are used to establish changes in the quantities and composition of nuclear material.
- The data obtained from the calibration of tanks and instruments and from sampling and analyses, the procedures to control the quality of measurements, and the derived estimates of random and systematic error.
- A description of the sequence of the actions taken in preparing for, and in taking, a physical inventory in order to ensure that it is correct and complete.
- A description of the actions taken in order to ascertain the cause and magnitude of any accidental or unmeasured loss that might occur.

If the state makes detailed records in every one of these areas, it would have a very high likelihood of detecting whether any nuclear materials have been diverted or stolen.[24]

Part III: IAEA Documents and Treaties that Help Establish Standards for Physical Protection of Fissile Materials

While INFCIRC/153 establishes standards for MC&A (albeit only in the NNWSs), it says nothing about physical protection.[25] There are two major IAEA documents that establish the standards for physical protection: INFCIRC/274/Rev.1, which was the result of the 1979 Convention on the

Physical Protection of Fissile Materials (PPC); and INFCIRC/225/Rev.4, *The Physical Protection of Nuclear Material and Nuclear Facilities*.[26] The PPC entered into force in 1987, and sixty states are now members of the treaty.[27] Although the PPC establishes some standards for physical protection, it only covers the transfer of materials for peaceful purposes across international borders, and it has no provision for verification or enforcement.

INFCIRC/225/Rev.4 is the document in which the IAEA systematically lays out its recommendations for physical protection during use, storage, and transportation. INFCIRC/225 was originally published in 1975, but it was revised several times afterward.[28] The latest version, INFCIRC/225/Rev.4, was published in 1998. This is the document that I use as a standard for assessing the adequacy of the physical protection systems in the NWSs.[29]

Although INFCIRC/225 has never actually been implemented, a number of IAEA documents refer to it. For example, the Nuclear Suppliers Group (INFCIRC/254/Rev.2) states that all items listed in their "trigger group" should be placed under physical protection that takes into account all international standards and refers to INFCIRC/225 as a "useful basis for guiding recipient States in designing a system of physical protection measures and procedures."[30]

Another important IAEA document that refers to INFCIRC/225 is the *Guidelines for the Management of Plutonium* (GMP). This document, codified in INFCIRC/549, was opened for signature in March 1998. It presents rigorous requirements for the management and disposition for excess plutonium used for peaceful purposes. It establishes MC&A standards similar to INFCIRC/153, and says that states should implement physical protection regulations "taking into account" INFCIRC/225/Rev.3.[31]

Part IV: Specific Physical Protection Recommendations in INFCIRC/225

While INFCIRC/153 establishes standards for control and accounting (albeit only in the NNWSs), it says nothing about physical protection. The standards for the physical protection of SNM are established by INFCIRC/225. INFCIRC/225 is intended to "establish conditions which would minimize the possibilities for unauthorized removal of nuclear material or for sabotage."[32] To achieve this end, it provides "a set of recommendations on requirements for the physical protection of nuclear material in use, transit, and storage and of nuclear facilities."[33]

INFCIRC/225 establishes a set of guidelines for the categorization of fissile materials and what physical protection measures should correspond to the different classification levels. Materials are divided into three categories, depending on the type of material, the physical and chemical form, the degree of dilution, the radiation level, and the quantity of the material present. The three categories are outlined in table A.1:

Table A.1. IAEA Categorization of Nuclear Material

Material	Form	Category I	Category II	Category III
1. Plutonium	Unirradiated	2 kg or more	Less than 2 kg but more than 500 g	500 g or less but more than 15 g
2. Uranium-235	Unirradiated: -uranium enriched to 20% U-235 or more	5 kg of more	Less than 5 kg but more than 1 kg	1 kg or less but more than 15g
	-uranium enriched to 10% U-235 but less than 20% U-235		10 kg or more	Less than 10 kg but more than 1 kg
	-uranium enriched above natural, but less than 10% U-235			10 kg or more
3. Uranium-233	Unirradiated	2 kg or more	Less than 2 kg but more than 500 g	500 g or less but more than 25 g
4. Irradiated Fuel			Depleted or natural uranium, thorium or low-enriched fuel (less than 10% fissile content)	

After INFCIRC/225 establishes the three categories for fissile material, it recommends the corresponding guidelines for physical protection. The physical protection guidelines "should take into account the category of nuclear material, its location (use, transit, storage) and the particular circumstances prevailing either in the State or along the transportation route."[34] The physical protection measures that correspond to each category for fissile materials in use storage are summarized in Section A below, and the measures for materials in transit are then summarized in Section B.

A. Physical Protection Recommendations for Special Nuclear Materials in Use and Storage

Requirements for Category I Materials in Use and Storage

During use and storage, Category I materials should be contained in at least two complete, reliable areas, an outer "protected area" and a more secure "inner area." I will discuss the physical protection recommendations for each of these areas in turn.[35]

Inner Area(s)

- All Category I material should be used or stored within the inner area or inner areas.
- Access to the inner area should be restricted to employees whose duties require access to this area. These employees should carry badges demonstrating authorization.
- There should be a limited number of entrances to the inner area. All emergency exits should be fitted with alarms.
- Fissile materials should be stored in a vault in the inner area. The vault should be protected by alarms and adequate locks, and the issue of keys or key-cards should be closely controlled.
- Whenever persons are present in inner areas, those areas should be under constant surveillance. The surveillance can be effected by mutual observation between two or more co-workers (e.g., a two-person rule).
- Material should be protected by guards at all times. An external and internal patrol should be provided.

Protected Area(s)

- The protected area should be under constant surveillance (by a guard or by electronic means). The perimeter of the protected area should normally consist of a physical barrier (a fence, wall, or a similar impediment approved by a security survey) in addition to and outside the walls of the building itself.
- Access to the protected area should be restricted to those whose duties require access to this area.
- Entry of private motor vehicles into the protected area should be minimized and limited to authorized parking areas. Private motor vehicles should be prohibited from access to inner areas.

Requirements for Category II Material in Use and Storage:

- Category II material should be used or stored within a protected area or protected areas. The protected area should be under constant surveillance (by a guard or by electronic means). The perimeter of the protected area should normally consist of a physical barrier (a fence or wall or a similar impediment approved by a security survey) in addition to and outside the walls of the building.

- All persons entering the protected area should be issued either special passes or badges and be appropriately registered, and access to the protected area should be kept to the minimum necessary. A record should be kept of all persons having access to or possession of keys or key-cards concerned with the containment or storage of nuclear material.
- Vehicles and all large objects entering the protected area should be checked to ensure that no unauthorized persons or articles of sabotage are introduced. Entry of private motor vehicles into the protected area should be minimized and limited to authorized parking areas.

Requirements for Category III Material in Use and Storage:

- Category III material should be used or stored within an area to which access is controlled.
- Provision should be made for detecting unauthorized intrusion and for appropriate action by guards or off-site response forces to attempted intrusion.

B. Physical Protection Recommendations for Nuclear Materials in Transit

Since nuclear material is probably the most vulnerable during transit, it is extremely important to have specific regulations governing its protection during these times. But international standards for the physical protection of nuclear materials during transit have been very weak. Before the publication of INFCIRC/225, the only regulations governing the transport of nuclear materials were those established by the Convention on the Physical Protection of Fissile Materials (PPC). As we have seen, however, the PPC only applies to the transport of fissile materials used for peaceful purposes, and only governs the transport of fissile materials across international borders. It says nothing about the transport of weapons-usable materials, or nuclear materials within a given state. The standards established by INFCIRC/225 over the transport of fissile materials are therefore extremely important, since they apply to the transport of all types of nuclear material, and also establish standards for the transport of materials within states.

General Techniques for the Protection of Nuclear Material in Transit

- Minimizing the total time during which the nuclear material is in transit.
- Protecting nuclear material in temporary storage in a manner consistent with the category of that material.
- Avoiding the use of regular movement schedules.
- Requiring predetermination of trustworthiness of all individuals involved in transport of nuclear material.
- Limiting advance knowledge of transport information to the minimum number of persons necessary.

Requirements for Category I Material in Transit

- *Advance notification to receiver.* The shipper should give the receiver advance notice of the planned shipment, specifying the mode of transport (road/rail/sea/air), the estimated time of arrival of the shipment, and the exact point of hand-over if this is done before the ultimate destination.
- *Selection of transportation and routing.* In choosing the route, consideration should be given to the security of passage, in particular, arranging the route in such a way as to avoid areas of natural disasters or civil disorders. The mode of transport for any consignment should be such as to keep to a minimum the number of cargo transfers and the length of time the cargo remains in transit.
- *Provision of locks and seals.* Unless there are overriding safety considerations, the packages containing nuclear material should be carried in closed, locked vehicles, compartments, or freight containers. Checks should be made before dispatch to confirm the integrity of the locks and seals on the package, vehicle, compartment, or freight container.
- *Search of load vehicle.* There should be a detailed search of the load vehicle prior to loading and shipment, to ensure that sabotage devices have not been implanted or that sabotage has not been initiated.
- *Measures after shipment.* The receiver should check the integrity of the packages, locks, and seals and accept the shipment immediately upon arrival.
- *Communication.* Domestic physical protection measures should include provision of continuous two-way radio communication or frequent telephone communication between the vehicle and shipper/receiver/state designee.

- *Guards.* Guards should accompany each shipment to protect the material against hostile acts. States are encouraged to use armed guards to the extent that laws and regulations permit.
- *Agreements for international transit.* In contracts or agreements between shippers and receivers involving international transit of material, the point at which responsibility for physical protection is transferred from the shipper to the receiver should be clearly stated.

Requirements for Category II Material in Transit

- *Advance notification to receiver.* The shipper should give the receiver advance notice of the planned shipment, specifying the mode of transport (road/rail/sea/air), the estimated time of arrival of the shipment, and the exact point of hand-over if this is done before the ultimate destination.
- *Selection of transportation and routing.* In choosing the route, consideration should be given to the security of passage, in particular, arranging the route in such a way as to avoid areas of natural disasters or civil disorders. The mode of transport for any consignment should be such as to keep to a minimum the number of cargo transfers and the length of time the cargo remains in transit.
- *Provision of locks and seals.* Unless there are overriding safety considerations, the packages containing nuclear material should be carried in closed, locked vehicles, compartments, or freight containers. Checks should be made before dispatch to confirm the integrity of the locks and seals on the package, vehicle, compartment, or freight container.
- *Search of load vehicle.* There should be a detailed search of the load vehicle prior to loading and shipment, to ensure that sabotage devices have not been implanted or that sabotage has not been initiated.
- *Measures after shipment.* The receiver should check the integrity of the packages, locks, and seals and accept the shipment immediately upon arrival.
- *Communication.* Domestic physical protection measures should include provision of frequent communication between the vehicle and shipper/receiver/state designee.
- *Agreements for international transit.* In contracts or agreements between shippers and receivers involving international transit of material, the point at which responsibility for physical protection is transferred from the shipper to the receiver should be clearly stated.

Requirements for Category III Material in Transit

- *Advance notification to receiver.* The shipper should give the receiver advance notice of the planned shipment, specifying the mode of transport (road/rail/sea/air), the estimated time of arrival of the shipment, and the exact point of hand-over if this is done before the ultimate destination.
- *Provision of locks and seals.* Where practicable, locks and seals should be applied to vehicles or freight containers.
- *Search of load vehicle.* There should be a detailed search of the load vehicle prior to loading and shipment, to ensure that sabotage devices have not been implanted or that sabotage has not been initiated.

Notes

1. Introduction: The Proliferation Debate

1. U.S. National Security Council and White House Office of Homeland Security, *National Strategy to Combat Weapons of Mass Destruction,* December 2002, <http://www.whitehouse.gov/news/releases/2002/12/WMDStrategy.pdf>, p. 1. Nor is opposition to WMD proliferation unique to the Bush administration. In the 1999 National Security Strategy, then-President Bill Clinton stated, "We have identified a new security agenda that addresses contemporary threats such as the proliferation of nuclear, chemical, and biological weapons, terrorism, and international crime. New efforts must continue to build on initiatives such as the extension of the Non-Proliferation Treaty, the containment of nations seeking to acquire and use weapons of mass destruction, [and] increased antiterrorism cooperation." (William J. Clinton, preface, *A National Security Strategy for a Global Age,* December 2000, <http://www.globalsecurity.org/military/library/policy/national/nss-0012.pdf>).

2. For convenience, I use the term *nuclear weapons state* (NWS) to refer to any country that possesses nuclear weapons (including India, Pakistan, and Israel), not just the five officially recognized nuclear weapons states (United States, Russia, China, Great Britain, and France).

3. Scott D. Sagan, "Sagan Responds to Waltz," in Scott D. Sagan and Kenneth N. Waltz, *The Spread of Nuclear Weapons: A Debate Renewed* (New York: W.W. Norton, 2003), p. 157.

4. George Tenet, Director of U.S. Central Intelligence, "The Worldwide Threat in 2003: Evolving Dangers in a Complex World," speech delivered before the Senate Select Committee on Intelligence, February 11, 2003, <http://www.cia.gov/cia/public_affairs/speeches/2003/dci_speech_02112003.html>. Since this speech, a few of those proliferation concerns appear to have been addressed. The 2003 war with Iraq, which resulted in the removal of Saddam Hussein from power, has eliminated Iraq's nuclear program. In addition, on December 22, 2003, after reportedly being caught importing nuclear weapons technologies, Libyan leader Moammar Gaddafi declared that he would give up his nuclear program and that he would allow weapons inspectors into Libya's nuclear facilities. In January 2004, the International Atomic Energy Agency inspected nine nuclear weapons facilities in Libya, four of which had been previously unknown to the agency. The inspections revealed technologies for enriching uranium, which could have provided key ingredients for a nuclear weapon.

While this is encouraging progress, it may take some time to verify that Libya has completely given up its nuclear program. See Daniel Williams, "Nuclear Program In Libya Detailed," *Washington Post*, December 30, 2003, p. A01; Andrew Purvis and Douglas Waller, "Lessons From Libya," *Time* 163, no. 2 (January 12, 2004), p. 18.

5. John J. Mearsheimer and Stephen M. Walt, "An Unnecessary War," *Foreign Policy,* no. 134 (January/February 2003): pp. 50–59; Kenneth M. Pollack, "A Last Chance to Stop Iraq," *New York Times,* February 21, 2003, p. A27; Joseph Cirincione and Dipali Mukhopadhyay, "Why Pollack Is Wrong: We Have Contained Saddam," *Carnegie Issue Brief,* February 21, 2003, <http://www.ceip.org/files/nonprolif/templates/article.asp?NewsID=4379>; Mark Strauss, "Think Again: Attacking Iraq," *Foreign Policy,* no. 129 (March–April 2002): pp. 14–19.

6. The specific definitions for accidental, unauthorized, and inadvertent use are discussed below.

7. Radiological devices are discussed below.

8. For an excellent summary of the history of the proliferation debate since the 1940s, see Peter R. Lavoy, "The Strategic Consequences of Nuclear Proliferation," *Security Studies* 4, no. 4 (summer 1995): pp. 699–711.

9. The proceedings of the conference where Vinier made this argument are summarized in Glenn T. Seabord, *Stemming the Tide: Arms Control in the Johnson Years* (Lexington, Mass.: D.C. Health, 1987), p. 63. Cited in "Lavoy, "The Strategic Consequences of Nuclear Proliferation," p. 701.

10. F.H. Hinsley, *Power and the Pursuit of Peace* (Cambridge: Cambridge University Press, 1963); Richard N. Rosecrance, *Action and Reaction in World Politics* (Boston: Little, Brown, 1963); Pierre Gallois, *The Balance of Terror: Strategy for the Nuclear Age* (Boston: Houghton Mifflin, 1961). These arguments are summarized in Lavoy, "Strategic Consequences of Nuclear Proliferation," pp. 701–702.

11. Thomas C. Schelling, *Arms and Influence* (New Haven: Yale University Press, 1966), p. 71.

12. See, for example, Albert Wohlstetter, "Nuclear Sharing: NATO and the N+1 Country," *Foreign Affairs* 39, no. 3 (April 1961): pp. 355–387; Fred C. Iklé, "Nth Countries and Disarmament," *Bulletin of the Atomic Scientists* 16 (1960): pp. 391–394; Alastair Buchan, "Introduction," in The American Assembly, *A World of Nuclear Powers?* (Englewood Cliffs: Prentice-Hall, 1966), pp. 1–12; Herman Kahn, "The Arms Race and Some of Its Hazards," *Daedalus* 89, no. 4 (fall 1960): pp. 776–778; Paul Doty, "The Role of Smaller Powers," *Daedalus* 89, no. 4 (fall 1960): pp. 818–830; Howard Simons, "World-Wide Capabilities for Production and Control of Nuclear Weapons," *Daedalus* 88, no. 3 (summer 1959): pp. 385–409; Oskar Morgenstern, "The N-Country Problem," *Fortune* 63, no. 3 (March 1961): pp. 136–137, 205–209.

13. Kenneth N. Waltz, *The Spread of Nuclear Weapons: More May Be Better,* Adelphi Paper, No. 171 (London: International Institute for Strategic Studies [IISS], 1981). This paper was later published as "More May Be Better," in Scott D. Sagan and Kenneth N. Waltz, *The Spread of Nuclear Weapons: A Debate* (New York: W.W. Norton, 1995), pp. 1–45. A second, revised version of this book was published in 2003, *The Spread of Nuclear Weapons: A Debate Renewed* (New York: W.W. Norton, 2003).

14. Waltz, "More May Be Better," p. 5.

15. Ibid., pp. 4–8.

16. Ibid., p. 7.

17. For example, Bruce Bueno de Mesquita and William Riker conclude, "Once half the nations in the system have nuclear weapons, the number of possible nuclear attacks diminishes, going to zero when all countries have sufficient capabilities to deter their relevant adversaries," though they do note that the likelihood of preemptive strikes is higher when a small number of states possess nuclear weapons. Martin van Creveld argues that the effect of proliferation would be to "push war itself into the nooks and crannies of the international system." And John Mearsheimer argues that "well-managed" nuclear proliferation in Europe "might provide the best hope of maintaining stability on the continent." See Bruce Bueno de Mesquita and William H. Riker, "An Assessment of the Merits of Selective Nuclear Proliferation," *Journal of Conflict Resolution* 26, no. 2 (June 1982): p. 287; Martin van Creveld, "Military Strategy for an Era of Transition," in *Turning Point: The Gulf War and U.S. Military Strategy,* ed. L. Benjamin Ederington and Michael J. Mazarr (Boulder, Colo.: Westview, 1994), p. 269; John Mearsheimer, "Back to the Future: Instability in Europe After the Cold War," *International Security* 15, no. 1 (summer 1990): p. 37.

18. For a brief, but important discussion of what "rational" might mean in "rational deterrence theory," see James G. Blight and David A. Welch, "Risking the Destruction of Nations: Lessons of the Cuban Missile Crisis for New and Aspiring Nuclear States," *Security Studies* 4, no. 4 (summer 1995): p. 815 n. 12.

19. Waltz, "More May Be Better," p. 21.

20. See, most notably, Bruce G. Blair, *The Logic of Accidental Nuclear War* (Washington, D.C.: Brookings Institution, 1993); Bruce G. Blair, *Global Zero Alert for Nuclear Forces* (Washington, D.C.: Brookings Institution, 1995); Scott D. Sagan, *The Limits of Safety: Organizations, Accidents, and Nuclear Weapons* (Princeton: Princeton University Press, 1993); Peter D. Feaver, *Guarding the Guardians: Civilian Control of Nuclear Weapons in the United States* (Ithaca: Cornell University Press, 1992); Peter D. Feaver, "Command and Control in Emerging Nuclear Nations," *International Security* 17, no. 3 (winter 1992/1993): pp. 163–168; James G. Blight and David A. Welch, *On the Brink: Americans and Soviets Reexamine the Cuban Missile Crisis,* 2nd ed. (New York: Noonday, 1990); Blight and Welch, "Risking the Destruction of Nations," pp. 811–850.

21. For the introduction of the term "neopessimist," see David J. Karl, "Proliferation Pessimism and Emerging Nuclear Powers," *International Security* 21, no. 3 (winter 1996/97): pp. 93–95; and Peter D. Feaver, "Neooptimists and the Enduring Problem of Nuclear Proliferation," *Security Studies* 6, no. 4 (summer 1997): pp. 93–99.

22. Scott D. Sagan, "The Perils of Proliferation: Organization Theory, Deterrence Theory, and the Spread of Nuclear Weapons," *International Security* 18, no. 4 (spring 1994): p. 71; Scott D. Sagan, "More Will Be Worse," in Sagan and Waltz, *The Spread of Nuclear Weapons: A Debate,* pp. 47–91. An updated version of this chapter was published in *The Spread of Nuclear Weapons: A Debate Renewed* (New York: W.W. Norton, 2003), pp. 46–87. For an additional criticism of "rational deterrence theory," see Blight and Welch, "Risking the Destruction of Nations," pp. 811–850.

23. Sagan, "The Perils of Proliferation," pp. 90–93.

24. Sagan, "More Will Be Worse," p. 78.

25. Sagan, "The Perils of Proliferation," p. 72. As Sagan argues, "the biases, routines, and parochial interests of powerful military organizations, not the 'objective' interests of the state, can determine state behavior" (Sagan, "More Will Be Worse," p. 48).

26. Sagan, "Sagan Responds to Waltz," pp. 170–173.

27. Sagan, "The Perils of Proliferation," p. 74; Sagan, "Sagan Responds to Waltz," p. 166. The problems arising from bureaucratic parochialism will be very important in this study. For example, there is significant evidence that parochialism caused Russia's Ministry of Atomic Energy (Minatom) to refuse to admit that there was a problem with Russia's nuclear controls. According to Allison et al.: "To date, key players in Russia—particularly including Minatom and its head, Viktor Mikhailov—have been unenthusiastic about and even often unwilling to engage in cooperation with the United States to improve nuclear security. In fact, they have been reluctant even to concede that there is a problem (since such acknowledgment amounts to self-condemnation)." Graham T. Allison, Owen R. Coté, Richard A. Falkenrath, and Steven E. Miller, *Avoiding Nuclear Anarchy* (Cambridge: MIT Press, 1996), p. 75; see also pp. 124–126.

28. See, for example, Karl, "Proliferation Pessimism and Emerging Nuclear Powers," pp. 87–119; Jordan Seng, "Less Is More: Command and Control Advantages of Minor Nuclear States," *Security Studies* 6, no. 4 (summer 1997): pp. 50–92; Peter R. Lavoy, "Civil-Military Relations, Strategic Conduct, and the Stability of Nuclear Deterrence in South Asia," in *Civil-Military Relations and Nuclear Weapons,* ed. Scott D. Sagan (Stanford: CISAC, 1994), pp. 79–109; George Perkovich, "A Nuclear Third Way in South Asia," *Foreign Policy,* no. 91 (summer 1993): pp. 85–104; Devin Hagerty, "Nuclear Deterrence in South Asia: The 1990 Indo-Pakistani Crisis," *International Security* 20, no. 3 (winter 1995/96): pp. 79–114; Bradley Thayer, "The Risk of Nuclear Inadvertence: A Review Essay," *Security Studies* vol. 3, no. 3 (spring 1994): pp. 428–493; Mario E. Carranza, "An Impossible Game: Stable Nuclear Deterrence after the Indian and Pakistani Tests," *Nonproliferation Review* 6, no. 3 (spring–summer 1999): pp. 11–24; Clayton P. Bowen and Daniel Wolvén, "Command and Control Challenges in South Asia," *Nonproliferation Review* 6, no. 3 (spring–summer 1999): pp. 25–35.

29. Karl, "Proliferation Pessimism and Emerging Nuclear Powers," pp. 87–119; Seng, "Less Is More," pp. 50–92. These articles formulated what became known as the "neooptimist" position, though this characterization is somewhat misleading, since earlier optimists such as Waltz make these arguments as well. See Kenneth N. Waltz, "Waltz Responds to Sagan," in Sagan and Waltz, *The Spread of Nuclear Weapons: A Debate Renewed,* p. 154.

30. Sagan, "More Will Be Worse," p. 78; Scott D. Sagan, "Correspondence: Proliferation Pessimism and Emerging Nuclear Powers," *International Security* 22, no. 2 (fall 1997): p. 200; Feaver, "Neooptimists and the Enduring Problem of Nuclear Proliferation," pp. 99–104; Peter D. Feaver, "Correspondence: Proliferation Pessimism and Emerging Nuclear Powers," *International Security* 22, no. 2 (fall 1997): p. 190.

31. Peter Stein and Peter D. Feaver, *Assuring Control of Nuclear Weapons: The Evolution of Permissive Action Links* (Lanham, Md.: University Press of America, 1987), pp. 7–8. See also Feaver, "Command and Control in Emerging Nuclear Nations," pp. 163–168.

32. Stein and Feaver, *Assuring Control of Nuclear Weapons,* p. 8.

33. Feaver, "Command and Control in Emerging Nuclear Nations," p. 164.

34. Rumsfeld Commission to Assess the Ballistic Missile Threat, Report to Congress, section IIC2, July 15, 1998, <http://www.house.gov/hasc/testimony/105thcongress/BMThreat.htm> .

35. Waltz, "More May Be Better," p. 21.

36. Ibid., pp. 5–6.

37. For example, Ralph Clough et al. speculate that the United States might consider such a preemptive attack on China for exactly this reason: "concern that Chinese missiles might be launched by accident, or fear that Peking might misread our intentions and launch its missiles first, might tempt some U.S. leaders to consider a preemptive strike in order to limit damage to this nation." See Ralph A. Clough, Doak Barnett, Morton Halperin, and Jerome Kahan, *The United States, China, and Arms Control* (Washington, D.C.: Brookings Institution, 1975), p. 34.

38. Waltz, "More May Be Better," p. 20.

39. Lewis A. Dunn, *Controlling the Bomb: Nuclear Proliferation in the 1980s* (New Haven: Yale University Press, 1982), p. 72; Feaver, "Correspondence: Proliferation Pessimism and Emerging Nuclear Powers," p. 191.

40. Dunn, *Controlling the Bomb,* p. 72. See also Sagan, "Perils of Proliferation," p. 98 and Feaver, "Correspondence: Proliferation Pessimism and Emerging Nuclear Powers," p. 191.

41. Karl, "Proliferation Pessimism and Emerging Nuclear Powers," p. 109.

42. Sagan, "Correspondence: Proliferation Pessimism and Emerging Nuclear Powers," p. 200; Feaver, "Neooptimism and Nuclear Proliferation's Enduring Problems," pp. 105, 115; Feaver, "Correspondence: Proliferation Pessimism and Emerging Nuclear Powers," p. 189

43. Blair, *The Logic of Accidental Nuclear War,* p. 254; Feaver, "Neooptimism and Nuclear Proliferation's Enduring Problems," pp. 176–177; Feaver, "Correspondence: Proliferation Pessimism and Emerging Nuclear Powers," p. 191

44. Waltz, "More May Be Better," p. 21

45. Ibid., p. 154; Karl, "Proliferation Pessimism and Emerging Nuclear Powers," pp. 112–115.

46. Feaver, "Neooptimists and the Enduring Problem of Nuclear Proliferation," p. 103.

47. Ibid., p. 101.

48. Ibid., p. 105.

49. Ibid., p. 107.

50. Waltz, "More May Be Better," p. 20. See also Seng, "Less Is More," p. 78.

51. Although the United States and the Soviet Union developed such capabilities and use-doctrines, optimists dismiss these actions as reflecting "decades of fuzzy thinking." See Kenneth N. Waltz, "Nuclear Myths and Political Realities," *American Political Science Review* 84, no. 3 (September 1990): p. 731.

52. Mearsheimer, "Back to the Future," p. 37. Mearsheimer argues that the bipolar nuclear order of the Cold War would be more stable than a multipolar nuclear order because there would be fewer fingers on triggers and fewer chances of confusion or misperception. Thus, while Mearsheimer recognizes some problems that could arise from proliferation, he does not think that they outweigh the advantages of

increased deterrence that would arise from carefully managed proliferation. For a similar argument in favor of only carefully managed proliferation, see Bueno de Mesquita and Riker, "Selective Nuclear Proliferation," p. 303.

53. Waltz, "More May Be Better," p. 41.

54. It is widely accepted that the most difficult part of developing a nuclear weapon is producing fissile materials. If a proliferating state were able to obtain large amounts of stolen fissile materials, its task would be much easier. Indeed, Iran, Iraq, Libya, and North Korea, among others, have all been reported to have sought to acquire stolen fissile materials for nuclear weapons. See Matthew Bunn, *The Next Wave: Urgently Needed New Steps to Control Warheads and Fissile Materials* (Washington, D.C., and Cambridge, Mass.: Carnegie Endowment for International Peace and Harvard University, 2000), pp. 14–15.

55. Waltz, "Waltz Responds to Sagan," p. 131.

56. Bueno de Mesquita and Riker, "Selective Nuclear Proliferation," p. 304.

57. Mearsheimer, "Back to the Future," p. 39.

58. Bueno de Mesquita and Riker, "Selective Nuclear Proliferation," p. 304. See also Mearsheimer, "Back to the Future," p. 39.

59. Some states might consider it to be in their interests to provide certain terrorist groups with nuclear weapons. See Leonard D. Spector, "Clandestine Nuclear Trade and the Threat of Nuclear Terrorism," in *Preventing Nuclear Terrorism,* ed. Paul Leventhal and Yonah Alexander (Lexington, Mass.: Lexington Books, 1987), p. 78. But it is in the interest of *even these* states to implement adequate MPC&A systems. After all, they would still want to maintain a strict control over which terrorist groups acquired a nuclear weapons capability. If there were significant nuclear leakage from the state, then this control would be lost, and terrorist groups directed against the state itself might also develop or obtain nuclear weapons.

60. Waltz, "Watz Responds to Sagan," p. 130.

61. Ibid., p. 129.

62. Ibid., p. 130. This argument is essentially the same as the one made in Brian Jenkins, "International Terrorism: A New Mode of Conflict," in *International Terrorism and World Security,* ed. David Carleton and Carlo Schaerf (London: Croom Helm, 1975), p. 15.

63. Bruce Hoffman, "Terrorism and WMD: Some Preliminary Hypotheses," *The Nonproliferation Review* 4, no. 3 (spring–summer 1997): p. 48.

64. Waltz, "Watz Responds to Sagan," p. 130.

65. Bunn, *The Next Wave,* pp. 14–15. Sagan also addresses Aum Shinrikyo in the 2003 edition of his debate with Waltz. See Sagan, "Sagan Responds to Waltz," p. 160.

66. Central Intelligence Agency, *Unclassified Report to Congress on the Acquisition of Technology Relating to Weapons of Mass Destruction and Advanced Conventional Munitions, 1 January through 30 June 2002,* April 10, 2003, <http://www.cia.gov/cia/reports/721_reports/jan_jun2002.html>. See also George Tenet, Director of U.S. Central Intelligence, "The Worldwide Threat in 2003: Evolving Dangers in a Complex World," speech delivered before the Senate Select Committee on Intelligence, February 11, 2003, <http://www.cia.gov/cia/public_affairs/speeches/2003/dci_speech_02112003.html>.

67. Benjamin Weiser, "Bin Laden Tried to Develop Nuclear Weapons, U.S. Says,"

New York Times, September 26, 1998; Michael Grunwald and Vernon Loeb, "Charges Filed Against Bin Laden," *Washington Post,* November 5, 1998, p. A17. A former member of Bin Laden's terrorist network reportedly told a federal jury on February 7, 2001, that Bin Laden's group had tried to buy uranium in 1993, presumably to aid in helping them construct a nuclear weapon. See Colum Lynch, "Bin Laden Sought Uranium, Jury Told," *Washington Post,* February 8, 2001, p. A02.

68. Central Intelligence Agency, "Terrorist CBRN: Materials and Effects," May 2003, <http://www.cia.gov/cia/reports/terrorist_cbrn/CBRN_threat.pdf>, p. 1; Mike Boettcher and Ingrid Arnesen, "Al Qaeda Documents Outline Serious Weapons Program: Terrorist Group Placed Heavy Emphasis on Developing Nuclear Device," *CNN.com,* January 25, 2002; John Lumpkin, "Diagrams Show Interest in Nuke Plants," *Associated Press,* January 30, 2002.

69. Don Van Natta Jr., "Running Terrorism as a Business," *New York Times,* November 11, 2001; Don Van Natta Jr. and Kate Zernike, "Hijackers' Meticulous Strategy of Brains, Muscle and Practice," *New York Times,* November 4, 2001; Kurt Eichenwald, "Terror Money Hard to Block, Officials Find," *New York Times,* December 10, 2001; Douglas Farah, "Al Qaeda Cash Tied to Diamond Trade: Sale of Gems from Sierra Leone Rebels Raised Millions, Sources Say," *Washington Post,* November 2, 2001, p. A1; Peter Finn, "Hijackers Depicted as Elite Group: European Officials See Greater Sophistication," *Washington Post,* November 5, 2001, p. A01.

70. George J. Tenet, Statement of the Director of Central Intelligence, prepared delivery before the Senate Armed Services Committee Hearing on Current and Projected National Security Threats, February 2, 1999, p. 4.

71. Oleg Bukharin, "Problems of Nuclear Terrorism," *The Monitor* 3, no. 2 (spring 1997): p. 9; Walter Laqueur, "Post-Modern Terrorism," *Foreign Affairs* 75, no. 5 (September–October 1996): p. 29.

72. For example, see Allison, et al., *Avoiding Nuclear Anarchy,* p. 54; Morten Bremer Maerli, "Relearning the ABCs: Terrorists and 'Weapons of Mass Destruction,'" *Nonproliferation Review* 7, no. 2 (summer 2000): pp. 108–119.

73. Iraq reportedly spent over $10 billion (U.S.) on its nuclear weapons program prior to the 1991 Gulf War. See "Between the Bomb and a Hard Place," *Economist* 334, no. 7907 (March 25, 1995): pp. 23–25.

74. This list is loosely based on the list of the types of nuclear terrorism in Konrad Kellen, "The Potential for Nuclear Terrorism: A Discussion," in *Preventing Nuclear Terrorism,* ed. Paul Leventhal and Yonah Alexander (Lexington, Mass.: Lexington Books, 1987), p. 106. Kellen does not identify radiological weapons as nuclear terrorism, though they have begun to be identified as nuclear terrorism in recent years.

75. The specific area that could be contaminated by a radiological device depends on a number of factors, including the type of radioactive material used, the amount of explosive used to disperse the radioactive material, weather conditions, and terrain. In addition, the number of people exposed to radiation by such a device would depend on the population density around the area and the emergency response taken after the attack. See Charles D. Ferguson, Tahseen Kazi, and Judith Perera, "Commercial Radioactive Sources: Surveying the Security Risks," Monterey Center for Nonproliferation Studies, Occasional Paper No. 11, January 2003, p. 20, <http://cns.miis.edu/pubs/opapers/op11/op11.pdf>. A well-placed and well-designed

radiological device would be capable of contaminating areas ranging from a few city blocks to a few square miles. In most cases the negative health effects would be small, though the psychological effects could be enormous (ibid., pp. 20–22).

76. Hoffman, "Terrorism and WMD," p. 50.

77. Guraraj Mutalik, Frank Barnaby, Peter Taylor, and David Sumner, *Crude Nuclear Weapons: Proliferation and the Terrorist Threat,* Global Health Watch Report, no. 1 (Cambridge, Mass.: International Physicians for the Prevention of Nuclear War, 1996), p. 34.

78. Bukharin, "Problems of Nuclear Terrorism," p. 9.

79. Ibid.

80. As stated above, notable exceptions include studies conducted by Bruce Blair, Scott Sagan, and Peter Feaver.

81. Karl, "Proliferation Pessimism and Emerging Nuclear Powers," p. 119; Sagan, "Perils of Proliferation," p. 98; Sagan, "Correspondence: Proliferation Pessimism and Emerging Nuclear Powers," p. 201; Peter D. Feaver, "Proliferation Optimism and Theories of Nuclear Operations," *Security Studies* 2, no. 3/4 (spring/summer 1993): p. 183; Feaver, "Neooptimists and the Enduring Problem of Nuclear Proliferation," pp. 122–123; Feaver, "Command and Control in Emerging Nuclear Nations," p. 160; Feaver, "Correspondence: Proliferation Pessimism and Emerging Nuclear Powers," p. 192; Jordan Seng, "Optimism in the Balance: A Response to Peter Feaver," *Security Studies* 6, no. 4 (summer 1997): p. 136.

82. Waltz, "More May Be Better," p. 21.

83. The risks of accidental launches are real. For example, in 1998, faulty wiring caused an accidental launch of a South Korean Nike-Hercules surface-to-air missile. The missile exploded 300 meters above the ground, injuring nine people and causing extensive damage to cars and residential homes. For reports on this incident, see *Seoul Yonhap,* December 4, 1998, in FBIS-EAS-98-338 (December 7, 1998), and *The Korea Times,* December 7, 1998, in FBIS-EAS-98-341 (December 11, 1998).

84. U.S. standards for one-point safety require that if the high explosive is detonated at any single point, the probability of producing a nuclear yield exceeding four pounds TNT equivalent is less than one in a million. See Donald R. Cotter, "Peacetime Operations: Safety and Security," in *Managing Nuclear Operations,* ed. Ashton B. Carter, John D. Steinbruner, Charles A. Zraket (Washington, D.C.: Brookings Institution, 1987), p. 43. Not all one-point safety designs would necessarily meet such a rigorous standard, however.

85. Robert S. Norris and William M. Arkin, "U.S. Nuclear Weapons Safety and Control Features," *Bulletin of the Atomic Scientists* 47, no. 8 (October 1991): p. 49.

86. Ibid.

87. Although it sounds similar, this precaution is different from keeping the warheads themselves disassembled. It is possible to store assembled warheads that are not mated to delivery vehicles.

88. Feaver, "Neooptimists and the Enduring Problem of Nuclear Proliferation," p. 114.

89. Feaver, "Command and Control in Emerging Nuclear Nations," p. 166.

90. As Peter Feaver points out, it is possible to imagine a code-management system in which the codes for the use-control devices were posted prominently on the

outside of each weapon. Regardless of how advanced or sophisticated the use-control hardware might be, such a code-management system would render the use-control devices useless against unauthorized use (ibid.).

91. For example, it will assess whether their early-warning systems experienced false alarms that could have sparked inadvertent nuclear wars.

92. In the context of the IAEA safeguards, MPC&A serves an additional purpose, namely detecting the diversion of nuclear materials by a given state from its peaceful nuclear program to an opaque nuclear weapons program. This issue is not directly related to the present study, however.

93. For the texts of INFCIRC/225/Rev.4 and INFCIRC/153, see the IAEA websites: <http://www.iaea.org/worldatom/Programmes/Protection/inf225rev4/rev4_content.html> and <http://www.iaea.org/Publications/Documents/Infcircs/Others/inf153.shtml>.

94. Mohamed ElBaradei, Director General of the IAEA, preface to INFCIRC/225/Rev.4.

95. Guidance and Considerations for Implementation of INFCIRC/225/Rev.3, par. 401–402.

96. *Integrated Demonstration of Materials, Protection, Control, and Accountability,* Los Alamos National Laboratory Unclassified Publication, June 1998, LALP-98-65, p. 6. See also Jason D. Ellis and Todd E. Perry, "Nunn-Lugar's Unfinished Agenda," *Arms Control Today* 27, no. 3 (October 1997): p. 16, <http://www.armscontrol.org/act/1997_10/nunnoct.asp>.

97. Ellis and Perry, "Nunn-Lugar's Unfinished Agenda," p. 16.

98. Because most nuclear facilities in NWSs would contain Category I materials, this chapter will only list the IAEA recommendations for Category I materials during use and storage. See the appendix for IAEA recommendations for Category II and Category III materials.

99. For the necessity of performance testing of physical protection systems, see INFCIRC/225/Rev.4, section 4.4.1, and Oleg Bukharin, Matthew Bunn, and Kenneth N. Luongo, *Renewing the Partnership: Recommendations for Accelerated Action to Secure Nuclear Material in the Former Soviet Union* (Washington, D.C.: Russian American Nuclear Security Advisory Council, 2000), pp. 79–86.

100. INFCIRC/153, section II.32.

101. *Integrated Demonstration of Materials, Protection, Control, and Accountability,* Los Alamos National Laboratory Unclassified Publication, June 1998, LALP-98-65, p. 6. See also Ellis and Perry, "Nunn-Lugar's Unfinished Agenda," p. 16.

102. IAEA, "Safeguards, Non-Proliferation and the Peaceful Uses of Nuclear Energy," IAEA Factsheet, <http://www.iaea.org/worldatom/Periodicals/Factsheets/English/safeguards-e.pdf>.

103. James E. Doyle and Stephen V. Mladineo, "Assessing the Development of a Modern Safeguards Culture in the NIS," *Nonproliferation Review* 5, no. 2 (winter 1998): p. 91.

104. Ibid., p. 92.

105. For the difficulties Russia has encountered with its nuclear controls since the Soviet collapse, see chapter 3.

106. As we will see, the Russian case is critical for demonstrating why an alter-

native system, one based primarily on guards, gates, and guns (known as the "3 G's"), is not sufficient for preventing thefts and sabotage, especially if the NWS encounters severe political, social, and economic upheavals. See chapter 3.

107. For a more detailed explanation of what the Russian case reveals for the optimism-pessimism debate, see Nathan Busch, "Russian Roulette: The Continuing Relevance of Russia to the Nuclear Proliferation Debate," *Security Studies* 11, no. 3 (spring 2002): pp. 44–90.

108. For example, Great Britain's nuclear weapons program appears to be heavily dependent on the U.S. program. The only nuclear weapon that Britain currently possesses is the Trident submarine-launched ballistic missile (SLBM), which is identical to the U.S. Trident SLBM (and is even drawn from the same reserve pool as the U.S. weapon). Moreover, the warhead for this weapon appears to be based on the U.S. W76 design. As such, British nuclear weapons would almost certainly have the same safety features and launch controls as U.S. weapons. The United States has also shared a great deal of information with the French on nuclear weapons safety and security designs. French nuclear weapons also utilize use-control devices equivalent to U.S. permissive action links to prevent accidental and unauthorized launches. For information on these systems, see Nicola Butler and Mark Bromley, *Secrecy and Dependence: The UK Trident System in the 21st Century,* BASIC Research Report, November 2001, <http://www.basicint.org/pubs/Research/UKtrident.pdf>; Stein and Feaver, *Assuring Control of Nuclear Weapons*; Nicola Butler, "Sharing Secrets," *Bulletin of the Atomic Scientists* 53, no. 1 (January/February 1997).

109. For the best discussion to date of Israel's nuclear weapons program and use doctrine, however, see Avner Cohen, "Nuclear Arms in Crisis under Secrecy: Israel and the Lessons of the 1967 and 1973 Wars," in *Planning the Unthinkable: How New Powers Will Use Nuclear, Biological, and Chemical Weapons,* ed. Peter R. Lavoy, Scott D. Sagan, and James Wirtz (Ithaca: Cornell University Press, 2000), pp. 104–124.

110. Waltz, "More May Be Better," p. 21.

111. Feaver, "Neooptimists and the Enduring Problem of Nuclear Proliferation," pp. 112–114, 118.

112. Gregory Giles, "Safeguarding the Undeclared Nuclear Arsenals," *Washington Quarterly* 16, no. 2 (spring 1993): pp. 173–179; Lewis A. Dunn, "Military Politics, Nuclear Proliferation, and the 'Nuclear Coup d'Etat,'" *Journal of Strategic Studies* 1 (May 1978): pp. 31–50.

113. Seng, "Less Is More," pp. 76–77, 81–83.

114. Avner Cohen and Benjamin Frankel, "Opaque Nuclear Proliferation," *Journal of Strategic Studies* 13, no. 3 (September 1990): p. 16.

115. Ibid., pp. 21–22.

116. Although India conducted a nuclear test in 1974, Cohen and Frankel argue that enough similarities existed in its behavior (prior to the 1998 test) to identify it as resembling the opaque "ideal-type" (ibid., p. 23). Indeed, at the time, India declared the 1974 test to be a "peaceful nuclear experiment" and not part of a weapons program.

117. Karl, "Proliferation Pessimism and Emerging Nuclear Powers," pp. 115–116.

118. Feaver, "Correspondence: Proliferation Pessimism and Emerging Nuclear Powers," p. 191.

119. Roy Godson and James J. Wirtz, "Strategic Denial and Deception," in *Strategic Denial and Deception: The Twenty-First Century Challenge,* ed. Roy Godson and James J. Wirtz (New Brunswick: Transaction Publishers, 2002), p. 1.

120. Jonathan B. Tucker, "Monitoring and Verification in a Noncooperative Environment: Lessons from the U.N. Experience in Iraq," *Nonproliferation Review* 3, no. 3 (spring–summer 1996): p. 9.

121. Godson and Wirtz, "Strategic Denial and Deception," p. 2.

122. Tucker, "Monitoring and Verification in a Noncooperative Environment," p. 9.

2. The United States

1. See, for example, Kenneth N. Waltz, "More May Be Better," in *The Spread of Nuclear Weapons: A Debate Renewed* (New York: W.W. Norton, 2003), pp. 21, 25–26, 35–36; John J. Mearsheimer, "Back to the Future: Instability in Europe After the Cold War," *International Security* 15, no. 1 (summer 1990): pp. 10–11.

2. For a history of the U.S. push to build these weapons, see Richard Rhodes, *The Making of the Atomic Bomb* (New York: Simon and Schuster, 1986).

3. Donald R. Cotter, "Peacetime Operations: Safety and Security," in *Managing Nuclear Operations,* ed. Ashton B. Carter, John D. Steinbruner, Charles A. Zraket (Washington, D.C.: Brookings Institution, 1987), p. 25.

4. Thomas Cochran, William M. Arkin, and Milton Hoenig, *Nuclear Weapons Databook, Vol. I: U.S. Nuclear Forces and Capabilities* (Cambridge, Mass.: Ballinger, 1984), p. 6.

5. Cotter, "Peacetime Operations," p. 26.

6. Cochran et al., *Nuclear Weapons Databook, Vol. I,* p. 6.

7. Ibid.

8. The term "strategic" generally refers to nuclear weapons whose capability and mission is to hit the heart of an adversary's homeland. Although the range of these weapons need not always be the key factor in their definition, in the U.S.-Russian dialogue on such weapons, geographical range has been the overriding feature in attempts to delineate tactical from strategic nuclear weapons. Thus, "strategic" generally refers to long-range weapons (including ICBMs, SLBMs, and long-range bombers and their weapons), while "tactical" generally refers to short-range missiles, short-range bombers, their nuclear weapons, nuclear land mines, nuclear artillery, etc.

9. Cochran et al., *Nuclear Weapons Databook, Vol. I,* p. 11. Atomic demolition munitions (ADMs) are small, low-yield nuclear weapons that were intended to be used behind enemy lines by special forces on sabotage and demolition missions. They could be used "to destroy tunnels, bridges, dams, and disrupt enemy troop movements." See "Atomic Demolition Munitions," in the U.S. Nuclear Weapons Cost Study Project, Brookings Institution, 1998, <http://www.brook.edu/FP/projects/nucwcost/madm.htm>.

10. Cochran et al., p. 12.

11. Thermonuclear (or fusion) devices produce much larger explosions than earlier, fission weapons (such as the weapons dropped on Hiroshima and Nagasaki).

Unlike fission weapons, which split atoms of highly-enriched uranium or plutonium, fission weapons produce massive amounts of energy by fusing atoms (typically of lithium and deuterium) together. For basic descriptions of fission and fusion weapons, see Rodney W. Jones and Mark G. McDonough, with Toby Dalton and Gregory Koblentz, *Tracking Nuclear Proliferation: A Guide in Maps and Charts, 1998* (Washington, D.C.: Carnegie Endowment for International Peace, 1998), pp. 317–318. The United States successfully completed its first test of a thermonuclear device on May 9, 1951, and tested its first operational thermonuclear bomb on May 21, 1956. For a history of the U.S. thermonuclear weapons project, see Richard Rhodes, *Dark Sun: The Making of the Hydrogen Bomb* (New York: Simon and Schuster, 1995).

12. Cochran et al., *Nuclear Weapons Databook, Vol. I,* p. 12.

13. Cotter, "Peacetime Operations," p. 29.

14. Cochran et al., *Nuclear Weapons Databook, Vol. I,* p. 6. Nuclear air defense weapons were intended to destroy groups of attack aircraft, specifically Soviet bombers. U.S. nuclear air defense weapons included surface-to-air missiles (SAMs), such as the Nike-Hercules and BOMARC missiles, or aircraft-launched air-to-air missiles, such as the Genie missile. Stephen I. Schwartz, "Four Trillion Dollars and Counting," *Bulletin of the Atomic Scientists* 51, no. 6, (November/December 1995): pp. 32–52.

15. Cotter, "Peacetime Operations," p. 17. For detailed discussions of the various nuclear weapons in the U.S. arsenal as of 1984, see Cochran et al., *Nuclear Weapons Databook, Vol. I,* pp. 2–311.

16. While the ABM treaty forbids the United States and the Soviet Union from creating a national missile defense, it does not ban all antiballistic missile systems. The original treaty permitted each side to build two operational ABM sites, each with one hundred ABM launchers and one hundred interceptor missiles, with associated radar, storage, and test facilities, but a 1974 amendment reduced the number of permitted operational ABM sites to one per side. For the texts of the 1972 treaty and the subsequent amendment, see <http://www.state.gov/www/global/arms/treaties/abm/abm2.html>.

17. David B. Thomson, *The START Treaties: Implementation and Status,* Center for International Security Affairs Publication, Los Alamos Laboratory, LA-UR-97–2045 (May 1997), p. 1.

18. Ibid.

19. Ibid., p. 3.

20. Philipp C. Bleek, "U.S., Russia Complete START I Reductions," *Arms Control Today* 32, no. 1 (January/February 2002): p. 33.

21. William M. Arkin, Robert S. Norris, and Joshua Handler, *Taking Stock: Worldwide Nuclear Deployments, 1998* (Washington, D.C.: Natural Resources Defense Council, 1998), p. 8.

22. Ibid., p. 9.

23. For a discussion of the Russian PNIs, see chapter 3.

24. Thomson, *The START Treaties,* pp. 3–8; Federation of American Scientists, "United States Nuclear Forces," <http://www.fas.org/nuke/guide/usa/forces.htm>.

25. Philipp C. Bleek, "Russia Ratifies START II, Extension Protocol; ABM-Related Agreements Also Approved," *Arms Control Today* 30, no. 4 (May 2000): pp. 39–42.

26. Wade Boese, "Russia Declares Itself No Longer Bound by START II," *Arms*

Control Today 31, no. 6 (July/August 2002), <http://www.armscontrol.org/act/2002_07–08/start2jul_aug02.asp>.

27. Philipp C. Bleek, "Bush, Putin Pledge Nuclear Cuts; Implementation Unclear," *Arms Control Today,* December 2001, <http://www.armscontrol.org/act/2001_12/stratreddec01.asp>.

28. "Letter of Transmittal and Article-by-Article Analysis of the Treaty on Strategic Offensive Reductions," *Arms Control Today* 32, no. 6 (July/August 2002): pp. 28–30.

29. Robert S. Norris, Hans M. Kristensen, and Joshua Handler, "U.S. Nuclear Forces, 2003," *Bulletin of the Atomic Scientists* 59, no. 3 (May/June 2003): p. 74; Bryan Bender, "Plan to Store Warheads Draws Fire of Arms-Control Backers," *Boston Globe,* February 24, 2002, p. A4; Michael Wines, "Russia Assails U.S. Stance on Arms Reductions," *New York Times,* March 12, 2002.

30. Helen Dewar, "Senate Backs U.S.-Russian Nuclear Pact," *Washington Post,* March 7, 2003, p. A1; Christine Kucia, "Senate Endorses Nuclear Reductions Treaty; Duma Delays," *Arms Control Today* 33. no. 3 (April 2003), <http://www.armscontrol.org/act/2003_04/sortratification_apr03.asp>; "U.S.-Russia: Duma Approves Moscow Treaty," *Global Security Newswire,* May 14, 2003, <http://www.nti.org/d_newswire/issues/newswires/2003_5_14.html>.

31. Norris and Kristensen, "U.S. Nuclear Forces, 2003," p. 76; Robert S. Norris et al., "U.S. Nuclear Forces, 2001," *Bulletin of the Atomic Scientists* 57, no. 2 (March/April 2001): p. 79.

32. Arkin et al., *Taking Stock,* p. 14. Nuclear weapons were withdrawn from Alaska, Arizona, Arkansas, Florida, Hawaii, Kansas, Maine, Michigan, New Hampshire, New Jersey, New York, South Carolina, and South Dakota (ibid., pp. 15–16). For a listing of the nuclear weapons stored in each state, see ibid., p. 15.

33. Norris, Kristensen, and Handler, "U.S. Nuclear Forces, 2003," p. 73; U.S. Air Force, "Minuteman Fact Sheet," <http://www.af.mil/factsheets/factsheet.asp?fsID=113>; U.S. Air Force, "MX Fact Sheet," <http://www.af.mil/factsheets/factsheet.asp?fsID=112>.

34. Norris, Kristensen, and Handler, "U.S. Nuclear Forces, 2003," p. 73; Arkin et al., *Taking Stock,* p. 14.

35. Norris, Kristensen, and Handler, "U.S. Nuclear Forces, 2003," p. 76.

36. Arkin et al., *Taking Stock,* p. 16.

37. Norris, Kristensen, and Handler, "U.S. Nuclear Forces, 2003," p. 76; Arkin et al., *Taking Stock,* p. 16.

38. Arkin et al., *Taking Stock,* p. 68.

39. Thomas B. Cochran, Robert S. Norris, Elliott Negin, and Christopher Paine, *Faking Nuclear Restraint: The Bush Administration's Secret Plan for Strengthening U.S. Nuclear Forces,* Natural Resources Defense Council, February 13, 2002, <http://www.nrdc.org/nuclear/restraint.asp>.

40. Arkin et al., *Taking Stock,* p. 69.

41. Bruce G. Blair, *The Logic of Accidental Nuclear War* (Washington, D.C.: The Brookings Institution, 1993), p. 168; Ashton B. Carter, "Assessing Command System Vulnerability," in *Managing Nuclear Operations,* ed. Carter, Steinbruner, and Zracket, p. 580; William Burr, *Launch on Warning: The Development of U.S. Capabilities, 1959–1979,* National Security Archive Electronic Briefing Book, April 2001,

<http://www.gwu.edu/~nsarchiv/NSAEBB/NSAEBB43/>. LOW remained the primary U.S. use doctrine at least until the mid-1990s, and probably remains so today. For example, in April 1994, Adm. Henry Chiles, then head of the U.S. Strategic Command, reportedly told the Senate Armed Services Committee that the U.S. military has no intention of risking the loss in striking power that might come from "riding out" a nuclear attack. See Frank N. von Hippel, "De-Alerting," *Bulletin of the Atomic Scientists* 53, no. 3 (May/June 1997): p. 35. LOW is also sometimes referred to as "launch-under-attack" (LUA).

42. John C. Toomay, "Warning and Assessment Sensors," in *Managing Nuclear Operations,* ed. Carter, Steinbruner, and Zracket, p. 287.

43. For a detailed discussion of U.S. BMEWS, see ibid., pp. 293–299.

44. PAVE PAWS stands for "precision acquisition of vehicle entry phased-array warning system."

45. U.S. Air Force, "PAVE PAWS Radar System," Air Force Fact Sheet, <http://www.af.mil/factsheets/factsheet.asp?fsID=168>.

46. Geoffrey Forden, Pavel (Paul) Podvig, and Theodore A. Postol, "False Alarm, Nuclear Danger," *IEEE Spectrum* 37, no. 3 (March 2000): pp. 31–39, reprinted at <http://www.armscontrol.ru/start/publications/spectrum-ews.htm>, p. 3.

47. Geostationary satellites stay above one spot on the Earth. They orbit at a distance of 37,000 kilometers from the surface of the Earth so that they complete one orbit in twenty-four hours.

48. Forden et al., "False Alarm, Nuclear Danger," p. 6.

49. "PAVE PAWS Radar System"; Senator Gary Hart and Senator Barry Goldwater, *Recent False Alerts from the Nation's Missile Attack Warning System,* U.S. House of Representatives, Committee on Armed Services, 96th Cong., 2nd session, October 9, 1980, p. 3.

50. Hart and Goldwater, *Recent False Alerts,* p. 5.

51. Ibid., p. 5. For additional information on the integrated U.S. early-warning system, see U.S. Air Force, "PAVE PAWS Radar System"; NORAD *North American Aerospace Defense Command,* <http://www.norad.mil>; Technical Sergeant Pat McKenna, "The Border Guards: NORAD: The Eyes and Ears of North America," *Airman Magazine* 40, no. 1 (January 1996), <http://www.af.mil/news/airman/0196/border.htm>.

52. NORAD, "Strategic Command Command Center," <http://www.stratcom.mil/factssheetshtml/commandctr.htm>.

53. Peter D. Feaver, *Guarding the Guardians: Civilian Control of Nuclear Weapons in the United States* (Ithaca: Cornell University Press, 1992), p. 30. The "combatant commanders" were previously referred to as CINCs of the various regions (e.g., CINC, U.S. Pacific Command, etc.), but in October 2002, Secretary of Defense Donald Rumsfeld announced that only the president would have the title of CINC, and the other commanders (with the exception of the CINC of NORAD) would be referred to as "combatant commanders." See Jim Garamone, "'CINC' Is Sunk," *DefenseLink.mil,* October 25, 2002, <http://www.defenselink.mil/news/Oct2002/n10252002_200210252.html>.

54. Feaver, *Guarding the Guardians,* p. 38. After the 1981 assassination attempt on President Reagan, the Federal Bureau of Investigation accidentally carried off this card along with Reagan's clothes (ibid., p. 38 n. 19).

55. Federation of American Scientists, "CINC Mobile Alternate Headquarters (CMAH), Cheyenne Mountain Alternate Headquarters (CMAH)," <http://www.fas.org/nuke/guide/usa/c3i/cmah.htm>; NORAD "Strategic Command Command Center."

56. Feaver, *Guarding the Guardians,* p. 38. For the specific order of the cabinet secretaries, see ibid., pp. 41–42.

57. Ibid., pp. 45–47.

58. Blair, *Logic of Accidental Nuclear War,* p. 46; Feaver, *Guarding the Guardians,* pp. 47–54.

59. National Security Archive, "First Documented Evidence that U.S. Presidents Predelegated Nuclear Weapons Release Authority to the Military," <http://www.gwu.edu/~nsarchiv/news/19980319.htm>.

60. Joint Chiefs of Staff, *Instructions for Expenditure of Nuclear Weapons in Emergency Conditions,* c. December 1959, p. 1, located in the National Security Archive, <http://www.gwu.edu/~nsarchiv/news/predelegation/predel.htm>.

61. Lyndon Johnson, *Memorandum for the Secretary of Defense,* March 26, 1964, p. 2, located in the National Security Archive, <http://www.gwu.edu/~nsarchiv/news/predelegation/pd16_02.htm>.

62. Blair, *Logic of Accidental Nuclear War,* p. 50.

63. Cotter, "Peacetime Operations," p. 61.

64. Cochran et al., *Nuclear Weapons Databook, Vol. I,* p. 30.

65. The improved controls were intended to provide assurances to both the United States and its NATO allies that all the weapons deployed in Europe were adequately controlled.

66. Dan Caldwell, "Permissive Action Links: A Description and Proposal," *Survival* 29, no. 3 (May/June 1987): p. 224.

67. Ibid., p. 225.

68. Cotter, "Peacetime Operations," pp. 46–49. See also Peter Stein and Peter D. Feaver, *Assuring Control of Nuclear Weapons: The Evolution of Permissive Action Links* (Lanham, Md.: University Press of America, 1987), p. 38. For the text of National Security Action Memorandum 160, see <http://www.interhack.net/people/cmcurtin/nsam-160/nsam160.html>.

69. There have been a number of similar descriptions of U.S. PALs. See Cotter, "Peacetime Operations," p. 49; Stein and Feaver, *Assuring Control of Nuclear Weapons,* pp. 56–57; Robert S. Norris and William M. Arkin, "U.S. Nuclear Weapons Safety and Control Features," *Bulletin of the Atomic Scientists* 47, no. 8 (October 1991): p. 49; Feaver, *Guarding the Guardians,* p. 17; Steven M. Bellovin, "Permissive Action Links," <http://www.research.att.com/~smb/nsam-160/pal.html>.

70. Norris and Arkin, "U.S. Nuclear Weapons Safety and Control Features," p. 48; Bellovin, "Permissive Action Links." Donald Cotter, however, does appear to suggest that CAT F PALs are theoretically impossible to bypass, which might imply that they incorporate more advanced electronic information processing. See Cotter, "Peacetime Operations," p. 49; and Bellovin, "Permissive Action Links." Although CAT F PALs were incorporated into Pershing II missiles, ground-launched cruise missiles, new gravity bombs, and lay-down bombs (which are bombs dropped from an airplane at low altitude and high speed), most of these weapons have been removed from the U.S. arsenal. Most available information suggests that no current U.S. nuclear weapons contain CAT F PALs. See table 2.3.

71. Cotter, "Peacetime Operations," p. 49.

72. Ibid.; Stein and Feaver, *Assuring Control of Nuclear Weapons,* p. 12.

73. Stein and Feaver, *Assuring Control of Nuclear Weapons,* p. 74.

74. Norris and Arkin, "U.S. Nuclear Weapons Safety and Control Features," p. 48

75. Feaver, *Guarding the Guardians,* p. 210. See also Stein and Feaver, *Assuring Control of Nuclear Weapons,* p. 60; and Shaun Gregory, *The Hidden Cost of Deterrence: Nuclear Weapons Accidents* (Washington: Brassey's, 1990), p. 34.

76. Federation of American Scientists, "Introduction," in *Special Weapons Primer,* <http://www.fas.org/nuke/intro/nuke/intro.htm>.

77. Norris and Arkin, "U.S. Nuclear Weapons Safety and Control Features," p. 48; Scott D. Sagan, *The Limits of Safety: Organizations, Accidents, and Nuclear Weapons* (Princeton: Princeton University Press, 1993), pp. 83–84.

78. Stein and Feaver, *Assuring Control of Nuclear Weapons,* p. 74.

79. Cotter, "Peacetime Operations," p. 52.

80. Ibid.

81. Department of Defense, 1995 Nuclear Posture Review, summarized by the Federation of American Scientists, <http://www.fas.org/nuke/guide/usa/doctrine/dod/95_npr.htm>, p. 9. See also Department of Defense, Office of the Executive Secretary, <http://www.defenselink.mil/execsec/adr95/npr_.html>.

82. Department of Defense, 1995 Nuclear Posture Review, p. 9.

83. Federation of American Scientists, "Introduction," in *Special Weapons Primer,* <http://www.fas.org/nuke/intro/nuke/intro.htm>.

84. Cotter, "Peacetime Operations," p. 27.

85. Ibid. See also Chuck Hansen, *U.S. Nuclear Weapons: The Secret History* (New York: Orion Books, 1988), pp. 226–227.

86. Cotter, "Peacetime Operations," p. 28. See also Stanley D. Spray, "History of U.S. Nuclear Weapon Safety Assessment: The Early Years," Sandia National Laboratories, SAND-96-1099C, p. 3.

87. Cotter, "Peacetime Operations," p. 43; David W. Plummer and William H. Greenwood, "The History of Nuclear Weapon Safety Devices," paper delivered at the 34th Joint Propulsion Conference, Cleveland Convention Center, Cleveland, Ohio, July 12–15, 1998, p. 2.

88. Plummer and Greenwood, "History of Nuclear Weapon Safety Devices," p. 2.

89. Cotter, "Peacetime Operations," p. 43; Stein and Feaver, *Assuring Control of Nuclear Weapons,* pp. 8, 22–24; Blair, *Logic of Accidental Nuclear War,* p. 107.

90. Cotter, "Peacetime Operations," p. 43.

91. Plummer and Greenwood, "History of Nuclear Weapon Safety Devices," p. 1.

92. This list is based on open-source reports. For a more comprehensive list of reported U.S. nuclear weapons accidents, see Hansen, *U.S. Nuclear Weapons,* pp. 227–228; and Chuck Hansen, "The Oops List," *Bulletin of the Atomic Scientists* 56, no. 6 (November/December 2000): pp. 64–66.

93. Hansen, *U.S. Nuclear Weapons,* p. 227.

94. Hansen, *U.S. Nuclear Weapons,* p. 228; Kidder, *Report to Congress: Assessment of the Safety of U.S. Nuclear Weapons,* p. E-2.

95. Plummer and Greenwood, "History of Nuclear Weapon Safety Devices," pp. 1–2; Cotter, "Peacetime Operations," p. 29.

96. Plummer and Greenwood, "History of Nuclear Weapon Safety Devices," p. 2.

97. Hansen, *U.S. Nuclear Weapons,* p. 229.

98. Cotter, "Peacetime Operations," p. 29.

99. Plummer and Greenwood, "History of Nuclear Weapon Safety Devices," p. 3.

100. S.D. Drell, J.S. Foster Jr., and C.H. Townes, *Report of the Panel on Nuclear Weapons Safety,* House Armed Services Committee, December 1990, pp. 29–30.

101. Norris and Arkin, "U.S. Nuclear Weapons Safety and Control Features," p. 48.

102. Spray, "History of U.S. Nuclear Weapon Safety Assessment," p. 9.

103. Norris and Arkin, "U.S. Nuclear Weapons Safety and Control Features," p. 49.

104. Ibid.

105. Plummer and Greenwood, "History of Nuclear Weapon Safety Devices," p. 3.

106. Ibid.

107. Ibid.

108. Cotter, "Peacetime Operations," p. 46.

109. Ibid.

110. Plummer and Greenwood, "History of Nuclear Weapon Safety Devices," p. 3.

111. The report argued, "For too long in the past the U.S. has retained older weapons that fail to meet the safety criteria proclaimed in 1968. . . . The SRAM-A is one example, but not the only one. It is not sufficient to pull such weapons off the [ready-alert aircraft] force but retain them in the war reserve stockpile in view of the hazards they will present under conditions of great stress should we ever need to generate strategic forces in times of heightened crisis." See Drell et al., *Report of the Panel on Nuclear Weapon Safety,* p. 32.

112. Ibid., p. 28.

113. Ibid., pp. 28–29. See also Sidney Drell and Bob Peurifoy, "Technical Issues of a Nuclear Test Ban," *Annual Review of Nuclear and Particle Science* 44 (1994): p. 313.

114. R.E. Kidder, *Report to Congress: Assessment of the Safety of U.S. Nuclear Weapons and Related Nuclear Test Requirements,* July 26, 1991, p. 5.

115. Ibid., pp. 4–5. The programs for the W89 warhead and the SRAM-II were scrapped by George H.W. Bush in 1991, in part because the SRAM-II was eliminated under the 1991–1992 Presidential Nuclear Initiatives. See David M. Kunsman and Douglas B. Lawson, *A Primer on U.S. Strategic Nuclear Policy,* Sandia National Laboratory Report, January 2001, <http://www.nti.org/e_research/official_docs/labs/prim_us_nuc_pol.pdf>.

116. Kidder, "Report to Congress," p. 1.

117. Ibid., p. 4.

118. Norris, Kristensen, and Handler, "U.S. Nuclear Forces, 2003," p. 76.

119. "Nuclear Posture Review [Excerpts]," Nuclear Posture Review Report, Submitted to Congress on December 31, 2001, available on the GlobalSecurity.org website: <http://www.globalsecurity.org/wmd/library/policy/dod/npr.htm>.

120. See the list of accidents above. Several other reported incidents involved intentional jettisoning of nuclear weapons during serious aircraft malfunctions or prior to airplane crashes. See Hansen, *U.S. Nuclear Weapons,* p. 228; Kidder, *Report to Congress: Assessment of the Safety of U.S. Nuclear Weapons,* p. E-2.

121. "U.S. Nuclear Weapons Accidents: Danger in Our Midst," *The Defense Monitor* 10, no. 5 (1981), <http://asms.k12.ar.us/armem/ha/cdiart.htm>. Between 1966 and 1991, about one-third of U.S. strategic bombers were maintained in a "strip alert" and could be launched within minutes, while the remaining bombers could take off in roughly an hour. In 1991, as part of the U.S. PNIs, President Bush ordered that all strategic bombers be taken off strip alert. See Cotter, "Peacetime Operations," p. 25. and Arkin et al., *Taking Stock,* p. 9.

122. Gregory, *The Hidden Cost of Deterrence,* p. 153.

123. Cotter, "Peacetime Operations," p. 50.

124. Plummer and Greenwood, "History of Nuclear Weapon Safety Devices," p. 2; Kidder, *Report to Congress: Assessment of the Safety of U.S. Nuclear Weapons,* p. E-2; Gregory, *The Hidden Cost of Deterrence,* p. 179.

125. Gregory, *The Hidden Cost of Deterrence,* p. 97.

126. Ibid., p. 97. As evidence for this incident, Gregory cites Cotter, "Peacetime Operations," p. 45, but I was unable to find any reference to this event in Cotter's article.

127. Gregory, *The Hidden Cost of Deterrence,* p. 184. No dates were provided for these reported incidents.

128. Feaver argues that while the submarine force would be highly survivable, surface ships are vulnerable to other ships and land-based anti-ship weapons. Moreover, he adds, the systems threatening specific nuclear-armed ships, such as an air base with Backfire bombers, could be in range of navy nuclear missiles. Thus, he concludes, navy commanders may have had at their disposal the very weapons needed to remove the threats they are facing, which is "the canonical recipe" for unauthorized use: a hard-pressed commander deciding to use nuclear weapons on his own authority because he fears the enemy will destroy him before he can get presidential authorization. See Feaver, *Guarding the Guardians,* p. 50. These risks were largely eliminated, however, with the removal of all nuclear weapons from surface ships in accordance with the 1991–1992 PNIs.

129. Feaver, *Guarding the Guardians,* p. 50.

130. Scott D. Sagan, "Nuclear Alerts and Crisis Management," *International Security* 9, no. 4 (spring 1985): p. 132.

131. Gregory, *The Hidden Cost of Deterrence,* p. 34. The danger of an unauthorized individual stealing an ICBM—or a warhead mated to an ICBM—deployed in a silo is generally considered negligible. See ibid, p. 34, and Stein and Feaver, *Assuring Control of Nuclear Weapons,* p. 60.

132. Stein and Feaver, *Assuring Control of Nuclear Weapons,* p. 23.

133. See especially Blair, *Logic of Accidental Nuclear War*; Bruce G. Blair, *Global Zero Alert for Nuclear Forces* (Washington, D.C.: Brookings Institution, 1995); Feaver, *Guarding the Guardians*; Sagan, *The Limits of Safety*; Scott D. Sagan, "More

Will Be Worse," and "Sagan Responds to Waltz," in Scott D. Sagan and Kenneth N. Waltz, *The Spread of Nuclear Weapons: A Debate Renewed* (New York: W.W. Norton, 2003); James G. Blight and David A. Welch, "Risking the Destruction of Nations: Lessons of the Cuban Missile Crisis for New and Aspiring Nuclear States," *Security Studies* 4, no. 4 (summer 1995): pp. 811–850.

134. Toomay, "Warning and Assessment Sensors," p. 276.

135. Hart and Goldwater, *Recent False Alerts,* p. 5.

136. Forden et al., "False Alarm, Nuclear Danger," p. 1; Hart and Goldwater, *Recent False Alerts,* p. 5; House Subcommittee of the Committee on Government Operations, *Failures of the North American Aerospace Defense Command's (NORAD) Attack Warning System,* 97th Cong., 1st session, May 19–20, 1981, p. 4.

137. Hart and Goldwater, *Recent False Alerts,* pp. 5–7.

138. James Woolsey, "Threats to United States National Security," testimony before the House of Representatives, Committee on National Security, February 12, 1998, <http://commdocs.house.gov/committees/security/has043000.000/has043000_1.htm>, p. 23.

139. Blair, *Logic of Accidental Nuclear War,* p. 194.

140. Sagan, *Limits of Safety,* pp. 98–99.

141. Ibid., pp. 99–100. As Sagan notes, the supposed saboteur turned out, ironically, to be a bear.

142. Ibid., pp. 130–131.

143. Ibid., p. 99.

144. For a detailed analysis of organizational difficulties during crises, see Sagan, "Nuclear Alerts and Crisis Management," pp. 99–139; and Sagan, *Limits of Safety.*

145. Sagan, *Limits of Safety,* pp. 79–80; Blight and Welch, "Risking the Destruction of Nations," p. 824.

146. Sagan, *Limits of Safety,* pp. 135–138; Blight and Welch, "Risking the Destruction of Nations," p. 824.

147. Institute for Science and International Security, <http://www.isis-online.org/mapproject/usa.html>.

148. David Albright and Mark Gorwitz, "Plutonium Watch: Tracking Civil Plutonium Inventories: End of 1999," issue brief, Institute for Science and International Security, October 2000, <http://www.isis-online.org/publications/puwatch/puwatch2000.html>; National Nuclear Security Administration, *Disposing of Surplus U.S. Highly Enriched Uranium,* Office of Fissile Material Disposition, National Nuclear Security Administration, U.S. Department of Energy, <http://www.nnsa.doe.gov/na-26/heu.htm>.

149. National Nuclear Security Administration, *Disposing of Surplus U.S. Highly Enriched Uranium.*

150. See National Nuclear Security Administration, *Disposing of Surplus U.S. Plutonium,* Office of Fissile Material Disposition, National Nuclear Security Administration, <http://www.nnsa.doe.gov/na-26/pu.htm>. The Department of Energy had originally planned to dispose of part of the excess plutonium by immobilizing it in ceramic and surrounding it with high-level radioactive waste. This plan was abandoned after Russian officials protested that this plutonium could be recovered and used to build new nuclear weapons (ibid.).

151. The gaseous diffusion facility for enriching uranium was located at the K-

25 site, while the plutonium production reactor was located at the Y-12 site. See Oak Ridge National Laboratory website, "Home of the First Nuclear Reactor," <http://www.ornl.gov/timeline/40/1940.shtml>, and "Yesterday at the Y-12 National Security Complex," Oak Ridge National Laboratory website, <http://www.y12.doe.gov/bwxt/y12/y12–yesterday.html>; U.S. Department of Energy, "Declassification of the United States Total Production of Highly Enriched Uranium," Office of the Press Secretary, <http://www.osti.gov/html/osti/opennet/document/press/pc13.html>.

152. Oak Ridge National Laboratory, "Yesterday at the Y-12 National Security Complex," <http://www.y12.doe.gov/bwxt/y12/y12–yesterday.html>; Rhodes, *The Making of the Atomic Bomb,* pp. 497–500.

153. D. Jayne Aaron and Judy A. Berryman, *Rocky Flats Site,* Historic American Engineering Record (HAER), 1998, <http://www.rfets.gov/haer/default.htm>.

154. The Portsmouth Gaseous Diffusion Plant continued to produce HEU until 1992, but these materials apparently were not used in nuclear weapons. In total, Oak Ridge produced 483 metric tons of HEU, and the Portsmouth facility produced 511 metric tons. See U.S. Department of Energy, "Declassification of the United States Total Production of Highly Enriched Uranium," Office of the Press Secretary, <http://www.osti.gov/html/osti/opennet/document/press/pc13.html>; Frans Berkhout, Anatoll Diakov, Harold Feiveson, Helen Hunt, Edwin Lyman, Marvin Miller, and Frank N. von Hippel, "Disposition of Separated Plutonium," *Science & Global Security* 3 (1993): p. 165.

155. Arjun Makhijani and Scott Saleska, "Hanford Cleanup: Explosive Solution," *Bulletin of the Atomic Scientists* 46, no. 8 (October 1990): p. 15; William Lanouette, "Weapons Plant at 40: Savannah River's Halo Fades," *Bulletin of the Atomic Scientists* 46, no. 10 (December 1990): p. 29.

156. Statement by Ambassador Robert T. Grey Jr., United States Representative to the Conference on Disarmament, Geneva, February 15, 2001, <http://www.us-mission.ch/press2001/0215grey.htm>.

157. Aaron and Berryman, *Rocky Flats Site.*

158. David Albright, Tom Zamora, and David Lewis, "Turn off Rocky Flats," *Bulletin of the Atomic Scientists* 46, no. 5 (June 1990): p. 15.

159. Ibid., p. 13.

160. Norris and Arkin, "U.S. Nuclear Forces, 2001," p. 78.

161. The United States generally refers to fissile materials as "special nuclear materials" (SNM). For specific definitions of the various types of SNM that the United States protects, see table 2.4.

162. William Desmond, Neil Zack, and James Tape, "The First 50 Years: A Review of the Department of Energy Domestic Safeguards and Security Program," paper presented at the Workshop on *A Comparative Analysis of Approaches to the Protection of Fissile Materials,* at Stanford University, July 28–30, 1997, p. 4.

163. Ibid., p. 1.

164. Ibid., p. 4.

165. John McPhee, *The Curve of Binding Energy* (New York, N.Y.: Farrar, Strauss, and Giroux, 1974), pp. 28, 48, 52–53. See also Mason Willrich and Theodore B. Taylor, *Nuclear Theft: Risks and Safeguards* (Cambridge, Mass.: Ballinger, 1974). These procedures are summarized in Matthew Bunn, "Security for Weapons-Usable Nuclear Materials: Expanding International Cooperation, Strengthening International Stan-

dards," in *A Comparative Analysis of Approaches to the Protection of Fissile Materials,* Proceedings of the Workshop at Stanford University, July 28–30, 1997, p. 16.

166. Desmond et al., "The First 50 Years," p. 2.

167. Ibid., p. 5.

168. Ibid., p. 7. For a discussion of destructive and nondestructive assay methods, see below.

169. It is worth asking how "politicized" these hearings were. On the one hand, some of the testimony in the hearings seems to exaggerate some of the vulnerabilities. On the other hand, the investigations did reveal procedural difficulties, missing sensors, and failures in performance tests. These are significant problems that would be difficult to exaggerate.

170. Gerry Sikorski, Representative of Minnesota, summarizing the findings of the 1982 Hearings, in *Safeguards at DOE's Nuclear Weapons Facilities,* Hearing before the Subcommittee on Oversight and Investigations of the Committee on Energy and Commerce, House of Representatives, 101st Congress, 1st session, p. 1.

171. John D. Dingell, Chairman of the Subcommittee on Oversight and Investigations, Congressional Testimony, in *Safeguards at DOE's Nuclear Weapons Facilities,* Hearing before the Subcommittee on Oversight and Investigations of the Committee on Energy and Commerce, House of Representatives, 101st Congress, 1st session, p. 7.

172. Cited in Bunn, "Security for Weapons-Usable Nuclear Material," p. 16.

173. Dingell, Congressional testimony, in *Safeguards at DOE's Nuclear Weapons Facilities,* p. 5.

174. Ibid., p. 2.

175. Ibid., pp. 5–6.

176. For the U.S. classification of Category I fissile materials, see table 2.4.

177. Dingell, *Safeguards at DOE's Nuclear Weapons Facilities,* Hearing before the Subcommittee on Oversight and Investigations of the Committee on Energy and Commerce, House of Representatives, 101st Congress, 1st session, July 20, 1989, p. 9.

178. Gerry Sikorski, Congressional testimony, in ibid., p. 1.

179. Matthew Bunn, "Measures to Modernize Security and Accounting for Nuclear Materials: Learning from Past U.S. Problems and Solutions," unpublished paper, 1995, p. 3. See also Bunn, "Security for Weapons-Usable Nuclear Material," p. 17.

180. Desmond et al., "The First 50 Years," p. 8.

181. C.A. Coulter, R. Shropshire, and K.E. Thomas, "The Structure of Nuclear Material Safeguards Systems," in *Fundamentals of Nuclear Materials Safeguards Systems,* Workshop at Los Alamos National Laboratory, April 12–16, 1999, pp. II-9–I-10.

182. For the specific regulations for protective forces, see DOE 5632 series and 10 CFR Parts 1046, 1047, and 1049. Security forces at U.S. nuclear facilities must meet rigorous requirements for physical fitness and training. See, for example, *Physical Fitness Training Reference Manual for Security Force Personnel at Fuel Cycle Facilities Possessing Formula Quantities of Special Nuclear Materials,* U.S. Nuclear Regulatory Commission, NUREG/CR-5690, September 1991.

183. A "security officer" is defined as "an unarmed individual who is employed for, and charged with, the protection of classified matter or Government Property," while a "security police officer" is defined as "an individual authorized to carry

firearms and make arrests who is employed for, and charged with, the protection of DOE assets and who is required to meet the requirements of Title 10, Code of Federal Regulations, Parts 1046, 1047, and 1049, as applicable, and DOE Order 5632.7A." See Coulter et al., "The Structure of Nuclear Material Safeguards Systems," p. II-6.

184. Ibid., pp. II-10–II-11.

185. Ibid., p. II-11.

186. For a detailed discussion of many of these physical barriers and U.S. government regulations for their installation, see *Personnel and Vehicle Barriers at Fuel Fabrication Facilities Using or Possessing Formula Quantities of Strategic Special Nuclear Material,* NUREG-1330, Division of Safeguards and Transportation, Office of Nuclear Material Safety and Security, U.S. Nuclear Regulatory Commission, Washington, D.C., December 1988.

187. Coulter et al., "The Structure of Nuclear Material Safeguards Systems," pp. II-12–II-13.

188. Ibid., p. II-14.

189. Ibid., pp. II-14–II-16. For an additional discussion of some of these technologies, see the website for the Cooperative Monitoring Center at Sandia National Laboratories, <http://www.cmc.sandia.gov>.

190. Coulter et al. "The Structure of Nuclear Material Safeguard Systems," p. II-17.

191. Ibid., p. II-19.

192. *Control and Accountability of Nuclear Materials,* U.S. Department of Energy, Washington, D.C., 1998, DOE O 474.1, p. 2.

193. J.T. Markin, "Fundamentals of Materials Accounting," in *Materials Accounting for Nuclear Safeguards,* Workshop at Los Alamos National Laboratory, April 12–16, 1999, p. I-1.

194. "Workshop on Materials Control and Accounting System Design," in *Materials Accounting for Nuclear Safeguards,* Workshop at Los Alamos National Laboratory, April 12–16, 1999, pp. XIII-5–XIII-7.

195. DOE, *Control and Accountability of Nuclear Materials,* DOE O 474.1, p. II-1.

196. Markin, "Fundamentals of Materials Accounting," pp. I-1–I-2.

197. Ibid., p. I-1.

198. Ibid., p. I-4.

199. Ibid., p. I-3. For a detailed discussion of bulk measurement techniques, see R.G. Gutmacher and D.D. Jackson, "Survey of Chemical and Bulk Measurements," in *Materials Accounting for Nuclear Safeguards,* Workshop at Los Alamos National Laboratory, April 12–16, 1999, pp. VIII-1–VIII-33.

200. Hastings A. Smith and Charles R. Hatcher, "Elements of Nondestructive Assay (NDA) Technology," in *Materials Accounting for Nuclear Safeguards,* Workshop at Los Alamos National Laboratory, April 12–16, 1999, pp. VII-1–VII-2.

201. For a more extensive discussion of NDA techniques, see ibid., pp. VII-1–VII-41.

202. DOE, *Control and Accountability of Nuclear Materials,* DOE O 474.1, pp. II-7–II-10. For an extensive discussion of measurement control, see D.D. Wolkey, N.R. Zack, and R.G. Gutmacher, "Measurement Control," in *Materials Accounting*

for Nuclear Safeguards, Workshop at Los Alamos National Laboratory, April 12–16, 1999, pp. IX-1–IX-34.

203. DOE, *Control and Accountability of Nuclear Materials,* DOE O 474.1, pp. II-12–II-16.

204. There are specific guidelines for determining what is an acceptable limit to the error in the measurements. For example, when assessing measurement discrepancies in inventory differences, the limit of error cannot exceed 2 percent of the total "throughput" of materials during the inventory period. Ibid., p. II-19.

205. Ibid., p. II-18.

206. See, for example, Department of Energy, "Guide for Implementation of DOE 5633.A," Office of Safeguards and Security, February 1993, and *Control and Accountability of Nuclear Materials,* DOE 5633.3B.

207. DOE, *Control and Accountability of Nuclear Materials,* DOE 5633.3B, p. III-2.

208. Ibid.

209. LANL, *Guidelines for Material Protection, Control and Accounting Upgrades at Russian Facilities* (DOE, September 28, 1998), p. 32.

210. Ibid., p. 8. See also DOE, *Control and Accountability of Nuclear Materials,* DOE 5633.3B, p. III-4.

211. DOE, *Control and Accountability of Nuclear Materials,* DOE 5633.3B, p. III-5.

212. Ibid., p. III-6.

213. For DOE-wide standards for tamper-indicating devices, see *Safeguards and Security (S&S) Standardization Program,* DOE 5630.17. For a discussion of some of the U.S.-designed tamper-indicating systems, see the website for the Cooperative Monitoring Center at Sandia National Laboratories, <http://www.cmc.sandia.gov>.

214. Coulter et al., "The Structure of Nuclear Material Safeguards Systems," pp. II-8–II-9. For the necessity of performance testing of MPC&A systems, see INFCIRC/225/Rev.4, and Oleg Bukharin, Matthew Bunn, and Kenneth N. Luongo, *Renewing the Partnership: Recommendations for Accelerated Action to Secure Nuclear Material in the Former Soviet Union* (Washington, D.C.: Russian American Nuclear Security Advisory Council, 2000), pp. 79–86.

215. Matthew Bunn, "Security for Weapons-Usable Nuclear Materials: Expanding International Cooperation, Strengthening International Standards," *A Comparative Analysis of Approaches to the Protection of Fissile Materials: Proceedings of the Workshop at Stanford University, July 28–30, 1997,* p. 17.

216. U.S. Department of Energy, *Plutonium: The First Fifty Years: United States Plutonium Production, Acquisition and Utilization from 1944 to 1994* (Washington, D.C.: Department of Energy, February 1996), section 10.2, <http://www.osti.gov/html/osti/opennet/document/pu50yrs/pu50y.html#ZZ0>.

217. David Albright, Frans Berkhout, and William Walker, *Plutonium and Highly Enriched Uranium, 1996: World Inventories, Capabilities and Policies* (Oxford: Oxford University Press, 1997), p. 45.

218. *Plutonium: The First Fifty Years,* section 10.2; Albright et al., *Plutonium and Highly Enriched Uranium,* p. 46.

219. Albright et al., *Plutonium and Highly Enriched Uranium,* p. 47.

220. For the text of Ridenour's resignation letter and an attached report on the difficulties he encountered as security chief at Rocky Flats, see <http://www.whistleblower.org>.

221. See Jim Carrier, "Flats Security Lax, Ex-Officials Warn, *The Denver Post,* May 20, 1997; Mark Eddy, "Flats Theft Risk Discounted—But DOE Confirms Security Problems," *The Denver Post,* June 10, 1997.

222. See U.S. Department of Energy, Office of Oversight, *Interim Report on the Status of Safeguards and Security in the Department of Energy,* November 1997. The above discussion is based on Matthew Bunn's summary of the reports on the security of Rocky Flats in "Security for Weapons-Usable Nuclear Materials," p. 28 n. 11.

223. Bunn, "Security for Weapons-Usable Nuclear Materials," p. 17.

224. Len Ackland, "Rocky Flats: Closing in on Closure," *Bulletin of the Atomic Scientists* 57, no. 6 (November/December 2001): pp. 52–56.

225. The United States General Accounting Office (GAO) also conducted several investigations of the security at DOE facilities. In one report in 1990, the GAO found that at Los Alamos National Laboratory, 78 percent of the security personnel failed a test of required skills. It reported that of the 54-member guard force, "42 failed to demonstrate adequate skill in using weapons, using a baton, or apprehending a person threatening the facility's security." See *Nuclear Safety: Potential Security Weaknesses at Los Alamos and Other DOE Facilities,* GAO/RCED-91-12, October 11, 1990. These findings are summarized in *Department of Energy: Key Factors Underlying Security Problems at DOE Facilities,* GAO/T-RCED-99-159, p. 8.

226. DOE, *Increasing Fissile Inventory Assurance within the U.S. Department of Energy,* Office of Independent Oversight and Performance Assurance, <https://www.oa.doe.gov/reports/ssevalstoc.html>, January 1995, p. ii.

227. DOE, *Follow-Up Review of Fissile Material Assurance in the Department of Energy Complex,* Office of Oversight, July 1998, p. 1, <https://www.oa.doe.gov/reports/ssevalstoc.html>.

228. Ibid., pp. 11–12.

229. U.S. Department of Energy, *Follow-Up Special Study of Nuclear Material Control and Accountability Programs Across the Department of Energy,* Office of Independent Oversight and Performance Assurance, November 2000, p. 1, <https://www.oa.doe.gov/reports/ssevalstoc.html>.

230. Ibid., pp. 1, 9–10.

231. "Nuclear Weapons Complex Vulnerable to Terrorist Attack," The Project on Government Oversight, October 15, 2001, <http://www.pogo.org>; Stephen Hedges and Jeff Zeleny, "Mock Terrorists Breached Security at Weapons Plants," *Chicago Tribune,* October 5, 2001, p. 10; Walter Pincus, "Report Finds 'Weakness' in Nuclear Controls," *Washington Post,* November 6, 2001, p. A7.

232. Eric Pianin and Bill Miller, "Nuclear Arms Plants' Security Lax, Report Says," *Washington Post,* January 23, 2002, p. A15; H. Josef Hebert, "Congressman: Nuke Weapons Vulnerable," *Associated Press,* January 23, 2002.

233. General Accounting Office, *Nuclear Security: NNSA Needs to Better Manage Its Safeguards and Security Program,* report to the Chairman, Subcommittee on National Security, Emerging Threats, and International Relations, Committee on Government Reforms, U.S. House of Representatives, May 2003.

234. Cochran et al., *Nuclear Weapons Databook, Vol. I,* p. 30.

235. DOE, *Increasing Fissile Inventory Assurance within the U.S. Department of Energy,* p. 1.

236. This figure does not include the additional amounts spent by the Department of Defense for securing nuclear warheads, or the amounts spent by commercial companies handling weapons-usable materials to meet regulations requiring effective security and accounting for these materials. See Bunn, "Measures to Modernize Security and Accounting for Nuclear Materials," p. 2.

237. See Avner Cohen and Benjamin Frankel, "Opaque Nuclear Proliferation," *Journal of Strategic Studies* 13, no. 3 (September 1990): p. 16.

3. Russia

1. Kenneth N. Waltz, *The Spread of Nuclear Weapons: More May Be Better,* Adelphi Paper, No. 171 (London: IISS, 1981); Kenneth N. Waltz, "More May Be Better," and "Waltz Responds to Sagan," in Scott D. Sagan and Kenneth N. Waltz, *The Spread of Nuclear Weapons: A Debate Renewed* (New York: W.W. Norton, 2003); Bruce Bueno de Mesquita and William H. Riker, "An Assessment of the Merits of Selective Nuclear Proliferation," *Journal of Conflict Resolution* 26, no. 2 (June 1982): pp. 283–306; John J. Mearsheimer, "Back to the Future: Instability in Europe After the Cold War," *International Security* 15, no. 1 (summer 1990): pp. 5–56.

2. Bruce G. Blair, *The Logic of Accidental Nuclear War* (Washington, D.C.: Brookings Institution, 1993); Bruce G. Blair, *Global Zero Alert for Nuclear Forces* (Washington, D.C.: Brookings Institution, 1995); Peter D. Feaver, *Guarding the Guardians: Civilian Control of Nuclear Weapons in the United States* (Ithaca: Cornell University Press, 1992); Scott D. Sagan, *The Limits of Safety: Organizations, Accidents, and Nuclear Weapons* (Princeton: Princeton University Press, 1993); Scott D. Sagan, "More Will Be Worse," and "Sagan Responds to Waltz," in Sagan and Waltz, *A Debate Renewed*; James G. Blight and David A. Welch, "Risking the Destruction of Nations: Lessons of the Cuban Missile Crisis for New and Aspiring Nuclear States," *Security Studies* 4, no. 4 (summer 1995): pp. 811–850.

3. David J. Karl, "Proliferation Pessimism and Emerging Nuclear Powers," *International Security* 21, no. 3 (winter 1996/1997): pp. 87–119; Jordan Seng, "Less Is More: Command and Control Advantages of Minor Nuclear States," *Security Studies* 6, no. 4 (summer 1997): pp. 50–92.

4. See, for example, Peter D. Feaver, "Neooptimists and the Enduring Problem of Nuclear Proliferation," *Security Studies* 6, no. 4 (summer 1997): pp. 93–99; Mario E. Carranza, "An Impossible Game: Stable Nuclear Deterrence after the Indian and Pakistani Tests," *Nonproliferation Review* 6, no. 3 (spring–summer 1999): pp. 11–24; Clayton P. Bowen and Daniel Wolvén, "Command and Control Challenges in South Asia," *Nonproliferation Review* 6, no. 3 (spring–summer 1999): pp. 25–35.

5. Amy F. Woolf, "Nuclear Weapons in Russia: Safety, Security, and Control Issues," Congressional Research Service Report to Congress, March 1, 1999 (updated June 25, 2003), p. 4.

6. Ibid. Although the vast majority remained in Russia, many strategic nuclear weapons remained in the former-Soviet republics of Belarus, Kazakhstan, and Ukraine.

Most of the tactical nuclear weapons outside of Russia reportedly remained in Belarus, Ukraine, and Kazakhstan, but there were also some remaining in Georgia, Kyrgyzstan, Tajikistan, Turkmenistan, and Uzbekistan.

7. On December 21, 1991, the leaders of eleven former-Soviet countries signed a treaty that gave Russia the sole custody over the former-Soviet nuclear weapons.

8. David B. Thomson, *The START Treaties: Implementation and Status,* Center for International Security Affairs Publication, Los Alamos Laboratory LA-UR-97–2045, May 1997, p. 4.

9. Although the warheads for all of the Soviet-era strategic weapons were returned to Russia in 1996, Ukraine retained a number of SS-19 and SS-24 ICBMs for several years after that. The last of the SS-19 missiles were eliminated in 1999, and the last SS-24 missiles were eliminated in 2001. Woolf, "Nuclear Weapons in Russia," p. 2.

10. William Arkin, Robert Norris, and Joshua Handler, *Taking Stock: Worldwide Nuclear Deployments, 1998* (Washington, D.C.: Natural Resources Defense Council, March 1998), p. 26.

11. A unique feature of Soviet and Russian industry is that each piece of military equipment has a finite service life. At the time that any piece of equipment is being produced, the production plant calculates its expected life span, maintenance schedule, and the number of spare parts it will need during its service life. The production plant then delivers all the spare parts along with the original equipment. At the end of the service life, the entire system is scrapped and replaced with a new one ("Interview with Minister of Defense Igor Sergeyev," *Itogi Weekly,* October 20, 1998, pp. 22–23). This method worked fairly well during the Soviet era, but it is now causing severe problems for the Russians. They often lack the resources to replace entire systems, and often therefore simply have to decommission old systems or try to extend their service lives without adequate maintenance or replacement parts. To make matters worse, many of Russia's weapons were produced in other former-Soviet republics, such as Ukraine. Russia is therefore encountering extreme difficulties in extending the operational life of these weapons, because the facilities for producing additional weapons or spare parts are no longer under Russian control.

12. In fact, because of its weakened conventional forces, Russia has changed its "no first use" policy and now reserves the right to use nuclear weapons in response to a conventional weapons attack (*OMRI Daily Digest,* no. 30, February 12, 1997; "Russia May Use Nukes First in Self-Defense," *Reuters,* February 11, 1997, p. 1).

13. For discussions of the current status and likely future deterioration of Russia's nuclear weapons, see Paul Podvig, "Russian Strategic Forces: Uncertain Future," *Breakthroughs* 7, no. 1 (spring 1998): pp. 11–21, <http://www.armscontrol.ru/transforming/podvig.htm>; Dean A. Wilkening, "The Evolution of Russia's Strategic Nuclear Force," CISAC Publication: Studies in International Security and Arms Control, July 1998, <http://iis-db.stanford.edu/pubs/10334/russianforces.pdf>, and Steve Zaloga, "Russia's Strategic Forces Stumble," *Jane's Intelligence Review* 12, no. 10 (October 2000): pp. 12–14; Robert Norris, William Arkin, Hans Kristensen, and Joshua Handler, "Russian Nuclear Forces, 2001," *Bulletin of the Atomic Scientists* 57, no. 3 (May/June 2001): pp. 78–79.

14. For a discussion of these treaties, see chapter 2.

15. For a discussion of the PNIs undertaken by the United States to reduce tactical weapons, see chapter 2.

16. Arkin et. al., *Taking Stock,* pp. 9–10.

17. Joseph Cirincione, with Jon B. Wolfsthal and Miriam Rajkumar, *Deadly Arsenals: Tracking Weapons of Mass Destruction* (Washington, D.C.: Carnegie Endowment for International Peace, 2002), p. 114; Robert S. Norris and Hans M. Kristensen, "Russian Nuclear Forces, 2003," *Bulletin of the Atomic Scientists* 59, no. 4 (July/August 2003): pp. 70–72. Estimates of the number of tactical nuclear weapons in Russia's arsenal vary widely, however. Jones and McDonough, for example, refer to estimates that "range from 15,000 to upward of 20,000." See Rodney W. Jones and Mark G. McDonough, with Toby Dalton and Gregory Koblentz, *Tracking Nuclear Proliferation: A Guide in Maps and Charts, 1998* (Washington, D.C.: Carnegie Endowment for International Peace, 1998), p. 43.

18. These "non-deployed" tactical weapons are not slated for destruction. See Nikolai Sokov, "Russia: Status and Trends in Tactical Weapon Deployment, 1998," web report, Monterey Center for Nonproliferation Studies, February 1999, <http://www.nti.org/db/nisprofs/over/tacnums.htm>, p. 1.

19. For a discussion of START II, see chapter 2.

20. For a discussion of SORT, see chapter 2.

21. See, for example, Vladimir Pavlovich Belousov, "Press Conference with Russian Experts Regarding START-2 Ratification Process," Speech given at the National Press Institute, October 15, 1998, p. 10.

22. Maslyukov, quoted in Joseph Pilat and Terence Taylor, "Amid Russia's Turmoil, Finishing START Remains a Priority," *Wall Street Journal Europe,* October 15, 1998, p. 1. Other Russian officials have made similar assessments. In 2000, Alexei G. Arbatov, deputy chairman of the Committee on Defense in Russia's Duma, said that Russia's nuclear forces would fall below 1,000 warheads, and in 2001, Russian President Putin pushed for bilateral cuts in U.S. and Russian weapons to 1,500 as part of SORT because that was the largest number Russia could hope to maintain. See Alexei G. Arbatov, "The Next Steps in Arms Control: A Russian Perspective," speech given at the Carnegie Endowment for International Peace, May 16, 2000, <http://www.ceip.org/programs/npp/arbatov051600.htm>; and "U.S. and Russia Make History," *CBS News.com,* May 13, 2002, <http://www.cbsnews.com/stories/2002/05/13/world/main508776.shtml>.

23. Until relatively recently, there was very little unclassified information on Russian C^{3}I. But several publications have allowed much more insight into the Russian C^{3}I system, particularly the works of Bruce Blair and Amy Woolf, and a Russian document: Paul Podvig, Oleg Bukharin, Timur Kadyshev, Eugene Miasnikov, Igor Sutiagin, Maxim Tarasenko, and Boris Zhelesov, *Russia's Strategic Nuclear Weapons* (Moscow: IzdAT, 1998).

24. Podvig et al., *Russia's Strategic Nuclear Weapons,* p. 52.

25. The Soviets chose to allow for the *option* of launch-on-warning; this does not mean that they would necessarily have responded to *all* attacks with such retaliations.

26. Blair, *Logic of Accidental Nuclear War,* pp. 115–167. The Natural Resources Defense Council also conducted a detailed assessment of the effects of a U.S. counterforce strike and determined that the United States could achieve high damage levels against Russian nuclear forces and C^{3}I with an arsenal of about 1,300 strategic weapons—fewer than contained in any of the proposals for the START III treaty. See

The U.S. Nuclear War Plan: A Time for Change (Natural Resources Defense Council, July 2001), <http://www.nrdc.org/nuclear/warplan/execsum.asp>.

27. Many U.S. analysts believed the Soviet policy was also implemented to allow for a first strike, which would also benefit from a C^{3}I system that gave them the ability to launch their nuclear weapons extremely rapidly.

28. Podvig et al., *Russia's Strategic Nuclear Weapons,* p. 409.

29. Ibid.

30. "Belarus Early Warning System to be Tested," *Interfax* (Russia), August 2, 1999; Vladislav Kuznetsov, "Early Warning Radar Undergoes Tests at Baranovichi, Belarus," *ITAR-TASS,* October 19, 2001; "Russian Radar Put into Operation in Belarus," *Pravda* (Russia), October 1, 2003, <http://newsfromrussia.com/world/2003/10/01/50289.html>.

31. "Azerbaijan Ratifies Radar Deal," *Russia Journal,* March 19, 2002.

32. Figures 3.1 and 3.2 are based on Podvig et al., *Russia's Strategic Nuclear Weapons,* pp. 411, 413; U.S. Department of Defense, *Soviet Military Power, 1987* (Washington, D.C.: U.S. Government Printing Office, 1987), pp. 48–49.

33. Podvig et al., *Russia's Strategic Nuclear Weapons,* pp. 414–415.

34. Ibid., pp. 415–416.

35. The Soviets actually launched one experimental geostationary satellite in 1975 but suspended further launches until 1984 (ibid., p. 415). For the definition of geostationary satellites, see note 2.45 above.

36. Valeriy Bogatrev, "Russian Antimissile Defense Cracks," *Kommersant-Daily,* July 15, 1998, p. 2 (translated in World News Connection, document no. FTS19980716000338). See also "Russia Loses New Early-Warning Satellite," *Aerospace Daily,* July 20, 1998, p. 104.

37. Jonathan McDowell, Harvard astrophysicist, interview by author, October 24, 2000; Amy F. Woolf, "Nuclear Weapons in Russia: Safety, Security, and Control Issues," Congressional Research Service Report, March 1, 1999, p. 5; Bogatrev, "Russian Antimissile Defense Cracks," p. 2; Zaloga, "Russia's Strategic Forces Stumble," pp. 12–14.

38. Jonathan McDowell, Harvard astrophysicist, interview by author, October 24, 2000. See also Bogatrev, "Russian Antimissile Defense Cracks," p. 2.

39. David Hoffman, "Shattered Shield: Russia's Myopic Missile Defense," *Washington Post,* February 10, 1999, p. 2. See also Geoffrey Forden, Pavel (Paul) Podvig, and Theodore A. Postol, "False Alarm, Nuclear Danger," *IEEE Spectrum* 37 (March 2000): pp. 31–39, <http://www.armscontrol.ru/start/publications/spectrum-ews.htm>; Zaloga, "Russia's Strategic Forces Stumble," pp. 13–14; Phillip Clark, "Decline of the Russian Early Warning Satellite Programme," *Jane's Intelligence Review* 13, no. 1 (January 2001): p. 17.

40. Philipp C. Bleek, "Fire Shuts Down Russian Early-Warning System," *Arms Control Today* 31, no. 5 (June 2001): p. 26; Pavel Podvig, "Russian Early-Warning System and Danger of Inadvertent Launch," *Physics and Society* 32, no. 1 (January 2003): pp. 7–8.

41. Podvig, "Russian Early-Warning System and Danger of Inadvertent Launch," p. 8.

42. Amy F. Woolf and Kara Wilson, "Russia's Nuclear Forces: Doctrine and Force Structure Issues," Congressional Research Service Report, May 23, 1997, pp. 25–26.

43. Steven Mufson, "Russia Summit of Lesser Accords Looming," *Washington Post,* June 2, 2000, p. A01.

44. Peter Baker, "Nuclear 'Milestone' Divides U.S., Russia: Failure to Construct Joint Warning Center Suggests Bigger Problems on Missile Defense," *Washington Post,* June 13, 2001, p. A23.

45. Amy F. Woolf, "Nuclear Weapons in Russia: Safety, Security, and Control Issues," updated June 25, 2003, p. 16; Rose Gottemoeller, "Nuclear Hangover: Addressing the Cold War Legacy," conference presentation given at *New American Strategies for Security and Peace,* Washington, D.C., October 28, 2003, <http://www.ceip.org/files/projects/npp/pdf/conference/NuclearHangover.pdf>, p. 2.

46. Podvig et al., *Russia's Strategic Nuclear Weapons,* p. 56; Amy F. Woolf, "Nuclear Weapons in the Former Soviet Union: Location, Command, and Control," Congressional Research Service Brief, No. 91144, November 27, 1996, <http://www.fas.org/spp/starwars/crs/91-144.htm>, p. 8; Gennadi Pavlov, Congressional Testimony, *Command and Control of Soviet Nuclear Weapons: Dangers and Opportunities Arising from the August Revolution,* Hearings before the Subcommittee on European Affairs, U.S. Senate, September 21, 1991, p. 5.

47. Woolf, "Nuclear Weapons in the Former Soviet Union," p. 8.

48. Blair, *Global Zero Alert,* p. 46.

49. Podvig et al., *Russia's Strategic Nuclear Weapons,* p. 58.

50. Ibid., p. 57.

51. Blair, *Logic of Accidental Nuclear War,* p. 73.

52. Podvig et al., *Russia's Strategic Nuclear Weapons,* p. 57.

53. Blair, *Global Zero Alert,* p. 48.

54. Ibid., pp. 50–51. See also Podvig et al., *Russia's Strategic Nuclear Weapons,* p. 167.

55. Blair, *Global Zero Alert,* pp. 20, 48–49; Bill Gertz, "Russian Renegades Pose Nuke Danger; CIA Says Arsenal Lacks Tight Controls," *Washington Times,* October 22, 1996, p. A1; David Hoffman, "Shattered Shield: Cold-War Doctrines Refuse to Die," *Washington Post,* March 15, 1998, p. A1. One report suggesting that the Chegets *are* necessary for strategic missile launches is Amy Woolf's 1996 Congressional Research Service Report (Woolf, "Nuclear Weapons in the Former Soviet Union," p. 8). But Woolf and Wilson appear to revise this assessment in a similar report a year later (Woolf and Wilson, "Russia's Nuclear Forces," pp. 22–23).

56. Podvig et al., *Russia's Strategic Nuclear Weapons,* p. 165.

57. Ibid., p. 166.

58. Ibid., p. 57.

59. Ibid., p. 167.

60. Blair, *Logic of Accidental Nuclear War,* p. 279.

61. Blair, *Global Zero Alert for Nuclear Forces,* p. 16.

62. Podvig et al., *Russia's Strategic Nuclear Weapons,* pp. 274–275.

63. Communications with Russian submarines on patrol are ensured by simultaneous transmission on a number of different frequencies, including at least two very-long-wave (VLW) frequencies, five short-wave (SW) frequencies, and five satellite frequencies (ibid., pp. 272–273).

64. Ibid., p. 275.

65. Ibid.

66. Ibid., p. 55.

67. Gertz, "Russian Renegades Pose Nuke Danger," p. A1.

68. Amy Woolf, on the other hand, argued in 1996 that submarine crews had to receive authorization codes from the national command authority before they could launch their SLBMs (Woolf, "Nuclear Weapons in the Former Soviet Union," p. 8).

69. Kathleen Bailey, testimony before the U.S. Senate Armed Services Committee, Subcommittee on Strategic Forces, March 31, 1998, <http://www.senate.gov/~armed_services/statemnt/980331kb.htm>, p. 7. Bailey appears to be referring only to SLBMs, rather than tactical nuclear weapons (particularly because Russian naval vehicles are no longer supposed to carry tactical nuclear weapons).

70. These storage facilities are guarded by special military units (Woolf, "Nuclear Weapons in the Former Soviet Union," p. 8).

71. As an additional precaution, the authorization to move the weapons would be transmitted through a different chain of command than that used for the order to increase the alert status of the bombers themselves (ibid.).

72. Podvig et al., *Russia's Strategic Nuclear Weapons,* p. 354.

73. Ibid., p. 354; See also Blair, *Logic of Accidental Nuclear War,* pp. 17, 101.

74. Blair, *Global Zero Alert for Nuclear Forces,* p. 17.

75. Ibid., p. 17 n. 32.

76. Woolf, "Nuclear Weapons in the Former Soviet Union," p. 8.

77. See earlier discussion of the PNI in this chapter.

78. Ibid.

79. Woolf, "Nuclear Weapons in the Former Soviet Union," p. 8.

80. See above discussion of strategic bomber use-control devices and launch procedures.

81. See "Theft of Nuclear Weapons" below.

82. Woolf, "Nuclear Weapons in the Former Soviet Union," p. 8.

83. Ibid.

84. Eugene Habiger, DOD News Briefing, June 16, 1998, <http://www.defenselink.mil/news/Jun1998/t06231998_t616hab2.html>, p. 7

85. Podvig et al., *Russia's Strategic Nuclear Weapons,* p. 169; Blair, *Global Zero Alert for Nuclear Forces,* p. 51.

86. Podvig et al., *Russia's Strategic Nuclear Weapons,* p. 61.

87. Ibid., p. 61. See also Blair, *Global Zero Alert for Nuclear Forces,* p. 53.

88. Podvig et al., *Russia's Strategic Nuclear Weapons,* p. 61.

89. Podvig et al. argue that the president and the minister of defense have to order the transmission of the command to launch Russia's weapons. They say Russia's command-and-control system was designed so that the military could prevent a situation in which the supreme commander (the president) alone could make the decision to deliver a first strike (Podvig et al., *Russia's Strategic Nuclear Weapons,* p. 59). This implies, however, that if the president and the minister of defense worked together, they could make the decision to deliver a first strike.

90. Blair, *Global Zero Alert for Nuclear Forces,* p. 54.

91. There might, for example, be some procedures that give the General Staff the ability and the authority to launch the Perimeter rockets if it has become clear that the president and minister of defense have been killed by an incoming nuclear attack (Podvig et al., *Russia's Strategic Nuclear Weapons,* p. 60).

92. Blair, *Global Zero Alert for Nuclear Forces,* p. 52.

93. Podvig et al., *Russia's Strategic Nuclear Weapons,* p. 61.

94. Blair, *Global Zero Alert for Nuclear Forces,* p. 52. The staff of the command node probably does not have the discretionary authority to decide whether or not to transmit the launch codes (ibid.).

95. Ibid. See also Steven J. Zaloga, "Russia's Doomsday Machine," *Jane's Intelligence Review* 8 (February 1, 1996): p. 55.

96. Podvig et al., *Russia's Strategic Nuclear Weapons,* p. 61.

97. Cf. Podvig et al., *Russia's Strategic Nuclear Weapons,* p. 61; Zaloga, "Russia's Doomsday Machine," pp. 54–56; Blair, *Global Zero Alert for Nuclear Forces,* pp. 51–56.

98. Bruce G. Blair, Harold A. Feiveson, and Frank N. von Hippel, "Taking Nuclear Weapons off Hair-Trigger Alert," *Scientific American* 277, no. 3 (November 1997): p. 75; Woolf and Wilson, "Russia's Nuclear Forces," p. 25; Zaloga, "Russia's Strategic Forces Stumble," pp. 13–14.

99. Blair, Feiveson, and von Hippel, "Taking Nuclear Weapons off Hair-Trigger Alert," p. 75; Patrick E. Tyler, "Power-Line Thieves Loot Russia, Often Risking Death or Maiming," *New York Times,* April 18, 2000.

100. Podvig, "Russian Strategic Forces: Uncertain Future," pp. 11–21; Wilkening, "The Evolution of Russia's Strategic Nuclear Force," pp. 1–64.

101. See reports of these events in Blair, Feiveson, and von Hippel, "Taking Nuclear Weapons off Hair-Trigger Alert," pp. 74–75; Thomas Nilsen, Igor Kudrik, and Alexandr Nikitin, "The Russian Northern Fleet," *Bellona Report,* no. 2 (1996), section 1.3.1, <http://www.bellona.no/imaker?sub=1&id=11092>; Sharon LaFraniere, "Power to Russian Nuclear Force Is Shut Off, Units on Border with China Go Dark Temporarily for Failure to Pay Bill," *Washington Post,* July 21, 1999, p. A15; Zaloga, "Russia's Strategic Forces Stumble," p. 12.

102. Blair, Feiveson, and von Hippel, "Taking Nuclear Weapons off Hair-Trigger Alert," p. 75.

103. For a similar assessment, see Woolf and Wilson, "Russia's Nuclear Forces," pp. 24–28.

104. Peter Stein and Peter D. Feaver, *Assuring Control of Nuclear Weapons: The Evolution of Permissive Action Links* (Lanham, Md.: University Press of America, 1987), p. 8.

105. Blair, *Logic of Accidental Nuclear War,* p. 107. Blair notes that ESDs also help control against unauthorized use, because these environmental conditions are almost impossible to imitate from the ground. For a more detailed discussion of the role of ESDs in protecting against unauthorized use, see Peter Stein and Peter D. Feaver, *Assuring Control of Nuclear Weapons: The Evolution of Permissive Action Links* (Lanham, Md.: University Press of America, 1987), p. 23.

106. The railway system allowed for the transportation of warheads from their deployment locations to warhead disassembly facilities.

107. U.S. experts involved in the CTR Program, interviews by author, 1999.

108. Ibid.

109. Podvig et al., *Russia's Strategic Nuclear Weapons,* p. 57.

110. Because some of Russia's nuclear weapons can be launched automatically, without the participation of launch crews (see above), either these weapons do not

have the components removed from their warheads, or the components can be re-installed automatically.

111. The United States definition of one-point safety is "when the weapon's high explosive is detonated at any single point, the probability of producing a nuclear yield greater than four pounds TNT equivalent is less than one in a million." See Donald R. Cotter, "Peacetime Operations: Safety and Security," in *Managing Nuclear Operations,* ed. Ashton B. Carter, John D. Steinbruner, and Charles A. Zraket (Washington, D.C.: Brookings Institution, 1987), p. 43. For a discussion of U.S. one-point safety designs, see chapter 2 above.

112. According to U.S. experts involved in the CTR Program, interviews by author.

113. John Dallman, interview with author, August 20, 1999.

114. This is the reason why the United States determined that IHE was necessary for its nuclear warheads. See Sidney Drell and Bob Peurifoy, "Technical Issues of a Nuclear Test Ban," *Annual Review of Nuclear and Particle Science* 44 (1994): pp. 306–309; Robert S. Norris and William Arkin, "U.S. Nuclear Weapons Safety and Control Features," *Bulletin of the Atomic Scientists* 47, no. 8 (October 1991): p. 49.

115. *Los Alamos National Laboratory Nuclear Weapons Program: Focus on the Stockpile,* November 1998, LALP-97-134, p. 15.

116. Ibid.

117. Podvig et al., *Russia's Strategic Nuclear Weapons,* p. 57. Of course, even an accidental launch of an *unarmed* ICBM could cause another state with an early-warning system and a launch-on-warning policy to retaliate.

118. Habiger, DOD News Briefing, June 16, 1998, p. 5.

119. James Woolsey, "Threats to United States National Security," testimony before the House of Representatives, Committee on National Security, February 12, 1998, <http://commdocs.house.gov/committees/security/has043000.000/has043000_1.htm>, p. 27. See also Bruce G. Blair, "Where Would All the Missiles Go?" *Washington Post,* October 15, 1996, p. A15.

120. For a discussion of risks of inadvertent launches of Russian weapons, see below.

121. Bruce G. Blair, quoted in Bill Gertz, "Missile Defense Fails to Take Spot among Campaign Issues; In Polls, 60 Percent Agree with Dole on Need for System," *Washington Times,* October 22, 1996, p. A17. General Eugene Habiger, former commander of the U.S. Strategic Command, reported that he was told that it takes ten minutes to re-enter launch coordinates into the Russian missiles. He made no mention of the missiles returning to their default settings (Habiger, DOD News Briefing, June 16, 1998, p. 5). The new default setting for U.S. missiles is the ocean, and an accidental launch of a U.S. missile would send it harmlessly out to sea. See Bruce G. Blair, Lachlan Forrow, Ira Helfand, George Lewis, Theodore A. Postol, Victor Sidel, Barry Levy, Herbert Abrams, and Christine Cassel, "Accidental Nuclear War—A Post–Cold War Assessment," *The New England Journal of Medicine* 338, no. 18 (April 30, 1998): p. 1326.

122. Woolsey, "Threats to United States National Security," p. 27.

123. The self-destruct mechanism on a test missile causes the missile to explode if it veers too far from its original trajectory or if its third booster rocket does not ignite properly (Yakovlev, quoted in *Moscow Interfax,* "Russian Forces to Get Topol-M Rockets Despite Launch Mishap," October 26, 1998, in FBIS-TAC-98-299). This statement differs from Bruce Blair's 1991 congressional testimony that Russia's de-

ployed ICBMs also have a self-destruct mechanism that would activate if a missile veered from its original launch trajectory. Blair does point out, however, that an accidentally launched missile would be most likely to follow its normal trajectory and would not self-destruct even if it had this mechanism (Bruce G. Blair, Congressional Testimony, *Command and Control of Soviet Nuclear Weapons: Dangers and Opportunities Arising from the August Revolution,* Hearings before the Subcommittee on European Affairs of the Committee on Foreign Relations, U.S. Senate, September 21, 1991). See also Bruce G. Blair, "Break-Up of the U.S.S.R.: Whither Nuclear Control?" *Transnational Law and Contemporary Problems* 2, no. 2 (fall 1992): pp. 534–535. A self-destruct mechanism should be distinguished from a command-destruct mechanism, which would allow a command center to cause a missile that has already been launched to explode before it hits its target. There is no evidence that Russian ICBMs or SLBMs contain command-destruct mechanisms, either.

124. Blair, Congressional testimony, *Command and Control of Soviet Nuclear Weapons,* p. 18; Blair, "Break-Up of the U.S.S.R.," pp. 534–535. If the United States successfully develops and deploys a national missile defense, it might be able to destroy an ICBM that was accidentally launched.

125. The most notable of these assessments are Robert Walpole, National Intelligence Officer for Strategic and Nuclear Programs, speech at the Carnegie Endowment for International Peace, September 17, 1998, <http://www.cia.gov/cia/public_affairs/speeches/1998/walpole_speech_091798.html>, p. 2; Rumsfeld Commission to Assess the Ballistic Missile Threat, Report to Congress, July 15, 1998, <http://www.house.gov/hasc/testimony/105thcongress/BMThreat.htm>, section IIC2; and Eugene Habiger, DOD News Briefing, November 4, 1997, p. 2, <http://www.defenselink.mil/news/Nov1997/t11071997_thabiger.html>.

126. Woolf, "Nuclear Weapons in the Former Soviet Union," p. 8.

127. Podvig et al., *Russia's Strategic Nuclear Weapons,* p. 56.

128. Ibid., p. 354. See also Blair, *Logic of Accidental Nuclear War,* p. 17.

129. In 1998, Russian deputy defense minister Vladimir Toporov stated that the air forces only received 57 percent of the standard flying practice hours. Military pilots had spent only twenty-one hours in flight by mid-November, and fighter pilots had received an average of ten hours ("Low Morale, Outdated Arms Reported in Russian Army," *Interfax* (Russia), November 11, 1998, in FBIS-UMA-98-315).

130. It is possible that these procedures could change if tensions with the United States or another country increased dramatically or if there were a breakdown in the Russian military structure.

131. See above.

132. See above.

133. Nilsen et al., "The Russian Northern Fleet," section 1.3.2; Christina Chuen, Michael Jasinski, and Bret Lortie, "Russia's Blue Water Blues," *Bulletin of the Atomic Scientists* 57, no. 1 (January/February 2001): pp. 65–69.

134. There has been increasing concern about such accidents occurring since the sinking of the Russian submarine *Kursk* on August 12, 2000. See Chuen et al., "Russia's Blue Water Blues," pp. 65–69.

135. Sokov, "Russia: Status and Trends in Tactical Weapon Deployment," pp. 1–2.

136. William C. Potter and Nikolai Sokov, "Nuclear Weapons That People Forget," *International Herald Tribune,* May 31, 2000, p. 6.

137. Woolf, "Nuclear Weapons in the Former Soviet Union," p. 8; Blair, *Logic of Accidental Nuclear War,* p. 96.

138. Blair, Feiveson, and von Hippel, "Taking Nuclear Weapons off Hair-Trigger Alert," pp. 74–76.

139. Ibid., pp. 74–75. See also "Low Morale, Outdated Arms Reported in Russian Army," *Interfax,* November 11, 1998 in FBIS-UMA-98-315; Nilsen et al., "The Russian Northern Fleet," section 1.3.2.

140. For example, aging circuitry was determined to be the cause of an accidental launch of a South Korean surface-to-air missile on December 4, 1998. The missile reportedly self-detonated in mid-flight, injuring a dozen civilians and damaging scores of cars and houses. See "More on Accidental Firing of ROK Missile," *Korea Times,* December 5, 1998, in FBIS-EAS-98-338, p. 1.

141. Peter D. Feaver, "Command and Control in Emerging Nuclear Nations," *International Security* 17, no. 3 (winter 1992/1993): p. 164.

142. Robert Walpole, speech at the Carnegie Endowment for International Peace, September 17, 1998, p. 2.

143. Rumsfeld Commission, Report to Congress, section IIC2.

144. Blair, *Global Zero Alert,* p. 17.

145. Ibid., p. 14. See also Paul Mann, "Nuclear Risks Mount in Besieged Russia," *Aviation Week and Space Technology* 149, no. 10 (September 7, 1998): pp. 60–62; Rumsfeld Commission, Report to Congress, section IIC2.

146. Podvig et al., *Russia's Strategic Nuclear Weapons,* p. 57.

147. A CIA document on Russian command and control reportedly says that the safeguards on all Russian nuclear devices can be defeated, "probably within weeks or days depending on the weapon involved" (quoted in Jim Wolf, "CIA Rates 'Low' the Risk of Unauthorized Use of Russian Nuclear Weapons," *Reuters,* October 23, 1996, p. A06).

148. Blair, *Global Zero Alert,* p. 20.

149. Blair, *Logic of Accidental Nuclear War,* p. 83.

150. Ibid., p. 82.

151. R. Jeffery Smith, "'Nuclear Suitcase' Disabled During Coup, Hill Told," *Washington Post,* September 25, 1991, p. A20; Blair, *Logic of Accidental Nuclear War,* p. 84.

152. Blair, *Logic of Accidental Nuclear War,* p. 86.

153. Matthew Evangelista, "Russia's Fragile Union," *Bulletin of the Atomic Scientists* 55, no. 3 (May/June 1999): pp. 50–55; Sharon LaFraniere, "A Crisis of Control in Russian Far East," *Washington Post,* May 2, 2000, p. A16.

154. Since his election as Russian president, Vladimir Putin has attempted to reconsolidate power, but it remains to be seen whether this attempt will be successful. Although in June 2001 Putin managed to push through legislation to strip regional leaders of their seats in parliament and replace them with appointed legislators, the regional leaders are still struggling to resist the central controls. See Associated Press, "Putin Suffers Setback in Effort to Rein in Regions," *New York Times,* June 28, 2000; Peter Baker and Susan B. Glasser, "Regions Resist Kremlin Control: Governors Cling to Power in Defiance of President," *Washington Post,* May 31, 2001, p. A01; Fred Wier, "Putin's Duel with the Bureaucrats," *Christian Science Monitor,* February 22, 2002.

155. See Aleksey Tarasov, "Again a Woman's Mutiny," *Izvestiya,* July 25, p. 1,

reported in *Yaderny Kontrol* 40 (July–August 1998): pp. 12–30 (translated in World News Connection, document no. FTS19981119000866); Pilvikki Kause, "Russian Military Shattered," *Helsingin Sanomat* (Internet version), October 1, 1998, pp. 1–3.

156. Daniel Gouré, quoted in Mann, "Nuclear Risks," p. 60.

157. Woolf, "Nuclear Weapons in the Former Soviet Union," p. 8.

158. See, for example, the testimony of General Eugene Habiger after he visited several Russian nuclear weapon facilities (Habiger, DOD News Briefings, November 4, 1997, and June 16, 1998).

159. Vladimir Orlov, "Nuclear Blackmail: Threats from 'Enemies Within' More Disturbing Than Conspiracies from Without," *Nezavismoye Voyennoye Obozreniye,* no. 32 (August 29–September 4, 1997): p. 2 (translated in World News Connection, document no. FTS19971001000544).

160. Ibid.

161. "Secretary Cohen Tours Russian Defense Facility, Nuclear Weapons Security Projects Viewed at Serviev Posad," DOD News Briefing, February 13, 1998, <http://www.defenselink.mil/news/Feb1998/b02131998_bt066–98.html>, p. 1.

162. Department of Defense, "The Cooperative Threat Reduction Program," in *Proliferation: Threat and Response,* 1997.

163. Orlov, "Nuclear Blackmail," p. 2.

164. Ibid.

165. John W.R. Lepingwell and Nikolai Sokov, "Strategic Offensive Arms Elimination and Weapons Protection, Control, and Accounting," *Nonproliferation Review* 7, no. 1 (spring 2000): p. 65.

166. Ibid., p. 65.

167. "Secretary Cohen Tours Russian Defense Facility," p. 1.

168. Woolf, "Nuclear Weapons in Russia," p. 6.

169. The Rumsfeld Commission determined that either a breakdown of control at the apex of power (at or above the level of the General Staff) or a revolt by a regional leader could increase the risk of an unauthorized use of nuclear weapons (Steve Maaranen, Rumsfeld Commission Staff, interview by author, May 14, 1999). Because the Rumsfeld Commission only studied the risks associated with strategic ballistic missiles, however, it did not address the risks of theft of nuclear cruise missiles or tactical nuclear weapons.

170. Woolf and Wilson, "Russia's Nuclear Forces," p. 27.

171. Ibid. For the risks associated with "delegative" command systems, see Feaver, "Command and Control in Emerging Nuclear Nations," pp. 168–170.

172. The author would like to thank Peter Lavoy for this suggestion.

173. David Harrison, "Revealed: Russia Spied on Blair for Saddam," *Sunday Telegraph* (London), April 13, 2003, p. 1.

174. Bill Nichols, "U.S.-Russian Relations Approach Chilliest since Cold War," *USA Today,* March 27, 2003, p. A10. See also Alan Cullision and Jeanne Whalen, "War Shows Fragility of U.S.-Russia Links," *Wall Street Journal,* April 1, 2003.

175. Waltz, "More May Be Better," p. 11.

176. Lewis A. Dunn, "Military Politics, Nuclear Proliferation, and the 'Nuclear Coup d'Etat,'" *Journal of Strategic Studies* 1 (May 1978): p. 46. For instance, the United States reportedly increased its alerts in "hundreds" of small ways during the 1991 coup attempt. See Blair, *Logic of Accidental Nuclear War,* pp. 56–57.

177. Moreover, deterrence would be largely ineffective against terrorists because they usually have no territory that can be targeted by nuclear weapons. See Bueno de Mesquita and Riker, "Selective Nuclear Proliferation," p. 304; Mearsheimer, "Back to the Future," p. 39. And terrorists would be quite likely to use a stolen nuclear weapon—either as a direct means of attack or as a tool for nuclear blackmail.

178. Hoffman, "Russia's Myopic Missile Defense," p. A1; David Hoffman, "I Had a Funny Feeling in My Gut," *Washington Post,* February 10, 1999, p. A19.

179. For a study of this incident and its implications, see Forden et al., "False Alarm, Nuclear Danger," pp. 1–12.

180. Hoffman, "Cold-War Doctrines Refuse to Die," p. A1.

181. Nikolai Devyanin, quoted in ibid.

182. Nikolai Sokov, "Could Norway Trigger a Nuclear War? Notes on the Russian Command and Control System," Program on New Approaches to Russian Security Policy, *PONARS Policy Memo,* no. 24, October 1997, <http://www.csis.org/ruseura/ponars/policymemos/pm_0024.pdf>.

183. Forden et al., "False Alarm, Nuclear Danger," pp. 1–12; Blair, *Global Zero Alert,* p. 47. Moreover, the Norwegian government reportedly had sent a letter to Russia notifying it of the impending rocket launch, but the letter was never given to the radar crews (Hoffman, "Cold-War Doctrines Refuse to Die," p. A1). If this report is true, there clearly were serious *bureaucratic* problems in Russia's BMEW system.

184. Forden et al., "False Alarm, Nuclear Danger," p. 3.

185. Ibid., p. 9.

186. James P. Rubin, Department of State Daily Briefing, February 10, 1999.

187. The Rumsfeld Commission concluded that the risks of an inadvertent launch could significantly increase during such scenarios, especially given Russia's deteriorating early-warning system (Rumsfeld Commission, Report to Congress, section IIC2; Steve Maaranen, Rumsfeld Commission Staff, interview by author, May 14, 1999).

188. Matthew Bunn, *The Next Wave: Urgently Needed New Steps to Control Warheads and Fissile Materials* (Carnegie Endowment for International Peace and Harvard University, 2000), p. 10.

189. Vladimir Kucherenko, "Russian Nuclear Material Monitoring System 'Far from Ideal,'" *Rossiyskaya Gazeta,* [translated], September 29, 2000, in RANSAC Nuclear News (October 4, 2000): p. 2.

190. Bunn, *The Next Wave,* pp. 16–17. See also William C. Potter, "Nuclear Leakage from the Post-Soviet States," Oral Presentation Before the Permanent Subcommittee on Investigations, U.S. Senate Committee on Governmental Affairs, March 13, 1996, <http://cns.miis.edu/pubs/reports/senoral.htm>.

191. Bunn, *The Next Wave,* p. 17. Months after the incident, Viktor Yerastov, director of the department of accounting and control of nuclear materials at the Russian Ministry of Atomic Energy (Minatom), confirmed that this attempted theft had taken place ("Nuclear Thieves Could Have Inflicted Serious Harm to the State," *Yaderny Kontrol,* November–December 1999, pp. 40–43, in the CNS Nuclear Trafficking Database, 19990950). Although Yerastov did not specify whether these materials were weapons-usable (i.e., whether they were HEU or Pu), Matthew Bunn argues that they were, based on Yerastov's comments and the types of materials in a nuclear weapon. See Bunn, *The Next Wave,* p. 17.

192. "Turkish Police Seize Enriched Uranium," *BBC News*, November 7, 2001; Steven Erlanger, "Lax Nuclear Security in Russia is Cited as Way for Bin Laden to Get Arms," *New York Times*, November 12, 2001.

193. Michael Dobbs, "Russian Official Reveals Attempt Made to Steal Nuclear Materials," *Washington Post*, November 13, 2001, p. A22.

194. For a discussion of these possibilities, see Emily Ewell, "NIS Nuclear Smuggling since 1995: A Lull in Significant Cases?" *Nonproliferation Review* 5, no. 3 (spring–summer 1998): pp. 119–125.

195. HEU is uranium enriched to a level of 20 percent or greater of the isotope uranium-235, the amount necessary for a nuclear explosion.

196. Although the Department of Energy previously estimated this amount to be 650 metric tons, the DOE's acting deputy undersecretary for defense and nuclear nonproliferation, Rose Gottemoeller, told a congressional subcommittee on March 21, 2000, that the actual amount was closer to 800 metric tons. See "More Russian Material at Risk Than Previously Thought," *Nuclear Weapons and Materials Monitor*, no. 4 (April 7, 2000): pp. 4–5. For assessments of the number of sites containing fissile materials, see Bunn, *The Next Wave*, p. 11; and Oleg Bukharin, Matthew Bunn, and Kenneth N. Luongo, *Renewing the Partnership: Recommendations for Accelerated Action to Secure Nuclear Material in the Former Soviet Union* (Washington, D.C.: Russian American Nuclear Security Advisory Council, 2000), p. 6.

197. For a chart listing all the Russian sites believed to contain weapons-usable fissile materials, see Jones et al., pp. 45–47.

198. For a list of main nuclear facilities in the former Soviet Union and their activities, see "Nuclear Facilities and Fissile Materials in the Former Soviet Union," in *Nuclear Status Report: Nuclear Weapons, Fissile Material, and Export Controls in the Former Soviet Union*, no. 6, ed. Jon Wolfsthal, Cristina-Astrid Chuen, and Emily Ewell Daughtry (Carnegie Endowment for International Peace and Monterey Institute of International Studies, June 2001), pp. 75–174.

199. For example, of the three plutonium production facilities, Chelyabinsk-65, Tomsk-7, and Krasnoyarsk-26, Tomsk-7 still has two functioning reactors and Krasnoyarsk-26 still has one. These reactors are being used to produce heat and electricity for their populations.

200. DOE, "US/Russian Cooperation on Protection, Control, and Accounting for Naval Nuclear Fuel," *Partnership for Nuclear Security*, Department of Energy Nuclear Material Security Task Force, December 1997, p. 43.

201. Ibid.

202. Oleg Bukharin and William C. Potter, "Potatoes were Guarded Better," *Bulletin of the Atomic Scientists* 51, no. 3 (May–June 1995): pp. 46–50, <http://www.bullatomsci.org/issues/1995/mj95/mj95.bukharin.html>.

203. Sergey Zelentsov (lieutenant general in the Russian Federation Ministry of Defense), "Nuclear Arsenal Must Be in the Same Hands," *Yaderny Kontrol*, no. 17 (May 1996): p. 20 (translated in World News Connection, document no. FTS19960501001994).

204. Arkin et al., *Taking Stock*, p. 29.

205. Oleg Bukharin, "Soft Landing for Bomb Uranium," *Bulletin of the Atomic Scientists* 49, no. 7 (September 1993): p. 46, <http://www.bullatomsci.org/issues/1993/

s93/s93Bukharin.html>. The distinction between MOD authority over nuclear weapons and Minatom's authority over fissile materials becomes somewhat blurred at the serial production facilities. MOD still oversees the nuclear weapons as they enter and exit the facilities, and maintains some presence at the facilities. At some point, responsibility is transferred to and from Minatom.

206. This distinction between defense- and civilian-related fissile materials is relatively new. During the Soviet era, there was no such distinction. During the early 1990s, there was a great deal of contention between Minatom and GAN over who had responsibility over defense-related nuclear materials.

207. For international standards for physical protection, see INFCIRC/225/Rev.4.

208. LANL, "Russian-American Collaborations to Reduce the Nuclear Danger," *Los Alamos Science,* no. 24, 1996, p. 82; Bukharin and Potter, "Potatoes Were Guarded Better," p. 48; Orlov, "Nuclear Blackmail," pp. 1–7; DOE, "U.S./Russian Program in Material, Protection, Control, and Accounting at the RRC Kurchatov Institute: 1996–1997," *Partnership for Nuclear Security,* Department of Energy Nuclear Material Security Task Force, December 1997, p. 55. While much of this presumably existed before the U.S.S.R. collapsed, it only became a problem after the other security systems failed.

209. Oleg Bukharin, "Security of Fissile Materials in Russia," *Annual Review of Energy and the Environment,* no. 21 (1996): p. 483.

210. Bukharin and Potter, "Potatoes Were Guarded Better," p. 49.

211. Orlov, "Nuclear Blackmail," p. 1

212. Ibid., p. 2

213. Bukharin, "Security of Fissile Materials in Russia," p. 483; Orlov, "Nuclear Blackmail," pp. 1–2.

214. Gennady Pshakin, "MPC&A Upgrades in Russia: Results, Problems, Perspectives," *Monitor* 5, no. 1–2 (winter–spring 1999): p. 20; David Hoffman, "Cure for Russia's Nuclear 'Headache' Proves to be Painful: Crisis, Spotty Data Hobble Bid to Secure Bomb Material," *Washington Post,* December 26, 1998, p. A01; Bukharin and Potter, "Potatoes Were Guarded Better," p. 48; DOE, "Cooperation between the Russian Federation and the United States to Enhance the Existing Nuclear Material, Protection, Control, and Accounting Systems at Mayak Production Association," *Partnership for Nuclear Security,* Department of Energy Nuclear Material Security Task Force, December 1997, p. 3.

215. *Report on Activities of the Federal Regulator of Russia on Nuclear and Radiation Safety in 1993,* Gosatomnadzor, RD-03-02-93, 1993, quoted in Bukharin, "Security of Fissile Materials in Russia," p. 483. For a similar assessment, see a 1998 DOE report, quoted in *Protecting Nuclear Materials in Russia,* National Research Council Publication, National Academy Press, <http://books.nap.edu/books/030906547X/html/index.html>, p. 10.

216. Alexander Roumiantsev, quoted in Yuri Volodin, Valentin Zakharov, Gennady Pshakin, and Alexander Roumiantsev, "On the Way to Establish an Effective State MPC&A System, Round Table Discussion," *Yaderny Kontrol* 5 (fall 1997): p. 20.

217. Ibid.

218. Ron Auguston, quoted in LANL, "Russian-American Collaborations," p. 34.

219. National Research Council, *Protecting Nuclear Weapons Material in Russia* (Washington, D.C.: National Academy Press, 1999), <http://books.nap.edu/books/030906547X/html/index.html>, pp. 8–9.

220. See the IAEA recommendations for the different categories of nuclear material in INFCIRC/225.

221. Roumiantsev, quoted in "Effective State MPC&A System," p. 20.

222. Ibid., p. 20. See also National Research Council, *Protecting Nuclear Weapons Material,* p. 10; Oleg Bukharin, "U.S.-Russian Cooperation in the Area of Nuclear Safeguards," *Nonproliferation Review* 2, no. 1 (fall 1994): p. 30.

223. Roumiantsev, quoted in "Effective State MPC&A System," p. 20; Bukharin, "Security of Fissile Materials in Russia," pp. 485–486; Bukharin, "U.S.-Russian Cooperation in the Area of Nuclear Safeguards," p. 30.

224. Ron Auguston, quoted in LANL, "Russian-American Collaborations to Reduce the Nuclear Danger," *Los Alamos Science,* Number 24, 1996, p. 34; National Research Council, *Protecting Nuclear Materials in Russia,* p. 7; Jessica Stern, "U.S. Assistance Programs for Improving MPC&A in the Former Soviet Union," *Nonproliferation Review* 3, no. 2 (winter 1996): p. 19.

225. Roumiantsev, quoted in "Effective State MPC&A System," p. 20; National Research Council, *Protecting Nuclear Weapons Material,* p. 10.

226. Alexander Roumiantsev, quoted in "On the Way to Establish an Effective State MPC&A System," *Yaderny Kontrol,* no. 5 (fall 1997): p. 18.

227. Bukharin, "Soft Landing for Bomb Uranium," p. 48; Matthew Bunn, "Security for Weapons-Usable Nuclear Materials: Expanding International Cooperation, Strengthening International Standards," *A Comparative Analysis of Approaches to the Protection of Fissile Materials: Proceedings of the Workshop at Stanford University, July 28–30, 1997,* p. 16. See also the summaries of MPC&A upgrades later performed at numerous facilities in DOE, *Partnership for Nuclear Security,* Department of Energy Nuclear Material Security Task Force, December 1997. Even on the rare occasion that a Russian facility *did* have portal monitors, they were less sensitive by a factor of twenty than commercial portal monitors in the West (Bukharin, "U.S.-Russian Cooperation in the Area of Nuclear Safeguards," p. 30).

228. Konstantin Dorofeev, head of the Russian MC&A program at K-26, interview by author, Los Alamos National Laboratory, May 25, 1999; Oleg Bukharin, "Security of Fissile Materials in Russia," *Annual Review of Energy and the Environment,* no. 21 (1996): p. 486; Bukharin and Potter, "Potatoes Were Guarded Better," p. 48.

229. *Report on Activities of the Federal Regulator of Russia on Nuclear and Radiation Safety in 1993,* Gosatomnadzor, RD-03-02-93, 1993, quoted in Oleg Bukharin, "Security of Fissile Materials in Russia," *Annual Review of Energy and the Environment,* no. 21 (1996): p. 486.

230. Quoted in LANL, "Russian-American Collaborations," p. 74.

231. Ibid.

232. Joseph Pilat, quoted in LANL, "Russian-American Collaborations," p. 37. For summaries of some of the delays within the U.S. government, see Jason D. Ellis, "Nunn-Lugar's Midlife Crisis," *Survival* 39, no. 1 (spring 1997): p. 94, and Paul White, quoted in LANL, "Russian-American Collaborations," p. 35.

233. White, quoted in LANL, "Russian-American Collaborations," p. 35.

234. General Accounting Office, "Weapons of Mass Destruction: Reducing the Threat from the Former Soviet Union: An Update," GAO/NSIAD-95-165, June 9, 1995, Appendix III: 0.2, p. 17.

235. Todd E. Perry, "Securing Russian Nuclear Materials: The Need for an Expanded U.S. Response," *Nonproliferation Review* 6, no. 2 (winter 1999): p. 87; Allison et al., *Avoiding Nuclear Anarchy,* pp. 122–126; C. Austin Reams, *Russia's Atomic Tsar: Viktor N. Mikhailov* (Center for International Security Affairs, Los Alamos National Laboratory, December 1996), pp. 12–13. For other instances of bureaucratic "turf wars" causing delays in the CTR program, see Lepingwell and Sokov, "Strategic Offensive Arms Elimination," p. 68.

236. Auguston, quoted in LANL, "Russian-American Collaborations," p. 34; White, quoted in ibid., p. 33; Katherine E. Johnson, "U.S.-FSU Nuclear Threat Reduction Programs: Effectiveness of Current Efforts and Prospects for Future Cooperation," Center for International Security Affairs Publication, Los Alamos National Laboratory, August 1995, p. 10; Allison et al., *Avoiding Nuclear Anarchy,* pp. 75–78, 119.

237. For summaries of the progress of the CTR program, see Ellis, "Nunn-Lugar's Midlife Crisis," p. 94; Lepingwell and Sokov, "Strategic Offensive Arms Elimination," pp. 59–75; and Kenneth N. Luongo and William E. Hoehn III, "Reform and Expansion of Cooperative Threat Reduction," *Arms Control Today* 33, no. 5 (June 2003), <http://www.armscontrol.org/act/2003_06/luongohoehn_june03.asp>.

238. LANL, "Russian-American Collaborations," p. 75.

239. Although the U.S. Department of Defense (DOD) initially had primary oversight of the program, the DOE was given official control of the program in 1996. See Jason D. Ellis and Todd E. Perry, "Nunn-Lugar's Unfinished Agenda," *Arms Control Today* 27, no. 3 (October 1997): p. 16.

240. Hecker, quoted in LANL, "Russian-American Collaborations," p. 37.

241. White, quoted in ibid., p. 35; Steven Younger, quoted in ibid., p. 36.

242. Hecker, quoted in ibid., p. 34.

243. Krasnoyarsk-26 was recently renamed as Zheleznogorsk.

244. The reactor burns the HEU, producing Np-239, which quickly decays to Pu-239.

245. For an explanation of the Purex process, see William P. Bebbington, "The Reprocessing of Nuclear Fuels," *Scientific American,* December 1976, pp. 32–33.

246. "Nuclear Nonproliferation," p. 7.

247. Matthew Bunn, Anthony Wier, and John P. Holdren, *Controlling Nuclear Warheads and Materials: A Report Card and Action Plan* (Washington, D.C.: Nuclear Threat Initiative and the Project on Managing the Atom, Harvard University, March 2003), p. vii.

248. William C. Potter, prepared remarks at the 7th Annual Carnegie International Non-Proliferation Conference, Washington, D.C. January 11–12, 1999, <http://www.ceip.org/programs/npp/potter.htm>, p. 2.

249. David Albright, quoted in Jørgen Wouters, "Peddling the Nuclear Arsenal: Should You Worry?" *ABCNEWS.com,* 1998, <http://archive.abcnews.go.com/sections/world/nuclear/nuclear2c.html>, p. 2.

250. Woolf, "Nuclear Weapons in Russia," p. 8; National Research Council, *Protecting Nuclear Weapons Material,* p. 3.

251. Woolf, "Nuclear Weapons in Russia," p. 8; Albright, quoted in Wouters, "Peddling the Nuclear Arsenal," p. 2; Carrie Smarto, Michael Haase, Mark Baumann, Katherine Garner, Nicole Nelson, and William Toth, "MPC&A Site Operations and Sustainability: A Policy Overview," paper presented to the 40th Annual Meeting of the Institute of Nuclear Material Management, Phoenix, Ariz., July 27, 1999, p. 1.

252. Perry, "Securing Russian Nuclear Materials," p. 88; Potter, 7th Annual Carnegie Non-Proliferation Conference, p. 2.

253. C. Ruth Kempf, "U.S. DOE Laboratory Views on U.S.-Russian Partnership for Nuclear Security," paper presented to the 39th Annual Meeting of the Institute of Nuclear Material Management, Naples, Fla., July 26, 1998, p. 3.

254. Bunn, *The Next Wave,* p. 13. See also Perry, "Securing Russian Nuclear Materials," p. 89.

255. Potter, 7th Annual Carnegie Non-Proliferation Conference, p. 2; Smarto et al., "MPC&A Site Operations and Sustainability," p. 4; David Wilkey and Charles Hatcher, "Implementation of Materials Accounting in Russia," in *Proceedings of the Institute of Nuclear Materials Management, 40th Annual Meeting,* Phoenix, Ariz., July 25–29, 1999; Bunn, *The Next Wave,* pp. 13, 34.

256. For a discussion of the necessity for a safeguards culture, see James E. Doyle and Stephen V. Mladineo, "Assessing the Development of a Modern Safeguards Culture in the NIS," *Nonproliferation Review* 5, no. 2 (winter 1998): p. 91.

257. Smarto et al., "MPC&A Site Operations and Sustainability," p. 1.

258. Valentin Zharokov, quoted in "Effective State MPC&A System," p. 21.

259. Bunn, *The Next Wave*, p. 11; Kenneth Sheely and Mary Alice Hayward, "New Strategic Directions in the MPC&A Program," paper presented at the 40th Annual Institute of Nuclear Material Management Conference, Phoenix, Ariz., 1999, p. 2.

260. Todd E. Perry, "From Triage to Long-Term Care: A U.S. NGO View on the Future of the MPC&A Program," paper presented at the 40th Annual Institute of Nuclear Material Management Conference, Phoenix, Ariz., 1999, p. 6.

261. Ibid.

262. Potter, 7th Annual Carnegie Non-Proliferation Conference; Albright, quoted in Wouters, "Peddling the Nuclear Arsenal," p. 2; National Research Council, *Protecting Nuclear Weapons Material,* p. 19; Doyle, "Improving Nuclear Materials Security," p. 2; William C. Potter and Fred Wehling, "Sustainability: A Vital Component of Nuclear Material Security in Russia," *Nonproliferation Review* 7, no. 1 (spring 2000): pp. 184–187.

263. Potter and Wehling, "Sustainability," pp. 184–187.

264. Dunn, "'Nuclear Coup d'Etat,'" pp. 36–50.

265. Sagan, "Sagan Responds to Waltz," pp. 169–170.

266. See Joseph Pilat, "Antinuclear Terrorism in the Advanced Industrial West," in *Political Terrorism and Energy,* ed. Yonah Alexander and Charles K. Ebinger (New York, N.Y.: Praeger, 1982), pp. 191–208.

267. For a similar though brief argument, see Feaver, "Correspondence," p. 113.

268. Bunn, "Security for Weapons-Usable Nuclear Materials," p. 16; Allison et al., *Avoiding Nuclear Anarchy,* p. 50; Bunn, *The Next Wave,* pp. 1–27.

4. China

1. See, for example, Waltz's argument that since poor states "can build sizeable forces only over long periods of time, they have time to learn how to care for them." Thus, Waltz implies, all a given NWS needs is time, and it will *necessarily* develop systems to ensure the safety and security of its nuclear weapons. See Kenneth N. Waltz, "Waltz Responds to Sagan," in Scott D. Sagan and Kenneth N. Waltz, *The Spread of Nuclear Weapons: A Debate Renewed* (New York: W.W. Norton, 2003), p. 131.

2. According to the CIA Factbook, China's per capita GDP in 2000 was $3,600. To put this figure in perspective, the per capita GDP of the United States was $36,200 in 2001, and Russia's was $7,700 (even after Russia's financial collapse in 1998, its per capita GDP was $4,000). See the CIA Factbook: <www.cia.gov/cia/publications/factbook/indexgeo.html>. These amounts are derived from purchasing power parity (PPP) calculations rather than from conversions of official currency exchange rates. The PPP method "involves the use of standardized international dollar price weights, which are applied to the quantities of final goods and services produced in a given economy" (ibid).

3. See Robert S. Norris, William M. Arkin, Hans M. Kristensen, and Joshua Handler, "Chinese Nuclear Forces, 2001," *Bulletin of the Atomic Scientists* 57, no. 5 (September/October 2001): p. 71; Joseph Cirincione, with Jon B. Wolfsthal and Miriam Rajkumar, *Deadly Arsenals: Tracking Weapons of Mass Destruction* (Washington, D.C.: Carnegie Endowment for International Peace, 2002), pp. 114–115. The Chinese reportedly define missile ranges as follows: short-range, less than 1,000 kilometers; medium-range, 1,000–3,000 kilometers; long-range, 3,000–8,000 kilometers; and intercontinental range, greater than 8,000 kilometers (Norris et al., "Chinese Nuclear Forces, 2001," p. 80).

4. See Robert Suro, "Study Sees a Possible China Nuclear Buildup," *Washington Post,* August 10, 2000, p. A2; Brad Roberts, Robert A. Manning, and Ronald N. Montaperto, "China: The Forgotten Nuclear Power," *Foreign Affairs* 79, no. 4 (July/August 2000): pp. 53–63; Charles Ferguson, "Sparking a Buildup: U.S. Missile Defense and China's Nuclear Arsenal," *Arms Control Today* 30, no. 2 (March 2000): pp. 13–18; "China Warns of Arms Race," *Associated Press,* May 3, 2001.

5. Colonel Victor Vasilyenvich Stefashin, "Chinese Nuclear Strategy and National Security," *Mirovaya Ekonomika I Mazhdunarodyye Otnosheniya,* no. 8 (August 19, 1995): p. 6 (translated in World News Connection, document no. FTS19970416001575); Robert S. Norris, Andrew S. Burrows, and Richard Fieldhouse, *Nuclear Weapons Databook, Vol. V: British, French and Chinese Nuclear Weapons* (Boulder: Westview Press, 1994), p. 365; Robert S. Norris and Hans M. Kristensen, "Chinese Nuclear Forces, 2003," *Bulletin of the Atomic Scientists* 59, no. 6 (November/December 2003): pp. 77–80. China has recently acquired about eighty of the two-seater, fighter-bomber Su-30MKKs from Russia and may intend these aircraft to have a nuclear role. See Norris and Kristensen, "Chinese Nuclear Forces, 2003," pp. 78–79.

6. The PLA does not appear to address the submarine by this name. They call it the "Type 092" (Harlan Jencks, an expert on China's weapons systems at Lawrence Livermore National Laboratory, interview by author, January 27, 1999).

7. Rodney W. Jones, Mark G. McDonough, with Toby Dalton and Gregory Koblentz, *Tracking Nuclear Proliferation: A Guide in Maps and Charts, 1998* (Washington, D.C.: Carnegie Endowment for International Peace, 1998), p. 63.

8. Ibid., p. 55.

9. Ibid., p. 63.

10. Norris et al., *Nuclear Weapons Databook, Vol. V,* p. 360.

11. Ibid.

12. For example, a reduced-range version of the DF-5 was first successfully flight-tested in 1971, but the DF-5 was not operationally deployed until 1981 (ibid., p. 361).

13. William Arkin and Robert S. Norris, "Chinese Nuclear Forces, 1999," *Bulletin of the Atomic Scientists* 55, no. 4 (1999): pp. 79–80. Norris and Arkin, "Chinese Nuclear Forces, 1999," p. 79.

14. Hua Di, "China's Security Dilemma to the Year 2010," Center for International Security and Cooperation report, Stanford University, October 1997, <http://iis-db.stanford.edu/pubs/10222/hua.pdf>, p. 10.

15. The "DF" is the Chinese designation for these missiles, standing for "Dong Feng," or "East Wind." "CSS" is the NATO designation for these weapons.

16. U.S. Department of Defense (DOD) Report to Congress, *Future Military Capabilities and Strategy of the People's Republic of China,* October 1998, Section 10. Although the 12,000-kilometer range missile is sometimes referred to as the DF-41, recent assessments have determined that it is an improved DF-31 and therefore refer to it as the DF-31A. According to Norris et al., the DF-41 program may have been canceled and another ICBM put under development instead. See Robert S. Norris, William M. Arkin, Hans M. Kristensen, and Joshua Handler, "Chinese Nuclear Forces, 2001," *Bulletin of the Atomic Scientists* 57, no. 5 (September/October 2001): p. 71.

17. Pamela Pun, "Top Missile Passes Test Simulations," *Hong Kong Standard,* October 15, 1999; Bill Gertz, "Pentagon Confirms China's Missile Test," *Washington Times,* December 13, 2000, p. 4; "China Tests DF-31 Missile," *Arms Control Today* 31, no. 1 (January/February 2001): p. 29; "DF-31," *GlobalSecurity.org,* <http://www.globalsecurity.org/wmd/world/china/df-31.htm>.

18. Norris and Arkin, "Chinese Nuclear Forces, 1999," p. 80; Robert A. Manning, "Op-Ed: China's New Nuclear Doctrine," *Los Angeles Times,* June 25, 1999, p. 1; Phillip C. Saunders and Jing-dong Yuan, "China's Strategic Force Modernization: Issues and Implications for the United States," in *Proliferation Challenges and Nonproliferation Opportunities for New Administrations,* ed. Michael Barletta, Center for Nonproliferation Studies, Occasional Paper No. 4, September 2000, p. 46.

19. This appears to be the range for the DF-11 with a 1,000-kilogram payload. Its range would be much longer with a reasonably sized nuclear warhead.

20. When used for export, the DF-15 is called the M-9 and the DF-11 is called the M-11 (the M stands for the English word "missile").

21. John W. Lewis and Hua Di, "China's Ballistic Missile Programs: Technologies, Strategies, Goals," *International Security* 17, no. 2 (fall 1992): p. 36.

22. Norris et al., *Nuclear Weapons Databook, Vol. V,* p. 370; Defense Intelligence Agency, "Nuclear Weapons Systems in China," *Defense Estimate Brief* (declassified), Defense Intelligence Agency, April 24, 1984, <http://www.gwu.edu/~nsarchiv/news/19990527/01–01.htm>.

23. Jones et al., *Tracking Nuclear Proliferation,* p. 55.
24. Norris et al., *Nuclear Weapons Databook, Vol. V,* p. 375.
25. Ibid.; Jones et al., *Tracking Nuclear Proliferation,* p. 65.
26. During the mid-1960s to the mid-1970s, China intentionally created duplicate facilities in order to increase the survivability of its nuclear-weapons complex during times of war. See Norris et al., *Nuclear Weapons Databook, Vol. V,* p. 349.
27. Ibid., p. 375.
28. Ibid.
29. Ibid.
30. Lewis and Hua, "China's Ballistic Missile Programs," p. 22.
31. Ibid., 24.
32. Norris et al., "Chinese Nuclear Forces, 2001," p. 71.
33. Ibid., p. 19.
34. Harlan Jencks, interview by author, Lawrence Livermore National Laboratory, January 27, 1999.
35. Cirincione et al., *Deadly Arsenals,* p. 143.
36. Lewis and Hua, "China's Ballistic Missile Programs," p. 25.
37. U.S. Department of Defense, "Report on the Military Power of the People's Republic of China," annual report to Congress, June 22, 2002, <http://www.defenselink.mil/news/Jun2000/china06222000.htm>.
38. Bates Gill, James C. Mulvenon, and Mark Stokes, "The Chinese Second Artillery Corps: Transition to Credible Deterrence," in James C. Mulvenon and Andrew N.D. Yang, eds., *The People's Liberation Army as Organization* (Santa Monica, Calif.: Rand, 2002), <http://www.rand.org/publications/CF/CF182/CF182.ch11.pdf>, p. 541. See also Norris and Kristensen, "Chinese Nuclear Forces, 2003," pp. 78–79.
39. Roberts et al., "China: The Forgotten Nuclear Power," p. 55.
40. The solid propellant is cast directly into the missile shell. The solid fuel actually provides some of the structural integrity of the rocket stage into which it is built.
41. Saunders and Yuan, "China's Strategic Force Modernization," p. 41; Federation of American Scientists, "DF-31," <http://www.fas.org/nuke/guide/china/icbm/df-31.htm>; Federation of American Scientists, "DF-41," <http://www.fas.org/nuke/guide/china/icbm/df-41.htm>; Pun, "Top Missile Passes Test Simulations"; Center for Nonproliferation Studies, "China's Nuclear Weapon Development, Modernization and Testing," available at the Nuclear Threat Initiative website, <http://www.nti.org/db/china/wnwmdat.htm>; Center for Nonproliferation Studies, "Chinese Ballistic Missile Designations and Characteristics," available at the Nuclear Threat Initiative website, <http://www.nti.org/db/china/wbmdat.htm>; Report of the Select Committee of U.S. National Security and Military/Commercial Concerns with the People's Republic of China, U.S. House of Representatives, Report 105–851, May 25, 1999, p. 193. This, of course, is not entirely certain. For example, Lewis and Hua state that the Second Artillery "will store the mobile DF-31 [a solid-fueled, road-mobile missile] in caves in peacetime and move it on a triple-purpose truck to a pre-selected launching site for rapid response in crises" (Lewis and Hua, "China's Ballistic Missile Programs," p. 29). If this is the method of storage, the chance of accidental launch will still be minimal during peacetime (but perhaps significantly increased during crises).
42. Mao Zedong, quoted in George Kominiak, Jane Eisenhauer, Kathryn Menaul,

and Tara Sather, *The "Command and Control" Philosophy of the Communist Party of China,* Sandia National Laboratories Publication, SAND96-2932, January 1996, p. 10.

43. Kominiak et al., *The "Command and Control" Philosophy of the Communist Party of China,* pp. 10–11.

44. Although there is very little open-source information on the chain of command in China's navy or air force, it is possible that they also have limited nuclear roles. Nevertheless, China primarily relies on the Second Artillery for its nuclear forces because the nation's air force is antiquated and China only possesses one ballistic missile submarine, which reportedly has constant operational difficulties. See Bates Gill and James Mulvenon, "The Chinese Strategic Rocket Forces: Transition to Credible Deterrence," paper presented at *China and Weapons of Mass Destruction: Implications for the United States,* conference sponsored by the National Intelligence Council and Federal Research Division, Washington, D.C., November 5, 1999, <http://www.fas.org/irp/nic/china_wmd.html>, pp. 6, 20.

45. Ibid., p. 20.

46. Mark A. Stokes, *China's Strategic Modernization: Implications for the United States* (Carlisle, Pa.: Strategic Studies Institute, U.S. Army War College, September 1999), <http://www.fas.org/nuke/guide/china/doctrine/chinamod.pdf>, p. 94.

47. "Counterforce" targeting refers specifically to the targeting of an adversary's nuclear forces and military apparatus, rather than its cities, in order to destroy them before they can be used against oneself. Thus, counterforce targeting requires rapid response times, precision targeting, and a large number of nuclear weapons capable of destroying numerous sites on the adversary's territory and military bases.

48. Iain Johnston, "China's New 'Old Thinking': The Concept of Limited Deterrence," *International Security* 20, no. 3 (winter 1995/1996): p. 20; Iain Johnston, "Prospects for Chinese Nuclear Force Modernization: Limited Deterrence Versus Multilateral Arms Control," *China Quarterly,* no. 146 (June 1996): pp. 556–557; Stokes, *China's Strategic Modernization,* p. 96.

49. Johnston has also discovered several prominent documents, however, that recommend abandoning the NFU doctrine. See Johnston, "China's New 'Old Thinking,'" pp. 22–23.

50. Ibid., p. 21.

51. Thus giving rise to what Johnston calls the "doctrine-capabilities gap" (ibid., pp. 31–38).

52. Bates Gill and James Mulvenon argue, however, that "these changes might signal a desire for eventual launch under attack (LUA) capability, but the current inventory of missiles and the next generation of replacements are not capable of the reaction times necessary for such a capability. More likely, the C^{3}I modernization program is meant to improve the credibility of China's minimal deterrent posture in the short to medium term. See Gill and Mulvenon, "The Chinese Strategic Rocket Forces," p. 21.

53. Federation of American Scientists, "DF-31," <http://www.fas.org/nuke/guide/china/icbm/df-31.htm>; Federation of American Scientists, "DF-41," <http://www.fas.org/nuke/guide/china/icbm/df-41.htm>; Pun, "Top Missile Passes Test Simulations"; Center for Nonproliferation Studies, "Nuclear Delivery System Modernization"; Center for Nonproliferation Studies, "Chinese Ballistic Missiles." One factor

that affects the launch times for these mobile missiles is how quickly the transporter erector launcher (TEL) vehicles can be moved and readied for launch. China is also reportedly devising means to modify its TEL to allow for missile erection within one minute and retraction within one minute. See Stokes, *China's Strategic Modernization,* p. 97; Bill Gertz, "Chinese Missile to Threaten U.S. by 2000," *Washington Times,* May 23, 1997.

54. The Associated Press, "China Warns of Arms Race," *New York Times,* May 3, 2001.

55. "Missile Launch 'All-Weather' Communications Secured," *People's Liberation Army Daily,* January 5, 1998, p. 2; "Military: New Digital Microwave Communications System," *Hong Kong Zhonggue Tongxun She,* January 6, 1998, (translated in World News Connection, document no. FTS19980106000368); Gill and Mulvenon, "Chinese Strategic Rocket Forces," p. 21.

56. DOD Report, *Future Military Capabilities and Strategy of the People's Republic of China,* section 11.

57. Stokes, *China's Strategic Modernization,* p. 109.

58. Ibid.

59. Ibid., p. 115.

60. Lewis and Hua, "China's Ballistic Missile Programs," p. 24.

61. Such a transition is not certain, however. For example, Bates Gill and James Mulvenon argue that technological constraints might prevent China from adopting a policy of LOW for some time. They argue that in the short- to mid-term, China might be developing more survivable forces to allow for a credible "minimal deterrence" for their strategic forces, while adopting the more offensive posture of "limited deterrence" for their theater nuclear forces. They therefore argue that limited deterrence is perhaps "the *aspirational* doctrine for a future Second Artillery, although the past production timelines of the missile industry should sober our expectations of its appearance anytime soon" (Gill and Mulvenon, "Chinese Strategic Rocket Forces," p. 28).

62. Saunders and Yuan, "China's Strategic Force Modernization," p. 41; Report of the Select Committee of U.S. National Security and Military/Commercial Concerns with the People's Republic of China, p. 193.

63. Dan Caldwell, "Permissive Action Links: A Description and Proposal," *Survival* 29, no. 3 (May/June 1987): p. 231.

64. See Federation of American Scientists, "Chinese Command and Control," <http://www.fas.org/nuke/guide/china/c3i/index.html>; and Institute for Foreign Policy Analysis, *Exploring U.S. Missile Defense Requirements in 2010: What Are the Policy and Technology Challenges?* April 1997, chapter 3, <http://www.fas.org/spp/starwars/advocate/ifpa/report696_ch3.htm>. China reportedly did receive some PAL technology from Russia, but the system was not very good. China therefore expressed interest in obtaining U.S. PALs in 1995. See Steve Coll and David B. Ottaway, "Will the United States, Russia and China be Nuclear Partners or Rivals in the 21st Century?" *Washington Post,* April 11, 1995, p. A01; and Danny B. Stillman, former intelligence analyst at Los Alamos National Laboratory, quoted in Steve Coll, "The Man Inside China's Bomb Labs: U.S. Blocks Memoir of Scientist Who Gathered Trove of Information," *Washington Post,* May 16, 2001, p. A01. The United States did not give China the PAL technology at that time, however (Dan Stillman, interview by author, December 2, 1998). It is also unlikely that the United States gave China assistance on

PALs in subsequent years. In 1996, due to concerns that some U.S.-China collaborative programs could provide China with classified information, the U.S. Congress included a prohibition in the FY1997 National Defense Authorization Act (NDAA) forbidding any funds to be given to DOE that relate to collaborative programs with China on nuclear weapons or nuclear weapons technology, "including stockpile stewardship, safety, and use control" (Title XXXI, Section 3137a, National Defense Authorization Act for Fiscal Year 1997). This prohibition was repeated in the FY1998 and FY1999 NDAA.

65. Gill and Mulvenon, "Chinese Strategic Rocket Forces," pp. 21, 24. For the distinction between "positive" and "negative" control, see Peter D. Feaver, "Command and Control in Emerging Nuclear Nations," *International Security* 17, no. 3 (winter 1992/93): pp. 163–168.

66. Federation of American Scientists, "Chinese Command and Control."

67. Robert Walpole, National Intelligence Officer for Strategic and Nuclear Programs, speech at the Carnegie Endowment for International Peace, September 17, 1998, <http://www.cia.gov/cia/public_affairs/speeches/1998/walpole_speech_091798.html>, p. 2.

68. Lewis and Hua, "China's Missile Programs," p. 23; Gill and Mulvenon, "Chinese Strategic Rocket Forces," p. 20; Johnston, "China's New 'Old Thinking,'" p. 31.

69. Terry Hawkins, Director of the Nonproliferation and International Security Division of Los Alamos National Laboratory, interview by author, November 4, 1998.

70. For a similar argument, especially related to "opaque" proliferating countries, see Feaver, "Neooptimists and the Enduring Problem of Nuclear Proliferation," p. 115.

71. Although Gill and Mulvenon argue that China might not be pushing as strongly for rapid-response capabilities in their strategic forces, they conclude that China might be developing these capabilities for its theater nuclear forces (Gill and Mulvenon, "Chinese Strategic Rocket Forces," p. 26).

72. Terry Hawkins, interview by author, November 4, 1998.

73. Walpole, speech at the Carnegie Endowment for International Peace, September 17, 1998, p. 2.

74. There is a great deal of overlap between the protection against unauthorized use and MPC&A. See the discussion of China's MPC&A in part two of this chapter.

75. John W. Lewis and Xue Litai, *China Builds the Bomb* (Stanford: Stanford University Press, 1988), p. 247.

76. Evan Feigenbaum, *The Military Transforms China: The Politics of Strategic Technology from the Nuclear Age to the Information Age,* Ph.D. dissertation, Stanford University, 1997, pp. 219–220.

77. Norris et al., *Nuclear Weapons Databook, Vol. V,* p. 333; Federation of American Scientists, "Nuclear Weapons Tests," <http://www.fas.org/nuke/guide/china/nuke/tests.htm>.

78. Nie Rongzhen, quoted in Lewis and Xue, *China Builds the Bomb,* p. 203.

79. Lewis and Xue, *China Builds the Bomb,* pp. 203–204; Feigenbaum, *The Military Transforms China,* p. 220.

80. For discussions of this incident, see: Donald G. Brennan, "The Risks of Spreading Weapons: A Historical Case," *Arms Control and Disarmament* 1 (1968):

pp. 59–60; Dan Caldwell and Peter D. Zimmerman, "Reducing the Risk of Nuclear War with Permissive Action Links," in *Technology and the Limitation of International Conflict,* ed. Barry M. Blechman (Washington, D.C.: John Hopkins Foreign Policy Institute, School of Advanced International Studies, 1989): pp. 151–175; Leonard Spector, *Going Nuclear: The Spread of Nuclear Weapons 1986–1987* (Cambridge, Mass.: Ballinger, 1987), pp. 32–37; C.L. Sulzberger, "Foreign Affairs: The Nuclear Pawn," *New York Times,* February 5, 1967, p. E-8; Richard Hughes, "Mao Calls Truce with Rebel General in Bomb Province," *London Sunday Times,* July 2, 1967; H.M. Jones, "China: Autonomous Wang," *Far Eastern Economic Review* 58 (December 28, 1967): pp. 569–570.

81. For an excellent summary and analysis of the Lin Biao Affair, see Philip Bridgham, "The Fall of Lin Piao," *China Quarterly* 55 (July/September 1973): pp. 427–449. A declassified CIA report suggests that the reports of Lin Baio's fleeing to the Soviet Union were spread by the Chinese government to discredit Lin Baio. See Central Intelligence Agency, *Special National Intelligence Estimate: Security Conditions in China,* February 10, 1972, in the National Security Archive, <http://www.gwu.edu/%7Ensarchiv/NSAEBB/NSAEBB19/04-02.htm>, p. 5.

82. Bridgham, "The Fall of Lin Piao," p. 440.

83. CIA, *Security Conditions in China,* pp. 3–4. Indeed, the air force was reportedly forced to stand down for two months as a result of the Lin Baio affair (ibid., p. 4).

84. Caldwell, "Permissive Action Links," p. 231.

85. Ibid.

86. Jonathan D. Pollack, "The Future of China's Nuclear Weapons Policy," in *Strategic Views from the Second Tier: The Nuclear Weapons Policies of France, Britain, and China,* ed. John C. Hopkins and Weixing Hu (New Brunswick, N.J.: Transaction Publishers, 1994), p. 164.

87. Ibid.

88. Coll and Ottaway, "Will the United States, Russia and China be Nuclear Partners or Rivals in the 21st Century?" p. A01. On several occasions, Chinese officials admitted to Danny B. Stillman, a former intelligence analyst at Los Alamos National Laboratory, that "splits in their military during the Tiananmen crisis brought home the potential danger of unauthorized control of nuclear weapons, and they wanted the United States to provide older PAL technology that would make Chinese bombs safer but not jeopardize U.S. bomb security." See Coll, "The Man Inside China's Bomb Labs," p. A01. The author has also verified the accuracy of these reports in several interviews with U.S. government officials, conducted from 1998 to 2001.

89. For example, Qin Jiwei, the minister of defense at the time, was known to have opposed using force against the students. During the crackdown, Zhou Yibing, Qin's long-time deputy and the commander of the Beijing Military Region, appeared to side with Qin. As a result, Zhou's troops also appeared reluctant to use force against the students. In another case, Hong Xuezhi, a former director of the PLA's General Logistics Department also opposed the use of force, and the personnel of the Logistics Department appeared to side with Hong against the government. For a summary of these events, see June Teufel Dreyer, "The Role of the PLA in China's Political Struggle," in *The PLA and the Tiananmen Crisis,* ed. Richard H. Yang, SCPS Papers, no. 1 (Taiwan: The Sun Yat-Sen Center for Policy Studies, National Sun Yat-Sen University, 1989), p. 4.

90. Dreyer, "The Role of the PLA in China's Political Struggle," p. 4; Harlan W. Jencks "China's Army, China's Future," in *China in the Nineties: Crisis Management and Beyond,* ed. David S.G. Goodman and Gerald Segal (Oxford: Clarendon Press, 1991), p. 144.

91. On May 21, Nie Rongzhen told the students that no one wanted to use force against them and even reportedly published statements advising against the use of force. See Yi Mu and Mark V. Thompson, *Crisis at Tiananmen: Reform and Reality in Modern China* (San Francisco: China Books and Periodicals, 1989), p. 69; Michael Oksenberg, Lawrence Sullivan, and Marc Lambert, *Beijing Spring, 1989: Confrontation and Conflict* (Armonk, New York: M.E. Sharp, Inc., 1990), pp. 316–317; June Teufel Dreyer, "The People's Liberation Army and the Power Struggle of 1989," *Problems of Communism* 38, no. 5 (September–October 1989): p. 42; Jencks, "China's Army, China's Future," p. 144.

On the same day, Zhang Aiping, along with six other senior military officers, wrote a letter to the Martial Law Enforcement Headquarters of the People's Liberation Army, saying that the army belonged to the people and must never be used against the people. See Theodore Han and John Li, *Tiananmen Square, Spring 1989: A Chronology of the Chinese Democracy Movement* (Berkeley, Calif.: Institute of East Asian Studies, University of California, Berkeley, 1992), p. 41; Jane's Information Group, *China in Crisis: The Role of the Military* (Jane's Information Group Ltd., 1989), p. 81; Jencks, "China's Army, China's Future," p. 144.

92. Lewis and Xue, *China Builds the Bomb,* p. 247.

93. Zhang was still the minister of defense in July 1987, less than two years before the Tiananmen crisis (J. Mohan Malik, "Chinese Debate on Military Strategy: Trends and Portents," *Journal of Northeast Asian Studies* 9, no. 2 (summer 1990): p. 8.

94. Some evidence for this is that in March 1990 General Li Xuge (Second Artillery commander at the time) wrote an article in China's *Liberation Army Daily* that further political and ideological work was necessary to ensure the troops in the Second Artillery are "always qualified politically" (quoted in George Kominiak, Jane Eisenhauer, Kathryn Menaul, and Tara Sather, *The "Command and Control" Philosophy of the Communist Party of China,* Sandia National Laboratories Publication, SAND96-2932, January 1996, p. 17).

95. Eric Eckholm, "China Inner Circle Admits Big Unrest," *New York Times,* June 2, 2001.

96. There are, however, serious questions about the veracity of economic data provided by the Chinese government. According to research conducted by Thomas G. Rawski at the University of Pittsburgh, China's economy may have actually been contracting since 1998. Indeed, Chinese premier Zhu Rongji reportedly stated that China's economy would have collapsed in 1998 without the state stimulus spending program that is driving China's debt to record levels. See Arthur Waldron, "China's Economic Façade," *Washington Post,* March 21, 2002, p. A35; Frederik Balfour, *Business Week,* no. 3777 (April 8, 2002): p. 52; Thomas G. Rawski, "What's Happening to China's GDP Statistics?" *China Economic Review* 12, no. 4 (December 2001): pp. 347–354.

97. David E. Sanger, "Bush Plans to Prolong Trade Benefits for China," *New York Times,* May 30, 2001; Christopher Bodeen, "China Prepares for Economic Fallout as WTO Membership Begins," *Associated Press,* December 11, 2001.

98. Minxin Pei, "Future Shock: The WTO and Political Change in China," *Policy Brief* 1, no. 3 (Washington, D.C.: Carnegie Endowment for International Peace, February 2001), p. 1.

99. Ibid., p. 4.

100. This estimate, issued by the Hong Kong–Based Information Center of Human Rights and Democracy, was reported in "Drought Fuels Violence in China," *Washington Post,* July 16, 2000. Official Labor Ministry statistics, which were reportedly passed to a Western diplomat, indicated that there were 120,000 labor disputes in 1999—fourteen times the number of disputes in 1992 (reported in John Pomfret, "Chinese Workers Are Showing Disenchantment," *Washington Post,* April 23, 2000, p. A23).

101. David Murphy, "Nothing More to Lose," *Far Eastern Economic Review* 165, no. 44 (November 7, 2002): p. 33.

102. These incidents were reported in: Erik Eckholm, "Leaner Factories, Fewer Workers Bring Labor Unrest to China," *New York Times,* March 19, 2002, p. A1; John Pomfret, "In Rural China, Democracy Is Not All It Seems," *Washington Post,* August 25, 2000, p. A01; "Angry Investors Take Over Sichuan Railway Station," *Hong Kong AFP,* October 18, 1999, in FBIS-CHI-1999-1018 (October 18, 1999); Pomfret, "Chinese Workers Are Showing Disenchantment," p. A23; John Pomfret, "Miner Riot Symptom of China's New Direction," *Washington Post,* April 5, 2000, p. A01; "Regional Briefing," *Far Eastern Economic Review* 163, no. 37 (September 14, 2000): p. 13; Erik Eckholm, "Chinese Raid Defiant Village, Killing 2, Amid Rural Unrest," *New York Times,* April 20, 2001, p. A1; John Pomfret, "Seeds of Revolt in Rural China: 'Farmers' Heroes' Give a Voice to Besieged Taxpayers," *Washington Post,* May 8, 2001, p. A01. For additional reports of widespread public dissatisfaction with increasing economic difficulties, widespread corruption, and the impotence of the CCP, see Elizabeth Rosenthal, "Beijing Gets a Scolding for Official Corruption, and Applauds," *New York Times,* March 6, 2000, p. A10; "Social Combustion in China," editorial, *New York Times,* April 7, 2000, p. A22; John Pomfret, "Party Expels Top Official in Chinese Bribe Case," *Washington Post,* April 21, 2000, p. A17; Erik Eckholm, "Unrest Grows in China's Old State Plants," *New York Times,* May 17, 2000, p. A12; John Pomfret, "Many Chinese Distrust Party's Idea of Reform," *Washington Post,* July 1, 2000, p. A18; Erick Eckholm, "Chinese Find Power Abuse Isn't Limited to the Cities," *New York Times,* December 3, 2000, p. A4; Phillip Pan, "Top Judicial Officials Say China's Corruption Is Deep," *Washington Post,* March 11, 2001, p. A18.

103. For excellent discussions of many of these risks, see Gordon Chang, *The Coming Collapse of China* (New York: Random House, 2001), and Minxin Pei, "China's Governance Crisis," *Foreign Affairs* 81, no. 5 (September–October 2002, pp. 96–109). See also Minxin Pei, "Will China Become Another Indonesia?" *Foreign Policy,* no. 116 (fall 1999): pp. 94–109; Gerry Groot, "Crises in China and Potential Dangers for Asia," in *Crisis and Conflict in Asia: Local, Regional and International Responses,* ed. P. Jain, G. O'Leary, F. Patrikeeff (Huntington, N.Y.: Nova Science Publishers, 2002), pp. 115–136); William H. Overholt, "China's Economic Squeeze," *Orbis* 44, no. 1 (winter 2000): pp. 13–33; Arthur Waldron, "The Making of Contemporary China," *Orbis* 46, no. 2 (spring 2002): pp. 391–407.

104. Hua, "China's Security Dilemma," p. 3.

105. Ibid.

106. Kal-Alexander Schlevogt, "China's Western Campaign," *Far Eastern Economic Review* 163, no. 33 (August 17, 2000): p. 29. See also Gerald Segal, *China Changes Shape: Regionalism and Foreign Policy,* Adelphi Paper, No. 287 (London: International Institute for Strategic Studies [IISS], 1994), pp. 3–72.

107. For excellent summaries of the Xinjiang separatist movement, see Paul George, "Islamic Unrest in the Xinjiang Uighur Autonomous Region," *Commentary, Canadian Security Intelligence Service,* no. 73 (spring 1998): pp. 1–9; P.B. Sinha, "Islamic Militancy and Separatism in Xinjiang," *Strategic Analysis* 20, no. 3 (June 1997): pp. 451–460; "Asia: Glimpse of a Troubled Land," *Economist* 351, no. 8117 (May 1, 1999): p. 39.

108. Yossef Bodansky, "Beijing Prepares for a New War Front in Xinjiang," *Defense and Foreign Affairs Strategic Policy* 28, no. 9 (September 2000): p. 4. On January 21, 2002, China officially declared that the separatists in Xinjiang have direct connections with al Qaeda. See Elizabeth Rosenthal, "Beijing Says Chinese Muslims Were Trained as Terrorists with Money from Bin Laden," *New York Times,* January 22, 2002, p. A11.

109. For example, on February 4, 1999, 9,000 armed police were sent to Xinjiang to suppress anti-Beijing rioting. Official Chinese reports said that ten people died in the rioting, but overseas reports place the death toll at over one hundred (*Inside China Today,* February 4, 1999). See also John Pomfret, "Separatists Defy Chinese Crackdown," *Washington Post,* January 26, 2000, p. A17. For additional accounts of the continuing violence associated with the Xinjiang separatist movement, see Ahmed Rashid and Susan V. Lawrence, "Joining Foreign Jihad," *Far Eastern Economic Review* 163, no. 36 (September 7, 2000): p. 24; "Jiang Says Hard Work Still Needed to Counter Separatism," *BBC News,* March 7, 1998; Duncan Hewitt, "China Clampdown on Muslim Region," *BBC News,* May 29, 2000; Ahmad Faruqui, "China-Pakistan: Fraying Ties," *Far Eastern Economic Review* 164, no. 2 (January 18, 2001): p. 33; Schlevogt, "China's Western Campaign," p. 29; Susan V. Lawrence, "Where Beijing Fears Kosovo," *Far Eastern Economic Review* 163, no. 36 (September 7, 2000): p. 24.

110. George, "Islamic Unrest," p. 2.

111. Susan Lawrence, "Breathing Space," *Far Eastern Economic Review* 163, no. 22 (June 1, 2000): pp. 17–18.

112. Jones et al., *Tracking Nuclear Proliferation,* p. 54. For a similar account of China's current internal problems, see DOD Report, *Future Military Capabilities and Strategy of the People's Republic of China,* section 1; Kenneth Lieberthal, *Governing China: From Revolution through Reform* (New York: W.W. Norton, 1995), pp. 267–269.

113. The warheads could possibly be assembled inside the cave, but they would need to be erected and fueled outside.

114. The Chinese have reportedly been quite concerned that U.S. spy satellites would enable the United States to identify where the assembly of missiles is taking place. See Lewis and Hua, "China's Ballistic Missile Programs," p. 23.

115. Harlan Jencks, interview with author, January 27, 1999.

116. Such an action would obviously require China to violate its declared doctrine of no first use, but given the limited survivability of its current nuclear forces,

China might nevertheless decide that such a violation would be justified. Indeed, Iain Johnston has discovered documents by Chinese military analysts calling for a first strike under some circumstances. See Johnston, "China's New 'Old Thinking,'" pp. 22–23.

117. Johnston, "China's New 'Old Thinking,'" p. 21.

118. Sections of this discussion of China's MPC&A are based on Nathan Busch, "China's Fissile Material Protection, Control, and Accounting: The Case for Renewed Collaboration," *Nonproliferation Review* 9, no. 3 (fall/winter 2002): pp. 89–106. For production and stockpile information, see: U.S. Department of Defense, *Proliferation: Threat and Response,* January 2001 (Washington, D.C.: U.S. Government Printing Office, 2001), <www.defenselink.mil/pubs/ptr20010110.pdf>, p. 14; Cirincione et al., *Deadly Arsenals,* p. 145; Lisbeth Gronlund, David Wright, and Yong Liu, "China and a Fissile Material Production Cut-Off," *Survival* 37, no. 4 (winter 1995–1996): p. 148.

119. Jones et al., *Tracking Nuclear Proliferation,* p. 54; David Albright, Frans Berkhout, and William Walker, *Plutonium and Highly Enriched Uranium, 1996: World Inventories, Capabilities and Policies* (Oxford: Oxford University Press, 1997), p. 422; David Wright and Lisbeth Gronlund, "Estimating China's Production of Plutonium for Weapons," Technical Working Paper, Union of Concerned Scientists (paper provided by authors, January 7, 1999), p. 13. Because China has provided no independent verification of the size of its fissile materials stockpile, however, the stockpile could be significantly larger or smaller than these estimates.

120. For a detailed discussion of this conversion, see Yitzhak Sichor, "Peaceful Fallout: The Conversion of China's Military-Nuclear Complex to Civilian Use," *Brief 10* (Bonn: Bonn International Center for Conversion, November 1997), <http://www.bicc.de/publications/briefs/brief10/brief10.pdf>, pp. 1–60.

121. Cirincione et al., *Deadly Arsenals,* p. 145.

122. Ibid.

123. For excellent discussions of the bureaucratic restructuring as of 1999, see Harlan Jencks, "COSTIND Is Dead. Long Live COSTIND!" in *The People's Liberation Army in the Information Age,* ed. James C. Mulvenon and Richard H. Yang (Santa Monica: RAND Corporation, 1999), p. 59; and Wen Hsu, "The Impact of Government Restructuring on Chinese Nuclear Arms Control and Nonproliferation Policymaking," *Nonproliferation Review* 6, no. 4 (fall 1999): pp. 152–167. Both scholars indicate that the full restructuring would continue for several years after they wrote their articles, however.

124. In the case of China's nuclear reactors and MPC&A issues, formal authority is usually more important. However, informal authority may nevertheless be relevant to some key issues, such as the acquisition of resources for MPC&A improvements and an individual plant or factory's ability to market services. (The author thanks an anonymous reviewer for this clarification.)

125. "Rules for Implementation of the Regulations on Nuclear Materials Control of the People's Republic of China," National Nuclear Safety Administration, Ministry of Energy, and the Commission of Science, Technology, and Industry for National Defense, September 25, 1990.

126. Lawrence Livermore National Laboratory, Sandia National Laboratories, Los Alamos National Laboratory, *Foreign Trip Report,* Beijing, China, June 23–July 2, 1995, pp. 5–6.

127. Hui Zhang, research fellow, Belfer Center for Science and International Affairs, Harvard University, Cambridge, Mass., telephone conversation with author, October 4, 2002. The CAEA currently has authority for "carrying out nuclear material control, nuclear export supervision and management," CAEA website, <www.caea.gov.cn/english/index.htm>.

128. Wen Hsu, Distinguished Member of the Technical Staff at Sandia National Laboratory, Livermore, Calif., telephone conversation with author, August 6, 1999.

129. Matthew Bunn, "Security for Weapons-Usable Nuclear Materials: Expanding International Cooperation, Strengthening International Standards," in *A Comparative Analysis of Approaches to the Protection of Fissile Materials,* Proceedings of the Workshop at Stanford University, July 28–30, 1997, p. 16.

130. For a similar argument, see Evan A. Feigenbaum, "China's Strategy of Weakness," *Far Eastern Economic Review* 164, no. 8 (March 1, 2001): p. 29.

131. The author would like to thank Dr. Gavin Cameron of the University of Salford, United Kingdom, for bringing this incident to his attention. The following section is based on an unpublished, untitled discussion paper by Dr. Cameron.

132. Hermann-Josef Tenhagen, "Uiguren Gegen Atomtests," *Die Tageszeitung,* August 17, 1995, p. 7.

133. "Nuclear Test Site Attacked," *Eastern Turkestan Information Bulletin* 3, no. 3 (June 1993), <http://www.taklamakan.org/etib/etib3_3.html#1>, p. 1. See also Andre Grabot, "The Uighurs—Sacrificed on Central Asia's Chess Board," *Agence France Presse,* April 25, 1996.

134. George, "Islamic Unrest," p. 2. See also Greg Austin, "The Strategic Implications of China's Public Order Crisis," *Survival* 37, no. 2 (summer 1995): pp. 7–23.

135. To view INFCIRC/369, see the Nuclear Threat Initiative website: <http://www.nti.org/db/china/engdocs/iaea369.htm>.

136. International Atomic Energy Agency, *IAEA Annual Report for 2001,* <www.iaea.org/worldatom/Documents/Anrep/Anrep2001/table_3.pdf>; "China and the International Atomic Energy Agency," <www.nti.org/db/china/iaeaorg.htm>.

137. Cirincione et al., *Deadly Arsenals,* pp. 160, 162 n. 8.

138. To view INFCIRC/274, see the IAEA website: <http://www.iaea.org/Publications/Documents/Infcircs/2000/infcirc274r1a7.pdf>.

139. To view INFCIRC/549, see the IAEA website: <http://www.iaea.org/Publications/Documents/Infcircs/1998/infcirc549.pdf>.

140. To view INFCIRC/153 and INFCIRC/225, see the IAEA websites: <http://www.iaea.org/Publications/Documents/Infcircs/Others/inf153.shtml> and <http://www.iaea.or.at/worldatom/Programmes/Protection/inf225rev4/rev4_content.html>.

141. These guidelines also state that the officially recognized NWSs should submit to safeguards by the IAEA all the plutonium that they no longer consider necessary for their national defense purposes. But it only requires that they take these steps as soon as it is "practicable" and places no deadline by which this transfer should occur.

142. Quinsheng Zhu, *A Brief Overview on State Systems of China Nuclear*

Material Control, China Atomic Energy Authority (Agency), Office of Nuclear Material Control, June 1994, p. 1.

143. 1987 "Regulations," p. 3. Although the 1987 "Regulations" originally gave the National Nuclear Safety Administration responsibility for approving licenses for nuclear materials (ibid., p. 2), the 1990 "Rules" clearly gave the China National Nuclear Corporation responsibility for approving and issuing these licenses (1990 "Rules," p. 1). It is not entirely clear what agency is responsible for licensing after China's 1998 restructuring of its nuclear bureaucracy, but it is probably the CAEA.

144. 1990 "Rules," p. 2.

145. MUF is calculated by the following formula:

$$MUF = BI\ (\textit{beginning inventory}) + A\ (\textit{additions}) - EI\ (\textit{ending inventory}) - R\ (\textit{removals}) - KL\ (\textit{known loss}).$$

The 1990 document also established the following regulations for acceptable standard error of MUF:

Facility Type	Relative Standard Error of MUF (%)
Uranium enrichment:	0.2%
Uranium processing:	0.3%
Plutonium processing:	0.5%
Uranium reprocessing:	0.8%
Plutonium reprocessing:	0.1%

146. "China's Attitudes Toward Nuclear Material Protection, Control, and Accounting," Nuclear Threat Initiative database, <www.nti.org/db/china/mpcapos.htm>.

147. To view the specific categories of fissile materials (Category I, II, and III materials) and the physical protection measures for each category recommended by INFCIRC/225, go to the IAEA website: <http://www.iaea.org/worldatom/Programmes/Protection/inf225rev4/rev4_content.html>.

148. Hsu, "The Impact of Government Restructuring," p. 158.

149. Nancy Hayden Prindle, "U.S. and China on Nuclear Arms Control and Nonproliferation: Building on Common Technical Interests," in *Arms Control Issues for the Twenty-First Century,* ed. James Brown (Sandia National Laboratory Publication, SAND97-2619, 1997), p. 322.

150. Albright, Berkhout and Walker, *Plutonium and Highly Enriched Uranium, 1996,* p. 422.

151. Tang Bin, "Major Advances Realized in Nation's Nuclear Fuel Accounting System," *China Nuclear Industry News,* September 11, 1996, in FBIS-CST-96-019 (November 26, 1996), p. 1.

152. Jones et al., *Tracking Nuclear Proliferation,* p. 55.

153. Annette Schaper, "The Case for Universal Full-Scope Safeguards on Nuclear Material," *Nonproliferation Review* 5, no. 2 (winter 1998): p. 75. This concern was also raised in Gronlund, Wright, and Liu, "China and a Fissile Material Production Cut-Off," p. 160.

154. The three Chinese nuclear facilities that are under full IAEA safeguards

would have this MC&A equipment, but those facilities that China designed indigenously probably do not have similar MC&A systems.

155. Xingqiang Zhang, "China's Practice of Nuclear Materials Control," *A Comparative Analysis of Approaches to the Protection of Fissile Materials,* Proceedings of the Workshop at Stanford University, July 28–30, CONF-9707121, p. 87.

156. Patrick E. Tyler, "Crime (and Punishment) Rages Anew in China," *New York Times,* July 11, 1996, p. A1; John Pomfret, "Chinese Executions Top Rest of World," *Washington Post,* February 2, 2000, p. A17; Lieberthal, *Governing China,* pp. 262, 267–269, 299, 301; Austin, "China's Public Order Crisis," pp. 7–14; Elizabeth Rosenthal, "China's Fierce War on Smuggling Uproots a Vast Hidden Economy," *New York Times,* March 6, 2000.

157. Hsu, "The Impact of Government Restructuring," p. 159.

158. The author would like to thank an anonymous reviewer for this suggestion. See also Jones and et al., *Tracking Nuclear Proliferation,* p. 54

159. This was certainly the case during the Cultural Revolution, though the political crisis did eventually affect the nuclear sector as well. See Lewis and Xue, *China Builds the Bomb,* pp. 203–204.

160. See above for a discussion of the major political crises that occurred while China possessed nuclear weapons.

161. Jones et al., *Tracking Nuclear Proliferation,* p. 54.

162. The loosening of the strict societal controls of the CCP have also allowed more opportunities for thefts and organized crime. In recent years, there have been numerous reports of skyrocketing crime rates in China. See, for example, Elizabeth Rosenthal, "China's Fierce War on Smuggling Uproots a Vast Hidden Economy," *New York Times,* March 6, 2000.

163. See, for example, Segal, *China Changes Shape,* pp. 3–72; Hua, "China's Security Dilemma," p. 3; Jones et al., *Tracking Nuclear Proliferation,* p. 54; and Austin, "China's Public Order Crisis," pp. 7–23.

164. *Integrated Demonstration of Materials Protection, Control, and Accountability,* Los Alamos National Laboratory Unclassified Publication, June 1998, LALP-98-65, p. 1

165. Nancy Prindle, "The U.S.-China Lab-to-Lab Technical Exchange Program," *Nonproliferation Review* 5, no. 3 (spring/summer 1998): p. 111.

166. Prindle, "The U.S.-China Lab-to-Lab Technical Exchange Program," p. 114.

167. *Integrated Demonstration of Materials Protection, Control, and Accountability,* Los Alamos National Laboratory Unclassified Publication, June 1998, LALP-98-65, p. 2.

168. Ibid., pp. 7–22.

169. See Prindle, "The U.S.-China Lab to Lab Technical Exchange Program," pp. 111–118.

170. To view the allegations of Chinese espionage in "U.S. National Security and Military/Commercial Concerns with the People's Republic of China," otherwise known as the "Cox report," see <www.access.gpo.gov/congress/house/hr105851/VI-06-Chap2.pdf>.

171. U.S. national laboratory official (name withheld by request), correspondence with author, October 2002.

172. Ibid.

173. See note 2 of this chapter (372n2) for a stastical comparison of China's per capita GDP against those of the United States and Russia.

174. For example, in the United States, a perimeter intrusion detection and assessment system (PIDAS) for the physical protection of facilities containing Category I materials costs nearly $1,000 per foot. A PIDAS would include the following: (a) fences and intrusion sensors, (b) alarm assessment video cameras and lights, (c) central and secondary alarm stations, and (d) an access control portal with nuclear material detection sensors.

175. Hsu, "The Impact of Government Restructuring," p. 165; see also pp. 152, 154

176. Prindle, "U.S. and China on Nuclear Arms Control and Nonproliferation," p. 322.

177. Ibid.

5. India and Pakistan

1. See, for example, Peter R. Lavoy, "Arms Control in South Asia," in *Arms Control Toward the Twenty-First Century,* ed. Jeffrey A. Larson and Gregory J. Rattray (Boulder: Lynne Reinner, 1995); Peter R. Lavoy, "Civil-Military Relations, Strategic Conduct, and the Stability of Nuclear Deterrence in South Asia," in *Civil-Military Relations and Nuclear Weapons,* ed. Scott D. Sagan (Stanford: CISAC Publication, June 1994), pp. 79–109; George Perkovich, "A Nuclear Third Way in South Asia," *Foreign Policy,* no. 91 (summer 1993): pp. 85–104; Devin Hagerty, "The Power of Suggestion: Opaque Proliferation, Existential Deterrence, and the South Asian Nuclear Arms Competition," in *The Proliferation Puzzle,* ed. Zachary Davis and Benjamin Frankel (Portland, Oreg.: Frank Cass Publishing Co., 1993), pp. 256–283; Sumit Ganguly, "India's Pathway to Pokhran II: The Prospects and Sources of New Delhi's Nuclear Weapons Program," *International Security* 23, no. 4 (spring 1999): pp. 148–177; Sumit Ganguly, "Correspondence: Debating New Delhi's Nuclear Decision," *International Security* 24, no. 4 (spring 2000): pp. 187–189.

2. See, for example, Samina Ahmed, "Security Dilemmas of Nuclear-Armed Pakistan," *Third World Quarterly* 21, no. 5 (October 2000): pp. 781–793; Clayton P. Bowen and Daniel Wolvén, "Command and Control Challenges in South Asia," *Nonproliferation Review* 6, no. 3 (spring–summer 1999): pp. 25–35; Mario E. Carranza, "Dangerous Optimism: Non-Weaponized Deterrence and Regional Peace in South Asia," *International Politics* 35 (June 1998): pp. 107–134; Mario E. Carranza, "An Impossible Game: Stable Nuclear Deterrence After the Indian and Pakistani Tests," *Nonproliferation Review* 6, no. 3 (spring–summer 1999): pp. 11–24; Amartya Sen, "India and the Bomb," *New Republic* 223, no. 13 (September 25, 2000): pp. 32–37.

3. U.S. Department of Defense, *Proliferation: Threat and Response,* January 2001 (Washington, D.C.: U.S. Government Printing Office, 2001), <http://www.defenselink.mil/pubs/ptr20010110.pdf>, p. 22.

4. Ibid.

5. Typically, an interstate conflict is classified as a war if there were over 1,000

battle deaths. See the J. David Singer and Melvin Small, "The Correlates of War Project," University of Michigan, <http://www.umich.edu/~cowproj/>. For the numbers of Indian and Pakistani troops killed in the Kargil war, see Sen, "India and the Bomb," p. 36; Raj Chengappa, "Kargil: Holding the Heights," *India Today,* August 16, 1999, p. 46; Rahul Bedi, "The Real Cost of Victory," *Asiaweek,* August 13, 1999.

6. Carranza, "Dangerous Optimism," p. 116.

7. Neil Joeck, *Maintaining Nuclear Stability in South Asia,* Adelphi Paper, No. 312 (London: International Institute for Strategic Studies [IISS], September 1997), p. 20; Kanti Bajpai, P.R. Chari, Pervaiz Iqbal Cheema, Stephen Cohen, and Sumit Ganguly, *Brasstacks and Beyond: Perception and Management of Crisis in South Asia* (New Delhi: Manohar Publishers, 1995), p. 101.

8. Carranza, "Dangerous Optimism," p. 116.

9. Joeck, "Maintaining Nuclear Stability in South Asia," pp. 24–25. For an additional explanation of this crisis, see Bajpai et al., *Brasstacks and Beyond.*

10. Carranza, "Dangerous Optimism," p. 116.

11. Ibid.

12. Ibid., p. 117.

13. See especially Devin Hagerty, *The Consequences of Nuclear Proliferation: Lessons from South Asia* (Cambridge, Mass.: MIT Press, 1998), pp. 92–116.

14. Carranza, "Dangerous Optimism," p. 116.

15. Joeck, "Maintaining Nuclear Stability in South Asia," p. 18.

16. Carranza, "Dangerous Optimism," p. 118.

17. Ibid., pp. 117–118.

18. George Perkovich, *India's Nuclear Bomb: The Impact on Global Proliferation* (Berkeley: University of California Press, 1999), pp. 308–309.

19. Joeck, "Maintaining Nuclear Stability in South Asia," p. 18.

20. See especially Devin Hagerty, "Nuclear Deterrence in South Asia: The 1990 Indo-Pakistani Crisis," *International Security* 20, no. 3 (winter 1995/1996): pp. 79–114.

21. Perkovich, *India's Nuclear Bomb,* p. 311.

22. Ibid., p. 308.

23. Joeck, "Maintaining Nuclear Stability in South Asia," p. 20.

24. Center for Contemporary Conflict, "War in Kargil," Project on "Asymmetric Conflict in South Asia: The Cause and Consequences of the 1999 Limited War in Kargil," Naval Postgraduate School, <http://www.ccc.nps.navy.mil/research/kargil/war_in_kargil.pdf>.

25. Waheguru Pal Singh Sidhu, "India's Nuclear Use Doctrine," in *Planning the Unthinkable: How New Powers Will Use Nuclear, Biological, and Chemical Weapons,* ed. Peter R. Lavoy, Scott D. Sagan, and James J. Wirtz (Ithaca: Cornell University Press, 2000), p. 142.

26. Samina Ahmed, "Learning from Nuclear Crises: Pakistan," paper presented at conference at Stanford University, December 1999, p. 8.

27. Ibid.; "1999 Kargil Conflict," *Globalsecurity.org,* <http://www.globalsecurity.org/military/world/war/kargil-99.htm>.

28. John Lancaster, "Kashmir Crisis Was Defused on Brink of War As U.S. Reviews Showdown," *Washington Post,* July 26, 1999, p. A01.

29. Bruce Reidel, "American Diplomacy and the 1999 Kargil Summit at Blair House," Center for the Advanced Study of India, *Policy Paper Series* (May 2002), <http://www.sas.upenn.edu/casi/reports/RiedelPaper051302.pdf>.

30. Ibid., pp. 8–9.

31. Lancaster, "Kashmir Crisis Was Defused on Brink of War," p. A01.

32. Sidhu, "India's Nuclear Use Doctrine," p. 144.

33. Reidel, "American Diplomacy and the 1999 Kargil Summit at Blair House," pp. 8–9.

34. "India's Nuclear Dilemmas," *Economist* 357, no. 8195 (November 6, 2000): p. 45.

35. See P.K. Balachanddran, "N-Strike Advised During Kargil War: Ramdas," *Hindustan Times,* December 9, 2000; The Acronym Institute, "Disturbing Portents in South Asia," *Disarmament Diplomacy* 53 (December 2000/January 2001), <http://www.acronym.org.uk/53sasia.htm>; Admiral L. Ramdas, "Myths and Realities of Nuclear Command and Control in India and Pakistan," *Disarmament Diplomacy* 54 (February 2001), <http://www.acronym.org.uk/54ramdas.htm>.

36. Rama Lakshmi, "Pakistan's New Role Riles Indian Leaders: Actions in Kashmir Called 'Terrorist,'" *Washington Post,* September 27, 2001, p. A15.

37. "Car Bomb Kills 21 Outside Kashmir Assembly," *Reuters,* October 1, 2001; "At Least 31 Die in Latest Kashmiri Clashes," *Reuters,* November 2, 2001.

38. Celia W. Dugger, "India Shells Pakistani Area, Imperiling Delicate Balance," *New York Times,* October 16, 2001; Rajiv Chandrasekaran, "Tension Rises in Volatile Kashmir," *Washington Post,* October 16, 2001, p. A11.

39. "India Says Pakistani Troops Fire in Kashmir," *Reuters,* October 18, 2001; "Islamic Fighters Exchange Fire with Soldiers in Kashmir," *Associated Press,* October 25, 2001.

40. Celia W. Dugger, "India Rejects Pakistani Bid for Talks, Citing Attack in Kashmir," *New York Times,* October 23, 2001.

41. "At Least 31 Die in Latest Attacks," *Reuters,* November 2, 2001.

42. "Suicide Squad Attacks Indian Parliament," *Reuters,* December 13, 2001.

43. Prashant Pandey, "Jaish, Lashkar Carried Out Attack with ISI Guidance: Police," *The Hindu* (India), December 17, 2001; Celia W. Dugger, "India Says Arrests Link Militants in Pakistan to Attack," *New York Times,* December 17, 2001.

44. George Fernandez, India's defense minister, quoted in Rajiv Chandrasekaran, "Indian Missiles Put 'in Position': Tensions Rise on Pakistani Border," *Washington Post,* December 27, 2001, p. A1. For suggestions that some of the missile deployments may have been nuclear, see Robert E. Rehbein, "Managing Proliferation in South Asia: A Case for Assistance to Unsafe Nuclear Arsenals," *Nonproliferation Review* 9, no. 1 (spring 2002): p. 95; Bill Gertz, "India, Pakistan Prepare for War," *Washington Times,* December 31, 2001, p. 1.

45. "Pakistan to Grant Amnesty to some Detained Militants," *Washington Post,* March 10, 2002, p. A28.

46. Rajiv Chandrasekaran and Rama Lakshimi, "Fugitive List Becomes Central Issue for India: Pakistan Pressed to Hand Over 20 Suspects," *Washington Post,* January 22, 2002, p. A10.

47. George J. Tenet, "Worldwide Threat—Converging Dangers in a Post 9/11

World," Testimony of Director of Central Intelligence before the Senate Select Committee on Intelligence, February 6, 2002.

48. George J. Tenet, "The Worldwide Threat in 2003: Evolving Dangers in a Complex World," Testimony of Director of Central Intelligence before the Senate Select Committee on Intelligence, February 11, 2003, <http://www.cia.gov/cia/public_affairs/speeches/2003/dci_speech_02112003.html>.

49. "Search for Kashmir Killers," *BBC News,* March 24, 2003, <http://news.bbc.co.uk/1/hi/world/south_asia/2879607.stm>.

50. Swati Pandey and Teresita C. Schaffer, "Building Confidence in India and Pakistan," *South Asia Monitor,* no. 49 (August 1, 2002), <http://www.csis.org/saprog/sam49.pdf>, p. 1.

51. Ibid.

52. Bajpai et al., *Brasstacks and Beyond,* p. 110.

53. For similar assessments, see DOD, *Proliferation: Threat and Response,* p. 22; Perkovich, *India's Nuclear Bomb,* p. 281; Kamal, "Pakistani Perceptions," p. 26; and Joeck, "Maintaining Nuclear Stability in South Asia," p. 31; Anton Le Guardia and Rahul Bedi, "Nuclear Threat over Kashmir," *Telegraph* (London), May 22, 2002.

54. For the text of the Lahore Declaration and the Memorandum of Understanding, see "The Lahore Declaration," *Disarmament Diplomacy,* no. 34 (February 1999), <http://www.acronym.org.uk/34doc3.htm>.

55. Howard Diamond, "India, Pakistan Agree on Security, Confidence Building Measures," *Arms Control Today* 29, no. 1, (January/February 1999): p. 21.

56. Center for Contemporary Conflict, "War in Kargil," Project on "Asymmetric Conflict in South Asia: The Cause and Consequences of the 1999 Limited War in Kargil," Naval Postgraduate School, <http://www.ccc.nps.navy.mil/research/kargil/war_in_kargil.pdf>.

57. "India's Nuclear Dilemmas," *Economist,* p. 46. There were some contacts at the diplomatic level, but none at the political leadership level.

58. Pamela Constable, "India, Pakistan Can't Reach Deal: Talks Appeared to Have Fatally Snagged on the Sensitive Issue of Kashmir," *Washington Post,* July 16, 2001; Celia W. Dugger, "Kashmir and A-Arms Defeat Leaders of India and Pakistan," *New York Times,* July 17, 2001.

59. Rose Gordon, "India, Pakistan Trade Tit-for-Tat Missile Tests," *Arms Control Today* 33, no. 3 (April 2003): p. 41.

60. Amy Waldman, "India Announces Steps in Effort to End Its Conflict with Pakistan," *New York Times,* May 3, 2003, p. A1.

61. "India: New Ambassador to Pakistan," *New York Times,* May 14, 2003, p. A8.

62. Miriam Rajkumar, "Spring Thaw in South Asia," *Carnegie Analysis,* Carnegie Endowment for International Peace, May 20, 2003, <http://www.ceip.org/files/nonprolif/templates/article.asp?NewsID=4822>; David Rohde, "India: Bus Service to Pakistan to Resume," *New York Times,* May 27, 2003, p. A8.

63. Tenet, "Worldwide Threat in 2003"; Šumit Ganguly, "The Slide Continues," *Foreign Affairs,* April 2003, <http://www.foreignaffairs.org/20030401faupdate11286/sumit-ganguly/the-slide-continues.html>. For a detailed assessment of Musharraf's continuing support of Islamic political parties and marginalization of Pakistan's mainstream political parties, see International Crisis

Group, "Pakistan: The Mullahs and the Military," *ICG Asia Report,* no. 49 (March 20, 2003).

64. "As Kashmir Peace Talk Grows, Indian Army Kills 12 Infiltrators," *New York Times,* May 23, 2003, p. A4.

65. Tenet, "Worldwide Threat—Converging Dangers in a Post 9/11 World."

66. For a discussion of these incidents and their risks of conventional and nuclear escalation, see James G. Blight and David A. Welch, "Risking the Destruction of Nations: Lessons of the Cuban Missile Crisis for New and Aspiring Nuclear States," *Security Studies* 4, no. 4 (summer 1995): pp. 811–850; and Scott D. Sagan, "Nuclear Alerts and Crisis Management," *International Security* 9, no. 4 (spring 1985): pp. 99–139.

67. Eric Arnett made this argument in 1997, even before the Kargil conflict. See Eric Arnett, "Nuclear Stability and Arms Sales to India: Implications for U.S. Policy," *Arms Control Today* 27, no. 5 (August 1997): pp. 7–11.

68. In May 2001, India conducted a large-scale military exercise explicitly intended to demonstrate India's ability to fight battles in the backdrop of nuclear weapons.

69. Samina Ahmed, "Security Dilemmas of Nuclear-Armed Pakistan," *Third World Quarterly* 21, no. 5 (October 2000): p. 781.

70. Ahmed, "Learning from Nuclear Crises," p. 3.

71. Quoted in Z. Hussain, "On the Brink," *Newsline,* June 1999, pp. 24–25, cited in Ahmed, "Security Dilemmas of Nuclear-Armed Pakistan," p. 789.

72. Ahmed, "Security Dilemmas in Nuclear-Armed Pakistan," p. 789. See also Arnett, "Nuclear Stability and Arms Sales to India," p. 8.

73. Ahmed, "Leaning from Nuclear Crises," p. 10.

74. Statements by Indian defense minister George Fernandes, quoted in Ahmed, "Learning from Nuclear Crises," p. 10. See also "Army Chief Fears Rising Tension on China borders," *Asian Age* (New Delhi), February 11, 1999, quoted in Farah Zhara, "Pakistan's Road to a Minimum Nuclear Deterrent," *Arms Control Today* 29, no. 5 (July/August 1999): p. 10.

75. Brigadier A.R. Siddiqi (Ret.), "Indian Army: Change of Guard," *The Nation* (Islamabad), October 4, 2000.

76. Quoted in DOD, *Proliferation: Threat and Response,* p. 23.

77. Independent analysis of the seismic data gathered from the tests has indicated that the actual yields of the tests fell far short of the official announcements. In particular, the seismic data collected during the May 11 test appears to rule out a successful detonation of a thermonuclear device. See Brian Barker and Terry Wallace, "Monitoring Nuclear Tests," *Science* 281, no. 5385 (September 25, 1998): pp. 1967–1968.

78. Farah Zhara estimates that Pakistan has about 50 nuclear-capable bombers and India has 250–300 fighter-bombers, while François Heisbourg states that Pakistan has 34 F-16–A/-B and 15 Mirage IIEP aircraft and that India has roughly 88 Jaguar and 147 MiG-27 nuclear-capable fighter-bombers. See Zhara, "Pakistan's Road to a Minimum Nuclear Deterrent," p. 10, and François Heisbourg, "The Prospects for Nuclear Stability between India and Pakistan," *Survival* 40, no. 4 (winter 1998–1999): p. 80.

79. Heisbourg, "Prospects for Nuclear Stability Between India and Pakistan," p. 81.

80. DOD, *Proliferation: Threat and Response,* p. 22.

81. Pravin Sawhney, "Pakistan Scores over India in Ballistic Missile Race," *Jane's Intelligence Review* 12, no. 11 (November 2000): p. 33.

82. DOD, *Proliferation: Threat and Response,* p. 25.

83. Carnegie Non-Proliferation Project; quoted in Joeck, "Nuclear Relations in South Asia," p. 139.

84. Gordon, "Tit-for-Tat Missile Tests," p. 41.

85. DOD, *Proliferation: Threat and Response,* p. 25.

86. Ibid.; Joseph Cirincione, with Jon B. Wolfsthal and Miriam Rajkumar, *Deadly Arsenals: Tracking Weapons of Mass Destruction* (Washington, D.C.: Carnegie Endowment for International Peace, 2002), p. 197.

87. Sawhney, "Pakistan Scores over India," p. 33; Gaurav Kampani, "Prithvi: The Case for 'No-First-Deployment,'" *Rediff on the Net,* August 25, 1998, <http://www.rediff.com/news/jul/10kamp.htm>; *CDISS Missile News,* Centre for Defence and International Security Studies, February 1997.

88. Eric Arnett, "Current Nuclear Weapon Capabilities in South Asia," SIPRI website, January 6, 1998, <http://projects.sipri.se/technology/Facts.html>.

89. *CDISS Missile News,* February 1997.

90. DOD, *Proliferation: Threat and Response,* p. 25.

91. Ibid.

92. See the discussion of the SLV below.

93. Allison Barr, "Chronology of Indian Missile Development," web report, Center for Nonproliferation Studies, Monterey Institute of International Studies, July 7, 2000, available at <http://cns.miis.edu/research/india/indiach2.htm>.

94. Alex Wagner, "India Tests Short-Range Agni Ballistic Missile," *Arms Control Today* 31, no. 2 (March 2002): p. 29; Rose Gordon, "India Conducts Four Missile Tests," *Arms Control Today* 33, no. 2 (March 2003).

95. "China's Fear over India Missile Test," BBC News, January 18, 2001.

96. DOD, *Proliferation: Threat and Response,* p. 25; "Report: India Tests Missile," *Associated Press,* January 17, 2001.

97. Rahul Bedi, "Indian Army Will Control Agni II," *Jane's Defense Weekly,* August 22, 2001, p. 5.

98. Indian Defense Research and Development Organization (DRDO) sources, quoted in Sawhney, "Pakistan Scores over India," p. 33.

99. DOD, *Proliferation: Threat and Response,* p. 25.

100. Ibid. See also Center for Nonproliferation Studies, "Chronology of Indian Missile Development," <http://cns.miis.edu/research/india/indiach2.htm>.

101. Jim Hackett, "The Ballistic Missile Threat: India and Pakistan, Centre for Defence and International Security Studies, *CDISS Missile News,* <http://www.cdiss.org/column3.htm>.

102. Ibid.

103. Ibid.

104. CIA Semi-Annual Report, quoted in Sawhney, "Pakistan Scores over India," p. 35.

105. J. Peter Scoblic, "China Issues Missile Export Pledge; U.S. Says It Will Waive Sanctions," *Arms Control Today* 30, no. 10 (December 2000): p. 23; Central Intelligence Agency, *Unclassified Report to Congress on the Acquisition of Technology Relating to Weapons of Mass Destruction and Advanced Conventional Munitions, 1 January through 30 June 2003,* November 2003, <http://www.cia.gov/cia/reports/721_reports/jan_jun2003.htm>; Tenet, "Worldwide Threat in 2003."

106. DOD, *Proliferation: Threat and Response,* p. 30; Joeck, "Nuclear Relations in South Asia," p. 140.

107. DOD, *Proliferation: Threat and Response,* p. 30.

108. Table prepared by Carnegie Non-Proliferation Project, quoted in Joeck, "Nuclear Relations in South Asia," p. 140; Peter R. Lavoy and Maj. Stephen A. Smith, "The Risk of Inadvertent Nuclear Use between India and Pakistan," *Strategic Insight,* Center for Contemporary Conflict, Naval Postgraduate School, February 3, 2003, <http://www.ccc.nps.navy.mil/rsepResources/si/feb03/southAsia2.pdf>, p. 3.

109. Lavoy and Smith, "The Risk of Inadvertent Nuclear Use between India and Pakistan," p. 3.

110. Sawhney, "Pakistan Scores over India," p. 35.

111. Ibid., p. 35; see also table prepared by Carnegie Non-Proliferation Project, quoted in Joeck, "Nuclear Relations in South Asia," p. 140.

112. Sawhney, "Pakistan Scores over India," p. 35.

113. Ibid.

114. Lavoy and Smith, "The Risk of Inadvertent Nuclear Use Between India and Pakistan," p. 3.

115. Central Intelligence Agency, *Unclassified Report to Congress on the Acquisition of Technology Relating to Weapons of Mass Destruction and Advanced Conventional Munitions, 1 January through 30 June 2001,* January 2002, <http://www.cia.gov/cia/reports/721_reports/jan_jun2001.htm>; "Pakistan to Test-Fire Ballistic Missiles," *Dawn* (Pakistan), January 21, 2001.

116. DOD, *Proliferation: Threat and Response,* p. 30; Lavoy and Smith, "The Risk of Inadvertent Nuclear Use Between India and Pakistan," p. 3.

117. Cirincione et al., *Deadly Arsenals,* p. 82.

118. Lavoy and Smith, "The Risk of Inadvertent Nuclear Use Between India and Pakistan," p. 3.

119. Federation of American Scientists, "Shaheen-II," Special Weapons website, <http://www.fas.org/nuke/guide/pakistan/missile/shaheen-2.htm>.

120. Ibid.

121. Central Intelligence Agency, *Unclassified Report to Congress on the Acquisition of Technology Relating to Weapons of Mass Destruction and Advanced Conventional Munitions, 1 January through 30 June 2002,* April 10, 2003, <http://www.cia.gov/cia/reports/721_reports/jan_jun2002.html>.

122. "The Ghauri: A Technical Snapshot," CDISS, <http://www.cdiss.org/98may5a.htm>; Bowen and Wolvén, "Command and Control Challenges in South Asia," p. 31; Andrew Koch and Waheguru Pal Singh Sidhu, "Subcontinental Missiles," *Bulletin of the Atomic Scientists* 54, no. 4 (July/August 1998): p. 44.

123. *CDISS Missile News,* May 1998, <http://www.cdiss.org/98may5a.htm>.

124. DOD, *Proliferation: Threat and Response,* p. 30.

125. Ibid. See also *CDISS Missile News,* May 1998, <http://www.cdiss.org/98may5a.htm>; Sawhney, "Pakistan Scores over India," p. 35.

126. *CDISS Missile News,* May 1998, <http://www.cdiss.org/98may5a.htm>; Koch and Sidhu, "Subcontinental Missiles," p. 45.

127. Ibid., p. 30.

128. "Pakistan Hands Nuclear Arms to Army," *BBC News,* January 8, 2003.

129. DOD, *Proliferation: Threat and Response,* pp. 23, 27.

130. Samina Ahmed, interview by author, December 10, 2000; Rehbein, "Managing Proliferation in South Asia," p. 95.

131. DOD, *Proliferation: Threat and Response,* pp. 23.

132. Howard Diamond, "India Releases Nuclear Doctrine, Looks to Emulate P-5 Arsenals," *Arms Control Today* 29, no. 5 (July/August 1999): p. 23. For the text of the doctrine, see "India's Draft Nuclear Doctrine," *Arms Control Today* 29, no. 5 (July/August 1999): pp. 33–34.

133. Nevertheless, the Indian Army chief, General Sunderajan, stated on January 16, 2001, that the Army at least is proceeding as if the draft doctrine were official policy, including weapon deployment and a nuclear triad. See "Indian Army Chief Plans Nuclear-Proof, Hi-Tech Force," *Asian Age,* January 6, 2001, pp. 1–2 in FBIS-CHI-2001-0116.

134. See Samina Ahmed and David Cortright, "Preventing a Nuclear Arms Race in South Asia: U.S. Policy Options," Kroc Institute Occasional Paper No. 18 (January 2000): p. 1.

135. Samina Ahmed, "Pakistan's Nuclear Weapons Program: Moving Forward or Tactical Retreat?" Kroc Institute Occasional Paper No. 18:OP:2, February 2000; Diamond, "India Releases Nuclear Doctrine," p. 2; Michael R. Gordon and Steven Myers, "Risk of Arms Race Seen in U.S. Design of Missile Defense," *New York Times,* May 27, 2000; Carranza, "Impossible Game," p. 17.

136. Lavoy and Smith, "The Risk of Inadvertent Nuclear Use between India and Pakistan," p. 5.

137. Zhara, "Pakistan's Road to a Minimum Nuclear Deterrent," p. 10.

138. Bowen and Wolvén, "Command and Control Challenges in South Asia," p. 31.

139. Ibid., p. 33. See also Lavoy and Smith, "The Risk of Inadvertent Nuclear Use between India and Pakistan," p. 5.

140. Sawhney, "Pakistan Scores over India," pp. 31–35; Arnett, "Current Nuclear Weapon Capabilities in South Asia"; Cirincione et al., *Deadly Arsenals,* p. 196.

141. P.R. Chari, "India's Slow-Motion Nuclear Deployment," *Carnegie Proliferation Brief* 3, no. 26 (September 7, 2000), <http://www.ceip.org/files/Publications/ProliferationBrief326.asp>.

142. Ganguly, "New Delhi's Nuclear Decision," p. 188; U.S. Department of State Briefing Paper, "Pakistani Nuclear Program," June 23, 1983, available in the National Security Archive, <http://www.gwu.edu/~nsarchiv/NSAEBB/NSAEBB6/ipn22_6.htm>.

143. See, for example, "Indian Defense Panel Urges Speeding up Indigenous Missile Production," *Asian Age,* December 29, 2000, p. 2, in FBIS-NES-2000-1229; Rahul Bedi, "Indian Nuclear Submarine Project Expected to Gather Momentum under New Leader," *Asian Age,* November 3, 2000, p. 3, in FBIS-NES-2000-1103.

144. DOD, *Proliferation: Threat and Response,* January 2001 (Washington, D.C.: U.S. Government Printing Office, 2001), p. 25. Rahul Bedi, "Indian Nuclear Submarine Project Expected to Gather Momentum Under New Leader," *Asian Age,* November 3, 2000, p. 3, in FBIS-NES-2000-1103; Central Intelligence Agency, *Unclassified Report to Congress on the Acquisition of Technology Relating to Weapons of Mass Destruction and Advanced Conventional Munitions, 1 January through 30 June 2003,* November 2003, <http://www.cia.gov/cia/reports/721_reports/jan_jun2003.htm>.

145. Joeck, "Nuclear Relations in South Asia," p. 141.

146. "India's Nuclear Dilemmas," *Economist,* p. 45.

147. Joeck, "Nuclear Relations in South Asia," p. 141.

148. Joeck, "Maintaining Nuclear Stability in South Asia," p. 31. See also Bajpai et al., *Brasstacks and Beyond,* p. 88.

149. "India's Nuclear Dilemmas," *Economist,* p. 46; Seema Mustafa, "Vajpayee's Illness Exposes Lack of Proper Nuclear Command," *Asian Age,* October 13, 2000, p. 1 in FBIS-NES-2000-1013, October 13, 2000.

150. For the text of this announcement, see Office of the Prime Minister of India, "Cabinet Committee on Security Reviews Progress in Operationalizing India's Nuclear Doctrine," press release, Press Information Bureau, January 4, 2003, <http://pib.nic.in/archieve/lreleng/lyr2003/rjan2003/04012003/r040120033.html>.

151. Office of the Prime Minister of India, "Cabinet Committee on Security Reviews Progress in Operationalizing India's Nuclear Doctrine."

152. Ibid.

153. "Strategic Forces Command (SFC)," *GlobalSecurity.org,* web report, August 12, 2003, <http://www.globalsecurity.org/wmd/world/india/sfc.htm>.

154. Kerry Boyd, "India Establishes Formal Nuclear Command Structure," *Arms Control Today* 33, no. 1 (January/February 2003): p. 31.

155. P.R. Chari, speech summarized in "Nuclear Command Authority and Strategic Forces Command," Report of the IPCS panel discussion, February 8, 2003, <http://www.ipcs.org/ipcs/ipcsSeminars2.jsp?action=showView&kValue=945>.

156. Zafar Nawaz Jaspal, "The Indian Nuclear Command Authority," *Defense Journal,* April 2003, <http://www.defencejournal.com/2003/apr/ind-nuclear.htm>; M.V. Ramana and Zia Mian, "The Nuclear Confrontation in South Asia," in *SIPRI Yearbook, 2003: Armaments, Disarmament and International Security* (Oxford: Oxford University Press, 2003), <http://editors.sipri.org/pubs/yb03/ch05.html>.

157. Boyd, "India Establishes Formal Nuclear Command Structure," p. 31.

158. Shakil Shaikh, "Pakistan's National Command Authority to Control All Strategic Organizations," *The News* (Islamabad), November 28, 2000, p. 1, in FBIS-NES-2000-1128; "Pakistan Established Nuclear Control Body," *Arms Control Today* 30, no. 2 (March 2000): p. 27.

159. "Pakistan Established Nuclear Control Body,"; M.A. Niazi, "NCA: But with Military Tinge," *The Nation* (Islamabad), February 4, 2000; "Pakistan Sets up Weapons Control Authority," *The Times of India,* February 4, 2000.

160. "Pakistan Sets up Nuclear Command Authority," *The News* (Islamabad), February 3, 2000.

161. Shaikh, "Pakistan's National Command Authority to Control All Strategic Organizations," p. 1

162. One could argue, of course, that the hands of a leader who seized power in a military coup already *are* the wrong hands. But the alternative could be worse, if the regime were to collapse.

163. Zinni, quoted in "Musharraf Says Nuclear Arsenal Secure, U.S. Not So Sure: CBS's Report," *Dawn,* October 16, 2000. Joseph Cirincione, the head of the Carnegie Endowment for International Peace, expressed similar concerns in an interview on "The Year 2015: The CIA Report," *Nightline,* January 17, 2001, <http://www.abcnews.go.com/sections/nightline/nightline/transcripts/nl010117_trans.html>.

164. Carranza, "Impossible Game," p. 18.

165. Mario E. Carranza, "An Impossible Game: Stable Nuclear Deterrence after the Indian and Pakistani Tests," *Nonproliferation Review* 6, no. 3 (spring–summer 1999): p. 19; Clayton P. Bowen and Daniel Wolvén, "Command and Control Challenges in South Asia," *Nonproliferation Review* 6, no. 3 (spring–summer 1999): pp. 25–35; Neal Joeck, "Nuclear Relations in South Asia," paper presented at the 6th Annual Carnegie International Non-Proliferation Conference, December 1998, pp. 9–10; Scott D. Sagan, "Nuclear Safety and Security in South Asia," in *Proliferation Challenges and Nonproliferation Opportunities for New Administrations,* ed. Michael Barletta, Monterey Center for Nonproliferation Studies, Occasional Paper No. 4, September 2000, <http://www.cns.miis.edu/pubs/opapers/op4/op4.pdf>, pp. 37–39; Anwer Sindhu, "Pakistan Rejects U.S. Nuclear Technology Offer," *The Nation* (Islamabad), November 16, 2000.

166. Carranza, "Impossible Game," p. 19; Joeck, "Maintaining Nuclear Stability in South Asia," p. 54; Joeck, "Nuclear Relations in South Asia," pp. 9–10.

167. Sagan, "Nuclear Safety and Security in South Asia," pp. 38–39.

168. Raj Chengappa, "The Bomb Makers," *India Today,* June 22, 1998, <http://India today.com/itoday/22061998/cover.html>.

169. Raj Chengappa, *Weapons of Peace: The Secret Story of India's Quest to Be a Nuclear Power* (New Delhi: HarperCollins Publishers India, 2000), pp. 420–421.

170. Manoj Joshi, "Safety Measures: Handle with Care," *India Today,* November 2, 1998, p. 52.

171. These questions are raised by P.R. Chari, "Protection of Fissile Materials: The Indian Experience," Arms Control, Disarmament, and International Security Program, University of Illinois, ACDIS Occasional Paper, September 1998, <http://www.acdis.uiuc.edu/homepage_docs/pubs_docs/PDF_Files/Chari%20OP.pdf>, p. 6.

172. Ibid.

173. Praful Bidwai and Achin Vanaik, *South Asia on a Short Fuse: Nuclear Politics and the Future of Global Disarmament* (Karachi: Oxford University Press, 2000), pp. 190–194.

174. Ibid., p. 193.

175. Ibid.

176. Eric Arnett, "India's Nuclear Brownout," *Bulletin of the Atomic Scientists* 52, no. 6 (November/December, 1996): pp. 15–16. For reports of serious continuing safety problems, see V.K. Shashikumar, "Leaks at India's Nuclear-Power Plants: Cause for Concern?" *Christian Science Monitor,* October 11, 2002.

177. Arnett, "India's Nuclear Brownout," p. 16. See also "Regulator: India Failing in Nuke Safety," *United Press International,* June 18, 1996.

178. "Regulator: India Failing in Nuke Safety," *United Press International,* June 18, 1996.

179. Ibid. See also T.S. Gopi Rethinaraj, "In the Comfort of Secrecy," *Bulletin of the Atomic Scientists* 55, no. 6 (November/December 1999): pp. 52–57.

180. A. Gopalakrishnan, "US-India Relations: Where Do We Go From Here?" lecture at Harvard University, March 1, 2001; Ramola Talwar Badam, "India's Nuke Program More Secretive," *Associated Press,* May 31, 2000; "Wisdom of Action Questioned," *The Hindu,* June 2, 2000.

181. Rethinaraj, "In the Comfort of Secrecy," pp. 54–57.

182. "Limiting Nuclear Hazards," editorial, *Dawn* (Karachi), January 24, 2001.

183. "Pakistan Enacts Law for Nuclear Safety," *The News* (Islamabad), January 23, 2001, reported in FBIS-NES-2001-0123.

184. "Limiting Nuclear Hazards," *Dawn,* January 24, 2001.

185. Ibid.

186. Zia Mian and A.H. Nayyar, "Pakistan's Chashma Nuclear Power Plant," Report No. 321, Center for Science and Global Security, Princeton University, December 1999, <http://www.princeton.edu/~globsec/publications/pdf/chashma.pdf>.

187. Ibid.

188. Dr. Nayyar, a professor of physics at Pakistan's Quaid-i-Azam University, quoted in ibid.

189. Samina Ahmed and David Cortright, "Going Nuclear: The Weaponization Option," in *Pakistan and the Bomb: Public Opinion and Nuclear Options,* ed. Samina Ahmed and David Cortright (New York: Oxford University Press, 1998), p. 96.

190. Ibid.

191. The Ojheri explosion could also have potentially sparked an inadvertent war. See below.

192. Lewis A. Dunn, *Controlling the Bomb: Nuclear Proliferation in the 1980s* (New Haven: Yale University Press, 1982), p. 72; Scott D. Sagan, "The Perils of Proliferation: Organization Theory, Deterrence Theory, and the Spread of Nuclear Weapons," *International Security* 18, no. 4 (spring 1994): p. 98; and Peter D. Feaver, "Correspondence: Proliferation Pessimism and Emerging Nuclear Powers," *International Security* 22, no. 2 (fall 1997): p. 191.

193. Joeck, "Nuclear Relations in South Asia," p. 138.

194. For similar concerns about dangers arising from rapid assembly of nuclear weapons during crises, see Peter D. Feaver, "Neooptimists and the Enduring Problems of Nuclear Proliferation," *Security Studies* 6, no. 4 (summer 1997): p. 115.

195. Some reports have referred to some safety features related to the nuclear triggers, but it is not clear what these safety features are, or how reliable they may be. See Chengappa, *Weapons of Peace,* p. 418.

196. Joeck, "Nuclear Relations in South Asia," p. 138.

197. Statement by Jaswant Singh in *The Hindu,* quoted in "India's Nuclear Dilemmas," p. 46.

198. There is some question whether India would remain satisfied with such a deployment option, given the deployments called for in India's Draft Nuclear Doctrine and India's repeated statements that its nuclear weapons are also intended to deter China.

199. Because India has a no first-use doctrine, they might choose to keep their weapons unmated until after a first strike were to occur. This seems rather unlikely,

however. Indeed, some reports indicate that India put its nuclear forces on alert during the Kashmir crisis. See "India's Nuclear Dilemmas," p. 45.

200. For similar concerns, see Joeck, "Nuclear Relations in South Asia," p. 141, and Lavoy, "Security in South Asia," p. 51.

201. Joeck, "Nuclear relations in South Asia," pp. 137–138.

202. "Asia: The Crumbling of Pakistan," *Economist* 349, no. 8090 (October 17, 1998): pp. 45–46; National Intelligence Council, *Global Trends 2015: A Dialogue about the Future with Nongovernmental Experts,* December 2000, <http://www.cia.gov/cia/reports/globaltrends2015/index.html#link13b>; Pamela Constable, "Great Expectations Fade in Pakistan," *Washington Post,* September 30, 2000, p. A17.

203. Jane Perlez, "A Nation Challenged: Cooperation; U.S. Sanctions on Islamabad Will Be Lifted," *New York Times,* September 22, 2001; Carter Dougherty, "Bush Proposes Lifting Sanctions on Pakistan; Effort Seen Tied to War on Terrorism," *Washington Times,* September 22, 2001, p. C1; Pakistan's Needs Run Deep," Editorial, *Los Angeles Times,* November 8, 2001; Teresita C. Schaffer, "Reviving Pakistan's Economy," report from *Pakistan's Future and U.S. Policy Options,* Center for Strategic and International Studies, January 17, 2002; Sushma Ramachandran, "South Asian Economic Outlook Bleak: Report," *The Hindu,* January 12, 2002.

204. For similar concerns, see Cirincione, interviewed in "The Year 2015: The CIA Report," *CBS Nightline.*

205. "Tear Gas Used Against Muslim Militants in Pakistan," *Associated Press,* October 14, 2001; At Least 3 Killed in Crackdown on Pakistan Protestors," *Reuters,* November 9, 2001; Pamela Constable, "'Jihad Is My First Obligation': Muslims in Pakistan's Tribal North Ready to Fight Alongside Taliban," *Washington Post,* November 6, 2001, p. A01; James Risen and Judith Miller, "Pakistani Intelligence Had Links to Al Qaeda, U.S. Officials Say," *New York Times,* October 29, 2001; Norimitsu Onishi, "Pakistan Tries to Split Army from Mullahs," *New York Times,* November 9, 2001.

206. Rick Bragg, "Pakistan Is 2 Worlds: One Urbane, One Enraged," *New York Times,* October 1, 2001; Steven Mufson, "U.S. Worries about Pakistan Nuclear Arms: Officials Try to Guard Against Arsenal, Radioactive Material Going to Terrorists," *Washington Post,* November 4, 2001, p. A21; Barry Bearak, "In Pakistan, a Shaky Ally," *New York Times,* October 2, 2001; Corey Hinderstein, "The First Casualty of the War on Terrorism Must Not Be Pakistan: Pakistan's Nuclear Weapons Must Not Fall into Terrorists' Hands," *ISIS Issue Brief,* September 18, 2001; David Albright, Kevin O'Neill, and Corey Hinderstein, "Securing Pakistan's Nuclear Arsenal: Principles for Assistance," *ISIS Issue Brief,* October 4, 2001, <http://www.isis-online.org/publications/terrorism/pakassist.html>; Jon Wolfsthal, "U.S. Needs a Contingency Plan for Pakistan's Nuclear Arsenal," *Los Angeles Times,* October 16, 2001; Jon Wolfshal, "Yet Another Worry: Pakistan's Nukes," *Newsday,* October 17, 2001, p. A39; Seymour M. Hersh, "Watching the Warheads: The Risks to Pakistan's Nuclear Arsenal," *New Yorker,* November 5, 2001, pp. 48–54; Mansoor Ijaz, "How Secure Is Pakistan's Plutonium?" *New York Times,* November 28, 2001.

207. Molly Moore and Kamran Khan, "Pakistan Moves Nuclear Weapons: Musharraf Says Arsenal Is Now Secure," *Washington Post,* November 11, 2001, p.

A01; Douglas Frantz, "U.S. and Pakistan Discuss Nuclear Security," *New York Times,* October 1, 2001; Greg Myre, "US Wants to Advise Pakistan on Nukes," *Associated Press,* November 3, 2001; Alex Wagner, "U.S. Offers Nuclear Security Assistance to Pakistan," *Arms Control Today* 31, no. 10 (December 2001): p. 24.

208. Joeck, "Maintaining Nuclear Stability in South Asia," pp. 27–28.

209. A few recent events vividly illustrate this point. On March 1, 2001, Pakistan's Criminal Investigation Department reportedly seized a large number of weapons from a terrorist group in Pakistan's Chaghai district. These weapons included five antitank mines and eleven missiles. On March 16, 2001, Pakistani police reportedly seized some sixty rockets from terrorists at Killi Badshah in Chaman. On April 10, 2001, "anti-national elements" planted a bomb in the parking lot of the high-security North Block in New Delhi, which houses the Home and Finance Ministries. On May 2, 2001, a bomb was discovered in a park in the heart of the capital. And on May 10, 2001, suspected militants set off two bombs within a gap of minutes. One bomb detonated in the high-security Sena Bhawan Complex, which houses the Army headquarters, and the other detonated behind South Block, where the prime minister's office is located. For a discussion of these incidents, see "Blasts Rock Army HQs," *The Nation* (New Delhi), May 10, 2001; "Pakistan Police Seize Antitank Mines, Missiles, Other Weapons in Chagai District," *The News* (Islamabad), March 1, 2001, in FBIS-NES-2001-0304; "Police in Quetta Arrest Two Persons, Seize 60 Rockets," *The News* (Islamabad), March 16, 2001, in FBIS-NES-2001-0316.

210. P.R. Chari, "Protection of Fissile Materials: The Indian Experience," pp. 4–5; Zafar Iqbal Cheema, "The Experience in Pakistan," in *A Comparative Analysis of Approaches to the Protection of Fissile Materials,* Proceedings of the Workshop at Stanford University, July 28–30, 1997, p. 114.

211. Bramha Chellaney and Paul Leventhal, "Nuclear Terrorism: Threat, Perception, and Response in South Asia," *Terrorism* 11, no. 6 (1988): p. 465.

212. These risks were obviously much more severe before the weapons were delivered to the military. As Neil Joeck wrote in 1997, "Keeping the military ignorant does not ensure against unauthorized use. It only guarantees that if and when nuclear capabilities are handed over to military units—in a crisis, most likely—they will be no better prepared to use the weapons than they would be to avoid using them." See Joeck, "Nuclear Relations in South Asia," p. 141.

213. Colonel Brian Cloughley (Ret.), "Transition Time in Pakistan's Army," *Jane's Intelligence Review* 12, no. 2 (April 2000): p. 26.

214. Carranza, "Impossible Game," pp. 17–19.

215. Ibid., p. 18. Insofar as India is concerned about a pre-emptive attack from China, it might also adopt a "delegative" command system.

216. For the risks associated with "delegative" command systems, see Peter D. Feaver, "Command and Control in Emerging Nuclear Nations," *International Security* 17, no. 3 (winter 1992/1993): pp. 168–170.

217. George Perkovich, quoted in Miller and Risen, "United States Is Worried about an Increased Threat of Nuclear Conflict over Kashmir," p. A8.

218. Arnett, "Nuclear Stability and Arms Sales to India," pp. 7–10; Ahmed, "Security Dilemmas of Nuclear-Armed Pakistan," pp. 784–785.

219. Samina Ahmed, interview with author, January 20, 2001.

220. There is also some evidence that there were serious Indian intelligence fail-

ures in the 1990 Kashmir crisis. Neil Joeck refers to a paper in which a U.S. intelligence representative "commented that it would take years for the whole story to emerge, that 1990 and 1987 represented cases of dreadful Indian and Pakistani intelligence, and that the Gates mission was dispatched after highest-level U.S. intelligence assessments. These comments suggested to [Indian] authorities that something had indeed been under way which U.S. intelligence sources had discovered—but which had escaped Indian attention." See Joeck, "Maintaining Nuclear Stability in South Asia," p. 32.

221. Lavoy and Smith, "The Risk of Inadvertent Nuclear Use between India and Pakistan," p. 4; Gaurav C. Sawant, "Smart Drones Silently Scan Enemy," *Indian Express,* June 8, 2002, <http://www.indianexpress.com/full_story.php?content_id=4068>.

222. Sagan, "Nuclear Safety and Security in South Asia," p. 38.

223. Bowen and Wolvén, "Command and Control Challenges in South Asia," pp. 32–33. For a similar account, see Zhara, "Pakistan's Road to a Minimum Nuclear Deterrent," p. 11.

224. Arnett, "Nuclear Stability and Arms Sales to India," pp. 9–10. Moreover, because India might be capable of destroying much of Pakistan's rudimentary C^3I network, Pakistan could fear that it faced a "use them or lose them" scenario, even if it actually did not (ibid.).

225. Nazir Kamal, "Pakistani Perceptions and Prospects of Reducing the Nuclear Danger in South Asia," Cooperative Monitoring Center, Occasional Paper No. 6, January 1999, SAND98-0505/6, p. 23 n. 52; Heisbourg, "Prospects for Nuclear Stability between India and Pakistan," p. 86.

226. Carranza, "An Impossible Game," p. 20.

227. Heisbourg, "Prospects for Nuclear Stability between India and Pakistan," p. 86.

228. One might expect that a crisis such the Brasstacks incident would have caused each side to realize the importance of CBMs, just as the Cuban missile crisis caused the United States and the Soviet Union to establish a hotline between the two countries. The fact that India and Pakistan did not use the hotlines in the 1990 Kashmir crisis or the 1999 Kargil war is very troubling indeed.

229. Perkovich, "*India's Nuclear Bomb,*" p. 281.

230. See the discussion of the Ojheri incident above.

231. Ahmed and Cortright, "Going Nuclear: The Weaponization Option," p. 96.

232. Ibid.

233. Karl, "Proliferation Pessimism and Emerging Nuclear Powers," p. 114; Sagan, "More Will Be Worse," pp. 86–87.

234. For excellent suggestions about how the United States might encourage India and Pakistan to move in this direction, see Samina Ahmed, *Countering Nuclear Risks in South Asia* (Washington, D.C.: Council for a Livable World), December 2001. This issue will be examined in greater detail in the final chapter of this work.

235. DOD, *Proliferation: Threat and Response,* pp. 23–24.

236. Andrew Koch, "Selected Indian Nuclear Facilities," Center for Nonproliferation Studies, Monterey Institute of International Studies, July 7, 2000, <http://cns.miis.edu/research/india/index.htm>.

237. Ibid.

238. Ibid.

239. Rodney W. Jones, Mark G. McDonough, with Toby Dalton and Gregory Koblentz, *Tracking Nuclear Proliferation: A Guide in Maps and Charts, 1998* (Washington, D.C.: Carnegie Endowment for International Peace, 1998), p. 112.

240. Ibid.

241. Ibid. See also Koch, "Selected Indian Nuclear Facilities."

242. Jones et al., *Tracking Nuclear Proliferation,* p. 112.

243. The reactors that are under construction include Kaiga-3, Kaiga-4, Kudankulam-1, Kudankulam-2, Rajasthan-5, Rajashan-6, Tarapar-3, and Tarapar-4. They are all expected to be completed between 2005 and 2007. See International Atomic Energy Agency, "India: Nuclear Power Reactors," Power Reactor Information System, <http://www.iaea.org/programmes/a2/index.html>.

244. DOD, *Proliferation: Threat and Response,* pp. 23–24.

245. Andrew Koch, "Nuclear Testing in South Asia and the CTBT," *Nonproliferation Review* 3, no. 3 (spring–summer 1996): p. 99; Jones et al., *Tracking Nuclear Proliferation,* p. 112.

246. For an explanation of the desirability of the various "grades" of plutonium for use in nuclear weapons, see Albright et al., *Plutonium and Highly Enriched Uranium, 1996* (Oxford: Oxford University Press, 1997), pp. 18–25.

247. Jones et al., *Tracking Nuclear Proliferation,* p. 120 n. 18; IAEA, "India: Nuclear Power Reactors."

248. Jones et al., *Tracking Nuclear Proliferation,* p. 99.

249. Koch, "Selected Indian Nuclear Facilities." For a discussion of "boosted" nuclear weapons, see "Nuclear Weapons—A Primer," in Jones et al., *Tracking Nuclear Proliferation,* Appendix I, p. 317.

250. DOD, *Proliferation: Threat and Response,* p. 24.

251. Ibid.

252. Andrew Koch and Jennifer Topping, "Pakistan's Nuclear-Related Facilities," web report, Center for Nonproliferation Studies, Monterey Institute of International Studies, p. 4, <http://cns.miis.edu/pubs/reports/pdfs/9707paki.pdf>.

253. Ibid.

254. Ibid., p. 1.

255. David Albright, "India's and Pakistan's Fissile Material and Nuclear Weapons Inventories, End of 1999," Institute for Science and International Security Occasional Paper, October 11, 2000, <http://www.isis-online.org/publications/southasia/stocks1000.html>, p. 1.

256. Andrew Koch and Jennifer Topping, "Pakistan's Nuclear Weapons Program: A Status Report," *Nonproliferation Review* 4, no. 3 (spring–summer 1997): p. 111.

257. Ibid.

258. Albright, "India's and Pakistan's Fissile Material and Nuclear Weapons Inventories, End of 1999," p. 2.

259. Ibid., p. 1.

260. Ibid., p. 3. An issue of *The Times of India* quotes "strategic thinkers," who estimate that Pakistan currently has a stockpile of 720 kilograms of weapons-grade uranium, which roughly fits with Albright's assessment, since Albright's assessment was for stockpiles at the end of 1999. See "Pak Has Enough Uranium for 36 N-Weapons," *The Times of India,* November 19, 2000.

261. Albright, "India's and Pakistan's Fissile Material and Nuclear Weapons Inventories, End of 1999," p. 3.

262. Ibid., p. 1.

263. According to a 1997 report by the U.S. Department of Defense, "The disadvantage of reactor-grade plutonium is not so much in the effectiveness of the nuclear weapons that can be made from it as in the increased complexity in designing, fabricating, and handling them. The possibility that either a state or a sub-national group would choose to use reactor-grade plutonium, should sufficient stocks of weapon-grade plutonium not be readily available, cannot be discounted. In short, reactor-grade plutonium is weapons-usable, whether by unsophisticated proliferators or by advanced nuclear weapon states." U.S. Department of Energy, Office of Arms Control and Nonproliferation, "Final Nonproliferation and Arms Control Assessment of Weapons-Usable Fissile Material Storage and Excess Plutonium Disposition Alternatives," (Washington, D.C.: DOE, DOE/NN-0007, January 13, 1997), pp. 66–68.

264. Albright, "India's and Pakistan's Fissile Material and Nuclear Weapons Inventories, End of 1999," p. 1.

265. Ibid., p. 3.

266. Interviews by author, November 15–18, 2000.

267. Cheema, "The Experience in Pakistan," p. 114.

268. Abdul Sattar, Pakistani foreign minister, speech at the Carnegie International Non-Proliferation Conference, June 18, 2001, <http://www.ceip.org/files/projects/npp/resources/Conference%202001/sattar.htm>.

269. For a discussion of China's aid to Pakistan's nuclear program, see David Albright and Mark Hibbs, "Pakistan's Bomb: Out of the Closet," *Bulletin of the Atomic Scientists* 48, no. 6 (July–August 1992): pp. 38–44.

270. Cheema, "The Experience in Pakistan," p. 115.

271. Chellaney and Leventhal, "Nuclear Terrorism: Threat, Perception, and Response in South Asia," *Terrorism* 11 (1988): p. 453.

272. S. Rajagopal, "Review of the Indian Nuclear Experience," *A Comparative Analysis of Approaches to the Protection of Fissile Materials,* Proceedings of the Workshop at Stanford University, July 28–30, 1997, pp. 111–112.

273. Ibid.

274. Interviews by author, November 15–18, 2000.

275. A. Gopalakrishnan, interview by author, Harvard University, October 1, 2000.

276. For the necessity of performance testing of MPC&A systems, see INFCIRC/225/Rev.4 and Oleg Bukharin, Matthew Bunn, and Kenneth N. Luongo, *Renewing the Partnership: Recommendations for Accelerated Action to Secure Nuclear Material in the Former Soviet Union* (Washington, D.C.: Russian-American Nuclear Security Advisory Council, 2000), pp. 79–86.

277. INFCIRC/225/Rev.4, section 4.4.

278. Annette Schaper, "The Case for Universal Full-Scope Safeguards on Nuclear Material," *Nonproliferation Review* 5, no. 2 (winter 1998): p. 75.

279. Interviews by author, November 15–18, 2000.

280. Adinarayantampi Gopalakrishnan, email correspondence with author, October 31, 2000.

281. Several U.S. officials have raised this objection to the author in private correspondence, October 27–31, 2000.

282. Albright, "India's and Pakistan's Fissile Material and Nuclear Weapons Inventories, end of 1999," p. 1.

283. James E. Doyle and Stephen V. Mladineo, "Assessing the Development of a Modern Safeguards Culture in the NIS," *Nonproliferation Review* 5, no. 2 (winter 1998): p. 91.

284. Ibid., pp. 91–92.

285. A. Gopalakrishnan, quoted in Nayan Chanda and Kathy Wilhelm, "Doomsday Averted," *Far Eastern Economic Review* 162, no. 5 (February 4, 1999): p. 16.

286. See the above section: "Lack of Safety Cultures in India and Pakistan."

287. For similar concerns, see Chellaney and Leventhal, "Nuclear Terrorism in South Asia," pp. 449, 465.

288. "Four Arrested in Shillong on Charge of Uranium Smuggling," *All India Radio Network* [the Indian Government's Official News Network], October 17, 1994, in "Operation Launched to Trace 'Huge' Uranium Quantity," JPRS-TND-94-020, p. 13; Programme for Promoting Nuclear Non-Proliferation Newsbrief, no. 28 (Fourth Quarter 1994), p. 18, <http://www.soton.ac.uk/~ppnn/nb28.pdf>; "India: Smugglers Caught," *Nucleonics Week,* November 3, 1994, p. 17.

289. "Police Arrest Two, Seize Uranium in Southern India," *Reuters,* November 7, 2000.

290. Mansoor Ijaz and R. James Woolsey, "How Secure Is Pakistan's Plutonium?" *New York Times,* November 28, 2001.

291. Kamran Khan and Molly Moore, "2 Nuclear Experts Briefed Bin Laden, Pakistanis Say," *Washington Post,* December 12, 2001, p. A01.

292. David E. Sanger, "Nuclear Experts in Pakistan May Have Links to Al Qaeda," *New York Times,* December 9, 2001, p. A1; Julian Borger, "Pakistan Nuclear Experts Advised Bin Laden: Pair Discussed Weapons of Mass Destruction," *Guardian,* December 13, 2001.

293. The possible weaknesses in Pakistan's controls over fissile materials are similar to the potential weaknesses in its controls over nuclear weapons discussed above.

294. Tenet, "Worldwide Threat in 2003."

295. Ganguly, "The Slide Continues."

296. Bryan Bender, "Pakistan: U.S. Visit Finds Continuing Obstacles to Nuclear Cooperation," *Global Security Newswire,* October 8, 2002, <http://www.nti.org/d_newswire/issues/2002/10/8/4p.html>.

6. Newly Proliferating States: Iraq, North Korea, and Iran

1. For a recent CIA intelligence assessment of the nuclear weapons programs in these countries, see Central Intelligence Agency, *Unclassified Report to Congress on the Acquisition of Technology Relating to Weapons of Mass Destruction and Advanced Conventional Munitions, 1 January through 30 June 2002,* April 10, 2003, <http://www.cia.gov/cia/reports/721_reports/jan_jun2002.html>.

2. George Tenet, Director of U.S. Central Intelligence, "The Worldwide Threat in 2003: Evolving Dangers in a Complex World," speech delivered before the Senate Select Committee on Intelligence, February 11, 2003, <http://www.cia.gov/cia/public_affairs/speeches/2003/dci_speech_02112003.html >.

3. John J. Mearsheimer and Stephen M. Walt, "An Unnecessary War," *Foreign*

Policy, no. 134 (January/February 2003): pp. 50–59; Kenneth M. Pollack, "A Last Chance to Stop Iraq," *New York Times,* February 21, 2003, p. A27; Joseph Cirincione and Dipali Mukhopadhyay, "Why Pollack Is Wrong: We Have Contained Saddam," *Carnegie Issue Brief,* February 21, 2003, <http://www.ceip.org/files/nonprolif/templates/article.asp?NewsID=4379>; Mark Strauss, "Think Again: Attacking Iraq," *Foreign Policy,* no. 129 (March–April 2002): pp. 14–19.

4. This is a point that Scott Sagan has long made in the context of the debate. See, for example, Scott D. Sagan, "More Will Be Worse," in *The Spread of Nuclear Weapons: A Debate Renewed* ed. Scott D. Sagan and Kenneth N. Waltz (New York: W.W. Norton, 2003), pp. 53–72.

5. Recent U.S. policy statements have explicitly introduced preventive strikes against WMD facilities in proliferating countries. See, for example, U.S. National Security Council and White House Office of Homeland Security, *National Strategy to Combat Weapons of Mass Destruction,* December 2002, <http://www.whitehouse.gov/news/releases/2002/12/WMDStrategy.pdf>.

6. Roy Godson and James J. Wirtz, "Strategic Denial and Deception," in *Strategic Denial and Deception: The Twenty-First Century Challenge,* ed. Roy Godson and James J. Wirtz (New Brunswick: Transaction Publishers, 2002), p. 1.

7. Jonathan B. Tucker, "Monitoring and Verification in a Noncooperative Environment: Lessons from the U.N. Experience in Iraq," *Nonproliferation Review* 3, no. 3 (spring–summer 1996), <http://www.cns.miis.edu/pubs/npr/vol03/33/tucker33.pdf>, p. 9.

8. Godson and Wirtz, "Strategic Denial and Deception," p. 2.

9. Tucker, "Monitoring and Verification in a Noncooperative Environment," p. 9.

10. For example, this is precisely the calculation that Iraq made after Israel destroyed the Osirak reactor. See Khidir Hamza, "Saddam's Bombmaker," presentation at the Carnegie Endowment for International Peace, November 2, 2000, <http://www.ceip.org/files/projects/npp/resources/hamzatranscript.htm>.

11. See, for example, the safety concerns at Indian and Pakistani nuclear facilities in chapter 5 above. For a much more extensive discussion of environmental and safety risks at current nuclear weapons facilities, see Jeffrey W. Knopf, "Recasting the Proliferation Optimism-Pessimism Debate," *Security Studies* 12, no. 1 (autumn 2003): pp. 41–96.

12. Knopf, "Recasting the Proliferation Optimism-Pessimism Debate," p. 85.

13. Lewis A. Dunn, *Controlling the Bomb: Nuclear Proliferation in the 1980s* (New Haven: Yale University Press, 1982), p. 72. See also Peter D. Feaver, "Correspondence: Proliferation Pessimism and Emerging Nuclear Powers," *International Security* 22, no. 2 (fall 1997): p. 191.

14. Though, if the long lead-up to the U.S. invasion of Iraq in 2003 (which included lengthy negotiations in the United Nations and a huge military buildup) are any indication, proliferating states might not need to fear strikes out of the blue.

15. Anthony H. Cordesman, "The New Iraqi 'Shell Game': The Strategy Iraq May Employ to Defeat UNMOVIC and IAEA Efforts," Center for Strategic and International Studies, December 5, 2002, <http://www.csis.org/burke/iraqishellgame.pdf>, p. 3.

16. David A. Kay, "Denial and Deception Practices of WMD Proliferators: Iraq and Beyond," *Washington Quarterly* 18, no. 1 (winter 1995): pp. 86–88.

17. Khidir Hamza with Jeff Stein, *Saddam's Bombmaker: The Terrifying Inside*

Story of the Iraqi Nuclear and Biological Weapons Agenda (New York: Scribner, 2000), p. 120.

18. Hamza, "Saddam's Bombmaker."

19. Joseph Cirincione, with Jon B. Wolfsthal and Miriam Rajkumar, *Deadly Arsenals: Tracking Weapons of Mass Destruction* (Washington, D.C.: Carnegie Endowment for International Peace, 2002), p. 274.

20. Kay, "Denial and Deception Practices," p. 86.

21. For an illuminating discussion of the disputes leading up to the withdrawal of inspectors in 1998, see Richard Butler, *The Greatest Threat: Iraq, Weapons of Mass Destruction, and the Growing Crisis of Global Security* (New York: Public Affairs, 2000).

22. Precise estimates vary on how long it would have taken Iraq to produce the fissile materials necessary for building nuclear weapons. In January 2001, the U.S. Department of Defense estimated that Iraq would require five or more years and foreign assistance to produce enough fissile materials for a nuclear weapon. See U.S. Department of Defense (DOD), *Proliferation: Threat and Response,* January 2001, <http://www.defenselink.mil/pubs/ptr20010110.pdf>, p. 40. The U.S. CIA estimated that Iraq would have been unlikely to produce indigenously enough weapons-grade material for a deliverable nuclear weapon until the last half of this decade, but that Iraq could produce a nuclear weapon within a year if it were able to acquire weapons-grade fissile material from abroad. It also warns that Baghdad may have acquired uranium enrichment capabilities that could shorten substantially the time necessary for producing a nuclear weapon. See Central Intelligence Agency, *Iraq's Weapons of Mass Destruction Programs,* October 2002, <http://www.cia.gov/cia/reports/iraq_wmd/Iraq_Oct_2002.pdf>, p. 6.

23. Central Intelligence Agency, *Iraq's Weapons of Mass Destruction Programs,* p. 2.

24. Mohammed ElBaradei, "Transcript of ElBaradei's U.N. Presentation," *CNN.com,* March 7, 2003, <http://www.cnn.com/2003/US/03/07/sprj.irq.un.transcript.elbaradei>; David Albright, "The CIA's Aluminum Tubes' Assessment: Is the Nuclear Case Going Down the Tubes?" *ISIS Issue Brief,* March 10, 2003, <http://www.isis-online.org/publications/iraq/al_tubes.html>.

25. ElBaradei, "Transcript of ElBaradei's U.N. Presentation."

26. Secretary of State Colin Powell, "Showdown: Iraq," *CNN Late Edition with Wolf Blitzer,* March 9, 2003 <http://www.cnn.com/TRANSCRIPTS/0303/09/le.00.html>.

27. Tenet, "The Worldwide Threat in 2003."

28. David A. Kay, "Statement on the Interim Progress Report on the Activities of the Iraq Survey Group," Congressional testimony before the House Permanent Select Committee on Intelligence, the House Committee on Appropriations, Subcommittee on Defense, and the Senate Select Committee on Intelligence, October 2, 2003, <http://www.cia.gov/cia/public_affairs/speeches/2003/david_kay_10022003.html>. Although Kay resigned his position in January 2004, the ISG and other U.S. intelligence agencies continue to share his conclusions about Iraq's nuclear weapons program. For example, Charles Duelfer, the new director of the ISG, stated in testimony to Congress on March 30, 2004, that "the ISG has developed information that suggests Iraqi interest in preserving and expanding the knowledge needed to design and develop nuclear weapons." And George Tenet, the Director of U.S. Central Intelligence,

stated in February 2004: "My provisional bottom line today: Saddam did not have a nuclear weapon. He still wanted one and Iraq intended to reconstitute a nuclear program at some point. But we have not yet found clear evidence that the dual-use items Iraq sought were for nuclear reconstitution. We do not know if any reconstitution efforts had begun but we may have overestimated the progress Saddam was making." See Charles Duelfer, Director of Central Intelligence Special Advisor for Strategy regarding Iraqi Weapons of Mass Destruction (WMD) Programs, Testimony to the U.S. Congress, March 30, 2004, <http://www.cia.gov/cia/public_affairs/speeches/2004/tenet_testimony_03302004.html>; George Tenet, "Iraq and Weapons of Mass Destruction," speech given at Georgetown University, February 5, 2004, <http://www.cia.gov/cia/public_affairs/speeches/2004/tenet_georgetownspeech_02052004.html>.

29. Kay, "Denial and Deception Practices," pp. 85, 98–104.

30. Ibid., p. 94. See also Jay C. Davis and David A. Kay, "Iraq's Secret Nuclear Weapons Program," *Physics Today* 45, no. 7 (July 1992): pp. 21–27; and Office of Technology Assessment, U.S. Congress, *Technologies Underlying Weapons of Mass Destruction,* OTA-BP-ISC-115 (Washington, D.C.: U.S. Government Printing Office, December 1993): pp. 168–169.

31. Davis and Kay, "Iraq's Secret Nuclear Weapons Program," p. 24; David Kay, "Iraqi Inspections: Lessons Learned," speech given at the Center for Nonproliferation Studies, February 10, 1993, <http://cns.miis.edu/research/iraq/kay.htm>.

32. Judith Miller, "Secret Sites: Iraqi Tells of Renovations at Sites for Chemical and Nuclear Arms," *New York Times,* December 20, 2001, p. A3.

33. "Saddam's Deadly Subway Scheming," *CBS News,* February 21, 2003, <http://www.cbsnews.com/stories/2003/02/21/60minutes/main541565.shtml>.

34. Deputy Secretary of Defense Paul Wolfowitz, "Iraq: What Does Disarmament Look Like?" speech given at the Council on Foreign Relations, New York City, January 23, 2003.

35. Timothy V. McCarthy and Jonathan B. Tucker, "Saddam's Toxic Arsenal: Chemical and Biological Weapons in the Gulf Wars," in *Planning the Unthinkable: How New Powers Will Use Nuclear, Biological, and Chemical Weapons*, ed. Peter R. Lavoy, Scott D. Sagan, and James J. Wirtz (Ithaca: Cornell University Press, 2000), p. 54; Kay, "Statement on the Interim Progress Report on the Activities of the Iraq Survey Group."

36. McCarthy and Tucker, "Saddam's Toxic Arsenal," pp. 74–75.

37. Amatzia Baram, "An Analysis of Iraqi WMD Strategy," *Nonproliferation Review* 8, no. 2 (summer 2001): p. 34.

38. McCarthy and Tucker, "Saddam's Toxic Arsenal," p. 52.

39. Ibid., p. 60.

40. Ibid., p. 61.

41. Gregory F. Giles, "The Islamic Republic of Iran and Nuclear, Biological, and Chemical Weapons," in *Planning the Unthinkable,* p. 83.

42. McCarthy and Tucker, "Saddam's Toxic Arsenal," p. 62.

43. Norman Cigar, "Iraq's Vision of the Nuclear Battlefield," *Contributions to War Studies,* no. 3 (Quantico, Va.: Marine Corps University Foundation, March 2003), <http://www.globalsecurity.org/wmd/library/news/iraq/2003/iraq-nuclear-battlefield-study.pdf >, p. v.

44. Cigar, "Iraq's Vision of the Nuclear Battlefield," p. 6.

45. Ibid., p. 18.
46. Ibid., p. 6.
47. Ibid., p. 5.
48. McCarthy and Tucker, "Saddam's Toxic Arsenal," p. 73.
49. Ibid., p. 48.
50. Ibrahim Al-Marashi, "Command and Control of Iraq's CW Arsenal," Center for Nonproliferation Studies, March 26, 2003, <http://www.cns.miis.edu/research/iraq/cocchem.htm>; Baram, "An Analysis of Iraqi WMD Strategy," p. 34; McCarthy and Tucker, "Saddam's Toxic Arsenal," p. 75.
51. McCarthy and Tucker, "Saddam's Toxic Arsenal," p. 75.
52. Ibid., p. 61.
53. Ibid., p. 73.
54. Ibid., p. 72.
55. Baram, "An Analysis of Iraqi WMD Strategy," p. 34
56. Cigar, "Iraq's Vision of the Nuclear Battlefield," p. 12.
57. Ibid.
58. Ibid.
59. Ibid.
60. Kenneth Waltz argues that dictators like Hussein are deterrable. They may be brutal, but they are neither "irrational" nor stupid, and they recognize what is necessary to survive. See Kenneth N. Waltz, "More May Be Better," in Scott D. Sagan and Kenneth N. Waltz, *The Spread of Nuclear Weapons: A Debate Renewed* (New York: W.W. Norton, 2003), pp. 13–14.
61. Mearsheimer and Walt, "An Unnecessary War," p. 54.
62. Ibid., p. 54.
63. Pollack, "A Last Chance to Stop Iraq," p. A27.
64. Baram, "An Analysis of Iraqi WMD Strategy," p. 34
65. "UK: Iraq Torches Seven Oil Wells," *CNN.com,* March 21, 2003, <http://www.cnn.com/2003/WORLD/meast/03/21/sprj.irq.oil.wells>.
66. Molly Moore, "Israeli Defenses Much Improved since Gulf War," *Washington Post,* January 5, 2003, p. A01.
67. Pollack, *Threatening Storm,* pp. 36–39.
68. Butler, *The Greatest Threat,* p. 39.
69. Pollack, "A Last Chance to Stop Iraq," p. A27.
70. Ibid.
71. Such a rapid effort to acquire nuclear weapons could introduce safety and security risks. And, as Waltz himself acknowledges, a rapid spread could also, in itself, be destabilizing. See Waltz, "More May Be Better," p. 41.
72. Cigar, "Iraq's Vision of the Nuclear Battlefield," p. v.
73. Ibid., p. 17.
74. Tenet, "The Worldwide Threat in 2003."
75. Secretary of State Colin L. Powell, "Remarks to the United Nations Security Council," February 5, 2003, <http://www.state.gov/secretary/rm/2003/17300.htm>.
76. Inigo Gilmore, "The Proof that Saddam Worked with Bin Laden," *London Telegraph,* April 27, 2003.
77. Ibid.
78. Stephen F. Hayes, "Case Closed," *Weekly Standard* 9, no. 11 (November 24,

2003); pp. 20-25; Stephen F. Hayes, "The Saddam-Osama Memo (cont.): A Close Examination of the Defense Department's Latest Statement," *The Daily Standard*, November 19, 2003, <http://www.weeklystandard.com/Content/Public/Articles/000/000/003/396hflxy.asp>. For additional reported links between the Ba'ath party and al Qaeda, see William Safire, "Missing Links Found," *New York Times*, November 24, 2003, p. A23.

79. Mearsheimer and Walt, "An Unnecessary War," p. 58.

80. Tucker, "Monitoring and Verification in a Noncooperative Environment," p. 10.

81. Ibid., p. 9

82. Ibid., p. 10.

83. Ibid.

84. Peter D. Zimmerman, "Technical Barriers to Nuclear Proliferation," *Security Studies* 2, nos. 3/4 (spring/summer 1993): p. 348.

85. Anthony H. Cordesman, *Iraq and the War of Sanctions: Conventional Threats and Weapons of Mass Destruction* (Westport, Conn.: Praeger, 1999), p. 622.

86. Ibid., p. 625.

87. Ibid.

88. Gary Milhollin, "Building Saddam Hussein's Bomb," *New York Times Magazine*, March 8, 1992, p. 32. This passage is also quoted in Scott D. Sagan, "More Will Be Worse," in *The Spread of Nuclear Weapons: A Debate Renewed* (New York: W.W. Norton, 2003), p. 70.

89. Cigar, "Iraq's Vision of the Nuclear Battlefield," p. 12.

90. Ibid., p. 12.

91. Sagan, "More Will Be Worse," pp. 80–81.

92. Amatzia Baram, "An Analysis of Iraqi WMD Strategy," p. 35.

93. Barton Gellman, "U.S. Reaps New Data on Weapons," *Washington Post*, March 20, 2003, p. A1. See also Stephen Fidler, "Securing of Arms Sites Will Be the Top Priority for US," *Financial Times*, March 20, 2003, p. 3; and Judith Miller, "Threats and Responses: Disarming Saddam Hussein; Teams of Experts to Hunt Iraqi Arms," *New York Times*, March 19, 2003, p. A1.

94. Bob Drogin, "War with Iraq/Nuclear Weapons Site; Nuclear Site Stood Unguarded for Days," *Los Angeles Times*, April 11, 2003, p. A1.

95. The weakening of Hussein's central authority had been an explicit goal of U.S. policy since the passage of the "Iraq Liberation Act of 1998." See William J. Clinton, "The Iraq Liberation Act," Statement by the President of the United States, Office of the Press Secretary, October 31 1998, <http://www.library.cornell.edu/colldev/mideast/libera.htm>.

96. Gregg Easterbrook, "American Power Moves Beyond the Mere Super," *New York Times*, April 27, 2003. This lesson might be driven home by the radically differing U.S. responses to Iraq and North Korea. Because North Korea has the ability to destroy Seoul, South Korea (with conventional and possibly nuclear weapons), the United States is effectively deterred from carrying out a preventive strike on North Korea or its nuclear facilities.

97. Tucker, "Monitoring and Verification in a Noncooperative Environment," p. 12.

98. Central Intelligence Agency, "North Korea," in the *CIA World Factbook,* 2002, <http://www.cia.gov/cia/publications/factbook/geos/kn.html>.

99. Cirincione et al., *Deadly Arsenals,* p. 244.

100. Ibid., p. 245.

101. Ibid., p. 246.

102. Ibid.

103. Larry A. Niksch, "North Korea's Nuclear Weapons Program," Congressional Research Service Brief for Congress, December 6, 2001, p. 6.

104. Ibid., p. 8. For a more detailed discussion of the Agreed Framework, see Cirincione, *Deadly Arsenals,* pp. 246–249, and David Albright and Kevin O'Neill, *Solving the North Korean Nuclear Puzzle* (Washington, D.C.: Institute for Science and International Security, 2000), pp. 31–55.

105. Dipali Mukhopadhyay and Jon Wolfsthal, "North Korea's Secret Nuclear Weapons Program: A Serious Violation of North Korea's International Commitments?" *Carnegie Analysis* (Washington, D.C.: Carnegie Endowment for International Peace), October 25, 2002, <http://www.ceip.org/files/nonprolif/templates/article.asp?NewsID=3877>.

106. David E. Sanger, "In North Korea and Pakistan, Deep Roots of Nuclear Barter," *New York Times,* November 24, 2002.

107. Seth Mydans, "North Korea Says It Is Withdrawing from Arms Treaty," *New York Times,* January 10, 2003.

108. Doug Struck, "Reactor Restarted, North Korea Says: Plutonium Could Be Used for Bombs," *Washington Post,* February 6, 2003, p. A31.

109. David E. Sanger and Eric Schmitt, "Satellites Said to See Activity at North Korean Nuclear Site," *New York Times,* January 31, 2003, p. A1.

110. "North Korea Reactivates Nuclear Facilities," *New York Times,* February 5, 2003.

111. Timothy L. O'Brien, "Atom Agency Finds Pyongyang in Violation of Arms Accords," *New York Times,* February 12, 2003.

112. Glenn Kessler and John Pomfret, "North Korea's Threats a Dilemma for China: Ally's Nuclear Gamesmanship Rankles Beijing," *Washington Post,* April 26, 2003, p. A01; David E. Sanger and Howard W. French, "North Korea Prompts U.S. to Investigate Nuclear Boast," *New York Times,* May 1, 2003, p. A20.

113. Joseph Kahn, "Korea Arms Talks Close with Plans for a New Round," *New York Times,* August 30, 2003, p. A1.

114. James Brooke, "Korean Claim Leaves U.S. Concerned, But Skeptical," *New York Times,* October 3, 2003, p. A6.

115. David E. Sanger, "Intelligence Puzzle: North Korean Bombs," *New York Times,* October 14, 2003, p. A9.

116. Ibid.

117. James Brooke and David E. Sanger, "North Koreans, in Shift, to Mull Security Offer," *New York Times,* October 26, 2003, p. A1.

118. Central Intelligence Agency, written responses to "Questions for the Record," posed by the Senate Select Committee on Intelligence following the February 2003 Worldwide Threat Briefing by the Director of Central Intelligence, August 18, 2003, <http://www.fas.org/irp/congress/2003_hr/021103qfr-cia.pdf>, p. 144.

119. Ibid.

120. Timothy L. Savage, "Crisis in 2003?: North Korea's WMD Program," *The Monitor: International Perspectives on Nonproliferation* 8, no. 3 (summer 2002): p. 25.

121. DOD, *Proliferation: Threat and Response,* p. 9. See also Center for Nonproliferation Studies, "Kumchangri Underground Facility," available on the Nuclear Threat Initiative website, <http://www.nti.org>.

122. Cirincione et al., *Deadly Arsenals,* pp. 249–250.

123. Niksch, "North Korea's Nuclear Weapons Program," p. 2; Cirincione et al., *Deadly Arsenals,* pp. 249–250.

124. Cirincione et al., *Deadly Arsenals,* p. 250.

125. Michael Levi, "Off Target: North Korea's Hidden Menace," *New Republic* 228, no. 11 (March 24, 2003): pp. 13–14.

126. John Diamond, "N. Korea Keeps U.S. Intelligence Guessing," *USA Today,* March 11, 2003, p. A1.

127. "U.S. Source Confirms North Korea Reprocessing Nuclear Fuel—Japanese Agency," *BBC Monitoring International Reports,* July 12, 2003; Jonathan Watts and Julian Borger, "Secret Nuclear Plant Detected in North Korea," *Guardian,* July 21, 2003, p. 10.

128. Thom Shanker and David E. Sanger, "North Korea Hides New Nuclear Site, Evidence Suggests," *New York Times,* July 20, 2003, p. A1; Watts and Borger, "Secret Nuclear Plant Detected in North Korea," p. 10.

129. David Albright, "North Korea's Current and Future Plutonium and Nuclear Weapon Stocks," *ISIS Issue Brief,* January 15, 2003, <http://www.isis-online.org/publications/dprk/currentandfutureweaponsstocks.html>.

130. Albright, "North Korea's Current and Future Plutonium and Nuclear Weapon Stocks."

131. Ibid.

132. Ibid.

133. Larry A. Niksch, "North Korea's Nuclear Weapons Program," Congressional Research Service, Issue Brief for Congress (updated August 27, 2003), <http://fas.org/spp/starwars/crs/IB91141.pdf>, p. 2.

134. Central Intelligence Agency, *Unclassified Report to Congress on the Acquisition of Technology Relating to Weapons of Mass Destruction and Advanced Conventional Munitions, 1 January through 30 June 2002,* April 10, 2003, <http://www.cia.gov/cia/reports/721_reports/jan_jun2002.html>.

135. See James A. Kelly, Assistant Secretary of State for East Asian and Pacific Affairs, testimony before the Senate Foreign Relations Committee, Regional Implications of the Changing Nuclear Equation on the Koran Peninsula, U.S. Senate Hearings, March 12, 2003. See also Carol Giacomo, "U.S. Sees Faster North Korea Uranium Production," *Washington Post,* March 12, 2003.

136. Albright, "North Korea's Current and Future Plutonium and Nuclear Weapon Stocks."

137. Joseph Bermudez Jr., "The Democratic People's Republic of Korea and Unconventional Weapons," in *Planning the Unthinkable,* p. 192.

138. Ibid., p. 193.

139. "N. Korea Test-Fires Missile into Sea of Japan," *Washington Post,* March 10, 2003, p. A17.

140. Bermudez, "The Democratic People's Republic of Korea and Unconventional Weapons," p. 198–199.

141. Cirincione et al., *Deadly Arsenals,* p. 251.

142. DOD, *Proliferation: Threat and Response,* p. 11.

143. Ibid.; Cirincione et al., *Deadly Arsenals,* p. 251.

144. DOD, *Proliferation: Threat and Response,* p. 11; "Nodong-1," *GlobalSecurity.org,* <http://www.globalsecurity.org/wmd/world/dprk/nd-1.htm>.

145. DOD, *Proliferation: Threat and Response,* p. 11; Cirincione et al., *Deadly Arsenals,* p. 251.

146. DOD, *Proliferation: Threat and Response,* p. 11.

147. Diamond, "N. Korea Keeps U.S. Intelligence Guessing," p. A1.

148. According to U.S. Secretary of Defense Donald Rumsfeld, North Korea has made tremendous strides in shielding sensitive military communications by installing underground fiber-optic cables for these communications. Ibid., p. A1.

149. Lynn M. Hansen, "Arms Control: Focus on Denial and Deception," in *Strategic Denial and Deception: The Twenty-First Century Challenge,* ed. Roy Godson and James J. Wirtz (New Brunswick: Transaction Publishers, 2002), pp. 177–178.

150. Maj. James M. Minnich, *North Korean Military Tactics* (Ft. Leavenworth, Kans.: U.S. Army Command and General Staff College, September 2001), <http://www.globalsecurity.org/wmd/library/news/dprk/2001/korea.pdf>, p. 9.

151. Bruce Bennett, "N. Korea's Threat to S. Korea," *United Press International,* March 7, 2003.

152. Ibid.

153. Ibid. See also Bermudez, "The Democratic People's Republic of Korea and Unconventional Weapons," p. 198.

154. Bermudez, "The Democratic People's Republic of Korea and Unconventional Weapons," p. 199.

155. Ibid., p. 195.

156. It is highly unlikely that Pyongyang could afford any kind of advanced security systems because it would be using up all of its available resources in acquiring the nuclear weapons in the first place. This is an argument that has been made about proliferating states generally, and it certainly applies to North Korea. See Dunn, *Controlling the Bomb,* p. 72; Feaver, "Correspondence: Proliferation Pessimism and Emerging Nuclear Powers," p. 191.

157. Bermudez, "The Democratic People's Republic of Korea and Unconventional Weapons," p. 199.

158. Knopf, "Recasting the Proliferation Optimism-Pessimism Debate," p. 85.

159. Ibid.

160. Ibid.

161. David Albright, "North Korea's Corroding Fuel," ISIS Occasional Report, Institute for Science and International Security, August 1, 1994, <http://www.isis-online.org/publications/dprk/ir080194.html>.

162. Knopf, "Recasting the Proliferation Optimism-Pessimism Debate," p. 85.

163. Richard Armitage, Testimony before the Senate Foreign Relations Committee, Hearings on WMD Developments on the Korean Peninsula, February 4, 2003. Assistant Secretary of State James Kelly reconfirmed these fears in congressional testimony on March 12, 2003. See James A. Kelly, Assistant Secretary of State for East Asian and Pacific Affairs, testimony before the Senate Foreign Relations Committee,

Regional Implications of the Changing Nuclear Equation on the Korean Peninsula, U.S. Senate Hearings, March 12, 2003.

164. Stephen Bosworth, Testimony before the Senate Foreign Relations Committee, Hearings on WMD Developments on the Korean Peninsula, February 4, 2003.

165. Kessler and Pomfret, "North Korea's Threats a Dilemma for China," p. A01; David E. Sanger, "Bush Shifts Focus to Nuclear Sales by North Korea," *New York Times,* May 5, 2003, p. A1.

166. Ashton B. Carter, William J. Perry, and John M. Shalikashvili, "A Scary Thought: Loose Nukes in North Korea," *Wall Street Journal,* February 6, 2003, p. A18; Bermudez, "The Democratic People's Republic of Korea and Unconventional Weapons," p. 200.

167. See, for example, Scott Snyder, "North Korea's Challenge of Regime Survival: Internal Problems and the Implications for the Future," *Pacific Affairs* 73, no. 4 (winter 2000/2001): pp. 517–533; Samuel S. Kim, "Does North Korea Have a Chance?" *Columbia East Asian Review* (fall 1997), <http://www.columbia.edu/cu/ccba/cear/issues/fall97/graphics/forum/kim/kim.htm>; Douglas Waller, "Ready to Implode?" *Time* 149, no. 18 (May 5, 1997): p. 60.

168. Rupert Wingfield-Hayes, "The Plight of North Korea's Refugees," *BBC News,* September 5, 2002; George Wehrfritz and Hideko Takayama, "Riding the Seoul Train: An Underground Railroad Leads North Korean Refugees to the South," *Newsweek International,* March 5, 2001, p. 26.

169. Snyder, "North Korea's Challenge of Regime Survival," pp. 524–533.

170. Moon Ihlwan and Brian Bremmer, "The Other Korean Crisis," *Business Week,* no. 3816 (January 20, 2003): p. 45.

171. Stephen Bosworth, Testimony before the Senate Foreign Relations Committee, Hearings on WMD Developments on the Korean Peninsula, February 4, 2003.

172. Nicholas Eberstadt, *The End of North Korea* (Washington, D.C.: The AEI Press, 1999), p. 120.

173. John Larkin, "Mysterious Reform," *Far Eastern Economic Review* 165, no. 31 (August 8, 2002): pp. 18–19; David Murphy, "Own Goal," *Far Eastern Economic Review* 165, no. 40 (October 10, 2002): p. 26.

174. Murphy, "Own Goal," p. 26.

175. "N. Korea Trade Zone Leader Detained," *BBC News Online,* October 4, 2002, <http://news.bbc.co.uk/2/hi/business/2298003.stm>.

176. John Larkin, "North Korea: Why Refugees Flee," *Far Eastern Economic Review* 166, no. 9 (March 6, 2003): pp. 14–16.

177. "Without Aid, They Starve," *Far Eastern Economic Review* 166, no. 9 (March 6, 2003): p. 16. Nicholas Eberstadt, "Korea," in *Strategic Asia 2001–2002* (Seattle, Wash.: National Bureau of Asian Research, 2001), <http://strategicasia.nbr.org/report>, p. 136; Norbert Vollersten, "Prisoner Nation: Why North Koreans Cheered Bush's 'Axis of Evil' Designation," *Wall Street Journal,* February 5, 2003, p. A18.

178. Vollersten, "Prisoner Nation," p. A18.

179. Central Intelligence Agency, *CIA World Factbook 2002,* <http://www.cia.gov/cia/publications/factbook/geos/kn.html>.

180. Ibid.; Ihlwan and Bremmer, "The Other Korean Crisis," p. 45.

181. Larkin, "North Korea: Why Refugees Flee," p. 14.

182. For details on North Korea's brutal labor camps, see John Larkin, "Ex-

posed—Kim's Slave Camps," *Far Eastern Economic Review* 165, no. 49 (December 12, 2002): pp. 14–18.

183. Larkin, "North Korea: Why Refugees Flee," p. 15.

184. Vollersten, "Prisoner Nation," p. A18.

185. "Without Aid, They Starve," p. 17.

186. Maj. David S. Maxwell, "Catastrophic Collapse of North Korea: Implications for the United States Military, a Monograph" (Fort Leavenworth, Kans., 1996, Doc. call no.: M-U 42022-2 M4652c), <http://www.kimsoft.com/korea/maxwell.htm#II>; Ihlwan and Bremmer, "The Other Korean Crisis," p. 45.

187. Snyder, "North Korea's Challenge of Regime Survival," p. 519; Vollersten, "Prisoner Nation," p. A18.

188. Maxwell, "Catastrophic Collapse of North Korea," <http://www.kimsoft.com/korea/maxwell.htm#II>.

189. Martin Chulov and Cameron Stewart, "N Korean Scientists Defect," *Australian,* April 19, 2003, p. 1.

190. Jei Guk Jeon, "North Korean Leadership: Kim Jong Il's Balancing Act in the Ruling Circle," *Third World Quarterly* 21, no. 5 (October 2000): pp. 761–779.

191. Ibid, p. 761.

192. Ibid., p. 775.

193. Ibid., p. 775.

194. "Without Aid, They Starve," *Far Eastern Economic Review,* 166, no. 9 (March 6, 2003): p. 16; Nicholas Eberstadt, "Korea," in *Strategic Asia 2001–02: Power and Purpose* (Seattle, Wash.: National Bureau of Asian Research, 2001), <http://strategicasia.nbr.org/report>, p. 136; Vollersten, "Prisoner Nation," p. A18.

195. Eberstadt, "Korea," p. 136.

196. James Dao, "U.S. to Resume Food Aid to North Korea, at a Reduced Level," *New York Times,* February 26, 2003, p. A11.

197. Ibid.

198. David Lague, "Beijing's Tough Korea Call," *Far Eastern Economic Review* 166, no. 9 (March 6, 2003): pp. 12–14.

199. Brent Scowcroft and Arnold Kanter, "A Surprising Success on North Korea," *New York Times,* May 1, 2003, p. A35; Kessler and Pomfret, "North Korea's Threats a Dilemma for China," p. A01.

200. Bertil Lintner, "It's Hard to Help Kim Jong Il," *Far Eastern Economic Review* 166, no. 12 (March 27, 2003): pp. 20–22; Matake Kamiya, "A Disillusioned Japan Confronts North Korea," *Arms Control Today* 33, no. 3 (May 2003): pp. 19–22; Richard Stevenson, "U.S. and Japan Warn North Korea on Nuclear Standoff," *New York Times,* May 24, 2003, p. A3.

201. For a discussion of Kim Dae Jung's Sunshine Policy, see Nicholas Eberstadt, "Our Other Korea Problem," *National Interest,* no. 69 (fall 2002): pp. 110–118.

202. Daniel A. Pinkston, "South Korean Electoral Politics and Seoul's Position on the North Korean Nuclear Crisis," Center for Nonproliferation Studies, April 25, 2003, <http://www.cns.miis.edu/pubs/week/pdf/030425.pdf>, p. 2.

203. Howard French, "North Korea Tests Missile," *New York Times,* February 25, 2003.

204. Pinkston, "South Korean Electoral Politics," p. 4.

205. For example, Marcus Noland argued in 1997 that North Korea will be able

to "muddle through" with only minor adjustments to the system, but he has more recently argued that "North Korea may be reaching the end of its muddling through period." Cf. Marcus Noland, "Why North Korea Will Muddle Through," *Foreign Affairs* 76, no. 4 (July/August 1997): pp. 105–118; and Marcus Noland, quoted in Ihlwan and Bremmer, "The Other Korean Crisis," p. 45.

206. Ihlwan and Bremmer, "The Other Korean Crisis," p. 45.

207. Bermudez, "The Democratic People's Republic of Korea and Unconventional Weapons," p. 200.

208. DOD, *Proliferation: Threat and Response,* pp. 34–35.

209. Giles, "The Islamic Republic of Iran and Nuclear, Biological, and Chemical Weapons," pp. 83–86.

210. DOD, *Proliferation: Threat and Response,* pp. 34–35.

211. Joby Warrick and Glenn Kessler, "Iran Had Secret Nuclear Program, U.N. Agency Says," *Washington Post,* November 11, 2003, p. A1.

212. Ibid.

213. Brenda Shaffer, "Iran at the Nuclear Threshold," *Arms Control Today* 33, no. 9 (November 2003), <http://www.armscontrol.org/act/2003_11/Shaffer.asp>.

214. Report by the Director General of the International Atomic Energy Agency, *Implementation of the NPT Safeguards Agreement by the Islamic Republic of Iran,* November 10, 2003, GOV/2003/75, <http://www.iaea.org/Publications/Documents/Board/2003/gov2003-75.pdf>, p. 10.

215. Ibid.

216. Ibid.

217. John Wolf, speech to the Second Session of the Preparatory Committee for the 2005 Review Conference of the Parties to the Treaty on the Non-Proliferation of Nuclear Weapons, *Washington File,* April 28, 2003.

218. Cirincione, et al., *Deadly Arsenals,* p. 258.

219. Ibid.

220. Ibid., p. 261.

221. "Iran Nuclear-Related Sites," Monterey Center for Nonproliferation Studies, <http://cns.miis.edu/research/iran/nucsites.htm>.

222. David Albright and Corey Hinderstein, "The Iranian Gas Centrifuge Uranium Enrichment Plant at Natanz: Drawing from Commercial Satellite Images," web report, Institute for Science and International Security (ISIS), March 14, 2003, <http://www.isis-online.org/publications/iran/natanz03_02.html>.

223. Shaffer, "Iran at the Nuclear Threshold."

224. Joby Warrick and Glenn Kessler, "Iran's Nuclear Program Speeds Ahead," *Washington Post,* March 10, 2003, p. A1.

225. David Albright and Corey Hinderstein, "Iran Building Nuclear Fuel Cycle Facilities: International Transparency Needed," *ISIS Issue Brief,* Institute for Science and International Security, December 12, 2002, <http://www.isis-online.org/publications/iran/iranimages.html>.

226. Seymour M. Hersh, "The Iran Game: How Will Tehran's Nuclear Ambitions Affect Our Budding Partnership?" *New Yorker* 77, no. 38 (December 3, 2001): pp. 42–50.

227. Parisa Hafezi, "Iran Reveals Plans to Make Fuel for Nuclear Plants," *Washington Post,* February 10, 2003, p. A13.

228. Peter Slevin and Joby Warrick, "U.S. Wary of Iranian Nuclear Aims: Tehran Insists Program Is Solely for Electricity," *Washington Post,* February 11, 2003, p. A12.

229. "Iran: Agreement to Return Spent Russian Fuel Still Unsigned," *Global Security Newswire,* March 12, 2003, <http://www.nti.org/d_newswire/issues/newswires/2003_3_12.html>.

230. Shaffer, "Iran at the Nuclear Threshold." David Albright explains the suspect nature of Iran's production of uranium metal: "The production of uranium metal is unusual and can indicate a nuclear weapons effort that uses metallic forms of natural uranium or highly enriched uranium. The IAEA has asked Iran about its planned use for the material. Iranian officials have stated that the purpose of the uranium metal is as shielding against radiation in containers that store irradiated fuel or materials. Such a use is suspect, however, because the uranium metal appears too refined for shielding material." David Albright and Corey Hinderstein, "Iran, Player or Rogue?" *Bulletin of the Atomic Scientists* 59, no. 5 (September/October 2003): pp. 55–56.

231. Central Intelligence Agency, *Unclassified Report to Congress on the Acquisition of Technology Relating to Weapons of Mass Destruction and Advanced Conventional Munitions, 1 January through 30 June 2002,* April 10, 2003, <http://www.cia.gov/cia/reports/721_reports/jan_jun2002.html>.

232. Cirincione et al., *Deadly Arsenals,* p. 255.

233. Ibid.

234. DOD, *Proliferation: Threat and Response,* pp. 37–38; Cirincione et al., *Deadly Arsenals,* p. 225.

235. CIA, *Acquisition of Technology Relating to Weapons of Mass Destruction and Advanced Conventional Munitions, 1 January through 30 June 2002.*

236. Giles, "The Islamic Republic of Iran and Nuclear, Biological, and Chemical Weapons," p. 92.

237. Ibid., p. 97.

238. Ibid., p. 101.

239. Ibid.

240. Ibid.

241. Ibid.

242. John L. Esposito, "Introduction: from Khomeini to Khatami," in *Iran at the Crossroads,* ed. John L. Esposito and R.K. Ramazani (New York, N.Y.: Palgrave, 2001), p. 1.

243. Ibid., p. 2

244. Ibid.

245. George Tenet, Director of U.S. Central Intelligence, "The Worldwide Threat in 2003: Evolving Dangers in a Complex World," speech delivered before the Senate Select Committee on Intelligence, February 11, 2003, <http://www.cia.gov/cia/public_affairs/speeches/2003/dci_speech_02112003.html >.

246. Shahram Chubin, *Whither Iran? Reform, Domestic Politics and National Security,* Adelphi Paper, No. 342 (New York, N.Y.: Oxford University Press, 2002), p. 20.

247. Bijan Khajehpour, "Iran's Economy: Twenty Years after the Islamic Revolution," in *Iran at the Crossroads,* ed. Esposito and Ramazani, p. 111.

248. Chubin, *Whither Iran?* p. 19.

249. Ibid.

250. Stanley Reed and Rose Brady, “Iran: Will Economic Reforms Keep the Mullahs on Top?” *Business Week,* no. 3815 (January 13, 2003): p. 57.

251. Chubin, *Whither Iran?* p. 19.

252. Ibid.

253. Mark Downes, *Iran's Unresolved Revolution* (Aldershot, England: Ashgate Publishing Company, 2002), p. 133.

254. Ibid.

255. Ibid., pp. 133–134.

256. Ibid., p. 133.

257. Mohsen Milani, “Reform and Resistance in the Islamic Republic of Iran,” in *Iran at the Crossroads,* ed. Esposito and Ramazani, p. 30.

258. Chubin, *Whither Iran?* p. 20.

259. Esposito, “From Khomeini to Khatami,” p. 5.

260. Chubin, *Whither Iran?* p. 13.

261. Milani, “Reform and Resistance in the Islamic Republic of Iran,” p. 29.

262. Ibid., p. 43.

263. Downes, *Iran's Unresolved Revolution,* p. 140.

264. Jonathan Manthorpe, “Anger at Clerics Threatens to Bring Iran to the Boil,” *Vancouver Sun,* November 23, 2002, p. A27.

265. “Clashes Between Students and Islamists in Teheran,” *Deutsche Presse-Agentur,* December 9, 2002.

266. Ibid.

267. Ibid.

268. Wendell Steavenson, “Iranian Protest Widens: 10,000 at Demo.,” *Gazette* (Montreal, Quebec), December 9, 2002, p. A13.

269. Ibid.

270. Manthorpe, “Anger at Clerics Threatens to Bring Iran to the Boil,” p. A27.

271. “News Analysis: No Real Winners in Iran's Municipal Elections,” *Deustche Presse-Agentur,* March 2, 2003.

272. “A Tested Theocracy,” *Economist.com,* June 12, 2003, <http://www.economist.com/agenda/displayStory.cfm?story_id=1840707>.

273. Karl Vick, “Iranian Apathy May Hinder U.S. Bid to Foment Unrest,” *Washington Post,* May 29, 2003, p. A14.

274. “Iran Arrests Pro-Clergy Militants,” *CBS News,* June 14, 2003, <http://www.cbsnews.com/stories/2003/06/15/world/main558755.shtml>. The militants who carried out the attacks were reportedly arrested the next day. The arrests of these hard-line militants, who normally act with impunity, suggest that Iran's ruling clerics were very concerned that the violence would only stoke the antigovernment protests (ibid.).

275. Ali Akbar Dareini, “Clashes Continue in Tehran; Ayatollah Warns of Major Crackdown,” *Associated Press,* June 14, 2003.

276. David Warren, “Iranian Regime Not Close to Falling,” *The Ottawa Citizen,* July 12, 2003.

277. “Analysis: Despite Another Ban, the Protests Continue in Iran,” *Deutsche Presse-Agentur,* July 11, 2003.

278. Ibid.

279. Chubin, *Whither Iran?* p. 18.

280. Vince Cannistraro, "The Iran Debate: Pentagon Eyes Massive Covert Attack on Iran," *ABCNews.com,* May 29, 2003, <http://abcnews.go.com/sections/us/DailyNews/ITeamInsider030529.html>; "Special Report: Next on the List?—Dealing with Iran," *Economist* 367, no. 8328 (June 14, 2003): p. 23.

281. Anthony H. Cordesman, "Weapons of Mass Destruction in the Middle East," Center for Strategic and International Studies, October 4, 1999, <http://www.csis.org/mideast/reports/WMDinMETrends.pdf>, p. 30.

282. According to the Nuclear Threat Initiative, "facilities known as Shahid Meisam were reportedly built alongside the Tehran-Karaj expressway as storage for artillery shells. These were filled with chemical products en route to Revolutionary Guard units. Due to lax safety measures, a significant portion of the 1,000 workers in the storage facilities are said to have fallen ill and died." See Nuclear Threat Initiative, "Chemical Facilities: Special Industries Organization (SIO)," Iran Profile, Internet Database, <http://www.nti.org/e_research/profiles/Iran/Chemical/2337_2412.html>.

283. Knopf, "Recasting the Proliferation Optimism-Pessimism Debate," p. 72.

284. Glenn Kessler, "Contacts with Tehran Ended: Terrorists in Iran Suspected of Role in Riyadh Blasts," *Washington Post,* May 25, 2003, p. A01.

285. Office of the Secretary of State, *Patterns of Global Terrorism, 2002* (Washington, D.C.: U.S. Department of State, April 2003), <http://www.state.gov/s/ct/rls/pgtrpt/2002>, p. 77.

286. Ibid.

287. Jessica Stern, "The Protean Enemy," *Foreign Affairs* 82, no. 4 (July/August 2003): p. 32.

288. Dana Priest and Douglas Farah, "Iranian Force has Long Ties to Al Qaeda," *Washington Post,* October 14, 2003, p. A17.

289. Kessler, "Contacts with Tehran Ended," p. A01.

290. Office of the Secretary of State, *Patterns of Global Terrorism, 2002,* p. 81. In the 1987 incident, the DPRK is believed to have been behind an in-flight bombing of a Korean Air Lines passenger jet that killed all 115 people on board. According to the Department of State report, while the DPRK has not sponsored a terrorist attack since 1987, it has sold weapons to several terrorist groups and has provided safe haven to several Japanese Red Army Faction members who participated in the hijacking of a Japanese Airlines flight to North Korea in 1970 (ibid.). For details on the DPRK's association with terrorism, see also Council on Foreign Relations, "North Korea," in *Terrorism: Questions and Answers,* <http://www.terrorismanswers.com/sponsors/northkorea2.html>.

7. Conclusions

1. Kenneth N. Waltz, "More May Be Better," in Scott D. Sagan and Kenneth N. Waltz, *The Spread of Nuclear Weapons: A Debate Renewed* (New York: W.W. Norton, 2003), p. 20.

2. Bruce G. Blair, *The Logic of Accidental Nuclear War* (Washington, D.C.: Brookings Institution, 1993), pp. 115–167. For example, a declassified 1975 assessment stated that despite the highly sophisticated nature of some of the system's elements, U.S. command and control was "fragmented, inelastic, fragile, and highly

vulnerable to a surprise nuclear attack." See L. Wainstein et al., "The Evolution of U.S. Strategic Command and Control, and Warning, 1945–1972," Institute for Defense Analyses Study S-467, June 1975, in the National Security Archives, <http://www.gwu.edu/~nsarchiv/nsa/NC/nuchis.html#samp>.

3. For example, the massive explosion at the Ojheri weapons depot in Pakistan caused a temporary breakdown in the telecommunications in the federal capital and at military headquarters (see chapter 5). For an assessment of the vulnerability of Indian and Pakistani military bases and command structures to nuclear or conventional first strikes, see Eric Arnett, "Nuclear Stability and Arms Sales to India: Implications for U.S. Policy," *Arms Control Today* 27, no. 5 (August 1997): pp. 7–11.

4. Ibid., p. 9.

5. Phillip C. Saunders and Jing-done Yuan, "China's Strategic Force Modernization: Issues and Implications for the United States," in *Proliferation Challenges and Nonproliferation Opportunities for New Administrations,* ed. Michael Barletta, Center for Nonproliferation Studies, Occasional Paper No. 4, September 2000, p. 41. China has also warned that if the United States adopts a national missile defense system, it will engage in a rapid buildup of its nuclear arsenal. See Roberto Suro, "Study Sees Possible China Nuclear Buildup," *Washington Post,* August 10, 2000, p. A02.

6. Samina Ahmed, *Countering Nuclear Risks in South Asia* (Washington, D.C.: Council for a Livable World, December 2001), p. 14.

7. It must be noted that part of the reason why the United States created such a large nuclear force, especially the large number of tactical nuclear weapons deployed in Europe, was to help provide extended deterrence—that is, to maintain a credible nuclear deterrent for its allies as well as for itself.

8. See chapter 1.

9. For the discussion of these safety devices, see chapter 2.

10. This fact drew serious criticism in several congressional reviews of the safety of U.S. nuclear weapons, including the 1990 Drell report and the 1991 Kidder report.

11. See chapter 2.

12. For a discussion of these risks, see chapter 3.

13. Russia may be forced to decommission many of its weapons because they have passed their service lives, but so far it has continued to retain many of these weapons after their service lives have expired. See Paul Podvig, "Russian Strategic Forces: Uncertain Future," *Breakthroughs* 7, no. 1 (spring 1998): pp. 11–21, <http://www.armscontrol.ru/transforming/podvig.htm>; Dean A. Wilkening, "The Evolution of Russia's Strategic Nuclear Force," CISAC Publication: Studies in International Security and Arms Control, July 1998, <http://iis-db.stanford.edu/pubs/10334/russianforces.pdf>; and Steve Zaloga, "Russia's Strategic Forces Stumble," *Jane's Intelligence Review* 12, no. 10 (October 2000): pp. 13–14.

14. Neil Joeck, "Nuclear Relations in South Asia," in *Repairing the Regime,* ed. Joseph Cirincione (New York: Routledge, 2000), p. 138.

15. There have also been reports that India and Pakistan assembled their weapons during some crises. Pakistan reportedly assembled at least one weapon during the 1990 Kashmir crisis, and India reportedly placed its nuclear weapons on alert during the 1999 Kargil war. See George Perkovich, *India's Nuclear Bomb: The Impact on Global Proliferation* (Berkeley: University of California Press, 1999), pp. 308–309, and "India's Nuclear Dilemmas," *Economist* 357, no. 8195 (November 6, 2000): p. 45.

16. See chapter 6.

17. Neil Joeck, "Nuclear Relations in South Asia," in *Repairing the Regime,* ed. Joseph Cirincione (New York: Routledge, 2000), p. 141; Colonel Brian Cloughley (Ret.), "Transition Time in Pakistan's Army," *Jane's Intelligence Review,* April 2000, p. 26. The Indian military in particular could have extreme difficulty handling nuclear weapons if they were delivered to the military during a crisis because the military has been forbidden to handle the weapons (Joeck, "Nuclear Relations in South Asia," p. 141). It is also possible that China has not adequately trained its personnel to act under such crisis situations, since China is not believed to have done the extensive training and tests that the United States and Russia have conducted (Terry Hawkins, Director of the Nonproliferation and International Security Division of the Los Alamos National Laboratory, interview by author, November 4, 1998.)

18. See, in particular, Peter D. Feaver, *Guarding the Guardians: Civilian Control of Nuclear Weapons in the United States* (Ithaca: Cornell University Press, 1992), pp. 47–55; Blair, *Logic of Accidental Nuclear War,* pp. 46–52.

19. Amy F. Woolf, "Nuclear Weapons in Russia: Safety, Security, and Control Issues," CRS Issue Brief for Congress, Congressional Research Service, November 5, 2001, pp. 3–4.

20. Ibid. For the risks associated with "delegative" command systems, see Peter D. Feaver, "Command and Control in Emerging Nuclear Nations," *International Security* 17, no. 3 (winter 1992/1993): pp. 168–170.

21. See chapter 3.

22. For a similar argument, see Peter D. Feaver, "Neooptimists and the Enduring Problem of Proliferation," *Security Studies* 6, no. 4 (summer 1997): pp. 113–115.

23. David J. Karl, "Proliferation Pessimism and Emerging Nuclear Powers," *International Security* 21, no. 3 (winter 1996/97): p. 112; Jordan Seng, "Less Is More: Command and Control Advantages of Minor Nuclear States," *Security Studies* 6, no. 4 (summer 1997): pp. 62–67. For a similar argument, see Waltz, "More May Be Better," pp. 20–21, 154.

24. China's arsenal had an estimated twenty warheads at the time of the 1966 test launch, and had increased to roughly one hundred by the time of the Lin Baio Affair in 1971 (Norris et al., *Nuclear Weapons Databook, Vol. V,* p. 359). China's arsenal in 1989 is estimated to have contained 433 warheads (ibid.).

25. Hua Di, "China's Security Dilemma to the Year 2010," Center for International Security and Cooperation report, Stanford University, October 1997, <http://iis-db.stanford.edu/pubs/10222/hua.pdf>, p. 3; Gordon Chang, *The Coming Collapse of China* (New York: Random House, 2001); Minxin Pei, "Future Shock: The WTO and Political Change in China, *Policy Brief* 1, no. 3 (Washington, D.C.: Carnegie Endowment for International Peace, February 2001), pp. 1–7; Minxin Pei, "Will China Become Another Indonesia?" *Foreign Policy,* no. 116 (fall 1999): pp. 94–109; Nathan Busch, "China's Fissile Material Protection, Control, and Accounting: The Case for Renewed Collaboration," *The Nonproliferation Review* 9, no. 3 (fall/winter 2002): pp. 89–106.

26. See chapter 5.

27. See chapter 5.

28. See, for example, Zia Mian, "Walk Softly and Look Ahead in Nuclear South

Asia," *Foreign Policy in Focus,* October 31, 2001, <http://www.fpif.org/pdf/gac/0110seamil.pdf>.

29. Šumit Ganguly, "The Slide Continues," *Foreign Affairs,* April 2003, <http://www.foreignaffairs.org/20030401faupdate11286/sumit-ganguly/the-slide-continues.html>.

30. For example, Lewis Dunn pointed out in 1978 that nearly half of the most likely candidate NWSs had experienced attempted or successful military coups d'etat in the previous decade, and the prospects of long-term political, social, and economic stability for today's aspiring nuclear powers such as Pakistan, Iran, and North Korea remain very questionable at best. See Lewis A. Dunn, "Military Politics, Nuclear Proliferation, and the 'Nuclear Coup d'Etat,'" *Journal of Strategic Studies* 1 (May 1978): p. 31.

31. Kenneth Katzman, *Iraq's Opposition Movements,* CRS Issue Brief, Congressional Research Service, March 26, 1998, <http://www.fas.org/irp/crs/crs-iraq-op.htm>; Paul Reynolds, "Who's Who in Iraq," *BBC News,* August 6, 2002, <http://news.bbc.co.uk/2/hi/middle_east/2174293.stm>; "Iraq after Saddam Hussein," *BBC News,* February 12, 2003, <http://news.bbc.co.uk/1/hi/world/middle_east/1879841.stm>; Kenneth M. Pollack, "A Last Chance to Stop Iraq," *New York Times,* February 21, 2003, p. A27.

32. Indeed, some analysts have described the rapid success of the military invasion as more of a collapse of the regime than a war. See John Keegan, "Saddam's Utter Collapse Shows This Has Not Been a Real War," *Daily Telegraph,* April 8, 2003.

33. For risks of instability in North Korea and Iran, see chapter 6.

34. Joeck, "Nuclear Relations in South Asia," p. 141.

35. Cloughley, "Transition Time in Pakistan's Army," p. 26.

36. See especially Scott D. Sagan, "Nuclear Alerts and Crisis Management," *International Security* 9, no. 4 (spring 1985): pp. 106–124; Scott D. Sagan, *The Limits of Safety: Organizations, Accidents, and Nuclear Weapons* (Princeton: Princeton University Press, 1993), pp. 62–102, 117–155; James G. Blight and David A. Welch, "Risking the Destruction of Nations: Lessons of the Cuban Missile Crisis for New and Aspiring Nuclear States," *Security Studies* 4, no. 4 (summer 1995): pp. 811–850.

37. See chapter 3.

38. The Rumsfeld Commission concluded that Russia's current early-warning and command-and-control systems could increase risks of an inadvertent launch of Russian weapons, especially if relations between the United States and Russia were to worsen, or if Russia feared that the United States was trying to capitalize on a situation of acute civil strife in Russia (Rumsfeld Commission, Report to Congress, section IIC2; Steve Maaranen, Rumsfeld Commission Staff, interview by author, May 14, 1999). See chapter 3.

39. For a similar argument, see Ahmed, *Countering Nuclear Risks in South Asia,* pp. 14–16.

40. For a discussion of several such incidents and their implications, see chapter 5.

41. For example, India's fissile material stockpile was estimated to be somewhere between 240 and 395 kilograms of weapons-grade plutonium at the end of 1999, and Pakistan's stockpile was estimated to be somewhere between 585 and 800 kilograms of weapons-grade uranium. These stockpiles have almost certainly increased

since then, because both countries are believed to be producing fissile materials for their nuclear weapons as rapidly as possible. See David Albright, "India's and Pakistan's Fissile Material and Nuclear Weapons Inventories, End of 1999," Institute for Science and International Security Occasional Paper, October 11, 2000, <http://www.isis-online.org/publications/southasia/stocks1000.html>.

42. Nancy Hayden Prindle, "U.S. and China on Nuclear Arms Control and Nonproliferation: Building on Common Technical Interests," in *Arms Control Issues for the Twenty-First Century,* ed. James Brown (Sandia National Laboratory Publication, SAND97-2619, 1997), p. 322.

43. See chapter 5.

44. For a discussion of the link between inadequate MPC&A and increased risks of rapid, destabilizing proliferation and opportunities for nuclear terrorism, see chapter 1.

45. David E. Sanger, "In North Korea and Pakistan, Deep Roots of Nuclear Barter," *New York Times*, November 24, 2002, p. A1; Gaurav Kampani, "Second-Tier Proliferation: The Case of Pakistan and North Korea," *Nonproliferation Review* 9, no. 3 (fall/winter 2002), pp. 107–116; David E. Sanger and William J. Broad, "From Rogue Nuclear Programs, Web of Trails Leads to Pakistan," *New York Times*, January 4, 2004, p. A1.

46. See chapter 6.

47. See Waltz, "More May Be Better," p. 41; John J. Mearsheimer, "Back to the Future: Instability in Europe After the Cold War," *International Security* 15, no. 1 (summer 1990): p. 37; Bruce Bueno de Mesquita and William H. Riker, "An Assessment of the Merits of Selective Nuclear Proliferation," *Journal of Conflict Resolution* 26, no. 2 (June 1982): p. 303.

48. See chapter 6.

49. See chapter 5.

50. Scott D. Sagan, "Sagan Responds to Waltz," in *A Debate Renewed,* p. 157.

51. Waltz, "More May Be Better," p. 21; Waltz, "Waltz Responds to Sagan," p. 131; Scott D. Sagan, "The Perils of Proliferation: Organization Theory, Deterrence Theory, and the Spread of Nuclear Weapons," *International Security* 18, no. 4 (spring 1994): p. 71.

52. Sagan, "Sagan Responds to Waltz," p. 158.

53. See, for example, the assessment in U.S. Department of Energy, *Increasing Fissile Inventory Assurance within the U.S. Department of Energy,* Office of Independent Oversight and Performance Assurance, January 1995, p. ii, <https://www.oa.doe.gov/reports/ssevalstoc.html>.

54. John W.R. Lepingwell and Nikolai Sokov, "Strategic Offensive Arms Elimination and Weapons Protection, Control, and Accounting," *Nonproliferation Review* 7, no. 1 (spring 2000): p. 68.

55. Wen Hsu, "Chinese Government Restructuring: Organizational Impact on China's Nuclear Establishment and Its Key Players in Arms Control and Nonproliferation," *Nonproliferation Review* 6, no. 4 (fall 1999): p. 165.

56. Lynn M. Hansen, "Arms Control: Focus on Denial and Deception," in *Strategic Denial and Deception: The Twenty-First Century Challenge,* ed. Roy Godson and James J. Wirtz (New Brunswick: Transaction Publishers, 2002), pp. 167–168.

57. See, for example, U.S. National Security Council and White House Office of

Homeland Security, *National Strategy to Combat Weapons of Mass Destruction,* December 2002, <http://www.whitehouse.gov/news/releases/2002/12/WMD Strategy.pdf>.

58. Avner Cohen and Benjamin Frankel, "Opaque Nuclear Proliferation," *Journal of Strategic Studies* 13, no. 3 (September 1990): pp. 21–22.

59. Peter D. Feaver, "Correspondence: Proliferation Pessimism and Emerging Nuclear Powers," *International Security* 22, no. 2 (fall 1997): p. 191. Opacity will necessarily have a major impact on the risks of accidental detonation of nuclear weapons. The majority of the nuclear tests in the United States and the Soviet Union were conducted to assess and improve the safety and reliability of their nuclear weapons.

60. For a summary of the safety and security difficulties in the Indian and Pakistani nuclear programs, see chapter 5.

61. Praful Bidwai and Achin Vanaik, *South Asia on a Short Fuse: Nuclear Politics and the Future of Global Disarmament* (Karachi: Oxford University Press, 2000), pp. 190–194.

62. T.S. Gopi Rethinaraj, "In the Comfort of Secrecy," *Bulletin of the Atomic Scientists* 55, no. 6 (November/December 1999): pp. 52–57; "Limiting Nuclear Hazards," *Dawn,* January 24, 2001.

63. See chapter 5.

64. The Pakistani armed forces were placed on high alert after the August 10, 1999, downing of a Pakistani naval plane by Indian jet fighters, and India's armed forces were placed on high alert after the imposition of military rule in Pakistan on October 12, 1999, by army chief Pervez Musharraf. See Samina Ahmed and David Cortright, *South Asia at the Nuclear Crossroads,* a joint publication by the Managing the Atom Project at Harvard University, the Fourth Freedom Forum, and the Joan B. Kroc Institute for International Peace Studies at the University of Notre Dame, (March 2001), p. 33 n. 5.

65. Seng argues, "if, as pessimists worry, minor proliferators will tend to suffer from domestic instabilities, then central leaders are likely to keep nuclear control organizations as insulated and tightly held as possible" (Seng, "Less Is More," pp. 75–76).

66. See chapter 4.

67. Lewis A. Dunn, *Controlling the Bomb: Nuclear Proliferation in the 1980s* (New Haven: Yale University Press, 1982), p. 72; Scott D. Sagan, "The Perils of Proliferation: Organization Theory, Deterrence Theory, and the Spread of Nuclear Weapons," *International Security* 18, no. 4 (spring 1994): p. 98; and Feaver, "Correspondence," p. 191.

68. Waltz, "More May Be Better," p. 21.

69. See chapter 5.

70. Dunn, *Controlling the Bomb*, p. 72. See also Sagan, "Perils of Proliferation," p. 98, and Feaver, "Correspondence," p. 191.

71. David Karl, for example, asserts that emerging NWSs will never assemble their weapons, and Kenneth Waltz maintains that emerging NWSs will be unlikely to undertake such "irrational" actions as building massive arsenals. See Karl, "Proliferation Pessimism and Emerging Nuclear Powers," pp. 108–109; Waltz, "More May Be Better," pp. 31–32. See also Shaun Gregory, "A Formidable Challenge: Nuclear

Command and Control in South Asia," *Disarmament Diplomacy* 54 (February 2001), <http://www.acronym.org.uk/54greg.htm>.

72. See especially George Perkovich, "A Nuclear Third Way in South Asia," *Foreign Policy,* no. 91 (summer 1993): pp. 85–104; Peter R. Lavoy, "Civil-Military Relations, Strategic Conduct, and the Stability of Nuclear Deterrence in South Asia," in *Civil-Military Relations and Nuclear Weapons,* ed. Scott D. Sagan (Stanford: CISAC Publication, June 1994), pp. 79–109; and Devin Hagerty, "The Power of Suggestion: Opaque Proliferation, Existential Deterrence, and the South Asian Nuclear Arms Competition," in *The Proliferation Puzzle,* ed. Zachary Davis and Benjamin Frankel (Portland, Oreg.: Frank Cass Publishing Co., 1993), pp. 256–283.

73. Indian and Pakistani officials have also claimed, unconvincingly, that they will avoid the dangers of the Cold War. For example, the Indian Army's chief of staff said they "do not want to get into a situation" like "the old days of mutually assured destruction" in the very same speech in which he said that India will develop thermonuclear devices and adopt the deployment system recommended in India's Draft Nuclear Doctrine (which includes a triad of 300–400 weapons deployed in rapid-response configurations). See Rahul Bedi, "'Exclusive Interview' with General Sunderajan Padmanabhan, Indian Army Chief," *Asian Age,* January 16, 2001, pp. 1–2, in FBIS-CHI-2001-0116.

74. See Jack Levy, "Learning and Foreign Policy: Sweeping a Conceptual Minefield," *International Organization* 48, no. 2 (spring 1994): pp. 279–312.

75. Ibid., pp. 288–290.

76. They thus support Peter Feaver's argument that "opacity inhibits a broader public strategic discourse that would increase public scrutiny of these issues and allow for a thorough examination of command-and-control problems." See Feaver, "Correspondence," p. 191.

77. Karl, "Proliferation Pessimism and Emerging Nuclear Powers," p. 114.

78. William Hoehn, "Update on Legislation Affecting U.S.–Former Soviet Union Nonproliferation and Threat Reduction: Summary of Key Provisions in the Fiscal Year 2004 Energy and Water Appropriations and Defense Authorization Conference Agreements," RANSAC report, November 17, 2003, <http://www.ransac.org>.

79. Such assistance might *only* be desirable if it were highly demonstrable that it would be in the U.S. interest or that it would clearly increase international stability. But neither of these is certain, or even likely, as we discuss in the remainder of this section.

80. Feaver, "Correspondence: Proliferation Pessimism and Emerging Nuclear Powers," p. 192. This is especially the case, since the United States has had tempestuous, and at times even hostile relations with many of the states with nuclear ambitions, such as Iran, Syria, and North Korea.

81. See Peter D. Feaver, "Command and Control in Emerging Nuclear Nations," *International Security* 17, no. 3 (winter 1992/93): p. 185; Ahmed, *Countering Nuclear Risks in South Asia,* pp. 14–17.

82. Most optimists agree that a rapid, uncontrolled spread of nuclear weapons would be destabilizing. See Waltz, "More May Be Better," p. 41; John J. Mearsheimer, "Back to the Future: Instability in Europe After the Cold War," *International Security* 15, no. 1 (summer 1990): p. 37; Bruce Bueno de Mesquita and William H. Riker,

"An Assessment of the Merits of Selective Nuclear Proliferation," *Journal of Conflict Resolution* 26, no. 2 (June 1982): p. 303.

83. See, for example, the *Guidelines for IAEA International Physical Protection Advisory Service (IPPAS),* IAEA Services Series, no. 3 (February 1999), <http://www.iaea.org/worldatom/Programmes/Safeguards/Protection/guideline.html>.

84. John Holdren, head of the Science, Technology, and Public Policy Program at Harvard University, interview with author, Harvard University, October 2000.

85. For example, in the context of South Asia, the Pentagon emphasized in a 2001 report that "given the long-standing hostility between [India and Pakistan], even a minor conflict runs the risk of escalating" into a nuclear exchange. See DOD, *Proliferation: Threat and Response,* January 2001 (Washington, D.C.: U.S. Government Printing Office, 2001), p. 30.

86. For a discussion of the Additional Protocol and the "integrated safeguards," see the appendix.

87. For a discussion of Russia's assistance in constructing the Bushehr reactor, see chapter 6.

88. John Larkin, "Up to the Same Old Tricks," *Far Eastern Economic Review* 165, no. 4 (November 21, 2002): p. 16; "N. Korea's Foolish Gamble," editorial, *Los Angeles Times,* November 22, 2002; Anthony Lake and Robert Gallucci, "Negotiating with Nuclear North Korea," *Washington Post,* November 6 2002, p. A21.

89. See, for example, Scowcroft and Kanter, "A Surprising Success on North Korea," p. A35; and Larkin, "Up to the Same Old Tricks," p. 16.

90. See, for example, Daryl G. Kimball, "Fuzzy Nuclear Math," *Arms Control Today* 31, no. 10 (December 2001): p. 2. For a discussion of SORT, see chapters 2 and 3.

91. For some recommendations on preliminary steps toward such a treaty, see William C. Potter and Nikolai Sokov, "Tactical Nuclear Weapons: The Nature of the Problem," report prepared for a discussion session on tactical nuclear weapons organized by the United Nations Institute for Disarmament Research (UNIDIR), Geneva, March 21–22, 2000, <http://cns.miis.edu/pubs/reports/tnw_nat.htm>.

92. For a discussion of the U.S. and Russian Presidential Nuclear Initiatives (PNIs), see chapters 2 and 3.

93. Potter and Sokov, "Tactical Nuclear Weapons," p. 3

94. Steven Mufson, "Russia Summit of Lesser Accords Looming," *Washington Post,* June 2, 2000, p. A01.

95. For a discussion of the ongoing disputes over the JDEC, see chapter 3.

96. For a summary of such suggestions, see Geoffrey Forden, Pavel (Paul) Podvig, and Theodore A. Postol, "False Alarm, Nuclear Danger," *IEEE Spectrum* 37, no. 3 (March 2000): pp. 31–39.

97. See Bruce G. Blair, *Global Zero Alert* (Washington, D.C.: Brookings Institution, 1995); and Bruce G. Blair, Harold A. Feiveson, and Frank N. von Hippel, "Taking Nuclear Weapons off Hair-Trigger Alert," *Scientific American* 277, no. 3 (November 1997): pp. 74–82. Former U.S. senator Sam Nunn made a similar proposal in 2003. See Walter Pincus, "Nunn Urges U.S., Russia to Ease Hair-Trigger Nuclear Alerts," *Washington Post,* May 22, 2003, p. A23.

98. For a discussion of the Moscow Treaty, or SORT, see chapter 2.

99. For a summary of these suggestions, see Amy F. Woolf, "Nuclear Weapons

in Russia: Safety, Security, and Control Issues," Congressional Research Service Report, March 1, 1999, p. 15.

100. Ibid., p. 16.

101. Ibid.

102. Howard Baker and Lloyd Cutler, *A Report Card on the Department of Energy's Nonproliferation Programs with Russia,* Russia Task Force, the Secretary of Energy Advisory Board, U.S. Department of Energy, January 10, 2001, p. iv; Walter Pincus, "$30 Billion Urged for Russian Nuclear Security," *Washington Post,* January 9, 2001, p. A21.

103. Matthew Bunn, Oleg Bukharin, and Kenneth N. Luongo, "Renewing the Partnership: One Year Later," in *Proceedings of the 42nd Annual Meeting of the Institute for Nuclear Materials Management* (Northbrook, Ill.: INMM, 2001), pp. 1–2.

104. "Text: U.S., Russia to Step-Up Efforts to Safeguard Nuclear Materials," *Washington File,* U.S. Department of State, December 4, 2001.

105. Philipp C. Bleek, "DOE Threat Reduction Funding Cut, Programs Reorganized," *Arms Control Today,* December 2001.

106. Russian-American Nuclear Security Advisory Council (RANSAC), "Russian-American Experts Applaud Bush Administration Budget for Cooperative Nuclear Security Programs," February 4, 2002, <http://www.ransac.org/Projects%20and%20Publications/News/News%20Releases/pr_020702.html>.

107. RANSAC, "Preliminary Report: Anticipated FY2003 Budget Request for Department of Energy Cooperative Nuclear Security Programs in Russia," January 9, 2002, <http://www.ransac.org/>; William Hoehn, "Update on Legislation Affecting U.S.–Former Soviet Union Nonproliferation and Threat Reduction: Summary of Key Provisions in the Fiscal Year 2004 Energy and Water Appropriations and Defense Authorization Conference Agreements," RANSAC report, November 17, 2003, <http://www.ransac.org>.

108. See *The G8 Global Partnership Against the Spread of Weapons and Materials of Mass Destruction,* Statement by the Group of Eight Leaders, Kananaskis, Canada, June 27, 2002, <http://www.state.gov/e/eb/rls/othr/11514.htm>.

109. For an excellent discussion of the "10 plus 10 over 10" initiative, as well as the concerns about its implementation, see Richard Lugar, "The Next Steps in U.S. Nonproliferation Policy," *Arms Control Today* 32, no. 10 (December 2002): pp. 3–5.

110. Matthew Bunn, Oleg Bukharin, and Kenneth N. Luongo, "Renewing the Partnership: One Year Later," in *Proceedings of the 42nd Annual Meeting of the Institute for Nuclear Materials Management* (Northbrook, Ill.: INMM, 2001), p. 1.

111. Kenneth Baker, congressional testimony, Hearing of the International Security, Proliferation and Federal Services Subcommittee of the Senate Governmental Affairs Committee, November 29, 2001.

112. For a much more extensive set of policy recommendations, see National Research Council, *Protecting Nuclear Weapons Material in Russia,* pp. 17–36; William C. Potter and Fred Wehling, "Sustainability: A Vital Component of Nuclear Material Security in Russia," *Nonproliferation Review* 7, no. 1 (spring 2000): pp. 182–187; Matthew Bunn, *The Next Wave: Urgently Needed New Steps to Control Warheads and Fissile Materials* (Carnegie Endowment for International Peace and Harvard University, 2000); and Oleg Bukharin, Matthew Bunn, and Kenneth N.

Luongo, *Renewing the Partnership: Recommendations for Accelerated Action to Secure Nuclear Material in the Former Soviet Union* (Washington, D.C.: Russian American Nuclear Security Advisory Council, 2000).

113. Nathan Busch, Maria Katsva, Igor Khriponiv, and Dmiriy Nokonov, *The Human Factor and Security Culture: Challenges to Safeguarding Fissile Materials in Russia,* ed. Igor Khriponov and James Holmes, CITS Occasional Report (Athens, Ga.: University of Georgia, November 2002), pp. 24–28.

114. I make this case in Nathan Busch, "China's Fissile Material Protection, Control, and Accounting: The Case for Renewed Collaboration," *Nonproliferation Review* 9, no. 3 (fall/winter 2002): pp. 89–106. Some of the following recommendations are based on that discussion.

115. This is probably why the United States has refused to give China information about U.S. PALs.

116. Willy Wo-Lap Lam, "China, U.S. Boost Ties Against Terrorism," <http://www.cnn.com>, October 19, 2001; Embassy of the People's Republic of China in the United States, "China, US Reach Consensus on Anti-Terrorism," December 6, 2001, <http://www.china-embassy.org/eng/22013.html>; "What the Presidents Said," *CNN.com,* October 19, 2001, <http://www.cnn.com>.

117. Alternatively, it might be possible to expand the Cooperative Threat Reduction program to include countries other than Russia. Richard Lugar, one of the original cosponsors of the CTR Program, has proposed precisely this plan, particularly in order to improve nuclear security in India and Pakistan. (See Kerry Boyd, "India-Pakistan: Analysts Propose to Safeguard South Asian Arsenals," *Global Security Newswire,* March 18, 2002.) But it might be possible to include MPC&A collaborations with China under such a proposed plan as well. Indeed, in some ways, it might be easier to justify expanding CTR to include MPC&A collaborations with China, since these collaborations would not be complicated by risks of condoning the nuclear programs in non-NPT states, as it would with India and Pakistan.

118. The author would like to thank Wen Hsu for these suggestions.

119. This was the experience in the U.S.-Russia collaborative programs. After long denying U.S. scientists access to Russia's most sensitive facilities, Russia signed an agreement with the United States in 2001 to open most of its remaining facilities to rapid MPC&A improvements. Following on these provisions, the U.S. Department of Energy secretary Spencer Abraham and the Russian minister of atomic energy Alexander Rumyantsev announced an agreement on November 29, 2001, to expand and accelerate efforts to improve Russia's MPC&A. See Matthew Bunn, Oleg Bukharin, and Kenneth N. Luongo, "Renewing the Partnership: One Year Later," in *Proceedings of the 42nd Annual Meeting of the Institute for Nuclear Materials Management* (Northbrook, Ill.: INMM, 2001), pp. 1–2; and U.S. Department of State, "Text: U.S., Russia to Step-Up Efforts to Safeguard Nuclear Materials," *Washington File,* December 4, 2001, pp. 1–2.

120. For a discussion of inconsistent U.S. nonproliferation policies toward India and Pakistan during and after the Cold War, see Samina Ahmed and David Cortright, *South Asia at the Nuclear Crossroads,* a joint publication by the Managing the Atom Project at Harvard University, the Fourth Freedom Forum, and the Joan B. Kroc Institute for International Peace Studies at the University of Notre Dame (March 2001), pp. 4–18.

121. For a discussion of the easing of U.S. nonproliferation efforts in South Asia after September 11, 2001, see Ahmed, *Countering Nuclear Risks in South Asia,* pp. 9–14.

122. Ibid., p. 16.

123. Ibid.

124. For a discussion of the Lahore Declaration, see chapter 5.

125. See *Guidelines for IAEA International Physical Protection Advisory Service (IPPAS).*

126. Wolfsthal, "U.S. Needs A Contingency Plan," p. 17.

127. Peter Finn, "Experts Discuss Chances of Nuclear Terrorism," *Washington Post,* November 3, 2001, p. A19.

128. For a discussion of the limitations of the 1980 Convention and the necessity for strengthened physical protection regulations, see Bonnie D. Jenkins, "Establishing International Standards for Physical Protection of Nuclear Material," *Nonproliferation Review* 5, no. 3 (spring–summer 1998): pp. 98–110.

129. David Ruppe, "International Response: IAEA Board Approves New Security Plan," *Global Security Newswire,* March 20, 2002, <http://www.nti.org/d_newswire/issues/2002/3/20/6s.html>.

130. Waltz, "More May Be Better," p. 21.

131. Kenneth N. Waltz, *Theory of International Politics* (New York: McGraw-Hill, 1979), pp. 121–123. Although this statement specifically relates to Waltz's theory of structural realism, his arguments on nuclear proliferation are based on the same assumptions.

132. Jeffrey W. Knopf, "Recasting the Proliferation Optimism-Pessimism Debate," *Security Studies* 12, no. 1 (autumn 2003): pp. 47–54.

Appendix

1. Guidance and Considerations for Implementation of INFCIRC/225/Rev.3, par. 401.

2. Ibid. par. 402.

3. *Integrated Demonstration of Materials, Protection, Control, and Accountability,* Los Alamos National Laboratory Unclassified Publication, June 1998, LALP-98-65, p. 6; see also Jason D. Ellis and Todd E. Perry, "Nunn-Lugar's Unfinished Agenda," *Arms Control Today* 27, no. 3 (October 1997): p. 16, <http://www.armscontrol.org/act/1997_10/nunnoct.asp>.

4. Ellis and Perry, "Nunn-Lugar's Unfinished Agenda," p. 16.

5. In the context of the IAEA, "safeguards" are the collective system of audits and on-site inspections intended to verify that the use of nuclear energy is exclusively for peaceful purposes. See Rodney W. Jones, Mark G. McDonough, with Toby Dalton and Gregory Koblentz, *Tracking Nuclear Proliferation: A Guide in Maps and Charts, 1998* (Washington, D.C.: Carnegie Endowment for International Peace, 1998), p. 16.

6. David Fischer, *History of the International Atomic Energy Agency: The First Forty Years* (International Atomic Energy Agency, 1997), p. 246.

7. Quoted in Fischer, *History of the International Atomic Energy Agency,* p. 249.

8. Ibid.

9. "International Atomic Energy Agency," Center for Nonproliferation Studies web database, Monterey Institute for International Studies, <http://www.nti.org/db/china/iaeaorg.ht>. For the text of INFCIRC/66, see the IAEA web page: <http://www.iaea.org/Publications/Documents/Infcircs/Others/inf66r2.shtml>.

10. INFCIRC/66, Articles 33–40.

11. Cuba acceded to the treaty on November 4, 2002. See "Cuba Accedes to NPT, Joins Tlatelolco," *Arms Control Today* 32, no. 10 (December 2002), p. 26.

12. For a discussion of "opaque" nuclear weapons programs, see Avner Cohen and Benjamin Frankel, "Opaque Nuclear Proliferation," *Journal of Strategic Studies* 13, no.3 (September 1990): pp. 14–44.

13. These safeguards are quite similar to the safeguards set out in INCIFC/153, though with small differences (due to no risk of *diversion* of materials into a covert nuclear weapons program). For details in the commitments that the NWS undertook in these voluntary offers, see the IAEA website: "The Safeguards System of the International Atomic Energy Agency," <http://www.iaea.org/OurWork/SV/Safeguards/safeg_system.pdf> and Fischer, *History of the International Atomic Energy Agency,* pp. 271–272.

14. INFCIRC/153, section I.7.

15. INFCIRC/153, par. 72.

16. Ibid., par. 73.

17. For routine inspections, the inspections must occur at least twenty-four hours after notification; in special inspections, the inspections should take place "as soon as possible" after notification.

18. *Nuclear Nonproliferation: Uncertainties with Implementing IAEA's Strengthened Safeguards System,* GAO Report, July 1998, GAO/NSIAD/RCED-98-184, pp. 6–7.

19. Ibid., pp. 7–8. This document not only provides an excellent summary of the new measures included in the Strengthened Safeguards system, but it also assesses the feasibility of these measures, given current IAEA funding levels.

20. For a list of these countries, see the IAEA website: <http://www.iaea.org/OurWork/SV/Safeguards/sg_protocol.html>.

21. IAEA, "Strengthening the Effectiveness and Improving the Efficiency of the Safeguards System and Application of the Model Protocol," IAEA General Conference report, August 16, 2000, <http://www.iaea.org/About/Policy/GC/GC44/Documents/gc44-12.pdf>, p. 7.

22. Ibid., p. 8.

23. SSAC is sometimes distinguished from MC&A. When a distinction is made, the MC&A refers to the accounting and control over nuclear materials at a specific nuclear facility, while SSAC refers to the overall state coordination of the MC&A programs. See Annette Schaper, "The Case for Universal Full-Scope Safeguards on Nuclear Material," *Nonproliferation Review* 5, no. 2 (winter 1998): p. 74. I do not make a similar distinction, however, because these terms are in fact often used synonymously.

24. INFCIRC/153 does not describe any specific requirements for material control systems. While specific agreements between the IAEA and individual countries reportedly do contain provisions for material control, these agreements generally are confidential.

25. See Bonnie D. Jenkins, "Establishing International Standards for Physical

Protection of Nuclear Material," *Nonproliferation Review* 5, no. 3 (spring–summer 1998): p. 98.

26. Several additional documents help establish physical protection norms, although they do not explicitly create any physical protection regulations. For example, the Nuclear Safety Convention (which convened in 1994 and was codified in INFCIRC/449) establishes safety standards for "land-based civil nuclear power plants under [IAEA] jurisdiction including such storage, handling and treatment facilities for radioactive materials that are on the same site and are directly related to the operation of the nuclear power plant." This does not apply to weapons facilities, however.

27. Jenkins, "Establishing International Standards for Physical Protection of Nuclear Material," p. 100.

28. It was revised in 1977, 1989, 1993, and 1998. For a brief history of the PPC and INFCIRC/225, see Jenkins, "Establishing International Standards for Physical Protection of Nuclear Material," pp. 99–100.

29. Although this document is probably the best standard to use, there have been other, more rigorous, recommendations for physical protection. For example, the National Academy of Sciences recommends a separate standard for facilities that store weapons-useable plutonium. See National Academy of Sciences, *Management and Disposition of Excess Weapons Plutonium* (Washington, D.C.: National Academy Press, 1994), available at <http://www.nap.edu/books/0309050421/html/index.html>.

30. INFCIRC/254/Rev.2, Annex C.

31. For a more thorough discussion of international agreements that refer to INFCIRC/225, see Jenkins, "Establishing International Standards for Physical Protection of Nuclear Material," pp. 102–103.

32. Sabotage is defined as "Any deliberate act directed against a nuclear facility or nuclear material in use, storage or transport which could directly or indirectly endanger the health and safety of personnel, the public and the environment by exposure to radiation or release of radioactive substances" (INFCIRC/225/Rev.4, section 2.12).

33. Ibid., section 2.2.a.

34. Ibid., section 4.2.5.1.

35. The requirements outlined in INFCIRC/225 are more extensive than I can describe here. I try to summarize as many of the major points as possible.

Bibliography

Note: All Internet web pages were active as of December 1, 2003.

Primary Sources, Intelligence Reports, Congressional Testimony

1972 ABM treaty and subsequent amendment. <http://www.state.gov/www/global/arms/treaties/abm/abm2.html>.

Armitage, Richard. Testimony before the Senate Foreign Relations Committee. Hearings on WMD Developments on the Korean Peninsula. 108th Congress, February 4, 2003.

Bailey, Kathleen. U.S. Senate Armed Services Committee, Subcommittee on Strategic Forces. 105th Congress, March 31, 1998. <http://www.senate.gov/~armed_services/statemnt/980331kb.htm>.

Baker, Howard, and Lloyd Cutler. *A Report Card on the Department of Energy's Nonproliferation Programs with Russia.* Washington, D.C.: Russia Task Force, the Secretary of Energy Advisory Board, U.S. Department of Energy, January 10, 2001.

Baker, Kenneth. Hearing of the International Security, Proliferation and Federal Services Subcommittee of the Senate Governmental Affairs Committee. Congressional testimony, 107th Congress, November 29, 2001.

Bosworth, Stephen. Testimony before the Senate Foreign Relations Committee, Hearings on WMD Developments on the Korean Peninsula. 108th Congress, February 4, 2003.

Central Intelligence Agency. *Unclassified Report to Congress on the Acquisition of Technology Relating to Weapons of Mass Destruction and Advanced Conventional Munitions, 1 January through 30 June 2003.* November 2003. <http://www.cia.gov/cia/reports/721_reports/jan_jun2003.htm>.

———. *Unclassified Report to Congress on the Acquisition of Technology Relating to Weapons of Mass Destruction and Advanced Conventional Munitions, 1 January through 30 June 2002.* April 10, 2003. <http://www.cia.gov/cia/reports/721_reports/jan_jun2002.html>.

———. *Iraq's Weapons of Mass Destruction Programs.* Washington, D.C.: U.S. Central Intelligence Agency, October 2002. <http://www.cia.gov/cia/reports/iraq_wmd/Iraq_Oct_2002.pdf>.

———. *CIA World Factbook 2002*. <http://www.cia.gov/cia/publications/factbook/index.html>.

———. *Special National Intelligence Estimate: Security Conditions in China*. Washington, D.C.: Central Intelligence Agency, 1972. <http://www.gwu.edu/%7Ensarchiv/NSAEBB/NSAEBB19/04-02.htm>.

Clinton, William J. "The Iraq Liberation Act." Statement by the President of the United States, Office of the Press Secretary, October 31, 1998. <http://www.library.cornell.edu/colldev/mideast/libera.htm>.

Defense Intelligence Agency. "Nuclear Weapons Systems in China." *Defense Estimate Brief*. Defense Intelligence Agency, April 24, 1984. <http://www.gwu.edu/~nsarchiv/news/19990527/01–01.htm>.

Dingell, John D. (Chairman of the Subcommittee on Oversight and Investigations). Subcommittee on Oversight and Investigations of the Committee on Energy and Commerce. *Safeguards at DOE's Nuclear Weapons Facilities,* 101st Congress, 1st session, July 30, 1989.

Drell, S.D, J.S. Foster Jr., and C.H. Townes. *Report of the Panel on Nuclear Weapons Safety*. Washington, D.C.: House Armed Services Committee, December 1990.

ElBaradei, Mohammed. *Transcript of ElBaradei's U.N. Presentation,* March 7, 2003. <http://www.cnn.com/2003/US/03/07/sprj.irq.un.transcript.elbaradei>.

Duelfer, Charles. Testimony to the U.S. Congress. 30 March 2004. <http://www.cia.gov/cia/public_affairs/speeches/2004/tenet_testimony_03302004.html>.

Hart, Gary, and Barry Goldwater (Senators). Committee on Armed Services. *Recent False Alerts from the Nation's Missile Attack Warning System,* 96th Congress, 2nd session, October 9, 1980.

House Subcommittee of the Committee on Government Operations, *Failures of the North American Aerospace Defense Command's (NORAD) Attack Warning System,* 97th Cong., 1st session, U.S. House of Representatives, May 19–20, 1981.

General Accounting Office. *Nuclear Security: NNSA Needs to Better Manage Its Safeguards and Security Program*. Report to the Chairman, Subcommittee on National Security, Emerging Threats, and International Relations, Committee on Government Reforms. U.S. House of Representatives, May 2003.

———. "Nuclear Nonproliferation: Uncertainties with Implementing IAEA's Strengthened Safeguards System." Washington, D.C.: General Accounting Office Report, GAO/NSIAD/RCED-98-184, July 1998.

———. "Weapons of Mass Destruction: Reducing the Threat from the Former Soviet Union: An Update." Washington, D.C.: U.S. General Accounting Office. GAO/NSIAD-95-165. June 9, 1995.

———. "Nuclear Nonproliferation and Safety: Challenges Facing the International Atomic Energy Agency." Washington, D.C.: United States General Accounting Office, GAO/NSIAD/RCED-93-284, 1993.

———. "Nuclear Safety: Potential Security Weaknesses at Los Alamos and Other DOE Facilities." Washington, D.C.: General Accounting Office, GAO/RCED-91-12, October 11, 1990.

Grey, Robert T., Jr. (Ambassador). Statement at the Conference on Disarmament, Geneva, February 15, 2001. <http://www.us-mission.ch/press2001/0215grey.htm>.

International Atomic Energy Agency. *Guidelines for IAEA International Physical Protection Advisory Service (IPPAS).* IAEA Services Series, No. 3, February 1999. <http://www.iaea.org/worldatom/Programmes/Safeguards/Protection/guideline.html>.

———. "India: Nuclear Power Reactors." Power Reactor Information System. <http://www.iaea.org/programmes/a2/index.html>.

———. "China: Nuclear Power Reactors." Power Reactor Information System. <http://www.iaea.org/programmes/a2/index.html>.

———. INFCIRC/66/Rev.2. <http://www.iaea.org/Publications/Documents/Infcircs/Others/inf66r2.shtml>.

———. INFCIRC/153. <http://www.iaea.org/Publications/Documents/Infcircs/Others/inf153.shtml>.

———. INFCIRC/225/Rev.4 <http://www.iaea.org/worldatom/Programmes/Protection/inf225rev4/rev4_content.html>

———. INFCIRC/274. <http://www.iaea.org/Publications/Documents/Infcircs/2000/infcirc274r1a7.pdf>.

———. INFCIRC/369. <http://www.nti.org/db/china/engdocs/iaea369.htm>.

———. INFCIRC/549. <http://www.iaea.org/Publications/Documents/Infcircs/1998/infcirc549.pdf>.

———. "The Safeguards System of the International Atomic Energy Agency." <http://www.iaea.org/OurWork/SV/Safeguards/safeg_system.pdf>.

———. "Strengthening the Effectiveness and Improving the Efficiency of the Safeguards System and Application of the Model Protocol." IAEA General Conference report, August 16, 2000. <http://www.iaea.org/About/Policy/GC/GC44/Documents/gc44-12.pdf>.

Johnson, Lyndon. *Memorandum for the Secretary of Defense,* March 26, 1964. <http://www.gwu.edu/~nsarchiv/news/predelegation/pd16_02.htm>.

Joint Chiefs of Staff. *Instructions for Expenditure of Nuclear Weapons in Emergency Conditions,* c. December 1959, <http://www.gwu.edu/~nsarchiv/news/predelegation/predel.htm>.

Kay, David A. "Statement on the Interim Progress Report on the Activities of the Iraq Survey Group." Congressional testimony before the House Permanent Select Committee on Intelligence, the House Committee on Appropriations, Subcommittee on Defense, and the Senate Select Committee on Intelligence. October 2, 2003. <http://www.cia.gov/cia/public_affairs/speeches/2003/david_kay_10022003.html>.

Kelly, James A. (Assistant Secretary of State for East Asian and Pacific Affairs). Testimony before the Senate Foreign Relations Committee, Regional Implications of the Changing Nuclear Equation on the Korean Peninsula. U.S. Senate Hearings. March 12, 2003.

Kidder, R.E. *Report to Congress: Assessment of the Safety of U.S. Nuclear Weapons and Related Nuclear Test Requirements.* Washington, D.C., July 26, 1991.

Los Alamos National Laboratory, *Los Alamos National Laboratory Nuclear Weapons Program: Focus on the Stockpile.* Los Alamos, N.M. LALP-97-134. November 1998. <http://www.ceip.org/files/nonprolif/templates/article.asp?NewsID=3877>.

———. "Russian-American Collaborations to Reduce the Nuclear Danger." *Los Alamos Science,* no. 24 (1996): pp. 1–82.

———. *Integrated Demonstration of Materials Protection, Control, and Accountability.* Los Alamos National Laboratory Unclassified Publication, June 1998. LALP-98-65.

National Intelligence Council. *Global Trends 2015: A Dialogue about the Future with Nongovernmental Experts.* Washington, D.C.: National Intelligence Council, December 2000. <http://www.cia.gov/cia/reports/globaltrends2015/globaltrends2015.pdf>.

National Nuclear Security Administration. *Disposing of Surplus U.S. Highly Enriched Uranium.* Office of Fissile Material Disposition. <http://www.nnsa.doe.gov/na-26/heu.htm>.

———. *Disposing of Surplus U.S. Plutonium.* Office of Fissile Material Disposition. <http://www.nnsa.doe.gov/na-26/pu.htm>.

Niksch, Larry A. "North Korea's Nuclear Weapons Program." Congressional Research Service. Issue Brief for Congress. December 6, 2001 (updated August 27, 2003). <http://fas.org/spp/starwars/crs/IB91141.pdf>.

Nuclear Regulatory Commission."Physical Fitness Training Reference Manual for Security Force Personnel at Fuel Cycle Facilities Possessing Formula Quantities of Special Nuclear Materials." Washington, D.C.: U.S. Nuclear Regulatory Commission. NUREG/CR-5690. September 1991.

———. "Personnel and Vehicle Barriers at Fuel Fabrication Facilities Using or Possessing Formula Quantities of Strategic Special Nuclear Material." Washington, D.C.: Division of Safeguards and Transportation, Office of Nuclear Material Safety and Security, U.S. Nuclear Regulatory Commission. NUREG-1330. December 1988.

Office of Technology Assessment, U.S. Congress. *Technologies Underlying Weapons of Mass Destruction.* Washington, D.C.: U.S. Government Printing Office, OTA-BP-ISC-115, December 1993.

Office of the Prime Minister of India, "Cabinet Committee on Security Reviews Progress in Operationalizing India's Nuclear Doctrine," press release, Press Information Bureau, January 4, 2003. <http://pib.nic.in/archieve/lreleng/lyr2003/rjan2003/04012003/r040120033.html>.

Pavlov, Gennadi. Congressional Testimony before the Subcommittee on European Affairs of the Committee on Foreign Relations. *Command and Control of Soviet Nuclear Weapons: Dangers and Opportunities Arising from the August Revolution,* September 21, 1991.

Potter, William. Permanent Subcommittee on Investigations, U.S. Senate Committee on Governmental Affairs. "Nuclear Leakage from the Post-Soviet States," March 13, 1996. <http://cns.miis.edu/pubs/reports/senoral.htm>.

Powell, Colin (Secretary of State). Remarks to the United Nations Security Council, February 5, 2003. <http://www.state.gov/secretary/rm/2003/17300.htm>.

Rezendes, Victor S. "Key factors underlying security problems at DOE facilities." Statement of, Director, Energy, Resources, and Science Issues, Resources, Community, and Economic Development Division: testimony before the Subcommittee on Oversight and Investigations, Committee on Commerce, House of Representatives. Washington, D.C.: U.S. General Accounting Office, (1999). Report Number: GAO/T-RCED-99-159.

Rubin, James. Paper presented at the Department of State Daily Briefing. February 10, 1999.

Rumsfeld Commission to Assess the Ballistic Missile Threat. Report to Congress, section IIC2. Washington, D.C., July 15, 1998. <http://www.house.gov/hasc/testimony/105thcongress/BMThreat.htm>

Sikorski, Gerry (Rep. of Minnesota), Hearing before the Subcommittee on Oversight and Investigations of the Committee on Energy and Commerce. *Summarizing the Findings of the 1982 Hearings, in Safeguards at DOE's Nuclear Weapons Facilities,* 101st Congress, 1st session, July 30, 1989.

Tenet, George. Speech given at Georgetown University. "Iraq and Weapons of Mass Destruction." February 5, 2004. <http://www.cia.gov/cia/public_affairs/speeches/2004/tenet_georgetownspeech_02052004.html>.

———. Senate Select Committee on Intelligence. *The Worldwide Threat in 2003: Evolving Dangers in a Complex World.* February 11, 2003. <http://www.cia.gov/cia/public_affairs/speeches/dci_speech_02112003.html>.

———. Senate Select Committee on Intelligence. "The Worldwide Threat in 2003: Evolving Dangers in a Complex World." February 11, 2003. <http://www.cia.gov/cia/public_affairs/speeches/2003/dci_speech_02112003.html>.

———. Testimony before the Senate Select Committee on Intelligence. "Worldwide Threat—Converging Dangers in a Post 9/11 World." February 6, 2002.

———. Senate Armed Services Committee Hearing on Current and Projected National Security Threats. February 2, 1999.

Thomson, David B. *The START Treaties: Implementation and Status.* Los Alamos, N.M.: Center for International Security Affairs Publication, Los Alamos National Laboratory. LA-UR-97–2045. May 1997.

U.S. Department of Defense. "Report on the Military Power of the People's Republic of China." Annual report to Congress. June 22, 2002. <http://www.defenselink.mil/news/Jun2000/china06222000.htm>.

———. "2001 Nuclear Posture Review." Department of Defense Report to Congress, December 31, 2001. <http://www.globalsecurity.org/wmd/library/policy/dod/npr.htm>.

———. *Proliferation: Threat and Response.* U.S. Department of Defense Report. Washington, D.C.: U.S. Government Printing Office, January 2001. <http://www.defenselink.mil/pubs/ptr20010110.pdf>.

———. *Future Military Capabilities and Strategy of the People's Republic of China.* Department of Defense Report to Congress, October 1998.

———. "The Cooperative Threat Reduction Program." *Proliferation: Threat and Response.* Washington, D.C.: U.S. Government Printing Office, 1997.

———. *1995 Annual Defense Report,* available at the Federation of American Scientists website, "Department of Defense Nuclear Posture Review." <http://www.fas.org/nuke/guide/usa/doctrine/dod/95_npr.htm>.

———. *1995 Nuclear Posture Review,* Office of the Executive Secretary. <http://www.defenselink.mil/execsec/adr95/npr_.html>.

———. *Soviet Military Power, 1987.* Washington, D.C.: U.S. Government Printing Office, 1987.

U.S. Department of Energy. *Follow-Up Special Study of Nuclear Material Control and Accountability Programs Across the Department of Energy.* Office of Independent Oversight and Performance Assurance, U.S. Department of Energy, November 2000. <https://www.oa.doe.gov/reports/ssevalstoc.html>.

———. "Control and Accountability of Nuclear Materials." Washington, D.C.: DOE O 474.1, 1998.

———. Office of Oversight. *Follow-Up Review of Fissile Material Assurance in the Department of Energy Complex.* July 1998. <https://www.oa.doe.gov/reports/ssevalstoc.html>.

———. "Cooperation between the Russian Federation and the United States to Enhance the Existing Nuclear Material, Protection, Control, and Accounting Systems at Mayak Production Association." *Partnership for Nuclear Security.* Washington, D.C.: Department of Energy Nuclear Material Security Task Force. December 1997.

———. "US/Russian Cooperation on Protection, Control, and Accounting for Naval Nuclear Fuel." *Partnership for Nuclear Security.* Washington, D.C.: Department of Energy Nuclear Material Security Task Force. December 1997.

———. "U.S./Russian Program in Material, Protection, Control, and Accounting at the RRC Kurchatov Institute: 1996–1997." *Partnership for Nuclear Security.* Washington, D.C.: Department of Energy Nuclear Material Security Task Force. December 1997.

———. *Interim Report on the Status of Safeguards and Security in the Department of Energy.* Washington, D.C.: U.S. Department of Energy, Office of Oversight, November 1997. <https://www.oa.doe.gov/reports/ssevalstoc.html>.

———. Office of Arms Control and Nonproliferation. "Final Nonproliferation and Arms Control Assessment of Weapons-Usable Fissile Material Storage and Excess Plutonium Disposition Alternatives." Washington, D.C.: DOE, DOE/NN-0007, January 13, 1997, pp. 66–68.

———. *Plutonium: The First Fifty Years: United States Plutonium Production, Acquisition and Utilization from 1944 to 1994.* Section 10.2. Washington, D.C.: Department of Energy. February 1996. <http://www.osti.gov/html/osti/opennet/document/pu50yrs/pu50y.html#ZZ0>.

———. *Increasing Fissile Inventory Assurance within the U.S. Department of Energy.* Washington, D.C.: Office of Independent Oversight and Performance Assurance, U.S. Department of Energy. January 1995. <http://tis.eh.doe.gov/iopa/reports/specrevs/9501fissile/fis_rep.pdf>.

———. "Guide for Implementation of DOE 5633.A." Office of Safeguards and Security, U.S. Department of Energy, February 1993. <http://tis.eh.doe.gov/iopa/reports/specrevs/9807followup/fissile.pdf>.

———. *Safeguards and Security (S&S) Standardization Program.* U.S. Department of Energy, DOE 5630.17, September 29, 1992.

———. "Declassification of the United States Total Production of Highly Enriched Uranium." Office of the Press Secretary, U.S. Department of Energy. <http://www.osti.gov/html/osti/opennet/document/press/pc13.html>.

U.S. Department of State, *Patterns of Global Terrorism, 2002.* Washington, D.C.: Office of the U.S. Department of State, April 2003. <http://www.state.gov/s/ct/rls/pgtrpt/2002>.

———. "Text: U.S., Russia to Step-Up Efforts to Safeguard Nuclear Materials." *Washington File:* U.S. Department of State, December 4, 2001.

———. "Pakistani Nuclear Program," State Department Briefing Paper. June 23, 1983. <http://www.gwu.edu/~nsarchiv/NSAEBB/NSAEBB6/ipn22_6.htm>.

U.S. House of Representatives. Select Committee on U.S. National Security and Military/Commercial Concerns with the People's Republic of China. *U.S. National Security and Military/Commercial Concerns with the People's Republic of China.* U.S. House of Representatives. Submitted by Rep. Christopher Cox. Washington, D.C.: Government Printing Office, 1999. <www.access.gpo.gov/congress/house/hr105851/>.

U.S. National Security Council and White House Office of Homeland Security. *National Strategy to Combat Weapons of Mass Destruction.* December 2002. <http://www.whitehouse.gov/news/releases/2002/12/WMDStrategy.pdf>.

U.S. White House. *A National Security Strategy for a Global Age.* December 2000. <http://www.globalsecurity.org/military/library/policy/national/nss-0012.pdf>.

Wainstein, L., C.D. Cremeans, J.K. Moriarity, and J. Ponturo. "The Evolution of U.S. Strategic Command and Control, and Warning, 1945–1972." Arlington, Va.: Institute for Defense Analyses, June 1975. <http://www.gwu.edu/~nsarchiv/nsa/NC/nuchis.html#samp>.

Wolf, John. Speech to the Second Session of the Preparatory Committee for the 2005 Review Conference of the Parties to the Treaty on the Non-Proliferation of Nuclear Weapons. *Washington File.* April 28, 2003.

Wolfowitz, Paul (Deputy Secretary of Defense). "Iraq: What Does Disarmament Look Like?" Speech given at the Council on Foreign Relations, New York, N.Y., January 23, 2003.

Woolf, Amy. "Nuclear Weapons in Russia: Safety, Security, and Control Issues." Congressional Research Service Report to Congress. March 1, 1999 (updated June 25, 2003).

———. "Nuclear Weapons in the Former Soviet Union: Location, Command, and Control." Congressional Research Service Brief, no. 91144. November 27, 1996. <http://www.fas.org/spp/starwars/crs/91–144.htm>.

Woolf, Amy F., and Kara Wilson. "Russia's Nuclear Forces: Doctrine and Force Structure Issues." Washington, D.C.: Congressional Research Service Report. May 23, 1997.

Woolsey, James. Congressional Testimony before the Committee on National Security. "Threats to United States National Security," February 12, 1998. <http://commdocs.house.gov/committees/security/has043000.000/has043000_1.htm>.

Newspapers and Periodicals

Aerospace Daily

AFP (Agence France-Presse)

All India Radio Network (New Delhi)

Asian Age (New Delhi)

Asiaweek

The Associated Press (New York)

The Australian (Sydney)

BBC News (London)

Boston Globe

CBS News.com

Dawn (Karachi)

The Denver Post

Deutsche Presse-Agentur (Hamburg)

Die Tageszeitung (Berlin)

The Economist (London)

Far Eastern Economic Review (Hong Kong)

Financial Times (London)

Global Security Newswire (Washington)

The Guardian (London)

Helsingin Sanomat (Helsinki)

The Hindu (New Delhi)

The Hindustan Times (New Delhi)

Hong Kong Standard (Hong Kong)

Hong Kong Zhonggue Tongxun She (Hong Kong)

Indian Express

India Today

Interfax (Russia)

International Herald Tribune (Neuilly Cedex, France)

ITAR-TASS (Moscow)

Itogi Weekly (Moscow)

Izvestiya (Moscow)
Kommersant-Daily (Moscow)
The Korea Times (Seoul)
London Sunday Times (London)
London Telegraph (London)
Los Angeles Times
The Nation (Islamabad)
The News (Islamabad)
Newsday
Newsweek
The New Yorker
New York Sun
New York Times
Nightline
The Ottowa Citizen (Ottowa)
People's Liberation Army Daily (Beijing)
Pravda.ru (Russia)
The Russia Journal (Moscow)
Seoul Yonhap (Seoul)
Time
The Times of India (New Delhi)
United Press International (Washington, D.C.)
The Vancouver Sun (Vancouver)
The Wall Street Journal Europe (Brussels)
Washington Post
Washington Times

Journals and Books

Ahmed, Samina. "Security Dilemmas of Nuclear-Armed Pakistan." *Third World Quarterly* 21, no. 5 (October 2000): pp. 781–793.

Ahmed, Samina, and David Cortright. "Going Nuclear: The Weaponization Option." In *Pakistan and the Bomb: Public Opinion and Nuclear Options*, edited by Samina Ahmed and David Cortright. New York: Oxford University Press, 1998.

Albright, David, Frans Berkhout, and William Walker. *Plutonium and Highly Enriched Uranium, 1996: World Inventories, Capabilities and Policies*. Oxford: Oxford University Press, 1997.

Albright, David, and Mark Hibbs. "Pakistan's Bomb: Out of the Closet." *Bulletin of the Atomic Scientists* 48, no. 6 (July–August 1992): pp. 38–44.

Albright, David, and Corey Hinderstein. "Iran, Player or Rogue?" *Bulletin of the Atomic Scientists* 59, no. 5 (September/October 2003): pp. 52–58.

Albright, David, and Kevin O'Neill. *Solving the North Korean Nuclear Puzzle*. Washington, D.C.: Institute for Science and International Security, 2000.

Albright, David, Tom Zamora, and David Lewis. "Turn off Rocky Flats." *Bulletin of the Atomic Scientists* 46, no. 5 (June 1990): pp. 12–18.

Allison, Graham T., Owen R. Coté, Richard A. Falkenrath, and Steven E. Miller. *Avoiding Nuclear Anarchy.* Cambridge, Mass.: MIT Press, 1996.

Arkin, William M., Robert S. Norris, and Joshua Handler. *Taking Stock: Worldwide Nuclear Deployments, 1998*. Washington, D.C.: Natural Resources Defense Council, 1998.

Arnett, Eric. "Nuclear Stability and Arms Sales to India: Implications for U.S. Policy." *Arms Control Today* 27, no. 5 (August 1997): pp. 7–11.

———. "India's Nuclear Brownout." *Bulletin of the Atomic Scientists* 52, no. 6 (November/December 1996): pp. 15–16.

Austin, Greg. "The Strategic Implications of China's Public Order Crisis." *Survival* 37, no. 2 (summer 1995): pp. 7–23.

Bajpai, Kanti, P.R. Chari, Pervaiz Iqbal Cheema, Stephen Cohen, and Šumit Ganguly. *Brasstacks and Beyond: Perception and Management of Crisis in South Asia*. New Delhi: Manohar Publishers, 1995.

Baram, Amatzia. "An Analysis of Iraqi WMD Strategy." *Nonproliferation Review* 8, no. 2 (summer 2001): pp. 25–39.

Barker, Brian, and Terry Wallace. "Monitoring Nuclear Tests." *Science* 281, no. 5385 (September 25, 1998): pp. 1967–1969.

Bebbington, William P. "The Reprocessing of Nuclear Fuels." *Scientific American* 235, no. 6 (December 1976): pp. 30–41.

Berkhout, Frans, Anatoll Diakov, Harold Feiveson, Helen Hunt, Edwin Lyman, Marvin Miller, and Frank von Hippel. "Disposition of Separated Plutonium." *Science & Global Security* 3 (1993): pp. 161–213.

Bidwai, Praful, and Achin Vanaik. *South Asia on a Short Fuse: Nuclear Politics and the Future of Global Disarmament.* Karachi: Oxford University Press, 2000.

Bin, Tang. "Major Advances Realized in Nation's Nuclear Fuel Accounting System." *China Nuclear Industry News* (September 11, 1996), in FBIS-CST-96-019 (November 26, 1996), p. 1.

Blair, Bruce G. *Global Zero Alert for Nuclear Forces.* Washington, D.C.: Brookings Institution, 1995.

———. *The Logic of Accidental Nuclear War.* Washington, D.C.: Brookings Institution, 1993.

———. "Break-Up of the U.S.S.R.: Whither Nuclear Control?" *Transnational Law and Contemporary Problems* 2, no. 2 (1992): pp. 517–536.

Blair, Bruce, Harold Feiveson, and Frank von Hippel. "Taking Nuclear Weapons off Hair-Trigger Alert." *Scientific American* 277, no. 3 (November 1997): pp. 74–81.

Blair, Bruce, Lachlan Forrow, Ira Helfand, George Lewis, Theodore Postol, Victor Sidel, Barry Levy, Herbert Abrams, and Christine Cassel. "Accidental Nuclear War—A Post–Cold War Assessment." *The New England Journal of Medicine* 338, no. 18 (April 30, 1998): pp. 1326–1332.

Bleek, Philipp C. "U.S., Russia Complete START I Reductions." *Arms Control Today* 32, no. 1 (January/February 2002): p. 33.

———. "Fire Shuts Down Russian Early-Warning System." *Arms Control Today* 31, no. 5 (June 2001): p. 26.

———. "DOE Threat Reduction Funding Cut, Programs Reorganized." *Arms Control Today* 31, no. 10 (December 2001): p. 23.

———. "Russia Ratifies START II, Extension Protocol; ABM-Related Agreements Also Approved." *Arms Control Today* 30, no. 4 (May 2000): pp. 39–42.

Blight, James G., and David A. Welch. "Risking the Destruction of Nations: Lessons of the Cuban Missile Crisis for New and Aspiring Nuclear States." *Security Studies* 4, no. 4 (summer 1995): pp. 811–850.

———. *On the Brink: Americans and Soviets Reexamine the Cuban Missile Crisis,* 2nd ed. New York: Noonday, 1990.

Bodansky, Yossef. "Beijing Prepares for a New War Front in Xinjiang." *Defense and Foreign Affairs Strategic Policy* 28, no. 9 (September 2000): pp. 4–6.

Bogatrev, Valeriy. "Russian Antimissile Defense Cracks." *Kommersant-Daily* (July 15, 1998), translated in World News Connection, document no. FTS19980716000338, p. 2

Bowen, Clayton P., and Daniel Wolvén. "Command and Control Challenges in South Asia." *Nonproliferation Review* 6, no. 3 (spring–summer 1999): pp. 25–35.

Boyd, Kerry. "India Establishes Formal Nuclear Command Structure." *Arms Control Today* 33, no. 1 (January/February 2003): p. 31.

Brennan, Donald G. "The Risks of Spreading Weapons: A Historical Case." *Arms Control and Disarmament* 1 (1968): pp. 59–60.

Bridgham, Philip. "The Fall of Lin Piao." *China Quarterly* 55 (July/September 1973): pp. 427–449.

Buchan, Alastair. "Introduction," in The American Assembly, *A World of Nuclear Powers?* Englewood Cliffs, N.J.: Prentice Hall, 1966. pp. 1–12.

Bueno de Mesquita, Bruce, and William H. Riker. "An Assessment of the Merits of Selective Nuclear Proliferation." *Journal of Conflict Resolution* 26, no. 2 (June 1982): pp. 283–306.

Bukharin, Oleg. "Problems of Nuclear Terrorism." *The Monitor* 3, no. 2 (spring 1997): pp. 8–10.

———. "Security of Fissile Materials in Russia." *Annual Review of Energy and the Environment* 21 (1996): pp. 467–496.

———. "Soft Landing for Bomb Uranium." *Bulletin of the Atomic Scientists* 49, no. 7 (September 1993): pp. 44–49.

Bukharin, Oleg, Matthew Bunn, and Kenneth N. Luongo. *Renewing the Partner-*

ship: Recommendations for Accelerated Action to Secure Nuclear Material in the Former Soviet Union. Washington, D.C.: Russian-American Nuclear Security Advisory Council, 2000.

Bukharin, Oleg, and William Potter. "Potatoes Were Guarded Better." *Bulletin of the Atomic Scientists* 51, no. 3 (1995): pp. 46–50.

Bunn, Matthew. *The Next Wave: Urgently Needed New Steps to Control Warheads and Fissile Materials.* Washington, D.C., and Cambridge, Mass.: Carnegie Endowment for International Peace and Harvard University, 2000.

Bunn, Mathew, Oleg Bukharin, and Kenneth N. Luongo. "Renewing the Partnership: One Year Later." In *Proceedings of the 42nd Annual Meeting of the Institute for Nuclear Materials Management.* Northbrook, Ill.: INMM, 2001.

Butler, Richard. *The Greatest Threat: Iraq, Weapons of Mass Destruction, and the Growing Crisis of Global Security.* New York: Public Affairs, 2000.

Caldwell, Dan. "Permissive Action Links: A Description and Proposal." *Survival* 29, no. 3 (May/June 1987): pp. 224–238.

Caldwell, Dan, and Peter D. Zimmerman. "Reducing the Risk of Nuclear War with Permissive Action Links." In *Technology and the Limitation of International Conflict,* edited by Barry M. Blechman (Washington, D.C.: John Hopkins Foreign Policy Institute, School of Advanced International Studies, 1989), pp. 151–175.

Carranza, Mario E. "An Impossible Game: Stable Nuclear Deterrence after the Indian and Pakistani Tests." *Nonproliferation Review* 6, no. 3 (spring–summer 1999): pp. 11–24.

———. "Dangerous Optimism: Non-Weaponized Deterrence and Regional Peace in South Asia." *International Politics* 35 (June 1998): pp. 107–134.

Carter, Ashton B. "Assessing Command System Vulnerability." In *Managing Nuclear Operations,* edited by Ashton B. Carter, John D. Steinbruner, Charles A. Zraket. Washington, D.C.: Brookings Institution, 1987.

Center for Defense Information. "U.S. Nuclear Weapons Accidents: Danger in Our Midst." *The Defense Monitor* 10, no. 5 (1981). <http://asms.k12.ar.us/armem/ha/cdiart.htm>.

Chanda, Nayan, and Kathy Wilhelm. "Doomsday Averted." *Far Eastern Economic Review* 162, no. 5 (February 4, 1999): pp. 12–17.

Chellaney, Bramha, and Paul Leventhal. "Nuclear Terrorism: Threat, Perception, and Response in South Asia." *Terrorism* 11, no. 6 (1988): pp. 447–470.

Chengappa, Raj. *Weapons of Peace: The Secret Story of India's Quest to Be a Nuclear Power.* New Delhi: HarperCollins Publishers India, 2000.

Chuen, Christina, Michael Jasinski, and Bret Lortie. "Russia's Blue Water Blues." *Bulletin of the Atomic Scientists* 57, no. 1 (January/February 2001): pp. 65–69.

Cirincione, Joseph, with Jon B. Wolfsthal and Miriam Rajkumar. *Deadly Arsenals: Tracking Weapons of Mass Destruction.* Washington, D.C.: Carnegie Endowment for International Peace, 2002.

Clark, Phillip. "Decline of the Russian Early Warning Satellite Programme." *Jane's Intelligence Review* 13, no. 1 (January 2001): pp. 14–17.

Clough, Ralph A., Doak Barnett, Morton Halperin, and Jerome Kahan, *The United States, China, and Arms Control.* Washington, D.C.: Brookings Institution, 1975.

Cloughley, Col. Brian (Ret.). "Transition Time in Pakistan's Army." *Jane's Intelligence Review* 12, no. 4 (April 2000): pp. 24–29.

Cochran, Thomas, William M. Arkin, and Milton Hoenig. *Nuclear Weapons Databook, Vol. I: U.S. Nuclear Forces and Capabilities.* Cambridge, Mass.: Ballinger, 1984.

Cohen, Avner, and Benjamin Frankel. "Opaque Nuclear Proliferation." *Journal of Strategic Studies* 13, no. 3 (September 1990): pp. 14–44.

Cordesman, Anthony H. *Iraq and the War of Sanctions: Conventional Threats and Weapons of Mass Destruction.* Westport, Conn.: Praeger, 1999.

Cotter, Donald R. "Peacetime Operations: Safety and Security." In *Managing Nuclear Operations,* edited by Ashton B. Carter, John D. Steinbruner, Charles A. Zraket. Washington, D.C.: Brookings Institution, 1987.

Davis, Jay C., and David A. Kay. "Iraq's Secret Nuclear Weapons Program." *Physics Today* 45, no. 7 (July 1992): pp. 21–27.

Diamond, Howard. "India Releases Nuclear Doctrine, Looks to Emulate P-5 Arsenals." *Arms Control Today* 29, no. 5 (July/August 1999): p. 23.

———. "India, Pakistan Agree on Security, Confidence Building Measures." *Arms Control Today* 29, no. 1 (January/February 1999): p. 21.

Doty, Paul. "The Role of Smaller Powers." *Daedalus* 89, no. 4 (fall 1960): pp. 818–830.

Doyle, James E., and Stephen V. Mladineo. "Assessing the Development of a Modern Safeguards Culture in the NIS." *Nonproliferation Review* 5, no. 2 (winter 1998): pp. 91–100.

Drell, Sidney, and Bob Peurifoy. "Technical Issues of a Nuclear Test Ban." *Annual Review of Nuclear and Particle Science* 44 (1994): pp. 285–327.

Dreyer, June Teufel. "The People's Liberation Army and the Power Struggle of 1989." *Problems of Communism* 38, no. 5 (September–October 1989): pp. 41–48.

———. "The Role of the PLA in China's Political Struggle." In *The PLA and Tiananmen Crisis,* edited by Richard H. Yang. Taiwan: The Sun Yat-Sen Center for Policy Studies, National Sun Yat-Sen University, 1989.

Dunn, Lewis A. *Controlling the Bomb: Nuclear Proliferation in the 1980s.* New Haven: Yale University Press, 1982.

———. "Military Politics, Nuclear Proliferation, and the 'Nuclear Coup d'Etat.'" *Journal of Strategic Studies* 1 (May 1978): pp. 31–50.

Eberstadt, Nicholas. "Our Other Korea Problem." *National Interest* 69 (fall 2002): pp. 110–118.

———. *The End of North Korea.* Washington, D.C.: The AEI Press, 1999.

Ellis, Jason D., and Todd E. Perry. "Nunn-Lugar's Unfinished Agenda." *Arms Control Today* 27, no. 3 (October 1997): pp. 14–22.

Evangelista, Matthew. "Russia's Fragile Union." *Bulletin of the Atomic Scientists* 55, no. 3 (May/June 1999): pp. 50–55.

Ewell, Emily. "NIS Nuclear Smuggling since 1995: A Lull in Significant Cases?" *Nonproliferation Review* 5, no. 3 (spring–summer 1998): pp. 119–125.

Faruqui, Ahmad. "China-Pakistan: Fraying Ties." *Far Eastern Economic Review* 164, no. 2 (January 18, 2001): p. 33.

Feaver, Peter D. "Correspondence: Proliferation Pessimism and Emerging Nuclear Powers." *International Security* 22, no. 2 (fall 1997): pp. 87–119.

———. "Neooptimists and the Enduring Problem of Nuclear Proliferation." *Security Studies* 6, no. 4 (summer 1997): pp. 93–125.

———. "Proliferation Optimism and Theories of Nuclear Operations." *Security Studies* 2, no. 3/4 (spring/summer 1993): pp. 159–191.

———. "Command and Control in Emerging Nuclear Nations." *International Security* 17, no. 3 (winter 1992/1993): pp. 160–187.

———. *Guarding the Guardians: Civilian Control of Nuclear Weapons in the United States*. Ithaca: Cornell University Press, 1992.

Feigenbaum, Evan A. "China's Strategy of Weakness." *Far Eastern Economic Review* 164, no. 8 (March 1, 2001): p. 29.

Ferguson, Charles. "Sparking a Buildup: U.S. Missile Defense and China's Nuclear Arsenal." *Arms Control Today* 30, no. 2 (March 2000): pp. 13–18.

Fischer, David. *History of the International Atomic Energy Agency: The First Forty Years*. Vienna: International Atomic Energy Agency, 1997.

Forden, Geoffrey, Pavel (Paul) Podvig, and Theodore A. Postol. "False Alarm, Nuclear Danger." *IEEE Spectrum* 37, no. 3 (March 2000): pp. 31–39.

Gallois, Pierre. *The Balance of Terror: Strategy for the Nuclear Age*. Boston: Houghton Mifflin, 1961.

Ganguly, Šumit. "The Slide Continues." *Foreign Affairs*, April 2003. <http://www.foreignaffairs.org/20030401faupdate11286/sumit-ganguly/the-slide-continues.html>.

———. "Correspondence: Debating New Delhi's Nuclear Decision." *International Security* 24, no. 4 (spring 2000): pp. 181–189.

———. "India's Pathway to Pokhran II: The Prospects and Sources of New Delhi's Nuclear Weapons Program." *International Security* 23, no. 4 (spring 1999): pp. 148–177.

George, Paul. "Islamic Unrest in the Xinjiang Uighur Autonomous Region." *Commentary, Canadian Security Intelligence Service* 73 (1998): pp. 1–9.

Giles, Gregory. "The Islamic Republic of Iran and Nuclear, Biological, and Chemical Weapons." In *Planning the Unthinkable: How New Powers Will Use Nuclear, Biological, and Chemical Weapons*, edited by Peter R. Lavoy, Scott D. Sagan, and James J. Wirtz. Ithaca: Cornell University Press, 2000.

———. "Safeguarding the Undeclared Nuclear Arsenals." *Washington Quarterly* 16, no. 2 (spring 1993): pp. 173–186.

Gill, Bates, James C. Mulvenon, and Mark Stokes. "The Chinese Second Artillery Corps: Transition to Credible Deterrence." In *The People's Liberation Army as*

Organization, edited by James C. Mulvenon and Andrew N.D. Yang. Santa Monica, Calif.: Rand, 2002. <http://www.rand.org/publications/CF/CF182/CF182.ch11.pdf>.

Godson, Roy, and James J. Wirtz. "Strategic Denial and Deception." In *Strategic Denial and Deception: The Twenty-First Century Challenge*, edited by Roy Godson and James J. Wirtz. New Brunswick: Transaction Publishers, 2002.

Gordon, Rose. "India, Pakistan Trade Tit-for-Tat Missile Tests." *Arms Control Today* 33, no. 3 (April 2003): p. 41.

———. "India Conducts Four Missile Tests." *Arms Control Today* 33, no. 2 (March 2003). <http://www.armscontrol.org/act/2003_03/indiamissiletests_mar03.asp>.

Gregory, Shaun. "A Formidable Challenge: Nuclear Command and Control in South Asia." *Disarmament Diplomacy* 54 (February 2001). <http://www.acronym.org.uk/54greg.htm>.

———. *The Hidden Cost of Deterrence: Nuclear Weapons Accidents.* Washington: Brassey's, 1990.

Gronlund, Lisbeth, David Wright, and Yong Liu. "China and a Fissile Material Production Cut-Off." *Survival* 37, no. 4 (winter 1995–1996): pp. 147–167.

Hagerty, Devin. *The Consequences of Nuclear Proliferation: Lessons from South Asia.* Cambridge, Mass.: MIT Press, 1998.

———. "Nuclear Deterrence in South Asia: The 1990 Indo-Pakistani Crisis." *International Security* 20, no. 3 (winter 1995/96): pp. 79–114.

———. "The Power of Suggestion: Opaque Proliferation, Existential Deterrence, and the South Asian Nuclear Arms Competition." In *The Proliferation Puzzle*, edited by Zachary Davis and Benjamin Frankel. Portland, Oreg.: Frank Cass Publishing Co., 1993.

Hamza, Khidir, with Jeff Stein. *Saddam's Bombmaker: The Terrifying Inside Story of the Iraqi Nuclear and Biological Weapons Agenda.* New York: Scribner, 2000.

Han, Theodore, and John Li. *Tiananmen Square, Spring 1989: A Chronology of the Chinese Democracy Movement.* Berkeley, Calif.: Institute of East Asian Studies, University of California, Berkeley, 1992.

Hansen, Chuck. "The Oops List." *Bulletin of The Atomic Scientists* 56, no. 6 (November/December 2000): pp. 64–66.

———. *U.S. Nuclear Weapons: The Secret History.* New York: Orion Books, 1988.

Hansen, Lynn M. "Arms Control: Focus on Denial and Deception." In *Strategic Denial and Deception: The Twenty-First Century Challenge*, edited by Roy Godson and James J. Wirtz. New Brunswick: Transaction Publishers, 2002.

Hayes, Stephen F. "Case Closed." *Weekly Standard* 9, no. 11 (November 24, 2003): pp. 20–25.

———. "The Saddam-Osama Memo (cont.): A Close Examination of the Defense Department's Latest Statement." November 19, 2003. <http://www.weeklystandard.com/Content/Public/Articles/000/000/003/396hflxy.asp>.

Heisbourg, François. "The Prospects for Nuclear Stability between India and Pakistan." *Survival* 40, no. 4 (winter 1998–1999): pp. 77–92.

Hinsley, F.H. *Power and the Pursuit of Peace.* Cambridge: Cambridge University Press, 1963.

Hoffman, Bruce. "Terrorism and WMD: Some Preliminary Hypotheses." *The Nonproliferation Review* 4, no. 3 (spring–summer 1997): pp. 45–53.

Hsu, Wen. "The Impact of Government Restructuring on Chinese Nuclear Arms Control and Nonproliferation Policymaking." *Nonproliferation Review* 6, no. 4 (fall 1999): pp. 152–167.

Hua Di, and John W. Lewis. "China's Ballistic Missile Programs: Technologies, Strategies, Goals." *International Security* 17, no. 2 (fall 1992): pp. 5–40.

Ihlwan, Moon, and Brian Bremmer, "The Other Korean Crisis," *Business Week* 3816 (January 20, 2003): p. 45.

Iklé, Fred C., "Nth Countries and Disarmament." *Bulletin of the Atomic Scientists* 16 (1960): pp. 391–394

International Crisis Group. "Pakistan: The Mullahs and the Military." *ICG Asia Report,* no. 49 (March 20, 2003).

Jane's Information Group. *China in Crisis: The Role of the Military.* London: Jane's Information Group Ltd., 1989.

Jencks, Harlan W. "China's Army, China's Future." In *China in the Nineties: Crisis Management and Beyond,* edited by David S.G. Goodman and Gerald Segal. Oxford: Clarendon Press, 1991.

Jenkins, Bonnie D. "Establishing International Standards for Physical Protection of Nuclear Material." *Nonproliferation Review* 5, no. 3 (spring–summer 1998): pp. 98–110.

Jenkins, Brian. "International Terrorism: A New Mode of Conflict." In *International Terrorism and World Security,* edited by David Carleton and Carlo Schaerf. London: Croom Helm, 1975.

Jeon, Jei Guk. "North Korean Leadership: Kim Jong Il's Balancing Act in the Ruling Circle." *Third World Quarterly* 21, no. 5 (October 2000): pp. 761–779.

Joeck, Neil. "Nuclear Relations in South Asia." In *Repairing the Regime,* edited by Joseph Cirincione. New York: Routledge, 2000.

———. *Maintaining Nuclear Stability in South Asia.* Adelphi Paper, No. 312. London: International Institute for Strategic Studies (IISS), September 1997.

Johnston, Iain. "Prospects for Chinese Nuclear Force Modernization: Limited Deterrence Versus Multilateral Arms Control." *China Quarterly* 146 (June 1996): pp. 548–576.

———. "China's New 'Old Thinking': The Concept of Limited Deterrence." *International Security* 20, no. 3 (winter 1995/1996): pp. 5–42.

Jones, H.M. "China: Autonomous Wang." *Far Eastern Economic Review* 58 (December 28, 1967): pp. 569–570.

Jones, Rodney W., and Mark G. McDonough, with Toby Dalton and Gregory Koblentz. *Tracking Nuclear Proliferation: A Guide in Maps and Charts, 1998.* Washington, D.C.: Carnegie Endowment for International Peace, 1998.

Kahn, Herman. "The Arms Race and Some of Its Hazards." *Daedalus* 89, no. 4 (fall 1960): pp. 744–780.

Kamiya, Matake. "A Disillusioned Japan Confronts North Korea." *Arms Control Today* 33, no. 3 (May 2003): pp. 19–22.

Karl, David J. "Proliferation Pessimism and Emerging Nuclear Powers." *International Security* 21, no. 3 (winter 1996/97): pp. 87–119.

Kay, David A. "Denial and Deception Practices of WMD Proliferators: Iraq and Beyond." *Washington Quarterly* 18, no. 1 (winter 1995): pp. 85–105.

Kellen, Konrad. "The Potential for Nuclear Terrorism: A Discussion." In *Preventing Nuclear Terrorism,* edited by Paul Leventhal and Yonah Alexander. Lexington: Lexington Books, 1987.

Kerr, Paul. "KEDO Suspends Oil Shipments to North Korea." *Arms Control Today* 32, no. 10 (December 2002): pp. 15, 23.

Khajehpour, Bijan. "Iran's Economy: Twenty Years after the Islamic Revolution." In *Iran at the Crossroads,* edited by John L. Esposito and R.K. Remazani. New York, N.Y.: Palgrave, 2001.

Kim, Samuel S. "Does North Korea Have a Chance?" *Columbia East Asian Review* (fall 1997). <http://www.columbia.edu/cu/ccba/cear/issues/fall97/graphics/forum/kim/kim.htm>.

Kimball, Daryl G. "Fuzzy Nuclear Math." *Arms Control Today* 31, no. 10 (December 2001): p. 2.

Knopf, Jeffrey. "Recasting the Proliferation Optimism-Pessimism Debate." *Security Studies* 12, no. 1 (autumn 2003): pp. 41–96.

Koch, Andrew. "Nuclear Testing in South Asia and the CTBT." *Nonproliferation Review* 3, no. 3 (summer 1996): pp. 98–104.

Koch, Andrew, and Waheguru Pal Singh Sidhu. "Subcontinental Missiles." *Bulletin of the Atomic Scientists* 54, no. 4 (July/August 1998): pp. 44–50.

Koch, Andrew, and Jennifer Topping. "Pakistan's Nuclear Weapons Program: A Status Report." *Nonproliferation Review* 4, no. 3 (spring–summer 1997): pp. 109–113.

Lague, David. "Beijing's Tough Korea Call." *Far Eastern Economic Review* 166, no. 9 (March 6, 2003): pp. 12–14.

"The Lahore Declaration." *Disarmament Diplomacy* 34 (February 1999). <http://www.acronym.org.uk/34doc3.htm>.

Lanouette, William. "Weapons Plant at 40: Savannah River's Halo Fades." *Bulletin of the Atomic Scientists* 46, no. 10 (December 1990): pp. 26–38.

Laqueur, Walter. "Post-Modern Terrorism." *Foreign Affairs* 75, no. 5 (September–October 1996): pp. 24–36.

Larkin, John. "North Korea: Why Refugees Flee." *Far Eastern Economic Review* 166, no. 9 (March 6, 2003): pp. 14–16.

———. "Exposed—Kim's Slave Camps." *Far Eastern Economic Review* 165, no. 49 (December 12, 2002): pp. 14–18.

———. "Mysterious Reform." *Far Eastern Economic Review* 165, no. 31 (August 8, 2002): pp. 18–19.

Lavoy, Peter R. "Arms Control in South Asia." In *Arms Control Toward the Twenty-First Century,* edited by Jeffrey A. Larson and Gregory J. Rattray. Boulder, Colo.: Lynne Reinner, 1995.

———. "The Strategic Consequences of Nuclear Proliferation," *Security Studies* 4, no. 4 (summer 1995): pp. 695–753.

———. "Civil-Military Relations, Strategic Conduct, and the Stability of Nuclear Deterrence in South Asia." In *Civil-Military Relations and Nuclear Weapons,* edited by Scott D. Sagan. Stanford: CISAC Publication, June 1994.

Lawrence, Susan V. "Where Beijing Fears Kosovo." *Far Eastern Economic Review* 163, no. 36 (September 7, 2000): pp. 22–24.

———. "Breathing Space." *Far Eastern Economic Review* 163, no. 22 (June 1, 2000): pp. 17–18.

Lawrence, Susan V., and Ahmed Rashid. "Joining Foreign Jihad." *Far Eastern Economic Review* 163, no. 36 (September 7, 2000): p. 24.

Lepingwell, John W.R., and Nikolai Sokov. "Strategic Offensive Arms Elimination and Weapons Protection, Control, and Accounting." *Nonproliferation Review* 7, no. 1 (spring 2000): pp. 55–79.

Levi, Michael. "Off Target: North Korea's Hidden Menace." *New Republic* 228, no. 11 (March 24, 2003): pp. 13–14.

Levy, Jack. "Learning and Foreign Policy: Sweeping a Conceptual Minefield." *International Organization* 48, no. 2 (spring 1994): pp. 279–312.

Lewis, John W., and Xue Litai. *China Builds the Bomb.* Stanford: Stanford University Press, 1988.

Lieberthal, Kenneth. *Governing China: From Revolution through Reform.* New York: W.W. Norton, 1995.

Lintner, Bertil. "It's Hard to Help Kim Jong Il." *Far Eastern Economic Review* 166, no. 12 (March 27, 2003): pp. 20–22.

Litovkin, Dmitriy. "Viktor Yerastov: Nuclear Thieves in Chelyabinsk Oblast Could Have Inflicted Serious Harm to the State." *Yaderny Kontrol,* no. 6 (November–December 1999): pp. 40–43.

Maerli, Morten Bremer. "Relearning the ABCs: Terrorists and 'Weapons of Mass Destruction.'" *Nonproliferation Review* 7, no. 2 (summer 2000): pp. 108–119.

Makhijani, Arjun, and Scott Saleska. "Hanford Cleanup: Explosive Solution." *Bulletin of the Atomic Scientists* 46, no. 8 (October 1990): pp. 14–20.

Malik, J. Mohan. "Chinese Debate on Military Strategy: Trends and Portents." *Journal of Northeast Asian Studies* 9, no. 2 (summer 1990): pp. 3–32.

Mann, Paul. "Nuclear Risks Mount in Besieged Russia." *Aviation Week and Space Technology* 149, no. 10 (September 7, 1998): pp. 60–62.

McCarthy, Timothy V., and Jonathan B. Tucker. "Saddam's Toxic Arsenal: Chemical and Biological Weapons in the Gulf Wars." In *Planning the Unthinkable: How*

New Powers Will Use Nuclear, Biological, and Chemical Weapons, edited by Peter R. Lavoy, Scott D. Sagan, and James J. Wirtz. Ithaca: Cornell University Press, 2000.

McKenna, T/Sgt. Pat. "The Border Guards: NORAD: The Eyes and Ears of North America," *Airman Magazine* 40, no. 1 (January 1996), <http://www.af.mil/news/airman/0196/border.htm>.

McPhee, John. *The Curve of Binding Energy.* New York: Farrar, Strauss, and Giroux, 1974.

Mearsheimer, John J. "Back to the Future: Instability in Europe After the Cold War." *International Security* 15, no. 1 (summer 1990): pp. 5–55.

Mearsheimer, John J., and Stephen M. Walt. "An Unnecessary War." *Foreign Policy* 134 (January/February 2003): pp. 50–59.

Mian, Zia. "Walk Softly and Look Ahead in Nuclear South Asia." *Foreign Policy in Focus* (October 31, 2001). <http://www.fpif.org/pdf/gac/0110seamil.pdf>.

Morgenstern, Oskar. "The N-Country Problem." *Fortune* 63, no. 3 (March 1961): pp. 136–137, 205–209.

Mu, Yi, and Mark V. Thompson. *Crisis at Tiananmen: Reform and Reality in Modern China.* San Francisco: China Books and Periodicals, 1989.

Murphy, David. "Own Goal." *Far Eastern Economic Review* 165, no. 40 (October 10, 2002): p. 26.

Mutalik, Guraraj, Frank Barnaby, Peter Taylor, and David Sumner. *Crude Nuclear Weapons: Proliferation and the Terrorist Threat.* Global Health Watch Report, no. 1. Cambridge, Mass.: International Physicians for the Prevention of Nuclear War, 1996.

National Academy of Sciences. *Management and Disposition of Excess Weapons Plutonium.* Washington, D.C.: National Academy Press, 1994. <http://www.nap.edu/readingroom/reader.cgi?auth=free&label=ul.book.0309050421>.

National Research Council. *Protecting Nuclear Materials in Russia.* Washington, D.C.: National Academy Press, 1999. <http://books.nap.edu/books/030906547X/html/index.html>.

Nilsen, Thomas, Igor Kudrik, and Alexandr Nikitin. "The Russian Northern Fleet." *Bellona Report* 2 (1996): section 1.3.1. <http://www.bellona.no/imaker?sub=1&id=11092>.

Noland, Marcus. "Why North Korea Will Muddle Through." *Foreign Affairs* 76, no. 4 (July/August 1997): pp. 105–118.

Norris, Robert S., and William M. Arkin. "U.S. Nuclear Forces, 2000." *Bulletin of the Atomic Scientists* 56, no. 3 (May/June 2000): pp. 69–71.

———. "Chinese Nuclear Forces, 1999." *Bulletin of the Atomic Scientists* 55, no. 4 (May/June 1999): pp. 79–80.

———. "U.S. Nuclear Weapons Safety and Control Features." *Bulletin of the Atomic Scientists* 47, no. 8 (1991): pp. 48–50.

Norris, Robert S., William M. Arkin, Hans M. Kristensen, and Joshua Handler. "Chinese Nuclear Forces, 2001." *Bulletin of the Atomic Scientists* 57, no. 5 (September/October 2001): p. 71

———. "Russian Nuclear Forces, 2001." *Bulletin of the Atomic Scientists* 57, no. 3 (May/June 2001): pp. 78–79.

———. "U.S. Nuclear Forces, 2001." *Bulletin of the Atomic Scientists* 57, no. 2 (March/April 2001): pp. 77–79.

Norris, Robert S., Andrew S. Burrows, and Richard Fieldhouse. *Nuclear Weapons Databook, Vol. V: British, French and Chinese Nuclear Weapons.* Boulder, Colo.: Westview Press, 1994.

Norris, Robert S., and Hans M. Kristensen. "Chinese Nuclear Forces, 2003." *Bulletin of the Atomic Scientists* 59, no. 6 (November/December 2003): pp. 77–80.

———. "Russian Nuclear Forces, 2003." *Bulletin of the Atomic Scientists* 59, no. 4 (July/August 2003): pp. 70–72.

———. "U.S. Nuclear Forces, 2003." *Bulletin of the Atomic Scientists* 59, no. 3 (May/June 2003): pp. 73–76.

Oksenberg, Michael, Lawrence Sullivan, and Marc Lambert. *Beijing Spring, 1989: Confrontation and Conflict.* Armonk, New York: M.E. Sharp, 1990.

Orlov, Vladimir. "Nuclear Blackmail: Threats from 'Enemies Within' More Disturbing Than Conspiracies from Without." *Nezavismoye Voyennoye Obozreniye* 32 (1997), translated in World News Connection, document no. FTS19971001000544 (August 29, 1997): p. 2.

Pandey, Swati, and Teresita C. Schaffer. "Building Confidence in India and Pakistan." *South Asia Monitor* 49 (August 1, 2002): p. 1. <http://www.csis.org/saprog/sam49.pdf>.

Pei, Minxin. "Will China Become Another Indonesia?" *Foreign Policy* 116 (fall 1999): pp. 94–109.

Pendley, Robert E. "Is Further Proliferation of Nuclear Weapons Irrelevant to U.S. National Security." In *The Proliferation Predicament,* edited by Joseph Pilat. New Brunswick: Transaction Books, 1985.

Perkovich, George. *India's Nuclear Bomb: The Impact on Global Proliferation.* Berkeley: University of California Press, 1999.

———. "A Nuclear Third Way in South Asia." *Foreign Policy* 91 (summer 1993): pp. 85–104.

Perry, Todd. "Securing Russian Nuclear Materials: The Need for an Expanded U.S. Response." *Nonproliferation Review* 6, no. 2 (winter 1999): pp. 84–97.

Pilat, Joseph. "Antinuclear Terrorism in the Advanced Industrial West." In *Political Terrorism and Energy,* edited by Yonah Alexander and Charles K. Ebinger. New York: Praeger, 1982.

Podvig, Paul, Oleg Bukharin, Timur Kadyshev, Eugene Miasnikov, Igor Sutiagin, Maxim Tarasenko, and Boris Zhelesov. *Russia's Strategic Nuclear Weapons.* Moscow: IzdAT, 1998.

Podvig, Pavel (Paul). "Russian Early-Warning System and Danger of Inadvertent Launch," *Physics and Society* 32, no. 1 (January 2003): pp. 7–8.

———. "Russian Strategic Forces: Uncertain Future." *Breakthroughs* 7, no. 1 (1998): pp. 11–21. <http://www.armscontrol.ru/transforming/podvig.htm>.

Pollack, Jonathan D. "The Future of China's Nuclear Weapons Policy." In *Strategic Views from the Second Tier: The Nuclear Weapons Policies of France, Britain, and China,* edited by John C. Hopkins and Weixing Hu. New Brunswick, N.J.: Transaction Publishing, 1994.

Potter, William, and Fred Wehling. "Sustainability: A Vital Component of Nuclear Material Security in Russia." *Nonproliferation Review* 7, no. 1 (spring 2000): pp. 180–188.

Prindle, Nancy Hayden. "The U.S.-China Lab-to-Lab Technical Exchange Program." *Nonproliferation Review* 5, no. 3 (spring/summer 1998): pp. 111–118.

———. "U.S. and China on Nuclear Arms Control and Nonproliferation: Building on Common Technical Interests." In *Arms Control Issues for the Twenty-First Century,* edited by James Brown. Albuquerque, N.M.: Sandia National Laboratory Publication, SAND97-2619, 1997.

Pshakin, Gennady. "MPC&A Upgrades in Russia: Results, Problems, Perspectives." *Monitor* 5, no. 1–2 (winter–spring 1999): pp. 18–20.

Ramana, M.V., and Zia Mian. "The Nuclear Confrontation in South Asia." *SIPRI Yearbook, 2003: Armaments, Disarmament and International Security.* Oxford: Oxford University Press, 2003. <http://editors.sipri.org/pubs/yb03/ch05.html>.

Ramdas, L., Admiral. "Myths and Realities of Nuclear Command and Control in India and Pakistan." *Disarmament Diplomacy* 54 (February 2001). <http://www.acronym.org.uk/54ramdas.htm>.

Rehbein, Robert E. "Managing Proliferation in South Asia: A Case for Assistance to Unsafe Nuclear Arsenals." *Nonproliferation Review* 9, no. 1 (spring 2002): pp. 92–107.

Rethinaraj, T.S. Gopi. "In the Comfort of Secrecy." *Bulletin of the Atomic Scientists* 55, no. 6 (November/December 1999): pp. 52–57.

Rhodes, Richard. *Dark Sun: The Making of the Hydrogen Bomb.* New York: Simon and Schuster, 1995.

———. *The Making of the Atomic Bomb.* New York: Simon and Shuster, 1986.

Roberts, Brad, Robert A. Manning, and Ronald N. Montaperto. "China: The Forgotten Nuclear Power." *Foreign Affairs* 79, no. 4 (July/August 2000): pp. 53–63.

Rosecrance, Richard N. *Action and Reaction in World Politics.* Boston: Little, Brown, 1963.

Sagan, Scott. "Correspondence: Proliferation Pessimism and Emerging Nuclear Powers." *International Security* 22, no. 2 (1997): pp. 185–207.

———. "The Perils of Proliferation: Organization Theory, Deterrence Theory, and the Spread of Nuclear Weapons." *International Security* 18, no. 4 (spring 1994): pp. 66–107.

———. *The Limits of Safety: Organizations, Accidents, and Nuclear Weapons.* Princeton, N.J.: Princeton University Press, 1993.

———. "Nuclear Alerts and Crisis Management." *International Security* 9, no. 4 (spring 1985): pp. 99–139.

Sagan, Scott D., and Kenneth N. Waltz. *The Spread of Nuclear Weapons: A Debate Renewed.* New York: W.W. Norton, 2003.

———. *The Spread of Nuclear Weapons: A Debate.* New York: W.W. Norton, 1995.

Savage, Timothy L. "Crisis in 2003?: North Korea's WMD Program." *The Monitor* 8, no. 3 (summer 2002): pp. 24–27.

Sawhney, Pravin. "Pakistan Scores over India in Ballistic Missile Race." *Jane's Intelligence Review* 12, no. 11 (November 2000): pp. 31–35.

Schaper, Annette. "The Case for Universal Full-Scope Safeguards on Nuclear Material." *Nonproliferation Review* 5, no. 2 (winter 1998): pp. 69–80.

Schelling, Thomas C. *Arms and Influence.* New Haven: Yale University Press, 1966.

Schlevogt, Kal-Alexander. "China's Western Campaign." *Far Eastern Economic Review* 163, no. 33 (August 17, 2000): p. 29.

Schwartz, Stephen I. "Four Trillion Dollars and Counting." *Bulletin of the Atomic Scientists* 51, no. 6, (November/December 1995): pp. 32–52.

Scoblic, J. Peter. "China Issues Missile Export Pledge; U.S. Says It Will Waive Sanctions." *Arms Control Today* 30, no. 10 (December 2000): p. 23.

Seabord, Glenn T. *Stemming the Tide: Arms Control in the Johnson Years.* Lexington, Mass.: D.C. Health, 1987.

Segal, Gerald. *China Changes Shape: Regionalism and Foreign Policy.* Adelphi Paper, No. 287. London: International Institute for Strategic Studies (IISS), 1994.

Sen, Amartya. "India and the Bomb." *New Republic* 223, no. 13 (September 25, 2000): pp. 32–37.

Seng, Jordan. "Less Is More: Command and Control Advantages of Minor Nuclear States." *Security Studies* 6, no. 4 (summer 1997): pp. 50–92.

———. "Optimism in the Balance: A Response to Peter Feaver." *Security Studies* 6, no. 4 (summer 1997): pp. 126–136

Shaffer, Brenda. "Iran at the Nuclear Threshold." *Arms Control Today* 33, no. 9 (November 2003). <http://www.armscontrol.org/act/2003_11/Shaffer.asp>.

Sidhu, Waheguru Pal Singh. "India's Nuclear Use Doctrine." In *Planning the Unthinkable: How New Powers Will Use Nuclear, Biological, and Chemical Weapons,* edited by Peter R. Lavoy, Scott D. Sagan, and James J. Wirtz. Ithaca: Cornell University Press, 2000.

Simons, Howard. "World-Wide Capabilities for Production and Control of Nuclear Weapons." *Daedalus* 88, no. 3 (summer 1959): pp. 385–409.

Sinha, P.B. "Islamic Militancy and Separatism in Xinjiang." *Strategic Analysis* 20, no. 3 (June 1997): pp. 451–460.

Snyder, Scott. "North Korea's Challenge of Regime Survival: Internal Problems and the Implications for the Future." *Pacific Affairs* 73, no. 4 (winter 2000/2001): pp. 517–533.

Spector, Leonard D. "Clandestine Nuclear Trade and the Threat of Nuclear Terrorism." In *Preventing Nuclear Terrorism,* edited by Paul Leventhal and Yonah Alexander. Lexington: Lexington Books, 1987.

———. *Going Nuclear: The Spread of Nuclear Weapons, 1986–1987.* Cambridge, Mass.: Ballinger, 1987.

Stefashin, Victor Vasilyenvich. "Chinese Nuclear Strategy and National Security." *Mirovaya Ekonomika I Mazhdunarodyye Otnosheniya* 8 (August 19, 1995), translated in World News Connection, document no. FTS19970416001575, p. 6.

Stein, Peter, and Peter Feaver. *Assuring Control of Nuclear Weapons: The Evolution of Permissive Action Links.* Lanham, Md.: University Press of America, 1987.

Steinhausler, Fritz, and George Bunn. "Guarding Nuclear Reactors and Materials from Terrorists and Thieves." *Arms Control Today* (October 2001): pp. 8–12.

Stern, Jessica. "The Protean Enemy." *Foreign Affairs* 82, no. 4 (July/August 2003): pp. 27–40.

———. "U.S. Assistance Programs for Improving MPC&A in the Former Soviet Union." *Nonproliferation Review* 3, no. 2 (winter 1996): pp.17–32.

Strauss, Mark. "Think Again: Attacking Iraq." *Foreign Policy* 129 (March–April 2002): pp. 14–19.

Thayer, Bradley. "The Risk of Nuclear Inadvertence: A Review Essay." *Security Studies* 3, no. 3 (spring 1994): pp. 428–493.

Toomay, John C. "Warning and Assessment Sensors." In *Managing Nuclear Operations,* edited by Ashton B. Carter, John D. Steinbruner, Charles A. Zraket. Washington, D.C.: Brookings Institution, 1987.

Tucker, Jonathan B. "Monitoring and Verification in a Noncooperative Environment: Lessons from the U.N. Experience in Iraq." *Nonproliferation Review* 3, no. 3 (spring–summer 1996): pp. 1–14.

van Creveld, Martin. "Military Strategy for an Era of Transition." In *Turning Point: The Gulf War and U.S. Military Strategy,* edited by Benjamin Ederington and Michael J. Mazarr. Boulder, Colo.: Westview, 1994.

Volodin, Yuri, Valentin Zakharov, Gennady Pshakin, and Alexander Roumiantsev, "On the Way to Establish an Effective State MPC&A System, Round Table Discussion." *Yaderny Kontrol 5* (fall 1997): pp. 2–20.

von Hippel, Frank N. "De-Alerting." *Bulletin of the Atomic Scientists* 53, no. 3 (May/June 1997): p. 35

Wagner, Alex. "India Tests Short-Range Agni Ballistic Missile." *Arms Control Today* 31, no. 2 (March 2002): p. 29.

———. "U.S. Offers Nuclear Security Assistance to Pakistan." *Arms Control Today* 31, no. 10 (December 2001): p. 24.

Waltz, Kenneth N. "Nuclear Myths and Political Realities." *American Political Science Review* 84, no. 3 (September 1990): pp. 731–745.

———. *The Spread of Nuclear Weapons: More May Be Better.* Adelphi Paper, No. 171. London: International Institute for Strategic Studies (IISS), 1981.

———. *Theory of International Politics*. New York: McGraw-Hill, 1979.

Willrich, Mason, and Theodore B. Taylor. *Nuclear Theft: Risks and Safeguards*. Cambridge, Mass.: Ballinger, 1974.

Wohlstetter, Albert. "Nuclear Sharing: NATO and the N+1 Country." *Foreign Affairs* 39, no. 3 (April 1961): pp. 355–387.

Zaloga, Steve. "Russia's Strategic Forces Stumble." *Jane's Intelligence Review* 12, no. 10 (October 2000): pp. 12–14.

Zelentsov, Sergey. "Nuclear Arsenal Must Be in the Same Hands." *Yaderny Kontrol* 17 (May 1996): p. 20.

Zhara, Farah. "Pakistan's Road to a Minimum Nuclear Deterrent." *Arms Control Today* 29, no. 5 (July/August 1999): pp. 9–13.

Zimmerman, Peter D. "Technical Barriers to Nuclear Proliferation." *Security Studies* 2, no. 3/4 (spring/summer 1993): pp. 345–355.

Internet Resources, Issue Briefs, Dissertations, and Conference Papers

Aaron, D. Jayne, and Judy A. Berryman. *Rocky Flats Site*. Historic American Engineering Record (HAER), 1998. <http://www.rfets.gov/haer/default.htm>.

Ahmed, Samina. *Countering Nuclear Risks in South Asia*. Washington, D.C.: Council for a Livable World, December 2001.

———. "Nuclear Weapons Program: Moving Forward or Tactical Retreat?" Occasional Paper No. 18:OP:2. Notre Dame, Ind.: Kroc Institute, January 2000.

———. "Learning from Nuclear Crises: Pakistan." Paper presented at a conference at Stanford University, December 1999.

Ahmed, Samina, and David Cortright. *South Asia at the Nuclear Crossroads*. A joint publication by the Managing the Atom Project at Harvard University, the Fourth Freedom Forum, and the Joan B. Kroc Institute for International Peace Studies at the University of Notre Dame, March 2001.

———. "Preventing a Nuclear Arms Race in South Asia: U.S. Policy Options." Notre Dame, Ind.: Kroc Institute, January 2000.

Albright, David. "The CIA's Aluminum Tubes' Assessment: Is the Nuclear Case Going Down the Tubes?" *ISIS Issue Brief*. March 10, 2003. <http://www.isis-online.org/publications/iraq/al_tubes.html>.

———. "North Korea's Current and Future Plutonium and Nuclear Weapon Stocks." *ISIS Issue Brief*. January 15, 2003. <http://www.isis-online.org/publications/dprk/currentandfutureweaponsstocks.html>.

———. "India's and Pakistan's Fissile Material and Nuclear Weapons Inventories, End of 1999." Occasional Paper. Washington, D.C.: Institute for Science and International Security, October 11, 2000. <http://www.isis-online.org/publications/southasia/stocks1000.html>.

Albright, David, and Mark Gorwitz. "Plutonium Watch: Tracking Civil Plutonium Inventories: End of 1999." Issue brief. Institute for Science and International Security. October 2000. <http://www.isis-online.org/publications/puwatch/puwatch2000.html>.

Albright, David, and Corey Hinderstein. "The Iranian Gas Centrifuge Uranium Enrichment Plant at Natanz: Drawing from Commercial Satellite Images." Web report. Institute for Science and International Security. March 14, 2003. <http://www.isis-online.org/publications/iran/natanz03_02.html>.

———. "Iran Building Nuclear Fuel Cycle Facilities: International Transparency Needed." *ISIS Issue Brief,* Institute for Science and International Security. December 12, 2002. <http://www.isis-online.org/publications/iran/iranimages.html>.

Albright, David, Kevin O'Neill, and Corey Hinderstein. "Securing Pakistan's Nuclear Arsenal: Principles for Assistance." *ISIS Issue Brief.* Institute for Science and International Security. October 4, 2001. <http://www.isis-online.org/publications/terrorism/pakassist.html>.

Al-Marashi, Ibrahim. "Command and Control of Iraq's CW Arsenal." Web report. Center for Nonproliferation Studies. March 26, 2003. <http://www.cns.miis.edu/research/iraq/cocchem.htm>.

Arbatov, Alexei G. "The Next Steps in Arms Control: A Russian Perspective." Speech given at the Carnegie Endowment for International Peace. Washington, D.C. May 16, 2000. <http://www.ceip.org/programs/npp/arbatov051600.htm>.

Arnett, Eric. "Current Nuclear Weapon Capabilities in South Asia." SIPRI Web report. January 6, 1998. <http://projects.sipri.se/technology/Facts.html>.

Bellovin, Steven M. *Permissive Action Links.* <http://www.research.att.com/~smb/nsam-160/pal.html>.

Belousov, Vladimir Pavlovich. "Press Conference with Russian Experts Regarding START-2 Ratification Process." Speech at the National Press Institute, October 15, 1998.

Brookings Institution. "Atomic Demolition Munitions." The U.S. Nuclear Weapons Cost Study Project. 1998. <http://www.brook.edu/FP/projects/nucwcost/madm.htm>.

Bunn, Mathew. "Security for Weapons-Usable Nuclear Materials: Expanding International Cooperation, Strengthening International Standards." *A Comparative Analysis of Approaches to the Protection of Fissile Materials.* Stanford, Calif.: Workshop at Stanford University, July 28–30, 1997.

Burr, William. *Launch on Warning: The Development of U.S. Capabilities, 1959–1979.* National Security Archive Electronic Briefing Book. April 2001. <http://www.gwu.edu/~nsarchiv/NSAEBB/NSAEBB43/>.

Center for Contemporary Conflict. "War in Kargil." Web report. Project on "Asymmetric Conflict in South Asia: The Cause and Consequences of the 1999 Limited War in Kargil." Naval Postgraduate School. <http://www.ccc.nps.navy.mil/research/kargil/war_in_kargil.pdf>.

Center for Defense Information. "Nuclear Weapon Database: United States Arsenal." <http://www.cdi.org/issues/nukef&f/database/usnukes.html>.

Center for Nonproliferation Studies. "Chinese Ballistic Missile Designations and

Characteristics." China Profiles Database. <http://www.nti.org/db/china/wbmdat.htm>.

———. "Chronology of Indian Missile Development." Resources on India and Pakistan. <http://cns.miis.edu/research/india/indiach2.htm>.

———. "Iran Nuclear-Related Sites." Iran Special Collection. <http://cns.miis.edu/research/iran/nucsites.htm>.

———. "Kumchangri Underground Facility." North Korea Profiles Database. <http://www.nti.org/e_research/profiles/NK/45_564.html>.

———. "Nuclear Delivery System Modernization." China Profiles Database. <http://www.nti.org/db/china/wdsmdat.htm>.

Centre for Defence and International Security Studies. "The Ghauri: A Technical Snapshot." Web report. <http://www.cdiss.org/98may5a.htm>.

———. *National Briefings: China.* Web report. <http://www.cdiss.org/chinab.htm>.

Chari, P.R. "India's Slow-Motion Nuclear Deployment." *Carnegie Proliferation Brief* 3, no. 26 (September 7, 2000). <http://www.ceip.org/files/Publications/ProliferationBrief326.asp>.

———. "Protection of Fissile Materials: The Indian Experience." Champaign, Ill.: Arms Control, Disarmament, and International Security Program, ACDIS Occasional Paper, University of Illinois, September 1998.

Cheema, Zafar Iqbal. "The Experience in Pakistan." *A Comparative Analysis of Approaches to the Protection of Fissile Materials.* Stanford, Calif.: Workshop at Stanford University, July 28–30, 1997.

Cigar, Norman. "Iraq's Vision of the Nuclear Battlefield." Quantico, Va.: Marine Corps University Foundation, March 2003. <http://www.globalsecurity.org/wmd/library/news/iraq/2003/iraq-nuclear-battlefield-study.pdf>.

Cirincione, Joseph, and Dipali Mukhopadhyay. "Why Pollack Is Wrong: We Have Contained Saddam." *Carnegie Issue Brief,* February 21, 2003. <http://www.ceip.org/files/nonprolif/templates/article.asp?NewsID=4379>.

Cochran, Thomas B., Robert S. Norris, Elliott Negin, and Christopher Paine. *Faking Nuclear Restraint: The Bush Administration's Secret Plan for Strengthening U.S. Nuclear Forces.* Natural Resources Defense Council. February 13, 2002. <http://www.nrdc.org/nuclear/restraint.asp>.

Cordesman, Anthony H. "The New Iraqi 'Shell Game': The Strategy Iraq May Employ to Defeat UNMOVIC and IAEA Efforts." Web report, Washington, D.C.: Center for Strategic and International Studies, December 5, 2002. <http://www.csis.org/burke/iraqishellgame.pdf>.

———. "Weapons of Mass Destruction in the Middle East." Center for Strategic and International Studies. October 4, 1999. <http://www.csis.org/mideast/reports/WMDinMETrends.pdf>.

Coulter, C.A., R. Shropshire, and K.E. Thomas. "The Structure of Nuclear Material Safeguards Systems." Paper presented at the Fundamentals of Nuclear Materials Safeguards Systems Conference, Los Alamos, N.M., Los Alamos National Laboratory, April 12–16, 1999.

Desmond, William, Neil Zack, and James Tape. "The First 50 Years: A Review of the Department of Energy Domestic Safeguards and Security Program." Paper presented at the Workshop on *A Comparative Analysis of Approaches to the Protection of Fissile Materials*, Stanford University, July 28–30, 1997.

Di, Hua. "China's Security Dilemma to the Year 2010." Web report. Center for International Security and Arms Control. 1997. <http://iis-db.stanford.edu/pubs/10222/hua.pdf>.

Eberstadt, Nicholas. "Korea." *Strategic Asia, 2001–2002*. Seattle, Wash.: National Bureau of Asian Research, 2001. <http://strategicasia.nbr.org/report>.

Federation of American Scientists. "Chinese Command and Control." <http://www.fas.org/nuke/guide/china/c3i/index.html>.

———. "CINC Mobile Alternate Headquarters (CMAH), Cheyenne Mountain Alternate Headquarters (CMAH)." <http://www.fas.org/nuke/guide/usa/c3i/cmah.htm>.

———. "DF-31." <http://www.fas.org/nuke/guide/china/icbm/df-31.htm>.

———. "DF-41." <http://www.fas.org/nuke/guide/china/icbm/df-41.htm>.

———. "Nuclear Weapons Tests." <http://www.fas.org/nuke/guide/china/nuke/tests.htm>.

———. "Shaheen-I." Special Weapons website. <http://www.fas.org/nuke/guide/pakistan/missile/hatf-4.htm>.

———. "Shaheen-II." Special Weapons website. <http://www.fas.org/nuke/guide/pakistan/missile/shaheen-2.htm>.

———. "Introduction." *Special Weapons Primer.* <http://www.fas.org/nuke/intro/nuke/intro.htm>.

———. "United States Nuclear Forces." Web factsheet. <http://www.fas.org/nuke/guide/usa/forces.htm>.

Feigenbaum, Evan. *The Military Transforms China: The Politics of Strategic Technology from the Nuclear Age to the Information Age.* Ph.D. diss., Stanford University, 1997.

Ferguson, Charles D., Tahseen Kazi, and Judith Perera. "Commercial Radioactive Sources: Surveying the Security Risks." Monterey Center for Nonproliferation Studies. Occasional Paper No. 11. January 2003. <http://cns.miis.edu/pubs/opapers/op11/op11.pdf>.

Gill, Bates, and James Mulvenon. "The Chinese Strategic Rocket Forces: Transition to Credible Deterrence." Paper presented at *China and Weapons of Mass Destruction: Implications for the United States*, conference sponsored by the National Intelligence Council and Federal Research Division, Washington, D.C., November 5, 1999. <http://www.fas.org/irp/nic/china_wmd.html>.

GlobalSecurity.org. "Nodong-1." Web report. <http://www.globalsecurity.org/wmd/world/dprk/nd-1.htm>.

———. "Strategic Forces Command (SFC)." Web report. August 12, 2003. <http://www.globalsecurity.org/wmd/world/india/sfc.htm>.

Gopalakrishnan, A. "US-India Relations: Where Do We Go From Here?" Lecture at Harvard University, March 1, 2001.

Gottemoeller, Rose. "Nuclear Hangover: Addressing the Cold War Legacy." Conference presentation given at *New American Strategies for Security and Peace,* Washington, D.C.. October 28, 2003. <http://www.ceip.org/files/projects/npp/pdf/conference/NuclearHangover.pdf>.

Gutmacher, R.G., and D.D. Jackson. "Survey of Chemical and Bulk Measurements." Paper presented at the Materials Accounting for Nuclear Safeguards Conference, Los Alamos, N.M., Los Alamos National Laboratory, April 12–16, 1999.

Habiger, Eugene. DOD News Briefing, June 16, 1998. <http://www.defenselink.mil/news/Jun1998/t06231998_t616hab2.html>.

Hackett, Jim. "The Ballistic Missile Threat: India and Pakistan." *CDISS Missile News.* Centre for Defence and International Security Studies. <http://www.cdiss.org/column3.htm>.

Hamza, Khidir. "Saddam's Bombmaker." Presentation at the Carnegie Endowment for International Peace, November 2, 2000. <http://www.ceip.org/files/projects/npp/resources/hamzatranscript.htm>.

Hatcher, Charles R., and Hastings A. Smith. "Elements of Nondestructive Assay (NDA) Technology." Paper presented at the Materials Accounting for Nuclear Safeguards Conference, Los Alamos National, N.M., Los Alamos National Laboratory, April 12–16, 1999.

Hinderstein, Corey. "The First Casualty of the War on Terrorism Must Not Be Pakistan: Pakistan's Nuclear Weapons Must Not Fall into Terrorists' Hands." *ISIS Issue Brief,* September 18, 2001.

Hoehn, William. "Update on Legislation Affecting U.S.–Former Soviet Union Nonproliferation and Threat Reduction: Summary of Key Provisions in the Fiscal Year 2004 Energy and Water Appropriations and Defense Authorization Conference Agreements." Web report. Russian-American Nuclear Security Advisory Council (RANSAC). November 17, 2003. <http://www.ransac.org>.

Institute for Foreign Policy Analysis. *Exploring U.S. Missile Defense Requirements in 2010: What Are the Policy and Technology Challenges?* Washington, D.C.: Institute for Foreign Policy Analysis, April 1997. <http://www.fas.org/spp/starwars/advocate/ifpa/report696_ch3.htm>.

International Atomic Energy Agency. "Safeguards, Non-Proliferation and the Peaceful Uses of Nuclear Energy." IAEA Factsheet. <http://www.iaea.org/worldatom/Periodicals/Factsheets/English/safeguards-e.pdf>.

Joeck, Neal. "Nuclear Relations in South Asia." Paper presented at the 6th Annual Carnegie International Non-Proliferation Conference, Washington, D.C., December 1998.

Johnson, Katherine E. "U.S.-FSU Nuclear Threat Reduction Programs: Effectiveness of Current Efforts and Prospects for Future Cooperation." Los Alamos, N.M.: Center for International Security Affairs Publication, Los Alamos National Laboratory, 1995.

Kamal, Nazir. "Pakistani Perceptions and Prospects of Reducing the Nuclear Danger in South Asia." Occasional Paper No. 6, SAND98-0505/6, Albuquerque, N.M.: Cooperative Monitoring Center, January 1999.

Kay, David. "Iraqi Inspections: Lessons Learned." Speech given at the Center for Nonproliferation Studies, Monterey Institute for International Studies, February 10, 1993. <http://cns.miis.edu/research/iraq/kay.htm>.

Kempf, C. Ruth. "U.S. DOE Laboratory Views on U.S.-Russian Partnership for Nuclear Security." Paper presented at the 39th Annual Meeting of the Institute of Nuclear Material Management, Naples, Fla., July 26, 1998.

Koch, Andrew. "Selected Indian Nuclear Facilities." Web report. Center for Nonproliferation Studies, Monterey Institute of International Studies. July 7, 2000. <http://cns.miis.edu/research/india/index.htm>.

Koch, Andrew, and Jennifer Topping. "Pakistan's Nuclear-Related Facilities." Web report. Center for Nonproliferation Studies, Monterey Institute of International Studies. <http://cns.miis.edu/pubs/reports/pdfs/9707paki.pdf>.

Kominiak, George, Jane Eisenhauer, Kathryn Menaul, and Tara Sather. *The "Command and Control" Philosophy of the Communist Party of China*. Albuquerque, N.M.: Sandia National Laboratories. SAND96-2932. January 1996.

Kunsman, David M., and Douglas B. Lawson. *A Primer on U.S. Strategic Nuclear Policy*. Sandia National Laboratory Report. January 2001. <http://www.nti.org/e_research/official_docs/labs/prim_us_nuc_pol.pdf>.

Lavoy, Peter R., and Maj. Stephen A. Smith. "The Risk of Inadvertent Nuclear Use between India and Pakistan." *Strategic Insight*. Center for Contemporary Conflict, Naval Postgraduate School. February 3, 2003. <http://www.ccc.nps.navy.mil/rsepResources/si/feb03/southAsia2.pdf>, p. 3.

Lawrence Livermore National Laboratory, Sandia National Laboratories, and Los Alamos National Laboratory. "Foreign Trip Report." Beijing, China, June 23–July 2, 1995.

Los Alamos National Laboratory. "Workshop on Materials Control and Accounting System Design." *Materials Accounting for Nuclear Safeguards*. Workshop at Los Alamos National Laboratory, April 12–16, 1999, chapter 13.

Markin, J.T. "Fundamentals of Materials Accounting." Paper presented at the Accounting for Nuclear Safeguards Conference, Los Alamos, N.M., Los Alamos National Laboratory, April 12–16, 1999.

Maxwell, Maj. David S. "Catastrophic Collapse of North Korea: Implications for the United States Military, a Monograph." Fort Leavenworth, Kans.: United States Army Command and General Staff College, 1996. Doc. call no.: M-U 42022-2 M4652c. <http://www.kimsoft.com/korea/maxwell.htm#II>.

Minnich, Maj. James M. *North Korean Military Tactics*. Ft. Leavenworth, Kans.: U.S. Army Command and General Staff College, September, 2001. <http://www.globalsecurity.org/wmd/library/news/dprk/2001/korea.pdf>.

Mukhopadhyay, Dipali, and Jon Wolfsthal. "North Korea's Secret Nuclear Weapons Program: A Serious Violation of North Korea's International Commitments?"

Carnegie Analysis. Washington, D.C.: Carnegie Endowment for International Peace, October 25, 2002, <http://www.ceip.org/files/nonprolif/templates/article.asp?NewsID=3877>.

National Security Archive. "First Documented Evidence that U.S. Presidents Predelegated Nuclear Weapons Release Authority to the Military." Web report. <http://www.gwu.edu/~nsarchiv/news/19980319.htm>.

Natural Resources Defense Council. "The U.S. Nuclear War Plan: A Time for Change." Web report. July 2001. <http://www.nrdc.org/nuclear/warplan/execsum.asp>.

———. "Table of USSR/Russian Strategic Bomber Forces, 1956-2002." Archive of Nuclear Data. <http://www.nrdc.org/nuclear/nudb/datab8.asp>.

North American Aerospace Defense Command (NORAD). *North American Aerospace Defense Command.* Web factsheet. <http://www.norad.mil>.

———. *Strategic Command Command Center.* Web factsheet. <http://www.stratcom.mil/factsheetshtml/commandctr.htm>.

Nuclear Threat Initiative. "Chemical Facilities: Special Industries Organization (SIO)." Iran Profile. Internet Database. <http://www.nti.org/e_research/profiles/Iran/Chemical/2337_2412.html>.

Oak Ridge National Laboratory. "Home of the First Nuclear Reactor." Oak Ridge website. <http://www.ornl.gov/info/timeline/40/1940.shtml>.

———. "Yesterday at the Y-12 National Security Complex." Oak Ridge website. <http://www.y12.doe.gov/bwxt/y12/y12–yesterday.html>.

Pei, Minxin. "Future Shock: The WTO and Political Change in China." *Policy Brief,* no. 1. Washington, D.C.: Carnegie Endowment for International Peace, February 2001.

Perry, Todd E. "From Triage to Long-Term Care: A U.S. NGO View on the Future of the MPC&A Program." Paper presented at the 40th Annual Institute of Nuclear Material Management Conference, Phoenix, Ariz., July 25–29, 1999.

Pinkston, Daniel A. "South Korean Electoral Politics and Seoul's Position on the North Korean Nuclear Crisis." Web report. Center for Nonproliferation Studies. April 25, 2003. <http://www.cns.miis.edu/pubs/week/pdf/030425.pdf>.

Plummer, David W., and William H. Greenwood. "The History of Nuclear Weapon Safety Devices." 34th Joint Propulsion Conference, Cleveland Convention Center, Cleveland, Ohio, July 12–15, 1998.

Potter, William. Paper presented at the 7th Annual Carnegie International Non-Proliferation Conference, Washington, D.C., January 11–12, 1999. <http://www.ceip.org/programs/npp/potter.htm>.

Potter, William, and Nikolai Sokov. "Tactical Nuclear Weapons: The Nature of the Problem." Presentation for a seminar hosted by the United Nations Institute for Disarmament Research (UNIDIR). Geneva, March 21–22, 2000.

Rajagopal, S. "Review of the Indian Nuclear Experience." *A Comparative Analysis of Approaches to the Protection of Fissile Materials.* Stanford, Calif.: Workshop at Stanford University, July 28–30, 1997.

Rajkumar, Miriam. "Spring Thaw in South Asia." *Carnegie Analysis*. Carnegie Endowment for International Peace. May 20, 2003. <http://www.ceip.org/files/nonprolif/templates/article.asp?NewsID=4822>.

Reams, C. Austin. *Russia's Atomic Tsar: Viktor N. Mikhailov.* Los Alamos, N.M.: Center for International Security Affairs, Los Alamos Laboratory, December 1996.

Reidel, Bruce. "American Diplomacy and the 1999 Kargil Summit at Blair House." Center for the Advanced Study of India. *Policy Paper Series*. May 2002. <http://www.sas.upenn.edu/casi/reports/RiedelPaper051302.pdf>.

Russian-American Nuclear Security Advisory Council. "Russian-American Experts Applaud Bush Administration Budget for Cooperative Nuclear Security Programs." RANSAC web report. February 4, 2002. <http://www.ransac.org/Projects%20and%20Publications/News/News%20Releases/pr_020702.html>.

———. "Preliminary Report: Anticipated FY2003 Budget Request for Department of Energy Cooperative Nuclear Security Programs in Russia." RANSAC web report. January 9, 2002. <http://www.ransac.org/new-web-site/whatsnew/fy03budget.html>.

Sagan, Scott. "Nuclear Safety and Security in South Asia." *Proliferation Challenges and Nonproliferation Opportunities for New Administrations,* edited by Michael Barletta. Monterey Center for Nonproliferation Studies, Occasional Paper No. 4, September 2000, pp. 37–39. <http://www.cns.miis.edu/pubs/opapers/op4/op4.pdf>.

Sattar, Abdul (Pakistani foreign minister). Paper presented at the Carnegie International Non-Proliferation Conference, Washington, D.C., June 18, 2001.

Saunders, Phillip C., and Jing-dong Yuan. "China's Strategic Force Modernization: Issues and Implications for the United States." *Proliferation Challenges and Nonproliferation Opportunities for New Administration,* edited by Michael Barletta. Monterey Center for Nonproliferation Studies, Occasional Paper No. 4, September 2000, <http://www.cns.miis.edu/pubs/opapers/op4/op4.pdf>, pp. 40–46.

Schaffer, Teresita C. "Reviving Pakistan's Economy." *Pakistan's Future and U.S. Policy Options*. Washington, D.C.: Center for Strategic and International Studies, January 17, 2002.

Sheely, Kenneth, and Mary Alice Hayward. "New Strategic Directions in the MPC&A Program." Paper presented at the 40th Annual Institute of Nuclear Material Management Conference, Phoenix, Ariz., July 25–29, 1999.

Sichor, Yitzhak. "Peaceful Fallout: The Conversion of China's Military-Nuclear Complex to Civilian Use." *Brief 10*. Bonn: Bonn International Center for Conversion, November 1997. <http://www.bicc.de/industry/brief10/brief10.pdf>.

Singer, J. David, and Melvin Small. "The Correlates of War Project." University of Michigan. <http://www.umich.edu/~cowproj/>.

Smarto, Carrie, Michael Haase, Mark Baumann, Katherine Garner, Nicole Nelson, and William Toth. "MPC&A Site Operations and Sustainability: A Policy Overview." Paper presented at the 40th Annual Meeting of the Institute of Nuclear Material Management, Phoenix, Ariz., July 27, 1999.

Sokov, Nikolai. "Could Norway Trigger a Nuclear War? Notes on the Russian Command and Control System." *PONARS Policy Memo,* no. 24, October 1997. <http://www.csis.org/ruseura/ponars/policymemos/pm_0024.pdf>.

———. "Russia: Status and Trends in Tactical Weapon Deployment, 1998." Web report. Monterey Center for Nonproliferation Studies. February 1999. <http://www.nti.org/db/nisprofs/over/tacnums.htm>.

Spray, Stanley D. "History of U.S. Nuclear Weapon Safety Assessment: The Early Years." Albuquerque, N.M.: Sandia National Laboratories. SAND-96-1099C. June 1996.

Stokes, Mark A. *China's Strategic Modernization: Implications for the United States.* Carlisle, Pa.: Strategic Studies Institute, U.S. Army War College, September 1999. <http://www.fas.org/nuke/guide/china/doctrine/chinamod.pdf>.

U.S. Air Force. "Minuteman Fact Sheet." Air Force Fact Sheet. <http://www.af.mil/factsheets/factsheet.asp?fsID=113>.

———. "MX Fact Sheet." Air Force Fact Sheet. <http://www.af.mil/factsheets/factsheet.asp?fsID=112>.

———. "PAVE PAWS Radar System." Air Force Fact Sheet. <http://www.af.mil/factsheets/factsheet.asp?fsID=168>.

———. "B-2 SPIRIT." U.S. Air Force Fact Sheet. <http://www.af.mil/factsheets/factsheet.asp?fsID=82>.

———. "B-52 STRATOFORTRESS." Air Force Fact Sheet. <http://www.af.mil/factsheets/factsheet.asp?fsID=83>.

U.S. Navy. "Trident Fleet Ballistic Missile." Web factsheet. United States Navy Factfile. <http://www.chinfo.navy.mil/navpalib/factfile/missiles/wep-d5.html>.

———. "Tomahawk Cruise Missile." Web factsheet, United States Navy Factfile. <http://www.chinfo.navy.mil/navpalib/factfile/missiles/wep-toma.html>.

Walpole, Robert. Speech at Carnegie Endowment for International Peace. September 17, 1998. <http://www.cia.gov/cia/public_affairs/speeches/1998/walpole_speech_091798.html>.

Wilkening, Dean. "The Evolution of Russia's Strategic Nuclear Force." CISAC Publication: Studies in International Security and Arms Control, July 1998. <http://iis-db.stanford.edu/pubs/10334/russianforces.pdf>.

Wilkey, David, and Charles Hatcher. "Implementation of Materials Accounting in Russia." Paper presented at the Institute of Nuclear Materials Management, 40th Annual Meeting, Phoenix, Ariz., July 25–29, 1999.

Wolfsthal, Jon, Cristina-Astrid Chuen, and Emily Ewell Daughtry. "Nuclear Facilities and Fissile Materials in the Former Soviet Union," in *Nuclear Status Report: Nuclear Weapons, Fissile Material, and Export Controls in the Former Soviet Union,* no. 6, edited by Jon Wolfsthal, Cristina-Astrid Chuen, and Emily Ewell Daughtry. Carnegie Endowment for International Peace and Monterey Institute of International Studies, June 2001, pp. 75–174.

Wolkey, D.D., N.R. Zack, and R.G. Gutmacher. "Measurement Control." Paper presented at the Materials Accounting for Nuclear Safeguards Conference, Los Alamos, N.M., Los Alamos National Laboratory, April 12–16, 1999.

Wright, David, and Lisbeth Gronlund. "Estimating China's Production of Plutonium for Weapons." Technical Working Paper, Union of Concerned Scientists, 1999.

Zhang, Xingqiang. "China's Practice of Nuclear Materials Control." *A Comparative Analysis of Approaches to the Protection of Fissile Materials.* Stanford: Workshop at Stanford University, July 28–30, 1997.

Zhu, Quinsheng. *A Brief Overview on State Systems of China Nuclear Material Control.* China Atomic Energy Authority (Agency), Office of Nuclear Material Control, June 1994.

Index